Rails 3 in Action

Rails 3 in Action

RYAN BIGG
YEHUDA KATZ

MANNING
SHELTER ISLAND

For online information and ordering of this and other Manning books, please visit
www.manning.com. The publisher offers discounts on this book when ordered in quantity.
For more information, please contact

>   Special Sales Department
>   Manning Publications Co.
>   20 Baldwin Road
>   PO Box 261
>   Shelter Island, NY 11964
>   Email: orders@manning.com

♾ Recognizing the importance of preserving what has been written, it is Manning's policy to have
the books we publish printed on acid-free paper, and we exert our best efforts to that end.
Recognizing also our responsibility to conserve the resources of our planet, Manning books
are printed on paper that is at least 15 percent recycled and processed without the use of
elemental chlorine.

Manning Publications Co.	Development editor: Cynthia Kane
20 Baldwin Road	Copyeditors: Kevin Hobson, Linda Kern
PO Box 261	Proofreader: Tiffany Taylor
Shelter Island, NY 11964	Typesetter: Dottie Marsico
	Cover designer: Marija Tudor

ISBN 978-1-935182-27-6
Printed in the United States of America
1 2 3 4 5 6 7 8 9 10 – MAL – 16 15 14 13 12 11

brief contents

v

contents

preface

This book has been through quite the development process! It began in 2008 with Michael Ivey, Yehuda Katz, and Ezra Zygmuntowicz and was called *Merb in Action*. Since then it has changed name and hands a couple of times, winding up with people such as James Cox and the great Mike Gunderloy, the latter of whom is probably most famous for his work on Factsheet Five and many .NET books, not to mention being one of the founding members of the RailsBridge (http://railsbridge.org) organization.

Then, somehow, I became involved with this book.

I received an email on a cold April morning in 2010 from Christina Rudloff at Manning asking if I would have any interest in joining the project. I was exceptionally excited! I had been writing short blog posts about Rails for years, and the idea of focusing that effort into writing a book made me extremely happy. Long story short: Yehuda Katz liked what he saw on my blog and wanted me to join the project. Working with Yehuda has been brilliant. He's got to be one of the smartest and most patient people I have ever met.

Shortly after receiving that initial email from Christina, I talked with another person from Manning, Michael Stephens, first via email and then very late at night over the phone (we are on different continents) about the project. I worked out the initial chapter layout, and I distinctly remember one thing that Michael asked me: "You know what you're getting yourself into, right?" I thought "Sure, I've written blog posts before, how hard could it be?" and replied in much the same manner. How little did I know!

Since then, I have learned a lot about the book-writing process. For starters, it involves a lot more than just the two people and the publishing company on the front cover. It also takes a very long time to write a book. This book has been my life for the past year and a bit. I've spent many weekends, mornings before work, and evenings after work (and way too often, time even in my dreams) writing chapters for this book. I've talked about it (perhaps too much) as well. It's become such a running joke among people I know that when I'm introduced, they ask, "Do you know he's writing a book?"

Writing is sometimes easy, but other times it can be a struggle to come up with anything at all. There have been bad days, sure, but the good days outnumber those massively. The feeling of achievement you get when you finish a chapter, or even a section, is awesome. Receiving positive feedback from people has been a huge boon to completing this book.

Now, in 2011, the book is finally done, and what an amazing feeling that is! I'd like to think that it offers a unique perspective on developing a full Ruby on Rails application from scratch in the same (or at least, similar) manner that people are developing Rails applications at this time. It's also the first book to cover the latest features of Rails found in version 3.1.

RYAN BIGG

acknowledgments

This has been an amazing process, full of amazing people. A large portion of this book would not have been possible without the support of my employer, Mikel Lindsaar, and company, RubyX, allowing me to take time off to write the book. The support of the community at large has also been enormous in helping me complete this book. Winning the Ruby Hero award at RailsConf, partially due to my work on this very book, was the highlight of my career so far. After I won the award, Mikel also provided me with a new laptop at no expense to replace my previous one that was three years old. Bloody champion!

Of course, a lot of this wouldn't have been as easy if it wasn't for the Rails Core Team's valiant efforts on their maintenance of the framework over the years and their constant focus on improving people's lives on an almost daily basis. Also there are Yehuda Katz, Carl Lerche, and André Arko to thank for their work on an important part of developing not only Rails applications, but also Ruby libraries such as Bundler and Thor. These people are my idols, and I love them dearly.

Through a Rails-based review system called Twist that I built myself over a single day, I've collected more than 1,200 notes from people from around the world who have been reviewing the book as I have been writing it. A special mention goes to the three people who've left the most notes in Twist: Roy Hacker, Deryl Doucette, and Peter Ley. An almost-as-special mention goes to the 33 other people who've also left notes. Without your help, this book wouldn't be half as brilliant as it is today.

Also thanks to Tim McEwan for the ideas for the engines chapter, Chris Darroch for an initial read-through of the first chapters, and Rob Zolkos for helping with some gnarly ePub Ruby and XLST code. And yes, thanks to Andrew Snow for assisting with a difficult moral problem in chapter 16 at Railscamp in June 2011.

In addition to those who've been leaving notes in Twist, there are the people at Manning. First, thanks to Christina Rudloff for the initial contact and Michael Stephens for the late-night chats and management of the process. Candace Gillhooley and Nick Chase have also been enormously helpful.

Cynthia Kane, my development editor at Manning, is particularly special. Her job was to tell me when I was doing things wrong, such as not segueing between sections or making the text flow too fast, and to leave me notes such as "FIGURE!!!" when I needed an image to go along with the text. Our almost weekly catch-ups were well worthwhile; it was great always having someone there, prodding me for more content and talking through the process. Marjan Bace, fearless leader of Manning Publications, should also be credited for supporting this project for as long as it has been around.

The production team at Manning, including Troy Mott, has been great throughout this process too. The extreme focus they've shown in finishing this book is stunning. I also need to mention the wonderful work by Doug Warren in the final technical proofing of the book, as well as Manning's copyeditors, who touched up basically every single paragraph in the book.

Special thanks to the reviewers who took time out of their busy schedules to provide feedback on the manuscript at different stages during development. They include Jason Rogers, Craig Smith, Emmanuel Asante, Chad Moone, Dr. Jamie P. Finlay, Dave Nicolette, Grant Oladipo, Jean-Philippe Castro, Americo Savinon, Thomas Athanas, Chris Kelly, Greg Vaughn, Pete Helgren, Joshua R Cronemeyer, Peter Melo, Robby O'Connor, Philip Hallstrom, Curtis Miller, Patrick Peak, Anthony J. Topper, Brian Rose, Daniel Bretoi, Wesley Moxam, and David Workman

Finally, my friends and family have been amazing throughout my entire life, all the way from my parents—who supported my career choice in Ruby on Rails and technical writing, even though they paid for me to study Network Admin at TAFE and always told me that I should "get out the house more"—to my current housemate, who accepts that we don't see much of each other (or at least I think so). You're all wonderful people, and I hope now that the book is over I will see more of you. I would list you all here if only it didn't require this book to be printed in a multivolume series.

RYAN BIGG

Rails 3 in Action is a long-time coming. To give you some perspective, the book was originally called *Merb in Action*, and it managed a perpetual beta through the Merb merge, the release of Rails 3.0, and is finally ready just in time for Rails 3.1.

I can say with confidence that *Rails 3 in Action* would not exist without the hard, tireless work of Ryan Bigg. It was Ryan's idea to focus the book around real-world testing from the ground up, and it makes *Rails 3 in Action* the first book for Rails practitioners that teaches Rails the way professional Rails developers do it.

Since we merged Merb with Rails, I have had the benefit of not insignificant support from friends and family, who helped keep me on course in the long process that eventually delivered Rails 3.0. I want to especially call out Aaron Patterson, José Valim, Santiago Pastorino, and Xavier Noria, who stepped up and brought life back to a community that was starting to show signs of age by the time Rails 2.3 hit the shelves. And Carl Lerche, who helped me keep focus on doing things right, even when it was tempting not to.

Finally, I would be remiss if I didn't thank my wife, Leah, who has been there for me through the amazing trajectory of my development career, through good times and bad. Without her, I would have given up long ago.

YEHUDA KATZ

about this book

Ruby on Rails is a leading web application framework built on top of the fantastic Ruby programming language. Both the language and the framework place an extreme emphasis on having a principle of least surprise and getting out of the way of the developers using it.

Ruby on Rails has been growing at a rapid pace, with large internet companies such as Yellow Pages and Groupon using it for their core functionality. With the latest release of Rails, version 3.1, comes a set of changes that improve the already brilliant framework that has been constructed over the past seven years. The fantastic community around the framework has also been growing at a similar pace.

This book is designed to take you through developing a full-featured Rails application from step one, showing you exactly how professionals in the real world are developing applications right now.

Who should read this book

This book is primarily for those who are looking to begin working with the Ruby on Rails framework and who have some prior experience with Ruby, although that is not entirely necessary.

Later chapters, such as chapter 13, "Designing an API," chapter 17, "Engines," and chapter 18, "Rack-based applications," delve into more advanced topics, so these chapters are suitable for people who already have a foundation with Rails and are looking to expand their skillset a little further.

If you're looking for a book that teaches you the same practices that are used in the real world, then this is the book you are looking for.

Roadmap

Chapter 1 introduces the Ruby on Rails framework and begins to show how you can develop the beginnings of an application.

Chapter 2 shows off test-driven development and behavior-driven development, which are two core concepts in this book and for developing Rails applications. By testing the code you write, you can be assured that it's always working that way.

Chapters 3 and 4 discuss the application you develop in this book—a project-management app of sorts—and delve into the core concepts of a Rails application. They also look at developing the first core features of your application.

Chapter 5 begins an introduction to nested resources, building on top of the features developed in the previous two chapters.

Chapter 6 introduces authentication, requiring users to sign in to the application before they can perform certain tasks.

Chapter 7 builds on the work in chapter 6 by adding new areas of the application that are accessible only to users with a certain flag set in the database. You also use namespaces for the first time.

Chapter 8 builds on the basic authorization created in chapter 7, fleshing it out into something neater and more scalable.

In chapter 9, you learn about file uploading using the Paperclip gem. In this chapter you also learn about testing parts of your application that use JavaScript and about CoffeeScript, a neater language that compiles down to JavaScript.

Chapter 10 builds not one but two new features for the application, adding the ability to comment on a ticket as well as track the ticket's lifecycle through varying states.

In chapter 11, you add a feature that lets users assign tags to tickets so they can be easily grouped. You also add a feature to allow users to search for tickets matching a certain state or tag, or both.

Chapter 12 begins our foray into dealing with email in a Rails application. You'll see not only how to send email but also how to receive messages and parse them into meaningful data in your application.

Chapter 13 involves creating an API for the project resources in an application that provide other applications with a standardized way to access your application's data. We also look at token-based authentication and how to create multiple versions of an API.

In chapter 14, you deploy the application to an Ubuntu box and set it up to act like a normal web server using a RubyGem called Passenger and a web server called nginx.

In chapter 15, you create a "nice to have" feature: the ability to sign up or sign in using either Twitter or GitHub. When this is complete, people are no longer required to provide you with an email and password when they sign up; instead, they can use GitHub and Twitter as authentication providers.

By chapter 16, your application is all grown up and needs to handle any kind of performance issues it encounters. We cover basic performance enhancements, such as pagination, database indexing, and page and fragment caching.

Chapter 17 introduces a new feature for Rails 3: engines. You develop one of your own from scratch—a forum system—and then integrate it with the existing application.

Chapter 18 delves into the depths of Rack, explaining how Rack applications are made and can be tied into Rails. The chapter also explains, and contains examples of, middleware being used in Rails.

Code conventions and downloads

Code conventions in the book follow the style of other Manning books in the *In Action* series. All code in listings and in text appears in a monospaced font like this to separate it from ordinary text. In some cases, the original source code has been reformatted to fit on the pages. In general, the original code was written with page-width limitations in mind, but sometimes you may find a slight formatting difference between the code in the book and that provided in the source download. In a few rare cases, where long lines could not be reformatted without changing their meaning, the book listings contain line-continuation markers. Code annotations accompany many of the listings, highlighting important concepts. In many cases, numbered bullets link to explanations that follow in the text.

Source code for all the working examples in this book is available for download from the publisher's website at www.manning.com/Rails3inAction.

Author Online

The purchase of *Rails 3 in Action* includes free access to a private forum run by Manning Publications where you can make comments about the book, ask technical questions, and receive help from the authors and other users. To access and subscribe to the forum, point your browser to www.manning.com/Rails3inAction, and click the Author Online link. This page provides information on how to get on the forum once you are registered, what kind of help is available, and the rules of conduct in the forum.

Manning's commitment to our readers is to provide a venue where a meaningful dialogue between individual readers and between readers and the authors can take place. It's not a commitment to any specific amount of participation on the part of the authors, whose contribution to the book's forum remains voluntary (and unpaid). We suggest you try asking the authors some challenging questions, lest their interest stray!

The Author Online forum and the archives of previous discussions will be accessible from the publisher's website as long as the book is in print.

about the authors

RYAN BIGG has been developing Ruby on Rails since version 1.2 and can be found helping out the community by answering questions on IRC or StackOverflow or writing documentation. He currently works for a web consultancy based in Sydney called RubyX.

YEHUDA KATZ is well known not only for his work on this third version of Ruby on Rails, but also for other web-related projects such as jQuery, Bundler, Merb, and SproutCore. He currently works for Strobe in San Francisco as a lead developer on SproutCore and is the coauthor of Manning's *jQuery in Action, Second Edition.*

about the cover illustration

The figure on the cover of *Rails 3 in Action* is captioned "A Soldier." The illustration is taken from a nineteenth-century edition of Sylvain Maréchal's four-volume compendium of regional and military dress customs published in France. Each illustration is finely drawn and colored by hand. The rich variety of Maréchal's collection reminds us vividly of how culturally apart the world's towns and regions were just 200 years ago. Isolated from each other, people spoke different dialects and languages. In the streets or in the countryside, it was easy to identify where they lived and what their trade or station in life was just by their dress.

Dress codes have changed since then and the diversity by region, so rich at the time, has faded away. It is now hard to tell apart the inhabitants of different continents, let alone different towns or regions. Perhaps we have traded cultural diversity for a more varied personal life—certainly for a more varied and fast-paced technological life.

At a time when it is hard to tell one computer book from another, Manning celebrates the inventiveness and initiative of the computer business with book covers based on the rich diversity of regional life of two centuries ago, brought back to life by Maréchal's pictures.

Ruby on Rails, the framework

1

Welcome aboard! It's great to have you with us on this journey through the world of Ruby on Rails. Ruby on Rails is known throughout the lands as a powerful web framework that helps developers rapidly build modern web applications. In particular, it provides lots of niceties to help you in your quest to develop a full-featured real-world application and be happy doing it. Great developers are happy developers. There's much more to the Rails world than might appear at first glance, but not overwhelmingly too much. And what a first glance! Oh, you two haven't met? Well, time for some introductions then!

1.1   *What is Ruby on Rails?*

Ruby on Rails is a framework built on the Ruby language, hence the name Ruby on Rails. The Ruby language was created back in 1993 by Yukihiro "Matz" Matsumoto of Japan. Ruby was released to the general public in 1995. Since then, it has earned both a reputation and an enthusiastic following for its clean design, elegant syntax, and wide selection of tools available in the standard library and via a package management system called *RubyGems*. It also has a worldwide community and many active contributors constantly improving the language and the ecosystem around it.

Ruby on Rails was created in 2004 by David Heinemeier Hansson during the development of 37signals' flagship product: Basecamp. When Rails was needed for other 37signals projects, the team extracted the Rails code from it, crafted the beginnings of the framework, and released it as open source under the MIT license.[1] Since then, Ruby on Rails has quickly progressed to become one of the leading web development frameworks. This is in no small part due to the large community surrounding it who are constantly working on submitting patches to add new features or to fix existing bugs. Version 3 of this framework indicates yet another significant milestone in the project's history and introduces some new concepts, but won't leave those already familiar with the framework in the dark. The latest version of Rails is the primary focus of this book.

1.1.1   *Benefits*

Ruby on Rails allows for rapid development of applications by using a concept known as *convention over configuration*. When you begin writing a Ruby on Rails application, you run an application generator, which creates a basic skeleton of directories and files for your application. These files and directories provide categorization for pieces of your code, such as the app/models directory for containing files that interact with the database and the public/images directory for images. Because all of this is already there for you, you won't be spending your time configuring the way your application is laid out. It's done for you.

How rapidly can you develop a Ruby on Rails application? Take the annual *Rails Rumble* event. This event aims to bring together small teams of one to four developers around the world to develop Ruby on Rails[2] applications in a 48-hour period. Using Rails, these teams can deliver amazing web applications in just two days.[3] Another great example of rapid development of a Rails application is the 20-minute blog screencast recorded by Yehuda Katz.[4] This screencast takes you from a no-application state to having a basic blogging and commenting system.

Ruby on Rails affords you a level of productivity unheard of in other web frameworks because every Ruby on Rails application starts out the same way. The similarity

---

[1]   The MIT license: http://en.wikipedia.org/wiki/MIT_License.

[2]   And now other Ruby-based web frameworks, such as Sinatra.

[3]   To see an example of what has come out of previous Rails Rumbles, take a look at their alumni archive: http://r09.railsrumble.com/entries.

[4]   20-minute blog screencast: http://vimeo.com/10732081.

between the applications is so close that the paradigm shift between different Rails applications is not tremendous. If and when you jump between Rails applications, you don't have to relearn how it all connects—it's mostly the same.

The core features of Rails are a conglomerate of many different parts called Railties (when said aloud it rhymes with "bowties"), such as *Active Record*, *Active Support*, *Action Mailer*, and *Action Pack*.[5] These different Railties provide a wide range of methods and classes that help you develop your applications. They prevent you from performing boring, repetitive tasks—such as coding how your application hooks into your database—and let you get right down to writing valuable code for your business.

Ever wished for a built-in way of writing automated tests for your web application? Ruby on Rails has you covered with *Test::Unit*, part of Ruby's standard library. It's incredibly easy to write automated test code for your application, as you'll see throughout this book. Test::Unit saves your bacon in the long term, and that's a fantastic thing. We touch on Test::Unit in the next chapter before moving on to RSpec and Cucumber, two other test frameworks that are preferred over Test::Unit and a little easier on the eyes too.

In addition to testing frameworks, the Ruby community has produced several high-quality libraries (called RubyGems, or gems for short) for use in your day-to-day development with Ruby on Rails. Some of these libraries add additional functionality to Ruby on Rails; others provide ways to turn alternative markup languages such as Markdown and Textile into HTML. Usually, if you can think it, there's a gem out there that will help you do it.

Noticing a common pattern yet? Probably. As you can see, Ruby on Rails (and the great community surrounding it) provides code that performs the trivial application tasks for you, from setting up the foundations of your application to handling the delivery of email. The time you save with all these libraries is immense! And because the code is open source, you don't have to go to a specific vendor to get support. Anybody who knows Ruby can help you if you're stuck.

1.1.2 Common terms

You'll hear a few common Ruby on Rails terms quite often. This section explains what they mean and how they relate to a Rails application.

MVC

The *Model-View-Controller* (*MVC*) paradigm is not unique to Ruby on Rails but provides much of the core foundation for a Ruby on Rails application. This paradigm is designed to keep the logically different parts of the application separate while providing a way for data to flow between them.

In applications that don't use MVC, the directory structure and how the different parts connect to each other is commonly left up to the original developer. Generally,

---

[5] Railties share the same version number as Rails, which means when you're using Rails 3.1, you're using the 3.1 version of the Railtie. This is helpful to know when you upgrade Rails because the version number of the installed Railties should be the same as the version number of Rails.

this is a bad idea because different people have different opinions on where things should go. In Rails, a specific directory structure makes all developers conform to the same layout, putting all the major parts of the application inside an app directory. This app directory has three main subdirectories: models, controllers, and views.

Domain logic—how the records in your database are retrieved—is kept in models. In Rails applications, models define the code that interacts with the database's tables to retrieve and set information in them. Domain logic also means things such as validations or particular actions to perform on the data.

Controllers interact with the models to gather information to send to the view. They call methods on the model classes, which can return single objects representing rows in the database or collections (arrays) of these objects. Controllers then make these objects available to the view through instance variables.

Views display the information gathered by the controller, by referencing the instance variables set there, in a user-friendly manner. In Ruby on Rails, this display is done by default with a templating language known as *Embedded Ruby* (*ERB*). ERB allows you to embed Ruby (hence the name) into any kind of file you wish. This template is then preprocessed on the server side into the output that's shown to the user.

The assets, helpers, and mailers directories aren't part of the MVC paradigm, but they are important parts of Rails. The assets directory is for the static assets of the application, such as JavaScript files, images, and Cascading Style Sheets (CSS) for making the application look pretty. We look more closely at this in chapter 3.

The helpers directory is a place to put Ruby code (specifically, modules) that provides helper methods for just the views. These helper methods can help with complex formatting that would otherwise be messy in the view or is used in more than one place.

Finally, mailers is a home for the classes of your application that deal with sending email. In previous versions of Rails, these classes were grouped with models but have since been given their own home. We look at them in chapter 11.

REST

MVC in Rails is aided by REST, a routing paradigm. *Representational State Transfer* (*REST*) is the convention for *routing* in Rails. When something adheres to this convention, it's said to be *RESTful*. Routing in Rails refers to how requests are routed within the application itself. You benefit greatly by adhering to these conventions, because Rails provides a lot of functionality around RESTful routing, such as determining where a form can, or will, send to.

1.1.3   *Rails in the wild*

A question sometimes asked by people new to Rails is, "Is Rails ready?" Of course it is! The evidence is stacked mightily in Rails' favor with websites such as Twitter, Yellow Pages, and of course Basecamp, serving millions and millions of page requests daily.[6]

---

[6] Some of the more well-known applications that run on Ruby on Rails can be found at http://rubyonrails.org /applications.

If any site is a testament to the power of Ruby on Rails, Twitter is it. Even though Twitter suffered from scaling problems back in 2008 (due to its massive growth and other technological problems, *not* due to Rails), it is now the eleventh most popular website, according to Alexa, and is exceptionally stable.

Another well-known site that runs Ruby on Rails is GitHub, a hosting service for Git repositories. This site was launched in February 2008 and is now the leading Git web-hosting site. GitHub's massive growth was in part due to the Ruby on Rails community quickly adopting it as their de facto repository hosting site. Now GitHub is home to over a million repositories for just about every programming language on the planet. It's not exclusive to programming languages either; if it can go in a Git repository, it can go on GitHub. As a matter of fact, this book and its source code are kept on GitHub!

Now that you know what other people have accomplished with this framework, let's dive into creating your own application.

1.2 Developing your first application

We covered the theory behind Rails and showed how quickly and easily you can develop an application. Now it's your turn to get an application going.

1.2.1 Installing Rails

To get started, you must have these three things installed:

- Ruby
- RubyGems
- Rails

If you're on a UNIX-based system (Linux or Mac), we recommend you use RVM (http://rvm.beginrescueend.com) to install Ruby and RubyGems. It is the preferred solution of the community because it works so simply. Installing from a package management system such as Ubuntu's Aptitude has been known to be broken.[7] After installing RVM, you must run this command to install a 1.9.2 version of Ruby:

```
rvm install 1.9.2
```

To use this version of Ruby, you would need to use `rvm use 1.9.2` every time you wished to use it or else set up a .rvmrc file in the root of your project, which is explained on the RVM site in great detail. Alternatively, you can set this version of Ruby as the default with the command `rvm use --default 1.9.2`, and use `rvm use system` if you ever want to swap back to the system-provided Ruby install if you have one.

If you're on Windows, you can't use RVM and you can't use a 1.9.* version of Ruby, but that's okay. Rails 3 works with Ruby 1.8 versions of Rails too. We would recommend the use of the Rails Installer program (http://railsinstaller.org) from Engine Yard, or installing the Ruby 1.8.7-p352 binary from ruby-lang.org as an alternative.

---

[7] Broken Ubuntu Ruby explained here: http://ryanbigg.com/2010/12/ubuntu-ruby-rvm-rails-and-you/.

Next, you need to install the `rails` gem. The following command installs both Rails and its dependencies. If you're using the Rails installer you will not need to run this command because Rails will already be installed:

```
gem install rails -v 3.1.0
```

1.2.2 *Generating an application*

With Rails now installed, to generate an application, you run the `rails` command and pass it the `new` argument and the name of the application you want to generate: *things_i_bought*. When you run this command, it creates a new directory called things_i_bought, which is where all your application's code will go. You can call your application anything you wish, but it can't be given the same name as a reserved word in Rails. For example, you wouldn't call your application rails because it defines a Rails *constant*, which is internal to Rails, and the two constants would clash.

The application that you're going to generate will be able to record purchases you have made. You can generate it using this command:

```
rails new things_i_bought
```

The output from this command may seem a bit overwhelming at first, but rest assured: it's for your own good. All of the directories and files generated here provide the building blocks for your application, and you'll get to know each of them as we progress. For now, let's get rolling and learn by doing, which is the best way of learning.

1.2.3 *Starting the application*

To get the server running, you must first change into the newly created application's directory and then run these commands to start the application server:

```
cd things_i_bought
bundle install
rails server
```

The `bundle install` command installs all the gems required for your application. This is explained in further detail in chapter 3.

This starts a web server on your local address on port 3000 using a Ruby standard library web server known as WEBrick. It will say it's "starting in development on http://0.0.0.0:3000," which indicates to you that the server will be available on port 3000 on all network interfaces of this machine.[8] To connect to this server, go to http://localhost:3000 in your favorite browser. You'll see the "Welcome aboard" page, which is so famous in Rails (see figure 1.1).

If you click About Your Application's Environment, you'll find your Ruby, Ruby-Gems, Ruby on Rails, and Rack versions and other environmental data. One of the things to note here is that the output for Environment is Development. Rails provides

---

[8] This is what the `0.0.0.0` address represents. It is not an actual address, so to speak, and so `localhost` or `127.0.0.1` should be used.

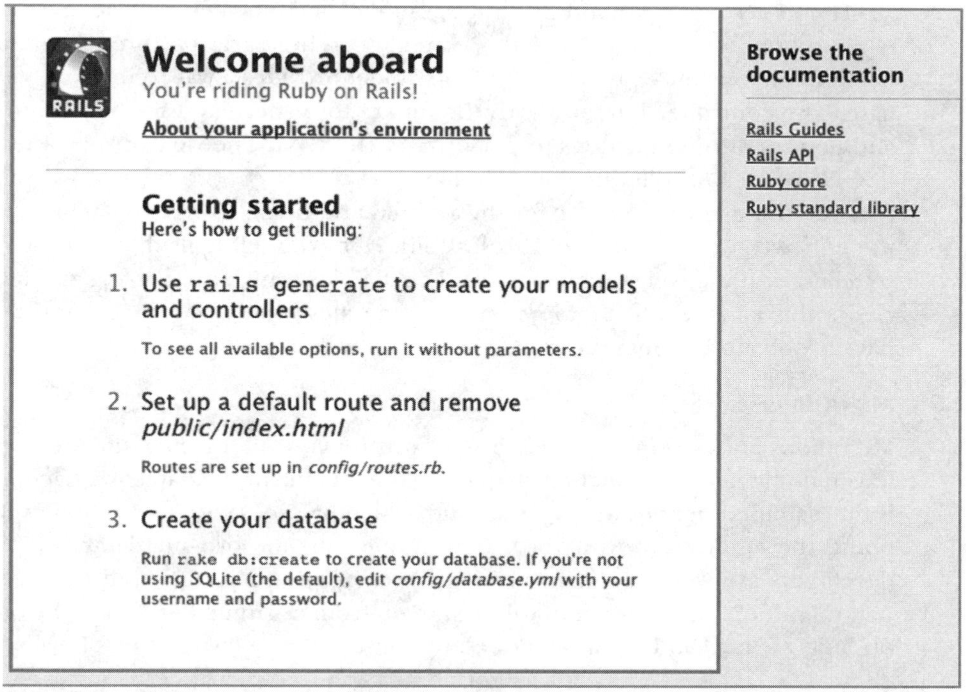

Welcome aboard
You're riding Ruby on Rails!

About your application's environment

Getting started
Here's how to get rolling:

1. Use rails generate to create your models and controllers

   To see all available options, run it without parameters.

2. Set up a default route and remove *public/index.html*

   Routes are set up in *config/routes.rb*.

3. Create your database

   Run rake db:create to create your database. If you're not using SQLite (the default), edit *config/database.yml* with your username and password.

Browse the documentation

Rails Guides
Rails API
Ruby core
Ruby standard library

Figure 1.1 Welcome aboard!

three environments for running your application: development, test, and production. How your application functions can depend on the environment in which it is running. For example, in the development environment, classes are not cached; so if you make a change to a class when running an application in development mode, you don't need to restart the server, but the same change in the production environment would require a restart.

1.2.4 Scaffolding

To get started with this Rails application, you generate a *scaffold*. Scaffolds in Rails provide a lot of basic functionality but are generally not used for full-scale development because you may want something more customized, in which case you'd build it yourself. But for this example of what Rails can do, let's generate a scaffold by running this command:

```
rails generate scaffold purchase name:string cost:float
```

When you used the rails command earlier, it generated an entire Rails application. You can use this command inside of an application to generate a specific part of the application by passing the generate argument to the rails command, followed by what it is you want to generate.

The scaffold command generates a model, a controller, and views based on the name passed after scaffold in this command. These are the three important parts needed for your purchase tracking. The model provides a way to interact with a database. The controller interacts with the model to retrieve and format its information and defines different actions to perform on this data. The views display the information from the controller in a neat format.

Everything after the name for the scaffold are the fields for the database table and the *attributes* for the objects of this scaffold. Here you tell Rails that the table for your purchase scaffold will contain name and cost fields, which are a string and a float.[9] To create this table, the scaffold generator generates what's known as a *migration*. Let's have a look at what migrations are.

1.2.5 *Migrations*

Migrations are used in Rails as a form of version control for the database, providing a way to implement incremental changes to the schema of the database. Each migration is timestamped right down to the second, which provides you (and anybody else developing the application with you) an accurate timeline of your database. When two developers are working on separate features of an application and both generate a new migration, this timestamp will stop them from clashing. Let's open the only file in db/migrate now and see what it does. Its contents are shown in the following listing.

> **Listing 1.1 db/migrate/[date]_create_purchases.rb**

```
class CreatePurchases < ActiveRecord::Migration
  def self.up
    create_table :purchases do |t|
      t.string :name
      t.float :cost

      t.timestamps
    end
  end

  def self.down
    drop_table :purchases
  end
end
```

Migrations are Ruby classes that inherit from ActiveRecord::Migration. Inside the class, two class methods are defined: up and down. Inside the up method is the code you want to be run when you run the migration, and inside the down method is the code that runs when you roll the migration back.

Inside both of these methods you use database-agnostic commands to create and drop a table. In the up method, you create a table and specify the fields you want in

---

[9] Usually you wouldn't use a float for storing monetary amounts because it can lead to incorrect-rounding errors. Generally, you store the amount in cents as an integer and then do the conversion back to a full dollar amount. This example uses a float because it's easier to not have to define the conversion at this point.

that table by calling methods on the t block variable. The string and float methods create fields of those particular types on any Rails-compatible database system.[10] You specified these fields when you used the scaffold command. The timestamps method is special; it creates two fields called created_at and updated_at, which have their values set when records are created and updated automatically by Rails.

To run the migration, type this command into the console:

```
rake db:migrate
```

This command run the self.up part of this migration. Because this is your first time running migrations in your Rails application, and because you're using a SQLite3 database, Rails first creates the database in a new file at db/development.sqlite3 and then creates the purchases table inside that. When you run rake db:migrate, it doesn't just run the self.up method from the latest migration but runs any migration that hasn't yet been run, allowing you to run multiple migrations sequentially.

Your application is, by default, already set up to talk to this new database, so you don't need to change anything. If you ever want to roll back this migration, you'd use rake db:rollback, which rolls back the latest migration by running the self.down method of the migration.[11]

Rails keeps track of the last migration that was run by storing it using this line in the db/schema.rb file:

```
ActiveRecord::Schema.define(:version => [timestamp]) do
```

This version should match the prefix of the migration you just created,[12] and Rails uses this value to know what migration it's up to. The remaining content of this file shows the combined state of all the migrations to this point. This file can be used to restore the last-known state of your database if you run the rake db:schema:load command.

With your database set up with a purchases table in it, let's look at how you can add rows to it through your application

1.2.6 *Viewing and creating purchases*

Start your browser now and go to http://localhost:3000/purchases. You'll see the scaffolded screen for purchases, as shown in figure 1.2. No purchases are listed yet, so let's add a new purchase by clicking New Purchase.

Listing purchases

Name Cost

New Purchase

Figure 1.2   Purchases

---

[10] So far, MySQL, PostgreSQL, SQLite3, Oracle, Frontbase, and IBM DB.

[11] If you want to roll back more than one migration, use the rake db:rollback STEP=3 command, which rolls back the three most recent migrations.

[12] Where [timestamp] in this example is an actual timestamp formatted like YYYYmmddHHMMSS.

In figure 1.3, you see two inputs for the fields you generated. This page is the result of the new action from thePurchasesController controller. What you see on the page comes from the view located at app/views/purchases/new.html.erb, and it looks like the following listing.

Listing 1.2   app/views/purchases/new.html.erb

```
<h1>New purchase</h1>

<%= render 'form' %>

<%= link_to 'Back', purchases_path %>
```

This is an ERB file, which allows you to mix HTML and Ruby code to generate dynamic pages. The beginning of an ERB tag indicates that the result of the code inside the tag will be output to the page. If you want the code to be evaluated but not output, you use the <% tag, like this:

Figure 1.3   A new purchase

```
<% some_variable = "foo" %>
```

If you were to use <%= some_variable = "foo" %> here, the some_variable variable would be set and the value output to the screen. By using <%=, the Ruby code is evaluated but not output.

The render method, when passed a string as in this example, renders a *partial*. A partial is a separate template file that you can include in other templates to repeat similar code. We'll take a closer look at these in chapter 3.

The link_to method generates a link with the text of the first argument (Back) and with an href attribute specified by the second argument (purchases_path), which is simply /purchases.

This particular partial is at app/views/purchases/_form.html.erb, and the first half of it looks like the following listing.

Listing 1.3   First half of app/views/purchases/_form.html.erb

```
<%= form_for(@purchase) do |f| %>
  <% if @purchase.errors.any? %>
    <div id="error_explanation">
      <h2><%= pluralize(@purchase.errors.count, "error") %> prohibited this
        purchase from being saved:</h2>

      <ul>
      <% @purchase.errors.full_messages.each do |msg| %>
        <li><%= msg %></li>
      <% end %>
      </ul>
    </div>
  <% end %>
```

This half is responsible for defining the form by using the `form_for` helper. The `form_for` method is passed one argument—an instance variable called `@purchase`—and with `@purchase` it generates a form. This variable comes from the Purchases-Controller's new action, which is shown in the following listing.

Listing 1.4   app/controllers/purchases_controller.rb

```ruby
def new
  @purchase = Purchase.new

  respond_to do |format|
    format.html # new.html.erb
    format.xml  { render :xml => @purchase }
  end
end
```

The first line in this action sets up a new `@purchase` variable by calling the `new` method on the `Product` model, which initializes a new object of this model. The variable is then automatically passed through to the view by Rails.

Next in the controller is the `respond_to` method that defines what formats this action responds to. Here, the controller responds to the `html` and `xml` formats. The `html` method here isn't given a block and so will render the template from app/views/purchases/new.html.erb, whereas the `xml` method, which is given a block, will execute the code inside the block and return an XML version of the `@purchase` object. You'll be looking at what the `html` response does from here forward because that is the default format requested.

So far, all of this functionality is provided by Rails. You've coded nothing yourself. With the `scaffold` generator, you get an awful lot for free.

Going back to the view, the block for the `form_for` is defined between its `do` and the `%>` at the end of the file. Inside this block, you check the `@purchase` object for any errors by using the `@purchase.errors.any?` method. These errors will come from the model if the object did not pass the validation requirements set in the model. If any errors exist, they're rendered by the content inside this `if` statement. Validation is a concept covered shortly.

The second half of this partial looks like the following listing.

Listing 1.5   Second half of app/views/purchases/_form.html.erb

```erb
  <div class="field">
    <%= f.label :name %><br />
    <%= f.text_field :name %>
  </div>
  <div class="field">
    <%= f.label :cost %><br />
    <%= f.text_field :cost %>
  </div>
  <div class="actions">
    <%= f.submit %>
  </div>
<% end %>
```

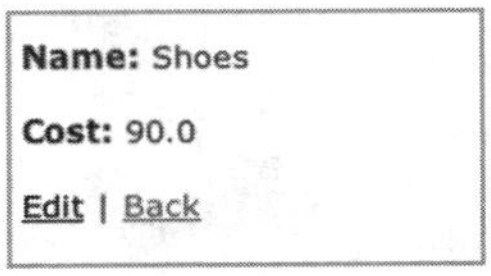

Here, the f object from the `form_for` block is used to define labels and fields for your form. At the end of this partial, the `submit` method provides a dynamic submit button.

Let's fill in this form now and click the submit button. You should see something similar to figure 1.4.

What you see here is the result of your posting: a successful creation of a `Purchase`. Let's see how it got there. The submit button posts the data from the form to the `create` action, which looks like the following listing.

Name: Shoes
Cost: 90.0
Edit	Back

Figure 1.4
Your first purchase

Listing 1.6   app/controllers/purchases_controller.rb

```ruby
def create
  @purchase = Purchase.new(params[:purchase])

  respond_to do |format|
    if @purchase.save
      format.html { redirect_to(@purchase, :notice => 'Purchase was successfu
      lly created.') }
      format.xml  { render :xml => @purchase, :status => :created, :location
      => @purchase }
    else
      format.html { render :action => "new" }
      format.xml  { render :xml => @purchase.errors, :status => :unprocessabl
      e_entity }
    end
  end
end
```

Here, you use the `Purchase.new` you first saw used in the `new` action. But this time you pass it an argument of `params[:purchase]`. `params` (short for *parameters*) is a method that returns the parameters sent from your form in a `Hash`-like object. When you pass this `params` hash into `new`, Rails sets the *attributes*[13] to the values from the form.

Inside the `respond_to` is an `if` statement that calls `@purchase.save`. This method *validates* the record, and if it's valid, the method saves the record to the database and returns `true`.

If the return value is `true`, the action responds by redirecting to the new `@purchase` object using the `redirect_to` method, which takes either a path or an object that it turns into a path (as seen in this example). The `redirect_to` method interprets what the `@purchase` object is and determines that the path required is `purchase_path` because it's an object of the `Purchase` model. This path takes you to the `show` action for this controller. The `:notice` option passed to the `redirect_to` sets up a *flash message*. A flash message is a message that can be displayed on the next request.

You've seen what happens when the purchase is valid, but what happens when it's invalid? Well, it uses the `render` method to show the `new` action's template again. We

---

[13] The Rails word for fields.

should note here that this doesn't call the new action/method again[14] but only renders the template.

You can make the creation of the @purchase object fail by adding a validation. Let's do that now.

1.2.7 Validations

You can add validations to your model to ensure that the data conforms to certain rules or that data for a certain field must be present or that a number you enter must be above a certain other number. You're going to write your first code for this application and implement both of these things now.

Open up your Purchase model and change the whole file to what's shown in the following listing.

Listing 1.7 app/models/purchase.rb

```ruby
class Purchase < ActiveRecord::Base
  validates_presence_of :name
  validates_numericality_of :cost, :greater_than => 0
end
```

You use the validates_presence_of method to define a validation that does what it says on the box: validates that the field has a value. The other validation method, validates_numericality_of, does more than what it initially claims: it validates that the cost attribute is a number and that it is greater than 0.

Let's test out these validations by going back to http://localhost:3000/purchases, clicking New Purchase, and clicking Create Purchase. You should see the errors shown in figure 1.5.

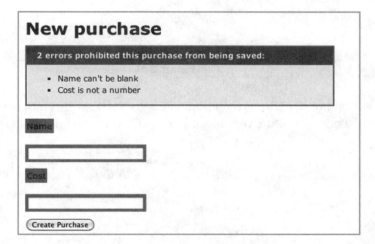

**Figure 1.5
Errors on purchase**

---

[14] To do that, you call redirect_to new_purchase_path, but that wouldn't persist the state of the @purchase object to this new request without some seriously bad hackery. By rerendering the template, you can display information about the object if the object is invalid.

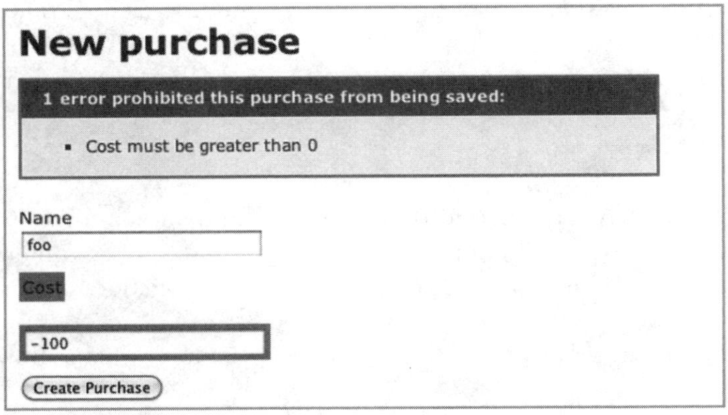

New purchase

1 error prohibited this purchase from being saved:

- Cost must be greater than 0

Name

`foo`

Cost

`-100`

(Create Purchase)

Figure 1.6   Cost must be greater than 0

Great! Here, you're told that Name can't be blank and that the value you entered for Cost isn't a number. Let's see what happens if you enter `foo` for the Name field and `-100` for the Cost field, and click Create Purchase. You should get a different error for the Cost field now, as shown in figure 1.6.

Good to see! Both of your validations are working now. When you change Cost to `100` and click Create Purchase, it should be considered valid by the validations and take you to the `show` action. Let's look at what this particular action does now.

1.2.8   Showing off

This action displays the content such as shown in figure 1.7.

← → C ☆ http://localhost:3000/purchases/2

Name: foo

Cost: 100.0

Edit | Back

Figure 1.7   A single purchase

The number at the end of the URL is the unique numerical ID for this purchase. But what does it mean? Let's look at the view for this `show` action now, as shown in the following listing.

Listing 1.8   app/views/purchases/show.html.erb

```erb
<p id="notice"><%= notice %></p>

<p>
  <b>Name:</b>
  <%= @purchase.name %>
</p>

<p>
  <b>Cost:</b>
```

```
  <%= @purchase.cost %>
</p>


<%= link_to 'Edit', edit_purchase_path(@purchase) %> |
<%= link_to 'Back', purchases_path %>
```

On the first line is the notice method, which displays the notice set on the redirect_to from the create action. After that, field values are displayed in p tags by simply calling them as methods on your @purchase object. This object is defined in your PurchasesController's show action, as shown in the following listing.

Listing 1.9   app/controllers/purchases_controller.rb

```
def show
  @purchase = Purchase.find(params[:id])

  ...
end
```

The find method of the Purchase class is used to find the record with the ID of params[:id] and instantiate a new Purchase object from it with params[:id] as the number on the end of the URL.

Going back to the view (app/views/purchases/show.html.erb) now, at the end of this file you see link_to, which generates a link using the first argument as the text for it and the second argument as the href for that URL. The second argument for link_to is a method itself: edit_purchase_path. This method is provided by a method call in config/routes.rb, which we now look at.

1.2.9   Routing

The config/routes.rb file of every Rails application is where the application routes are defined in a succinct Ruby syntax. The methods used in this file define the pathways from requests to controllers. If you look in your config/routes.rb while ignoring the commented-out lines for now, you'll see what's shown in the following listing.

Listing 1.10   config/routes.rb

```
ThingsIBought::Application.routes.draw do
  resources :purchases
end
```

Inside the block for the draw method is the resources method. Collections of similar objects in Rails are referred to as *resources*. This method defines the routes and routing helpers (such as the edit_purchase_path method) to your purchases resources. Look at table 1.1 for a list of the helpers and their corresponding routes.

In this table, :id can be substituted for the ID of a record. Each routing helper has an alternative version that will give you the full URL to the resource. Simply use the _url extension rather than _path, and you'll get a URL such as http://localhost:3000/purchases for purchases_url.

Helper	Route
purchases_path	/purchases
new_purchase_path	/purchases/new
edit_purchase_path	/purchases/:id/edit
purchase_path	/purchases/:id

Table 1.1 Routing helpers and their routes

From this table, two of these routes will act differently depending on how they're requested. The first route, /purchases, takes you to the index action of Purchases-Controller if you do a GET request. GET requests are the standard type of requests for web browsers, and this is the first request you did to this application. If you do a POST request to this route, it will go to the create action of the controller. This is the case when you submit the form from the new view. Let's go to http://localhost:3000/purchases/new now and look at the source of the page. You should see the beginning tag for your form looking like the following listing.

Listing 1.11   The HTML source of app/views/purchases/new.html.erb

```
<form action="/
    purchases" class="new_purchase" id="new_purchase" method="post">
```

The two attributes to note here are the action and method attributes. The action dictates the route to where this form goes, and the method tells the form what kind of HTTP request to make.

How'd this tag get rendered in the first place? Well, as you saw before, the app/views/purchases/new.html.erb template uses the form partial from app/views/purchases/_form.html.erb, which contains this as the first line:

```
<%= form_for(@purchase) do |f| %>
```

This one simple line generates that form tag. When we look at the edit action shortly, you'll see that the output of this tag is different, and you'll see why.

The other route that responds differently is the /purchases/{id} route, which acts in one of three ways. You already saw the first way: it's the show action to which you're redirected (a GET request) after you create a purchase. The second of the three ways is when you update a record, which we look at now.

1.2.10   *Updating*

Let's change the cost of the foo purchase now. Perhaps it only cost 10. To change it, go back to http://localhost:3000/purchases and click the Edit link next to the foo record. You should now see a page that looks similar to the new page, shown in figure 1.8.

This page looks similar because it re-uses the partial used in the new action. Such is the power of partials: you can use the same code for two different requests to your application. The template for this action can be seen in the following listing.

Figure 1.8   Editing a purchase

Listing 1.12   app/views/purchases/edit.html.erb

```
<h1>Editing purchase</h1>

<%= render 'form' %>

<%= link_to 'Show', @purchase %> |
<%= link_to 'Back', purchases_path %>
```

For this action, you're working with a pre-existing object rather than a new object, which you used in new. This pre-existing object is found by the edit action in PurchasesController, shown in the next listing.

Listing 1.13   app/controllers/purchases_controller.rb

```
# GET /purchases/1/edit
def edit
  @purchase = Purchase.find(params[:id])
  ...
end
```

The code to find the @purchase object here is identical to what you saw earlier in the show action.

Back in the view for a moment, at the bottom of it you can see two uses of link_to. The first creates a Show link, linking to the @purchase object, which is set up in the edit action of your controller. Clicking this link would take you to purchase_path(@purchase) or /purchases/:id. Rails will figure out where the link needs to go according to the class of the object. Using this syntax, it will attempt to call the purchase_path method because the object has a class of Purchase and will pass the object along to that call, generating the URL.[15]

The second use of link_to in this view generates a Back link, which uses the routing helper purchases_path. It can't use an object here because it doesn't make sense to; calling purchases_path is the easy way to go back to the index action.

---

[15] This syntax is exceptionally handy if you have an object and are not sure of its type but still want to generate a link for it. For example, if you had a different kind of object called Order and it was used instead, it would use order_path rather than purchase_path.

In the beginning...

In really early versions of Rails, you had to generate links like this:

```
link_to "Back", { :controller => "purchases",
:action => "show",
:id => @purchase.id }
```

This hash was then interpreted and matched to a route, like /purchases/1. You can still use it today in Rails 3 if you wish, but it's not best practice. The hash can be shortened:

```
link_to "Back", "/purchases/#{@purchase.id}"
```

These days, the following is best:

```
link_to "Back", @purchase
```

By using the routing helpers introduced in Rails 2 and still available in Rails 3.1, you can have much shorter `link_to` calls in your application, increasing the readability of the code throughout.

Let's try filling in this form now, for example, by changing the cost from 100 to 10 and clicking Update Purchase. You now see the show page but with a different message, shown in figure 1.9.

Clicking Update Purchase brought you back to the show page. How did that happen? Click the back button on your browser and view the source of this page, specifically the form tag and the tags directly underneath, shown in the following listing.

Listing 1.14   The HTML source of app/views/purchases/edit.html.erb

```
form action="/purchases/
    2" class="edit_purchase" id="edit_purchase_2" method="post"
  div style="margin:0;padding:0;display:inline"
    input name="_method" type="hidden" value="put" /
  /div
...
```

This `form`'s `action` points at /purchases/2, which is the route to the `show` action in `PurchasesController`. You should also note two other things. The `method` attribute of this form is a `post`, but there's also the `input` tag underneath.

The `input` tag passes through the _method parameter with the value set to `"put"`. Rails catches this parameter and turns the request from a POST into a PUT. This is the

Figure 1.9   Viewing an updated purchase

second (of three) ways the /purchases/{id} responds according to the method. By making a PUT request to this route, you're taken to the update action in Purchases-Controller. Let's take a look at this in the following listing.

Listing 1.15   app/controllers/purchases_controller.rb

```ruby
def update
  @purchase = Purchase.find(params[:id])

  respond_to do |format|
    if @purchase.update_attributes(params[:purchase])
      format.html { redirect_to(@purchase,
                    :notice => 'Purchase was successfully updated.') }
      format.xml  { head :ok }
    else
      format.html { render :action => "edit" }
      format.xml  { render :xml => @purchase.errors,
                    :status => :unprocessable_entity }
    end
  end
end
```

Just as in the show and edit actions, you fetch the object first by using the find method. The parameters from the form are sent through in the same fashion as they were in the create action, coming through as params[:purchase]. Rather than instantiating a new object by using the new class method, you use update_attributes on the @purchase object. This does what it says on the tin: updates the attributes. What it doesn't say on the tin, though, is that it validates the attributes and, if the attributes are valid, saves the record and returns true. If they aren't valid, it returns false.

When update_attributes returns true, you're redirected back to the show action for this particular purchase by using redirect_to.

If it returns false, you're shown the edit action's template again, just as back in the create action where you were shown the new template again. This works in the same fashion and displays errors if you enter something wrong. Let's try editing a purchase and setting the name to blank and then clicking Update Purchase. It should error exactly like the create method did, as shown in figure 1.10.

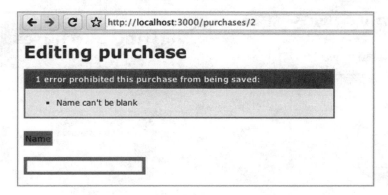

Figure 1.10
Update fails!

As you can see by this example, the validations you defined in your `Purchase` model take effect for both the creation and updating of records automatically.

Now what would happen if, rather than update a purchase, you wanted to delete it? That's built in to the scaffold too.

1.2.11 *Deleting*

In Rails, delete is given a much more forceful name: *destroy*. This is another sensible name because to destroy a record is to put an end to its existence.[16] Once this record's gone, it's gone, baby, gone.

You can destroy a record by going to http://localhost:3000/purchases and clicking the Destroy link shown in figure 1.11 and then clicking OK on the confirmation box that pops up.

When that record's destroyed, you're taken back to the Listing Purchases page. You'll see that the record no longer exists. You should now only have one record, as shown in figure 1.12.

How does all of this work? Let's look at the `index` template in the following listing to understand, specifically the part that's used to list the purchases.

Listing 1.16   app/views/purchases/index.html.erb

```
<% @purchases.each do |purchase| %>
  <tr>
    <td><%= purchase.name %></td>
    <td><%= purchase.cost %></td>
    <td><%= link_to 'Show', purchase %></td>
    <td><%= link_to 'Edit', edit_purchase_path(purchase) %></td>
    <td><%= link_to 'Destroy', purchase, :confirm => 'Are you sure?',
                                  :method => :delete %></td>
  </tr>
<% end %>
</table>

<br />

<%= link_to 'New Purchase', new_purchase_path %>
```

Listing purchases

Name Cost
Shoes 90.0 Show **Edit** Destroy
foo   100.0 Show **Edit** Destroy ◄───

New Purchase

Figure 1.11   Destroy!

Listing purchases

Name Cost
Shoes 90.0 Show **Edit** Destroy

New Purchase

Figure 1.12   Last record standing

---

[16] Mac OS X dictionary.

In this template, @purchases is a collection of all the objects from the Purchase model, and each is used to iterate over each, setting purchase as the variable used in this block.

The methods name and cost are the same methods used in app/views/purchases/ show.html.erb to display the values for the fields. After these, you see the three uses of link_to.

The first link_to passes in the purchase object, which links to the show action of PurchasesController by using a route such as/purchases/{id}, where {id} is the ID for this purchase object.

The second link_to links to the edit action using edit_purchase_path and passes the purchase object as the argument to this method. This routing helper determines the path is /purchases/{id}/edit.

The third link_to links seemingly to the purchase object exactly as the first, but it doesn't go there. The :method option on the end of this route specifies the method of :delete, which is the third and final way the /purchases/{id} route can be used. If you specify :delete as the method of this link_to, Rails interprets this request and takes you to the destroy action in the PurchasesController. This action is shown in the following listing.

Listing 1.17   app/controllers/purchases_controller.rb

```ruby
def destroy
  @purchase = Purchase.find(params[:id])
  @purchase.destroy

  respond_to do |format|
    format.html { redirect_to(purchases_url) }
    format.xml  { head :ok }
  end
end
```

Just as in the show, edit, and update actions shown earlier, this action finds the @purchase object by using Purchase.find and then destroys the record by calling destroy on it, which permanently deletes the record. Then it uses redirect_to to take you to the purchases_url, which is the route helper defined to take you to http:// localhost:3000/purchases. Note that this action uses the purchases_url method rather than purchases_path, which generate a full URL back to the purchases listing, such as http://localhost:3000/purchases/1.

That wraps up our application run-through!

1.3   *Summary*

In this chapter you learned what Rails is and how to get an application started with it, the absolute bare, bare, *bare* essentials of a Rails application. But look how fast you got going! It took only a few simple commands and an entire two lines of your own code to get the bones of a Rails application going. From this basic skeleton, you can keep adding on bits and pieces to develop your application, and all the while you get things for free from Rails. You don't have to code the logic of what happens when Rails receives a request or specify what query to execute on your database to insert a record—Rails does it for you.

You also saw that some big-name players—such as Twitter and GitHub—use Ruby on Rails. This clearly answers the question "Is Rails ready?" Yes, it very much is. A wide range of companies have built successful websites on the Rails framework, and a lot more will do so in the future.

Still wondering if Ruby on Rails is right for you? Ask around. You'll hear a lot of people singing its praises. The Ruby on Rails community is passionate not only about Rails but also about community building. Events, conferences, user group meetings, and even camps are held all around the world for Rails. Attend these and discuss Ruby on Rails with the people who know about it. If you can't attend these events, you can explore the IRC channel on Freenode *#rubyonrails*, the mailing list *rubyonrails-talk* on Google Groups, not to mention Stack Overflow and a multitude of other areas on the internet where you can discuss with experienced people what they think of Rails. Don't let this book be the only source for your knowledge. There's a whole world out there, and no book could cover it all!

The best way to answer the question "What is Rails?" is to experience it for yourself. This book and your own exploration can eventually make you a Ruby on Rails expert.

When you added validations to your application earlier, you manually tested that they were working. This may seem like a good idea for now, but when the application grows beyond a couple of pages, it becomes cumbersome to manually test them. Wouldn't it be nice to have some automated way of testing your applications? Something to ensure that all the individual parts always work? Something to provide the peace of mind that you crave when you develop anything? You want to be sure that it's continuously working with the most minimal effort possible, right?

Well, Ruby on Rails does that too. There are several testing frameworks for Ruby and Ruby on Rails, and in chapter 2 we look at three of them: Test::Unit, RSpec, and Cucumber.

Testing saves your bacon

2

This chapter covers

- Writing tests with RSpec and Cucumber
- Maintaining code through tests
- Test- and behavior-driven development

Chapter 1 presented an extremely basic layout of a Rails application and an example of the scaffold generator.[1] One question remains, though: how do you make your Rails applications maintainable?

The answer is that you write automated tests for the application as you develop it, and you write these all the time.

By writing automated tests for your application, you can quickly ensure that your application is working as intended. If you didn't write tests, your alternative would be to check the entire application manually, which is time consuming and error prone. Automated testing saves you a ton of time in the long run and leads to fewer bugs. Humans make mistakes; programs (if coded correctly) do not. We're going to be doing it right from step one.[2]

---

[1] We won't use the scaffold generator for the rest of the book because people tend to use it as a crutch, and it generates extraneous code.

[2] Unlike certain other books.

2.1   *Test- and behavior-driven development*

In the Ruby world a huge emphasis is placed on testing, specifically on *test-driven development* (TDD) and *behavior-driven development* (BDD). This chapter covers three testing tools, Test::Unit, RSpec, and Cucumber, in a basic fashion so you can quickly learn their format.

By learning good testing techniques now, you've got a solid way to make sure nothing is broken when you start to write your first real Rails application. If you didn't test, there's no telling what could go wrong in your code.

TDD is a methodology consisting of writing a failing test case first (usually using a testing tool such as *Test::Unit*), then writing the code to make the test pass, and finally refactoring the code. This process is commonly called *red-green-refactor*. The reasons for developing code this way are twofold. First, it makes you consider how the code should be running before it is used by anybody. Second, it gives you an automated test you can run as often as you like to ensure your code is still working as you intended. We'll be using the Test::Unit tool for TDD.

BDD is a methodology based on TDD. You write an automated test to check the interaction between the different parts of the codebase rather than testing that each part works independently.

The two tools used for BDD are *RSpec* and *Cucumber*, both of which this book uses heavily.

Let's begin by looking at TDD and Test::Unit.

2.2   *Test-driven development*

A cryptic yet true answer to the question "Why should I test?" is "because you are human." Humans—the large majority of this book's audience—make mistakes. It's one of our favorite ways to learn. Because humans make mistakes, having a tool to inform them when they make one is helpful, isn't it? Automated testing provides a quick safety net to inform developers when they make mistakes. By they, of course, we mean you. We want you to make as few mistakes as possible. We want you to save your bacon!

TDD and BDD also give you time to think through your decisions before you write any code. By first writing the test for the implementation, you are (or, at least, you should be) thinking through the implementation: the code you'll write *after* the test and how you'll make the test passes. If you find the test difficult to write, then perhaps the implementation could be improved. Unfortunately, there's no clear way to quantify the difficulty of writing a test and working through it other than to consult with other people who are familiar with the process.

Once the test is implemented, you should go about writing some code that your test can pass. If you find yourself working backward—rewriting your test to fit a buggy implementation—it's generally best to rethink the test and scrap the implementation. Test first, code later.

2.2.1   Why test?

Automated testing is much, much easier than manual testing. Have you ever gone through a website and manually filled in a form with specific values to make sure it conforms to your expectations? Wouldn't it be faster and easier to have the computer do this work? Yes, it would, and that's the beauty of automated testing: you won't spend your time manually testing your code because you'll have written test code to do that for you.

On the off chance you break something, the tests are there to tell you the what, when, how, and why of the breakage. Although tests can never be 100% guaranteed, your chances of getting this information without first having written tests are 0%. Nothing is worse than finding out something is broken through an early-morning phone call from an angry customer. Tests work toward preventing such scenarios by giving you and your client peace of mind. If the tests aren't broken, chances are high (though not guaranteed) that the implementation isn't either.

You'll likely at some point face a situation in which something in your application breaks when a user attempts to perform an action you didn't consider in your tests. With a base of tests, you can easily duplicate the scenario in which the user encountered the breakage, generate your own failed test, and use this information to fix the bug. This commonly used practice is called *regression testing*.

It's valuable to have a solid base of tests in the application so you can spend time developing new features *properly* rather than fixing the old ones you didn't do quite right. An application without tests is most likely broken in one way or another.

2.2.2   *Writing your first test*

The first testing library for Ruby was Test::Unit, which was written by Nathaniel Talbott back in 2000 and is now part of the Ruby core library. The documentation for this library gives a fantastic overview of its purpose, as summarized by the man himself:

> *The general idea behind unit testing is that you write a test method that makes certain assertions about your code, working against a test fixture. A bunch of these test methods are bundled up into a test suite and can be run any time the developer wants. The results of a run are gathered in a test result and displayed to the user through some* UI.
>
> —Nathaniel Talbott

The UI Talbott references could be a terminal, a web page, or even a light.[3]

A common practice you'll hopefully by now have experienced in the Ruby world is to let the libraries do a lot of the hard work for you. Sure, you *could* write a file yourself that loads one of your other files and runs a method and makes sure it works, but why do that when Test::Unit already provides that functionality for such little cost? Never re-invent the wheel when somebody's done it for you.

Now you're going to write a test, and you'll write the code for it later. Welcome to TDD.

---

[3]   Such as the one GitHub has made: http://github.com/blog/653-our-new-build-status-indicator.

To try out Test::Unit, first create a new directory called example and in that directory make a file called example_test.rb. It's good practice to suffix your filenames with _test so it's obvious from the filename that it's a test file. In this file, you're going to define the most basic test possible, as shown in the following listing.

Listing 2.1   example/example_test.rb

```
require 'test/unit'

class ExampleTest < Test::Unit::TestCase
  def test_truth
    assert true
  end
end
```

To make this a Test::Unit test, you begin by requiring test/unit, which is part of Ruby's standard library. This provides the Test::Unit::TestCase class inherited from on the next line. Inheriting from this class provides the functionality to run any method defined in this class whose name begins with test. Additionally, you can define tests by using the test method:

```
test "truth" do
  assert true
end
```

To run this file, you run ruby example_test.rb in the terminal. When this command completes, you see some output, the most relevant being two of the lines in the middle:

```
.
1 tests, 1 assertions, 0 failures, 0 errors, 0 skips
```

The first line is a singular period. This is Test::Unit's way of indicating that it ran a test and the test passed. If the test had failed, it would show up as an F; if it had errored, an E. The second line provides statistics on what happened, specifically that there was one test and one assertion, and that nothing failed, there were no errors, and nothing was skipped. Great success!

The assert method in your test makes an assertion that the argument passed to it evaluates to true. This test passes given anything that's not nil or false. When this method fails, it fails the test and raises an exception. Go ahead, try putting 1 there instead of true. It still works:

```
.
1 tests, 1 assertions, 0 failures, 0 errors, 0 skips
```

In the following listing, you remove the test_ from the beginning of your method and define it as simply a truth method.

Listing 2.2   example/example_test.rb, alternate truth test

```
def truth
  assert true
end
```

Test::Unit tells you there were no tests specified by running the `default_test` method internal to Test::Unit:

```
No tests were specified.
1 tests, 1 assertions, 1 failures, 0 errors
```

Remember to always prefix Test::Unit methods with `test`!

2.2.3 Saving bacon

Let's make this a little more complex by creating a bacon_test.rb file and writing the test shown in the following listing.

Listing 2.3 example/bacon_test.rb

```
require 'test/unit'
class BaconTest < Test::Unit::TestCase
  def test_saved
    assert Bacon.saved?
  end
end
```

Of course, you want to ensure that your bacon[4] is always saved, and this is how you do it. If you now run the command to run this file, `ruby bacon_test.rb`, you get an error:

```
NameError: uninitialized constant BaconTest::Bacon
```

Your test is looking for a constant called `Bacon` and cannot find it because you haven't yet defined the constant. For this test, the constant you want to define is a `Bacon` class. You can define this new class before or after the test. Note that in Ruby you usually must define constants and variables before you use them. In Test::Unit tests, the code is only run when it finishes evaluating it, which means you can define the `Bacon` class after the test. In the next listing, you follow the more conventional method of defining the class above the test.

Listing 2.4 example/bacon_test.rb

```
require 'test/unit'
class Bacon

end
class BaconTest < Test::Unit::TestCase
  def test_saved
    assert Bacon.saved?
  end
end
```

Upon rerunning the test, you get a different error:

```
NoMethodError: undefined method `saved?' for Bacon:Class
```

---

[4] Both the metaphorical and the crispy kinds.

Progress! It recognizes there's now a `Bacon` class, but there's no `saved?` method for this class, so you must define one, as in the following listing.

```
class Bacon
  def self.saved?
    true
  end
end
```

One more run of `ruby bacon_test.rb` and you can see that the test is now passing:

```
.
1 tests, 1 assertions, 0 failures, 0 errors, 0 skips
```

Your bacon is indeed saved! Now any time that you want to check if it's saved, you can run this file. If somebody else comes along and changes that `true` value to a `false`, then the test will fail:

```
F

  1) Failure:
test_saved(BaconTest) [bacon_test.rb:11]:
Failed assertion, no message given.
```

Test::Unit reports "Failed assertion, no message given" when an assertion fails. You should probably make that error message clearer! To do so, you can specify an additional argument to the `assert` method in your test, like this:

```
assert Bacon.saved?, "Our bacon was not saved :("
```

Now when you run the test, you get a clearer error message:

```
  1) Failure:
test_saved(BaconTest) [bacon_test.rb:11]:
Our bacon was not saved :(
```

And that, my friend, is the basics of TDD using Test::Unit. Although we don't use this method in the book, it's handy to know about because it establishes the basis for TDD in Ruby in case you wish to use it in the future. Test::Unit is also the default testing framework for Rails, so you may see it around in your travels. From this point on, we focus on RSpec and Cucumber, the two gems you'll be using when you develop your next Rails application.

2.3   *Behavior-driven development*

BDD is similar to TDD, but the tests for BDD are written in an easier-to-understand language so that developers and clients alike can clearly understand what is being tested. The two tools we cover for BDD are RSpec and Cucumber.

RSpec tests are written in a Ruby domain-specific language (DSL), like this:

```
describe Bacon do
  it "is edible" do
```

```
      Bacon.edible?.should be_true
    end
  end
```

The benefits of writing tests like this are that clients can understand precisely what the test is testing and then use these steps in acceptance testing;[5] a developer can read what the feature should do and then implement it; and finally, the test can be run as an automated test. With tests written in DSL, you have the three important elements of your business (the clients, the developers, and the code) all operating in the same language.

RSpec is an extension of the methods already provided by Test::Unit. You can even use Test::Unit methods inside of RSpec tests if you wish. But we're going to use the simpler, easier-to-understand syntax that RSpec provides.

Cucumber tests are written in a language called *Gherkin*, which goes like this:

```
Given I am reading a book
When I read this example
Then I should learn something
```

Each line indicates a *step*. The benefit of writing tests in the Gherkin language is that it's closer to English than RSpec is, making it even easier for clients and developers to read.

2.3.1 RSpec

RSpec is a BDD tool written by Steven R. Baker and now maintained by David Chelimsky as a cleaner alternative to Test::Unit, with RSpec being built as an extension to Test::Unit. With RSpec, you write code known as *specs* that contain *examples*, which are synonymous to the *tests* you know from Test::Unit. In this example, you're going to define the Bacon constant and then define the edible? method on it.

Let's jump right in and install the rspec gem by running gem install rspec. You should see the following output:

```
Successfully installed rspec-core-2.6.4
Successfully installed rspec-expectations-2.6.4
Successfully installed rspec-mocks-2.6.4
Successfully installed rspec-2.6.4
```

You can see that the final line says the rspec gem is installed, with the version number specified after the name. Above this line, you also see a thank-you message and, underneath, the other gems that were installed. These gems are dependencies of the rspec gem, and as such, the rspec gem won't work without them.

When the gem is installed, create a new directory for your tests called bacon anywhere you like, and inside that, create another directory called spec. If you're running a UNIX-based operating system such as Linux or Mac OS X, you can run the mkdir -p bacon/spec command to create these two directories. This command will

---

[5] A process whereby people follow a set of instructions to ensure a feature is performing as intended.

generate a bacon directory if it doesn't already exist, and then generate in that directory a spec directory.

Inside the spec directory, create a file called bacon_spec.rb. This is the file you use to test your currently nonexistent Bacon class. Put the code from the following listing in spec/bacon_spec.rb.

Listing 2.6   bacon/spec/bacon_spec.rb

```
describe Bacon do
  it "is edible" do
    Bacon.edible?.should be_true
  end

end
```

You describe the (undefined) Bacon class and write an example for it, declaring that Bacon is edible. The describe block contains tests (examples) that describe the behavior of bacon. In this example, whenever you call edible? on Bacon, the result should be true. should serves a similar purpose to assert, which is to assert that its object matches the arguments passed to it. If the outcome is not what you say it should be, then RSpec raises an error and goes no further with that spec.

To run the spec, you run rspec spec in a terminal in the root of your bacon directory. You specify the spec directory as the first argument of this command so RSpec will run all the tests within that directory. This command can also take files as its arguments if you want to run tests only from those files.

When you run this spec, you get an uninitialized constant Object::Bacon error, because you haven't yet defined your Bacon constant. To define it, create another directory inside your Bacon project folder called lib, and inside this directory, create a file called bacon.rb. This is the file where you define the Bacon constant, a class, as in the following listing.

Listing 2.7   bacon/lib/bacon.rb

```
class Bacon

end
```

You can now require this file in spec/bacon_spec.rb by placing the following line at the top of the file:

```
require 'bacon'
```

When you run your spec again, because you told it to load bacon, RSpec has added the lib directory on the same level as the spec directory to Ruby's load path, and so it will find the lib/bacon.rb for your require. By requiring the lib/bacon.rb file, you ensure the Bacon constant is defined. The next time you run it, you get an undefined method for your new constant:

```
1) Bacon is edible
   Failure/Error: Bacon.edible?.should be_true
```

```
NoMethodError:
  undefined method `edible?' for Bacon:Class
```

This means you need to define the edible? method on your Bacon class. Re-open lib/
bacon.rb and add this method definition to the class:

```
def self.edible?
  true
end
```

Now the entire file looks like the following listing.

Listing 2.8   bacon/lib/bacon.rb

```
class Bacon
  def self.edible?
    true
  end
end
```

By defining the method as self.edible?, you define it for the class. If you didn't prefix the method with self., it would define the method for an instance of the class
rather than for the class itself. Running rspec spec now outputs a period, which indicates the test has passed. That's the first test—done.

   For the next test, you want to create many instances of the Bacon class and have the
edible? method defined on them. To do this, open lib/bacon.rb and change the
edible? class method to an instance method by removing the self. from before the
method, as in the next listing.

Listing 2.9   bacon/lib/bacon.rb

```
class Bacon
  def edible?
    true
  end
end
```

When you run rspec spec again, you get the familiar error:

```
1) Bacon edible?
   Failure/Error: its(:edible?) { should be_true }
     expected false to be true
```

Oops! You broke a test! You should be changing the spec to suit your new ideas before
changing the code! Let's reverse the changes made in lib/bacon.rb, as in the following
listing.

Listing 2.10   bacon/lib/bacon.rb

```
class Bacon
  def self.edible?
    true
  end
end
```

When you run `rspec spec`, it passes. Now let's change the spec first, as in the next listing.

Listing 2.11   bacon/spec/bacon_spec.rb

```
describe Bacon do
  it "is edible" do
    Bacon.new.edible?.should be_true
  end
end
```

In this code, you instantiate a new object of the class rather than using the `Bacon` class. When you run `rspec spec`, it breaks once again:

```
NoMethodError in 'Bacon is edible'
undefined method `edible?' for #<Bacon:0x101deff38>
```

If you remove the `self.` from the `edible?` method, your test will now pass, as in the following listing.

Listing 2.12   Terminal

```
$ rspec spec
.
1 example, 0 failures
```

Now you can go about breaking your test once more by adding additional functionality: an `expired!` method, which will make your bacon inedible. This method sets an instance variable on the `Bacon` object called `@expired` to `true`, and you use it in your `edible?` method to check the bacon's status.

First you must test that this `expired!` method is going to actually do what you think it should do. Create another example in spec/bacon_spec.rb so that the whole file now looks like the following listing.

Listing 2.13   bacon/spec/bacon_spec.rb

```
require 'bacon'
describe Bacon do
  it "is edible" do
    Bacon.new.edible?.should be_true
  end

  it "expired!" do
    bacon = Bacon.new
    bacon.expired!
    bacon.should be_expired
  end
end
```

When you find you're repeating yourself, stop! You can see here that you're defining a bacon variable to `Bacon.new` and that you're also using `Bacon.new` in the first example. You shouldn't be repeating yourself like that!

A nice way to tidy this up is to move the call to `Bacon.new` into a `subject` block. `subject` calls allow you to create an object to reference in all specs inside the `describe` block,[6] declaring it the subject (both literally and figuratively) of all the tests inside the `describe` block. You can define a subject like this:

```
subject { Bacon.new }
```

In the context of the entire spec, it looks like the following listing.

Listing 2.14   bacon/spec/bacon_spec.rb

```
require 'bacon'

describe Bacon do

  subject { Bacon.new }

  it "is edible" do
    Bacon.new.edible?.should be_true
  end

  it "expired!" do
    bacon = Bacon.new
    bacon.expired!
    bacon.expired.should be_true
  end
end
```

Now that you have the subject, you can cut a lot of the code out of the first spec and refine it:

```
its(:edible?) { should be_true }
```

First, the `its` method takes the name of a method to call on the subject of these tests. The block specified should contain an assertion for the output of that method. Unlike before, you're not calling `should` on an object, as you have done in previous tests, but rather on seemingly nothing at all. If you do this, RSpec figures out that you mean the subject you defined, so it calls `should` on that.

You can also reference the `subject` manually in your tests, as you'll see when you write the `expired!` example shown in the following listing.

Listing 2.15   bacon/spec/bacon_spec.rb

```
it "expired!" do
  subject.expired!
  subject.should_not be_edible
end
```

Here, the `expired!` method must be called on the `subject` because it is only defined on your `Bacon` class. For readability's sake, you explicitly call the `should_not` method on the `subject` and specify that `edible?` should return `false`.

---

[6] Or inside a `context` block, which we use later. It works in a similar way to the `describe` blocks.

If you run `rspec spec` again, your first spec still passes, but your second one fails because you have yet to define your `expired!` method. Let's do that now in lib/bacon.rb, as shown in the following listing.

Listing 2.16   bacon/lib/bacon.rb

```
class Bacon
  def edible?
    true
  end

  def expired!
    self.expired = true
  end
end
```

By running `rspec spec` again, you get an `undefined method` error:

```
NoMethodError in 'Bacon expired!'
undefined method `expired=' for #<Bacon:0x101de6578>
```

This method is called by the following line in the previous example:

```
self.expired = true
```

To define this method, you can use the `attr_accessor` method provided by Ruby, as shown in listing 2.17; the `attr` prefix of the method means attribute. If you pass a `Symbol` (or collection of symbols) to this method, it defines methods for setting (expired=) and retrieving the attribute `expired` values, referred to as a *setter* and a *getter* respectively. It also defines an instance variable called @expired on every object of this class to store the value that was specified by the `expired=` method calls.

> **WARNING**   In Ruby you can call methods without the `self.` prefix. You specify the prefix because otherwise the interpreter will think that you're defining a *local variable*. The rule for setter methods is that you should always use the prefix.

Listing 2.17   bacon/lib/bacon.rb

```
class Bacon
  attr_accessor :expired
  ...
end
```

With this in place, if you run `rspec spec` again, your example fails on the line following your previous failure:

```
Failure/Error: subject.should_not be_edible
  expected edible? to return false, got true
```

Even though this sets the `expired` attribute on the `Bacon` object, you've still hard-coded true in your `edible?` method. Now change the method to use the attribute method, as in the following listing.

Listing 2.18   bacon/lib/bacon.rb

```
def edible?
  !expired
end
```

When you run `rspec spec` again, both your specs will pass:

```
..

2 examples, 0 failures
```

Let's go back in to lib/bacon.rb and remove the `self.` from the `expired!` method:

```
def expired!
  expired = true
end
```

If you run `rspec spec` again, you'll see your second spec is now broken:

```
Failure/Error: Bacon expired!
expected edible? to return false, got true
```

Tests save you from making mistakes such as this. If you write the test first and then write the code to make the test pass, you have a solid base and can refactor the code to be clearer or smaller and finally ensure that it's still working with the test you wrote in the first place. If the test still passes, then you're probably doing it right.

If you change this method back now

```
def expired!
  self.expired = true
end
```

and then run your specs using `rspec spec`, you'll see that they once again pass:

```
..

2 examples, 0 failures
```

Everything's normal and working once again, which is great!

That ends our little foray into RSpec for now. You'll use it again later when you develop your application. If you'd like to know more about RSpec, *The RSpec Book: Behavior-Driven Development with RSpec, Cucumber, and Friends* (David Chelimsky et al., Pragmatic Bookshelf, 2010) is recommended reading.

2.3.2   *Cucumber*

For this section, we retire the `Bacon` example and go for something more formal with Cucumber.

> **NOTE**   This section assumes you have RSpec installed. If you don't, use this command to install it: `gem install rspec`.

Whereas RSpec and Test::Unit are great for *unit testing* (testing a single part), Cucumber is mostly used for testing the entire integration stack.

Cucumber's history is intertwined with RSpec, so the two are similar. In the beginning of BDD, as you know, there was RSpec. Shortly thereafter, there were RSpec Stories, which looked like the following listing.

Listing 2.19 Example

```
Scenario "savings account is in credit" do
  Given "my savings account balance is", 100 do |balance|
    @account = Account.new(balance)
  end
  ...
end
```

The idea behind RSpec Stories is that they are code- and human-readable stories that can be used for automated testing as well as quality assurance (QA) testing by stakeholders. Aslak Hellesoy rewrote RSpec Stories during October 2008 into what we know today as Cucumber. The syntax remains similar, as seen in the following listing.

Listing 2.20 Example

```
Scenario: Taking out money
  Given I have an account
  And my account balance is 100
  When I take out 10
  Then my account balance should be 90
```

What you see here is known as a *scenario* in Cucumber. Under the scenario's title, the remainder of the lines are called *steps*, which are read by Cucumber's parser and matched to *step definitions*, where the logic is kept. Scenarios are found inside a *feature*, which is a collection of common scenarios. For example, you may have one feature for dictating what happens when a user creates projects and another for when a user creates tickets.

Notice the keywords `Given`, `And`, `When`, and `Then`. These are just some of the keywords that Cucumber looks for to indicate that a line is a step. If you're going to be using the same keyword on a new line, it's best practice to instead use the `And` keyword because it reads better. Try reading the first two lines aloud from the previous listing, then replace the `And` with `Given` and try it again. It just sounds *right* to have an `And` there rather than a `Given`.

`Given` steps are used for setting up the scene for the scenario. This example sets up an account and gives it a balance of 100.

`When` steps are used for defining actions that should happen during the scenario. The example says, `When I take out 10`.

`Then` steps are used for declaring things that take place after the `When` steps have completed. This example says, `When I take out 10 Then my account balance should be 90`.

These different step types add a great deal of human readability to the scenarios in which they're used, even though they can be used interchangeably. You could define all the steps as `Givens`, but it's not really readable. Let's now implement this example scenario in Cucumber. First, run `mkdir -p accounts/features`, which, much as in the RSpec example, creates a directory called accounts and a directory inside of that called features. In this features directory, create a file called account.feature. In this file, you write a feature definition, as shown in the following listing.

Listing 2.21   accounts/features/account.feature

```
Feature: My Account
  In order to manage my account
  As a money minder
  I want to ensure my money doesn't get lost
```

This listing lays out what this feature is about and is more useful to human readers (such as stakeholders) than it is to Cucumber.

Next, you put in your scenario underneath the feature definition, as in the following listing.

Listing 2.22   accounts/features/account.feature

```
Scenario: Taking out money
  Given I have an account
  And it has a balance of 100
  When I take out 10
  Then my balance should be 90
```

The whole feature should now look like the following listing.

Listing 2.23   accounts/features/account.feature

```
Feature: My Account
  In order to manage my account
  As a money minder
  I want to ensure my money doesn't get lost

  Scenario: Taking out money
    Given I have an account
    And it has a balance of 100
    When I take out 10
    Then my balance should be 90
```

As you can see in listing 2.23, it's testing the whole stack of the transaction rather than a single unit. This process is called *integration testing*. You set the stage by using the `Given` steps, play out the scenario using `When` steps, and ensure that the outcome is as you expected by using `Then` steps. The `And` word is used when you want a step to be defined in the same way as the previous step, as seen in the first two lines of this scenario.

To run this file, you first need to ensure Cucumber is installed, which you can do by installing the Cucumber gem: `gem install cucumber`. When the Cucumber gem is installed, you can run this feature file by going into the accounts directory and running `cucumber features`, as in the next listing.

Listing 2.24   Terminal

```
Feature: My Account
  In order to manage my account
  As a money minder
  I want to ensure my money doesn't get lost

  Scenario: Taking out money
    Given I have an account
    And it has a balance of 100
    When I take out 10
    Then my balance should be 90
```

This output appears in color in the terminal with the steps of the scenario in yellow,[7] followed by a summary of this Cucumber run, and then a list of what code you used to define the missing steps (not shown in this example output), again in yellow. What this output doesn't tell you is *where* to put the step definitions. Luckily, this book does. All these step definitions should go into a new file located at features/step_definitions/account_steps.rb. The file is called account_steps.rb and not account.rb to clearly separate it from any other Ruby files, so when looking for the steps file, you don't get it confused with any other file. In this file, you can copy and paste in the steps Cucumber gave you, as in the following listing.

Listing 2.25   features/step_definitions/account_steps.rb

```
Given /^I have an account$/ do
  pending # express the regexp above with the code you wish you had
end

Given /^it has a balance of (\d+)$/ do |arg1|
  pending # express the regexp above with the code you wish you had
end

When /^I take out (\d+)$/ do |arg1|
  pending # express the regexp above with the code you wish you had
end

Then /^my balance should be (\d+)$/ do |arg1|
  pending # express the regexp above with the code you wish you had
end
```

If you run cucumber features again, you'll see that all your steps are defined but not run (signaled by their blue coloring) except the very first one, which is yellow because it's pending. Now you're going to restructure the first step to make it not pending. It will now instantiate an Account object that you'll use for the rest of this scenario.

---

[7] If you're running Windows, you may need to install ANSICON in order to get the colored output. This process is described at https://github.com/adoxa/ansicon, and you can download ANSICON from http://adoxa.110mb.com/ansicon/.

Listing 2.26   features/step_definitions/account_steps.rb

```
Given /^I have an account$/ do
  @account = Account.new
end
```

Steps are defined by using *regular expressions,* which are used when you wish to match strings. In this case, you're matching the *step* in the feature with this *step definition* by putting the text after the `Given` keyword into a regular expression. After the regular expression is the do Ruby keyword, which matches up with the `end` at the end. This syntax indicates a *block*, and this block is run ("called") when this step definition is matched.

With this step defined, you can try running `cucumber features/account.feature` to see if the feature will pass. No—it fails with this error:

```
Given I have an account
  uninitialized constant Object::Account (NameError)
```

Similar to the beginning of the RSpec showcase, create a lib directory inside your accounts directory. To define this constant, you create a file in this new directory called account.rb. In this file you put code to define the class, shown in the following listing.

Listing 2.27   accounts/lib/account.rb

```
class Account

end
```

This file is not loaded automatically, of course: you have to require it just as you did in RSpec with lib/bacon.rb. Cucumber's authors already thought of this and came up with a solution. Any file inside of features/support is automatically loaded, with one special file being loaded before all the others: features/support/env.rb. This file should be responsible for setting up the foundations for your tests. Now create features/support/env.rb and put these lines inside it:

```
$LOAD_PATH << File.expand_path('../../../lib', __FILE__)
require 'account'
```

When you run this feature again, the first step passes and the second one is pending:

```
Scenario: Taking out money
  Given I have an account
  And it has a balance of 100
    TODO (Cucumber::Pending)
```

Go back into features/step_definitions/account_steps.rb now and change the second step's code to set the balance on your `@account` object, as shown in the next listing. Note in this listing that you change the block argument from `arg1` to `amount`.

Listing 2.28   features/step_definitions/account_steps.rb

```ruby
Given /^it has a balance of (\d+)$/ do |amount|
  @account.balance = amount
end
```

With this step, you've used a *capture group* inside the regular expression. The capture group captures whatever it matches. In Cucumber, the match is returned as a variable, which is then used in the block. An important thing to remember is that these variables are always `String` objects.

When you run this feature again, this step fails because you haven't yet defined the method on the `Account` class:

```
And it has a balance of 100
  undefined method `balance=' for #<Account:0xb7297b94> (NoMethodError)
```

To define this method, open lib/account.rb and change the code in this file to look exactly like the following listing.

Listing 2.29   accounts/lib/account.rb

```ruby
class Account
  def balance=(amount)
    @balance = amount
  end
end
```

The method is defined as `balance=`. In Ruby, these methods are called *setter* methods and, just as their name suggests, they're used for setting things. Setter methods are defined *without* the space between the method name and the = sign, but they can be called with or without the space, like this:

```ruby
@account.balance=100
# or
@account.balance = 100
```

The object after the equals sign is passed in as the single argument for this method. In this method, you set the `@balance` instance variable to that value. Now when you run your feature, this step passes and the third one is the pending one:

```
Scenario: Taking out money
  Given I have an account
  And it has a balance of 100
  When I take out 10
    TODO (Cucumber::Pending)
```

Go back into features/step_definitions/account_steps.rb and change the third step to take some money from your account:

```ruby
When /^I take out (\d+)$/ do |amount|
  @account.balance = @account.balance - amount
end
```

Now when you run this feature, it'll tell you there's an undefined method `balance`, but didn't you just define that?

```
When I take out 10
  undefined method `balance' for #<Account:0xb71c9a8c
                                    @balance=100> (NoMethodError)
```

Actually, the method you defined was `balance=` (with an equals sign), which is a setter method. `balance` (*without* an equals sign) in this example is a *getter* method, which is used for retrieving the variable you set in the setter method. Not all methods without equal signs are getter methods, however. To define this method, switch back into lib/account.rb and add this new method directly under the setter method, as shown in the following listing.

Listing 2.30   accounts/lib/account.rb

```
def balance=(amount)
  @balance = amount
end
def balance
  @balance
end
```

Here you define the `balance=` and `balance` methods you need. The first method is a *setter* method, which is used to set the @balance instance variable on an `Account` object to a specified value. The `balance` method returns that specific balance. When you run this feature again, you'll see a new error:

```
When I take out 10
  String can't be coerced into Fixnum (TypeError)
  ./features/step_definitions/account_steps.rb:10:in `-'
```

This error occurred because you're not storing the balance as a `Fixnum` but as a `String`. As mentioned earlier, the variable returned from the capture group for the second step definition is a `String`. To fix this, you coerce the object into a `Fixnum` by calling `to_i`[8] inside the setter method, as shown in the following listing.

Listing 2.31   accounts/lib/account.rb

```
def balance=(amount)
  @balance = amount.to_i
end
```

Now anything passed to the `balance=` method will be coerced into an integer. You also want to ensure that the other value is also a `Fixnum`. To do this, open features/step_definitions/account_steps.rb and change the third step to look exactly like the following listing.

---

[8] For the sake of simplicity, we use `to_i`. Some will argue that `to_f` (converting to a floating-point number) is better to use for money. They'd be right. This is not a real-world system, only a contrived example. Chill.

Listing 2.32   features/step_definitions/account_steps.rb

```
When /^I take out (\d+)$/ do |amount|
  @account.balance -= amount.to_i
end
```

That makes this third step pass, because you're subtracting a `Fixnum` from a `Fixnum`. When you run this feature, you'll see that this step is definitely passing and the final step is now pending:

```
Scenario: Taking out money
  Given I have an account
  And it has a balance of 100
  When I take out 10
  Then my balance should be 90
    TODO (Cucumber::Pending)
```

This final step asserts that your account balance is now 90. You can implement it in features/step_definitions/account_steps.rb, as shown in the following listing.

Listing 2.33   features/step_definitions/account_steps.rb

```
Then /^my balance should be (\d+)$/ do |amount|
  @account.balance.should eql(amount.to_i)
end
```

Here you must coerce the `amount` variable into a `Fixnum` again so you're comparing a `Fixnum` with a `Fixnum`. With this fourth and final step implemented, your entire scenario (which also means your entire feature) passes:

```
Scenario: Taking out money
  Given I have an account
  And it has a balance of 100
  When I take out 10
  Then my balance should be 90

1 scenario (1 passed)
4 steps (4 passed)
```

As you can see from this example, Cucumber allows you to write tests for your code in syntax that can be understood by developers, clients, and parsers alike. You'll see a lot more of Cucumber when you use it in building your next Ruby on Rails application.

2.4   Summary

This chapter demonstrated how to apply TDD and BDD principles to test some rudimentary code. You can (and should!) apply these principles to all code you write, because testing the code ensures it's maintainable from now into the future. You don't have to use the gems shown in this chapter to test your Rails application; they are just preferred by a large portion of the community.

You'll apply what you learned in this chapter to building a Rails application from scratch in upcoming chapters. You'll use Cucumber from the outset by developing features to describe the behavior of your application and then implementing the necessary steps to make them pass. Thankfully, there's another gem that generates some of these steps for you.

When you wish to test that a specific controller action is inaccessible, you use RSpec because it's better suited for single-request testing. You use Cucumber when you want to test a series of requests, such as when creating a project. You'll see plenty of examples of when to use Cucumber and when to use RSpec in later chapters.

Let's get into it!

Developing a real
Rails application

This chapter covers

- Building the foundation for a major app
- Diving deep into app foundations
- Generating the first functionality for an app

This chapter gets you started on building a Ruby on Rails application from scratch using the techniques covered in the previous chapter plus a couple of new ones. With the techniques you learned in chapter 2, you can write features describing the behavior of the specific actions in your application and then implement the code you need to get the feature passing.

For the remainder of the book, this application is the main focus. We guide you through it in an Agile-like fashion. Agile focuses largely on iterative development, developing one feature at a time from start to finish, then refining the feature until it's viewed as complete before moving on to the next one.[1]

---

[1] More information about Agile can be found on Wikipedia: http://en.wikipedia.org/wiki/Agile_software _development.

Some of the concepts covered in this chapter were explained in chapter 1. Rather than using scaffolding, as you did previously, you write this application from the ground up using the behavior-driven development (BDD) process and other generators provided by Rails.

The scaffold generator is great for prototyping, but it's less than ideal for delivering simple, well-tested code that works precisely the way you want it to work. The code provided by the scaffold generator often may differ from the code you want. In this case, you can turn to Rails for lightweight alternatives to the scaffold code options, and you'll likely end up with cleaner, better code.

First, you need to set up your application!

3.1 Application setup

Chapter 1 explained how to quickly start a Rails application. This chapter explains a couple of additional processes that improve the flow of your application development. One process uses BDD to create the features of the application; the other process uses version control. Both will make your life easier.

3.1.1 The application story

Your client may have a good idea of the application they want you to develop. How can you transform the idea in your client's brain into beautifully formed code? First, you sit down with your client and talk through the parts of the application. In the programming business, we call these parts *stories*, and we use Cucumber to develop the stories.

Start with the most basic story and ask your client how they want it to behave. Then write the Cucumber scenario for it using the client's own terms. You define the step definitions when it's time to implement the *function* of the story. The client can also provide helpful information about the *form*—what the application should look like. With the function and form laid out, you have a pretty good idea of what the client wants.

You may find it helpful to put these stories into a system such as Pivotal Tracker (http://pivotaltracker.com) so you can keep track of them. Pivotal Tracker allows you to assign points of difficulty to a story and then, over a period of weeks, estimate which stories can be accomplished in the next iteration on the basis of how many were completed in previous weeks. This tool is exceptionally handy to use when working with clients because the client can enter stories and then follow the workflow process. In this book, we don't use Pivotal Tracker because we aren't working with a real client, but this method is highly recommended.

For this example application, your imaginary client, who has limitless time and budget (unlike those in the real world), wants you to develop a ticket-tracking application to track the company's numerous projects. You'll develop this application using the methodologies outlined in chapter 2: you'll work iteratively, delivering small working pieces of the software to the client and then gathering the client's feedback to improve the application as necessary. If no improvement is needed, then you can move on to the next prioritized chunk of work.

BDD is used all the way through the development process. It provides the client with a stable application, and when (not if) a bug crops up, you have a nice test base you can use to determine what is broken. Then you can fix the bug so it doesn't happen again, a process called *regression testing* (mentioned in chapter 2).

As you work with your client to build the Cucumber stories, the client may ask why all of this prework is necessary. This can be a tricky question to answer. Explain that writing the tests before the code and then implementing the code to make the tests pass creates a safety net to ensure that the code is always working. Note: Tests will make your code more maintainable, but they won't make your code bug-proof.

Features also give you a clearer picture of what the clients *really* want. By having it all written down in features, you have a solid reference to point to if clients say they suggested something different. Story-driven development is simply BDD with emphasis on things a user can actually do with the system.

By using story-driven development, you know what clients want, clients know you know what they want, you have something you can run automated tests with to ensure that all the pieces are working, and finally if something *does* break, you have the test suite in place to catch it. It's a win-win-win situation.

To start building the application you'll be developing throughout this book, run the good old `rails` command, preferably outside the directory of the previous application. Call this app *ticketee*, the Australian slang for a person who checks tickets on trains. It also has to do with this project being a ticket-tracking application, and a Rails application, at that. To generate this application, run this command:

```
rails new ticketee
```

Presto, it's done! From this bare-bones application, you'll build an application that

- Tracks tickets (of course) and groups them into projects
- Provides a way to restrict users to certain projects
- Allows users to upload files to tickets
- Lets users tag tickets so they're easy to find
- Provides an API on which users can base development of their own applications

You can't do all of this with a command as simple as `rails new [application_name]`, but you can do it step by step and test it along the way so you develop a stable and worthwhile application.

Throughout the development of the application, we advise you to use a version control system. The next section covers that topic using Git. You're welcome to use any other, but this book uses Git exclusively.

> **Help!**
> If you want to see what else you can do with this `new` command (hint: there's a lot!), you can use the `--help` option:
> ```
> rails new --help
> ```
> The `--help` option shows you the options you can pass to the `new` command to modify the output of your application.

3.1.2 Version control

It is wise during development to use version control software to provide checkpoints in your code. When the code is working, you can make a commit, and if anything goes wrong later in development, you can revert to the commit. Additionally, you can create branches for experimental features and work on those independently of the main code base without damaging working code.

This book doesn't go into detail on how to use a version control system, but it does recommend using Git. Git is a distributed version control system that is easy to use and extremely powerful. If you wish to learn about Git, we recommend reading *Pro Git*, a free online book by Scott Chacon.[2]

Git is used by most developers in the Rails community and by tools such as Bundler, discussed shortly. Learning Git along with Rails is advantageous when you come across a gem or plugin that you have to install using Git. Because most of the Rails community uses Git, you can find a lot of information about how to use it with Rails (even in this book!) should you ever get stuck.

If you do not have Git already installed, GitHub's help site offers installation guides for Mac,[3] Linux,[4] and Windows.[5] The precompiled installer should work well for Macs, and the package distributed versions (APT, eMerge, and so on) work well for Linux machines. For Windows, the *msysGit* application does just fine.

For an online place to put your Git repository, we recommend GitHub,[6] which offers free accounts. If you set up an account now, you can upload your code to GitHub as you progress, ensuring that you don't lose it if anything were to happen to your computer. To get started with GitHub, you first need to generate a secure shell (SSH) key, which is used to authenticate you with GitHub when you do a git push to GitHub's servers.[7] Once you generate the key, copy the public key's content (usually found at ~/.ssh/id_rsa.pub) into the SSH Public Key field on the Signup page or, if you've already signed up, click the Account Settings link (see figure 3.1) in the menu at the top, select SSH Public Keys, and then click Add Another Public Key to enter it there (see figure 3.2).

Figure 3.1 Click Account Settings.

---

[2] http://progit.org/book/.
[3] http://help.github.com/mac-set-up-git/. Note this lists four separate ways, not four separate steps, to install Git.
[4] http://help.github.com/linux-set-up-git/.
[5] http://help.github.com/win-set-up-git/.
[6] http://github.com.
[7] A guide for this process can be found at http://help.github.com/linux-key-setup/.

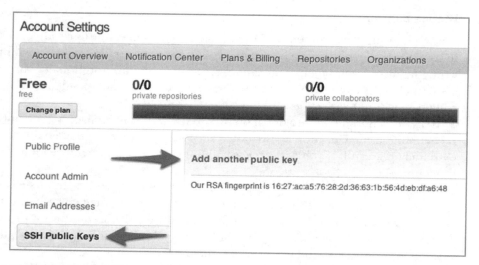

Figure 3.2   Add an SSH key.

Now that you're set up with GitHub, click the New Repository button on the dashboard to begin creating a new repository (see figure 3.3).

Figure 3.3   Create a new repository.

On this page, enter the Project Name as *ticketee* and click the Create Repository button to create the repository on GitHub. Now you are on your project's page. Follow the instructions, especially concerning the configuration of your identity. In listing 3.1, replace "Your Name" with your real name and you@example.com with your email address. The email address you provide should be the same as the one you used to sign up to GitHub. The git commands should be typed into your terminal or command prompt.

Listing 3.1   Configuring your identity in GitHub

```
git config --global user.name "Your Name"
git config --global user.email you@example.com
```

You already have a ticketee directory, and you're probably inside it. If not, you should be. To make this directory a git repository, run this easy command:

```
git init
```

Your ticketee directory now contains a .git directory, which is your git repository. It's all kept in one neat little package

To add all the files for your application to this repository's *staging area*, run

```
git add .
```

The staging area for the repository is the location where all the changes for the next commit are kept. A commit can be considered as a checkpoint of your code. If you make a change, you must stage that change before you can create a commit for it. To create a commit with a message, run

```
git commit -m "Generated the Rails 3 application"
```

This command generates quite a bit of output, but the most important lines are the first two:

```
Created initial commit cdae568: Generated the Rails 3 application
35 files changed, 9280 insertions(+), 0 deletions(-)
```

`cdae568` is the short commit ID, a unique identifier for the commit, so it changes with each commit you make. The number of files and insertions may also be different. In Git, commits are tracked against *branches*, and the default branch for a git repository is the master branch, which you just committed to.

The second line lists the number of files changed, insertions (additional line count), and deletions. If you modify a line, it's counted as both an insertion and a deletion because, according to Git, you've removed the line and replaced it with the modified version.

To view a list of commits for the current branch, type `git log`. You should see an output similar to the following listing.

Listing 3.2   Viewing the commit log

```
commit cdae568599251137d1ee014c84c781917b2179e1
Author: Your Name <you@example.com>
Date:    [date stamp]

    Generated the Rails 3 application
```

The hash after the word `commit` is the *long commit ID*; it's the longer version of the previously sighted short commit ID. A commit can be referenced by either the long or the short commit ID in Git, providing no two commits begin with the same short ID.[8] With that commit in your repository, you have something to push to GitHub, which you can do by running

```
git remote add origin git@github.com:yourname/ticketee.git
git push origin master -u
```

The first command tells Git that you have a remote server called `origin` for this repository. To access it, you use the `git@github.com:[your github username]/ticketee.git` path, which connects to the repository using SSH. The next command pushes the named branch to that remote server, and the `-u` option tells Git to always pull from this remote server for this branch unless told differently. The output from this command is similar to the following listing.

---

[8]   The chances of this happening are 1 in 268,435,456.

Listing 3.3   Terminal

```
Counting objects: 73, done.
Compressing objects: 100% (58/58), done.
Writing objects: 100% (73/73), 86.50 KiB, done.
Total 73 (delta 2), reused 0 (delta 0)
To git@github.com:rails3book/ticketee.git
 * [new branch]      master -> master
Branch master set up to track remote branch master from origin.
```

The second to last line in this output indicates that your push to GitHub succeeded because it shows that a new branch called master was created on GitHub. Next, you must set up your application to use RSpec and Cucumber.

3.1.3   *The Gemfile and generators*

The Gemfile is used for tracking which gems are used in your application. The Bundler gem is responsible for everything to do with this file; it's the Bundler's job to ensure that all the gems are installed when your application is initialized. Let's look at the following listing to see how this looks inside (commented lines are removed for simplicity).

Listing 3.4   Gemfile

```
source 'http://rubygems.org'

gem 'rails', '3.1.0'

gem 'sqlite3'

group :assets do
  gem 'sass-rails', "  ~> 3.1.0"
  gem 'coffee-rails', "~> 3.1.0"
  gem 'uglifier'
end

gem 'jquery-rails'

group :test do
  # Pretty printed test output
  gem 'turn', :require => false
end
```

In this file, Rails sets a source to be http://rubygems.org (the canonical repository for Ruby gems). All gems you specify for your application are gathered from the source. Next, it tells Bundler it requires version 3.1.0.beta of the rails gem. Bundler inspects the dependencies of the requested gem as well as all gem dependencies of those dependencies (and so on), then does what it needs to do to make them available to your application.

This file also requires the sqlite3 gem, which is used for interacting with SQLite3 databases, the default when working with Rails. If you were to use another database system, you would need to take out this line and replace it with the relevant gem, such as mysql2 for MySQL or pg for PostgreSQL.

The assets group inside the Gemfile contains two gems called sass-rails and coffee-rails. The sass-rails gem provides a bridge into the sass gem, which provides much better templating for stylesheets, and the `coffee-rails` gem provides a similar bridge between Rails and the CoffeeScript templating languages. We'll look at these in further detail when they're required.

Finally, at the bottom of the Gemfile, the `turn` gem is specified. This gem is for making the Test::Unit output a lot prettier, but you're not going to be using Test::Unit, you can remove these lines:

```
group :test do
  # Pretty printed test output
  gem 'turn', :require => false
end
```

While you're removing Test::Unit things, remove the test directory too: you won't need that either. You'll be using the spec directory for your tests instead.

Chapter 2 focused on BDD and, as was more than hinted at, you'll be using it to develop this application. First, alter the Gemfile to ensure you have the correct gems for RSpec and Cucumber for your application. Add the lines from the following listing to the bottom of the file.

Listing 3.5 Check for RSpec and Cucumber gems

```
group :test, :development do
  gem 'rspec-rails', '~> 2.5'
end

group :test do
  gem 'cucumber-rails'
  gem 'capybara'
  gem 'database_cleaner'
end
```

In the Gemfile, you specify that you wish to use the latest 2.x release of RSpec in the `test` and `development` groups. You put this gem inside the `development` group because without it, the tasks you can use to run your specs will be unavailable. Additionally, when you run a generator for a controller or model, it'll use RSpec, rather than the default Test::Unit, to generate the tests for that class.

With `rspec-rails`, you specified a version number with `~> 2.5`, which tells Ruby-Gems you want RSpec 2.5 *or higher.* This means when RSpec releases 2.5.1 or 2.6 and you go to install your gems, RubyGems will install the latest version it can find rather than only 2.5.

A new gem is used in listing 3.5: *Capybara.* Capybara is a browser simulator in Ruby that is used for *integration testing.* Cucumber and Capybara are two distinct entities. Cucumber is the testing tool that interacts with Capybara to perform tasks on a simulated application. Integration testing using Cucumber and Capybara ensures that when a link is clicked in your application, it goes to the correct page, or when you fill in a form and click the Submit button, an onscreen message tells you it was successful.

Capybara also supports real browser testing by launching an instance of Firefox. You can then test your application's JavaScript, which you'll use extensively in chapter 8.

An alternative to Capybara is Webrat, which is now less preferred because of the cleaner syntax and real browser testing features of Capybara. Capybara is the better alternative, hands down.[9]

Another new gem in listing 3.5 is the `database_cleaner` gem, which is used by `cucumber_rails` to clear out the database at the end of each test run to ensure you're working with a pristine state each time.

Groups in the Gemfile are used to define gems that should be loaded in specific scenarios. When using Bundler with Rails, you can specify a gem group for each Rails *environment*, and by doing so, you specify which gems should be required by that environment. A default Rails application has three standard environments: *development*, *test*, and *production*.

Development is used for your local application, such as when you're playing with it in the browser. In development mode, page and class caching is turned off, so requests may take a little longer than they do in production mode. Don't worry. This is only the case for larger applications. We're not there yet.

Test is used when you run the automated test suite for the application. This environment is kept separate from the development environment so your tests start with a clean database to ensure predictability.

Production is used when you finally deploy your application. This mode is designed for speed, and any changes you make to your application's classes are not effective until the server is restarted.

This automatic requiring of gems inside the Rails environment groups is done by this line in config/application.rb:

```
Bundler.require(:default, Rails.env) if defined?(Bundler)
```

To install these gems to your system, run `bundle install --binstubs` at the root of your application. It tells the Bundler gem to read your `Gemfile` and install the gems specified in it.

The `--binstubs` option stores executable files in the bin directory for the gems that have executables. Without it, you'd have to type `bundle exec rspec spec` to run your RSpec tests. With it, you can just run `bin/rspec spec`. Much better! You don't need to run `bundle install --binstubs` every time because Bundler remembers this configuration option for later.

You don't even have to run `bundle install`! Just `bundle` will do the same thing.

> **NOTE** If you're running Ubuntu, you must install the `build-essential` package because some gems build native extensions and require the make utility. You may also have to install the `libxslt1-dev` package because the `nokogiri` gem (a dependency of Cucumber) depends on it. You'll also need to install the `libsqlite3-dev` package to allow the `sqlite3` gem to install.

---

[9] As of this writing, Webrat has an open bug: https://github.com/brynary/webrat/pull/46. If we were using Webrat, we could run into it and be stuck in the mud (so to speak).

This command installs not only the `rspec-rails`, `cucumber`, and `capybara` gems but also their dependencies (and so on)! How great is *that*? You're just getting started.

The `bundle install --binstubs` command also creates a Gemfile.lockfile that contains a list of the gems and their relative versions. Once `Gemfile.lock` is created, whenever you run `bundle install`, Bundler reads *this* file rather than Gemfile to work out the dependencies of the application and installs from it. You commit this file to your repository so that when other people work on your project and run `bundle install`, they get exactly the same versions that you have.

Next, you want to generate the skeleton for Cucumber. A *generator* can generate either static or dynamic content, depending on the generator. For the Cucumber skeleton generator, it's set content. To run this generator, you use the `rails` command

```
rails generate cucumber:install
```

or simply

```
rails g cucumber:install
```

Rails doesn't mind if you use `generate` or `g`: it's all the same to Rails.

Let's not mind too much about all the files it has generated at the moment; they're explained in time. With the Cucumber skeleton now generated, you have a base on which to begin writing your features.

While you're generating things, you may as well run the RSpec generator too:

```
rails generate rspec:install
```

With this generated code in place, you should make a commit so you have another base to roll back to if anything goes wrong:

```
git add .
git commit -m "Ran the cucumber and rspec generators"
git push
```

3.1.4 Database configuration

By default, Rails uses a database system called SQLite3, which stores each environment's database in separate files inside the db directory. SQLite3 is the default database system because it's the easiest to set up. Out of the box, Rails also supports the MySQL and PostgreSQL databases, with gems available that can provide functionality for connecting to other database systems such as Oracle.

If you want to change which database your application connects to, you can open config/database.yml (development configuration shown in the following listing) and alter the settings to the new database system.

Listing 3.6   config/database.yml

```
development:
  adapter: sqlite3
  database: db/development.sqlite3
  pool: 5
  timeout: 5000
```

For example, if you want to use PostgreSQL, you change the settings to read like the following listing. It's common convention, but not mandatory, to call the environment's database [app_name]_[environment].

Listing 3.7   config/database.yml

```
development:
  adapter: postgresql
  database: ticketee_development
  username: root
  password: t0ps3cr3t
```

You're welcome to change the database if you wish. Rails will go about its business. It's good practice to develop and deploy on the same database system to avoid strange behavior between two different systems. Systems such as PostgreSQL perform faster than SQLite, so switching to it may increase your application's performance. Be mindful, however, that switching database systems doesn't automatically switch your data over for you.

It's generally wise to use different names for the different database environments because if you use the same database in development and test, the database will be emptied of all data when the tests are run, eliminating anything you may have set up in development mode. You should never work on the live production database directly unless you are absolutely sure of what you're doing, and even then extreme care should be taken.

Finally, if you're using MySQL, it's wise to set the encoding to `utf8` for the database, using this setup in the config/database.yml file:

```
development:
  adapter: mysql2
  database: ticketee_development
  username: root
  password: t0ps3cr3t
  encoding: utf8
```

This way, the database is set up automatically to work with UTF-8 (UCS Transformation Format–8-bit), eliminating any potential encoding issues that may be encountered otherwise.

That's database configuration in a nutshell. Now we look at how to use a pre-prepared stylesheet to make an application look prettier than its unstyled brethren.

3.1.5   *Applying a stylesheet*

So that your application looks good as you're developing it, we have a pre-prepared stylesheet you can use to style the elements on your pages. You can download the stylesheet from http://github.com/rails3book/ticketee/raw/master/app/assets/stylesheets/application.css and put it in the app/stylesheets directory. By default, your Rails application includes this stylesheet; you can configure it in the app/views/layouts/application.html.erb file using this line:

```
<%= stylesheet_link_tag "application" %>
```

No further configuration is necessary: just drop and use. Simple.

With a way to make your application decent looking, let's develop your first feature to use this new style: creating projects.

3.2 *First steps*

You now have version control for your application, and you're hosting it on GitHub. You also cheated a little and got a pre-prepared stylesheet.[10]

It's now time to write your first Cucumber feature, which isn't nearly as daunting as it sounds. We explore things such as models and RESTful routing while we do it. It'll be simple, promise!

3.2.1 *Creating projects*

The CRUD (*c*reate, *r*ead, *u*pdate, *d*elete) acronym is something you see all the time in the Rails world. It represents the creation, reading, updating, and deleting of something, but it doesn't say what that something is.

In the Rails world, CRUD is usually referred to when talking about *resources*. Resources are the representation of the information from your database throughout your application. The following section goes through the beginnings of generating a CRUD interface for a resource called *Project* by applying the BDD practices learned in chapter 2 to the application you just bootstrapped. What comes next is a sampler of how to apply these practices when developing a Rails application. Throughout the remainder of the book, you continue to apply these practices to ensure you have a stable and maintainable application. Let's get into it!

The first story for your application is the creation (the C in CRUD). You create a resource representing projects in your application by writing a feature, creating a controller and model, and adding a resource route. Then you add a validation to ensure that no project can be created without a name.

First, you generate a feature file at features/creating_projects.feature, and in this file, you put the story you would have discussed with the client, as shown in the following listing.

> **Listing 3.8 features/creating_projects.feature**

```
Feature: Creating projects
  In order to have projects to assign tickets to
  As a user
  I want to create them easily

  Scenario: Creating a project
    Given I am on the homepage
    When I follow "New Project"
    And I fill in "Name" with "TextMate 2"
    And I press "Create Project"
    Then I should see "Project has been created."
```

---

[10] You wouldn't have a pre-prepared stylesheet in the real world, where designers would design at the same time you're developing features.

To run all features for your application, run `rake cucumber:ok`. This command causes the following error message:

```
...db/schema.rb doesn't exist yet. Run "rake db:migrate" to
create it then try again. If you do not intend to use a database,
you should instead alter ...ticketee/config/application.rb to limit
the frameworks that will be loaded
```

The db/schema.rb file referenced here (when generated) will contain a Ruby version of your database's schema, which can be used to import the structure of your database. The great thing is that this file is database agnostic, so if you choose to switch databases during the life of your project, you won't have to re-create this schema file. To generate this file, run this command:

```
rake db:migrate
```

For now, this command prints out the standard first line of rake output, the path to the application:

```
(in /home/us/ticketee)
```

When you run any Rake task, the first line will be this line. Its only purpose is to indicate which directory you're running inside. When you run this particular task, it generates the db/schema.rb file your feature required. Therefore, you can run `rake cucumber:ok` again to have it fail on the second step of your feature:

```
When I follow "New Project"
  no link with title, id or text 'New Project' found
```

The first step here passes, but you haven't written a step definition for it, as you did in chapter 2! It nevertheless passes because of the features/step_definitions/web_steps.rb file, which was generated when you ran the `rails generate cucumber:install` command. This file contains a step definition that matches your first step:

```
Given /^(?:|I )am on (.+)$/ do |page_name|
  visit path_to(page_name)
end
```

First, Cucumber interprets this step on the basis of the definition from within this file. The `visit` method inside this definition comes from Capybara and emulates going to a specific path in a virtual browser. The `path_to` method is also defined, but it's in the features/support/paths.rb file inside the `NavigationHelpers` module, again provided by Cucumber:

```
module NavigationHelpers
...
  def path_to(page_name)
    case page_name

    when /the home\s?page/
      '/'
  ...
```

Therefore, the path that Capybara will visit is /. If you start the server for the application by running `rails server` (or `rails s`) and navigate to http://localhost:3000 in

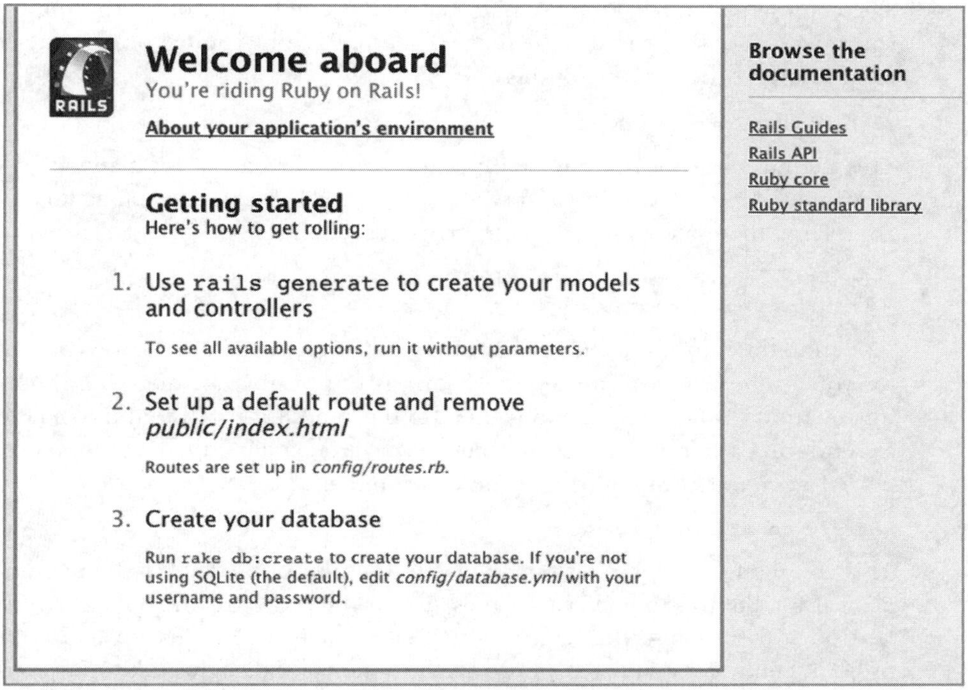

Welcome aboard
You're riding Ruby on Rails!

About your application's environment

Browse the documentation

Rails Guides
Rails API
Ruby core
Ruby standard library

Getting started
Here's how to get rolling:

1. **Use rails generate to create your models and controllers**

   To see all available options, run it without parameters.

2. **Set up a default route and remove** *public/index.html*

   Routes are set up in *config/routes.rb*.

3. **Create your database**

   Run rake db:create to create your database. If you're not using SQLite (the default), edit *config/database.yml* with your username and password.

Figure 3.4   Welcome aboard: take #2

your browser, you'll see the famous Welcome Aboard page from Rails (the same one you saw when you generated your first application in chapter 1), shown in figure 3.4.

This is the page Capybara sees, and the reason the first step passes is that Capybara can go to the homepage successfully. This Welcome Aboard page lives at public/index.html in your application. To proceed, delete this file using this command:

```
git rm public/index.html
```

Run rake cucumber:ok again. This time you'll see that the first step fails:

```
Given I am on the homepage
  No route matches [GET] "/" (ActionController::RoutingError)
```

The first step fails because you removed the public/index.html file that Rails was originally serving up at the root path, so the task goes to Rails. Rails claims it can't handle that route and throws an exception. You have to tell Rails what to do with a request for /, or the *root route* comes in. You can do this easily in config/routes.rb. At the moment, this file has the content seen in the following listing (comments removed).

Listing 3.9   config/routes.rb

```
Ticketee::Application.routes.draw do
end
```

The comments are good for a read if you're interested in the other routing syntax, but you needn't look at these right now. To define a root route, you put the following directly under the first line of this file:

```
root :to => "projects#index"
```

This defines the root route to point at the `ProjectsController`'s `index` action. This controller doesn't exist yet, and when you run `rake cucumber:ok` again, Cucumber complains about a missing constant, `ProjectsController`:

```
Given I am on the homepage
  uninitialized constant ProjectsController ...
```

To define this constant, you generate a *controller.* The controller is the first port of call for your routes (as you can see now!) and is responsible for querying the model for information inside an action and then doing something with that information (such as rendering a template). (Lots of new terms are explained later. Patience, grasshopper.) To generate this controller, run this command:

```
rails g controller projects
```

This command produces output similar to the output produced when you ran `rails new` earlier, but this time it creates files just for the projects controller, the most important of these being the controller itself, which is housed in app/controllers/projects_controller.rb. This is where all the actions will live, just like your app/controllers/purchases_controller.rb back in chapter 1. Before we dive into that, a couple of notes about the output.

app/views/projects contains the views relating to your actions (more on this shortly).

`invoke helper` shows that the `helper` generator was called here, generating a file at app/helpers/projects_helper.rb. This file defines a `ProjectsHelper` module. Helpers generally contain custom methods to use in your view, and they come as blank slates when they are first created.

`invoke erb` signifies that the Embedded Ruby (ERB) generator was invoked. Actions to be generated for this controller have corresponding ERB views located in app/views/projects.

`invoke rspec` shows that the RSpec generator was invoked at this point also. This means that RSpec has generated a new file at spec/controllers/projects_controller.rb, which you can use to test your controller; you won't use this for the time being. By generating RSpec tests rather than Test::Unit tests, a long-standing issue within Rails has been fixed. (In previous versions of Rails, even if you specified the RSpec gem, all the default generators would still generate Test::Unit tests. With Rails 3, the testing framework you use is just one of a large number of configurable things in your application.)

As mentioned previously when you ran `rails generate rspec:install`, this generator has generated an RSpec controller spec for your controller, spec/controllers/projects_controller_spec.rb, rather than a Test::Unit functional test. This file is used for testing the individual actions in your controller.

Now, you've just run the generator to generate a new `ProjectsController` class and all its goodies. This should fix the "uninitialized constant" error message. If you run `rake cucumber:ok` again, it declares that the index action is missing:

```
Given I am on the homepage
  The action 'index' could not be found for ProjectsController ...
```

To define the `index` action in your controller, you must define a method inside the `ProjectsController` class, just as you did when you generated your first application, shown in the following listing.

Listing 3.10   app/controllers/projects_controller.rb

```
class ProjectsController < ApplicationController
  def index

  end
end
```

If you run `rake cucumber:ok` again, this time Rails complain of a missing template `projects/index`:

```
Given I am on the homepage
Missing template projects/index, application/index
  with {:handlers=>[:erb, :builder],
        :formats=>[:html],
        :locale=>[:en, :en]}.

  Searched in:
    * ".../ticketee/app/views"
```

The error message isn't the most helpful, but it's quite detailed. If you know how to put the pieces together, you can determine that it's trying to look for a template called projects/index or application/index, but it's not finding it. These templates are primarily kept at app/views, so it's fair to guess that it's expecting something like app/views/projects/index.

The extension of this file is composed of two parts: the format followed by the handler. In your output, you've got a handler of either `:erb` or `:builder` and a format of `:html`, so it's fair to assume from this that the file it's looking for is either index.html.erb or index.html.builder. Either of these is fine, but we'll use the first one for consistency's sake.

The first part, *index*, is the name of the action; that's the easy part. The second part, *html*, indicates the format of this template. Actions in Rails can respond to different formats (using `respond_to`, which you saw in chapter 1); the default format is *html*. The third part, *erb*, indicates the templating language you're using, or the handler for this specific template. Templates in Rails can use different templating languages/handlers, but the default in Rails is ERB, hence the *erb* extension.

You could also create a file at app/views/application/index.html.erb to provide the view for the `index` action. This would work because the `ProjectsController` inherits from the `ApplicationController`. If you had another controller inherit from

ProjectsController, you could put an action's template at app/views/application, app/views/projects, or app/views/that_controller, and Rails would still pick up on it. This allows different controllers to share views in a simple fashion.

To generate this view, create the app/views/projects/index.html.erb file for now. When you run rake cucumber:ok again, you get back to what looks like the original error:

```
Given I am on the homepage
    When I follow "New Project"
      no link with title, id or text 'New Project' found
```

Although this looks like the original error, it's actually your first step *truly* passing now. You've defined a homepage for your application by generating a controller, putting an action in it, and creating a view for that action. Now Cucumber (via Capybara) can navigate to it. That's the first step in the first feature passing for your first application, and it's a great first step!

The second step in your features/creating_projects.feature file is now failing, and it's up to you to fix it. You need a link on the root page of your application that reads "New Project". Open app/views/projects/index.html.erb, and put the link in by using the link_to method:

```
<%= link_to "New Project", new_project_path %>
```

This single line re-introduces two old concepts and one new one: ERB *output* tags, the link_to method (both of which you saw in chapter 1), and the mysterious new_project_path method.

As a refresher, in ERB, when you use <%= (known as an ERB output tag), you are telling ERB that whatever the output of this Ruby is, put it on the page. If you only want to evaluate Ruby, you use an ERB evaluation tag: <%, which doesn't output content to the page but only evaluates it. Both of these tags end in %>.

The link_to method in Rails generates an <a> tag with the text of the first argument and the href of the second argument. This method can also be used in block format if you have a lot of text you want to link to:

```
<%= link_to new_project_path do %>
  bunch
  of
  text
<% end %>
```

Where new_project_path comes from deserves its own section. It's the very next one.

3.2.2   *RESTful routing*

The new_project_path method is as yet undefined. If you ran rake cucumber:ok, it would still complain of an undefined method or local variable, 'new_project_path'. You can define this method by defining a route to what's known as a *resource* in Rails. Resources are collections of objects that all belong in a common location, such as projects, users, or tickets. You can add the projects resource in config/routes.rb by using the `resources` method, putting it directly under the `root` method in this file, as shown in the following listing.

Listing 3.11   config/routes.rb

```
resources :projects
```

This is called a *resource* route, and it defines the routes to the seven *RESTful* actions in your projects controller. When something is said to be RESTful, it means it conforms to the Representational State Transfer (REST) standard. In Rails, this means the related controller has seven actions:

- `index`
- `show`
- `new`
- `create`
- `edit`
- `update`
- `destroy`

These seven actions match to just four request paths:

- /projects
- /projects/new
- /projects/:id
- /projects/:id/edit

How can four be equal to seven? It can't! Not in this world, anyway. Rails will determine what action to route to on the basis of the HTTP method of the requests to these paths. Table 3.1 lists the routes, HTTP methods, and corresponding actions to make it clearer.

The routes listed in the table are provided when you use `resources :projects`. This is yet another great example of how Rails takes care of the configuration so you can take care of the coding.

Table 3.1   RESTful routing matchup

HTTP method	Route	Action
GET	/projects	index
POST	/projects	create
GET	/projects/new	new
GET	/projects/:id	show
PUT	/projects/:id	update
DELETE	/projects/:id	destroy
GET	/projects/:id/edit	edit

To review the routes you've defined, you can run the `rake routes` command and get output similar to the following.

```
root                   /
  {:controller=>"projects", :action=>"index"}
projects      GET      /projects(.:format)
  {:action=>"index", :controller=>"projects"
              POST     /projects(.:format)
  {:action=>"create", :controller=>"projects"}
new_project   GET      /projects/new(.:format)
  {:action=>"new", :controller=>"projects"
edit_project  GET      /projects/:id/edit(.:format)
  {:action=>"edit", :controller=>"projects"}
project       GET      /projects/:id(.:format)
  {:action=>"show", :controller=>"projects"}
              PUT      /projects/:id(.:format)
  {:action=>"update", :controller=>"projects"}
              DELETE   /projects/:id(.:format)
  {:action=>"delete", :controller=>"projects"}
```

The words in the leftmost column of this output are the beginnings of the method names you can use in your controllers or views to access them. If you want just the path to a route, such as /projects, then use `projects_path`. If you want the full URL, such as http://yoursite.com/projects, use `projects_url`. It's best to use these helpers rather than hardcoding the URLs; doing so makes your application consistent across the board. For example, to generate the route to a single project, you would use either `project_path` or `project_url`:

```
project_path(@project)
```

This method takes one argument and generates the path according to this object. You'll see later how you can alter this path to be more user friendly, generating a URL such as /projects/1-our-project rather than the impersonal /projects/1.

The four paths mentioned earlier match up to the helpers in table 3.2. Running `rake cucumber:ok` now produces a complaint about a missing `new` action:

```
When I follow "New Project"
  The action 'new' could not be found for ProjectsController
```

In the following listing, you define the `new` action in your controller by defining a `new` method directly underneath the `index` method.

URL	Helper
GET /projects	projects_path
/projects/new	new_project_path
/projects/:id	project_path
/projects/:id/edit	edit_project_path

Table 3.2
RESTful routing matchup

Listing 3.13   app/controllers/projects_controller.rb

```
class ProjectsController < ApplicationController

  def index

  end

  def new

  end

end
```

Running `rake cucumber:ok` now results in a complaint about a missing `new` template, just as it did with the `index` action:

```
When I follow "New Project"
    Missing template projects/new with {
      :handlers=>[:erb, :builder, :sass, :scss],
      :formats=>[:html],
      :locale=>[:en, :en]
    } in view paths "/home/rails3/ticketee/app/views"
```

You can create the file at app/views/projects/new.html.erb to make this step pass, although this is a temporary solution. You come back to this file later to add content to it. The third step should now be the failing step, given the second one is passing, so run `rake cucumber:ok` to see if this is really the case:

```
And I fill in "Name" with "TextMate 2"
  cannot fill in, no text field, text area or password field with
    id, name, or label 'Name' found (Capybara::ElementNotFound)
```

Now Capybara is complaining about a missing `"Name"` field on the page it's currently on, the new page. You must add this field so that Capybara can fill it in. Before you do that, however, fill out the `new` action in the `ProjectsController` so you have an object to base the fields on. Change the `new` to this:

```
def new
  @project = Project.new
end
```

The `Project` constant is going to be a class, located at app/models/project.rb, thereby making it a *model*. A model is used to retrieve information from the database. Because this model inherits from Active Record, you don't have to set up anything extra. Run the following command to generate your first model:

```
rails g model project name:string
```

This syntax is similar to the controller generator's syntax except that you specified you want a model, not a controller. The other difference is that you gave it one further argument comprising a field name and a field type separated by a colon. When the generator runs, it generates not only the model file but also a *migration* containing the code to create this table and the specified field. You can specify as many fields as you like after the model's name.

Migrations are effectively version control for the database. They are defined as Ruby classes, which allows them to apply to multiple database schemas without having to be altered. All migrations have a `change` method in them when they are first defined. For example, the code shown in the following listing comes from the migration that was just generated.

Listing 3.14 db/migrate/[date]_create_projects.rb

```
class CreateProjects < ActiveRecord::Migration
  def change
    create_table :projects do |t|
      t.string :name

      t.timestamps
    end
  end
end
```

The `change` method is a new addition to Rails 3.1. When you run the migration forward (using `rake db:migrate`), it creates the table. When you roll the migration back (with `rake db:rollback`), it deletes (or drops) the table from the database. In previous versions of Rails, this migration would have been written as follows:

```
class CreateProjects < ActiveRecord::Migration
  def self.up
    create_table :projects do |t|
      t.string :name

      t.timestamps
    end
  end

  def self.down
    drop_table :projects
  end
end
```

Here, the `self.up` method would be called if you ran the migration forward, and the `self.down` method if you ran it backward.

In Rails 3.1, you can still use this syntax if you wish, but instead of `self.up` and `self.down`, you simply define the up and down methods:

```
class CreateProjects < ActiveRecord::Migration
  def up
    # code
  end

  def down
    # code
  end
end
```

This syntax is especially helpful if the migration does something that has a reverse function that isn't clear, such as removing a column:

```
class CreateProjects < ActiveRecord::Migration
  def up
    remove_column :projects, :name
  end

  def down
    add_column :projects, :name, :string
  end
end
```

This is because ActiveRecord won't know what type of field to re-add this column as, so you must tell it what to do in the case of this migration being rolled back.

The first line tells Active Record you want to create a table called `projects`. You call this method in the block format, which returns an object that defines the table. To add fields to this table, you call methods on the block's object (called t in this example and in all model migrations), the name of which usually reflects the type of column it is, and the first argument is the name of that field. The `timestamps` method is special: it creates two fields, the `created_at` and `updated_at` datetime fields, which are by default set to the current time in coordinated universal time (UTC) by Rails when a record is created and updated, respectively.

A migration doesn't automatically run when you create it—you must run it yourself using `rake db:migrate`. This command migrates the database up to the latest migration, which for now is the only migration. If you create a whole slew of migrations at once, this command migrates them in the order they were created.

With this model created and its related migration run, you can now run the feature and have the second step passing once again and the third one failing:

```
When I follow "New Project"
And I fill in "Name" with "TextMate 2"
  cannot fill in, no text field, text area or password field with
    id, name, or label 'Name' found (Capybara::ElementNotFound)
```

Now you are back to the missing field error. To add this field to the new action's view, you use a *partial*. Partials allow you to render dynamic content chunks in your views and are helpful for reducing duplicate code. You put this form in a partial because you must use it later in the `edit` action of your controller. To create a partial for your projects, create a new file called app/views/projects/_form.html.erb; the underscore prefix to this file's name indicates that it's a partial. You fill this file with the content from the following listing.

Listing 3.15 app/views/projects/_form.html.erb

```erb
<%= form_for(@project) do |f| %>
  <p>
    <%= f.label :name %>
    <%= f.text_field :name %>
  </p>
  <%= f.submit %>
<% end %>
```

So many new things! The `form_for` call allows you to specify the values for the attributes of your new `Project` object when this partial is rendered under the `new` action, and it allows you to edit the values for an existing object when you're on the `edit` action. This works because you'll set `@project` in both of these actions to point to new and existing objects respectively.

The `form_for` method is passed the `@project` object as the first argument, and with this, the helper does more than simply place a form tag on the page. `form_for` inspects the `@project` object and creates a form builder specifically for that object. The two main things it inspects are (1) whether or not it's a new record and (2) what the class name is.

Determining what `action` attribute the form has (where the form sends to) is dependent on whether the object is a new record. A record is classified as new when it hasn't been saved to the database, and this check is performed internally to Rails using the `persisted?` method, which returns `true` if the record is stored in the database or `false` if it's not. The class of the object also plays a pivotal role in where the form is sent. Rails inspects this class and from it determines what the route should be. In this case, it is /projects. Because the record is new, the path is /projects and the method for the form is `post`. Therefore, a request is sent to the `create` action in `ProjectsController`.

After that part of `form_for` is complete, you use the block syntax to receive an `f` variable, which is a `FormBuilder` object. You can use this object to define your forms fields. The first element you define is a `label`. `label` tags correspond to their field elements on the page and serve two purposes in the application. First, they give users a larger area to click rather than just the field, radio button, or check box. The second purpose is so you can reference the label's text in the Cucumber story, and Cucumber will know what field to fill in.

> **TIP** If you want to customize a label, you can pass a second argument:
> ```
> <%= f.label :name, "Project name" %>
> ```

After the label, you put the `text_field`, which renders an `input` tag corresponding to the label and the field. The output tag looks like this:

```
<input id="project_name" name="project[name]"
    size="30" type="text">
```

Then you use the `submit` method to provide users with a Submit button for your form. Because you call this method on the `f` object, a check is made regarding checks whether or not the record is new and sets the text to read "Create Project" if the record is new or "Update Project" if it is not.

The great thing about this partial is that later on, you can use it to implement your `edit` action. To use this partial for the `new` action, put the following code inside the app/views/projects/new.html.erb:

```
<h2>New project</h2>
<%= render "form" %>
```

The `render` method in this variation renders the app/views/projects/_form.html.erb partial at this location.

Now, running `rake cucumber:ok` once more, you can see that your feature is one step closer to finishing: the field is filled in. How did Capybara know where to find the correct field to fill in? Simple. When you defined the field inside app/views/projects/_form.html.erb, you used the syntax shown in the following listing.

Listing 3.16 app/views/projects/_form.html.erb

```
<%= f.label :name %>
<%= f.text_field :name %>
```

Capybara finds the label containing the `"Name"` text you ask for in your scenario and fills out the corresponding field. Capybara has a number of ways to locate a field, such as by the name of the corresponding label, the `id` attribute of the field, or the `name` attribute. The last two look like this:

```
When I fill in "project_name" with "TextMate 2"
# or
When I fill in "project[name]" with "TextMate 2"
```

These aren't human friendly ways to find a field, so let's use `"Name"` instead.

When you run the feature again with `rake cucumber:ok`, you get this error:

```
And I press "Create Project"
  The action 'create' could not be found for ProjectsController
```

The feature now complains of a missing action called `create`. To define this action, you define the `create` method underneath the new method in the `Projects-Controller`, as in the following listing.

Listing 3.17 app/controllers/projects_controller.rb

```
def create
  @project = Project.new(params[:project])
  @project.save
  flash[:notice] = "Project has been created."
  redirect_to @project
end
```

The new method takes the argument `params`, which is available inside controller methods and returns the parameters passed to the action, such as those from the form, as a `HashWithIndifferentAccess` object. These are different from normal `Hash` objects, because you can reference a `String` key by using a matching `Symbol` and vice versa. In this case, the `params` hash is

```
{
  "commit"      => "Create Project",
  "action"      => "create",
  "project"     => {
    "name" => "TextMate 2"
```

```
  },
  "controller" => "projects"
}
```

> **TIP** If you'd like to inspect the `params` hash at any point in time, you can put `p params` in any action and then run the action either by accessing it through `rails server` or by running a scenario that will run an action containing this line. This outputs to the console the `params` hash and is equivalent to doing `puts params.inspect`.

All the hashes nested inside this hash are also `HashWithIndifferentAccess` hashes. If you want to get the name key from the `project` hash here, you can use either `{ :name => "TextMate 2" }[:name]`, as in a normal `Hash` object, or `{ :name => "TextMate 2" }['name']`; you may use either the `String` or the `Symbol` version—it doesn't matter.

The first key in the `params` hash, `commit`, comes from the Submit button, which has the value Create Project. This is accessible as `params[:commit]`. The second key, `action`, is one of two parameters always available, the other being `controller`. These represent exactly what their names imply: the controller and action of the request, accessible as `params[:controller]` and `params[:action]` respectively. The final key, `project`, is, as mentioned before, a `HashWithIndifferentAccess`. It contains the fields from your form and is accessible via `params[:project]`. To access the name field, use `params[:project][:name]`, which calls the `[]` method on `params` to get the value of the `:project` key and then, on the result, calls `[]` again, this time with the `:name` key to get the name of the project passed in.

When `new` receives this `HashWithIndifferentAccess`, it generates a new `Project` object with the attributes based on the parameters passed in. The `Project` object will have a `name` attribute set to the value from `params[:project][:name]`.

You call `@project.save` to save your new `Project` object into the `projects` table.

The `flash` method in your `create` action is a way of passing messages to the next request, and it's also a `HashWithIndifferentAccess`. These messages are stored in the session and are cleared at the completion of the next request. Here you set the `:notice` key to be *Project has been created.* to inform the user what has happened. This message is displayed later, as is required by the final step in your feature.

The `redirect_to` method takes either an object, as in the `create` action, or a path to redirect to as a string. If an object is given, Rails inspects that object to determine what route it should go to, in this case, `project_path(@project)` because the object has now been saved to the database. This method generates the path of something such as /projects/:id, where `:id` is the record `id` attribute assigned by your database system. The `redirect_to` method tells the browser to begin making a new request to that path and sends back an empty response body; the HTTP status code will be a 302 Redirected to /projects/1, which is the currently nonexistent `show` action.

Upon running `rake cucumber:ok` again, you are told that your app doesn't know about a `show` action:

```
And I press "Create Project"
  The action 'show' could not be found for ProjectsController
```

Combining redirect_to and flash

You can combine `flash` and `redirect_to` by passing the `flash` as an option to the `redirect_to`. If you want to pass a success message, you use the `notice` flash key; otherwise you use the `alert` key. By using either of these two keys, you can use this syntax:

```
redirect_to @project,
:notice => "Project has been created."
# or
redirect_to @project,
:alert => "Project has not been created."
```

If you do not wish to use either `notice` or `alert`, you must specify `flash` as a hash:

```
redirect_to @project,
:flash => { :success => "Project has been created."}
```

The `show` action is responsible for displaying a single record's information. To retrieve a record, you need an ID to fetch. You know the URL for this page is going to be something like /projects/1, but how do you get the 1 from that URL? Well, when you use resource routing, as you have done, this 1 is available as `params[:id]`, just as `params[:controller]` and `params[:action]` are also automatically made available by Rails. You can then use this `params[:id]` parameter in your `show` action to find a specific `Project` object.

Put the code from the following listing into app/controllers/projects_controller.rb to do this right now.

Listing 3.18 app/controllers/projects_controller.rb

```
def show
  @project = Project.find(params[:id])
end
```

You pass the `params[:id]` object to `Project.find` here, which gives you a single `Project` object that relates to a record in the database, which has its `id` field set to whatever `params[:id]` is. If Active Record cannot find a record matching that ID, it raises an `ActiveRecord::RecordNotFound` exception.

When you run `rake cucumber:ok`, you get an error telling you the `show` action's template is missing:

```
And I press "Create Project"
  Missing template projects/show, application/show
  with { :handlers=>[:erb, :builder],
         :formats=>[:html],
         :locale=>[:en, :en]}.

  Searched in:
        * "/Users/ryanbigg/Sites/book/edge-ticketee/app/views"
```

You can create the file app/views/projects/show.html.erb with the following content for now:

```
<h2><%= @project.name %></h2>
```

When you run `rake cucumber:ok`, you see this message:

```
And I press "Create Project"
  Then I should see "Project has been created."
  expected #has_content?("Project has been created.")
  to return true, got false
```

This error message shows the `has_content?` method from Capybara, which is used to see if the page has specific content on it. It's checking for `"Project has been created."` and is not finding it. Therefore, you must put it somewhere, but where? The best location is in the application layout, located at app/views/layouts/application.html.erb. This file provides the layout for all templates in your application, so it's a great spot for the flash message.

Here is quite the interesting file:

```
<html>
<head>
  <title>Ticketee</title>
  <%= stylesheet_link_tag    "application" %>
  <%= javascript_include_tag "application" %>
  <%= csrf_meta_tags %>
</head>
<body>

<%= yield %>

</body>
</html>
```

The first line sets up the doctype to be HTML for the layout, and three new methods are used: `stylesheet_link_tag`, `javascript_include_tag`, and `csrf_meta_tags`.

`stylesheet_link_tag` is for including stylesheets from the app/assets/stylesheets directory. Using this tag results in the following output:

```
<link href="/assets/application.css"
      media="screen"
      rel="stylesheet"
      type="text/css" />
```

The `/assets` path is served by a gem called `sprockets`. In this case, you're specifying the /assets/application.css path, so Sprockets looks for a file called app/assets/application.css, which would usually act as a *manifest file* listing the Cascading Style Sheets (CSS) files that need to be included for the application. The current manifest file just provides a stylesheet for the entire application.

For your CSS files, you can use the Sass language to produce more powerful stylesheets. Your application depends on the `sass-rails` gem, which itself depends on sass, the gem for these stylesheets. We don't go into detail here because the Sass site covers most of that ground: http://sass-lang.com/. Rails automatically generates stylesheets for each controller that uses Sass, as indicated by its .css.scss extension. This final extension tells Sprockets to process the file using Sass before serving it as CSS.

javascript_include_tag is for including JavaScript files from the public/javascripts directory. When the application string is specified here, Rails loads the application JavaScript manifest file, app/assets/javascripts/application.js, which looks like this:

```
//= require jquery
//= require jquery_ujs
//= require_tree .
```

This file includes the jquery.js and jquery_ujs.js files located in the jquery-rails gem that your application depends on (see the Gemfile) and compiles them into one super-file called application.js, which is referenced by this line in the output of your pages:

```
<script src="/assets/application.js" type="text/javascript"></script>
```

This file is also served through the sprockets gem. As with your CSS stylesheets, you can use an alternative syntax called CoffeeScript (http://coffeescript.org), which provides a simpler JavaScript syntax that compiles into proper JavaScript. Just as with the Sass stylesheets, Rails generates CoffeeScript files inside app/assets/javascripts with the extension .js coffee, indicating to Sprockets they are to be parsed by a CoffeeScript interpreter first, then served as JavaScript. We use CoffeeScript a little later, in chapter 9.

csrf_meta_tags is for protecting your forms from cross-site request forgery (CSRF)[11] attacks. It creates two meta tags, one called csrf-param and the other csrf-token. This unique token works by setting a specific key on forms that is then sent back to the server. The server checks this key, and if the key is valid, the form is submitted. If the key is invalid, an ActionController::InvalidAuthenticityToken exception occurs.

Later in the file is the single line

```
<%= yield %>
```

This line indicates to the layout where the current action's template is to be rendered. Create a new line just before <%= yield %> and place the following code on it:

```
<% flash.each do |key, value| %>
  <div class='flash' id='<%= key %>'>
    <%= value %>
  </div>
<% end %>
```

---

[11] http://en.wikipedia.org/wiki/CSRF.

This code renders all the `flash` messages that get defined, regardless of their name. It displays the `flash[:notice]` you set up in the controller. Run `rake cucumber:ok` again and see that not only the last step in your scenario is passing,

```
Then I should see "Project has been created."
```

but the entire scenario is passing!

```
1 scenario (1 passed)
5 steps (5 passed)
```

Yippee! You have just written your first BDD feature for this application! That's all there is to it. If this process feels slow, that's how it's supposed to feel when you're new to any process. Remember when you were learning to drive a car? You didn't drive like Michael Schumacher first off. You learned by doing it slowly and methodically. As you progress, it becomes quicker, as all things do with practice.

3.2.3   Committing changes

You're at a point where all (just the one for now) your features are running, and points like this are great times to make a commit:

```
git add .
git commit -m "Creation of projects feature complete"
```

You should commit often because commits provide checkpoints you can revert back to if anything goes wrong. If you're going down a path where things aren't working and you want to get back to the last commit, you can revert all your changes by using

```
git checkout .
```

> **WARNING**   This command doesn't prompt you to ask whether you're sure you want to take this action. You should be incredibly sure that you want to destroy your changes. If you're not sure and want to keep your changes while reverting back to the previous revision, it's best to use the `git stash` command. This command stashes your unstaged changes to allow you to work on a clean directory and allows you to restore the changes using `git stash apply`.

With the changes committed to your local repository, you can push them off to the GitHub servers. If for some reason the code on your local machine goes missing, you have GitHub as a backup. Run `git push` to put it up to GitHub's servers. You don't need to specify the remote or branch because you did that the first time you pushed.

Commit early. Commit often.

3.2.4   Setting a page title

Before you completely finish working with this story, there is one more thing to point out: the templates are rendered *before* the layout. You can use this to your benefit by setting an instance variable such as `@title` in the `show` action's template; then you can reference it in your application's layout to show a title for your page at the top of the tab or window.

To test that the page title is correctly implemented, add an addendum to your Cucumber scenario for it. At the bottom of the scenario in features/creating _projects.feature, add the two lines shown in the following listing.

Listing 3.19 features/creating_projects.feature

```
And I should be on the project page for "TextMate 2"
And I should see "TextMate 2 - Projects - Ticketee"
```

The first line ensures that you're in the `ProjectsController`'s show action, or at least it would if you had defined the path to it. If you run `rake cucumber:ok` now, this first step fails:

```
Can't find mapping from "the project page for "TextMate 2"" to a path.
Now, go and add a mapping in .../ticketee/features/support/paths.rb
```

Then it tells you to add a mapping in features/support/paths.rb, which is what you should do. You visited this file at the beginning of your feature when you saw that it had this path to the home page defined:

```
when /the home\s?page/
  '/'
```

To define your own path, simply add another `when` directly underneath this one, as in the following listing.

Listing 3.20 features/support/paths.rb

```
when /the project page for "([^\"]*)"/
  project_path(Project.find_by_name!($1))
```

These two `when`s together should now look like the following listing.

Listing 3.21 features/support/paths.rb

```
when /the home\s?page/
  '/'
when /the project page for "([^\"]*)"/
  project_path(Project.find_by_name!($1))
```

When the `when` is fully matched to whatever `page_name` is, the part in the quotation marks is captured and stored as the variable $1. This is referred to as a *capture group*.

You then use this variable to find the project by the given name so that `project_path` has a record to act on, thereby returning the path to the project. You find this record by using a *dynamic method*. This `find_by_name!` method doesn't exist, and in Ruby when methods don't exist, another method named `method_missing` is called.

The `method_missing` method is passed the name of the method that cannot be found, and any arguments passed to it are passed as additional arguments to method_missing. These are then used to construct a real method call and make Ruby act as though the method exists. When you use the *bang* (find_by_name! with an exclamation mark as opposed to find_by_name) version of this method, Active Record raises an ActiveRecord::RecordNotFound exception if the record isn't found. This can prove helpful if, for example, you misspell a project's name when trying to use this step. The exception raised if you don't capitalize the *M* in TextMate (thereby making it Textmate) is this:

```
Then I should be on the project page for "Textmate 2"
Couldn't find Project with name = Textmate 2 (ActiveRecord::RecordNotFound)
```

If you don't use the bang version of this method, the finder returns nil. If project_path is passed nil, you get a hard-to-debug error:

```
Then I should be on the project page for "Textmate 2"
No route matches {:action => "show", :controller => "projects"}
```

This error claims that no route matches up to the ProjectsController's show action, but there actually is one: /projects/:id. The difference is that this route requires you to pass through the id parameter too; otherwise the error occurs.

To debug something like this, you check and double check what values were being passed where, particularly what $1 was coming back as, and whether Project.find_by_name was returning any record. If you checked those two things, you'd find that Project.find_by_name isn't returning what you think it should be returning, and hopefully you'd realize you were passing in the wrong name.

Upon running rake cucumber:ok, you now see that a step passes, but the rest of the feature fails:

```
And I should be on the project page for "TextMate 2"
And I should see "TextMate 2 - Projects - Ticketee"
expected #has_content?("TextMate 2 - Projects - Ticketee")
to return true, got false
```

Why are you getting an error seemingly from *RSpec*? Because Capybara uses its helpers internally to determine if it can find content. This error therefore means that Capybara can't find the content it's looking for. What content? Have a look at the last line of the backtrace:

```
features/creating_projects.feature:13:
```

Line 13 of features/creating_projects.feature is the And I should see "TextMate 2 - Projects - Ticketee" step, which checks for content shown on the page. To make this step pass, you need to define the content it should see. Write the code from the following listing into app/views/projects/show.html.erb.

Listing 3.22 app/views/projects/show.html.erb

```
<% @title = "TextMate 2 - Projects - Ticketee" %>
```

Then enter the following code in app/views/layouts/application.html.erb where the title tag currently is.

```
<title><%= @title || "Ticketee" %></title>
```

In Ruby, instance variables that aren't set return nil as their values. If you try to access an instance variable that returns a nil value, you can use || to return a different value, as in this example.

With this in place, your step passes when you run rake cucumber:ok:

```
And I should see "TextMate 2 - Projects - Ticketee"
```

With this scenario now passing, you can change your code and have a solid base to ensure that whatever you change works as you expect. To demonstrate this point, change the code in show to use a *helper* instead of setting a variable.

Helpers are methods you can define in the files inside app/helpers, and they are made available in your views. Helpers are for extracting the logic from the views, as views should just be about displaying information. Every controller that comes from the controller generator has a corresponding helper, and another helper exists for the entire application. Now open app/helpers/application_helper.rb and insert the code from the following listing.

```
module ApplicationHelper
  def title(*parts)
    unless parts.empty?
      content_for :title do
        (parts << "Ticketee").join(" - ") unless parts.empty?
      end
    end
  end
end
```

When you specify an argument in a method beginning with the splat operator (*), any arguments passed from this point will be available inside the method as an array. Here that array can be referenced as parts. Inside the method, you check to see if parts is empty? by using the opposite keyword to if: unless. If no arguments are passed to the title method, parts will be empty and therefore empty? will return true.

If parts are specified for the title method, then you use the content_for method to define a named block of content, giving it the name of "title". Inside this content block, you join the parts together using a hyphen (-), meaning this helper will output something like "TextMate 2 - Projects - Ticketee".

With this, you can slightly alter the title code inside the app/views/projects/show.html.erb page to look like "TextMate 2 - Projects - Ticketee", perhaps getting it to show the name of the project rather than Show in the title. Before you do that, though, you should change the line in the feature that checks for the title on the page to the following:

```
And I should see "TextMate 2 - Projects - Ticketee"
```

When you run this feature, it should be broken:

```
expected #has_content?("TextMate 2 - Projects - Ticketee")
to return true, got false
```

Now you can fix it by replacing the line that sets @title in your show template with this one:

```
<% title(@project.name, "Projects") %>
```

You don't need Ticketee here any more because the method puts it in for you. Let's replace the title tag line with this:

```
<title>
  <% if content_for?(:title) %>
    <%= yield(:title) %>
  <% else %>
    Ticketee
  <% end %>
</title>
```

This code uses a new method called content_for?, which checks that the specified content block is defined. If it is, you use yield and pass it the name of the content block, which causes the content for that block to be rendered. If it isn't, then you just output the word Ticketee, and that becomes the title.

When you run this feature again, it passes:

```
...
And I should see "TextMate 2 - Projects - Ticketee"

1 scenario (1 passed)
7 steps (7 passed)
```

That's a lot neater now, isn't it? Let's create a commit for that functionality and push your changes:

```
git add .
git commit -m "Added title functionality for show page"
git push
```

Next up, we look at how to stop users from entering invalid data into your forms.

3.2.5 *Validations*

The next problem to solve is preventing users from leaving a required field blank. A project with no name isn't useful to anybody. Thankfully, Active Record provides *validations* for this issue. Validations are run just before an object is saved to the database, and if the validations fail, then the object isn't saved. When this happens, you want to tell the user what went wrong, so you write a feature that looks like the following listing.

Listing 3.25   features/creating_projects.feature

```
Scenario: Creating a project without a name
  Given I am on the homepage
  When I follow "New Project"
  And I press "Create Project"
  Then I should see "Project has not been created."
  And I should see "Name can't be blank"
```

The first two steps are identical to the ones you placed inside the other scenario. You should eliminate this duplication by making pour code DRY (*Don't Repeat Yourself!*). This is another term you'll hear a lot in the Ruby world. It's easy to extract common code from where it's being duplicated and into a method or a module you can use instead of the duplication. One line of code is 100 times better than 100 lines of duplicated code. To DRY up your code, before the first scenario, you define a *background*. For Cucumber, backgrounds have a layout identical to scenarios but are executed before *every* scenario inside the feature. Delete the two steps from the top of both of these scenarios so that they now look like the following listing.

Listing 3.26   features/creating_projects.feature

```
Scenario: Creating a project
  And I fill in "Name" with "TextMate 2"
  And I press "Create Project"
  Then I should see "Project has been created."
  And I should be on the project page for "TextMate 2"
  And I should see "TextMate 2 - Projects - Ticketee"

Scenario: Creating a project without a name
  And I press "Create Project"
  Then I should see "Project has not been created."
  And I should see "Name can't be blank"
```

Then on the line before the first `Scenario`, define the `Background`, as in the next listing.

Listing 3.27   features/creating_projects.feature

```
Background:
  Given I am on the homepage
  When I follow "New Project"
```

Now when you run `rake cucumber:ok`, this will fail because it cannot see the error message on the page:

```
Then I should see "Project has not been created."
```

To get this feature to do what you want it to do, add a validation. Validations are defined on the model and typically are run before the data is put into the database, but this can be made optional, as you'll see later. To define a validation ensuring the name attribute is there, open the app/models/project.rb file and make it look like the following listing.

Listing 3.28 app/models/project.rb

```
class Project < ActiveRecord::Base
  validates :name, :presence => true
end
```

This `validates` method tells the model that you want to validate the `name` field and that you want to validate its presence. There are other kinds of validations as well, such as the `:uniqueness` key, which, when passed `true` as the value, validates the uniqueness of this field as well. In prior versions of Rails, to do this you would have to use the `validates_presence_of` method instead:

```
class Project < ActiveRecord::Base
  validates_presence_of :name
end
```

This syntax is still supported in Rails 3, but with the new syntax in Rails 3, you can specify multiple validation types for multiple fields on the same line, thereby reducing duplication in your model.

Beware race conditions with the uniqueness validator

The `validates_uniqueness_of` validator works by checking to see if a record matching the validation criteria exists already. If this record doesn't exist, the validation will pass.

A problem arises if two connections to the database both make this check at almost exactly the same time. Both connections will claim that a record doesn't exist and therefore will allow a record to be inserted for each connection, resulting in non-unique records.

A way to prevent this is to use a database uniqueness index so the database, not Rails, does the uniqueness validation. For information about how to do this, consult your database's manual.

Although this problem doesn't happen all the time, it *can* happen, so it's something to watch out for.

With the presence validation in place, you can experiment with the validation by using the Rails console, which allows you to have all the classes and the environment from your application loaded in a sandbox environment. You can launch the console with this command

```
rails console
```

or with its shorter alternative:

```
rails c
```

If you're familiar with Ruby, you may realize that this is effectively *IRB* with some Rails sugar on top. For those of you new to both, IRB stands for *Interactive Ruby*, and it provides an environment for you to experiment with Ruby without having to create new files. The console prompt looks like this:

```
Loading development environment (Rails 3.1.0.beta)
irb(main):001:0>
```

At this prompt,[12] you can enter any valid Ruby and it'll be evaluated. But for now, the purpose of opening this console is to test the newly appointed validation. To do this, try to create a new project record by calling the `create` method. The `create` method is similar to the `new` method, but it attempts to create an object and then a database record for it rather than just the object. You use it identically to the `new` method:

```
irb(main):001:0> Project.create
=> #<Project id: nil,
           name: nil,
           created_at: nil,
           updated_at: nil>
```

Here you get a new `Project` object with the `name` attribute set to `nil`, as you should expect because you didn't specify it. The `id` attribute is `nil` too, which indicates that this object is not persisted (saved) in the database.

If you comment out or remove the validation from inside the `Project` class and type `reload!` in your console, the changes you just made to the model are reloaded. When the validation is removed, you have a slightly different outcome when you call `Project.create`:

```
irb(main):001:0> Project.create
=> #<Project id: 1,
           name: nil,
           created_at: "2010-05-06 01:00:15",
           updated_at: "2010-05-06 01:00:15">
```

Here, the `name` field is still expectedly `nil`, but the other three attributes have values. Why? When you call `create` on the `Project` model, Rails builds a new `Project` object with any attributes you pass it[13] and checks to see if that object is valid. If it is, Rails sets the `created_at` and `updated_at` attributes to the current time and then saves it to the database. After it's saved, the `id` is returned from the database and set on your object. This object is valid, according to Rails, because you removed the validation, and therefore Rails goes through the entire process of saving.

The `create` method has a bigger, meaner brother called `create!` (pronounced *create BANG!*). Re-add or uncomment the validation from the model and type `reload!` in the console, and you'll see what this mean variant does with this line:

```
irb(main):001:0> Project.create!
ActiveRecord::RecordInvalid: Validation failed: Name can't be blank
```

---

[12] Although you may see something similar to `ruby-1.9.2-p180 :001 >` too, which is fine.

[13] The first argument for this method is the attributes. If there is no argument passed, then all attributes default to their default values.

The create! method, instead of nonchalantly handing back a Project object regardless of any validations, raises an ActiveRecord::RecordInvalid exception if any of the validations fail, showing the exception followed by a large stacktrace, which you can safely ignore for now. You are notified which validation failed. To stop it from failing, you must pass in a name attribute, and it will happily return a saved Project object:

```
irb(main):002:0> Project.create!(:name => "TextMate 2")
=> #<Project id: 2,
            name: "TextMate 2",
            created_at: "[timestamp]",
            updated_at: "[timestamp]">
```

That's how to use create to test it in the console, but in your ProjectsController, you use the method shown in the following listing instead.

Listing 3.29   app/controllers/projects_controller.rb

```
@project = Project.new(params[:project])
@project.save
```

save doesn't raise an exception if validations fail, as create! did, but instead returns false. If the validations pass, save returns true. You can use this to your advantage to show the user an error message when this returns false by using it in an if statement. Make the create action in the ProjectsController, as in the following listing.

Listing 3.30   app/controllers/projects_controller.rb

```
def create
  @project = Project.new(params[:project])
  if @project.save
    flash[:notice] = "Project has been created."
    redirect_to @project
  else
    flash[:alert] = "Project has not been created."
    render :action => "new"
  end
end
```

Now if the @project object is valid, then save returns true and executes everything between the if and the else. If it isn't valid, then everything between the else and the following end is executed. In the else, you specify a different key for the flash message because you'll want to style alert messages differently from notices later in the application's lifecycle.

When you run rake cucumber:ok here, the second step of your second scenario passes because you now have the flash[:alert] set:

```
Then I should see "Project has not been created."
And I should see "Name can't be blank"
  expected #has_content?("Name can't be blank")
  to return true, got false

  ...

12 steps (1 failed, 11 passed)
```

This scenario passes because of the changes you made to the controller and application layout, where you display all the `flash` messages. Of course, the third step is now failing. To display error messages in the view, you need to install the `dynamic_form` gem. To install it, add this line to your Gemfile underneath the line for the `coffee-rails` gem:

```
gem 'coffee-rails'
gem 'dynamic_form'
```

Then you must run `bundle install` to install it. Alternatively, you could install it as a plugin by using this command:

```
rails plugin install git://github.com/rails/dynamic_form.git
```

This command executes a `git clone` on the URL passed in and creates a new folder called vendor/plugins/dynamic_form in your application, putting the plugin's code inside of it. Installing it as a plugin would lead to a "polluted" repository, so installing it as a gem is definitely preferred here. Also, when it's installed as a gem, RubyGems and Bundler provide an exceptionally easy way of keeping it up to date, whereas the plugin architecture in Rails doesn't. This is a good reason to try to use gems instead of plugins.

The helpful method you're installing this gem for is the `error_messages` method on the `FormBuilder` object—that is, what f represents when you use `form_for` in your app/views/projects/_form.html.erb view:

```
<%= form_for(@project) do |f| %>
```

Directly under this `form_for` line, on a new line, insert the following to display the error messages for your object inside the form:

```
<%= f.error_messages %>
```

Error messages for the object represented by your form, the `@project` object, will now be displayed. When you run `rake cucumber:ok`, you get this output:

```
2 scenarios (2 passed)
12 steps (12 passed)
```

Commit and push, and then you're done with this story!

```
git add .
git commit -m "Add validation to ensure names are
                specified when creating projects"
git push
```

3.3 *Summary*

We first covered how to version-control an application, which is a critical part of the application development cycle. Without proper version control, you're liable to lose valuable work or be unable to roll back to a known working stage. We used Git and GitHub as examples, but you may use alternatives, such as SVN or Mercurial, if you prefer. This book covers only Git, because covering everything would result in a multi-volume series, which is difficult to transport.

Next we covered the basic setup of a Rails application, which started with the `rails new` command that initializes an application. Then we segued into setting up the Gemfile to require certain gems for certain environments, such as RSpec in the test environment, and then running the installers for these gems so your application is fully configured to use them. For instance, after running `rails g rspec:install`, your application is set up to use RSpec and so will generate RSpec specs rather than the default Test::Unit tests for your models and controllers.

Finally, you wrote the first story for your application, which involved generating a controller and a model as well as an introduction to RESTful routing and validations. With this part of your application covered by Cucumber features, you can be notified if it is broken by running `rake cucumber:ok`, a command that runs all the features of the application and lets you know if everything is working or if anything is broken. If something is broken, the feature fails, and then it's up to you to fix it. Without this automated testing, you would have to do it all manually, and that just isn't any fun.

Now that you've got a first feature under your belt, let's get into writing the next one!

Oh CRUD!

This chapter covers

- Expanding on the functionality of your app
- Building a RESTful resource
- Creating, updating, and deleting a resource

In chapter 3, you began writing stories for a CRUD (create, read, update, delete) interface for your Project resource. Here, you continue in that vein, beginning with writing a story for the *R* part of CRUD: reading. We often refer to reading as *viewing* in this and future chapters—we mean the same thing, but sometimes viewing is just a better word.

For the remainder of the chapter, you'll round out the CRUD interface for projects, providing your users with ways to edit, update, and delete projects too. Best of all, you'll be doing this using behavior-driven development the whole way through.

4.1 Viewing projects

The show action generated for the story in chapter 3 was only half of this part of CRUD. The other part is the index action, which is responsible for showing a list of the projects. From this list, you can navigate to the show action for a particular project. The next story is about adding functionality to allow you to do that.

83

4.1.1   *Writing a feature*

Create a new file in the features directory called viewing_projects.feature, shown in the following listing.

Listing 4.1   features/viewing_projects.feature

```
Feature: Viewing projects
  In order to assign tickets to a project
  As a user
  I want to be able to see a list of available projects

  Scenario: Listing all projects
    Given there is a project called "TextMate 2"
    And I am on the homepage
    When I follow "TextMate 2"
    Then I should be on the project page for "TextMate 2"
```

If you run rake cucumber:ok here, all the features will run. Instead, you want to run just the feature you're working on because you don't want the other feature to be altered by what you do here. When you're done, you'll run rake cucumber:ok to ensure that everything is still working.

To run just this one feature, use the bin/cucumber executable, which was added to your project when you ran bundle install --binstubs. If you didn't use the --binstubs option, you would have to use bin/cucumber instead, and typing all of that gets a bit boring after a while.

Now, to run this single feature, you run the following command:

```
bin/cucumber features/viewing_projects.feature
```

You should always use bin/cucumber rather than straight cucumber to run the bundled version of your gems because you could be using different versions of the same gem across separate projects. By running the bin/cucumber command, you ensure that you're loading the version of the gem specified by your bundle rather than the system version of that gem.

The first line of the only scenario in the feature fails, all because you haven't defined the "there is a project" step yet, as Cucumber informs you in the output:

```
3 scenarios (1 undefined, 2 passed)
15 steps (3 skipped, 1 undefined, 11 passed)

You can implement step definitions for
undefined steps with these snippets:

Given /^there is a project called "([^"]*)"$/ do |arg1|
  pending # express the regexp above with the code you wish you had
end
```

As you can see in the step output, you've got one undefined step. Underneath that, Cucumber very handily gives you a step definition you can use to define this step. In this step, you need to create a new Project object. Rather than doing it manually by calling Project.create everywhere you need it, you can set up a little thing called *factories*.

Factories allow you to create new example objects for all of your models in a simple and elegant syntax. This functionality doesn't come with Rails, unfortunately, so you must rely on a gem for it: `factory_girl`.

4.1.2　*The Factory Girl*

The `factory_girl`, created by thoughtbot,[1] provides an easy way to use *factories* to create new objects for your tests. Factories define a bunch of default values for an object, allowing you to have easily craftable objects you can use to run your tests on.

Before you can use this gem, you need to add it to the `:test` group in your Gemfile. Now the whole group looks like this:

```
group :test do
  gem 'cucumber-rails'
  gem 'capybara'
  gem 'database_cleaner'
  gem 'factory_girl'
end
```

To install, run `bundle`. You'll now use Factory Girl in your new step definition.

Create a new file at features/step_definitions/project_steps.rb, and add this small chunk of code:

```
Given /^there is a project called "([^\"]*)"$/ do |name|
  Factory(:project, :name => name)
end
```

The `Factory` method[2] looks for the `:project` factory and generates a new object based on the details it contains. You don't have a factory defined yet, but you will shortly.

When you define the factory, you give it a default name. The `:name => name` part of this method call changes the default name to the one passed in from your feature. You use factories here because you needn't be concerned about any other attribute on the `Project` object. If you weren't using factories, you'd have to use this method to create the object instead:

```
Project.create(:name => name)
```

Although this code is about the same length as its `Factory` variant, it isn't future-proof. If you were to add another field to the `projects` table and add a validation (say, a presence one) for that field, you'd have to change all occurrences of the `create` method to contain this new field. When you use factories, you can change it in one place—where the factory is defined. If you cared about what that field was set to, you could modify it by passing it as one of the key-value pairs in the `Factory` call.

That's a lot of theory—now how about some practice? Let's see what happens when you run `bin/cucumber features/viewing_projects.feature`:

```
Not registered: project (ArgumentError)
```

---

[1]　Thoughtbot's website: http://thoughtbot.com.

[2]　Yes, methods can begin with a capital letter.

Aha! You're now told there's no such factory! Then you'd better get around to creating one. You use these factories not only in your Cucumber features but also later in your RSpec tests. Placing the factories inside the features directory isn't fair to the RSpec tests, and placing them inside the spec isn't fair to the Cucumber tests. So where do they go? Create a new folder at the root of your application for them, and name it factories. Inside this directory, create your Project factory by creating a new file called project_factory.rb and filling it with the following content:

```
Factory.define :project do |project|
  project.name 'Ticketee'
end
```

This small snippet defines your project factory, which creates a new instance of the Project class, defaulting the name attribute to Ticketee. These files aren't going to load themselves, so you must create a new file at features/support/factories.rb and put this content in it:

```
Dir[Rails.root + "factories/*.rb"].each do |file|
  require file
end
```

All .rb files in features/support are loaded automatically before Cucumber starts, so all the files in the factories are required, and they define all the factories in the files.

With this factory defined, your feature should have nothing to whine about. Let's look at the following listing to see what happens now when you run bin/cucumber features/viewing_projects.feature

Listing 4.2   features/viewing_projects.feature failure

```
Given there is a project called "TextMate 2"
And I am on the homepage
When I follow "TextMate 2"
  no link with title, id or text 'TextMate 2' found ...
```

A link appears to be missing. You'll add that right now.

4.1.3   Adding a link to a project

Capybara is expecting a link on the page with the words "TextMate 2" but can't find it. The page in question is the homepage, which is the index action from your ProjectsController. Capybara can't find it because you haven't yet put it there, which is what you're going to do now. Open app/views/projects/index.html.erb, and add the contents of the following listing underneath the first link.

Listing 4.3   app/views/projects/index.html.erb

```
<h2>Projects</h2>
<ul>
  <% @projects.each do |project| %>
    <li><%= link_to project.name, project %></li>
  <% end %>
</ul>
```

If you run the Cucumber feature again, you get this error, which isn't helpful at first glance:

```
Showing /[path to ticketee]/app/views/projects/index.html.erb
 where line #5
 raised:
You have a nil object when you didn't expect it!
You might have expected an instance of Array.
```

This error points at line 5 of your app/views/projects/index.html.erb file. From this you can determine that the error has something to do with the @projects variable. This variable isn't yet been defined, and because there's no each method on nil, you get this error. As mentioned in chapter 3, instance variables in Ruby return nil rather than raise an exception if they're undefined. Watch out for this in Ruby—as seen here, it can sting you hard.

To define this variable, open ProjectsController at app/controllers/projects_controller.rb and change the index method definition to look like the following listing.

Listing 4.4   app/controllers/projects_controller.rb

```
def index
  @projects = Project.all
end
```

By calling all on the Project model, you retrieve all the records from the database as Project objects, and they're available as an Array-like object. Now that you've put all the pieces in place, you can run the feature with bin/cucumber features/viewing_projects.feature, and all the steps should pass:

```
1 scenario (1 passed)
4 steps (4 passed)
```

The feature now passes. Is everything else still working, though? You can check by running rake cucumber:ok. At the bottom, you should see this:

```
3 scenarios (3 passed)
16 steps (16 passed)
```

All of your scenarios and their steps are passing, meaning all of the functionality you've written so far is working as it should. Commit and push this using

```
git add .
git commit -m "Added the ability to view a list of all projects"
git push
```

The reading part of this CRUD resource is done! You've got the index and show actions for the ProjectsController behaving as they should. Now you can move on to *updating*.

4.2   *Editing projects*

With the first two parts of CRUD (creating and reading) done, you're ready for the third part: updating. Updating is similar to creating and reading in that it has two actions for each part (creation has new and create, reading has index and show). The two actions for updating are edit and update. Let's begin by writing a feature and creating the edit action.

4.2.1   *The edit action*

As with the form used for creating new projects, you want a form that allows users to edit the information of a project that already exists. You first put an Edit Project link on the show page that takes users to the edit action where they can edit the project. Write the feature from the following listing into features/editing_projects.feature.

Listing 4.5   features/editing_projects.feature

```
Feature: Editing Projects
  In order to update project information
  As a user
  I want to be able to do that through an interface

  Scenario: Updating a project
    Given there is a project called "TextMate 2"
    And I am on the homepage
    When I follow "TextMate 2"
    And I follow "Edit Project"
    And I fill in "Name" with "TextMate 2 beta"
    And I press "Update Project"
    Then I should see "Project has been updated."
    Then I should be on the project page for "TextMate 2 beta"
```

In this story, you again use the bin/cucumber command to run just this one feature: bin/cucumber features/editing_projects.feature.

The first three steps pass for this feature because of the work you've already done, but it fails on the fourth step when it tries to follow the as-yet nonexistent Edit Project link on the show page:

```
no link with title, id or text 'Edit Project' found (Capybara::ElementNotFound)
```

To add this link, open app/views/projects/show.html.erb and add the link from the following listing underneath the code currently in that file.

Listing 4.6   app/views/projects/show.html.erb

```
<%= link_to "Edit Project", edit_project_path(@project) %>
```

The edit_project_path method generates the link to the Project object, pointing at the ProjectsController's edit action. This method is provided to you because of the resources :projects line in config/routes.rb.

If you run `bin/cucumber features/editing_projects.feature` again, it now complains about the missing `edit` action:

```
The action 'edit' could not be found for ProjectsController
```

You should now define this action in your `ProjectsController`, underneath the `show` action, as in the following listing.

Listing 4.7   app/controllers/projects_controller.rb

```ruby
def edit
  @project = Project.find(params[:id])
end
```

As you can see, this action works in an identical fashion to the `show` action, where the ID for the resource is automatically passed as `params[:id]`. Let's work on DRYing[3] this up once you're done with this controller. When you run feature again, you're told that the `edit` view is missing:

```
Given I am on the homepage
Missing template projects/edit, application/edit
  with {:handlers=>[:erb, :builder],
        :formats=>[:html],
        :locale=>[:en, :en]}.

  Searched in:
    * ".../ticketee/app/views"
```

It looks like you need to create this template. For this `edit` action's template, you can re-use the `form` partial (app/views/projects/_form.html.erb) you created in chapter 3 by putting the code from the following listing into app/views/projects/edit.html.erb.

Listing 4.8   app/views/projects/edit.html.erb

```erb
<h2>Edit project</h2>
<%= render "form" %>
```

When you pass a string to the `render` method, Rails looks up a partial in the current directory matching the string and renders that instead. Using the partial, the next step passes without any further intervention from you when you run `bin/cucumber features/editing_projects.feature`, but the output now says it can't find the `update` action:

```
And I fill in "Name" with "TextMate 2 beta"
    And I press "Update Project"
      The action 'update' could not be found for ProjectsController
```

Great! It looks like the `edit` action is working fine, so your next step is to define the `update` action.

---

[3] As a reminder: DRY = Don't Repeat Yourself!

4.2.2   *The update action*

As the following listing shows, you can now define this `update` action underneath the `edit` action in your controller.

Listing 4.9   app/controllers/projects_controller.rb

```
def update
  @project = Project.find(params[:id])
  @project.update_attributes(params[:project])
  flash[:notice] = "Project has been updated."
  redirect_to @project
end
```

Notice the new method here, `update_attributes`. It takes a hash of attributes identical to the ones passed to `new` or `create`, updates those specified attributes on the object, and then saves them to the database if they are valid. This method, like `save`, returns `true` if the update is valid or `false` if it is not.

Now that you've implemented the `update` action, let's see how the feature is going by running `bin/cucumber features/editing_projects.feature`:

```
1 scenario (1 passed)
8 steps (8 passed)
```

What happens if somebody fills in the name field with a blank value? The user receives an error, just as in the `create` action. You should move the first four steps from the first scenario in features/editing_projects.feature into a `Background` so the `Feature` now looks like the following listing.

Listing 4.10   features/editing_projects.feature

```
Feature: Editing Projects
  In order to update project information
  As a user
  I want to be able to do that through an interface

  Background:
    Given there is a project called "TextMate 2"
    And I am on the homepage
    When I follow "TextMate 2"
    And I follow "Edit Project"

  Scenario: Updating a project
    And I fill in "Name" with "TextMate 2 beta"
    And I press "Update Project"
    Then I should see "Project has been updated."
    Then I should be on the project page for "TextMate 2 beta"
```

Now you can add a new scenario, shown in the following listing, to test that the user is shown an error message for when the validations fail on `update` directly under the other scenario in this file.

Listing 4.11 features/editing_projects.feature

```
Scenario: Updating a project with invalid attributes is bad
    And I fill in "Name" with ""
    And I press "Update Project"
    Then I should see "Project has not been updated."
```

When you run `bin/cucumber features/editing_projects.feature`, the first step passes but the second doesn't:

```
expected there to be content "Project has not been updated." in "[text]"
```

Again, this error means that it was unable to find the text "Project has not been updated." on the page. This is because you haven't written any code to test for what to do if the project being updated is now invalid. In your controller, use the code in the following listing for the `update` action.

Listing 4.12 app/controllers/projects_controller.rb

```ruby
def update
  @project = Project.find(params[:id])
  if @project.update_attributes(params[:project])
    flash[:notice] = "Project has been updated."
    redirect_to @project
  else
    flash[:alert] = "Project has not been updated."
    render :action => "edit"
  end
end
```

And now you can see that the feature passes when you rerun it:

```
2 scenarios (2 passed)
15 steps (15 passed)
```

Again, you should ensure everything else is still working by running `rake cucumber :ok`; you should see this summary:

```
5 scenarios (5 passed)
31 steps (31 passed)
```

Let's make a commit and push now:

```
git add .
git commit -m "Added updating projects functionality"
git push
```

The third part of CRUD, updating, is done. The fourth and final part is *deleting*.

4.3 Deleting projects

We've reached the final stage of CRUD: deletion. This involves implementing the final action of your controller, the `destroy` action, which allows you to delete projects.

4.3.1   *Writing a feature*

You're going to need a feature to get going: a Delete Project link on the show page that, when clicked, prompts the user for confirmation. You put the feature at features/deleting_projects.feature using the following listing.

Listing 4.13   features/deleting_projects.feature

```
Feature: Deleting projects
  In order to remove needless projects
  As a project manager
  I want to make them disappear

  Scenario: Deleting a project
    Given there is a project called "TextMate 2"
    And I am on the homepage
    When I follow "TextMate 2"
    And I follow "Delete Project"
    Then I should see "Project has been deleted."
    Then I should not see "TextMate 2"
```

When you run this feature using bin/cucumber features/deleting_projects .feature, the first three steps pass, and the fourth fails:

```
And I follow "Delete Project"
  no link with title, id or text 'Delete Project' found ...
```

4.3.2   *Adding a destroy action*

Of course, you need to create a Delete Project link for the show action's template, app/views/projects/show.html.erb. You put this on the line after the Edit Project link using the following listing.

Listing 4.14   app/views/projects/show.html.erb

```
<%= link_to "Delete Project", @project, :method => :delete,
  :confirm => "Are you sure you want to delete this project?" %>
```

Here you pass two new options to the link_to method, :method and :confirm.

The :method option tells Rails what HTTP method this link should be using, and here's where you specify the :delete method. In the previous chapter, the four HTTP methods were mentioned; the final one is DELETE. When you developed your first application, chapter 1 explained why you use the DELETE method, but let's review why. If all actions are available by GET requests, then anybody can send you a link to, say, the destroy action for one of your controllers, and if you click that, it's bye-bye precious data.

By using DELETE, you protect an important route for your controller by ensuring that you have to follow the link from the site to make the proper request to delete this resource.

The :confirm option brings up a prompt, using JavaScript, that asks users if they're sure of what they clicked. Because Capybara doesn't support JavaScript by default, this prompt is ignored, so you don't have to tell Capybara to click OK on the prompt—there is no prompt because Rails has a built-in fallback for users without JavaScript enabled. If you launch a browser and follow the steps in the feature to get to this Delete Project link, and then click the link, you see the confirmation prompt. This prompt is exceptionally helpful for preventing accidental deletions.

When you run the feature again, it complains of a missing `destroy` action:

```
And I follow "Delete Project"
  The action 'destroy' could not be found for ProjectsController
```

The final action you need to implement is in your controller, and you'll put it underneath the `update` action. This action is shown in the following listing.

Listing 4.15 app/controllers/projects_controller.rb

```ruby
def destroy
  @project = Project.find(params[:id])
  @project.destroy
  flash[:notice] = "Project has been deleted."
  redirect_to projects_path
end
```

Here you call the `destroy` method on the `@project` object you get back from your `find`. No validations are run here, so no conditional setup is needed. Once you call `destroy` on that object, the relevant database record is gone for good but the object still exists. When it's gone, you set the `flash[:notice]` and redirect back to the project's index page by using the `projects_path` routing helper.

With this last action in place, your newest feature should pass when you run `bin/cucumber features/deleting_projects.feature`:

```
1 scenario (1 passed)
6 steps (6 passed)
```

Let's see if everything else is running with `rake cucumber:ok`:

```
6 scenarios (6 passed)
37 steps (37 passed)
```

Great! Let's commit that:

```
git add .
git commit -m "Implemented delete functionality for projects"
git push
```

Done! Now you have the full support for CRUD operations in your `ProjectsController`. Let's refine this controller into simpler code before we move on.

4.3.3 Looking for what isn't there

People sometimes poke around an application looking for things that are no longer there, or they muck about with the URL. As an example, launch your application's server by using `rails server` and try to navigate to http://localhost:3000/projects/not-here. You'll see the exception shown in figure 4.1.

ActiveRecord::RecordNotFound in ProjectsController#show

Couldn't find Project with ID=not-here

Figure 4.1 `ActiveRecord::RecordNotFound` **exception**

The `ActiveRecord::RecordNotFound` exception is Rails' way of displaying exceptions in development mode. Underneath this error, more information is displayed, such as the backtrace of the error.

If you were running in the *production* environment, you would see a different error. Stop the server that is currently running, and run these commands to start in production mode:

```
rake db:migrate RAILS_ENV=production
rails server -e production
```

Here you must specify the `RAILS_ENV` environment variable to tell Rails you want to migrate your production database. By default in Rails, the development and production databases are kept separate so you don't make the mistake of working with production data and deleting something you shouldn't. This problem is also solved by placing the production version of the code on a different server from the one you're developing on. You only have to run the migration command when migrations need to be run, not every time you need to start your server.

You also pass the `-e production` option to the `rails server` command, which tells it to use the production environment. Next, navigate to http://[our-local-ip]:3000/project/not-here, where [our-local-ip] is whatever the IP of your computer is on the *local* network, like 10.0.0.2 or 192.168.0.3. When you do this, you get the standard Rails 404 page (see figure 4.2), which, to your users, is unhelpful.

It's not the page that's gone missing, but rather the *resource* you're looking for isn't found. If users see this error, they'll probably have to click the Back button and then refresh the page. You could give users a much better experience by dealing with the error message yourself and redirecting them back to the home page.

To do so, you capture the exception and, rather than letting Rails render a 404 page, you redirect the user to the `index` action with an error message. To test that users are shown an error message rather than a "Page does not exist" error, you'll write an RSpec controller test rather than a Cucumber feature, because viewing projects that aren't there is something a users *can* do, but not something they *should* do. Plus, it's easier.

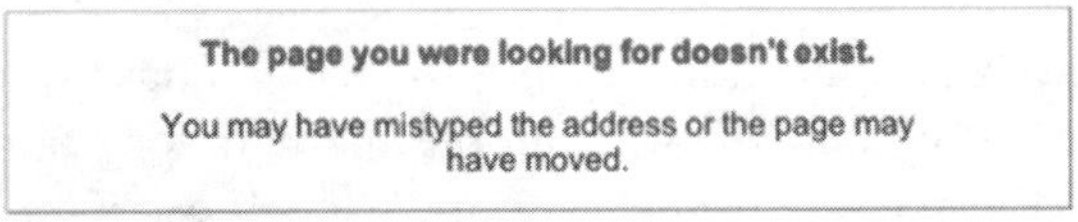

The page you were looking for doesn't exist.

You may have mistyped the address or the page may have moved.

Figure 4.2 **"Page does not exist" error**

The file for this controller test, spec/controllers/projects_controller_spec.rb, was automatically generated when you ran the controller generator because you have the rspec-rails gem in your Gemfile.[4] Open this controller spec file and take a look. It should look like the following listing.

Listing 4.16   spec/controllers/projects_controller_spec.rb

```
require 'spec_helper'

describe ProjectsController do

end
```

The spec_helper.rb file it references is located at spec/spec_helper.rb and it, like the previous examples of spec/spec_helper.rb (in chapter 2), is responsible for setting up the environment for your tests. This time, however, it already has code, which includes the Rails environment and the Rails-associated RSpec helpers as well as any file inside the spec/support directory or its subdirectories.

In this controller spec, you want to test that you get redirected to the Projects page if you attempt to access a resource that no longer exists. You also want to ensure that a flash[:alert] is set.

To do all this, you put the following code inside the describe block:

```
it "displays an error for a missing project" do
  get :show, :id => "not-here"
  response.should redirect_to(projects_path)
  message = "The project you were looking for could not be found."
  flash[:alert].should eql(message)
end
```

The first line *inside* this RSpec test—more commonly called an *example*—tells RSpec to make a GET request to the show action for the ProjectsController. How does it know which controller should receive the GET request? RSpec infers it from the class used for the describe block.

In the next line, you tell RSpec that you expect the response to take you back to the projects_path through a redirect_to call. If it doesn't, the test fails, and nothing more in this test is executed: RSpec stops in its tracks.

The final line tells RSpec that you expect the flash[:alert] to contain a useful messaging explaining the redirection to the index action.[5]

To run this spec, use the bin/rspec spec/controllers/projects_controller _spec.rb command.

It may seem like nothing is happening at first, because RSpec must load the Rails environment and your application, and loading takes time. The same delay occurs when you start running a Rails server.

---

[4] The rspec-rails gem automatically generates the file using a Railtie, the code of which can be found at https://github.com/rspec/rspec-rails/blob/master/lib/rspec-rails.rb.

[5] The lines for the flash[:alert] are separated into two lines to accommodate the page width of this book. You can put it on one line if you like. We won't yell at you.

When the test runs, you get a failure:

```
F

1) ProjectsController displays an error
   message when asked for a missing project
    Failure/Error: get :show, :id => "not-here"
    Couldn't find Project with ID=not-here
```

This is the same failure you saw when you tried running the application using `rails server`. Now that you have a failing test, you can fix it.

Open the app/controllers/projects_controller.rb file, and put the code from the following listing underneath the last action in the controller but before the end of the class.

Listing 4.17   app/controllers/projects_controller.rb

```
private
  def find_project
    @project = Project.find(params[:id])
    rescue ActiveRecord::RecordNotFound
    flash[:alert] = "The project you were looking" +
                    " for could not be found."
    redirect_to projects_path
  end
```

This method has the `private` method before it, so the controller doesn't respond to this method as an action. To call this method before every action, use the `before_filter` method. Place these lines directly under the `class Projects-Controller` definition:

```
before_filter :find_project, :only => [:show,
                                        :edit,
                                        :update,
                                        :destroy]
```

What does all this mean? Let's start with the `before_filter`. `before_filters` are run before all the actions in your controller unless you specify either the `:except` or `:only` option. Here you have the `:only` option defining actions you want the `before_filter` to run for. The `:except` option is the opposite of the `:only` option, specifying the actions you do not want the `before_filter` to run for. The `before_filter` calls the `find_project` method before the specified actions, setting up the `@project` variable for you. This means you can remove the following line from all four of your actions (show, edit, update, and destroy):

```
@project = Project.find(params[:id])
```

By doing this, you make the `show` and `edit` actions empty. If you remove these actions and run `rake cucumber:ok` again, all the scenarios still pass. Controller actions don't need to exist in the controllers if there are templates corresponding to those actions, which you have for these actions. For readability's sake, it's best to leave these in the controller so anyone who reads the code knows that the controller responds to these actions.

Back to the spec now: if you run `bin/rspec spec/controllers/projects _controller_spec.rb` once more, the test now passes:

```
.
1 example, 0 failures
```

Let's check to see if everything else is still working by running `rake cucumber:ok` and then `rake spec`. You should see these outputs:

```
6 scenarios (6 passed)
37 steps (37 passed)
# and
.
3 examples, 0 failures, 2 pending
```

The RSpec output shows two pending examples. These come from the spec files for `ProjectsHelper` (spec/helpers/projects_helper_spec.rb) and `Project` model (spec/ models/project_spec.rb) respectively. You can delete these files or remove the `pending` lines from them to make your RSpec output green instead of yellow when it passes. Other than that, these two specs have no effect on your test output.

It's great to see that everything is still going! Let's commit and push that!

```
git add .
git commit -m "Users should be redirected back to the projects page
                if they try going to a project that doesn't exist."
git push
```

This completes the basic `CRUD` implementation for your project's resource. Now you can create, read, update, and delete projects to your heart's content, and these features are all well covered with tests, which leads to greater maintainability.

4.4   *Summary*

This chapter covered developing the first part of your application using BDD practices and Cucumber and then making each step pass. Now you have an application that is truly maintainable. If you want to know if these features or specs are working later in the project, you can run `rake cucumber:ok` or `rake spec` and if something is broken, you'll know about it. Doesn't that beat manual testing? Just think of all the time you'll save in the long run.

You learned firsthand how rapidly you can develop the CRUD interface for a resource in Rails. There are even faster ways to do it (such as by using *scaffolding*, discussed in chapter 1), but to absorb how this whole process works, it's best to go through it yourself, step by step, as you did in this chapter.

So far you've been developing your application using BDD techniques, and as your application grows, it will become more evident how useful these techniques are. The main thing they'll provide is assurance that what you've coded so far is still working exactly as it was when you first wrote it. Without these tests, you may accidentally break functionality and not know about it until a user—or worse, a client—reports it. It's best that you spend some time implementing tests for this functionality now so that you don't spend even more time later apologizing for whatever's broken and fixing it.

With the basic project functionality done, you're ready for the next step. Because you're building a ticket-tracking application, it makes sense to implement functionality that lets you track tickets, right? That's precisely what you do in the next chapter. We also cover nested routing and association methods for models. Let's go!

Nested resources 5

This chapter covers

- Building a nested resource
- Declaring data associations between two database tables
- Working with objects within an association

With the project resource CRUD done, the next step is to set up the ability to create tickets within the scope of a given project. The term for performing actions for objects within the scope of another object is *nesting*. This chapter explores how to set up nested routing for `Ticket` resources by creating a CRUD interface for them, scoped underneath the projects resource that you just created.

5.1 Creating tickets

To add the functionality to create tickets underneath the projects, you first develop the Cucumber features and then implement the code required to make them pass. Nesting one resource under another involves additional routing, working with associations in Active Record, and using more `before_filters`. Let's get into this.

To create tickets for your application, you need an idea of what you're going to implement. You want to create tickets only for particular projects, so you need a

New Ticket link on a project's show page. The link must lead to a form where a title and a description for your ticket can be entered, and the form needs a button that submits it to a `create` action in your controller. You also want to ensure the data is valid, just as you did with the `Project` model. Start by using the code from the following listing in a new file.

Listing 5.1   features/creating_tickets.feature

```
Feature: Creating Tickets
In order to create tickets for projects
As a user
I want to be able to select a project and do that

Background:
  Given there is a project called "Internet Explorer"
  And I am on the homepage
  When I follow "Internet Explorer"
  And I follow "New Ticket"

Scenario: Creating a ticket
  When I fill in "Title" with "Non-standards compliance"
  And I fill in "Description" with "My pages are ugly!"
  And I press "Create Ticket"
  Then I should see "Ticket has been created."

Scenario: Creating a ticket without valid attributes fails
  When I press "Create Ticket"
  Then I should see "Ticket has not been created."
  And I should see "Title can't be blank"
  And I should see "Description can't be blank"
```

When you run the code in listing 5.1 using the `bin/cucumber features/creating_tickets.feature` command, your background fails, as shown here:

```
And I follow "New Ticket"
no link with title, id or text 'New Ticket' found ...
```

You need to add this New Ticket link to the app/views/projects/show.html.erb template. Add it underneath the Delete Project link, as shown in the following listing.

Listing 5.2   app/views/projects/show.html.erb

```
<%= link_to "New Ticket", new_project_ticket_path(@project) %>
```

This helper is called a *nested routing helper* and is just like the standard routing helper. The similarities and differences between the two are explained in the next section.

5.1.1 Nested routing helpers

In listing 5.2, you used a nested routing helper—`new_project_ticket_path`—rather than a standard routing helper such as `new_ticket_path` because you want to create a new ticket for a given project. Both helpers work in a similar fashion, except the nested routing helper takes one argument always, the `@project` object for which you want to create a new ticket: the object that you're nested inside. The route to any ticket URL is always scoped by /projects/:id in your application. This helper and its brethren are defined by changing this line in config/routes.rb

```
resources :projects
```

to the lines in the following listing.

Listing 5.3   config/routes.rb

```
resources :projects do
  resources :tickets
end
```

This code tells the routing for Rails that you have a tickets resource nested inside the projects resource. Effectively, any time you access a ticket resource, you access it within the scope of a project too. Just as the resources :projects method gave you helpers to use in controllers and views, this nested one gives you the helpers (where id represents the identifier of a resource) shown in table 5.1.

Table 5.1   Nested RESTful routing matchup

Route	Helper
/projects/:project_id/tickets	project_tickets_path
/projects/:project_id/tickets/new	new_project_ticket_path
/projects/:project_id/tickets/:id/edit	edit_project_ticket_path
/projects/:project_id/tickets/:id	project_ticket_path

As before, you can use the *_url alternatives to these helpers, such as project _tickets_url, to get the full URL if you so desire. The :project_id symbol here would normally be replaced by the project ID as well as the :id symbol, which would be replaced by a ticket's ID.

In the left column are the routes that can be accessed, and in the right, the routing helper methods you can use to access them. Let's make use of them by first creating your TicketsController.

5.1.2   Creating a tickets controller

Because you defined this route in your routes file, Capybara can now click the link in your feature and proceed before complaining about the missing TicketsController, spitting out an error followed by a stack trace:

```
And I follow "New Ticket"
    uninitialized constant TicketsController ...
```

Some guides may have you generate the model before you generate the controller, but the order in which you create them is not important. In Cucumber, you just follow the bouncing ball, and if Cucumber tells you it can't find a controller, then you generate the controller it's looking for next. Later, when you inevitably receive an error that it cannot find the Ticket model, as you did for the Project model, you generate that too.

To generate this controller and fix this uninitialized constant error, use this command:

```
rails g controller tickets
```

You may be able to pre-empt what's going to happen next if you run Cucumber: it'll complain of a missing new action that it's trying to get to by clicking the New Ticket link. Open app/controllers/tickets_controller.rb and add the new action, shown in the following listing.

Listing 5.4   app/controllers/tickets_controller.rb

```
def new
  @ticket = @project.tickets.build
end
```

The build method simply instantiates a new record for the tickets association on the @project object, working in much the same way as the following code would:

```
Ticket.new(:project_id => @project.id)
```

Of course, you haven't yet done anything to define the @project variable in Tickets-Controller, so it would be nil. You must define the variable using a before_filter, just as you did in the ProjectsController. Put the following line just under the class definition in app/controllers/tickets_controller.rb:

```
before_filter :find_project
```

You don't restrict the before_filter here: you want to have a @project to work with in all actions because the tickets resource is only accessible through a project. Underneath the new action, define the method that the before_filter uses:

```
private
  def find_project
    @project = Project.find(params[:project_id])
  end
```

Where does params[:project_id] come from? It's made available through the wonders of Rails's routing, just as params[:id] was. It's called project_id instead of id because you could (and later will) have a route that you want to pass through an ID for a ticket as well, and that would be params[:id]. Now how about that tickets method on your @project object? Let's make sure it doesn't already exist by running bin/cucumber features/creating_tickets.feature:

```
And I follow "New Ticket"
  undefined method 'tickets' for #<Project:0xb7461074> (NoMethodError)
```

No Rails magic here yet.

5.1.3 Defining a has_many association

The `tickets` method is defined by an association method in the `Project` class called `has_many`, which you can use as follows, putting it directly above the validation you put there earlier:

```
has_many :tickets
```

As mentioned before, this defines the `tickets` method you need but also gives you a whole slew of other useful methods, such as the `build` method, which you call on the association. The `build` method is equivalent to `new` for the `Ticket` class (which you create in a moment) but associates the new object instantly with the `@project` object by setting a foreign key called `project_id` automatically. Upon running the feature, you get this:

```
And I follow "New Ticket"
  uninitialized constant Project::Ticket (NameError)
```

You can determine from this output that the method is looking for the `Ticket` class, but why? The `tickets` method on `Project` objects is defined by the `has_many` call in the `Project` model. This method assumes that when you want to get the tickets, you actually want objects of the `Ticket` model. This model is currently missing; hence, the error. You can add this model now with the following command:

```
rails generate model ticket title:string description:text project:references
```

The `project:references` part defines an integer column for the `tickets` table called `project_id` in the migration. This column represents the project this ticket links to and is called a *foreign key*. You should now run the migration by using `rake db:migrate` and load the new schema into your test database by running `rake db:test:prepare`.

The `rake db:migrate` task runs the migrations and then dumps the structure of the database to a file called db/schema.rb. This structure allows you to restore your database using the `rake db:schema:load` task if you wish, which is better than running all the migrations on a large project again! The `rake db:test:prepare` task loads this schema into the test database, making the fields that were just made available on the development database by running the migration also now available on the test database.

Now when you run `bin/cucumber features/creating_tickets.feature`, you're told the new template is missing:

```
And I follow "New Ticket"
Missing template tickets/new, application/new
  with {:handlers=>[:erb, :builder],
        :formats=>[:html],
        :locale=>[:en, :en]}.

  Searched in:
    * ".../ticketee/app/views"
```

A file seems to be missing! You must create this file in order to continue.

5.1.4   *Creating tickets within a project*

Create the file at app/views/tickets/new.html.erb, and put the following inside:

```
<h2>New Ticket</h2>
<%= render "form" %>
```

This template renders a form partial, which will be relative to the current folder and will be placed at app/views/tickets/_form.html.erb, using the code from the next listing.

Listing 5.5   app/views/tickets/_form.html.erb

```
<%= form_for [@project, @ticket] do |f| %>
  <%= f.error_messages %>
  <p>
    <%= f.label :title %><br>
    <%= f.text_field :title %>
  </p>
  <p>
    <%= f.label :description %><br>
    <%= f.text_area :description %>
  </p>
  <%= f.submit %>
<% end %>
```

Note that form_for is passed an array of objects rather than simply

```
<%= form_for @ticket do |f| %>
```

This code indicates to form_for that you want the form to post to the nested route you're using. For the new action, this generate a route like /projects/1/tickets, and for the edit action, it generates a route like /projects/1/tickets/2. When you run bin/cucumber features/creating_tickets.feature again, you're told the create action is missing:

```
And I press "Create Ticket"
  The action 'create' could not be found for TicketsController
```

To define this action, put it directly underneath the new action but before the private method:

```
def create
  @ticket = @project.tickets.build(params[:ticket])
  if @ticket.save
    flash[:notice] = "Ticket has been created."
    redirect_to [@project, @ticket]                    ◁── ❶ Specify array
  else
    flash[:alert] = "Ticket has not been created."
    render :action => "new"
  end
end
```

Inside this action, you use redirect_to and specify an Array ❶—the same array you used in the form_for earlier—containing a Project object and a Ticket object. Rails inspects any array passed to helpers, such as `redirect_to` and `link_to`, and determines what you mean from the values. For this particular case, Rails determine that you want this helper:

```
project_ticket_path(@project, @ticket)
```

Rails determines this helper because, at this stage, `@project` and `@ticket` are both objects that exist in the database, and you can therefore route to them. The route generated would be /projects/1/tickets/2 or something similar. Back in the `form_for`, `@ticket` was new, so the route happened to be /projects/1/tickets.

You could have been explicit and specifically used `project_ticket_path` in the action, but using an array is DRYer.

When you run bin/cucumber features/creating_tickets.feature, both scenarios report the same error:

```
And I press "Create Ticket"
  The action 'show' could not be found TicketsController
```

Therefore, you must create a `show` action for the `TicketsController`, but when you do so, you'll need to find tickets only for the given project.

5.1.5   *Finding tickets scoped by project*

Currently, the first scenario is correct, but the second one is not.

Of course, now you must define the `show` action for your controller, but you can anticipate that you'll need to find a ticket for the `edit`, `update`, and `destroy` actions too and pre-empt those errors. You can also make this a `before_filter`, just as you did in the `ProjectsController` with the `find_project` method. You define this finder underneath the `find_project` method in the `TicketsController`:

```
def find_ticket
  @ticket = @project.tickets.find(params[:id])
end
```

`find` is yet another association method provided by Rails when you declared that your `Project` model has_many `:tickets`. This code attempts to find tickets only within the scope of the project. Put the `before_filter` at the top of your class, just underneath the one to find the project:

```
before_filter :find_project
before_filter :find_ticket, :only => [:show,
                                      :edit,
                                      :update,
                                      :destroy]
```

The sequence here is important because you want to find the `@project` before you go looking for tickets for it. With this `before_filter` in place, create an empty `show` action in your controller to show that it responds to this action:

```
def show
end
```

Then create the view for this action at app/views/tickets/show.html.erb using this code:

```
<div id='ticket'>
  <h2><%= @ticket.title %></h2>
  <%= simple_format(@ticket.description) %>
</div>
```

The new method, simple_format, converts the line breaks[1] entered into the description field into HTML break tags (<br>) so that the description renders exactly how the user intends it to.

Based solely on the changes that you've made so far, your first scenario should be passing. Let's see with a quick run of bin/cucumber features/creating_tickets .feature:

```
Then I should see "Ticket has been created."
...
2 scenarios (1 failed, 1 passed)
16 steps (1 failed, 2 skipped, 13 passed)
```

This means that you've got the first scenario under control and that users of your application can create tickets within a project. Next, you need to add validations to the Ticket model to get the second scenario to pass.

5.1.6   *Ticket validations*

The second scenario fails because the @ticket that it saves is valid, at least according to your application in its current state:

```
expected there to be content "Ticket has not been created" in "[text]"
```

You need to ensure that when somebody enters a ticket into the application, the title and description attributes are filled in. To do this, define the following validations inside the Ticket model.

Listing 5.6   app/models/ticket.rb

```
validates :title, :presence => true
validates :description, :presence => true
```

Now when you run bin/cucumber features/creating_tickets.feature, the entire feature passes:

```
2 scenarios (2 passed)
16 steps (16 passed)
```

Before we wrap up here, let's add one more scenario to ensure that what is entered into the description field is longer than 10 characters. You want the descriptions to be useful! Let's add this scenario to the features/creating_tickets.feature file:

```
Scenario: Description must be longer than 10 characters
  When I fill in "Title" with "Non-standards compliance"
  And I fill in "Description" with "it sucks"
```

---

[1]   Line breaks are represented as \n and \r\n in strings in Ruby rather than as visible line breaks.

Alternative validation syntax

You can use a slightly differently named method call to accomplish the same thing here:

```
validates_presence_of :title
validates_presence_of :description
```

Some people prefer this syntax because it's been around for a couple of years; others prefer the newer style. It's up to you which to choose. A number of other `validates_*` methods are available.

```
And I press "Create Ticket"
Then I should see "Ticket has not been created."
And I should see "Description is too short"
```

The final line here is written this way because you do not know what the validation message is, but you'll find out later. To implement this scenario, add another option to the end of the validation for the `description` in your `Ticket` model, as shown in the following listing.

Listing 5.7 app/models/ticket.rb

```
validates :description, :presence => true,
                        :length => { :minimum => 10 }
```

If you go into `rails console` and try to create a new `Ticket` object by using `create!`, you can get the full text for your error:

```
irb(main):001:0> Ticket.create!
ActiveRecord::RecordInvalid: ... Description is too short
(minimum is 10 characters)
```

That is the precise error message you are looking for in your feature. When you run `bin/cucumber features/creating_tickets.feature` again, you see that all three scenarios are now passing:

```
3 scenarios (3 passed)
25 steps (25 passed)
```

You should ensure that the rest of the project still works. Because you have both features and specs, you should run the following command to check everything:

```
rake cucumber:ok spec
```

The summary for these two tasks together is[2]

```
9 scenarios (9 passed)
62 steps (62 passed)
# and
5 examples, 0 failures, 4 pending
```

---

[2] The summary is altered to cut down on line noise with only the important parts shown.

Great! Everything's still working. Push the changes!

```
git add .
git commit -m "Implemented creating tickets for a project"
git push
```

This section covered how to create tickets and link them to a specific project through the foreign key called `project_id` on records in the `tickets` table.

The next section shows how easily you can list tickets for individual projects.

5.2   *Viewing tickets*

Now that you have the ability to create tickets, you use the `show` action to create the functionality to view them individually.

When displaying a list of projects, you use the `index` action of the `Projects-Controller`. For tickets, however, you use the `show` action because this page is currently not being used for anything else in particular. To test it, put a new feature at features/viewing_tickets.feature using the code from the following listing.

Listing 5.8 features/viewing_tickets.feature

```
Feature: Viewing tickets
In order to view the tickets for a project
As a user
I want to see them on that project's page

Background:
  Given there is a project called "TextMate 2"
  And that project has a ticket:
    | title          | description                    |
    | Make it shiny! | Gradients! Starbursts! Oh my!  |
  And there is a project called "Internet Explorer"
  And that project has a ticket:
    | title                | description    |
    | Standards compliance | Isn't a joke.  |

  And I am on the homepage

  Scenario: Viewing tickets for a given project
    When I follow "TextMate 2"
    Then I should see "Make it shiny!"
    And I should not see "Standards compliance"
    When I follow "Make it shiny!"
    Then I should see "Make it shiny" within "#ticket h2"        ❶  Check element
    And I should see "Gradients! Starbursts! Oh my!"                using CSS
                                                                    selector
    When I follow "Ticketee"
    And I follow "Internet Explorer"
    Then I should see "Standards compliance"
    And I should not see "Make it shiny!"
    When I follow "Standards compliance"
    Then I should see "Standards compliance" within "#ticket h2"
    And I should see "Isn't a joke."
```

Quite the long feature! We'll go through it piece by piece in just a moment. First, let's examine the within usage in your scenario. Rather than checking the entire page for content, this step checks the specific element using Cascading Style Sheets (CSS) selectors. The #ticket prefix finds all elements with an ID of ticket that contain an h2 element with the content you specified. This content should appear inside the specified tag only when you're on the ticket page, so this is a great way to make sure that you're on the right page and that the page is displaying relevant information.

The first step passes because you defined it previously; the next one is undefined. Let's see this by running bin/cucumber features/viewing_tickets.feature:

```
Undefined step: "that project has a ticket:" (Cucumber::Undefined)
```

The bottom of the output tells you how to define the step:

```
Given /^that project has a ticket:$/ do |table|
# table is a Cucumber::Ast::Table
pending # express the regexp above with the code you wish you had
end
```

This step in the scenario is defined using the following syntax:

```
| title         | description                  |
| Make it shiny! | Gradients! Starbursts! Oh my! |
```

For Cucumber, this syntax represents a table, which is what the step definition hints at. Using the code shown in the following listing, define this step inside a new file at features/step_definitions/ticket_steps.rb.

Listing 5.9 features/step_definitions/ticket_steps.rb

```
Given /^that project has a ticket:$/ do |table|
  table.hashes.each do |attributes|
    @project.tickets.create!(attributes)
  end
end
```

Because you used a table here, Cucumber provides a hashes method for the table object, which uses the first row in the table as keys and the rest of the rows (as many as you need) for the values of hashes stored in an array. In this step, you iterate through this array, and each hash represents the attributes for the tickets you want to create.

One thing that you haven't done yet is define the @project variable used inside this iterator. To do that, open features/step_definitions/project_steps.rb and change this line

```
Factory(:project, :name => name)
```

to the following:

```
@project = Factory(:project, :name => name)
```

Instance variables are available throughout the scenario in Cucumber, so if you define one in one step, you may use it in the following steps. If you run the feature again, you see that it can't find the text for the first ticket because you're not displaying any tickets on the show template yet:

```
expected there to be content "Make it shiny!" in "[text]"
```

5.2.1 *Listing tickets*

To display a ticket on the show template, you can iterate through the project's tickets by using the tickets method, made available by the has_many :tickets call in your model. Put this code at the bottom of app/views/projects/show.html.erb, as shown in the next listing.

Listing 5.10 app/views/projects/show.html.erb

```
<ul id='tickets'>
  <% @project.tickets.each do |ticket| %>
    <li>
      #<%= ticket.id %> - <%= link_to ticket.title, [@project, ticket] %>
    </li>
  <% end %>
</ul>
```

> **TIP** If you use a @ticket variable in place of the ticket variable in the link_to's second argument, it will be nil. You haven't initialized the @ticket variable at this point, and uninitialized instance variables are nil by default. If @ticket rather than the correct ticket is passed in here, the URL generated will be a projects URL, such as /projects/1, rather than the correct /projects/1/tickets/2.

Here you iterate over the items in @project.tickets using the each method, which does the iterating for you, assigning each item to a ticket variable inside the block. The code inside this block runs for every single ticket. When you run bin/cucumber features/viewing_tickets.feature, you get this error:

```
When I follow "Ticketee"
    no link with title, id or text 'Ticketee' found
```

The reasoning behind wanting this not-yet-existing link is that when users click it, it takes them back to the homepage, which is where you want to go in your feature to get back to the projects listing. To add this link, put it into app/views/layouts/application .html.erb (as shown in the following listing) so that it's available on every page, just above the <%= yield %>.

Listing 5.11 app/views/layouts/application.html.erb

```
<h1><%= link_to "Ticketee", root_path %></h1>
<%= yield %>
```

The call to yield should be used only once. If you put <%= yield %> then the content of the page would be rendered twice.

The `root_path` method is made available by the call to the `root` method in config/routes.rb. This simply outputs / when it's called, providing a path to the root of your application.

Running `bin/cucumber features/viewing_tickets.feature` again, you can see this is all working:

```
1 scenario (1 passed)
18 steps (18 passed)
```

Your code expressly states that inside the TextMate 2 project, you should see only the `"Make it shiny!"` ticket, and inside the Internet Explorer project, you should see only the `"Standards compliance"` ticket. Both statements worked.

Time to make sure everything else is still working by running `rake cucumber:ok spec`. You should see that everything is green:

```
10 scenarios (10 passed)
80 steps (80 passed)
# and
5 examples, 0 failures, 4 pending
```

Fantastic! Push!

```
git add .
git commit -m "Implemented features for displaying a list of relevant
               tickets for projects and viewing particular tickets"
git push
```

Now you can see tickets just for a particular project, but what happens when a project is deleted? The tickets for that project would not be deleted automatically. To implement this behavior, you can pass some options to the `has_many` association, which will delete the tickets when a project is deleted.

5.2.2 Culling tickets

When a project is deleted, its tickets become useless: they're inaccessible because of how you defined their routes. Therefore, when you delete a project, you should also delete the tickets for that project, and you can do that by using the `:dependent` option on the `has_many` association defined in your `Project` model.

This option has three choices that all act slightly differently from each other. The first one is the `:destroy` value:

```
has_many :tickets, :dependent => :destroy
```

If you put this in your `Project` model, any time you call `destroy` on a `Project` object, Rails iterates through each ticket for this project and calls `destroy` on them, then calls any destroy callbacks (such as any `has_manys` in the `Ticket` model, which also have the dependent option)[3] the `ticket` objects have on them, any destroy callbacks for those objects, and so on. The problem is that if you have a large number of tickets, `destroy` is called on each one, which will be slow.

---

[3] Or any callback defined with `after_destroy` or `before_destroy`.

The solution is the second value for this option:

```
has_many :tickets, :dependent => :delete_all
```

This simply deletes all the tickets using a SQL delete, like this:

```
DELETE FROM tickets WHERE project_id = :project_id
```

This operation is quick and is exceptionally useful if you have a large number of tickets that *don't* have callbacks. If you *do* have callbacks on `Ticket` for a destroy operation, then you should use the first option, `:dependent => :destroy`.

Finally, if you just want to disassociate tickets from a project and unset the `project_id` field, you can use this option:

```
has_many :tickets, :dependent => :nullify
```

When a project is deleted with this type of `:dependent` option defined, it will execute an SQL query such as this:

```
UPDATE tickets SET project_id = NULL WHERE project_id = :project_id
```

Rather than deleting the tickets, this option keeps them around, but their `project_id` fields are unset.

Using this option would be helpful, for example, if you were building a task-tracking application and instead of projects and tickets you had users and tasks. If you delete a user, you may want to reassign rather than delete the tasks associated with that user, in which case you'd use the `:dependent => :nullify` option instead.

In your projects and tickets scenario, though, you use `:dependent => :destroy` if you have callbacks to run on tickets when they're destroyed or `:dependent => :delete_all` if you have no callbacks on tickets.

This was a little bit of a detour for the work you're doing now, but it's a nice thing to know if you ever need to delete an associated object when the original object is deleted.

Let's look at how to edit the tickets in your application.

5.3   *Editing tickets*

You want users to be able to edit tickets, the *updating* part of this CRUD interface. This section covers creating the `edit` and `update` actions for the `TicketsController`.

The next feature you're going to implement is the ability to edit tickets. This functionality follows a thread similar to the projects edit feature where you follow an Edit link in the `show` template. With that in mind, you can write this feature using the code in the following listing and put it in a file at features/editing_tickets.feature.

Listing 5.12   features/editing_tickets.feature

```
Feature: Editing tickets
  In order to alter ticket information
  As a user
  I want a form to edit the tickets
```

```
Background:
  Given there is a project called "TextMate 2"
  And that project has a ticket:
    | title           | description                 |
    | Make it shiny!  | Gradients! Starbursts! Oh my! |
  Given I am on the homepage
  When I follow "TextMate 2"
  And I follow "Make it shiny!"
  When I follow "Edit Ticket"

Scenario: Updating a ticket
  When I fill in "Title" with "Make it really shiny!"
  And I press "Update Ticket"
  Then I should see "Ticket has been updated."
  And I should see "Make it really shiny!" within "#ticket h2"
  But I should not see "Make it shiny!"

Scenario: Updating a ticket with invalid information
  When I fill in "Title" with ""
  And I press "Update Ticket"
  Then I should see "Ticket has not been updated."
```

When you run this feature using bin/cucumber features/editing_tickets.feature, the first two steps pass, but the third fails:

```
When I follow "Edit"
no link with title, id or text 'Edit Ticket' found
```

To fix this, add the Edit Ticket link to the TicketsController's show template, because that's where you've navigated to in your feature. Put it on the line underneath the <h2> tag in app/views/tickets/show.html.erb:

```
<%= link_to "Edit Ticket", [:edit, @project, @ticket] %>
```

Here is yet another use of the Array argument passed to the link_to method, but rather than passing all Active Record objects, you pass a Symbol first. Rails, yet again, works out from this Array what route you wish to follow. Rails interprets this array to mean the edit_project_ticket_path method, which is called like this:

```
edit_project_ticket_path(@project, @ticket)
```

Now that you have an Edit Project link, you need to add the edit action to the TicketsController.

5.3.1 Adding the edit action

The next logical step is to define the edit action in your TicketsController, which you can leave empty because the find_ticket before filter does all the hard lifting for you (shown in the following listing).

Listing 5.13   app/controllers/tickets_controller.rb

```
def edit

end
```

Again, you're defining the action here so that anybody coming through and reading your `TicketsController` class knows that this controller responds to this action. It's the first place people will go to determine what the controller does, because it is the *controller*.

The next logical step is to create the view for this action. Put it at app/views/ tickets/edit.html.erb and fill it with this content:

```
<h2>Editing a ticket in <%= @project.name %></h2>
<%= render "form" %>
```

Here you re-use the `form` partial you created for the `new` action, which is handy. The `form_for` knows which action to go to. If you run the feature command here, you're told the `update` action is missing:

```
And I press "Update"
  The action 'update' could not be found TicketsController
```

5.3.2   Adding the update action

You should now define the `update` action in your `TicketsController`, as shown in the following listing.

> **Listing 5.14   app/controllers/tickets_controller.rb**

```
def update
  if @ticket.update_attributes(params[:ticket])
    flash[:notice] = "Ticket has been updated."
    redirect_to [@project, @ticket]
  else
    flash[:alert] = "Ticket has not been updated."
    render :action => "edit"
  end
end
```

Remember that in this action you don't have to find the `@ticket` or `@project` objects because a `before_filter` does it for the `show`, `edit`, `update`, and `destroy` actions. With this single action implemented, both scenarios in your ticket-editing feature pass:

```
2 scenarios (2 passed)
20 steps (20 passed)
```

Now check to see if everything works:

```
12 scenarios (12 passed)
100 steps (100 passed)
# and
5 examples, 0 failures, 4 pending
```

Great! Let's commit and push that:

```
git add .
git commit -m "Implemented edit action for the tickets controller"
git push
```

In this section, you implemented edit and update for the TicketsController by using the scoped finders and some familiar methods, such as update_attributes. You've got one more part to go: deletion.

5.4 *Deleting tickets*

We now reach the final story for this nested resource, the deletion of tickets. As with some of the other actions in this chapter, this story doesn't differ from what you used in the ProjectsController, except you'll change the name *project* to *ticket* for your variables and flash[:notice]. It's good to have the reinforcement of the techniques previously used: practice makes perfect.

Let's use the code from the following listing to write a new feature in features/deleting_tickets.feature.

Listing 5.15 features/deleting_tickets.feature

```
Feature: Deleting tickets
  In order to remove tickets
  As a user
  I want to press a button and make them disappear

  Background:
    Given there is a project called "TextMate 2"
    And that project has a ticket:
      | title         | description                    |
      | Make it shiny! | Gradients! Starbursts! Oh my! |
    Given I am on the homepage
    When I follow "TextMate 2"
    And I follow "Make it shiny!"

  Scenario: Deleting a ticket
    When I follow "Delete Ticket"
    Then I should see "Ticket has been deleted."
    And I should be on the project page for "TextMate 2"
```

When you run this using bin/cucumber features/deleting_tickets.feature, the first step fails because you don't yet have a Delete Ticket link on the show template for tickets:

```
When I follow "Delete Ticket"
no link with title, id or text 'Delete Ticket' found (Capybara::ElementNotFound)
```

You can add the Delete Ticket link to the app/views/tickets/show.html.erb file just under the Edit link (shown in the next listing), exactly as you did with projects.

Listing 5.16 app/views/tickets/show.html.erb

```
<%= link_to "Delete Ticket", [@project, @ticket], :method => :delete,
           :confirm => "Are you sure you want to delete this ticket?" %>
```

The :method => :delete is specified again, turning the request into one headed for the destroy action in the controller. Without this :method option, you'd be off to the show action because the link defaults to the GET method. Upon running bin/cucumber features/deleting_tickets.feature, you're told a destroy action is missing:

```
When I follow "Delete Ticket"
The action 'destroy' could not be found in TicketsController
```

The next step must be to define this action, right? Open app/controllers/tickets_controller.rb, and define it directly under the update action:

```
def destroy
  @ticket.destroy
  flash[:notice] = "Ticket has been deleted."
  redirect_to @project
end
```

With that done, your feature should now pass:

```
1 scenario (1 passed)
8 steps (8 passed)
```

Yet again, check to see that everything is still going as well as it should by using rake cucumber:ok spec. If it is, you should see output similar to this:

```
13 scenarios (13 passed)
108 steps (108 passed)
and
5 examples, 0 failures, 4 pending
```

Commit and push!

```
git add .
git commit -m "Implemented deleting tickets feature"
git push
```

You've now completely created another CRUD interface, this time for the tickets resource. This resource is accessible only within the scope of a project, so you must request it using a URL such as /projects/1/tickets/2 rather than /tickets/2.

5.5   *Summary*

In this chapter, you generated another controller, the TicketsController, which allows you to create records for your Ticket model that will end up in your tickets table. The difference between this controller and the ProjectsController is that the TicketsController is accessible only within the scope of an existing project because you used nested routing.

In this controller, you scoped the finds for the Ticket model by using the tickets association method provided by the association helper method has_many call in your Project model. has_many also provides the build method, which you used to begin to create new Ticket records that are scoped to a project.

In the next chapter, you learn how to let users sign up and sign in to your application using a gem called devise. You also implement a basic authorization for actions such as creating a project.

Authentication and basic authorization

6

This chapter covers

- Working with engine code and generators
- Building an authentication system with an engine
- Implementing basic authorization checking

You've now created two resources for your Ticketee application: projects and tickets. Now you'll use a gem called Devise, which provides authentication, to let users sign in to your application. With this feature, you can track which tickets were created by which users. A little later, you'll use these user records to allow and deny access to certain parts of the application.

The general idea behind having users for this application is that some users are in charge of creating projects (project owners) and others use whatever the projects provide. If they find something wrong with it or wish to suggest an improvement, filing a ticket is a great way to inform the project owner of their request. You don't want absolutely everybody creating or modifying projects, so you'll learn to restrict project creation to a certain subset of users.

To round out the chapter, you'll create another CRUD interface, this time for the users resource, but with a twist.

Before you start, you must set up Devise!

6.1   *What Devise does*

Devise is an authentication gem that provides a lot of the common functionality for user management, such as letting users sign in and sign up, in the form of a Rails *engine*. An engine can be thought of as a miniature application that provides a small subset of controllers, models, views, and additional functionality in one neat little package. You can override the controllers, models, and views if you wish, though, by placing identically named files inside your application. This works because Rails looks for a file in your application first before diving into the gems and plugins of the application, which can speed up the application's execution time.

6.1.1   *Installing Devise*

To install Devise, first add the following line to the Gemfile, right after the end for the :test group:

```
gem 'devise', '~> 1.4.3'
```

To install the Devise gem, run bundle. Once Devise is installed, you need to run the generator, but how do you know the name of it? Simple! You can run the generate command with no additional arguments to list all the generators:

```
rails generate
```

In this output, you'll see devise:install listed. Hey, that'll probably help you get things installed! Let's try it:

```
rails g devise:install
```

This code generates two files, config/initializers/devise.rb and config/locales/devise.en.yml:

- config/initializers/devise.rb sets up Devise for your application and is the source for all configuration settings for Devise.
- config/locales/devise.en.yml contains the English translations for Devise and is loaded by the internationalization (I18n) part of Rails. You can learn about internationalization in Rails by reading the official I18n guide: http://guides.rubyonrails.org/i18n.html.

The code also gives you three setup tips to follow. The first setup tip tells you to set up some Action Mailer settings, which you can place in your development environment's configuration at config/environments/development.rb and in your test environment's configuration at config/environments/test.rb:

```
config.action_mailer.default_url_options = { :host => 'localhost:3000' }
```

The files in config/environments are used for environment-specific settings, like the one you just added. If you wish to configure something across all environments for your application, you put it in config/application.rb.

The second tip tells you to set up a root route, which you have done already. The third tip tells you to add displays for `notice` and `alert` in your application layout, which you've also done, except with different code than what it suggests.

The next step to get Devise going is to run this command:

```
rails g devise user
```

This generator generates a model for your user and adds the following line to your config/routes.rb file:

```
devise_for :users
```

By default, this one simple line adds routes for user registration, signup, editing and confirmation, and password retrieval. The magic for this line comes from inside the User model that was generated, which contains the code from the following listing.

Listing 6.1 app/models/user.rb

```
class User < ActiveRecord::Base
  # Include default devise modules. Others available are:
  # :token_authenticatable, :encryptable, :confirmable,
  # :lockable, :timeoutable and :omniauthable
  devise :database_authenticatable, :registerable,
         :recoverable, :rememberable, :trackable, :validatable

  # Setup accessible (or protected) attributes for your model
  attr_accessible :email, :password,
                  :password_confirmation, :remember_me
end
```

The devise method here comes from the Devise gem and configures the gem to provide the specified functions. These modules are shown in the following two tables. Table 6.1 shows default functions, and table 6.2 shows the optional functions.

Table 6.1 Devise default modules

Module	Provides
`:database_authenticatable`	Adds the ability to authenticate via an email and password field in the database.
`:registerable`	Provides the functionality to let a user sign up.
`:recoverable`	Adds functionality to let the user recover their password if they ever lose it.
`:rememberable`	Provides a check box for users to check if they want their session to be remembered. If they close their browser and revisit the application, they are automatically signed in on their return.

Table 6.1 Devise default modules (*continued*)

Module	Provides
:trackable	Adds functionality to track users, such as how many times they sign in, when they last signed in, and the current and last IPs they signed in from.
:validatable	Validates the user has entered correct data, such as a valid email address and password.

Table 6.2 Devise optional modules (off by default)

Module	Provides
:token_authenticatable	Lets the user authenticate via a token; can be used in conjunction with :database_authenticatable
:encryptable	Adds support for other methods of encrypting passwords; by default, Devise uses bcrypt
:confirmable	When users register, sends them an email with a link they click to confirm they're a real person (you'll switch on this module shortly because it's one step to prevent automated signups)
:lockable	Locks the user out for a specific amount of time after a specific number of retries (configurable in the initializer); default is a lock-out time of 1 hour after 20 retries
:timeoutable	If users have no activity in their session for a specified period of time, they are automatically signed out; useful for sites that may be used by multiple people on the same computer, such as email or banking sites
:omniauthable	Adds support for the OmniAuth gem, which allows for alternative authentication methods using services such as OAuth and OpenID

The devise call is followed by a call to attr_accessible. This method defines fields that are accessible via *attribute mass-assignment*. Attribute mass-assignment happens when you pass a whole slew of attributes to a method such as create or update_attributes; because these methods take any and all parameters passed to them by default, users may attempt to hack the form and set an attribute they are not supposed to set, such as an admin boolean attribute. By using attr_accessible, you define a white list of fields you want the user to access. Any other fields passed through in an attribute mass-assignment are ignored.

The final step here is to run rake db:migrate to create the users table from the Devise-provided migration in your development database and run rake db:test:prepare so it's created in the test database too.

6.2 User signup

With Devise set up, you're ready to write a feature that allows users to sign up. The Devise gem provides this functionality, so this feature will act as a safeguard to ensure that if the functionality were ever changed, the feature would break.

To make sure this functionality is always available, you write a feature for it, using the following listing, and put it in a new file at features/signing_up.feature.

Listing 6.2 features/signing_up.feature

```
Feature: Signing up
In order to be attributed for my work
As a user
I want to be able to sign up

Scenario: Signing up
  Given I am on the homepage
  When I follow "Sign up"
  And I fill in "Email" with "user@ticketee.com"
  And I fill in "Password" with "password"
  And I fill in "Password confirmation" with "password"
  And I press "Sign up"
  Then I should see "You have signed up successfully."
```

When you run this feature using `bin/cucumber features/signing_up.feature`, you're told it can't find a Sign Up link, probably because you haven't added it yet:

```
no link with title, id or text 'Sign up' found
```

You should now add this link in a nav:[1]

```
<nav>
<%= link_to "Sign up", new_user_registration_path %>
</nav>
```

You previously used the `menu` on the app/views/tickets/show.html.erb page to style the links there. Here you use a `nav` tag because this is a major navigation menu for the entire application, not just a single page's navigation.

With this link now in place, the entire feature passes when you run it because Devise does all the heavy lifting for you:

```
1 scenario (1 passed)
7 steps (7 passed)
```

Because Devise has already implemented this functionality, you don't need to write any code for it. This functionality could be overridden in your application, and this feature is insurance against anything changing for the worse.

With the signup feature implemented, this is a great point to see if everything else is working by running `rake cucumber:ok spec`. You should see this output:

---

[1] nav is an HTML5 tag and may not be supported by some browsers. As an alternative, you could put `<div id='nav'>` instead, in app/views/layouts/application.html.erb, directly underneath the `h1` tag for your application's title.

```
14 scenarios (14 passed)
115 steps (115 passed)
# and
6 examples, 0 failures, 5 pending
```

Great! Commit that!

```
git add .
git commit -m "Added feature to ensure Devise signup is always working"
git push
```

In this section, you added a feature to make sure Devise is set up correctly for your application. When users sign up to your site, they'll receive an email as long as you configured your Action Mailer settings correctly. The next section covers how Devise automatically signs in users who click the confirmation link provided in the email they've been sent.

6.3   *Confirmation link sign-in*

With users now able to sign up to your site, you should make sure they're also able to sign in. When users are created, they should be sent a confirmation email in which they have to click a link to confirm their email address. You don't want users signing up with fake email addresses! Once confirmed, the user is automatically signed in by Devise.

6.3.1   *Testing email*

First, you enable the `confirmable` module for Devise because (as you saw earlier) it's one of the optional modules. With this module turned on, users will receive a confirmation email that contains a link for them to activate their account. You need to write a test that checks whether users receive a confirmation email when they sign up and can confirm their account by clicking a link inside that email.

For this test, you use another gem called `email_spec`. To install this gem, add the following line to your Gemfile inside the `test` group:

```
gem 'email_spec'
```

Now run `bundle` to install it.

Next, run the generator to get the steps for `email_spec` with the following command:

```
rails g email_spec:steps
```

This command generates steps in a file at features/step_definitions/email_steps.rb that you can use in your features to check whether a user received a specific email and more. This is precisely what you need to help you craft the next feature: signing in, receiving an email, and clicking the confirmation link inside it.

One additional piece you must set up is to require the specific files from the email_spec library. Create a new file at features/support/email.rb, which you use for requiring the `email_spec` files. Inside this file, put these lines:

```
# Email Spec helpers
require 'email_spec'
require 'email_spec/cucumber'
```

6.3.2 *Confirming confirmation*

With the `email_spec` gem now fully installed and set up, let's write a feature for signing users in when they click the confirmation link they should receive in their email. Insert the following listing at features/signing_in.feature.

Listing 6.3 features/signing_in.feature

```
Feature: Signing in
  In order to use the site
  As a user
  I want to be able to sign in

  Scenario: Signing in via confirmation
    Given there are the following users:
      | email             | password |
      | user@ticketee.com | password |
    And "user@ticketee.com" opens the email with subject
    "Confirmation instructions"
    And they click the first link in the email
    Then I should see "Your account was successfully confirmed"
    And I should see "Signed in as user@ticketee.com"
```

With this scenario, you make sure that when users are created, they receive an email called "Confirmation instructions" that should contain confirmation instructions. This email will contain a link, and when users click it, they should see two things: a message saying "Your account was successfully confirmed" and notification that they are now "Signed in as user@ticketee.com" where user@ticketee.com represents the username.

The first step in this scenario is currently undefined, so when you run this feature using `bin/cucumber features/signing_in.feature`, it fails with the undefined step:

```
Given /^there are the following users:$/ do |table|
  pending # express the regexp above with the code you wish you had
end
```

This step definition allows you to create as many users as you wish using Cucumber's table syntax. Put this step definition inside a new file called features/step_definitions/user_steps.rb, using the code from the following listing.

Listing 6.4 features/step_definitions/user_steps.rb

```
Given /^there are the following users:$/ do |table|
  table.hashes.each do |attributes|
    @user = User.create!(attributes)
  end
end
```

In this step definition, you use Cucumber's table format again to specify more than one user to create. To get to these attributes, iterate through `table.hashes`, storing each set of attributes as `attributes` for each iteration. Inside the iteration, the `create!` method creates the user record using these attributes. All of this should look pretty familiar—you used it to create tickets for a project.

The second step in this scenario is provided by the `email_spec` gem, and it fails when you run `bin/cucumber features/signing_in.feature` again:

```
And "user@ticketee.com" opens the email with subject "Confirmation
➥instructions"
Could not find email With subject "Confirmation instructions".
Found the following emails:

[]
```

This is `email_spec` telling you it can't find an email with the title "Confirmation instructions," which is what Devise would send out if you had told it you wanted users to be confirmable. You haven't yet done this, so no emails are being sent.

To make users confirmable, add the `:confirmable` symbol at the end of the `devise` call in app/models/user.rb:

```
devise :database_authenticatable, :registerable,
       :recoverable, :rememberable, :trackable,
       :validatable, :confirmable
```

Now Devise will send confirmation emails when users sign up. When you run `bin/cucumber features/signing_in.feature` again, your first step is failing:

```
Given there are the following users:
  | email              | password | unconfirmed |
  | user@ticketee.com  | password | true        |
  undefined local variable or method 'confirmed_at' for #<User:...>
```

The `confirmed_at` attribute is used by Devise to determine whether or not a user has confirmed their account. By default, this attribute is `nil`, indicating the user hasn't confirmed yet. The attribute doesn't exist at the moment, so you get this error.

You could add this attribute to the existing db/migrate/[timestamp] _devise_create_users.rb migration, but because you already pushed that migration, you should avoid changing it, as others will have to rerun the migration to get those changes. Even though it's just you working on the project at the moment, it's a good rule of thumb to not modify migrations that have already been pushed.

Instead, create a new migration to add the `confirmed_at` field and two others, `confirmation_token` and `confirmation_sent_at`. The `confirmation_token` is generated by Devise and used to identify users attempting to confirm their account when they click the confirmation link from the email. The `confirmation_sent_at` field is used also by Devise and tracks the time when the confirmation email was sent:

```
rails g migration add_confirmable_fields_to_users
```

Let's now open this migration and put the code from the following listing inside it.

Listing 6.5 db/migrate/[timestamp]_add_confirmable_fields_to_users.rb

```
class AddConfirmableFieldsToUsers < ActiveRecord::Migration
  def change
    add_column :users, :confirmation_token, :string
    add_column :users, :confirmed_at, :datetime
    add_column :users, :confirmation_sent_at, :datetime
  end
end
```

This migration adds the specified columns to the users table when you run rake db:migrate or removes them when you run rake db:rollback.

When users sign up, a confirmation token is generated for them. An email with a link containing this token is sent (and the confirmation_sent_at field is set). When users click the link, their account is confirmed, and the confirmed_at field is set to the current time in the process.

You now need to run rake db:migrate and rake db:test:prepare to update your test database with this latest change. With these fields in place, you should be much closer to having your scenario pass. Let's see with a quick run of bin/cucumber features/signing_in.feature:

```
Scenario: Signing in via confirmation
    Given there are the following users:
      | email             | password |
      | user@ticketee.com | password |
    And "user@ticketee.com" opens the email with subject "Confirmation
➥instructions"
    And they click the first link in the email
    Then I should see "Your account was successfully confirmed"
    Then I should see "Signed in as user@ticketee.com"
      expected there to be content "Created by user@ticketee.com" in "[text]"
```

Everything but the final step is passing. The final step checks for "Signed in as user@ticketee.com" somewhere on the page, but it can't find it. You must add it to your application's layout, replacing the Sign Up link with "Signed in as [username]" so users don't have the option to sign up if they're already signed in!

Let's open app/views/layouts/application.html.erb and change this line

```
<%= link_to "Sign up", new_user_registration_path %>
```

to the following:

```
<% if user_signed_in? %>
  Signed in as <%= current_user.email %>
<% else %>
  <%= link_to "Sign up", new_user_registration_path %>
<% end %>
```

The user_signed_in? and current_user methods are provided by Devise. The user_signed_in? method returns true if the user is signed in; otherwise it returns false. The current_user method returns a User object representing the current user, and from that object you can call the email method to display the user's email.

When you run `bin/cucumber features/signing_up.feature`, the entire feature is passing:

```
1 scenario (1 passed)
5 steps (5 passed)
```

In addition to signing-up facilities, Devise handles all the signing-in facilities too. All you need to add is the `:confirmable` symbol to the `devise` call in the model, the confirmation fields to the `users` table, and the message "Signed in as [user]" in your application—three easy steps.

Does everything else pass? Run `rake cucumber:ok spec`, and you should see the following output:

```
15 scenarios (15 passed)
120 steps (120 passed)
# and
6 examples, 0 failures, 5 pending
```

Great! Push that!

```
git add .
git commit -m "Added feature for ensuring that a user is signed in
              via a confirmation email by using email spec"
git push
```

Now that users can sign up and confirm their email addresses, what should happen when they return to the site? They should be able to sign in! Let's make sure this can happen.

6.4   *Form sign-in*

The previous story covered the automatic sign-in that happens when users follow the confirmation link from the email they receive when they sign up. Now you must write a story for users who have confirmed their account and are returning and need to sign in again.

Place the scenario in the following listing directly underneath the previous scenario in features/signing_in.feature.

Listing 6.6   features/signing_in.feature

```
Scenario: Signing in via form
Given there are the following users:
  | email             | password |
  | user@ticketee.com | password |
And I am on the homepage
When I follow "Sign in"
And I fill in "Email" with "user@ticketee.com"
And I fill in "Password" with "password"
And I press "Sign in"
Then I should see "Signed in successfully."
```

When you run `bin/cucumber features/signing_in.feature`, it complains about the missing Sign In link:

```
When I follow "Sign in"
no link with title, id or text 'Sign in' found (Capybara::ElementNotFound)
```

You should add the link directly under the Sign Up link in app/views/layouts /application.html.erb, as shown in the following listing.

Listing 6.7 app/views/layouts/application.html.erb

```
<%= link_to "Sign in", new_user_session_path %>
```

When you run the feature again, it still fails, but this time on the final step:

```
And I press "Sign in"
Then I should see "Signed in successfully."
  expected there to be content "Signed in successfully." in "[text]"
```

It fails because users who have not yet confirmed their account by clicking the link in the email can't sign in. To fix this, you could confirm the users with the first step in this scenario, but it would break the first scenario because it requires users to be unconfirmed.

To fix this, alter the first scenario in this feature to contain the following as its first step:

```
Given there are the following users:
| email              | password | unconfirmed |
| user@ticketee.com  | password | true        |
```

With this small change, the step now has an additional key available in the attributes hash in the step definition. If this step is called with an unconfirmed user, it doesn't confirm the user; otherwise it does. Let's alter this step definition in features/ step_definitions/user_steps.rb:

```
Given /^there are the following users:$/ do |table|
  table.hashes.each do |attributes|
    unconfirmed = attributes.delete("unconfirmed") == "true"
    @user = User.create!(attributes)
    @user.confirm! unless unconfirmed
  end
end
```

At the top of the iteration over table.hashes, you now call attributes .delete("unconfirmed"), which removes the unconfirmed key from the attributes hash, returning its value in the process. If that value is equal to true then unconfirmed is also set to true. If that's the case, the final line in the iterator isn't called and the user isn't confirmed. Otherwise, as in the case in the second scenario of the feature, the user is confirmed and allowed to sign in.

When you run bin/cucumber features/signing_in.feature again, both scenarios pass:

```
2 scenarios (2 passed)
12 steps (12 passed)
```

Run your tests again before you commit these changes with rake cucumber:ok spec. Even though you didn't change much code in this section, it's still a good habit to run your tests before every commit to stop unintentional regressions. You should see the following summaries:

```
16 scenarios (16 passed)
127 steps (127 passed)
# and
6 examples, 0 failures, 5 pending
```

Great, let's commit and push:

```
git add .
git commit -m "Added feature for signing in via the Devise-provided form"
git push
```

6.5   *Linking tickets to users*

Now that users can sign in and sign up to your application, it's time to link a ticket with a user when it's created automatically, clearly defining which user created the ticket. You also want to ensure that the user who created the ticket gets attribution on the ticket page.

That part is easy: you need a "Created by [user]" message displayed on the ticket page. The setup before it is a little more difficult, but you'll get through it.

You can test for this functionality by amending the Creating a Ticket scenario inside features/creating_tickets.feature to have the following line as the final line for the scenario:

```
Then I should see "Created by user@ticketee.com"
```

When you run the feature using bin/cucumber features/creating_tickets.feature, it fails on this new step because it isn't on the ticket show template:

```
expected #has_content?("Created by user@ticketee.com")
to return true, got false ...
```

You need to make sure the user is signed in before they can create a ticket; otherwise, you won't know who to make the owner of that ticket. When users go to a project page and click the New Ticket link, they should be redirected to the sign-in page and asked to sign in. Once they're signed in, they should be able to create the ticket. Change the Background of the Feature in features/creating_tickets.feature to ensure this process happens, using the code from the following listing.

Listing 6.8   features/creating_tickets.feature

```
Given there is a project called "Internet Explorer"
And there are the following users:
| email              | password |
| user@ticketee.com | password |
And I am on the homepage
When I follow "Internet Explorer"
And I follow "New Ticket"
```

```
Then I should see "You need to sign in or sign up before continuing."
When I fill in "Email" with "user@ticketee.com"
And I fill in "Password" with "password"
And I press "Sign in"
Then I should see "New Ticket"
```

The step that checks for the text "You need to sign in or sign up before continuing" fails because you're not ensuring the user is signed in before the new action in the TicketsController.

To do so, you can use the Devise-provided method authenticate_user! as a before_filter. Put this method directly underneath the class definition for Tickets-Controller inside app/controllers/tickets_controller.rb. The placement of this before_filter ensures that if it fails, the other two before_filters underneath it will not needlessly run, eventually saving valuable CPU cycles.

The line you put in the TicketsController is

```
before_filter :authenticate_user!, :except => [:index, :show]
```

This line ensures that users are authenticated before they go to any action in the controller that isn't the index or show, including the new and create actions.

By ensuring this authentication, you'll know which user created a ticket during the creation process, so let's link tickets to users.

6.5.1 Attributing tickets to users

To link tickets to specific users, you alter the build line in your create action in TicketsController from this line

```
@ticket = @project.tickets.build(params[:ticket])
```

to this:

```
@ticket = @project.tickets.build(params[:ticket].merge!(:user => current_user))
```

The merge! method here is a Hash and HashWithIndifferentAccess method, which merges the provided keys into the hash and overrides any keys already specified.[2] When you run the feature again using bin/cucumber features/creating_tickets .feature, it complains about an unknown attribute in all three scenarios:

```
unknown attribute: user (ActiveRecord::UnknownAttributeError)
```

This error occurs because you haven't added a belongs_to association between the Ticket and User. Let's open app/models/ticket.rb and add this line directly under the belongs_to :project line:

```
belongs_to :user
```

The belongs_to method defines methods for accessing the association, as has_many does, except here you retrieve only one record. Active Record knows which record to retrieve when you call either project or user on a Ticket object because it

---

[2] Which could happen if someone hacked the form and attempted to pass their own user attribute.

intelligently uses the name of the `belongs_to` association to imply that the fields are `project_id` and `user_id`, respectively. When looking up a user, Active Record performs a query like this:

```
SELECT * FROM users WHERE id = #{@ticket.user_id}
```

This query then returns a row from the database that matches the ID (if there is one), and Active Record creates a new `User` object from this result.

With these associations set up, you now need to add a field on the `tickets` table to store the ID of the user that a ticket links to. Run this command:

```
rails g migration add_user_id_to_tickets user_id:integer
```

Based solely on how you wrote the name of this feature, Rails will understand that you want to add a particular column to the `tickets` table. You specify the name and type of the column after the migration name, and Rails creates the migration with the field prefilled for you.

If you open the new migration file (it's the last one in the db/migrate directory), you'll see the output in the following listing.

Listing 6.9   db/migrate/[timestamp]_add_user_id_to_tickets.rb

```
class AddUserIdToTickets < ActiveRecord::Migration
  def change
    add_column :tickets, :user_id, :integer
  end
end
```

It's all done for you! You can close this file and then run the migration with `rake db:migrate` and prepare the test database by using `rake db:test:prepare`.

Let's rerun `bin/cucumber features/creating_tickets.feature` and see where it stands now:

```
Then I should see "Created by user@ticketee.com"
  expected there to be content "Created by user@ticketee.com" in "[text]"
```

> **Bash migrate alias**
>
> If you're using bash as a shell (which is probably the case if you're on a UNIX operating system), you could add an alias to your `~/.bashrc` to do both of these steps for you rather than having to type them out:
>
> ```
> alias migrate='rake db:migrate && rake db:test:prepare'
> ```
>
> Then type `source ~/.bashrc`, and the alias will be available to you in your current terminal window. It'll also be available in new terminal windows even if you didn't use `source`, because this file is processed every time a new bash session is started. If you don't like typing `source`, then `. ~/.bashrc` will do.

> **Make sure to run db:test:prepare**
>
> If you don't prepare the test database, the following error occurs when you run the feature:
>
> ```
> And I press "Create Ticket"
> undefined method 'email' for nil:NilClass (ActionView::Template::Error)
> ```
>
> Watch out for that one.

Only one scenario fails now. We're right back to the missing "Created by user@ticketee .com" text. Open app/views/tickets/show.html.erb and, above the ticket description, put the following line:

```
<br><small>Created by <%= @ticket.user.email %></small>
```

This line adds the text the feature needs to pass, so when you run `bin/cucumber features/creating_tickets.feature`, you get the following output:

```
3 scenarios (3 passed)
44 steps (44 passed)
```

You should run `rake cucumber:ok spec` as usual to ensure you haven't broken anything:

```
Failing Scenarios:
cucumber features/deleting_tickets.feature:15
cucumber features/editing_tickets.feature:16
cucumber features/viewing_tickets.feature:18
```

Oops, it looks like you did! If you didn't have these tests in place, you wouldn't have known about this breakage unless you tested the application manually or guessed (or somehow knew) that your changes would break the application in this way. Let's see if you can fix it.

6.5.2 *We broke something!*

Luckily, all the failed tests have the same error

```
When I follow "Make it shiny!"
  undefined method 'email' for nil:NilClass (ActionView::Template::Error)
  ...
  ./app/views/tickets/show.html.erb:4:in ...
```

Whatever is causing this error is on line 4 of app/views/tickets/show.html.erb:

```
Created by <%= @ticket.user.email %>
```

Aha! The error is `undefined method 'email' for nil:NilClass`, and the only place you call `email` on this line is on the `user` object from `@ticket`, so you can determine that `user` must be `nil`. But why? Let's have a look at how to set up the data in the features/viewing_tickets.feature feature, as shown in the following listing.

Listing 6.10   features/viewing_tickets.feature

```
Given there is a project called "TextMate 2"
And that project has a ticket:
  | title          | description                  |
  | Make it shiny! | Gradients! Starbursts! Oh my! |
```

No user is assigned to this ticket for the second step, and that's why `user` is `nil`. You should rewrite this feature to make it create a ticket and link it to a specific user.

6.5.3   *Fixing the Viewing Tickets feature*

The first step is to create a user you can link to, so change the first lines of the Background to this:

```
Given there are the following users:
  | email             | password |
  | user@ticketee.com | password |
And there is a project called "TextMate 2"
And that project has a ticket:
  | title          | description                  |
  |  Make it shiny! | Gradients! Starbursts! Oh my! |
```

Next, change the third step a little so it creates a ticket with a user:

```
And "user@ticketee.com" has created a ticket for this project:
  | title          | description                  |
  |  Make it shiny! | Gradients! Starbursts! Oh my! |
```

Also be sure to change the other ticket-creation lines further down:

```
And "user@ticketee.com" has created a ticket for this project:
  | title               | description   |
  | Standards compliance | Isn't a joke. |
```

When you run `bin/cucumber features/viewing_tickets.feature`, you get the new version of this step definition:

```
Given /^"([^\"]*)" has created a ticket for this project:$/ do |arg1, table|
  # table is a Cucumber::Ast::Table
  pending # express the regexp above with the code you wish you had
end
```

Copy the first line of this step definition, open features/step_definitions/ticket_steps.rb, and replace the first line in the file with this new line. Then replace `arg1` with `email`, making the entire step definition

```
Given /^"([^\"]*)" has created a ticket for this project:$/ do |email, table|
  table.hashes.each do |attributes|
    @project.tickets.create!(attributes)
  end
end
```

Next, link this new ticket to the user who has the email you pass in. Change the step definition as follows:

```
Given /^"([^\"]*)" has created a ticket for this project:$/ do |email, table|
  table.hashes.each do |attributes|
```

```
    attributes = attributes.merge!(:user => User.find_by_email!(email))
      @project.tickets.create!(attributes)
    end
end
```

With this step definition in place, the feature should pass. Let's do another run of
bin/cucumber features/viewing_tickets.feature:

```
1 scenario (1 passed)
19 steps (20 passed)
```

Let's now fix up the other two, beginning with the Editing Tickets feature.

6.5.4   *Fixing the Editing Tickets feature*

You can re-use the step definition you created in the previous section in the features/
editing_tickets.feature by changing the first few lines of the Background to be identical
to the next listing.

Listing 6.11   features/editing_tickets.feature

```
Given there are the following users:
  | email               | password |
  | user@ticketee.com   | password |
Given there is a project called "TextMate 2"
And "user@ticketee.com" has created a ticket for this project:
  | title          | description                   |
  |  Make it shiny! | Gradients! Starbursts! Oh my! |
```

When you run the feature—unlike the Viewing Tickets feature—it doesn't pass, complaining that it can't find the field called Title. Uh oh:

```
cannot fill in, no text field, text area or password field with id,
name, or label 'Title' found (Capybara::ElementNotFound)
```

Back in the TicketsController, you restricted some of the actions by using the
before_filter:

```
before_filter :authenticate_user!, :except => [:index, :show]
```

This before_filter restricts any access to the edit action for people who are not
signed in. In this feature then, you should sign in as the user you create so you can
edit this ticket. Change the first line of the Background to sign in as that user:

```
Background:
  Given there are the following users:
    | email               | password |
    | user@ticketee.com   | password |
  And I am signed in as them
```

When you run this feature, you see the last step in the example is undefined. You must
define this new step so you can sign in as the user set up in the first step of the
Background. Because you assigned @user in the there are the following users step,
you can reference this variable in the new step. Define this new step at the bottom of
features/step_definitions/user_steps.rb by copying the lines from features/signing_in
.feature and doing a couple of replacements, as shown in the following listing.

Listing 6.12   features/user_steps.rb

```
Given /^I am signed in as them$/ do
  steps(%Q{
    Given I am on the homepage
    When I follow "Sign in"
    And I fill in "Email" with "#{@user.email}"
    And I fill in "Password" with "password"
    And I press "Sign in"
    Then I should see "Signed in successfully."
  })
end
```

In this step definition, you use a method called `steps`. Because step definitions are written in Ruby, you can't use step definitions as you do in Cucumber features. To get around this restriction, use the `steps` method and specify each step you want to call inside `%Q{}`, a kind of super-`String` that allows you to use double and single quotes inside. The `steps` method then takes each of these steps and runs them as if they were inside a feature.

Because this step is essentially a duplicate of what's already in features/ signing_in.feature, you can remove the similar lines and turn the Signing in via Form scenario into what's shown in the following listing.

Listing 6.13   features/signing_in.feature

```
Scenario: Signing in via form
Given there are the following users:
  | email             | password |
  | user@ticketee.com | password |
  And I am signed in as them
```

Much simpler!

Now if you run `bin/cucumber features/editing_tickets.feature`, this feature passes because you're signing in as a user before attempting to edit a ticket!

```
2 scenarios (2 passed)
27 steps (27 passed)
```

One more feature to go: the Deleting Tickets feature.

6.5.5   *Fixing the Deleting Tickets feature*

To fix the Deleting Tickets feature, take the first couple of lines from features/ editing_tickets.feature and put them into features/deleting_tickets.feature so that the first few lines of the `Background` for this feature look like the following listing.

Listing 6.14   features/deleting_tickets.feature

```
Given there are the following users:
  | email             | password |
  | user@ticketee.com | password |
And I am signed in as them
Given there is a project called "TextMate 2"
```

```
And "user@ticketee.com" has created a ticket for this project:
  | title          | description                |
  |  Make it shiny! | Gradients! Starbursts! Oh my! |
```

When you run `bin/cucumber features/deleting_tickets.feature`, this feature passes once again:

```
1 scenario (1 passed)
11 steps (11 passed)
```

There! The last of the broken features is fixed.

Now that the known failing scenarios are working, let's check for any other breakages with `rake cucumber:ok spec`. You should see this output:

```
16 scenarios (16 passed)
148 steps (148 passed)
# and
6 examples, 0 failures, 4 pending
```

Great! Let's commit and push that to GitHub now:

```
git add .
git commit -m "When creating tickets, attribute them to the creator."
git push
```

You've added the feature to add attribution to the tickets so that when a ticket is created, you know who created it. You've also restricted certain actions in the `Tickets-Controller` on the basis of whether or not a user is signed in.

6.6   *Summary*

This chapter covered how to set up authentication so that users can sign up and sign in to your application to accomplish certain tasks.

We began with Devise, a gem that provides the signing up and signing in capabilities right out of the box by way of being a Rails engine. Using Devise, you tested the functionality provided by the gem in the same way you tested functionality you wrote yourself: by writing Cucumber features to go with it.

Then you moved into testing whether emails were sent out to the right people by using another gem called email_spec. The gem allows you to click a link in an email to confirm a user's account and then have Devise automatically sign in the user.

Then came linking tickets to users, so you can track which user created which ticket. This was done by using the setter method provided by the `belongs_to` method's presence on the `Ticket` class. You were also able to use `Hash`'s lovely `merge!` method in the `TicketsController`'s create action to link any ticket that was being created to the currently signed-in user.

In the next chapter, we look at restricting certain actions to only users who are signed in or who have a special attribute set on them.

Basic access control

As your application now stands, anybody, whether they're signed in or not, can create new projects. As you did for the actions in the `TicketsController`, you must restrict access to the actions in the `ProjectsController`. The twist here is that you'll allow only a certain subset of users—users with one particular attribute set in one particular way—to access the actions.

You'll track which users are administrators by putting a boolean field called `admin` in the users table. This is the most basic form of user *authorization*, which is not to be confused with *authentication*, which you implemented in chapter 6. Authentication is the process users go through to confirm their identity, whereas authorization is the process users go through to gain access to specific areas.

7.1   *Projects can be created only by admins*

To restrict the creation of projects to admins, you alter the existing `Background` in features/creating_projects.feature and insert the following listing as the first three lines.

Listing 7.1   features/creating_projects.feature

```
Given there are the following users:
| email             | password |
| admin@ticketee.com | password |
And I am signed in as them
```

This listing creates a user. The `Background` should now look like the following listing.

Listing 7.2   features/creating_projects.feature

```
Given there are the following users:
| email             | password | admin |
| admin@ticketee.com | password | true  |
And I am signed in as them
Given I am on the homepage
When I follow "New Project"
```

There's a problem here: the `admin` attribute for `User` objects isn't *mass-assignable*. You saw this issue in chapter 6 when the `attr_accessible` method was introduced. This restriction means that you can't assign the `admin` attribute along with other attributes using the `new`, `build`, `create`, or `update_attributes` method.

You have to set this attribute manually by using either `update_attribute` or the setter, `user.admin = [value]`. You use the latter here, so change this step in features/step_definitions/user_steps.rb

```
Given /^there are the following users:$/ do |table|
table.hashes.each do |attributes|
  unconfirmed = attributes.delete("unconfirmed") == "true"
  @user = User.create!(attributes)
  @user.confirm! unless unconfirmed
end
end
```

to this:

```
Given /^there are the following users:$/ do |table|
table.hashes.each do |attributes|
  unconfirmed = attributes.delete("unconfirmed") == "true"
  @user = User.create!(attributes)
  @user.update_attribute("admin", attributes["admin"] == "true")
  @user.confirm! unless unconfirmed
end
end
```

If you pass the `admin` attribute in your table, it'll be a string. You check whether the string is equal to `true`, and if it is, you use `update_attribute` to set the `admin` field manually to `true` or `false`, depending on whether or not `attributes["admin"]` is true.

When you run this feature, it can't find the `admin` field for your users table, because you haven't added it yet:

```
Given there are the following users:
| email              | password | admin |
| admin@ticketee.com | password | true  |
    undefined method `admin=' for #<User: ...>
```

7.2   *Adding the admin field to the users table*

You can generate a migration to add the `admin` field by running `rails generate migration add_admin_to_users admin:boolean`. You want to modify this migration so that when users are created, the `admin` field is set to `false` rather than defaulting to `nil`. Open the freshly generated migration and change this line

```
add_column :users, :admin, :boolean
```

to this:

```
add_column :users, :admin, :boolean, :default => false
```

When you pass in the `:default` option here, the `admin` field defaults to `false`, ensuring that users aren't accidentally created as admins.

The command `rake db:migrate db:test:prepare` runs the migration, adds the `admin` field to the users table, and sets up the test database. Now you see that the step is passing:

```
Given there are the following users:
| email              | password | admin |
| admin@ticketee.com | password | true  |
```

With this step definition implemented, run `rake cucumber:ok` and `rake spec` to make sure you haven't broken anything. According to this output, you haven't:

```
16 scenarios (16 passed)
152 steps (152 passed)
```

Great! Now you can go about restricting the acts of creating, updating, and destroying projects to only those users who are admins.

7.3   *Restricting actions to admins only*

For this step, you implement a `before_filter` that checks not only whether the user is signed in but also whether the user is an admin.

Before you write this `before_filter`, you write a controller spec rather than a Cucumber feature to test it. Cucumber features are great for defining a set of actions that a user can perform in your system, but controller specs are much better for quickly testing singular points, such as whether or not a user can go to a specific action in the controller. You used this same reasoning back in chapter 4 to test what happens when a user attempts to go to a project that doesn't exist.

You want to ensure that all visits to the `new`, `create`, `edit`, `update`, and `destroy` actions are done by admins and are inaccessible to other users. Open spec/controllers/

projects_controller_spec.rb, and add a `let` inside the `describe` so the top of the spec looks like the following listing.

Listing 7.3 spec/controllers/projects_controller_spec.rb

```
describe ProjectsController do
let(:user) do
  user = Factory(:user)
  user.confirm!
  user
end

context "standard users" do
  it "cannot access the new action" do
    sign_in(:user, user)
  end
end

...
end
```

Here you use a multilined block for the `let` method. This method defines a `user` method, which returns a newly created and confirmed user. You create this user using Factory Girl.

You then use this object in your test to sign in as that user. The benefit of using `let` over defining an instance variable in a `before` block is that the `let` code is called only when it's referenced, whereas all the code in a `before` is evaluated regardless. This is helpful if some of your tests don't need a `User` object.

Underneath the `let`, you add a short placeholder test that signs in as the user, attempting to use the `user` `let` method. With this test, the `let` block is called, and you should get an error when you run this spec using `bin/rspec spec/controllers/projects _controller_spec.rb`:

```
Not registered: user (ArgumentError)
```

Therefore, you should create a user factory that creates a `user` object with a random email address (because you may wish to create more than one user at a time using this factory), and the password should default to *password*. Define this factory in a new file called factories/user_factory.rb:

```
Factory.define :user do |user|
user.sequence(:email) { |n| "user#{n}@ticketee.com" }
user.password "password"
user.password_confirmation "password"
end
```

In this factory, you use the `sequence` method provided by Factory Girl, which passes a unique number to the block and makes your user's email addresses unique.

The files within the factories directory aren't yet required by RSpec, so their factories aren't available for you. To make RSpec load them, create a new file at spec/support /factories.rb and put this content in it:

```
Dir[Rails.root + "factories/*.rb"].each do |file|
require file
end
```

When the value of the `email` method is inside a block, it's evaluated every time this factory is called and generates a new (hopefully random) email address.

The next bit of code to write is in your spec and is the first example to ensure that users who are not admins (such as the `user` object) cannot access the `new` action. The code in the following listing should replace the placeholder `"cannot access the new action"` example you've already got.

Listing 7.4   spec/controllers/projects_controller_spec.rb

```
context "standard users" do
it "cannot access the new action" do
  sign_in(:user, user)
  get :new
  response.should redirect_to(root_path)
  flash[:alert].should eql("You must be an admin to do that.")
end
end
```

This spec is placed inside a `context` block because you'll have specs for standard users later. `context` blocks function similarly to `describe` blocks; they're mainly used to specify the context of an example rather than to describe what it does.

On the first line of the example, you use the `sign_in` method, which is available in Devise, but the appropriate part isn't yet included. This method takes two arguments: the scope and the resource. Because you have only one scope for Devise, you don't have to worry about what this means right now. What you do care about is that this method will sign in a user.

To add this method, you must include a module in your RSpec configuration: the `Devise::TestHelpers` module. Open spec/spec_helper.rb, and you'll see the `RSpec.configure` block (comments stripped) shown in the following listing.

Listing 7.5   spec/spec_helper.rb

```
RSpec.configure do |config|
config.mock_with :rspec
end
```

This `configure` method is responsible for setting up RSpec. To include the `Devise::TestHelpers` method, you could use it like this:

```
RSpec.configure do |config|
config.mock_with :rspec
config.include Devise::TestHelpers
end
```

But you may want to rerun the RSpec generator to update your spec/spec_helper.rb file and its associates when you update RSpec. If this file is updated, you'll lose your changes. To fix this problem, use `RSpec.configure` in another file: spec/support/devise.rb. RSpec automatically loads files in this directory. Let's create this file now and fill it with the content from the following listing.

Listing 7.6   spec/support/devise.rb

```
RSpec.configure do |config|
config.include Devise::TestHelpers
end
```

You should include this module only for controller tests by passing a `filter` to the end:

```
config.include Devise::TestHelpers, :type => :controller
```

If you don't restrict where this module is included, it could lead to problems further down the line. It's better to be safe than sorry.

> **TIP** You can specify `:type => :model` as a filter if you want to include a module only in your model specs. If you ever write any view specs, you can use `:type => :view` to include this module only in the view specs. Similarly, you can use `:controller` for controller specs.

Going back to your spec, you make a request on the third line to the `new` action in the controller. The `before_filter` that you haven't yet implemented should catch the request before it gets to the action; it won't execute the request but instead redirects the user to `root_path` and shows a `flash[:alert]` saying the user "must be an admin to do that."

  If you run this spec with `bin/rspec spec/controllers/projects_controller _spec.rb`, it fails as you expect:

```
Failure/Error: response.should redirect_to(root_path)
    Expected response to be a <:redirect>, but was <200>
```

This error message tells you that although you expected to be redirected, the response was actually a 200 response, indicating a successful response. This isn't what you want. Now let's get it to pass.

  The first step is to define a new method that checks whether a user is an admin, and if not, displays the "You must be an admin to do that" message and then redirects the requester to the `root_path`. First define this new method inside app/controllers/application_controller.rb, which is the base class for all controllers and makes any methods defined here available to all controllers. Define the method using the following listing inside the `ApplicationController` class.

Listing 7.7   app/controllers/application_controller.rb

```
private

def authorize_admin!
  authenticate_user!
  unless current_user.admin?
```

```
      flash[:alert] = "You must be an admin to do that."
      redirect_to root_path
    end
end
```

This method uses the `authenticate_user!` method (provided by Devise) to ensure that the user is signed in. If the user isn't signed in when this method is called, they're asked to sign in. If the user isn't an admin after signing in, they're shown the "You must be an admin to do that" message and redirected to the homepage.

To call this method, call `before_filter` at the top of your `ProjectsController`, as shown in the following listing.

Listing 7.8   app/controllers/projects_controller.rb

```
before_filter :authorize_admin!, :except => [:index, :show]
```

With that in place, you can rerun the spec `bin/rspec spec/controllers/projects _controller_spec.rb`, which should now pass:

```
2 examples, 0 failures
```

Great, now you know this is working for the new action, but does it work for `create`, `edit`, `update`, and `destroy`? You can replace the `"cannot access the new action"` example you just wrote with the code from the following listing.

Listing 7.9   spec/controllers/projects_controller_spec.rb

```
{ "new" => "get",
"create" => "post",
"edit" => "get",
"update" => "put",
"destroy" => "delete" }.each do |action, method|
it "cannot access the #{action} action" do
  sign_in(:user, user)
  send(method, action.dup, :id => project.id)
  response.should redirect_to(root_path)
  flash[:alert].should eql("You must be an admin to do that.")
end
end
```

In this example, you use a `project` variable, which you need to set up by using a `let`, as you did for user. Under the `let` for user, add one for `project`:

```
let(:project) { Factory(:project) }
```

The attributes of this `project` object are unimportant: you only need a valid object, and Factory Girl provides that for you.

The keys for the hash on the first line of listing 7.9 contain all the actions you want to ensure are protected; the values are the methods you use to make the request to the action. You use the action here to give your examples dynamic names, and you use them further down when you use the `send` method. The `send` method allows you to dynamically call methods and pass arguments to them. It's used here because for each key-value pair of the hash, the action[1] and method change. You pass in the :id parameter because, without it, the controller can't route to the edit, update, or destroy action. The new and create actions ignore this parameter.

The remainder of this spec is unchanged, and when you run bin/rspec spec/controllers/projects_controller_spec.rb, you should see all six examples passing:

```
6 examples, 0 failures
```

Now's a good time to ensure you haven't broken anything, so let's run rake cucumber :ok spec:

```
cucumber features/deleting_projects.feature:6
cucumber features/editing_projects.feature:12
cucumber features/editing_projects.feature:18
```

Oops. Three scenarios are broken. They failed because, for these features, you're not signing in as an admin user—or, in fact, as *any* user!—which is now required for performing the actions in the scenario. You can fix these scenarios by signing in as an admin user.

7.3.1 *Fixing three more broken scenarios*

For the features/deleting_projects.feature, add a new Background, as shown in the following listing.

Listing 7.10   features/deleting_projects.feature

```
Background:
Given there are the following users:
  | email             | password | admin |
  | admin@ticketee.com | password | true  |
And I am signed in as them
```

When you run this feature, it once again passes:

```
1 scenario (1 passed)
8 steps (8 passed)
```

For the editing_projects.feature, use the steps from listing 7.10 again, putting them at the top of the already existing Background:

```
Given there are the following users:
| email             | password | admin |
| admin@ticketee.com | password | true  |
And I am signed in as them
```

Now this feature also passes. Check it using bin/cucumber features/editing _projects.feature:

```
2 scenarios (2 passed)
21 steps (21 passed)
```

---

[1] The action variable is a frozen string in Ruby 1.9.2 (because it's a block parameter), so you need to duplicate the object because Rails forces the encoding on it to be UTF-8.

That should be the last of it. When you run `rake cucumber:ok`, everything once again passes:

```
16 scenarios (16 passed)
158 steps (158 passed)
```

Great! Now that accessing the actions is restricted, let's make a commit here:

```
git add .
git commit -m "Restrict access to project
          actions to admins only"
git push
```

You should also hide the links from the users who are not admins, because it's useless to show actions to people who can't perform them.

7.3.2 *Hiding the New Project link*

Next you'll learn how to hide certain links, such as the New Project link, from users who have no authorization to perform that action in your application. To begin, write a new feature called features/hidden_links.feature, which looks like the following listing.

Listing 7.11   features/hidden_links.feature

```
Feature: Hidden Links
In order to clean up the user experience
As the system
I want to hide links from users who can't act on them

Background:
  Given there are the following users:
    | email                | password | admin |
    | user@ticketee.com    | password | false |
    | admin@ticketee.com   | password | true  |
  And there is a project called "TextMate 2"

Scenario: New project link is hidden for non-signed-in users
  Given I am on the homepage
  Then I should not see the "New Project" link

Scenario: New project link is hidden for signed-in users
  Given I am signed in as "user@ticketee.com"
  Then I should not see the "New Project" link

Scenario: New project link is shown to admins
  Given I am signed in as "admin@ticketee.com"
  Then I should see the "New Project" link
```

When you run this feature using `bin/cucumber features/hidden_links.feature`, you're given three new steps to define:

```
Then /^I should not see the "([^\"]*)" link$/ do |arg1|
pending # express the regexp above with the code you wish you had
end
```

```
Given /^I am signed in as "([^\"]*)"$/ do |arg1|
pending # express the regexp above with the code you wish you had
end

Then /^I should see the "([^\"]*)" link$/ do |arg1|
pending # express the regexp above with the code you wish you had
end
```

Put the first and last steps in a new file called features/step_definitions/link_steps.rb, using the code from the next listing.

Listing 7.12 features/step_definitions/link_steps.rb

```
Then /^I should see the "([^\"]*)" link$/ do |text|
page.should(have_css("a", :text => text),
  "Expected to see the #{text.inspect} link, but did not.")
end

Then /^I should not see the "([^\"]*)" link$/ do |text|
page.should_not(have_css("a", :text => text),
  "Expected to not see the #{text.inspect} link, but did.")
end
```

These two steps use the `have_css` method provided by Capybara, which checks that a page has an element matching a Cascading Style Sheets (CSS) matcher, in this case an element called a. The option you pass after it (`:text => text`) tells Capybara that you're checking for an a element that contains the text specified. If this matcher fails, it outputs a custom error message that is the optional second argument to the `should` and `should_not` method calls here, with `have_css` being the first argument.

With these steps defined, you can now add the other new step to features/step_definitions/user_steps.rb using the code from the following listing.

Listing 7.13 features/step_definitions/user_steps.rb

```
Given /^I am signed in as "([^\"]*)"$/ do |email|
@user = User.find_by_email!(email)
steps("Given I am signed in as them")
end
```

This step finds the user mentioned and then calls the `"Given I am signed in as them"` step. Providing you always set up your users with "password" as their password, this new step will pass.

When you run your feature using `bin/cucumber features/hidden_links.feature`, the first two scenarios are failing:

```
Failing Scenarios:
cucumber features/hidden_links.feature:13
cucumber features/hidden_links.feature:17
```

They fail, of course, because you've done nothing yet to hide the link! Open app/views/projects/index.html.erb, and change the New Project link to the following:

```
<%= admins_only do %>
<%= link_to "New Project", new_project_path %>
<% end %>
```

You'll define the `admins_only` method soon, and it'll take a block. Inside this block, you specify all the content you want shown if the user is an admin. No content will be shown if the user is not an admin. To define the `admins_only` helper, open app/helpers /application_helper.rb and define the method inside the module using this code:

```
def admins_only(&block)
block.call if current_user.try(:admin?)
nil
end
```

The `admins_only` method takes a block, which is the code between the `do` and `end` in your view. To run this code inside the method, call `block.call`, which runs the specified block but only if `current_user.try(:admin?)` returns a value that evaluates to true. This `try` method tries a method on an object, and if that method doesn't exist (as it wouldn't if `current_user` were `nil`), then it returns `nil`. At the end of the method, you return `nil` so the content doesn't show again.

When you run this feature using bin/cucumber features/hidden_links.feature, it passes:

```
3 scenarios (3 passed)
12 steps (12 passed)
```

Now that you've got the New Project link hiding if the user isn't an admin, let's do the same thing for the Edit Project and Delete Project links.

7.3.3   *Hiding the edit and delete links*

Add this `admins_only` helper to the Edit Project and Delete Project links on the projects show view, but not before adding further scenarios to cover these links to features/ hidden_links.feature, as shown in the following listing.

> **Listing 7.14   features/hidden_links.feature**

```
Scenario: Edit project link is hidden for non-signed-in users
Given I am on the homepage
When I follow "TextMate 2"
Then I should not see the "Edit Project" link

Scenario: Edit project link is hidden for signed-in users
Given I am signed in as "user@ticketee.com"
When I follow "TextMate 2"
Then I should not see the "Edit Project" link

Scenario: Edit project link is shown to admins
Given I am signed in as "admin@ticketee.com"
When I follow "TextMate 2"
Then I should see the "Edit Project" link
```

```
Scenario: Delete project link is hidden for non-signed-in users
Given I am on the homepage
When I follow "TextMate 2"
Then I should not see the "Delete Project" link

Scenario: Delete project link is hidden for signed-in users
Given I am signed in as "user@ticketee.com"
When I follow "TextMate 2"
Then I should not see the "Delete Project" link

Scenario: Delete project link is shown to admins
Given I am signed in as "admin@ticketee.com"
When I follow "TextMate 2"
Then I should see the "Delete Project" link
```

To make these steps pass, change the ProjectsController's show template to wrap these links in the admins_only helper, as shown in the next listing.

Listing 7.15   app/views/projects/show.html.erb

```erb
<%= admins_only do %>
<%= link_to "Edit Project", edit_project_path(@project) %>
<%= link_to "Delete Project", project_path(@project), :method => :delete,
                :confirm => "Are you sure you want to delete this project?" %>
<% end %>
```

When you run this entire feature using bin/cucumber features/hidden_links .feature, all the steps should pass:

```
9 scenarios (9 passed)
42 steps (42 passed)
```

All right, that was a little too easy! But that's Rails.

This is a great point to ensure that everything is still working by running rake cucumber:ok spec. According to the following output, it is:

```
25 scenarios (25 passed)
200 steps (200 passed)
# and
11 examples, 0 failures, 5 pending
```

Let's commit and push that:

```
git add .
git commit -
    m "Lock down specific projects controller actions for admins only"
git push
```

In this section, you ensured that only users with the admin attribute set to true can get to specific actions in your ProjectsController as an example of basic authorization.

Next, you learn to "section off" part of your site using a similar methodology and explore the concept of namespacing.

7.4   *Namespace routing*

Although it's fine and dandy to ensure that admin users can get to special places in your application, you haven't yet added the functionality for *triggering* whether or not a user is an admin from within the application itself. To do so, you create a new *namespaced* section of your site called admin. The purpose of namespacing in this case is to separate a controller from the main area of the site so you can ensure that users accessing this particular controller (and any future controllers you create in this namespace) have the admin field set to true.

You begin by generating a namespaced controller with an empty index action by using this command:

```
rails g controller admin/users index
```

When the / separator is used between parts of the controller, Rails knows to generate a namespaced controller called Admin::UsersController at app/controllers/admin/users_controller.rb. The views for this controller are at app/views/admin/users, and the spec is at spec/controllers/admin/users_controller_spec.rb.

This command also inserts a new route into your config/routes.rb file. You don't want that, so remove this line:

```
get "users/index"
```

Now you must write a spec for this newly generated controller to ensure only users with the admin attribute set to true can access it. Open spec/controllers/admin/users_controller_spec.rb and write an example to ensure non-signed-in users can't access the index action, as shown in the following listing.

Listing 7.16   spec/controllers/admin/users_controller_spec.rb

```ruby
require 'spec_helper'

describe Admin::UsersController do
let(:user) do
  user = Factory(:user)
  user.confirm!
  user
end

context "standard users" do
  before do
    sign_in(:user, user)
  end

  it "are not able to access the index action" do
    get 'index'
    response.should redirect_to(root_path)
    flash[:alert].should eql("You must be an admin to do that.")
  end
end
end
```

The new RSpec method, `before`, takes a block of code that's executed before every spec inside the current `context` or `describe`.

You use the lengthy `let(:user)` block again, which is effectively the same as what you have in spec/controllers/projects_controller_spec.rb. Rather than duplicating the code inside this block, move it into a new file in your spec/support directory. Its job is to provide methods to help you seed your test data, so call it seed_helpers.rb. In this file, create a module called `SeedHelpers`, which contains a `create_user!` method that uses the code from the `let`. This file is shown in the following listing.

Listing 7.17   spec/support/seed_helpers.rb

```
module SeedHelpers
  def create_user!(attributes={})
    user = Factory(:user, attributes)
    user.confirm!
    user
  end
end

RSpec.configure do |config|
  config.include SeedHelpers
end
```

With this new spec/support/seed_helpers.rb file, you can now use `create_user!` rather than the three lines of code you're currently using. Let's change the `let(:user)` in spec/controllers/projects_controller_spec.rb to this:

```
let(:user) { create_user! }
```

Ah, much better! Let's also change it in the new spec/controllers/admin/users _controller_spec.rb file:

```
let(:user) { create_user! }
```

When you run this spec file using `bin/rspec spec/controllers/admin/users _controller_spec.rb`, you see that there's no route to the `index` action:

```
1) Admin::UsersController regular users are not able to access the
       ➥index action
  Failure/Error: get 'index'
  No route matches {:controller => "admin/users"}
```

In fact, there's no route to the controller at all! To define this route, open config/ routes.rb and insert the following code before the final `end` in the file.

Listing 7.18   config/routes.rb

```
namespace :admin do
  resources :users
end
```

This code defines similar routes to the vanilla `resources` but nests them under an admin/ prefix. Additionally, the routing helpers for these routes have an `admin` part to them: what would normally be `users_path` becomes `admin_users_path`, and `new_user_path` becomes `new_admin_user_path`.

With this namespace defined, when you run `bin/rspec spec/controllers/admin/users_controller_spec.rb`, you should see it fail with a different error:

```
Failure/Error: response.should redirect_to(root_path)
Expected response to be a <:redirect>, but was <200>
```

This error appears because you need to implement the `authorize_admin!` `before_filter` for your namespace. To apply it to all controllers in this namespace, you create a new *supercontroller* whose only job (for now) is to call the `before_filter`. You can also put methods that are common to the `admin` section here.

Create a new file at app/controllers/admin/base_controller.rb, and fill it with this code:

```
class Admin::BaseController < ApplicationController
before_filter :authorize_admin!
end
```

This file can double as an eventual homepage for the admin namespace and as a class that the other controllers inside the admin namespace can inherit from, which you'll see in a moment. You inherit from `ApplicationController` with this controller so you receive all the benefits it provides, like the `authorize_admin!` method and the Action Controller functionality.

Open app/controllers/admin/users_controller.rb, and change the first line of the controller from this

```
class Admin::UsersController < ApplicationController
```

to this:

```
class Admin::UsersController < Admin::BaseController
```

Because `Admin::UsersController` inherits from `Admin::BaseController`, the `before_filter` from `Admin::BaseController` now runs for every action inside `Admin::UsersController`, and therefore in your spec, should pass.

Run it with `bin/rspec  spec/controllers/admin/users_controller_spec.rb` now, and you should see this:

```
.
1 example, 0 failures
```

With that done, you should ensure that everything is working as expected by running `rake cucumber:ok spec`:

```
25 scenarios (25 passed)
200 steps (200 passed)
# and
14 examples, 0 failures, 7 pending
```

Great, everything is still green! Let's commit that:

```
git add .
git commit -m "Added admin namespaced users controller"
git push
```

7.5   *Namespace-based CRUD*

Now that only admins can access this namespace, you can create the CRUD actions for this controller too, as you did for the `TicketsController` and `ProjectsController` controllers. Along the way, you'll also set up a homepage for the admin namespace.

For this new CRUD resource, you first write a feature for creating a user and put it at features/creating_users.feature, as shown in the following listing.

Listing 7.19   features/creating_users.feature

```
Feature: Creating Users
In order to add new users to the system
As an admin
I want to be able to add them through the backend

Background:
 Given there are the following users:
    | email             | password | admin |
    | admin@ticketee.com | password | true  |
  And I am signed in as them
  Given I am on the homepage
  When I follow "Admin"
  And I follow "Users"
  When I follow "New User"

Scenario: Creating a new user
  And I fill in "Email" with "newbie@ticketee.com"
  And I fill in "Password" with "password"
  And I press "Create User"
  Then I should see "User has been created."

Scenario: Leaving email blank results in an error
 When I fill in "Email" with ""
 And I fill in "Password" with "password"
 And I press "Create User"
 Then I should see "User has not been created."
 And I should see "Email can't be blank"
```

When you run this feature using `bin/cucumber features/creating_users.feature`, the first four steps pass; but when you follow the Admin link, it fails because the link doesn't exist yet:

```
When I follow "Admin"
no link with title, id or text 'Admin' found (Capybara::ElementNotFound)
```

7.5.1   *Adding a namespace root*

Of course, you need this link for the feature to pass, but you want to show it only for admins. You can use the `admins_only` helper you defined earlier and put the link in app/views/layouts/application.html.erb in the `nav` element:

```
<%= admins_only do %>
<%= link_to "Admin", admin_root_path %><br>
<% end %>
```

At the moment, `admin_root_path` doesn't exist. To define it, open config/routes.rb and change the namespace definition from this

```
namespace :admin do
  resources :users
end
```

to this:

```
namespace :admin do
  root :to => "base#index"
  resources :users
end
```

When you rerun the feature, it fails because you don't have an `index` action for the `Admin::BaseController` controller:

```
When I follow "Admin"
The action 'index' could not be found for Admin::BaseController
```

Let's add that now.

7.5.2 *The index action*

Open app/controllers/admin/base_controller.rb, and add the `index` action so the class definition looks like the following listing.

> **Listing 7.20   app/controllers/admin/base_controller.rb**

```
class Admin::BaseController < ApplicationController
before_filter :authorize_admin!

def index

end
end
```

You define the action here to show users that this controller has an `index` action. The next step is to create the view for the `index` action by creating a new file at app/views/admin/base/index.html.erb and filling it with the following content:

```
<%= link_to "Users", admin_users_path %>
Welcome to Ticketee's Admin Lounge. Please enjoy your stay.
```

You needn't wrap the link in an `admins_only` here because you're inside a page that's visible only to admins. When you run the feature, you *don't* get a message saying The action 'index' could not be found even though you should. Instead, you get this:

```
When I follow "New User"
no link with title, id or text 'New User' found
```

This unexpected output occurs because the `Admin::UsersController` inherits from `Admin::BaseController`, where you just defined an `index` method. By inheriting from this controller, `Admin::UsersController` also inherits its views. When you inherit from a class like this, you get the methods defined in that class too. You can override the `index` action from `Admin::BaseController` by redefining it in `Admin::UsersController`, as in the following listing.

Listing 7.21   app/controllers/admin/users_controller.rb

```
class Admin::UsersController < Admin::BaseController
def index
  @users = User.all(:order => "email")
end
end
```

Next, you rewrite the template for this action, which lives at app/views/admin/users/index.html.erb, so it contains the New User link and lists all the users gathered up by the controller, as shown in the following listing.

Listing 7.22   app/views/admin/users/index.html.erb

```
<%= link_to "New User", new_admin_user_path %>
<ul>
<% @users.each do |user| %>
  <li><%= link_to user.email, [:admin, user] %></li>
<% end %>
</ul>
```

In this example, when you specify a `Symbol` as an element in the route for the `link_to`, Rails uses that element as a literal part of the route generation, making it use `admin_user_path` rather than `user_path`. You saw this in chapter 5 when you used it with `[:edit, @project, ticket]`, but it bears repeating here.

When you run `bin/cucumber features/creating_users.feature` again, you're told the `new` action is missing:

```
When I follow "New User"
The action 'new' could not be found for Admin::UsersController
```

7.5.3   *The new action*

Let's add the `new` action `Admin::UsersController` now by using this code:

```
def new
@user = User.new
end
```

And let's create the view for this action at app/views/admin/users/new.html.erb:

```
<h2>New User</h2>
<%= render "form" %>
```

Using the following listing, create the form partial that's referenced in this new view at
app/views/admin/users/_form.html.erb. It must contain the email and password
fields, which are the bare essentials for creating a user.

Listing 7.23   app/views/admin/users/_form.html.erb

```
<%= form_for [:admin, @user] do |f| %>
<%= f.error_messages %>
<p>
  <%= f.label :email %>
  <%= f.text_field :email %>
</p>

<p>
  <%= f.label :password %>
  <%= f.password_field :password %>
</p>
<%= f.submit %>
<% end %>
```

For this form_for, you use the array form you saw earlier with [@project, @ticket],
but this time you pass in a symbol rather than a model object. Rails interprets the
symbol literally, generating a route such as admin_users_path rather than
users_path, which would normally be generated. You can also use this array syntax
with link_to and redirect_to helpers. Any symbol passed anywhere in the array is
interpreted literally.

When you run the feature once again, you're told there's no action called create:

```
And I press "Create User"
The action 'create' could not be found for Admin::UsersController
```

7.5.4 *The create action*

Let's create that action now by using this code:

```
def create
@user = User.new(params[:user])
if @user.save
  flash[:notice] = "User has been created."
  redirect_to admin_users_path
else
  flash[:alert] = "User has not been created."
  render :action => "new"
end
end
```

With this action implemented, both scenarios inside this feature now pass:

```
2 scenarios (2 passed)
21 steps (21 passed)
```

This is another great middle point for a commit, so let's do so now. As usual, you
should run rake cucumber:ok spec to make sure everything's still working:

```
27 scenarios (27 passed)
221 steps (221 passed)
# and
14 examples, 0 failures, 7 pending
```

Great! Let's push that:

```
git add .
git commit -m "Added the ability to create users through the admin backend"
git push
```

Although this functionality allows you to create new users through the admin backend, it doesn't let you create admin users. That's up next.

7.6   *Creating admin users*

To create admin users, you need a check box on the form that, when clicked, sets the user's `admin` field to `true`. But, because the `admin` attribute isn't on the list of accessible attributes (`attr_accessible` inside app/models/user.rb), it can't be mass-assigned as the other fields can. Therefore, you must manually set this parameter in the controller before the user is saved.

To get started, let's add another scenario to the features/creating_users.feature using the code from the following listing.

Listing 7.24   features/creating_users.feature

```
Scenario: Creating an admin user
When I fill in "Email" with "newadmin@ticketee.com"
And I fill in "Password" with "password"
And I check "Is an admin?"
And I press "Create User"
Then I should see "User has been created"
And I should see "newadmin@ticketee.com (Admin)"
```

Now when you run `bin/cucumber features/creating_users.feature`, it fails on the `"Is an admin?"` step:

```
cannot check field, no checkbox with id, name,
or label 'Is an admin?' found (Capybara::ElementNotFound)
```

You want to add this check box to the form for creating users, which you can do by adding the following code to the `form_for` block inside app/views/admin/users/_form.html.erb:

```
<p>
<%= f.check_box :admin %>
<%= f.label :admin, "Is an admin?" %>
</p>
```

With this check box in place, when you run `bin/cucumber features/creating_users.feature`, you're told `"newadmin@ticketee.com (Admin)"` can't be found anywhere on the page:

```
expected #has_content?("newadmin@ticketee.com (Admin)")
to return true, got false
```

This failure occurs because `admin` isn't a mass-assignable attribute and therefore isn't set and because the user's admin status isn't displayed anywhere on the page. One thing at a time. First, change the `create` action in `Admin::UsersController` to set the `admin` field before you attempt to save the user, as shown in the following listing.

Listing 7.25   app/controllers/admin/users_controller.rb

```
...
@user = User.new(params[:user])
@user.admin = params[:user][:admin] == "1"
if @user.save
...
```

This code sets the `admin` attribute on the user, which is one of the two things you need to get this step to pass. The second problem is that only the user's email address is displayed: no text appears to indicate they're a user. To get this text to appear, change the line in app/views/admin/users/index.html.erb from this

```
<li><%= link_to user.email, [:admin, user] %></li>
```

to this:

```
<li><%= link_to user, [:admin, user] %></li>
```

By not calling any methods on the `user` object and attempting to write it out of the view, you cause Ruby to call `to_s` on this method. By default, this outputs something similar to the following, which isn't human friendly:

```
#<User:0xb6fd6054>
```

You can override the `to_s` method on the `User` model to provide the string containing the email and admin status of the user by putting the following code inside the class definition in app/models/user.rb, underneath the `attr_accessible` line:

```
def to_s
"#{email} (#{admin? ? "Admin" : "User"})"
end
```

Now that the `admin` field is set and displayed on the page, the feature should pass when you run `bin/cucumber features/creating_users.feature`:

```
3 scenarios (3 passed)
33 steps (33 passed)
```

This is another great time to commit, and again, run `rake cucumber:ok spec` to make sure everything works:

```
28 scenarios (28 passed)
288 steps (288 passed)
# and
14 examples, 0 failures, 7 pending
```

Good stuff. Push it:

```
git add .
git commit -
    m "Added the ability to create admin users through the admin backend"
git push
```

Now you can create normal and admin users through the backend. In the future, you may need to modify an existing user's details or delete a user, so we examine the *updating* and *deleting* parts of the CRUD next.

7.7   *Editing users*

This section focuses on creating the updating capabilities for the `Admin::Users-Controller`. Additionally, you need some functionality on the backend to enable users to confirm their account, and you can put it on the editing page.

As usual, you start by writing a feature to cover this functionality, placing the file at features/editing_users.feature and filling it with the content from the following listing.

Listing 7.26   features/editing_users.feature

```
Feature: Editing a user
In order to change a user's details
As an admin
I want to be able to modify them through the backend

Background:
Given there are the following users:
  | email              | password | admin |
  | admin@ticketee.com | password | true  |
And I am signed in as them

Given there are the following users:
  | email             | password |
  | user@ticketee.com | password |
Given I am on the homepage
When I follow "Admin"
And I follow "Users"
And I follow "user@ticketee.com"
And I follow "Edit User"

Scenario: Updating a user's details
When I fill in "Email" with "newguy@ticketee.com"
And I press "Update User"
Then I should see "User has been updated."
And I should see "newguy@ticketee.com"
And I should not see "user@ticketee.com"

Scenario: Toggling a user's admin ability
When I check "Is an admin?"
And I press "Update User"
Then I should see "User has been updated."
And I should see "user@ticketee.com (Admin)"

Scenario: Updating with an invalid email fails
```

```
When I fill in "Email" with "fakefakefake"
And I press "Update User"
Then I should see "User has not been updated."
And I should see "Email is invalid"
```

When you run this feature using `bin/cucumber features/editing_users.feature`, you discover the `show` action is missing:

```
And I follow "user@ticketee.com"
The action 'show' could not be found for Admin::UsersController
```

7.7.1   *The show action*

Define the `show` action in the `Admin::UsersController`, shown in listing 7.28, directly under the `index` action, because grouping the different parts of CRUD is conventional. The method you define is blank because you need to use a `before_filter` to find the user, as you've done in other controllers to find other resources.

> **Listing 7.27   app/controllers/admin/users_controller.rb**

```
def show

end
```

You call the method to find the user object `find_user` and define it under the actions in this controller, like this:

```
private
def find_user
  @user = User.find(params[:id])
end
```

You then need to call this method using a `before_filter`, which should run before the `show`, `edit`, `update`, and `destroy` actions. Put this line at the top of your class definition for `Admin::UsersController`:

```
before_filter :find_user, :only => [:show, :edit, :update, :destroy]
```

With this method in place, you can write the template for the `show` action to make this step pass. This file goes at app/views/admin/users/show.html.erb and uses the following code:

```
<h2><%= @user %></h2>
<%= link_to "Edit User", edit_admin_user_path(@user) %>
```

Now when you run `bin/cucumber features/editing_users.feature`, the step that previously failed passes, and you're on to the next step:

```
And I follow "user@ticketee.com"
And I follow "Edit User"
The action 'edit' could not be found for Admin::UsersController
```

Good, you're progressing nicely. You created the `show` action for the `Admin::Users-Controller`, which displays information for a user to a signed-in admin user. Now you need to create the `edit` action so admin users can edit a user's details.

7.7.2 *The edit and update actions*

Add the `edit` action directly underneath the `create` action in your controller. It should be another blank method like the `show` action:

```
def edit

end
```

With this action defined and the `@user` variable used in its view already set by the `before_filter`, you now create the template for this action at app/views/admin/users/edit.html.erb. This template renders the same form as the `new` template:

```
<%= render "form" %>
```

When you run `bin/cucumber features/editing_users.feature`, you're told the `update` action doesn't exist:

```
The action 'update' could not be found for Admin::UsersController
```

Indeed, it doesn't, so let's create it! Add the `update` action to your `Admin::Users-Controller`, as shown in the following listing. You needn't set up the `@user` variable here because the `find_user before_filter` does it for you.

> **Listing 7.28 app/controllers/admin/users_controller.rb**

```
def update
if @user.update_attributes(params[:user])
  flash[:notice] = "User has been updated."
  redirect_to admin_users_path
else
  flash[:alert] = "User has not been updated."
  render :action => "edit"
end
end
```

With this action in place, you need to delete the password parameters from `params[:user]` if they are blank. Otherwise, the application will attempt to update a user with a blank password, and Devise won't allow that. Above `update_attributes`, insert this code:

```
if params[:user][:password].blank?
params[:user].delete(:password)
end
```

Now the entire action looks like the following listing.

> **Listing 7.29 app/controllers/admin/users_controller.rb**

```
def update
if params[:user][:password].blank?
  params[:user].delete(:password)
  params[:user].delete(:password_confirmation)
end
if @user.update_attributes(params[:user])
```

```
    flash[:notice] = "User has been updated."
    redirect_to admin_users_path
  else
    flash[:alert] = "User has not been updated."
    render :action => "edit"
  end
end
```

When you run `bin/cucumber features/editing_users.feature` again, the first and third scenarios pass, but the second one fails because you haven't set the user's admin capabilities inside the `update` action, as you did in the `create` action. To do so, remove the following line from the `create` action:

```
@user.admin = params[:user][:admin] == "1"
```

Now define a method called `set_admin`, which you can use in both actions. This method goes directly underneath `find_user` under the `private` keyword, as shown in the following listing.

Listing 7.30   app/controllers/admin/users_controller.rb

```
private
def set_admin
  @user.admin = params[:user][:admin] == "1"
end
```

To use this method in the `update` action, place it directly above the call to `update_attributes`:

```
set_admin
if @user.update_attributes(params[:user])
```

Placing `set_admin` above `update_attributes` ensures that the user is made an admin directly before the `save` for `update_attributes` is triggered. You should also put it before the save in the `create` action:

```
set_admin
if @user.save(params[:user])
```

Now when you run the feature, all the scenarios pass:

```
3 scenarios (3 passed)
41 steps (41 passed)
```

In this section, you added two more actions to your `Admin::UsersController`: `edit` and `update`. Admin users can now update users' details if they please.

Run `rake cucumber:ok spec` to ensure nothing was broken by your latest changes. You should see this output:

```
31 scenarios (31 passed)
270 steps (270 passed)
# and
14 examples, 0 failures, 7 pending
```

Let's make a commit for this new feature:

```
git add .
git commit -m "Added ability to edit and update users"
git push
```

With the updating done, there's only one more part to go for your admin CRUD interface: deleting users.

7.8 *Deleting users*

There comes a time in an application's life when you need to delete users. Maybe they asked for their account to be removed. Maybe they were being pesky. Or maybe you have another reason to delete them. Whatever the case, having the functionality to delete users is helpful.

Keeping with the theme so far, you first write a feature for deleting users (using the following listing) and put it at features/deleting_users.feature.

Listing 7.31   features/deleting_users.feature

```
Feature: Deleting users
In order to remove users
As an admin
I want to click a button and delete them

Background:
  Given there are the following users:
    | email              | password | admin |
    | admin@ticketee.com | password | true  |
    | user@ticketee.com  | password | false |

  And I am signed in as "admin@ticketee.com"
  Given I am on the homepage
  When I follow "Admin"
  And I follow "Users"

Scenario: Deleting a user
  And I follow "user@ticketee.com"
  When I follow "Delete User"
  Then I should see "User has been deleted"
```

When you run this feature, you get right up to the first step with no issue and then it complains:

```
no link with title, id or text 'Delete' found (Capybara::ElementNotFound)
```

Of course, you need the Delete link! Add it to the show template at app/views/admin/users/show.html.erb, right underneath the Edit User link:

```
<%= link_to "Delete User", admin_user_path(@user), :method => :delete,
        :confirm => "Are you sure you want to delete this user?" %>
```

You need to add the destroy action next, directly under the update action in Admin::UsersController, as shown in the following listing.

Listing 7.32   app/controllers/admin/users_controller.rb

```
def destroy
@user.destroy
flash[:notice] = "User has been deleted."
 redirect_to admin_users_path
end
```

When you run `bin/cucumber features/deleting_users.feature`, the feature passes because you now have the Delete User link and its matching `destroy` action:

```
1 scenario (1 passed)
8 steps (8 passed)
```

There's one small problem with this feature, though: it doesn't stop you from deleting yourself!

7.8.1 *Ensuring you can't delete yourself*

To make it impossible to delete yourself, you must add another scenario to the deleting_users.feature, shown in the following listing.

Listing 7.33   features/deleting_users.feature

```
Scenario: Userscannot delete themselves
When I follow "admin@ticketee.com"
And I follow "Delete User"
Then I should see "You cannot delete yourself!"
```

When you run this feature with `bin/cucumber features/deleting_users.feature`, the first two steps of this scenario pass, but the third one fails, as you might expect, because you haven't added the message! Change the `destroy` action in the `Admin::UsersController` to the following listing.

Listing 7.34   app/controllers/admin/users_controller.rb

```
def destroy
if @user == current_user
  flash[:alert] = "You cannot delete yourself!"
else
  @user.destroy
  flash[:notice] = "User has been deleted."
end

redirect_to admin_users_path
end
```

Now, before the `destroy` method does anything, it checks to see if the user attempting to be deleted is the current user and stops it with the `"You cannot delete yourself!"` message. When you run `bin/cucumber features/deleting_users.feature` this time, the scenario passes:

```
2 scenarios (2 passed)
16 steps (16 passed)
```

Great! With the ability to delete users implemented, you've completed the CRUD for `Admin::UsersController` and for the users resource entirely. Now make sure you haven't broken anything by running `rake cucumber:ok spec`. You should see this output:

```
33 scenarios (33 passed)
286 steps (286 passed)
# and
14 examples, 0 failures, 7 pending
```

Fantastic! Commit and push that:

```
git add .
git commit -m "Added feature for deleting users,
            including protection against self-deletion"
```

With this final commit, you've got your admin section created, and it provides a great CRUD interface for users in this system so that admins can modify their details when necessary.

7.9   *Summary*

For this chapter, you dove into basic access control and added a field called `admin` to the users table. You used `admin` to allow and restrict access to a namespaced controller.

Then you wrote the CRUD interface for the users resource underneath the admin namespace. This interface is used in the next chapter to expand on the authorization that you've implemented so far: restricting users, whether admin users or not, to certain actions on certain projects. You rounded out the chapter by not allowing users to delete themselves.

The next chapter focuses on enhancing the basic permission system you've implemented so far, introducing a gem called `cancan`. With this permission system, you'll have much more fine-grained control over what users of your application can and can't do to projects and tickets.

More authorization

8

This chapter covers

- Expanding with a more advanced system
- Setting permissions to control user actions
- Implementing a seed of data for the app

At the end of chapter 7, you learned a basic form of authorization based on a boolean field on the users table called `admin`. If this field is set to `true`, identifying admin users, those users can access the CRUD functions of the `Project` resource as well as an admin namespace where they can perform CRUD on the `User` resource.

In this chapter, we expand on authorization options by implementing a broader authorization system using a `Permission` model. The records for this model's table define the actions specified users can take on objects from your system, such as projects. Each record tracks the user who has a specific permission, the object to which the permission applies, and the type of permission granted.

The authorization implemented in this chapter is *whitelist authorization*. Under whitelist authorization, all users are denied access to everything by default, and you must specify what the user can do. The opposite is *blacklist authorization,* under which all users are allowed access to everything by default and you must block what they may not access. You use whitelist authorization for your application because you may have a large number of projects and want to assign a user to only one of them. Whitelist authorization involves fewer steps in restricting a user to one project.

A good way to think about whitelist authorization is as the kind of list a security guard would have at an event. If you're not on the list, you don't get in. A blacklist comparison would be if the security guard had a list of people who *weren't* allowed in.

This chapter guides you through restricting access to the CRUD operations of `TicketsController` one by one, starting with reading and then moving into creating, updating, and deleting. Any time users want to perform one of these actions, they must be granted permission to do so, or added to "the list."

During this process, you'll see another gem called CanCan, which provides some methods for your controllers and views that help you check the current user's permission to perform a specific action.

You first set up permissions through the Cucumber features, and once you're done with restricting the actions in your controller, you'll generate functionality in the backend to allow administrators of the application to assign permissions to users.

8.1   Restricting read access

A time comes in every ticket-tracking application's life when it's necessary to restrict which users can see which projects. For example, you could be operating in a consultancy where some people are working on one application, and others are working on another. You want the admins of the application to be able to customize which projects each user can see.

First, you create a model called `Permission` that tracks which users have which permissions for which actions. Before you create that model, you must update one of your Viewing Projects features to make sure only users who have permission to view a project are able to do so.

Add a background and change the scenario in this feature to set up a user with the correct permissions, and then make the user visit that project, changing the code in the scenario in this feature to what is shown in the following listing.

Listing 8.1   features/viewing_projects.feature

```
Background:
  Given there are the following users:
    | email             | password |
    | user@ticketee.com | password |
  And I am signed in as them
  And there is a project called "TextMate 2"
  And "user@ticketee.com" can view the "TextMate 2" project     ❶ Let user
                                                                   view project
Scenario: Listing all projects
  And I am on the homepage
  When I follow "TextMate 2"
  Then I should be on the project page for "TextMate 2"
```

You've effectively rewritten a large portion of this feature, which is common practice when implementing such large changes.

Underneath the `there is a project` step in the `Background` for this feature is a new step ❶. It's responsible for giving the specified user access to the specified project, but not just any permission: permission to view the project. This step is currently undefined, so when you run `bin/cucumber features/viewing_projects.feature`, you get the step definition for it:

```
Given /^"([^"]*)" can view the "([^"]*)" project$/ do |arg1, arg2|
  pending # express the regexp above with the code you wish you had
end
```

To implement this step, you use the not-yet-existent `Permission` model, which stores the permissions in the database. This model needs a related table called `permissions`, which contains three fields.

The first field is the `action` field, which keeps track of the type of permission a user has on particular objects. The objects can be of different types, so you must create two fields to track the association to the object: `thing_type` and `thing_id`. This kind of association is called a *polymorphic association, poly* meaning "many" and *morphic* meaning "forms," which is fitting. You'll see more on these in a little while.

One more field you add to this `permissions` table is a `user_id` column linking that `Permission` to a `User`.

With all of that in mind, you can define this step in a new file at features/step_definitions/permission_steps.rb, as shown in the following listing.

Listing 8.2   features/step_definitions/permission_steps.rb

```
Given /^"([^"]*)" can view the "([^"]*)" project$/ do |user, project|
  Permission.create!(:user => User.find_by_email!(user),
                     :thing => Project.find_by_name!(project),
                     :action => "view")
end
```

In listing 8.2, you create a new `Permission` record with the action defined as `view` linking the project and user passed in. This record defines the users who can access the project. When you run this feature, you get an error because the `Permission` class is not yet defined:

```
And "user@ticketee.com" can view the "TextMate 2" project
  uninitialized constant Permission (NameError)
```

Define it now by generating the model using the following command, typed all on one line:

```
rails generate model permission user_id:integer thing_id:integer
  thing_type:string action:string
```

With this model and its related migration, you can run `rake db:migrate` and `rake db:test:prepare` to set up the development and test databases. When you run your feature again, you get this error message:

```
And "user@ticketee.com" can view the "TextMate 2" project
  unknown attribute: user (ActiveRecord::UnknownAttributeError)
```

This message occurs because you haven't defined a `belongs_to` association between the `Permission` objects and the users they relate to. To set up this association, open app/models/permission.rb and define it using a simple `belongs_to`:

```
belongs_to :user
```

That's the first association you need to define, and when you run this feature again, you get a second error that looks similar to the first:

```
And "user@ticketee.com" can view the "TextMate 2" project
  unknown attribute: thing (ActiveRecord::UnknownAttributeError)
```

This code represents a polymorphic association, which as mentioned earlier, needs to associate with many types of objects. A polymorphic association uses the `thing_type` and `thing_id` fields to determine what object a `Permission` object relates to.

To define this association in your model, use this line:

```
belongs_to :thing, :polymorphic => true
```

Figure 8.1 illustrates how this association works.

When you assign an object to the `thing` polymorphic association, instead of just saving `thing_id` as in a normal `belongs_to`, Rails also saves the `thing_type` field, which is the string version of the object's class, or `thing.class.to_s`. In this step of your application, the `thing_type` field is set to Project because you're assigning a `Project` object to `thing`. Therefore, the new record in the table has both `thing_type` and `thing_id` attributes set.

When Rails loads this object, it goes through the process shown in figure 8.2. Rails knows this is a polymorphic association because you told it in the `Permission` model, and it therefore uses the `thing_id` and `thing_type` fields to find the object. By knowing `thing_type`, Rails can figure out what model the association is and then use that

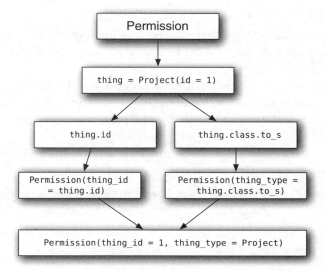

Figure 8.1 Polymorphic saving

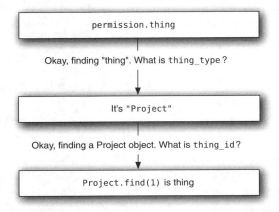

Figure 8.2   Polymorphic loading

model to load a specific object with the `id` of `thing_id`. Then, boom, you've got a `Project` object.

Now when you run `bin/cucumber features/viewing_projects.feature`, it passes:

```
1 scenario (1 passed)
7 steps (7 passed)
```

The feature should pass with or without the new permission step because, at the moment, the permission settings have no bearing on what projects a user can see.

The easiest way to specify which projects users can see is to restrict the scope of the projects the `show` action searches on so that projects the user doesn't have access to don't show up in this list. By default, a `find` on a model searches all records in the related table, but you can add a `scope` method to your model to allow you to search on restricted sets of records.

8.2   *Restricting by scope*

To restrict the `show` action to certain record sets, you implement a *scope* on the `Project` model that returns only the projects with related `Permission` records that declare the user is authorized to read them.

Before you scope down this `find`, you must write a spec to test that the `show` action in the `ProjectsController` really does scope down this `find`, and if the project can't be found, the controller should deny all knowledge of a project ever having existed.

The spec goes into spec/controllers/projects_controller_spec.rb directly under the spec for testing that standard users can't access specified actions, but still inside the `context` block for standard users. This spec is shown in the following listing.

> **Listing 8.3   spec/controllers/projects_controller_spec.rb**

```
it "cannot access the show action" do
  sign_in(:user, user)
  get :show, :id => project.id
```

```
    response.should redirect_to(projects_path)
    flash[:alert].should eql("The project you were looking for could not be fou
      nd.")
end
```

You use the same error message from the missing project spec because you don't want to acknowledge to unauthorized users that the project they're looking for exists when they don't have access to read it. When you run this spec using bin/rspec spec /controllers/projects_controller_spec.rb, it fails:

```
1) ProjectsController standard users cannot access the show action
    Failure/Error: response.should redirect_to(projects_path)
```

The spec fails because you haven't yet scoped down the find call in the find_project method, which is called using a before_filter in ProjectsController.

With a failing spec testing the nonexistent behavior, open app/controllers/ projects_controller.rb and change the find_project method to look for projects that the current user has access to so your spec will pass. But there's one problem: you're not restricting the show action to only users who are signed in now.

You must make it so that the user has to sign in before accessing the show action because you need to use the current_user method to check what permissions this user has access to within the find_project method.

To do so, call the authenticate_user! method as a before_filter in this controller, just as you did for certain actions in the TicketsController. Place this method above the find_project to ensure that a user is authenticated before find_project does its job. The filters in ProjectsController should now look like the following listing.

Listing 8.4 app/controllers/projects_controller.rb

```
before_filter :authorize_admin!, :except => [:index, :show]
before_filter :authenticate_user!, :only => [:show]
before_filter :find_project, :only => [:show, :edit, :update, :destroy]
```

Now alter the find_project method to check the permissions of the project before letting authorized users see it or refusing unauthorized users access. Change the line that defines the @project variable from this

```
@project = Project.find(params[:id])
```

to this:

```
@project = Project.readable_by(current_user).find(params[:id])
```

The readable_by method doesn't exist yet; you'll define it in just a moment. The readable_by method returns a scope of only the projects the user is allowed to view. This scope has exactly the same methods that an Active Record class has, so you can treat it just like one. You can define this method using the scope class method in your Project mode.

The `scope` method provides a method you can call on your class or on an association collection for this class that returns a subset of records. The following `scope` call, for example, defines a method called `admins`:

```
scope :admins, where(:admin => true)
```

If you wanted to, you could call this `admins` method on your `User` model to return all the users who are admins:

```
User.admins
```

If you didn't have the `scope` method, you'd have to specify the `where` manually on your queries everywhere you used them, like this:

```
User.where(:admin => true)
```

As you can see, manually specifying `where` isn't nearly as pretty as simply calling `User.admins`. This may seem like a contrived example, but trust us: it gets ugly when the conditions become more complex. Scopes are yet another great example of the DRY (Don't Repeat Yourself) convention seen throughout Rails. Because the `scope` method defines your scope's logic in one central location, you can easily change all uses of this scope by changing it in this one spot.

Scopes are also chainable. Imagine that you had another scope defined on your `User` model, such as the following, as well as a field for storing the gender, appropriately called `gender`:

```
scope :female, where(:gender => "Female")
```

You can call this scope by itself

```
User.female
```

which return all of your female users, or you can get all your female admins by doing either this

```
User.admin.female
```

or this

```
User.female.admin
```

Rails builds up the queries by applying the scopes one at a time, and calling them in any order will result in the same query.

Let's define a real scope now, along with the `permissions` association it needs to use. Put this scope under the validation inside the `Project` model, as shown in the following lines:

```
validates :name, :presence => true, :uniqueness => true

has_many :permissions, :as => :thing
scope :readable_by, lambda { |user|
  joins(:permissions).where(:permissions => { :action => "view",
                                              :user_id => user.id })
}
```

① Link to thing association

The :as option on the has_many :permissions association ❶ links your projects to the thing association on the Permission objects. You need this association defined here because it's used by the scope below it.

Usually, you use scope without passing a block (represented by the lambda), but here the outcome of this scope is dynamic according to which user is passed to it. You therefore use a block to be able to pass this argument to the method generated by the scope call, which then becomes available in the block for use in the where statement.

The joins method here joins the permissions table using a SQL INNER JOIN, allowing you to perform queries on columns from that table too. You do just that with the where method, specifying a hash that contains the permissions key, which points to another hash containing the fields you want to search on and their expected values.

This scope then returns all the Project objects containing a related record in the permissions table that has the action field set to view and the user ID equal to that of the passed-in user.

With this scope method in place, when you run this spec file again with bin/rspec spec/controllers/projects_controller_spec.rb, your tests pass because you're now scoping down the find in the find_project method. But you still have one failure:

```
7 examples, 1 failure
```

This failing spec is the last one in this file where you assert that users receive the message "The project you were looking for could not be found" if they attempt to access a project that is unknown to the system. It fails with this error:

```
Expected response to be a redirect to <http://test.host/projects>
but was a redirect to <http://test.host/users/sign_in>
```

Rather than redirecting back to /projects as it should, this code now redirects to the /users/sign_in path. This would happen only if the user attempted to access an action that you had locked down to be visible only to those who were signed in. Recent changes to the show action fit this bill: users are now required to sign in before you run the find_project method.

Therefore, you just need to make a small fix to this final spec: you must sign in as a user before you make the get :show request. Let's change the first two lines of this spec in spec/controllers/projects_controller.rb from this

```
it "displays an error for a missing project" do
  get :show, :id => "not-here"
```

to this:

```
it "displays an error for a missing project" do
  sign_in(:user, user)
  get :show, :id => "not-here"
```

Now when you run bin/rspec spec/controllers/projects_controller_spec.rb, all the examples pass:

```
. . . . . . .
7 examples, 0 failures
```

All right! The examples for this controller are passing, but how about the feature—the one you wrote previously to test that users *can* access this show action if they have the correct permissions? This spec tested the negative, making sure a user without permission *can't* access this project.

With the code you just implemented, this feature should still pass as it did the last time you ran it. Let's find out by running `bin/cucumber features/viewing _projects.feature`:

```
1 scenario (1 passed)
7 steps (7 passed)
```

Isn't that wonderful? You rewrote the feature and it still passed! You've tested both the granted and denied facets of this particular permission by writing a feature and spec respectively.

Now that you implemented that little chunk of functionality and everything seems to be going smoothly, let's make sure the entire application is going the same way by running `rake cucumber:ok spec`. Oh dear! You broke just about every feature in some way:

```
Failing Scenarios:
cucumber features/creating_projects.feature:14
cucumber features/creating_tickets.feature:20
cucumber features/deleting_projects.feature:12
cucumber features/deleting_tickets.feature:19
cucumber features/editing_projects.feature:16
cucumber features/editing_tickets.feature:20
cucumber features/hidden_links.feature:35
cucumber features/hidden_links.feature:50
cucumber features/viewing_tickets.feature:20

33 scenarios (9 failed, 4 skipped, 20 passed)
289 steps (9 failed, 87 skipped, 193 passed)
```

These features are all broken because you restricted the permissions on the `find_project` method, and all of these features depend on this functionality in one way or another. Let's fix these, from the top, one at a time.

8.3   *Fixing what you broke*

Currently, you have a whole bundle of features that are failing! When this happens, it may seem like everything's broken (and maybe some things are on fire), but in reality it's not as bad as it seems. The best way to fix a mess like this is to break it down into smaller chunks and tackle it one chunk at a time. The output from `rake cucumber:ok spec` provided a list of the broken features: they are your chunks. Let's go through them and fix them, starting with the Editing Projects feature.

8.3.1 Fixing Editing Projects

When you run `bin/cucumber features/editing_projects.feature:14`, Cucumber can't find the Edit Project link:

```
And I follow "Edit Project"
  no link with title, id or text 'Edit Project' found
    ➡ (Capybara::ElementNotFound)
```

This error occurs because when Cucumber follows the TextMate 2 link, it's taken to the `show` action, which redirects it to the `projects_path` because the user doesn't have access to this project, and the page the user would now be on doesn't have an Edit Project link. But the users for this feature are the all-seeing admins and therefore should be able to access all projects regardless of whether or not they have permission to do so. Therefore, you must change how you declare `@project` in the `find_project` method in `ProjectsController` to account for admins. Change it from this

```
@project = Project.readable_by(current_user).find(params[:id])
```

to this:

```
@project = if current_user.admin?
  Project.find(params[:id])
else
  Project.readable_by(current_user).find(params[:id])
end
```

As you can see, this code won't scope the find using the `readable_by` scope if the user is an admin, but it will if the user isn't. When you run `bin/cucumber features/editing_projects.feature`, it should now pass:

```
2 scenarios (2 passed)
19 steps (19 passed)
```

This change should fix a couple of other features as well, so rerun `rake cucumber:ok` to find the ones that are still broken. You have a much shorter list now:

```
cucumber features/creating_tickets.feature:20
cucumber features/deleting_tickets.feature:19
cucumber features/editing_tickets.feature:20
cucumber features/viewing_tickets.feature:20
```

You reduced your failing scenarios from nine to only four, which is pretty good. Let's fix the first of these, the Creating Tickets feature.

8.3.2 Fixing the four failing features

Let's run the first feature with `bin/cucumber features/creating_tickets.feature`. You'll see that it can't find the New Ticket link:

```
And I follow "New Ticket"
  no link with title, id or text 'New Ticket' found (Capybara::ElementNotFound)
```

This is the same problem as before: the user doesn't have permission to access that project. To fix this problem, alter the `Background`, put the permission step underneath the user-creation step, and sign in as that user, like this:

```
Given there are the following users:
  | email              | password |
  | user@ticketee.com  | password |
And "user@ticketee.com" can view the "Internet Explorer" project
And I am signed in as them
```

This `Background` also contains code that ensures users are asked to sign in if they click the New Ticket link when they're not signed in. Because you'll log in as a user before you get to this point, you can remove the last few lines from this `Background`:

```
Then I should see "You need to sign in or sign up before continuing."
When I fill in "Email" with "user@ticketee.com"
And I fill in "Password" with "password"
And I press "Sign in"
Then I should see "New Ticket"
```

When you run this feature again, all the scenarios pass:

```
3 scenarios (3 passed)
35 steps (35 passed)
```

One down, three to go. The next failing feature is the Deleting Tickets feature.

It fails for the same reason as the previous one: the user doesn't have access to the project to delete a ticket. Let's fix this now by putting the following line underneath where your project is created:

```
Given there is a project called "TextMate 2"
And "user@ticketee.com" can view the "TextMate 2" project
```

That's a little too easy! When you run `bin/cucumber features/deleting_tickets .feature`, this feature now passes:

```
1 scenario (1 passed)
11 steps (11 passed)
```

Next up is the Editing Tickets feature, which contains not one but two broken scenarios. The two scenarios in this feature, similar to the Editing Projects scenario, are broken because the feature can't find a link:

```
And I follow "Make it shiny!"
  no link with title, id or text 'Make it shiny!' found
  ➥ (Capybara::ElementNotFound)
```

Again, the error occurs because the user doesn't have permission to access this particular project. You must specify that this user has access to this project in the `Background`, just as you did for the Creating Tickets and Editing Tickets features. Add this line directly under the line that creates the project in the `Background`:

```
And "user@ticketee.com" can view the "TextMate 2" project
```

When you run `bin/cucumber features/editing_tickets.feature`, both scenarios should pass:

```
2 scenarios (2 passed)
26 steps (26 passed)
```

Great! You fixed another feature. The one remaining feature that fails is Viewing Tickets, which you fix in the same way as you fixed the previous features. Add this line again underneath where you create the TextMate 2 project, this time in features/viewing_tickets.feature:

```
And "user@ticketee.com" can view the "TextMate 2" project
```

You also need to add one for the Internet Explorer project:

```
And "user@ticketee.com" can view the "Internet Explorer" project
```

Also in this feature, you're not signing in as the user who has these permissions, so directly underneath the first step in your `Background`, add the following step:

```
And I am signed in as them
```

Running `bin/cucumber features/viewing_tickets.feature`, you'll see that this feature is passing:

```
1 scenario (1 passed)
23 steps (23 passed)
```

That was fast! All four failing features are fixed. Well, so we hope. You independently verified them, but run `rake cucumber:ok spec` to make sure nothing else is broken:

```
33 scenarios (33 passed)
287 steps (287 passed)
# and
16 examples, 0 failures, 8 pending
```

Great! Everything's working again! Let's commit that:

```
git add .
git commit -m "Made projects only visible to users with
permission to see them"
git push
```

In these first two sections, you added the restriction on the `ProjectsController` that projects should be accessible only to users with `Permission` records with the action set to `view`. In the process, you broke a couple of features, but fixing them was really simple.

However, these changes only protect the actions in the `ProjectsController` that use the `find_project` method and *not* those in the `TicketsController`. Before you make changes in the `TicketsController`, note that the links to all projects are still visible to all users through the `ProjectsController`'s `index`, which is definitely something you should fix first.

8.3.3   *One more thing*

As described previously, the links to all projects are still visible to all users on the homepage. The way to fix it is to write a new scenario to test that this behavior is always present. You don't have to write the whole scenario because you already have a scenario you can *modify* instead, the one inside features/viewing_projects.feature.

To test that the links are hidden on the index action, add a new step to the Background and one to the scenario. The one in the Background goes directly under the line that creates the TextMate 2 project, and it creates another project called Internet Explorer:

```
And there is a project called "Internet Explorer"
```

Place the line that goes in the scenario directly under the line that takes you to the homepage, making the first two lines of this scenario look like this:

```
And I am on the homepage
Then I should not see "Internet Explorer"
```

This feature will now ensure that the user who doesn't have permission to view the TextMate 2 project no longer can see the Internet Explorer project. When you run this feature using bin/cucumber features/viewing_projects.feature, it fails:

```
expected #has_no_content?("Internet Explorer")
 to return true, got false
```

To fix it, open app/controllers/projects_controller.rb and modify the index method to do exactly what the find_project method does: restrict. You could re-use the code from the find_project method in the index action, but that isn't very DRY. Instead, extract the code from find_project and move it into the Project model. Take the code from this method

```
@project = if current_user.admin?
  Project.find(params[:id])
else
  Project.readable_by(current_user).find(params[:id])
end
```

and change it to this much shorter version:

```
@project = Project.for(current_user).find(params[:id])
```

The model is a better place than the controller for this logic. Open app/models/project .rb and define this new for class method using the code shown next. You'll also refactor the method:

```
def self.for(user)
  user.admin? ? Project : Project.readable_by(user)
end
```

The first line of this method uses a *ternary statement*, which is a shorter version of this:

```
if current_user.admin?
  Project
```

```
else
  Project.readable_by(current_user)
end
```

This statement is useful when you have short conditional statements like this one, but it shouldn't be (ab)used for longer conditional statements. As a general rule of thumb, if the line for a ternary statement is longer than 80 characters, it's probably best to split it out over multiple lines for better readability.

In the `find_project` method, you can call `find` on what this new `for` method returns, and now in the `index` method, you can use it in an identical fashion, but just replace the call to `find` with `all`, like this:

```
def index
  @projects = Project.for(current_user).all
end
```

Because you are referencing `current_user` in this action, you must modify the `before_filter` line that references `authenticate_user!` to ensure that users are signed in before they visit this page. Let's change it to this:

```
before_filter :authenticate_user!, :only => [:index, :show]
```

When you run the feature again with `bin/cucumber features/viewing_projects .feature`, it passes:

```
1 scenario (1 passed)
9 steps (9 passed)
```

Ensure that everything is working as it should by running `rake cucumber:ok spec`. Oops! You broke some of the scenarios inside the Hidden Links feature, as shown by this output from the `cucumber:ok` part of the command you just ran:

```
cucumber features/hidden_links.feature:23
cucumber features/hidden_links.feature:27
cucumber features/hidden_links.feature:36
cucumber features/hidden_links.feature:40
```

If you run the first one of these features with `bin/cucumber features/hidden_links .feature:23`, you'll see that it can't find the TextMate 2 link.

```
When I follow "TextMate 2"
  no link with title, id or text 'TextMate 2' found (Capybara::ElementNotFound)
```

This error occurs because the user in this feature doesn't have permission to view the TextMate 2 project. But if you look at this scenario, it's for users who are not signed in—users who can no longer visit this page because, when they do, they are redirected to the sign-in page. This means that the following scenarios no longer apply and can be deleted:

```
Scenario: Edit project link is hidden for non-signed-in users
Scenario: Delete project link is hidden for non-signed-in users
```

Removing these scenarios removes two of the failing scenarios, but two more are still failing:

```
Failing Scenarios:
cucumber features/hidden_links.feature:21
cucumber features/hidden_links.feature:31
```

These two scenarios fail because user@ticketee.com doesn't have access to the Text-Mate 2 project. To give it access, you can put the permission step underneath the project-creation step in the `Background`, like this:

```
And there is a project called "TextMate 2"
And "user@ticketee.com" can view the "TextMate 2" project
```

When you run this feature again using `bin/cucumber features/hidden_links.feature`, it passes:

```
7 scenarios (7 passed)
39 steps (39 passed)
```

You fixed the scenarios in the Hidden Links feature, but the Signing Up feature still fails. These two features aren't closely related, so it's best to make a commit but *not* push it to GitHub now so you have all related changes in one commit and other changes in separate commits. For this commit, the `ProjectsController`'s index action is restricted to displaying projects only the user can see, so the commit commands are as follows:

```
git add .
git commit -m "Don't show projects that a
 user doesn't have permission to see"
```

Now let's see why the Signing Up feature is acting up. When you run it using `bin/cucumber features/signing_up.feature`, the final step fails:

```
Then I should see "You have signed up successfully"
expected #has_content?("You have signed up successfully.")
to return true, got false
```

When users sign up to your application, they're shown the "You have signed up successfully" message, as the feature says they should, and they're also redirected to the root of your application. The problem lies with this final step: people are redirected to the root of the application, the `ProjectsController`'s index action, which is now locked down to require that users be authenticated before they can view this action. This is problematic, but it's fixable.

8.3.4   *Fixing Signing Up*

The Signing Up feature is broken, and the problem lies solely with the latest changes you made to the `ProjectsController`. When users sign up, they're sent to the `root_path` in the application, which resolves to the `index` action in the `ProjectsController`. This controller has the `authenticate_user!` method called before all actions in it, checking if users are authenticated. If they aren't, they're redirected to the sign-in page.

You can see all of this in action if you start your server using `rails server` and attempt to sign up. Rather than being properly shown the "You have signed up successfully" message, you'll see the Sign In page, as shown in figure 8.3.

The configuration to send users to the `root_path` after sign-up is in Devise's `Devise::RegistrationsController`[1] and is defined in a method called after `_inactive_sign_up_path_for`:

```
# The path used after sign up for inactive accounts.
   ➥ You need to overwrite
# this method in your own RegistrationsController.
def after_inactive_sign_up_path_for(resource)
  root_path
end
```

As you can see, this method is hardcoded to return `root_path`. The comment above this method suggests that you override the method in your own `RegistrationsController`. It means you must create a new controller called `RegistrationsController`[2] and, inside this controller, override the `after_inactive_sign_up_path_for` method. To give this controller the same functionality as Devise's `Devise::Registrations Controller`, you need to inherit from that controller. Finally, you can no longer redirect to `root_path`, so you generate a new part of your application to present new users with a message telling them they must confirm their account.

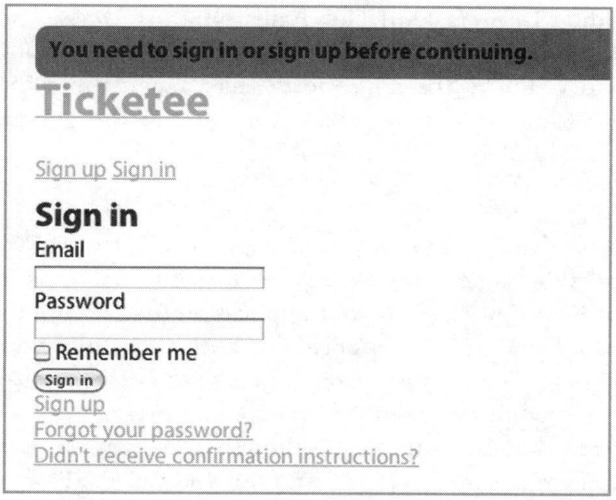

You need to sign in or sign up before continuing.

Ticketee

Sign up Sign in

Sign in
Email

Password

☐ Remember me
(Sign in)
Sign up
Forgot your password?
Didn't receive confirmation instructions?

Figure 8.3   Sign-in page

---

[1] The `Devise::RegistrationsController` can be found at https://github.com/plataformatec/devise/blob/v1.4.2/app/controllers/devise/registrations_controller.rb#L93-95.

[2] The controller could be called anything: it just needs a name so you can point Devise at it later.

Create a new controller now at app/controllers/registrations_controller.rb and fill it with this content:

```
class RegistrationsController < Devise::RegistrationsController

  private

  def after_inactive_sign_up_path_for(resource)
    confirm_user_path
  end
end
```

By defining this new controller as inheriting from `Devise::Registrations-Controller`, you inherit all the behavior from that controller and gain the ability to override things such as the `after_inactive_sign_up_path_for`, of which you take full advantage here. The `resource` argument is the `User` object representing who's signing up. You could use it, but in this context, don't. Next, you need to tell Devise to use this controller instead of its own. Alter the following line in config/routes.rb

```
devise_for :users
```

to this:

```
devise_for :users, :controllers => { :registrations => "registrations" }
```

The `:controllers` option tells Devise you want to customize the controllers it uses, and with this new hash, you tell it to use the `RegistrationsController` you defined for registrations. In this controller, you override `after_inactive_sign_up_path_for` to go to a new route: `confirm_user_path`.

Because you're overriding Devise's controller, Rails won't use Devise's views. You must copy the views from Devise into your application and move them into the app /views/registrations directory. Lucky for you, Devise has a generator that places Devise's views in your application: `devise:views`. You can run the generator with this command:

```
rails g devise:views
```

This command places Devise's views into the app/views/devise directory of your application. This directory shares the same name as the directory internal to Devise where these views came from, and if a view exists in your application first, then Rails doesn't look for it in the engines attached to the application. With these files copied over, move the app/views/devise/registrations directory out to app/views/registrations so you have some views to use for your new `RegistrationsController`.

Now you must address the problem that although the `confirm_users_path` method used in your `RegistrationsController` isn't defined yet, `redirect_to` takes users to that location. Define a route for it by opening config/routes.rb and inserting this line underneath `devise_for :users`:

```
get '/awaiting_confirmation',
  :to => "users#confirmation",
  :as => 'confirm_user'
```

> ### Post, put, delete, and anything
>
> You can define routes that respond only to POST, PUT, and DELETE requests using the `post`, `put`, and `delete` methods, respectively. All of these methods use the same syntax and work in similar manners, but they define routes that respond only to certain HTTP methods.
>
> If it doesn't matter which HTTP method a route responds to, you can use the `match` method:
>
> ```
> match '/some_route',
> :to => "some#where"
> ```
>
> This would respond to GET, POST, PUT and DELETE methods. This method is actually used by the `get`, `post`, `put`, and `delete` methods internally, except they call it like this:
>
> ```
> match '/some_route',
> :to => "some#where",
> :conditions => { :method => :get }
> ```
>
> You *could* use conditions to filter the HTTP methods to which a route would respond, but it's better to just use the relevant HTTP method's method.

The `get` method defines a new route in your application that responds to only GET requests to /awaiting_confirmation. This route goes to the `confirmation` action in UsersController, which you haven't created yet either. Soon!

The `:as` option tells Rails that you want routing helpers generated for this route and you want the helpers to have the prefix `confirm_user`. This generates `confirm_user_path`, which you use in your new `check_for_sign_up` action in ProjectsController as well as in a `confirm_user_url` method.

When you run the Signing Up feature again with `bin/cucumber features/signing _up.feature` you don't get the same error, but you get one that can be easily fixed:

```
Given I am on the homepage
  uninitialized constant UsersController
```

This is the controller you'll use to show users the confirmation page, so let's create it with a `confirmation` action that you'll need with this command:

```
rails g controller users confirmation
```

This command adds a route to your routes file that you don't want (because it overrides a route that Devise uses), so remove this line from config/routes.rb:

```
get "users/confirmation"
```

The added bonus of putting the action here is that you get a view for free at app/views/users/confirmation.html.erb. In this view you'll display the "You have signed up successfully" message as well as a "Please confirm your account before signing in" message. Before you add these messages to the template, add a line at the bottom of the scenario inside features/signing_up.feature to check for this confirmation message:

```
Then I should see "Please confirm your account before signing in."
```

This line ensures that you're always taken to the correct page upon sign-up. Now replace the code inside app/views/users/confirmation.html.erb with the following code to make this feature pass again:

```
<h1>You have signed up successfully.</h1>
```

Please confirm your account before signing in.

When users sign up, rather than seeing a confusing page telling them they must be signed in, they'll instead see the page shown in figure 8.4.

The Signing Up feature is probably fixed now, but the only true way to make sure it's working is to test it manually or to run the feature. Running the feature is easier, so let's do that with `bin/cucumber features/signing_up.feature`:

```
1 scenario (1 passed)
7 steps (7 passed)
```

Everything is green. Awesome! This feature is passing again. Let's make a commit for that:

```
git add .
git commit -m "Fix signing up feature,
  take user to alternative confirmation page"
```

Is everything else working, though? Let's check with `rake cucumber:ok spec`:

```
31 scenarios (31 passed)
285 steps (285 passed)
# and
19 examples, 0 failures, 10 pending
```

Now everything's working! Let's push those changes to GitHub:

```
git push
```

You've limited the ability of users to take action on things inside the Projects-Controller and fixed the Signing Up feature that broke because of the changes you made. But you haven't protected the TicketsController. This is a problem because users who can't view a project will still be able to view its tickets, which could pose a security risk. A project's most vital assets (for now) are the tickets associated with it, and users who don't have permission to see the project shouldn't be able to see the associated tickets. Let's add this restriction next.

Figure 8.4   "Please confirm your account"

8.4 Blocking access to tickets

When implementing permissions, you have to be careful to ensure that all users who should have access to something do, and all users who *shouldn't* have access to something don't. All of the `TicketsController`'s actions are still available to all users because it has no permission checking. If you leave it in that state, users who are unable to see the project can still make requests to the actions inside `Tickets-Controller`. They shouldn't be able to do anything to the tickets in a project if they don't have permission to view tickets for it. Let's implement permission checking to remedy this problem.

8.4.1 Locking out the bad guys

To prevent users from seeing tickets in a project they're unauthorized to see, you must lock down the `show` action of `TicketsController`.

To test that when you put this restriction in place, it's correct, write a spec in the spec/controllers/tickets_controller_spec.rb file, just as you did for the `Projects-Controller`. This file should now look like the following listing.

Listing 8.5 spec/controllers/tickets_controller_spec.rb

```
require 'spec_helper'

describe TicketsController do
  let(:user) { create_user! }
  let(:project) { Factory(:project) }
  let(:ticket) { Factory(:ticket, :project => project,
                                  :user => user) }

  context "standard users" do
    it "cannot access a ticket for a project" do
      sign_in(:user, user)
      get :show, :id => ticket.id, :project_id => project.id
      response.should redirect_to(root_path)
      flash[:alert].should eql("The project you were looking for could not be
      found.")
    end
  end
end
```

This test sets up a project, a ticket, and a user who has no explicit permission to view the project and therefore shouldn't be able to view the ticket. You test this spec by signing in as the unauthorized user and trying to go to the `show` action for this ticket, which requires you to pass through a `project_id` to help it find what project the ticket is in. The test should pass if the user is redirected to the `root_path` and if, upon the user seeing the `flash[:alert]`, the application denies all knowledge of this project ever having existed.

When you run this test using `bin/rspec spec/controllers/tickets_controller _spec.rb`, you see the `ticket` factory is undefined:

```
No such factory: ticket (ArgumentError)
```

Define this factory now in a new file called factories/ticket_factory.rb. This file will be automatically loaded by the code in spec/support/factories.rb:

```
Factory.define :ticket do |ticket|
  ticket.title "A ticket"
  ticket.description "A ticket, nothing more"
  ticket.user { |u| u.association(:user) }
  ticket.project { |p| p.association(:project) }
end
```

Here you set up some defaults for the title and description fields for a factory-provided ticket, but you do something new with the user method. You pass a block and call the association method on the object returned from the block, and the user for this ticket becomes one user factory-created object. Nifty. You do the same thing for the project method, so you can create tickets using this factory and have them related to a project automatically if you want. For this spec, however, you override it.

When you run bin/rspec spec/controllers/tickets_controller_spec.rb again, this test fails because the user can still access this action:

```
TicketsController standard users cannot access a ticket for a project
    Failure/Error: response.should redirect_to(root_path)
```

With this test failing correctly, you can work on restricting the access to only the projects the user has access to. Open app/controllers/tickets_controller.rb and remove the :except option from the authenticate_user! filter, so it goes from this

```
before_filter :authenticate_user!, :except => [:index, :show]
```

to this:

```
before_filter :authenticate_user!
```

Now users should always be asked to sign in before accessing the index and show actions for this controller, meaning that current_user will always return a User object.

You can reference the current_user method in find_project and use the for method to limit the project find scope to only the projects to which that user has access. You can change the find_project method to the following example:

```
def find_project
  @project = Project.for(current_user).find(params[:project_id])
  rescue ActiveRecord::RecordNotFound
    flash[:alert] = "The project you were looking for could not be found."
    redirect_to root_path
end
```

The rewritten find_project method will retrieve a Project only if the current_user has permission to view that project or is an admin. Otherwise, an ActiveRecord ::RecordNotFound exception will be thrown and rescued here, showing users "The project you were looking for could not be found."

When you run the spec again with `bin/rspec spec/controllers/tickets _controller_spec.rb`, it now passes because this user can no longer see this project and is shown the error:

```
.
1 example, 0 failures
```

You scoped the project find for the `TicketsController` in the same way you did for the `ProjectsController`, limiting it to only those projects to which the current user has access.

That's the end of that! Now ensure that all your specs and features are passing by running `rake cucumber:ok spec`. You should see this output:

```
31 scenarios (31 passed)
285 steps (285 passed)
# and
20 examples, 0 failures, 10 pending
```

In this section, you altered the `TicketsController` so that only users with permission to access a project can see the tickets inside it. Let's commit that:

```
git add .
git commit -m "Restrict reading tickets to correct project scope"
git push
```

Now let's add a new permission that restricts who can create tickets in a project.

8.5   *Restricting write access*

Sometimes when working on a project, you'll want to limit the creation of tickets to a certain person or a group of people, such as to only developers or only clients. For this, you want the New link to be hidden from people who don't have this permission, and you need both the `new` and `create` actions to reject such users.

8.5.1   *Rewriting a feature*

You're lucky to already have the feature for creating tickets, so you just need to add a step to the `Background` declaring that the user can create tickets in the project. Place this step directly under the one declaring that users can view the project. Open features/creating_tickets.feature, and modify the `Background` so it contains these two lines:

```
And "user@ticketee.com" can view the "Internet Explorer" project
And "user@ticketee.com" can create tickets in the "Internet Explorer" project
```

When you run `bin/cucumber features/creating_tickets.feature`, you're told this step is undefined:

```
Given /^"([^"]*)" can create tickets in the "([^"]*)"
    ➥ project$/ do |arg1, arg2|
  pending # express the regexp above with the code you wish you had
end
```

Define it in features/step_definitions/permission_steps.rb directly under the viewing projects step. This new step goes like this:

```
Given /^"([^"]*)" can create tickets in the "([^"]*)" project$/
    do |user, project|
  Permission.create!(:user => User.find_by_email!(email),
                     :thing => Project.find_by_name!(project),
                     :action => "create tickets")
end
```

This step is similar to the step before it. You changed the word *view* to *create tickets* and made a few other small changes, so you should DRY these steps up now. Change the steps to read exactly like the following listing.

Listing 8.6   features/step_definitions/permission_steps.rb

```
permission_step = /
    ^"([^"]*)" can ([^"]*?) ([o|i]n)?\s?the "([^"]*)" project$/
Given permission_step do |user, permission, on, project|
  create_permission(user, find_project(project), permission)
end

def create_permission(email, object, action)
  Permission.create!(:user => User.find_by_email!(email),
                     :thing => object,
                     :action => action)
end

def find_project(name)
  Project.find_by_name!(name)
end
```

Here we separated the regular expression onto its own line to make the line a little shorter. It can all be put on one line without any adverse effects; this just makes it neater.

Now you extract creating permissions, finding the user, and finding the project into separate methods, which means you won't have to change each step if you want to change the way a permission is created. You also combine the acts involved in creating permissions into one step that matches all currently defined step definitions using a regular expression that conforms to the style of other steps:

```
Given "user@ticketee.com" can create tickets on the "Ticketee" project
Given "user@ticketee.com" can view the "Ticketee" project
Given "user@ticketee.com" can edit tickets in the "Ticketee" project
```

This new step definition allows greater flexibility in how your steps are defined yet leaves them easy to parse.

With this permission step defined, run `bin/cucumber features/creating _tickets.feature`, and the entire feature passes:

```
3 scenarios (3 passed)
35 steps (35 passed)
```

This feature will pass whether the user has permission to create a ticket or not. You're now basically in the same situation you faced with the Viewing Tickets feature: the feature would pass either way. So, just like before, you use RSpec to test that users can't create a ticket if they don't have permission to do so.

8.5.2 Blocking creation

Let's write the specs to test that users *with* permission to view the project but *without* permission to create tickets can't create tickets. Put the specs shown in the following listing in spec/controllers/tickets_controller_spec.rb inside the standard users context block so all the examples are grouped nicely.

Listing 8.7 spec/controllers/tickets_controller_spec.rb

```
context "with permission to view the project" do

  before do
    sign_in(:user, user)
    Permission.create!(:user => user, :thing => project, :action => "view")
  end

  def cannot_create_tickets!
    response.should redirect_to(project)
    flash[:alert].should eql("You cannot create tickets on this project.")
  end

  it "cannot begin to create a ticket" do
    get :new, :project_id => project.id
    cannot_create_tickets!
  end

  it "cannot create a ticket without permission" do
    post :create, :project_id => project.id
    cannot_create_tickets!
  end
end
```

You first set up the specs using a before, signing in as a user, and defining a permission for that user to view the project. Next, you define a method called cannot _create_tickets! asserting that unauthorized users should be redirected to the project and shown an alert stating they're not allowed to create tickets. Rather than duplicating these two lines in each spec where you want to check that a user receives the correct message, you just call the cannot_create_tickets! method in that place. The two examples you just added ensure that unauthorized visitors to the new and create actions can't create tickets.

When you run this file with bin/rspec spec/controllers/tickets_controller _spec.rb, the specs fail, just as you might expect:

```
Failure/Error: response.should redirect_to(project)
Expected response to be a <:redirect>, but was <200>
```

To make the spec pass, you need to implement the permission checking on the `new` and `create` actions in your `TicketsController`.

Run a `before_filter` before the `new` action that checks whether the current user has permission; if not, then redirect the user to the project page and display the error described in the spec.

Now change the `before_filter` calls to include this new one, as shown in the following lines:

```
before_filter :authenticate_user!
before_filter :find_project
before_filter :find_ticket, :only => [:show, :edit, :update, :destroy]
before_filter :authorize_create!, :only => [:new, :create]
```

This `authorize_create!` `before_filter` is placed after the `authenticate_user!` and `find_project` `before_filters` because it uses the `current_user` object set up by the `authenticate_user!` method and the `@project` object from `find_project`.

In this new filter, you call a new method called `cannot?`, which returns `true` or `false` to indicate whether the currently signed-in user can't or can do a particular action. You define the `authorize_create!` method code shown next:

```
def authorize_create!
  if !current_user.admin? && cannot?("create tickets".to_sym, @project)
    flash[:alert] = "You cannot create tickets on this project."
    redirect_to @project
  end
end
```

In this example, you use `to_sym` to create a symbolized version of a string, which is required because the `cannot?` method takes only symbols. You also check whether or not the user is an admin; if so, the user should be allowed to create tickets. If you run the controller's spec again with `bin/rspec spec/controllers/tickets_controller _spec.rb`, the example fails because the `cannot?` method is undefined:

```
Failure/Error: get :new, :project_id => project.id
undefined method 'cannot?' for #<TicketsController:0xb651244c>
```

Rails doesn't come with a `cannot?` method, but a gem called cancan (stylized as Can-Can) does. This gem helps you tie together the `User` and `Permission` records. Let's install it now.

8.5.3   *What is CanCan?*

CanCan is a gem written by Ryan Bates of Railscasts fame; it provides some nice helper methods (such as the `cannot?` method and its antithesis, `can?`) to use in controllers and views.

The `can?` and `cannot?` methods use the same `permissions` table you created to check that a user has permission to perform a specific action on a specific object.

To install CanCan, add this line to your Gemfile directly underneath the line for Devise:

```
gem 'cancan'
```

(There's no particular reason to put this gem underneath Devise other than that it's sensible to group together gems dealing with similar functions.) To install the CanCan gem, run `bundle install`.

8.5.4 *Adding abilities*

When you run `bin/rspec spec/controllers/tickets_controller_spec.rb`, you get this output:

```
Failure/Error: get :new, :project_id => project.id
    uninitialized constant Ability
```

This error occurs because CanCan is now defining the `cannot?` method for the controller, which uses a CanCan in-built method called `current_ability`:

```
@current_ability ||= ::Ability.new(current_user)
```

The `||=` sets `@current_ability` if it isn't already set. The `::` before `Ability` indicates to Ruby that you want the `Ability` at the root namespace. This allows you to have a module called `CanCan::Ability` and a class at `Ability` and to differentiate between the two. In this example, it's trying to access just `Ability`, which is a class that doesn't yet exist.

This new `Ability` class will provide the link between users and their permissions. You define it in a new file at app/models/ability.rb exactly like the following listing.

> **Listing 8.8 app/models/ability.rb**

```
class Ability
  include CanCan::Ability

  def initialize(user)
    user.permissions.each do |permission|
      can permission.action.to_sym,
        permission.thing_type.constantize do |thing|
        thing.nil? ||
        permission.thing_id.nil? ||
        permission.thing_id == thing.id
      end
    end
  end
end
```

The `Ability` class's initialize method defines how `can?` and `cannot?` will act. In this example, you iterate over all the users' permissions and use the `can?` method to say that a user can perform a specific function. Users who shouldn't be able to perform that function won't have an entry in the `permissions` table for it. This is the *whitelist authorization* described at the beginning of the chapter.

When you run `bin/rspec spec/controllers/tickets_controller_spec.rb`, you get this error:

```
Failure/Error: get :new, :project_id => project.id
undefined method 'permissions' for #<User:0xb59dc528>
```

This error occurs because you haven't yet defined a `has_many` association on the `User` model to the `Permission` model. To do so, open app/models/user.rb and add this line within the class:

```
has_many :permissions
```

This is another case where there's no reason other than that it makes sense to put it directly underneath the line for the tickets association. It's best if you group all similar methods together. With this association in place, run `bin/rspec spec/controllers/tickets_controller_spec.rb`, and the whole spec file passes:

```
...
3 examples, 0 failures
```

Great! Now that the spec's passing, unauthorized users don't have access to the new and `create` actions. How about checking that those who have permissions can access these actions? Let's check on the Creating Tickets feature. With this permission checking in place, any user with the right permissions should still be able to create tickets. Run `bin/cucumber features/creating_tickets.feature` to make sure. It should pass:

```
3 scenarios (3 passed)
38 steps (38 passed)
```

Good. Users without permission to create tickets no longer can do so.

Now that you've implemented this story, it's time to commit. As usual, you should ensure that everything is still working by running `rake cucumber:ok spec`. Everything should pass:

```
31 scenarios (31 passed)
288 steps (288 passed)
# and
22 examples, 0 failures, 10 pending
```

Let's commit the changes:

```
git add .
git commit -m "Restricting creating tickets to only users
  ➡who have permissions to do it"
git push
```

In this section, you limited the creation of tickets to only those users who're granted permission to do so by using the `Permission` class and the CanCan gem.

8.6   *Restricting update access*

You just learned how to restrict access to the creation of tickets; your next step is to restrict which users can update tickets. Thankfully, you can re-use the framework that's already in place with CanCan to make this a cinch. You can also re-use the Editing Tickets feature to test the restriction.

For this feature, at features/editing_tickets.feature, you set up a `Permission` that says the user you sign in as has permission to update tickets. To do this, write a step in the `Background` directly under the other one that sets up read access, as shown here:

```
And "user@ticketee.com" can view the "TextMate 2" project
And "user@ticketee.com" can edit tickets in the "TextMate 2" project
```

When you run bin/cucumber features/editing_tickets.feature, it all passes, just as you expect. This step covers the scenario in which the user *has* permission to update tickets; to cover the scenario in which the user doesn't have permission, you need to write a couple of specs first.

8.6.1 *No updating for you!*

In this section, you restrict updating of tickets in the same way you restricted creating tickets. You start by writing two examples: one to test the `edit` action and the other to test the `update` action. Inside spec/controllers/tickets_controller_spec.rb, within the "with permission to view the project" context, define a `cannot_update_tickets!` method right under the `cannot_create_tickets!` method, as shown next:

```
def cannot_update_tickets!
  response.should redirect_to(project)
  flash[:alert].should eql("You cannot edit tickets on this project.")
end
```

Then, underneath the existing examples, put the specs, as shown in the following listing.

Listing 8.9 Update tests for spec/controllers/tickets_controller_spec.rb

```
it "cannot edit a ticket without permission" do
  get :edit, { :project_id => project.id, :id => ticket.id }
  cannot_update_tickets!
end

it "cannot update a ticket without permission" do
  put :update, { :project_id => project.id,
                 :id => ticket.id,
                 :ticket => {}
               }
  cannot_update_tickets!
end
```

These two examples make requests to their respective actions and assert that the user is redirected away from them with an error message explaining why. With both of these actions, you need to pass a `project_id` parameter so the `find_project` method can find a project and an `id` parameter so the `find_ticket` method can find a ticket. For the update action, you pass an empty hash so `params[:ticket]` is set. If you didn't do this, you would get a confusing error in your test:

```
NoMethodError:
  undefined method 'stringify_keys' for nil:NilClass
```

This error occurs because the update_attributes call in the update action would be passed nil, because that's what params[:ticket] defaults to if you don't pass it in here. This error would happen only if the user had permission to update a ticket, which all users have for now (but not for long).

When you run this file using bin/rspec spec/controllers/tickets_controller _spec.rb, these two examples fail:

```
1) TicketsController standard users with permission to view the project
   cannot edit a ticket without permission
    Failure/Error: response.should redirect_to(project)

2) TicketsController standard users with permission to view the project
   cannot update a ticket without permission
    Failure/Error: response.should redirect_to(project)
```

Now you can implement this feature in your controller!

8.6.2   *Authorizing editing*

Before the edit and update actions are run, you want to authorize the user for them. Write another before_filter for TicketsController: the before_filter list for this controller should now look like the following listing.

> **Listing 8.10   app/controllers/tickets_controller.rb**

```
before_filter :authenticate_user!
before_filter :find_project
before_filter :find_ticket, :only => [:show, :edit, :update, :destroy]
before_filter :authorize_create!, :only => [:new, :create]
before_filter :authorize_update!, :only => [:edit, :update]
```

At the bottom of this controller class, define the new method shown in the following listing:

```
def authorize_update!
  if !current_user.admin? && cannot?(:"edit tickets", @project)
    flash[:alert] = "You cannot edit tickets on this project."
    redirect_to @project
  end
end
```

Now check whether the specs pass by running bin/rspec spec/controllers/tickets _controller_spec.rb:

```
5 examples, 0 failures
```

Wasn't that easy? The edit and update actions in the TicketsController are now restricted, just like the create action. How's the feature going? Let's see if those with permission can still update tickets. Run bin/cucumber features/editing_tickets .feature:

```
2 scenarios (2 passed)
28 steps (28 passed)
```

Just like that, you're finished restricting updating tickets to only some users.

Now run `rake cucumber:ok spec` to make sure nothing is broken. Everything should be good:

```
31 scenarios (31 passed)
290 steps (290 passed)
# and
24 examples, 0 failures, 10 pending
```

Fantastic! Let's commit that:

```
git add .
git commit -m "Restricting ticket updating to only those who have permission"
git push
```

Good stuff. In this section, you learned how to restrict the `edit` and `update` actions using the permissions you implemented earlier. There's one last port of call for this restricting business: the `destroy` action.

8.7   *Restricting delete access*

The final action you restrict is the `destroy` action in the `TicketsController`. Again, you can re-use a feature to test this behavior: the Deleting Tickets feature.

As you did with the Creating Tickets and Updating Tickets features, you implement a step here in the Deleting Tickets feature to give the user permission to delete tickets. Under the line that grants users permission to view the TextMate 2 project, put another one to grant them permission to delete tickets, as shown here:

```
And "user@ticketee.com" can view the "TextMate 2" project
And "user@ticketee.com" can delete tickets in the "TextMate 2" project
```

When you run this feature, the whole thing passes because you already have the step that supports the different permissions you require:

```
1 scenario (1 passed)
12 steps (12 passed)
```

This feature ensures that anybody with permission can delete tickets for projects, but you need another spec to test that anybody *without* permission is prevented from deleting tickets.

8.7.1   *Enforcing destroy protection*

To ensure that users without permission to delete tickets can't do so, you write a spec (shown next) directly under the one for the `update` action in spec/controllers/tickets_controller_spec.rb:

```
it "cannot delete a ticket without permission" do
  delete :destroy, { :project_id => project.id, :id => ticket.id }
  response.should redirect_to(project)
  flash[:alert].should eql("You cannot delete tickets from this project.")
end
```

You don't have to put the last two lines in their own method because you won't use them more than once. When you run this spec, it fails on the final line rather than on the third line:

```
1) TicketsController standard users with permission to view the project
    cannot delete a ticket without permission
      Failure/Error: flash[:alert].should eql
    ➠("You cannot delete tickets from this project.")
```

This error occurs because the destroy action is actually being processed, and it redirects the user to the project once it's complete. The spec doesn't know the difference between a redirect from within the action or within the before_filter, nor should it.

To make this spec pass, define a new method called authorize_delete! at the bottom of the TicketsController:

```
def authorize_delete!
  if !current_user.admin? && cannot?(:"delete tickets", @project)
    flash[:alert] = "You cannot delete tickets from this project."
    redirect_to @project
  end
end
```

Then you can call this method in a before_filter too:

```
before_filter :authorize_delete!, :only => :destroy
```

When you run this spec using bin/rspec spec/controllers/tickets_controller _spec.rb, it's all passing:

```
6 examples, 0 failures
```

Now that you're stopping users without permission, how goes your feature? Run bin/ cucumber features/deleting_tickets.feature to find out:

```
1 scenario (1 passed)
12 steps (12 passed)
```

Great! With this last permission in place, all the actions in the TicketsController are restricted to their appropriate users. Let's make a commit:

```
git add .
git commit -m "Restrict destroy action to only people with permission"
git push
```

Because the controller's actions are restricted, the links associated with these actions should be hidden from users who are unable to perform these actions.

8.7.2 *Hiding links based on permission*

To ensure that these links are hidden from those who shouldn't be able to see them but are still visible to admins (because admins should be able to do everything), you use features/hidden_links.feature. Start with the New Ticket link by adding the scenarios from the following listing.

Listing 8.11 features/hidden_links.feature

```
Scenario: New ticket link is shown to a user with permission
  Given "user@ticketee.com" can view the "TextMate 2" project
  And "user@ticketee.com" can create tickets on the "TextMate 2" project
  And I am signed in as "user@ticketee.com"
  When I follow "TextMate 2"
  Then I should see "New Ticket"

Scenario: New ticket link is hidden from a user without permission
  Given "user@ticketee.com" can view the "TextMate 2" project
  And I am signed in as "user@ticketee.com"
  When I follow "TextMate 2"
  Then I should not see the "New Ticket" link

Scenario: New ticket link is shown to admins
  Given I am signed in as "admin@ticketee.com"
  When I follow "TextMate 2"
  Then I should see the "New Ticket" link
```

These three scenarios test all three permutations of users who could possibly see this page. Users with permission and admins should be able to see the link, and users without permission should not. When you run this feature with bin/cucumber features/ hidden_links.feature, the second scenario fails:

```
Expected to not see the "New Ticket" link, but did.
  (RSpec::Expectations::ExpectationNotMetError)
```

This error occurs because the link is visible independently of whether or not the user has permission. With these scenarios in place, you can work on making them pass. You can wrap the New Ticket in a helper method, similar to the admins_only helper used in chapter 6. Open app/views/projects/show.html.erb, and change the New Ticket link from this

```
<%= link_to "New Ticket", new_project_ticket_path(@project) %>
```

to this:

```
<%= authorized?("create tickets".to_sym, @project) do %>
  <%= link_to "New Ticket", new_project_ticket_path(@project) %>
<% end %>
```

Currently, this authorized? method is undefined. This is the method you need in views all across your application to determine if the user has permission to see the specific action and if that user is an admin. Because you'll use this helper everywhere, define it inside app/helpers/application_helper.rb, as shown here:

```
def authorized?(permission, thing, &block)
  block.call if can?(permission.to_sym, thing) ||
        current_user.try(:admin?)
  nil
end
```

This helper uses CanCan's can? method to check if the user is authorized to perform this action. If so, then all is fine and dandy. If not, then you check to see if the current_user is set (it won't be set if the user isn't signed in), and if it is, check to see if that user is an admin by using the try method, which returns nil. If the method specified can't be found on thing, try is called. If it's found, then you use block.call, which runs the passed-in block.

With this helper implemented, all three new scenarios should pass. Run bin/cucumber features/hidden_links.feature to find out:

```
10 scenarios (10 passed)
60 steps (60 passed)
```

Great! They're passing! Now let's implement another few for testing the Edit link for tickets. Add the three scenarios from the following listing to the bottom of features/hidden_links.feature.

Listing 8.12   features/hidden_links.feature

```
Scenario: Edit ticket link is shown to a user with permission
  Given "user@ticketee.com" can view the "TextMate 2" project
  And "user@ticketee.com" can edit tickets on the "TextMate 2" project
  And I am signed in as "user@ticketee.com"
  When I follow "TextMate 2"
  And I follow "Shiny!"
  Then I should see the "Edit" link

Scenario: Edit ticket link is hidden from a user without permission
  Given "user@ticketee.com" can view the "TextMate 2" project
  And I am signed in as "user@ticketee.com"
  When I follow "TextMate 2"
  And I follow "Shiny!"
  Then I should not see the "Edit" link

Scenario: Edit ticket link is shown to admins
  Given I am signed in as "admin@ticketee.com"
  When I follow "TextMate 2"
  And I follow "Shiny!"
  Then I should see the "Edit" link
```

When you run these scenarios using bin/cucumber feature/hidden_links.feature, the link to Shiny! can't be found for any of them:

```
And I follow "Shiny!"
  no link with title, id or text 'Shiny!' found (Capybara::ElementNotFound)
```

The Shiny! link should be a link to a ticket, but you haven't yet created this ticket. To do so, under the line where you created the TextMate 2 project in the Background, add the following to create a ticket:

```
And "user@ticketee.com" has created a ticket for this project:
  | title  | description        |
  | Shiny! | My eyes! My eyes!  |
```

Now when you run this feature, the middle scenario fails, just like when you implemented the Create link filtering:

```
Expected to see the "Edit" link, but did not.
  (RSpec::Expectations::ExpectationNotMetError)
```

This time, you edit the file app/views/tickets/show.html.erb. Change the Edit link from this

```
<%= link_to "Edit Ticket", [:edit, @project, @ticket] %>
```

to this:

```
<%= authorized?("edit tickets", @project) do %>
  <%= link_to "Edit Ticket", [:edit, @project, @ticket] %>
<% end %>
```

With this one small change to use the authorized? helper to check for the permission to edit tickets for the current project, the Hidden Links feature now passes when you run bin/cucumber features/editing_tickets.feature:

```
13 scenarios (13 passed)
97 steps (97 passed)
```

Great! You've got one last link to protect now: the Delete Project link on the tickets show page. Add another three scenarios to this feature, shown in the following listing.

Listing 8.13   features/deleting_tickets.feature

```
Scenario: Delete ticket link is shown to a user with permission
  Given "user@ticketee.com" can view the "TextMate 2" project
  And "user@ticketee.com" can delete tickets in the "TextMate 2" project
  And I am signed in as "user@ticketee.com"
  When I follow "TextMate 2"
  And I follow "Shiny!"
  Then I should see "Delete"

Scenario: Delete ticket link is hidden from a user without permission
  Given "user@ticketee.com" can view the "TextMate 2" project
  And I am signed in as "user@ticketee.com"
  When I follow "TextMate 2"
  And I follow "Shiny!"
  Then I should not see the "Delete" link

Scenario: Delete ticket link is shown to admins
  Given I am signed in as "admin@ticketee.com"
  When I follow "TextMate 2"
  And I follow "Shiny!"
  Then I should see the "Delete" link
```

When you run this feature, the middle scenario fails again:

```
Then I should not see "Delete"
  Expected to not see the "Delete" link, but did.
  (RSpec::Expectations::ExpectationNotMetError)
```

To fix it, open or switch back to app/views/tickets/show.html.erb and wrap the Delete Ticket link in the warm embrace of the authorized? method, just as you did with the Edit Ticket link:

```
<%= authorized?("delete tickets", @project) do %>
  <%= link_to "Delete Ticket",
              project_ticket_path(@project, @ticket),
              :method => :delete,
              :confirm => "Are you sure you want to delete this ticket?" %>
<% end %>
```

When you run `bin/cucumber features/hidden_links.feature`, all 15 scenarios pass:

```
16 scenarios (16 passed)
124 steps (124 passed)
```

Fantastic! Now you've stopped displaying links to the users who shouldn't see them and switched to displaying them only to people who should be able to see them.

What a whirlwind adventure! First you learned to check for permissions for all the actions in the `TicketsController`, and then you learned to hide links from users in the views. Let's make sure everything is working by running `rake cucumber:ok spec`:

```
40 scenarios (40 passed)
376 steps (376 passed)
# and
17 examples, 0 failures, 3 pending
```

Great! Now let's commit:

```
git add .
git commit -m "Restrict actions in TicketsController
    ➥based on permissions and hide links"
git push
```

With all that done, you now have the scaffold for setting up permissions but no interface to it! There's currently no way in the system for a user (in particular, an admin) to set up the permissions on other users. We now implement that.

8.8 *Assigning permissions*

In chapter 6, you added an `admin` field to the `users` table and then triggered it through the admin backend by checking or unchecking a check box. You're going to do the same thing with the permissions for the projects. When you're done, you'll see a permissions screen that allows you to pick and choose the permissions for the users and projects.

You implement this screen one check box at a time because you must confirm that the permissions you assign through this interface work just as well as when you use the step definitions in Cucumber. Let's get started with the permission to view projects.

8.8.1 *Viewing projects*

In this section, you implement the foundations for assigning the permissions through the admin backend, starting with the permission to view projects. Create a new feature called features/assigning_permissions.feature, and start it out with the code from the following listing.

Listing 8.14 features/assigning_permissions.feature

```
Feature: Assigning permissions
  In order to set up users with the correct permissions
  As an admin
  I want to check all the boxes

  Background:
    Given there are the following users:
      | email              | password | admin |
      | admin@ticketee.com | password | true  |
    And I am signed in as them

    And there are the following users:
      | email             | password |
      | user@ticketee.com | password |
    And there is a project called "TextMate 2"

    When I follow "Admin"
    And I follow "Users"
    And I follow "user@ticketee.com"
    And I follow "Permissions"

  Scenario: Viewing a project
    When I check "View" for "TextMate 2"
    And I press "Update"
    And I follow "Sign out"

    Given I am signed in as "user@ticketee.com"
    Then I should see "TextMate 2"
```

This scenario has two users: an admin user and a standard user. You sign in as the admin user, go to the permissions page, check a box, click Update, and then sign out. Then you sign in as the user who was just granted permission to test that permission, which you do in the next step. This ensures that the assigning of the permissions always works. For now, you're only testing the permission to view a project permission.

When you run bin/cucumber features/assigning_permissions.feature, it fails when it tries to follow the Permissions link:

```
And I follow "Permissions"
  no link with title, id or text 'Permissions' found
  ➥ (Capybara::ElementNotFound)
```

If you look at how the Background gets to this point, you can see that it follows the Admin link, which leads to the admin dashboard, then to Users to take you to the place where you can see users, and finally clicks a user, taking you to the Admin::Users-Controllershow action. Therefore, you need to add the missing Permissions link to the app/views/admin/users/show.html.erb directly underneath the Delete User link:

```erb
<%= link_to "Delete User", admin_user_path(@user),
                    :method => :delete,
                    :confirm => "Are you sure you want
                    ➥to delete this user?" %>
<%= link_to "Permissions", admin_user_permissions_path(@user) %>
```

The path for this `link_to` (which is not yet defined) takes you to the `Admin ::PermissionsController`'s index action. To get this `link_to` to work, define that permissions are nested under users in the config/routes.rb, and add the admin namespace in the definition using this code:

```
namespace :admin do
  root :to => "base#index"
  resources :users do
    resources :permissions
  end
end
```

With these changes in the config/routes.rb file, the `admin_user_permissions_path` used in the `link_to` will now be defined. When you run the feature using `bin/cucumber features/assigning_permissions.feature`, you see there's more to be done for this step:

```
And I follow "Permissions"
  uninitialized constant Admin::PermissionsController
  ➥(ActionController::RoutingError)
```

Ah, of course! You must create the controller for this link!

THE PERMISSIONS CONTROLLER

You can generate the `Admin::PermissionsController` file by running this command:

```
rails g controller admin/permissions
```

Along with an app/controllers/admin/permissions_controller.rb file, this command generates other goodies, such as a helper and a directory for the views at app/views/admin/permissions. Before you go further, you must modify this file to make the class inherit from the right place so that only admins can access it. Open the file, and change the first line to this:

```
class Admin::PermissionsController < Admin::BaseController
```

This line makes the controller inherit from the `Admin::BaseController` class, which restricts all actions in this controller to only admin users. When you run the feature again, the `index` action is missing from this controller:

```
And I follow "Permissions"
  The action 'index' could not be found for Admin::PermissionsController
```

Obviously, you need to define this action before you carry on. Inside this action, load all the permissions for the user you're currently looking at, and then, with the view, display a page from which an admin can choose what permissions this user has on each project. It'd be helpful if this user was loaded by a `before_filter` because you'll need it for the action that updates the permissions later. With all this in mind, update the entire controller to resemble the following listing.

Listing 8.15   app/controllers/admin/permissions_controller.rb

```ruby
class Admin::PermissionsController < Admin::BaseController
  before_filter :find_user

  def index
    @ability = Ability.new(@user)
    @projects = Project.all
  end

  private

    def find_user
      @user = User.find(params[:user_id])
    end
end
```

The new `Ability` instance created here lets you check the user's ability to perform specific actions on any project by simply calling this code:

```ruby
@ability.can?(:"view", @project)
```

This syntax may look similar to the syntax used in `TicketsController`—it is. In that controller, you used the `cannot?` method, which is the opposite of the `can?` method. These methods are added to the controller by CanCan and are just shorter helper methods to do almost exactly what you did in this controller. The only difference is that you're not acting on the `current_user` here, so you must define an `Ability` object yourself and use that instead.

THE PERMISSIONS SCREEN

Now that you have the `index` action up, you need to make its view look like what is shown in figure 8.5. Create a new file at app/views/admin/permissions/index.html.erb, and fill it with the content from the following listing.

Figure 8.5   The permissions screen

Listing 8.16   app/views/admin/permissions/index.html.erb

```erb
<h2>Permissions for <%= @user.email %></h2>
<%= form_tag update_user_permissions_path, :method => :put do %>
  <table>
    <thead>
      <th>Project</th>
      <% permissions.each do |name, text| %>
        <th><%= text %></th>
      <% end %>
    </thead>
    <tbody>
      <% @projects.each do |project| %>
        <tr class='<%= cycle("odd", "even") %>'>                ←①
          <td><%= project.name %></td>
          <% permissions.each do |name, text| %>               ←②

            <td>
              <%= check_box_tag "permissions[#{project.id}][#{name}]",
                  @ability.can?(name.to_sym, project) %>
            </td>
          <% end %>
        </tr>
      <% end %>
    </tbody>
  </table>
  <%= submit_tag "Update" %>
<% end %>
```

This template defines the table discussed earlier. It provides a header row of permission titles and rows for each project containing that project's name followed by check boxes for each of the permissions. In this view, you use the form_tag, which generates a form that points to the path specified by its first argument. You also use a permissions helper method ①, which isn't currently defined but will provide a list of permissions to iterate through to check on each project.

Right underneath where you use permissions, you use another helper method called cycle ①. This method is built into Rails and cycles through its given arguments for each iteration of whatever it's encapsulated in, so when this page displays the first project, the method sets the class of that tr tag to odd and the second one to even. It cycles between these two classes until it runs out of projects. This is how you can easily get different rows in this table to be styled differently.

Before we look at how to define the permissions method, run bin/cucumber cucumber features/assigning_permissions.feature:

```
undefined local variable or method
  'update_user_permissions_path' [...]
```

You get an error because you haven't yet defined the route for the form. The Admin::PermissionsController serves a different purpose than the standard REST controllers. For this controller, you use the update action to update a whole slew of permissions rather than a single one. To map to this action by using the update method, you must define another *named route* in your config/routes.rb file using the put method:

```
put '/admin/users/:user_id/permissions',
              :to => 'admin/permissions#update',
              :as => :update_user_permissions
```

With this method, you define a new route for your application that will only respond to PUT requests to this route. The :user_id inside the route is a variable and is passed to the action as params[:user_id]. The controller and action are defined using the :to symbol, and finally the method itself is given a name with the :as option.

Now when you run the feature again, this route method is defined, but the permissions method isn't:

```
And I follow "Permissions"
  undefined local variable or method 'permissions' [...]
  ➥(ActionView::Template::Error)
```

Great! It seems like your page just requires this permissions helper method.

DEFINING A HELPER METHOD

Back in chapter 6, you defined a helper method called admins_only in Application-Helper, which allowed you to show links only for admin users. This time, you define the permissions method, which contains a list of permissions to display check boxes on this page. Because this method is specific to views from the Admin ::Permissions-Controller controller, place it in app/helpers/admin/permissions _helper.rb and define it as shown in the following listing.

> **Listing 8.17   app/helpers/admin/permissions_helper.rb**

```
module Admin::PermissionsHelper
  def permissions
    {
      "view" => "View"
    }
  end
end
```

This permissions method returns a hash containing only one key-value pair at the moment because you're testing only one particular check box. You use this method to display all the permissions you want to be configurable by admins, and you revisit this method later to define more pairs. You use this method in your view twice; the first time, you iterate over it like this:

```
<% permissions.each do |name, text| %>
  <th><%= text %></th>
<% end %>
```

When you iterate over a Hash object with the each method, the key for the hash becomes the first block variable and the value becomes the second block variable; these variables change for each key-value pair of the Hash object. In this case, it renders headers for the table in this view. You use this helper later in the view too:

```
<% permissions.each do |name, text| %>
  <td>
    <%= check_box_tag "permissions[#{project.id}][#{name}]",
      @ability.can?(name.to_sym, project) %>
  </td>
<% end %>
```

Here you use just the key from the hash to define a uniquely identifiable name for this check box. The second argument is the value returned to the controller, which you use to determine whether or not this check box is checked. The third argument uses the `@ability` object to determine whether or not this check box is displayed as checked. By using this method, you get a tag like this:

```
<input id=\"permissions_1_view\"
  name=\"permissions[1][view]\"
  type=\"checkbox\"
  value=\"1\" />
```

You're given both the `id` and `name` attributes, which are generated from the first argument you passed to `check_box_tag`. The `id` attribute indicates not the permission's ID but the ID of the project that you're determining the permission is for. You use the `id` attribute shortly to check this box using Capybara and the parsed-into-`params` version of the `name` attribute just after that in your controller.

When you run `bin/cucumber features/assigning_permissions.feature` again, you reach the following undefined step:

```
When I check "View" for "TextMate 2"
  Undefined step: "I check "View" for "TextMate 2"" (Cucumber::Undefined)

...

When /^I check "([^"]*)" for "([^"]*)"$/ do |arg1, arg2|
  pending # express the regexp above with the code you wish you had
end
```

Take the snippet at the end of the output and put it in features/step_definitions/permission_steps.rb underneath the other step definitions but above the methods. You should end up with a step definition like this:

```
When /^I check "([^"]*)" for "([^"]*)"$/ do |permission, name|
  project = Project.find_by_name!(name)
  permission = permission.downcase.gsub(" ", "_")
  field_id = "permissions_#{project.id}_#{permission}"
  steps(%Q{When I check "#{field_id}"})
end
```

For this step definition, you must first find the project by its name so you can get its ID, because a later part of this step that checks the permission check box requires the ID of the project to compile the ID for the fields.[3] Then you use the handy `steps` method you used in chapter 7 to call another step where you pass in the `downcase`'d and

---

[3] The project name won't change, but the ID might, so you use the identifier that's unlikely to change.

gsub'd version of the permission string. The name passed in is the `titleize`'d version of the permission and should match the title in the permissions table heading.

When you run this feature again, it passes because this step is defined and because it can check this check box, but it fails because the form tries to go to the `update` action inside `Admin::PermissionsController`, which doesn't exist yet:

```
And I press "Update"
  The action 'update' could not be found for Admin::PermissionsController
```

This action's a little tricky. Not only do you want it to add permissions for users, you also want to delete those permissions.[4] This action receives `params[:permissions]` in this `Hash` format from the form:

```
{"1"=>{"view"=>"1"}}
```

The first key is the ID of the project, and the hash inside contains the permissions for that project. If no check boxes are checked for that project, then no hash exists in `params[:permissions]` for it. Therefore, you use this hash to update the permissions that a user can do now, as shown in the following listing.

Listing 8.18 update action inside app/controllers/admin/permissions_controller.rb

```
def update
  @user.permissions.clear
  params[:permissions].each do |id, permissions|
    project = Project.find(id)
    permissions.each do |permission, checked|
      Permission.create!(:user => @user,
                         :thing => project,
                         :action => permission)
    end
  end
  flash[:notice] = "Permissions updated."
  redirect_to admin_user_permissions_path
end
```

You first clear all the users' permissions using the association method `clear`. Next, you iterate through all the key-value pairs in `params[:permissions]` and find the project for each one. Then you iterate through the `permissions` for the parameter and create a new permission for every project. Finally, you set a `flash[:notice]` and redirect back to the permissions page. Now when you run this feature, the Sign Out link is missing:

```
no link with title, id or text 'Sign out' found (Capybara::ElementNotFound)
```

You didn't add this link in chapter 7 because you didn't need it, but in hindsight, you should have. Add this link now to app/views/layouts/application.html.erb directly under the `Signed in as` text:

---

[4] Which is possibly why the action is called `update`.

```
Signed in as <%= current_user.email %>
<%= link_to "Sign out", destroy_user_session_path, :method =>
:delete %>
```

This link now shows only to people who are signed in. The routing helper destroy_user_session_path is provided for free by Devise. When you rerun the Assigning Permissions feature with bin/cucumber features/assigning_permissions .feature, everything passes:

```
1 scenario (1 passed)
13 steps (13 passed)
```

Great! You created a way for admins to choose which users can see which projects through an interface of check boxes and confirmed that users can see the project they have access to and can't see the projects they aren't authorized to see. Let's run all the tests with rake cucumber:ok spec to make sure everything is working:

```
41 scenarios (41 passed)
389 steps (389 passed)
# and
26 examples, 0 failures, 11 pending
```

All systems green! Let's make a commit before you go any further:

```
git add .
git commit -m "Added permissions screen for admins"
```

Next, you implement this feature for the other permissions used.

8.8.2   *And the rest*

Now that you have the foundation in place for this check box screen, you can add the rest of the permissions you've implemented. The next permission you implemented after the restriction of read access was the restriction of write access, restricting which users could and couldn't perform the new and create actions on TicketsController. With an interface in place for admins to assign permissions through the backend, you should ensure that they can assign the permission to create tickets and that users to whom they assign this permission can perform that action.

CREATING TICKETS

Open features/assigning_permissions.feature, and add the scenario shown in the following listing right under the scenario currently in this file.

> **Listing 8.19   features/assigning_permissions.feature**

```
Scenario: Creating tickets for a project
  When I check "View" for "TextMate 2"
  When I check "Create tickets" for "TextMate 2"
  And I press "Update"
  And I follow "Sign out"

  Given I am signed in as "user@ticketee.com"
  When I follow "TextMate 2"
  And I follow "New Ticket"
```

```
And I fill in "Title" with "Shiny!"
And I fill in "Description" with "Make it so!"
And I press "Create"
Then I should see "Ticket has been created."
```

Just as in your first scenario, you check the View check box for the project. Otherwise, the user wouldn't be able to see the project where the new ticket link was. Then you check the Create Tickets check box, update the user's permissions, and sign out. Next, you sign in as that user and make sure you can do what you just gave that user permission to do. When you run this feature with `bin/cucumber features/assigning _permissions.feature`, the first step fails because it can't find the check box:

```
cannot check field, no checkbox with id, name,
or label 'permissions_1_create_tickets' found (Capybara::ElementNotFound)
```

Let's add this check box then! Open app/helpers/admin/permissions_helper.rb, and add the permission to your hash, changing this method from

```
def permissions
  {
    "view" => "View"
  }
end
```

to

```
def permissions
  {
    "view" => "View",
    "create tickets" => "Create Tickets"
  }
end
```

Keep in mind that the key *must* match the intended action for the `Permission` object; the value is just a label for this permission. The action is what you use in your `authorized?` helpers around the application.

When you another key-value pair in this hash, the code inside app/views/admin/ permissions/index.html.erb automatically shows a check box for this new permission. When you run this feature again, it passes because this new check box is visible and the permission is applied correctly:

```
2 scenarios (2 passed)
35 steps (35 passed)
```

Wasn't that a piece of cake? Let's move on to the next permission now: updating tickets. Actually, let's do both updating tickets and deleting tickets at the same time.

THE DOUBLE WHAMMY

Just to show the world how great you are at developing this application, you'll now write two scenarios and get them both to pass at the same time. Add both of these scenarios to the end of features/assigning_permissions.feature, as shown in the following listing.

Listing 8.20　features/assigning_permissions.feature

```
Scenario: Updating a ticket for a project
  When I check "View" for "TextMate 2"
  And I check "Edit tickets" for "TextMate 2"
  And I press "Update"
  And I follow "Sign out"

  Given I am signed in as "user@ticketee.com"
  When I follow "TextMate 2"
  And I follow "Shiny!"
  And I follow "Edit"
  And I fill in "Title" with "Really shiny!"
  And I press "Update Ticket"
  Then I should see "Ticket has been updated"

Scenario: Deleting a ticket for a project
  When I check "View" for "TextMate 2"
  And I check "Delete tickets" for "TextMate 2"
  And I press "Update"
  And I follow "Sign out"

  Given I am signed in as "user@ticketee.com"
  When I follow "TextMate 2"
  And I follow "Shiny!"
  And I follow "Delete"
  Then I should see "Ticket has been deleted."
```

The scenarios should be descriptive enough to understand—no particular magic going on here. But you're acting on a ticket in both these scenarios that doesn't exist: the Shiny! ticket. You need to create this ticket in your Background if you want these scenarios to pass. Add this step definition right under the line in the Background that creates the TextMate 2 project, as shown next:

```
And "user@ticketee.com" has created a ticket for this project:
  | title  | description     |
  | Shiny! | Eye-blindingly so |
```

Now when you run this feature, your two newest scenarios are failing, both with similar errors:

```
cannot check field, no checkbox with id, name,
or label 'permissions_1_update_tickets' found
# and
cannot check field, no checkbox with id, name,
or label 'permissions_1_delete_tickets' found
```

Of course! You have no check boxes for Capybara to check yet! Add them now by changing the permissions method in app/helper/admin/permissions_helper.rb from this

```
def permissions
  {
    "view" => "View",
    "create tickets" => "Create Tickets"
  }
end
```

to this:

```
def permissions
  {
    "view" => "View",
    "create tickets" => "Create Tickets",
    "edit tickets" => "Edit Tickets",
    "delete tickets" => "Delete Tickets"
  }
end
```

By adding these two permissions here, you display the check boxes that should make your scenarios all green. Let's run the feature with `bin/cucumber features/assigning _permissions.feature` to find out:

```
4 scenarios (4 passed)
72 steps (72 passed)
```

How great are you? Two features with one blow. Awesome stuff.

That's the final piece of the authorization puzzle. You now have a way for admins to assign permissions to users. But does everything work? Here's hoping! Let's run `rake cucumber:ok spec`:

```
44 scenarios (44 passed)
448 steps (448 passed)
# and
26 examples, 0 failures, 11 pending
```

Awesome! Let's commit this:

```
git add .
git commit -m "Added creating, editing, updating and deleting
              tickets to assigning permissions interface"
git push
```

Although it's great that you now have an interface for assigning permissions, you don't have a way to do it without first having an admin user set up. You can set up an admin user manually through the console, or you can do it by creating *seed data*.

8.9   *Seed data*

Seed data is records created for the purpose of providing the minimal viable requirements to get an application running. Before Rails 2.2, many applications implemented such records through using plugins such as *seed_fu*, but since 2.2, seed data is built in.

Seed data allows you to create records for your application to provide a usable base if you or anybody else wants to get set up with the application quickly and easily. For your application's seed data, you'll create an admin user and an example project. From there, anybody using the admin user will be able to perform all the functions of the application.

Seed data lives under db/seeds.rb, and you can run this file by running `rake db:seed`. The code for this rake task is this:

```
load Rails.root + "db/seeds.rb"
```

The `load` method works in a similar fashion to `require`, loading and executing the code inside the file. One difference, however, is that `load` expects the given string (or `Pathname`) to be the full path, with the extension, to the file.

First write a feature to ensure that when the seed data is loaded, you can sign in with the email admin@ticketee.com and the password *password* and you can get to the TicketeeBeta project. Put this feature in features/seed.feature, and write it as shown in the following listing.

Listing 8.21   features/seed.feature

```
Feature: Seed Data
  In order to fill the database with the basics
  As the system
  I want to run the seed task

  Scenario: The basics
    Given I have run the seed task
    And I am signed in as "admin@ticketee.com"
    Then I should see "Ticketee Beta"
```

It's a pretty basic feature, but your seed file will be equally basic. Before you create it, however, you should define the first step of this scenario. You can get the definition for this step by running `bin/cucumber features/seed.feature`. The step definition looks like this:

```
Given /^I have run the seed task$/ do
  pending # express the regexp above with the code you wish you had
end
```

Put this step definition in a new file called features/step_definitions/application_steps.rb because it doesn't really tie in with the other step files you've defined. If you have more steps like this, you can put them into this file later too. The code for this file is simple:

```
Given /^I have run the seed task$/ do
  load Rails.root + "db/seeds.rb"
end
```

Now when you run your feature again, it can't find the user your seed data is supposed to create:

```
And I am signed in as "admin@ticketee.com"
  Couldn't find User with email = admin@ticketee.com
  ➥(ActiveRecord::RecordNotFound)
```

It can't find this user because you haven't yet created one for this scenario. This user should be created by the db/seeds.rbfile. Open this file now, and add a couple of lines to create this user, set the user up as an admin, and confirm the user, as shown in the following listing.

Listing 8.22   db/seeds.rb

```
admin_user = User.create(:email => "admin@ticketee.com",
                         :password => "password")
admin_user.admin = true
admin_user.confirm!
```

Now run `bin/cucumber features/seed.feature` to ensure that you can sign in as this user. If you can, you should see the step passing and the next step failing:

```
And I am signed in as "admin@ticketee.com"
Then I should see "Ticketee Beta"
  Failed assertion, no message given. (MiniTest::Assertion)
```

To get this last step of the scenario to pass, you must add the project to db/seeds.rb by putting this line in there:

```
Project.create(:name => "Ticketee Beta")
```

Your entire seeds file should look like the following listing.

Listing 8.23   db/seeds.rb

```
admin_user = User.create(:email => "admin@ticketee.com",
                         :password => "password")
admin_user.admin = true
admin_user.confirm!

Project.create(:name => "Ticketee Beta")
```

This is all you need to get this feature to pass. Let's run it now with `bin/cucumber features/seed.feature` to make sure:

```
1 scenario (1 passed)
3 steps (3 passed)
```

Great! With this seeds file, you now have data to put in the database so you can bootstrap your application. Let's run `rake db:seed` to load this data. Start your application's server by typing `rails server` into a terminal, and then go to your server at http://localhost:3000 in your browser. Sign in as the admin user using the same email and password you set up in your seeds file. You should see the display shown in figure 8.6.

When you're signed in as a user, you should be able to do everything from creating a new ticket to creating a new user and setting up user permissions. Go ahead and play around with what you've created so far.

When you're done playing, run `rake cucumber:ok spec` for the final time this chapter:

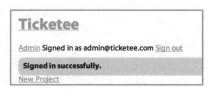

Figure 8.6   What admins see

```
45 scenarios (45 passed)
451 steps (451 passed)
# and
26 examples, 0 failures, 11 pending
```

Everything's still green, which means it's time for another commit:

```
git add .
git commit -m "Added a seeds file"
git push
```

Now you're done!

8.10   *Summary*

This chapter covered implementing authorization for your application and setting up a permissions-based system for both the ProjectsController and TicketsController.

You started with a Permission model, which you used in a scope on the Project model to show only the projects a user should be able to access. Then you used the CanCan plugin, which provided the can? and cannot? methods to use first in the controllers to stop users from accessing specified actions and then in the views, through the authorized? method, to stop users from seeing specified links.

You implemented a way for admins to change the permissions of a user through the admin backend of the system by displaying a series of check boxes. Here you used an update action that wasn't quite like the normal update action, and you had to define a custom-named route for it.

Finally, you learned how to set up seed data for your application so you have a solid base of objects to work from. Without using seed data, you'd have to manually set up the data not only for your local development environment but also for your production server, which can be tedious. Seed data saves you that effort. You also wrote a test for this data in the form of a feature that ensures the data from the seed file is always created when the seed task is run.

In chapter 9, you learn how to attach files to tickets. File uploading is an essential part of any ticket-tracking application because files can provide that additional piece of context required for a ticket, such as a screenshot, a patch, or any type of file. You also learn about restricting the availability of these files on the basis of users' permissions.

File uploading

9

This chapter covers

- Uploading files to the app
- Locking down file access based on declared permissions
- Uploading multiple files using JavaScript, jQuery, and CoffeeScript

In chapter 9, you learned how to restrict access to specific actions in your application, such as viewing projects and creating tickets, by defining a `Permission` model that keeps track of which users have access to which actions.

Ticketee's getting pretty useful now. This chapter focuses on file uploading, the next logical step in a ticket-tracking application. Sometimes, when people file a ticket on an application such as Ticketee, they want to attach a file to provide more information for that ticket, because words alone can only describe so much. For example, a ticket description saying, "This button should move up a bit," could be better explained with a picture showing where the button is now and where it should be. Users may want to attach any kind of file: a picture, a crash log, a text file, you name it. Currently, Ticketee has no way to attach files to the ticket: people would have to upload them elsewhere and then include a link with their ticket description.

213

By providing Ticketee the functionality to attach files to the ticket, you provide the project owners a useful context that will help them more easily understand what the ticket creator means. Luckily, there's a gem called Paperclip that allows you to implement this feature easily.

Once you're familiar with Paperclip, you'll change your application to accept multiple files attached to the same ticket using a JavaScript library called Prototype (which comes with Rails) and some custom JavaScript code of your own. Because you're using JavaScript, you have to alter the way you test parts of your application. To test JavaScript functionality, you'll be using WebDriver,[1] which is a framework built for automatic control of web browsers. WebDriver is especially useful because you can use the same steps you use for standard Cucumber and Capybara tests and because Capybara will take care of driving the browser. By running the tests inside the browser, you ensure the JavaScript on the page will be executed, and then you can run the tests on the results. Pretty handy!

Finally, you'll see how you can restrict access to the files contained within the projects of your application so that confidential information isn't shared with people who don't have access to a particular project.

File uploading is also useful in other types of applications. Suppose you wrote a Rails application for a book. You could upload the chapters to this application, and then people could provide notes on those chapters. Another example is a photo gallery application that allows you to upload images of your favorite cars for people to vote on. File uploading has many different uses and is a cornerstone of many Rails applications.

9.1   Attaching a file

You start off by letting users attach files when they begin creating a ticket. As explained before, files attached to tickets can provide useful context as to what feature a user is requesting or can point out a specific bug. A picture is worth a thousand words, as they say. It doesn't have to be an image; it can be any type of file. This kind of context is key to solving tickets.

To provide this functionality, you must add a file-upload box to the new ticket page, which allows users to select a file to upload. When the form is submitted, the file is submitted along with it. You use the Paperclip gem to store the file inside your application's directory.

9.1.1   A feature featuring files

You first need to write a scenario to make sure the functionality works. This scenario shows you how to deal with file uploads when creating a ticket. Users should be able to create a ticket, select a file, and upload it. Then they should be able see this file, along with the other ticket details, on the ticket's page. They may choose to click the filename, which would download the file. Let's test all this by adding a scenario at the

---

[1] There's a great post explaining WebDriver on the Google Open Source blog: http://google-opensource .blogspot.com/2009/05/introducing-webdriver.html.

bottom of features/creating_tickets.feature that creates a ticket with an attachment,[2] as shown in the following listing.

Listing 9.1 features/creating_tickets.feature

```
Scenario: Creating a ticket with an attachment
  When I fill in "Title" with "Add documentation for blink tag"
  And I fill in "Description" with "The blink tag has a speed attribute"
  And I attach the file "spec/fixtures/speed.txt" to "File"
  And I press "Create Ticket"
  Then I should see "Ticket has been created."
  Then I should see "speed.txt" within "#ticket .asset"
```

❶ Attach file

In this feature you introduce a new concept: the Attach the File step ❶ of this scenario, which attaches the file found at the specified path to the specified field. The path here is deliberately in the spec/fixtures directory because you may use this file for functional tests later. This directory would usually be used for test fixtures, except that at the moment, you don't have any.[3] Create the spec/fixtures/speed.txt file now, and fill it with some random filler text like this:

```
The blink tag can blink faster if you use the speed="hyper" attribute.
```

Try running this feature using bin/cucumber features/creating_tickets.feature :37 and see how far you get. It fails on the attaching step because the File field isn't yet available:

```
And I attach the file "spec/fixtures/speed.txt" to "File"
  cannot attach file, no file field with id, name,
  or label 'File' found (Capybara::ElementNotFound)
```

Add the File field to the ticket form partial directly underneath the p tag for the description field using the code in the following listing.

Listing 9.2 app/views/tickets/_form.html.erb

```
<p>
  <%= f.label :asset, "File" %>
  <%= f.file_field :asset %>
</p>
```

You call this field asset internally, but the user will see File. The reason for this is explained a little later.

In earlier versions of Rails, you were required to specify that this form is multipart. A multipart form should be used for any HTML form that contains a file-upload field. In earlier versions, if you didn't enable this form setting, you'd only get the filename from the field rather than the file itself. In Rails 3.1, you don't need to do this because it's done automatically if the form uses the file_field. But it's preferable to indicate

---

[2] Please note that although the blink tag was once a part of HTML, it should never be used. Same goes for the marquee tag.

[3] Nor will you ever, as factories replace them in your application.

that the form is multipart anyway, so you should do this now by changing the form_for line in app/views/tickets/_form.html.erb from this

```
<%= form_for [@project, @ticket] do |f| %>
```

to this:

```
<%= form_for [@project, @ticket], :html => { :multipart => true } do |f| %>
```

Now we come to a very interesting point in implementing file uploading. When you run `bin/cucumber features/creating_tickets.feature`, all of the scenarios are broken and all for the same reason:

```
And I press "Create Ticket"
  unknown attribute: asset (ActiveRecord::UnknownAttributeError)
```

Because you added this `file_field`, the `create` action's code dutifully tries to assign it as an attribute, only to find that it's not defined and so causes this error. Rather than running a migration to add an attribute by this name, you use the Paperclip gem to handle it.

9.1.2   *Enter stage right, Paperclip*

Just as you would use a normal paperclip to attach paper files together, in your application you use the Paperclip gem to provide the attachment functionality you need for tickets. This gem was created by thoughtbot,[4] which has a whole slew of other useful gems, such as Hoptoad.[5]

To install Paperclip, you need to add a line to the Gemfile to tell Bundler that you want to use this gem. Put this underneath the line specifying the CanCan gem, separated by a line because it's a different type of gem (CanCan has to do with users, paperclip has to do with files):

```
gem 'cancan'

gem 'paperclip'
```

Next, you must run `bundle install` to install this gem.

With Paperclip now installed, you can work on defining the asset attribute that your model wants. It's not really an attribute; the error message is misleading in that respect. All it needs is a setter method (`asset=`) and it would be happy. But you need this method to do more than set an attribute on this object; you need it to accept the uploaded file and store it locally. Paperclip lets you define this fairly easily with its `has_attached_file` method. This method goes in the `Ticket` model, defines the setter method you need, and gives four application the ability to accept and process this file. Add it to your `Ticket` model with this line:

```
has_attached_file :asset
```

Now this `asset=` method is defined, but it's not yet over!

---

4   http://thoughtbot.com.
5   For a full list of thoughtbot's gems, see its GitHub page: http://github.com/thoughtbot.

9.1.3 *Using Paperclip*

When you run `bin/cucumber features/creating_tickets.feature` again, you're told your model is missing one more thing:

```
When I press "Create Ticket"
  Ticket model missing required attr_accessor
  for 'asset_file_name' (Paperclip::PaperclipError)
```

`attr_accessor` references a Ruby method that defines a setter and a getter method named after its arguments, such as in the following listing.

Listing 9.3 `attr_accessor` **example**

```ruby
attr_accessor :foo

# is the same as...

def foo
  @foo
end

def foo=(value)
  @foo = value
end
```

These getter and setter methods are defined automatically by Active Model for the fields in your database. Paperclip wants the `asset_file_name` method defined on your `Ticket` instance's method. `asset_file_name` is one of four methods used by Paperclip to track details about the file. The other methods are `asset_content_type`, `asset_file_size`, and `asset_updated_at`. To define the `asset_file_name` method and its siblings, create a migration that adds them as attributes of the `Ticket` model by running this command:

```
rails g paperclip ticket asset
```

This `paperclip` generator (provided by the Paperclip gem) adds the proper fields to your `tickets` table. You tell it you want the attachment to be called `asset`.

By running this command, you get a new file in db/migrate that ends with _add_attachment_asset_to_ticket.rb. If you open this file now, you should see a pre-filled migration, as shown in the following listing.

Listing 9.4 **db/migrate/[time]_add_attachment_asset_to_ticket.rb**

```ruby
class AddAttachmentAssetToTicket < ActiveRecord::Migration
  def self.up
    add_column :tickets, :asset_file_name, :string
    add_column :tickets, :asset_content_type, :string
    add_column :tickets, :asset_file_size, :integer
    add_column :tickets, :asset_updated_at, :datetime
  end

  def self.down
    remove_column :tickets, :asset_file_name
    remove_column :tickets, :asset_content_type
```

```
      remove_column :tickets, :asset_file_size
      remove_column :tickets, :asset_updated_at
   end
end
```

Remember that you call the field asset internally, but to the user, it's called File? This column-naming convention is the reason for the different names. To ease confusion for people working on the application (you!), you call these fields with the asset prefix so that the column names are asset_file_name and not file_file_name. There's also another reason, which is explained in section 9.2.

To add these columns to your development environment's database, run rake db :migrate. Then run rake db:test:prepare to add them to your test environment's database. If you run the feature with bin/cucumber features/creating_tickets .feature, all the scenarios that were previously passing are still passing. But the scenario you just added fails with this error:

```
Then I should see "speed.txt" within "#ticket .asset"
```

You can see that the scenario failed because Capybara can't find the text within this element on the TicketsController's show page: this text and this element don't exist! You need to add at least the filename for your scenario to pass, so add it underneath the spot in the show view where you currently have the following:

```
Created by <%= @ticket.user.email %>
<%= simple_format(@ticket.description) %>
```

You must also wrap all the code in this view inside a div tag with the id attribute ticket and spice it up a little by adding the content type and file size there too, as shown in the following listing.

> **Listing 9.5   app/views/tickets/show.html.erb**

```
<small>Created by <%= @ticket.user.email %></small>
<%= simple_format(@ticket.description) %>

<% if @ticket.asset.exists? %>
  <h3>Attached File</h3>
  <div class="asset">
    <p>
      <%= link_to File.basename(@ticket.asset.path),      ❶ Provide
      @ticket.asset.url                                     download link
%>
    </p>
    <p><small><%= number_to_human_size(@ticket.asset.size) %>
      (<%= @ticket.asset.content_type %>)</small></p>
  </div>
<% end %>
```

Here you use the exists? method defined on the asset method (which was defined by Paperclip and returns a Paperclip::Attachment object); the exists? method returns true if the file exists. You use it because you don't want it trying to display the path or any other information of a file when there isn't one.

You use the `url` ❶ method here with `link_to` to provide the user with a link to download[6] this file. In this case, the URL for this file would be something like http://localhost:3000/system/assets/1/original/file.txt.

Where is this system route defined? Well, it's not a route. It's actually a directory inside the public folder of your application where Paperclip saves your files.

Requests to files from the public directory are handled by the server rather than by Rails, and anybody who enters the URL in their browser can access them. This is bad because the files in a project should be visible only to authorized users. You'll handle that problem a little later in the chapter.

Underneath the filename, you display the size of the file, which is stored in the database as the number of bytes. To convert it to a human-readable output (such as "71 Bytes," which will be displayed for your file), you use the `number_to_human_size` Action View helper.

With the file's information now being output in app/views/tickets/show.html.erb, this feature passes when you run `bin/cucumber features/creating_tickets .feature`:

```
4 scenarios (4 passed)
52 steps (52 passed)
```

Awesome! Your files are being uploaded and taken care of by Paperclip, which stores them at public/system/assets. Let's see if your changes have brought destruction or salvation by running `rake cucumber:ok spec`:

```
46 scenarios (46 passed)
466 steps (466 passed)
# and
26 examples, 0 failures, 11 pending
```

What I will say when I get through this book! Let's commit but not push this just yet:

```
git add .
git commit -m "Added the ability to attach a file to a ticket"
```

Have a look at the commit output. It contains this line:

```
create mode 100644 public/system/assets/1/original/speed.txt
```

This line is a leftover file from your test and shouldn't be committed to the repository because you could be testing using files much larger than this. You can tell Git to ignore the entire public/system directory by adding it to the .gitignore file. Open that file now and add this line to the bottom:

```
public/system
```

---

[6] Some browsers open certain files as pages rather than downloading them. Modern browsers do so for .txt files and the like.

This file tells Git which files you don't want versioned. The whole file should look like this now:

```
.bundle
db/*.sqlite3
log/*.log
tmp/**/*
public/system
```

By default, the .bundle directory (for Bundler's configuration), the SQLite3 databases, the logs for the application, and any files in tmp are ignored. With public/system added, this directory is now ignored by Git too. You should also remove this directory from your latest commit, and thankfully, Git provides a way to do so by using these two commands:

```
git rm public/system/assets/1/original/speed.txt
git commit --amend -m "Added the ability to attach a file to a ticket"
```

The first command removes the file from the filesystem and tells Git to remove it from the repository. The second command amends your latest commit to exclude this file, and it will be as if your first commit with this message never existed. Let's push this change:

```
git push
```

Great! Now you can attach a file to a ticket. There's still some work to do, however. What would happen if somebody wanted to add more than one file to a ticket? Let's take a look at how to do that.

9.2   *Attaching many files*

You have an interface for attaching a single file to a ticket but no way for a user to attach more than one. Let's imagine your pretend client asked you to boost the number of file-input fields on this page to three.

If you're going to add these three file-input fields to your view, you need some more fields in your database to handle them. You could define four fields for each file-upload field, but a much better way to handle this is to add another model.

Creating another model gives you the advantage of being able to scale it to not just three file-input fields but more if you ever need them. Call this model `Asset`, after the name you gave to the `has_attached_file` in the `Ticket` model.

When you're done with this feature, you should see three file-upload fields as shown in figure 9.1.

You can create new instances of this model through the ticket form by using *nested attributes*. Nested attributes have been a feature of Rails since version 2.3, and they allow the attributes of an association to be passed from the creation or update of a particular resource. In this case, you'll be passing nested attributes for new

Figure 9.1
File-upload boxes

asset objects while creating a new `Ticket` model. The best part is that the code to do all of this remains the same in the controller.

You need to modify the scenario for creating a ticket with an attachment in your Creating Tickets feature so it uploads two additional files.

9.2.1 *Two more files*

Let's take the scenario for creating a ticket with an attachment from features/ creating_tickets.feature and add these two additional file upload fields so the entire scenario looks like the following listing.

Listing 9.6   File attachment scenario, features/creating_tickets.feature

```
Scenario: Creating a ticket with an attachment
  When I fill in "Title" with "Add documentation for blink tag"
  And I fill in "Description" with "The blink tag has an undocumented
      ➥speed attribute"
  And I attach the file "spec/fixtures/speed.txt" to "File #1"
  And I attach the file "spec/fixtures/spin.txt" to "File #2"
  And I attach the file "spec/fixtures/gradient.txt" to "File #3"
  And I press "Create Ticket"
  Then I should see "Ticket has been created."
  And I should see "speed.txt" within "#ticket .assets"
  And I should see "spin.txt" within "#ticket .assets"
  And I should see "gradient.txt" within "#ticket .assets"
```

In this scenario, you attach three files to your ticket and assert that you see them within the `assets` element, which was previously called `#ticket .asset` but now has the pluralized name of `#ticket .assets`.

You download only the one file here and check for the content. It's not at all likely that the other two files wouldn't work in the same way given that they're interpreted and rendered identically.

Now run this single scenario using `bin/cucumber features/creating_tickets` `.feature:36`. It should fail on the first Attach the File step, because you renamed the label of this field:

```
And I attach the file "spec/fixtures/speed.txt" to "File #1"
  cannot attach file, no file field with id, name,
  or label 'File #1' found (Capybara::ElementNotFound)
```

To get this step to pass, you can change the label on the field in app/views/tickets/ _form.html.erb to "File #1":

```
<p>
  <%= f.label :asset, "File #1" %>
  <%= f.file_field :asset %>
</p>
```

While you're changing things, you may as well change app/views/tickets/ show.html.erb to reflect these latest developments. First, change the `if` around the asset field to use the assets method, because it'll need to check the assets of a ticket rather than the asset. You also need to change the h3 that currently reads Attached File so it reads Attached Files because there's more than one file. You should also change the div that encapsulates your assets to have the class attribute of assets. These three changes mean that you now have these three lines in app/views/tickets/show.html.erb:

```
<% if @ticket.assets.exists? %>
  <h3>Attached Files</h3>
  <div class="assets">
```

When you call exists? this time, it calls the ActiveRecord::Base association method, which checks if there are any assets on a ticket and returns true if there are. Although assets isn't yet defined, you can probably guess what you're about to do.

First, though, you need to change the lines underneath the ones you just changed to the following:

```
<% @ticket.assets.each do |asset| %>
  <p>
    <%= link_to File.basename(asset.asset_file_name), asset.asset.url %>
  </p>
  <p>
    <small><%= number_to_human_size(asset.asset.size) %></small>
  </p>
<% end %>
```

Here you switch to using the assets method and iterate through each element in the array, rendering the same output as you did when you had a single asset.

All of these changes combined will help your scenario pass, which is a great thing. When you run this scenario again, the first file field step passes, but the second fails:

```
And I attach the file "spec/fixtures/speed.txt" to "File #1"
And I attach the file "spec/fixtures/spin.txt" to "File #2"
  cannot attach file, no file field with id, name,
  or label 'File #2' found (Capybara::ElementNotFound)
```

You *could* add another field:

```
<p>
  <%= f.label :asset_2, "File #2" %>
  <%= f.file_field :asset_2 %>
</p>
```

But that's a messy way of going about it. The best way to handle this problem is through an associated model, a has_many association, and by using *nested attributes*. To use nested attributes in the view, you use the fields_for helper. This helper defines the fields for an association's records, as many as you like. Let's remove the file field completely and replace it with this:

```
<% number = 0 %>
<%= f.fields_for :assets do |asset| %>                    ◁———❶ Number increment
  <p>
```

```
      <%= asset.label :asset, "File ##{number += 1}" %>        ←— ❷ The assets
      <%= asset.file_field :asset %>
    </p>
  <% end %>
```

Directly before the `fields_for` call, you set a local variable called `number`, which is incremented whenever you render a `label` ❶.

You use `fields_for` much in the same way you use `form_for`. You call `fields_for` on the `f` block variable from `form_for`, which tells it you want to define nested fields inside this original form. The argument to `fields_for`—`:assets` ❷—tells Rails the name of the nested fields.

The file field inside this `fields_for` now has the `name` attribute of `ticket[assets][asset]` rather than simply `ticket[asset]`, meaning it will be available in the controller as `params[:ticket][:assets][:asset]`.

When you run this scenario with `bin/cucumber features   creating_tickets .feature:36`, it now fails because it still can't find the second file-upload field:

```
And I attach the file "spec/fixtures/spin.txt" to "File #2"
  cannot attach file, no file field with id, name,
  or label 'File #2' found (Capybara::ElementNotFound)
```

To make this appear, you must define an `assets` association in your `Ticket` model so the `fields_for` in your view will provide `file_fields` for three new `Asset` objects. If this method is available and you've declared that your model accepts nested attributes for this association, `fields_for` iterates through the output from this method and renders the fields from `fields_for` for each element.

You can define this `assets` method by defining a `has_many` association in your `Ticket` model:

```
has_many :assets
```

Underneath this `has_many`, you also define that a `Ticket` model accepts nested attributes for assets by using `accepts_nested_attributes_for`:

```
accepts_nested_attributes_for :assets
```

This little helper tells your model to accept asset attributes along with ticket attributes whenever you call methods like `new`, `build`, and `update`. It has the added bonus of switching how `fields_for` performs in your form, making it reference the association and calling the attributes it defines `assets_attributes` rather than `assets`.

When you run the scenario with `bin/cucumber features/creating_tickets .feature:38`, you see again that the `Asset` is not defined:

```
And I follow "New Ticket"
  uninitialized constant Ticket::Asset (ActionView::Template::Error)
```

You'd best get onto that then!

9.2.2   *Using nested attributes*

You used the term *Asset* rather than *File* throughout this application because of this model. You can't define a `File` model because there's already a `File` class in Ruby. `Asset` is an alternative name you can use. To define this `Asset` constant in your application, you can run the model generator:

```
rails g model asset
```

Each record for this model refers to a single file that has been uploaded to a ticket. Therefore, each record in the `assets` table must have the same `asset_*` fields that each `tickets` record currently has. Storing the asset references in the `assets` table now makes the references in the `tickets` table irrelevant, so you should remove them. You should also add a relationship between the asset records and the ticket records by adding a `ticket_id` field to the `assets` table. Open the migration this generates, and change it to the following listing to reflect these ideas.

> **Listing 9.7   db/migrate/[date]_create_assets.rb**

```ruby
class CreateAssets < ActiveRecord::Migration
  def change
    create_table :assets do |t|
      t.string :asset_file_name
      t.integer :asset_file_size
      t.string :asset_content_type
      t.datetime :asset_updated_at
      t.integer :ticket_id

      t.timestamps
    end

    [:asset_file_name,
     :asset_file_size,
     :asset_content_type,
     :asset_updated_at].each do |column|
      remove_column :tickets, column
    end
  end
end
```

Run this migration with `rake db:migrate` to migrate your development environment's database, and then run `rake db:test:prepare` to migrate the test environment's database. When you run the feature again with `bin/cucumber features/creating_tickets.feature:36`, your `File #1` field is once again missing:

```
And I attach the file "spec/fixtures/speed.txt" to "File #1"
  cannot attach file, no file field with id, name,
  or label 'File #1' found (Capybara::ElementNotFound)
```

You've gone backward! Or so it seems.

As mentioned earlier, `fields_for` detects that the `assets` method is defined on your `Ticket` object and then iterates through each object in this collection while rendering the fields inside `fields_for` for each. When you create a new ticket in

TicketsController's new action, however, you don't initialize any assets for this ticket, so assets returns an empty array and no fields at all are displayed.

To get this action to render three file input fields, you must initialize three Asset objects associated to the Ticket object the form uses. Change your new action inside TicketsController to this:

```
def new
  @ticket = @project.tickets.build
  3.times { @ticket.assets.build }
end
```

The final line of this action calls @ticket.assets.build three times, which creates the three Asset objects you need for your fields_for.

When you run the scenario again, the three fields are available, but the scenario now fails because it can't find a file to upload:

```
And I attach the file "spec/fixtures/speed.txt" to "File #1"
And I attach the file "spec/fixtures/spin.txt" to "File #2"
And I attach the file "spec/fixtures/gradient.txt" to "File #3"
And I press "Create Ticket"
  /home/you/ticketee/spec/fixtures/
      spin.txt file does not exist (RuntimeError)
```

Create this spin.txt file now inside the spec/fixtures directory, and give it the following content:

```
Spinning blink tags have a 200% higher click rate!
```

You also need to add the gradient.txt file to the same directory, and it contains this:

```
Everything looks better with a gradient!
```

These two text pieces are random filler meant only to provide some text if you ever need to reference it. Let's run the scenario again:

```
And I press "Create Ticket"
  unknown attribute: asset (ActiveRecord::UnknownAttributeError)
```

You got this message earlier when you were implementing single-file uploading because you didn't define has_attached_file on the Ticket class. Let's get more backtrace for this error by using the -b switch at the end of the command: bin/cucumber features/creating_tickets.feature:36 -b. This command provides the whole backtrace for an error. In this particular backtrace, you're after anything to do with assets, because that's the only thing that's changed since this feature was passing. You should see a line like the following about 10 lines down:

```
.../active_record/nested_attributes.rb:254:in 'assets_attributes='
```

This line indicates that the failure most likely has to do with the assets_attributes= method, which was kindly enough provided by Rails through the call to accepts_nested_attributes_for. If this error occurs *after* the assets_attributes= method, then it definitely has to do with this method. In fact, it's probably because you haven't yet defined the `has_attached_file` in the `Asset` model, right? Yup, you should do that!

Open app/models/asset.rb, and add this line:

```
has_attached_file :asset
```

Remove the same line from app/models/ticket.rb because you no longer need it. Having this `has_attached_file` defined in the `Asset` model is probably all you need. You've had all three file fields displaying, and now you've got your `Asset` model set up to receive these files. When you run the scenario again using `bin/cucumber features /creating_tickets.feature:38`, it all passes:

```
1 scenario (1 passed)
18 steps (18 passed)
```

Hooray, the scenario passed! In this section, you set up the form that creates new `Ticket` objects to also create three associated `Asset` objects by using nested attributes. This process was made possible by moving the responsibility of handling file uploads out of the `Ticket` model and into the associated `Asset` model.

Let's ensure that nothing is broken by running `rake cucumber:ok spec`:

```
46 scenarios (46 passed)
470 steps (470 passed)
# and
21 examples, 0 failures, 4 pending
```

Awesome, let's commit and push this:

```
git add .
git commit -m "Users can now upload 3 files at a time"
git push
```

Great. You're done with nested attributes! Earlier, it was mentioned that the files uploaded to your application are publicly available for anybody to access because these files are in the public directory. Any file in the public directory is served up automatically by any Rails server, bypassing all the authentication and authorization in your application. This is a bad thing. What if one of the projects in your application has files that should be accessed only by authorized users?

9.3   *Serving files through a controller*

You can solve this issue by serving the uploaded files through a controller for your application. Using a `before_filter` similar to the one you used previously in the `TicketsController`, this controller will check that the user attempting to access a file has permission to access that particular project.

When you implemented permission behavior before, you ensured that any unauthorized user would be blocked from accessing the resource you were trying to protect by writing a controller spec. You write this same kind of spec test for serving files.

9.3.1 Protecting files

You first need to generate the controller through which you'll serve the assets. Call it files, because assets is already reserved by Sprockets:

```
rails g controller files
```

Now write a spec to ensure that unauthorized users can't see the files inside it. For this spec test, you must create two users, a project, a ticket, and an asset. The first user should have permission to read this project, and the second user shouldn't.

Open spec/controllers/files_controller_spec.rb, and add let definitions that set up your users, project, ticket, and asset inside the describe for FilesController, as shown in the following listing.

Listing 9.8 spec/controllers/files_controller_spec.rb

```
describe FilesController do
  let(:project) { Factory(:project) }
  let(:ticket) { Factory(:ticket, :project => project) }
  let(:good_user) { create_user! }
  let(:bad_user) { create_user! }

  let(:path) { Rails.root + "spec/fixtures/speed.txt" }
  let(:asset) do
    ticket.assets.create(:asset => File.open(path))
  end

  before do
    good_user.permissions.create!(:action => "view",
                                  :thing => project)
  end
end
```

You used a let for setting up a project, two users, a ticket for this project, a path to the file that's served from the controller, and the asset for the ticket. This is the asset you'll be serving from the controller for this spec test.

You set up the permission in a before block because you won't be referencing it anywhere in your tests, so having it as a let block wouldn't work. You should use let blocks only when you're going to be referencing them inside your tests. If you need code set up beforehand, you should use a before block instead.

To serve the files from this controller, use the show action, using the id parameter to find the asset the user is requesting. When the application finds this asset, you want it to check that the user requesting the asset has permission to read the project this asset links to. The good_user object should be able to, and the bad_user object shouldn't. Now add the spec to test the good_user's ability to download this asset by using the code from the following listing.

Listing 9.9 spec/controllers/assets_controller_spec.rb

```
context "users with access" do

  before do
```

```
    sign_in(:user, good_user)
  end

  it "can access assets in a project" do
    get 'show', :id => asset.id
    response.body.should eql(File.read(path))
  end
end
```

If you're using Windows you may have to do this on the response.body line instead, because the line breaks on Windows are slightly different:

```
response.body.gsub!(/\r\n?/, "\n").should eql(File.read(path))
```

In this example, you sign in as the good_user by using another before block. Then you assert that when this user attempts to get this asset through the show action, the user should receive it as a response. Write another context and spec for the bad_user too, as shown in the following listing.

Listing 9.10   spec/controllers/assets_controller_spec.rb

```
context "users without access" do
  before do
    sign_in(:user, bad_user)
  end

  it "cannot access assets in this project" do
    get 'show', :id => asset.id
    response.should redirect_to(root_path)
    flash[:alert].should eql("The asset you were looking for
  ➥could not be found.")
  end
end
```

Here you sign in as the bad_user and then deny all knowledge of the asset's existence by redirecting to root and displaying an alert flash message. Let's run these specs now with bin/rspec spec/controllers/assets_controller_spec.rb. Both examples complain:

```
The action 'show' could not be found for FilesController
```

Well, that's no good. Now you need to define this show action.

9.3.2 *Showing your assets*

Open your FilesController file and define the show action, along with a before_filter to set the current_user variable, which you'll need for permission checking. This code is shown in the following listing.

Listing 9.11   app/controllers/files_controller.rb

```
class FilesController < ApplicationController
  before_filter :authenticate_user!
  def show
```

```
          asset = Asset.find(params[:id])
          send_file asset.asset.path, :filename      => asset.asset_file_name,
                                      :content_type => asset.asset_content_type
      end
end
```

In this action, you find the `Asset` object by using the `params[:id]` the action receives. Then you use the `asset` object in combination with the `send_file` method to send the file back as a response rather than a view in your application.

The first argument for `send_file` is the path to the file you're sending. The next argument is an options hash used to pass in the `filename` and `content_type` options so the browser receiving the file knows what to call it and what type of file it is.

To route requests to this controller, you need to define a route in your config/routes.rb file, which you can do with this line:

```
resources :files
```

When you run the specs for this controller again using `bin/rspec spec/controllers/files_controller_spec.rb`, the first spec passes, but the second one fails:

```
FilesController users without access cannot access assets in this project
...
Expected response to be a <:redirect>, but was <200>.
```

The `show` action doesn't redirect as this example expects because you're not doing any permission checking in your action, which is what this example is all about: "users without access cannot access assets in this project." To fix this problem, check that the user has permission to access this asset's project by using the CanCan helpers you used in chapter 8. You can use them in your `show` action now, as shown in the following listing.

> **Listing 9.12　app/controllers/files_controller.rb**

```
def show
  asset = Asset.find(params[:id])
  if can?(:view, asset.ticket.project)
    send_file asset.asset.path, :filename      => asset.asset_file_name,
                                :content_type => asset.asset_content_type
  else
    flash[:alert] = "The asset you were looking for could not be found."
    redirect_to root_path
  end
end
```

Now when you rerun these specs, you're missing a method:

```
undefined method 'ticket' for #<Asset:0x000001043d1e18>
```

This method is a simple `belongs_to`, which you must define inside the `Asset` model:

```
belongs_to :ticket
```

When you rerun your specs, they both pass because the authorized user (`good_user`) can get a file and the unauthorized user (`bad_user`) can't:

```
2 examples, 0 failures
```

Great! Now you've begun to serve the files from `FilesController` to only people who have access to the asset's relative projects. There's one problem, though: all users can still access these files without having to go through the `FilesController`.

9.3.3 *Public assets*

People can still get to your files as long as they have the link provided to them because the files are still stored in the public folder. Let's see how this is possible by starting up the server using `rails server`, signing in, and creating a ticket. Upload the spec/fixtures/spin.txt file as the only file attached to this ticket. You should see a ticket like the one in figure 9.2.

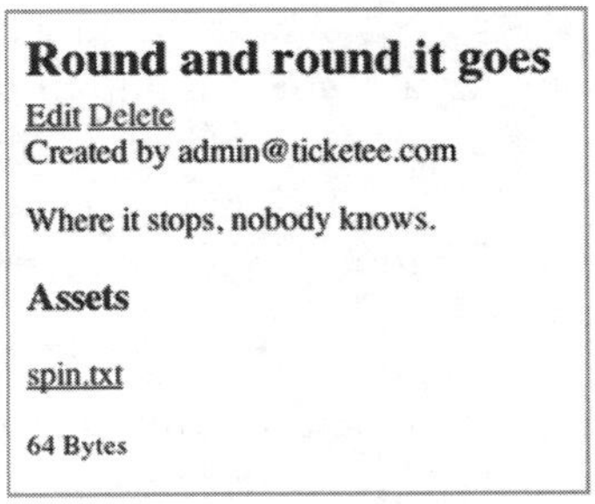
Round and round it goes
Edit Delete
Created by admin@ticketee.com
Where it stops, nobody knows.
Assets
spin.txt
64 Bytes

Figure 9.2 A ticket with spin!

Hover over the spin.txt link on this page, and you'll see a link like this:

```
http://localhost:3000/system/assets/5/original/spin.txt?1282564953
```

As you saw earlier in this chapter, this link is a route not to a controller in your application but to a file inside the public directory. Any file in the public directory is accessible to the public. Sensible naming schemes rock!

If you copy the link to this file, sign out, and then paste the link into your browser window, you can still access it. These files need to be protected, and you can do that by moving them out of the public directory and into another directory at the root of your application called files. You should create this directory now.

9.3.4 *Privatizing assets*

You can make these files private by storing them in the files folder. You don't have to move them there manually: you can tell Paperclip to put them there by default by passing the `:path` option to `has_attached_file` in app/models/asset.rb like this:

```
has_attached_file :asset, :path => (Rails.root + "files/:id").to_s
```

Now try creating another ticket and attaching the spec/fixtures/spin.txt file. This time when you use the link to access the file, you're told there's no route. This is shown in figure 9.3.

Routing Error
No route matches "/system/assets/6/original/spin.txt"

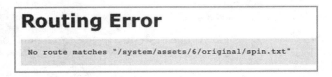

Figure 9.3 No route!

The URL generated for this file is incorrect because Paperclip automatically assumes all files are kept in the public folder. Because you changed the `path` of where the files are kept, the URL is out of sync. You should now tell Paperclip the new URL for your files, which is the URL for the `show` action for the `FilesController`:

```
has_attached_file :asset, :path => (Rails.root + "files/:id").to_s,
                          :url => "/files/:id"
```

A great test to see if you can still see assets after this change is to run the scenario from features/creating_tickets.feature, which creates a ticket with three attachments and then opens one of them. Run `bin/cucumber features/creating_tickets.feature :38` to see if this still works:

```
1 scenario (1 passed)
18 steps (18 passed)
```

Great! With this feature still passing, the files are being served through the `Files-Controller` controller correctly. You're done with implementing the functionality to protect assets from unauthorized access, so you should commit. First ensure that nothing is broken by running `rake cucumber:ok spec`:

```
44 scenarios (44 passed)
508 steps (508 passed)
# and
22 examples, 0 failures, 5 pending
```

It's great to see everything is still in working order. Now commit and push your changes:

```
git add .
git commit -m "Assets are now strictly served through FilesController"
git push
```

By serving these files through the `FilesController`, you can provide a level of control over who can see them and who can't by allowing only those who have access to the asset's project to have access to the asset.

Inevitably, somebody's going to want to attach more than three files to a ticket, and then what? Well, you could add more fields until people stop asking for them, or you could be lazy and code a solution to save time. This solution entails putting an Add Another File link underneath the final file field in your form that, when clicked, adds another file field. Users should be able to continue to do this ad infinitum. How do you implement this?

You use JavaScript. That's how.

9.4   *Using JavaScript*

You started this chapter with only one file field and then moved to three after you realized users may want to upload more than one file to your application. Although having three fields suits the purposes of many users, others may wish to upload yet more files.

You could keep adding file fields until all the users are satisfied, or you could be sensible about it and switch back to using one field and, directly underneath it, providing a link that, when clicked, adds another file field. Using this solution, you also clean up your UI a bit by removing possible extra file fields yet still allowing users to attach as many files as they like. This is where JavaScript comes in.

When you introduce JavaScript into your application, you have to run any scenarios that rely on it through another piece of software called WebDriver. WebDriver is a browser driver, which was installed when the Capybara gem was installed, so you don't have to do anything to set it up. Capybara without WebDriver won't run JavaScript because it doesn't support it by itself. By running these JavaScript-reliant scenarios through WebDriver, you ensure the JavaScript will be executed. One of the great things with this WebDriver and Capybara partnership is that you can use the same old, familiar Capybara steps to test JavaScript behavior.

9.4.1 *JavaScript testing*

Capybara provides an easy way to trigger WebDriver testing. You *tag* a scenario (or feature) with the @javascript tag, and it launches a new web browser window and tests your code by using the same steps as standard Capybara testing. Isn't that neat? To tag a scenario, place @javascript above it. Let's write a new scenario in the Creating Tickets feature for multifile uploading, as shown in the following listing.

> **Listing 9.13   features/creating_tickets.feature**

```
@javascript
Scenario: Creating a ticket with an attachment
  When I fill in "Title" with "Add documentation for blink tag"
  And I fill in "Description" with "The blank tag has an undocumented
  ➥speed attribute"
  And I attach the file "spec/fixtures/speed.txt" to "File #1"       ←┐ File
  And I follow "Add another file"                                    ❶ field
  And I attach the file "spec/fixtures/spin.txt" to "File #2"
  And I press "Create Ticket"
  Then I should see "Ticket has been created."
  And I should see "speed.txt" within "#ticket .assets"              ←┐ Create
  And I should see "spin.txt" within "#ticket .assets"              ❷ ticket
  When I follow "speed.txt"
```

The @javascript tag at the top of this scenario tells Cucumber that the scenario uses JavaScript, so it should be run using WebDriver. Also in this scenario, you've filled in only one file field ❶ because, as stated before, you're going to reduce the number of initial file fields to one. After filling in this field, you follow the Add Another File link that triggers a JavaScript event, which renders the second file field that you can then fill in. The rest of this scenario remains the same: ensuring that the ticket is created ❷ and that you can see the files inside the element with the class assets.

When you run this scenario with bin/cucumber features/creating_tickets .feature:36, it fails because the Add Another File link doesn't yet exist:

```
And I follow "Add another file"
  no link with title, id or text 'Add another file' found
```

Before you fix it, however, let's make the form render only a single asset field by changing this line in the new action in `TicketsController`

```
3.times { @ticket.assets.build }
```

to this:

```
@ticket.assets.build
```

By building only one asset to begin with, you show users that they may upload a file. By providing the link to Add Another File, you show them that they may upload more than one if they please. This is the best UI solution because you're not presenting the user with fields they may not use.

Now it's time to make the Add Another File link exist and do something useful!

9.4.2 Introducing jQuery

The Add Another File link, when clicked, triggers an asynchronous call to an action, which renders a second file field.

For the Add Another File link to perform an asynchronous request when it's clicked, you can use the JavaScript framework called jQuery. In earlier versions of Rails, a JavaScript framework called Prototype came with it, but a large portion of the community prefers jQuery to Prototype. Developers can choose whether to use Prototype or jQuery or any other kind of JavaScript framework, but we use jQuery here because it's favored in the community.[7]

To install jQuery in earlier versions of Rails, you would have had to go to http://jquery.com, download the latest version of jQuery, put it in your public/javascripts, and then include it in your application layout. Next, you would have had to install the `jquery-rails` gem. It was quite a lot of work for something that should have been simple!

With Rails 3.1, you don't need to download jQuery from the website or alter the default application in any way. With `jquery-rails` in the application's Gemfile, you are already set up.

Next, tell your application to include the JavaScript files from this gem if Rails hasn't done it already. Currently, you have this line in your app/views/layouts/application.html.erb file:

```
<%= javascript_include_tag "application" %>
```

It generates HTML like this:

```
<script src="/assets/application.js" type="text/javascript">
</script>
```

---

[7] Our choice totally has nothing to do with the fact that one of the authors is on the jQuery Core Team! We promise!

The /assets path here is handled by the sprockets gem, which comes standard with Rails 3.1. When this route is requested, the sprockets gem takes care of serving it. It begins by reading the assets/javascripts/application.js file, which specifies the following things:

```
// FIXME: Tell people that this is a manifest file, real code should go
into discrete files
// FIXME: Tell people how Sprockets and CoffeeScript works
//
//= require jquery
//= require jquery_ujs
//= require_tree .
```

The lines prefixed with // are comments, but the lines prefixed with //= are *directives* that tell Sprockets what to do. These directives require the jquery and jquery_ujs files from the jquery-rails gem. The jquery file is the jQuery framework itself, whereas the jquery-ujs file provides *unobtrusive JavaScript* helpers for things such as the confirmation box that pops up when you click on a link, which was defined using link_to's :confirm helper.

Rails has already required all the JavaScript files you need to get started here. Let's define the Add Another File link now.

9.4.3 *Adding more files with JavaScript*

You must add the Add Another File link to your tickets form at app/views/tickets/ _form.html.erb. Put it underneath the end for the fields_for so it's displayed below existing file fields:

```
<%= link_to "Add another file",
  new_file_path,
  :remote => true,            Remote  ❶
  :update => "files",         Update  ❷
  :position => "after"        Position ❸
%>
```

Here you use the link_to method to define a link, and you pass some options to it. The first option is :remote => true ❶, which tells Rails you want to generate a link that uses JavaScript to make a background request, called an *asynchronous request*, to the server. More precisely, the request uses the JavaScript provided by the jquery-ujs.js file that came with the jquery-rails gem.

This request then responds with some content, which is dealt with by the :update ❷ and :position ❸ options. The first option, :update, tells Rails to tell the JavaScript that handles the response that you want to insert the content from the background request into the element with the id attribute of files. The second, :position, tells it that you want to insert the content after any other content in the element, which would make your second file field appear after the first file field.

The element this updates doesn't currently exist, but you can easily create it by wrapping the `fields_for` inside a `div` with the `id` attribute set to `files`, as shown in the following listing.

Listing 9.14   app/views/tickets/_form.html.erb

```
<div id='files'>
  <%= f.fields_for :assets, :child_index => number do |asset| %>
    <p>
      <%= asset.label :asset, "File ##{number += 1}" %>
      <%= asset.file_field :asset %>
    </p>
  <% end %>
</div>
```

This `div` tag provides an element for your new `link_to` to insert a file field into. If you run this scenario with `bin/cucumber features/creating_tickets.feature:36`, the step that follows the Add Another File link passes, but the file field is still not visible:

```
And I follow "Add another file"
And I attach the file "spec/fixtures/spin.txt" to "File #2"
  cannot attach file, no file field with id, name, or label 'File #2'
```

The Add Another File link currently uses the `new_file_path` helper, which generates a route such as `/files/new`. This route points to the `new` action in `FilesController`. This action isn't defined at the moment, so the feature won't work. Therefore, the next step is to define the action you need.

9.4.4   *Responding to an asynchronous request*

The job of the `new` action inside the `FilesController` is to render a single file field for the ticket form so users may upload another file. This action needs to render the fields for an asset, which you already do inside app/views/tickets/_form.html.erb by using these lines:

```
<p>
  <%= f.fields_for :assets do |asset| %>
    <p>
      <%= asset.label :asset, "File ##{number += 1}" %>
      <%= asset.file_field :asset %>
    </p>
  <% end %>
</p>
```

To re-use this code for the `new` action in `FilesController`, move it into a partial located at app/views/files/_form.html.erb.

In app/views/tickets/_form.html.erb, you can replace the lines with this simple line:

```
<%= render :partial => "files/form",
           :locals  => { :number => number } %>
```

When you pass the `:locals` option to `render`, you can set local variables that can be used in the partial. Local variables in views are usable only in the views or partials in which they're defined unless you pass them through by using this `:locals`. You pass through the number of your file field and the `asset` object provided by `fields_for` `:assets`.

To get the `new` action to render this partial, you can use the same code in the `new` action in `FilesController` but with a small change:

```
def new
  asset = Asset.new
  render :partial => "files/form",
         :locals => { :asset => asset }
end
```

Here you must pass the name of the partial using the `:partial` option so the controller will attempt to render a partial. If you left it without the option, the controller would instead try to render the template at app/views/files/form.html.erb, which doesn't exist.

Before this line, you need to set up the `asset` variable that you reference. Add these two lines directly above the first line inside the `new` action:

```
@ticket = Ticket.new
asset = @ticket.assets.build
```

Because the `Ticket` object for your form is only a new record, it isn't important precisely what object it is: all new `Ticket` objects are the same until they're saved to the database and given a unique identifier. You can exploit this by creating another `Ticket` object and building your new asset from it.

It makes sense to do this because in your app/views/files/_form.html.erb file, you still reference the now-nonexistent f variable, which came from `form_for @ticket` in app/views/tickets/new.html.erb. Again, you can exploit the fact that all new `Ticket` objects are the same and use a `fields_for` instead of a `form_for` in this partial to get it to give the file field a proper name. Without this `fields_for`, the name of the field would be something like `asset[asset]`, and you need it to be something more like `ticket[asset_attributes][0][asset]`. Now change the app/views/files/_form .html.erb partial to look like the following listing.

Listing 9.15   app/views/files/_form.html.erb

```
<%= fields_for @ticket do |f| %>
  <%= f.fields_for :assets, :child_index => number do |asset| %>
    <p>
      <%= asset.label :asset, "File ##{number += 1}" %>
      <%= asset.file_field :asset %>
    </p>
  <% end %>
<% end %>
```

The `@ticket` object here could either be from the `new` action in the `Tickets-Controller` or from the `new` action in the `FilesController`: it doesn't matter.

What does matter here is the `number` variable that identifies the number of file fields you are currently up to. You specify the `child_index` option in your `fields_for` so that each time these fields are rendered, they're given different identifiers. The assets form partial gets this `number` variable only from the tickets partial; you've yet to set up a way the `new` action sets this variable. Without this variable set in the `new` action, you can't render the app/views/files/_form.html.erb for a new asset without knowing what number you're up to. Let's set that up now.

9.4.5 *Sending parameters for an asynchronous request*

The `number` variable indicates what file field you are up to, so you need a way to tell the `new` action in `FilesController` how many file fields are currently on the page. Previous versions of Rails had an option for this called `:with`, which has now, unfortunately, been removed. No matter, you can do it in JavaScript. It's better to put this code in JavaScript anyway, because it'll already be using some to determine the number to pass through. Rather than using pure JavaScript, you'll be using CoffeeScript, which comes with Rails 3.1 but can be used in any other language. Let's learn some CoffeeScript now.

LEARNING COFFEESCRIPT

CoffeeScript is, in the words of its website, "a little language that compiles into JavaScript." It's written in a simple syntax, like this:

```
square = (x) -> x * x
```

This code compiles into the following JavaScript code:

```
var square;
square = function(x) {
  return x * x;
};
```

In the CoffeeScript version, you define a variable called `square`. Because this isn't yet initialized, it is set up using `var square;` in the JavaScript output. You assign a function to this variable, specifying the arguments using parentheses `(x)` and then specifying the code of the function after `->`. The code inside the function in this case is converted into literal JavaScript, making this function take an argument, multiply it by itself, and `return` the result.

Although this is a pretty basic example of CoffeeScript, it shows off its power. What you would write on four lines of JavaScript requires just one line of extremely easy-to-understand CoffeeScript.

Each time you generate a controller using Rails, a new file called app/assets/javascripts/[controller_name].js.coffee is created.[8] This file is created so you have a location to put CoffeeScript code that is specific to views for the relevant controller. This is really helpful in your situation, because you're going to use some CoffeeScript to tell your Add Another File link what to do when it's clicked.

---

[8] If you have the `coffee-rails` gem in your Gemfile.

Open app/assets/javascripts/tickets.js.coffee, and we'll build up your function line by line so you can understand what you're doing. Let's begin by putting this line first:

```
$(->
```

It seems like a random amalgamation of characters, but this line is really helpful. It calls the jQuery $[9] function and passes it a function as an argument. This line runs the function only when the page has fully loaded.[10] You need this because the JavaScript otherwise would be executed before the link you're going to be referencing is loaded. Let's add a second line to this:

```
$(->
  $('a#add_another_file').click(->
```

This line uses jQuery's $ function to select an element on the page called a, which has an id attribute of add_another_file that will soon be your Add Another File link. This would happen only after the page is ready. After this, you call the click function on it and pass it a function that runs when you click on this link. Let's now add a third line:

```
$(->
  $('a#add_another_file').click(->
  url = "/files/new?number=" + $('#files input').length
```

The double-space indent here indicates to CoffeeScript that this code belongs inside the function passed to click.[11] Here, you define a variable called url, which will be the URL you use to request a new file field on your page. At the end of this URL you specify the number parameter with some additional jQuery code. This code selects all the input elements inside the element on the page with the id attribute of files and stores them in an array. To find out how many elements are in that array, you call length on it. The URL for the first time you click this link would now look something like /files/new?number=1, indicating that you already have one file field on your page.

Let's make the fourth line now:

```
$(->
  $('a#add_another_file').click(->
    url = "/files/new?number=" + $('#files input').length
    $.get(url,
```

This line is pretty simple; you call the jQuery function $, and then call the get[12] function on it, which starts an asynchronous request to the specified URL that is the first argument here, using the variable you set up on the previous line. Another line:

```
$(->
  $('a#add_another_file').click(->
    url = "/files/new?number=" + $('#files input').length
```

---

[9] Aliased from the jQuery function: http://api.jquery.com/jquery/.

[10] For the meaning of "loaded," see this: http://api.jquery.com/ready

[11] http://api.jquery.org/click.

[12] http://api.jquery.com/jQuery.get.

```
$.get(url,
  (data)->
```

This line is indented another two spaces again, meaning it is going to be an argument for the get function. This line defines a new function with an argument called data, which is called when the asynchronous request completes, with the data argument being the data sent back from the request. One more line:

```
$(->
  $('a#add_another_file').click(->
    url = "/files/new?number=" + $('#files input').length
    $.get(url,
      (data)->
        $('#files').append(data)
```

This final line takes the data received from the request and appends[13] it to the end of the element that has the id attribute of files on this page. That's the one with the single file-input field currently.

Finally, you need to close these functions you've defined, which you can do with three closing parentheses matching the levels of indentation, finalizing your code as this:

```
$(->
  $('a#add_another_file').click(->
    url = "/files/new?number=" + $('#files input').length
    $.get(url,
      (data)->
        $('#files').append(data)
    )
  )
)
```

That's all there is to it! When your server receives a request at /assets/application.js, the request will be handled by the Sprockets gem. The Sprockets gem will then combine jquery, jquery_ujs, and app/assets/javascripts/tickets.js.coffee into one JavaScript file, parsing the CoffeeScript into the following JavaScript:

```
$(function() {
  return $('a#add_another_file').click(function() {
    var url;
    url = "/files/new?number=" + $('#files input').length;
    return $.get(url, function(data) {
      return $('#files').append(data);
    });
  });
});
```

In the production environment, this file is compiled upon the first request and then cached to save valuable processing time.

---

[13] http://api.jquery.com/append.

This is a little more verbose than the CoffeeScript and another great demonstration of how CoffeeScript allows you to write more with less. For more information and usage examples of CoffeeScript, see the CoffeeScript site: http://coffeescript.org.

Let's now give your link the `id` attribute that's required to get this working so we can move on.

PASSING THROUGH A NUMBER

Open your app/views/tickets/_form.html.erb and replace the code for your Add Another File link with this:

```
<%= link_to "Add another file", 'javascript:',
  :id => "add_another_file" %>
```

This gives the element the `id` attribute you require. Let's witness this JavaScript in action now by running `rails server` to start up a server, signing in using the email address user@ticketee.com and the password *password*, and then creating a ticket on a project. Clicking the Add Another File link results in an error that you'll fix shortly. Click it anyway. Afterward, go back to the window where `rails server` is running.

This window shows information such as queries and results for every request, but you're only interested in the last request made. This request should begin with the following line:

```
Started GET "/files/new?number=1...
```

This line tells you that Rails has begun serving a `GET` request to the /files/new route with a bunch of URL parameters. Your `number` parameter is the first one in this example. The following lines show the URL that was requested as well as what action and controller served this request:

```
Started GET "/files/new?number=1" for 127.0.0.1 at [timestamps]
  Processing by FilesController#new as */*
  Parameters: {"number"=>"1"}
```

The line you're most interested in is the third line:

```
Parameters: {"number"=>"1", ... }
```

This is the `params` hash output in a semi-human-readable format. Here you can see it has the `number` parameter, so you can use this inside the `new` action. With all this in mind, you can change how you render the partial in the `new` action inside `Files-Controller` to this:

```
render :partial => "files/form",
       :locals => { :number => params[:number].to_i,
                    :asset => asset }
```

You must convert the `number` parameter to an integer using the `to_i` method because it'll be a `String` when it comes from `params`. It needs to be a `Fixnum` so the partial can add 1 to it.

Now if you refresh this page and attempt to upload two files, you should see that it works. Does your scenario agree? Let's find out by running `bin/cucumber features/creating_tickets.feature:38`:

```
1 scenario (1 passed)
18 steps (18 passed)
```

Yup, all working! Great. You've switched the ticket form back to only providing one file field but providing a link called Add Another File, which adds another file field on the page every time it's clicked. You originally had implemented this link using the `:remote` option for `link_to`, but switched to using CoffeeScript when you needed to pass the `number` parameter through. A couple of other small changes, and you got it all working very neatly again!

This is a great point to see how the application is faring before committing. Let's run the tests with `rake cucumber:ok spec`. You should see the following:

```
46 scenarios (46 passed)
469 steps (469 passed)
# and
30 examples, 0 failures, 13 pending
```

Awesome! Let's commit it:

```
git add .
git commit -m "Provide an 'Add another file link' that uses Javascript
              so that users can upload more than one file"
git push
```

This section showed how you can use JavaScript and CoffeeScript to provide the user with another file field on the page using some basic helpers. JavaScript is a powerful language and is a mainstay of web development that has gained a lot of traction in recent years thanks to libraries such as the two you saw here, jQuery and CoffeeScript, as well as others such as Prototype and Raphael.

By using JavaScript, you can provide some great functionality to your users. The best part? Just as you can test your Rails code, you can make sure JavaScript is working by writing tests that use WebDriver.

9.5 Summary

This chapter covered two flavors of file uploading: single-file uploading and multiple-file uploading.

You first saw how to upload a single file by adding the `file_field` helper to your view, making your form multipart, and using the Paperclip gem to handle the file when it arrives in your application.

After you conquered single-file uploading, you tackled multiple-file uploading. You off loaded the file handling to another class called `Asset`, which kept a record for each file you uploaded. You passed the files from your form by using nested attributes, which allowed you to create `Asset` objects related to the ticket being created through the form.

After multiple-file uploading, you learned how to restrict which files are served through your application by serving them through a controller. By using a controller, you can use CanCan's `can?` helper to determine if the currently signed-in user has access to the requested asset's project. If so, then you give the user the requested asset using the `send_file` controller method. If not, you deny all knowledge of the asset ever having existed.

Finally, you used a JavaScript library called jQuery, in combination with a simpler way of writing JavaScript called CoffeeScript, to provide users with an Add Another File link. jQuery does more than simple asynchronous requests, though, and if you're interested, the documentation[14] is definitely worth exploring.

In the next chapter, we look at giving tickets a concept of state, which enables users to see which tickets need to be worked on and which are closed. Tickets will also have a default state so they can be easily identified when they're created.

---

[14] http://jquery.com.

Tracking state

In a ticket-tracking application such as Ticketee, tickets aren't there to provide information about a particular problem or suggestion; rather, they're there to provide the workflow for it. The general workflow of a ticket is that a user will file it and it'll be classified as a "new" ticket. When the developers of the project look at this ticket and decide to work on it, they'll switch the state on the ticket to "open" and, once they're done, mark it as "resolved." If a ticket needs more information on it then they'll add another state, such as "needs more info." A ticket could also be a duplicate of another ticket or it could be something that the developers determine isn't worthwhile putting in. In cases such as this, the ticket may be marked as "duplicate" or "invalid," respectively.

The point is that tickets have a workflow, and that workflow revolves around state changes. You'll allow the admin users of this application to add states, but not to delete them. The reason for this is if an admin were to delete a state that was used, then you'd have no record of that state ever existing. It's best if, once states are created and used on a ticket, they can't be deleted.[1]

To track the states, you'll let users leave a comment. With a comment, users will be able to leave a text message about the ticket and may also elect to change the state of the ticket to something else by selecting it from a drop-down box. But not all users will be able to leave a comment and change the state. You'll protect both creating a comment and changing the state.

By the time you're done with all of this, the users of your application will have the ability to add comments to your tickets. Some users, due to permission restriction, will be able to change the state of a ticket through the comment interface.

You'll begin with creating that interface for a user to create a comment and then build on top of that the ability for the user to change the state of a ticket while adding a comment. Let's get into it.

10.1 Leaving a comment

Let's get started by adding the ability to leave a comment. When you're done you will have a simple form that looks like figure 10.1.

To get started with this you'll write a Cucumber feature that goes through the process of creating a comment. When you're done with this feature, you will have a comment form at the bottom of the show action for the TicketsController which you'll then use as a base for adding your state drop-down box later on. Put this feature in a new file at features/creating_comments.feature, and make it look like the following listing.

Figure 10.1   The comment form

Listing 10.1   features/creating_comments.feature

```
Feature: Creating comments
  In order to update a ticket's progress
  As a user
  I want to leave comments

  Background:
    Given there are the following users:
      | email             | password |
      | user@ticketee.com | password |
    And I am signed in as them
    And there is a project called "Ticketee"
    And "user@ticketee.com" can view the "Ticketee" project
    And "user@ticketee.com" has created a ticket for this project:
```

---

[1]   Alternatively, these states could be moved into an "archive" state of their own so they couldn't be assigned to new tickets but still would be visible on older tickets.

```
| title                    | description                               |
| Change a ticket's state  | You should be able to create a comment    |
  Given I am on the homepage
  And I follow "Ticketee"

Scenario: Creating a comment
  When I follow "Change a ticket's state"
  And I fill in "Text" with "Added a comment!"
  And I press "Create Comment"
  Then I should see "Comment has been created."
  Then I should see "Added a comment!" within "#comments"

Scenario: Creating an invalid comment
  When I follow "Change a ticket's state"
  And I press "Create Comment"
  Then I should see "Comment has not been created."
  And I should see "Text can't be blank"
```

Here you navigate from the homepage to the ticket page by following the respective links, fill in the box with the label Text, and create your comment. You've put the link to the ticket inside the scenarios rather than the `Background` because you'll use this feature for permission checking later on. Let's try running this feature now by running `bin/cucumber features/creating_comments.feature`.

10.1.1 Where's the ticket?

You'll see that, after it follows the Ticketee link on the page, it can't find the ticket. What?

```
And I follow "Change a ticket's state"
  no link with title, id or text 'Change a ticket's state'
  found (Capybara::ElementNotFound)
```

Uh oh, something's gone wrong and for some reason Capybara can't find the link. Before the failing step in the scenario you put this line:

```
Then show me the page
```

This step will show the exact page that Capybara sees when it tries to follow this link, providing a certain gem is installed. If you run this feature by using `bin/cucumber features/creating_comments.feature`, you'll be told to install the `launchy` gem:

```
Sorry, you need to install launchy to open pages: `gem install launchy`
```

> **WARNING** Launchy is known to be problematic on Windows and just may not work at all. As a replacement, you may have to manually open the pages created in the tmp directory called capybara-[date].

Launchy is the gem responsible for launching the browser to show you the page. Launchy also provides a common cross-platform of launching different applications. Rather than installing this using `gem install launchy`, you'll add this to your Gemfile inside the `cucumber` group because you only need this gem for your Cucumber features. The whole `cucumber` group for your Gemfile should now look like this:

```ruby
group :test do
  gem 'cucumber-rails'
  gem 'capybara'
  gem 'database_cleaner'
  gem 'factory_girl'
  gem 'email_spec'
  gem 'launchy'
end
```

When you run `bundle install`, it will install the `launchy` gem for you. Let's rerun your feature again. This time, a page pops up with your home page, as shown in figure 10.2.

See how there are two Ticketee links on this page? Capybara's dutifully following your instruction to click the Ticketee link, and it clicks the *first* link it finds on the page! You want it to click the *second* link. Let's change the line in your features/creating_comments.feature that follows this link to the following:

```
And I follow "Ticketee" within "#projects"
```

Here you use the `within` version of this step which will look up the link within the element with the `id` attribute set to "projects." No element currently has this attribute, so let's preempt the scenario failing on this step and add this `id` to the `ul` element in app/views/projects/index.html.erb, as shown in the following listing.

> **Listing 10.2   app/views/projects/index.html.erb**

```erb
<ul id='projects'>
  <% for project in @projects %>
    <li><%= link_to project.name, project %></li>
  <% end %>
</ul>
```

Good! That should make your scenario follow the correct link. Try rerunning it now. You should see this:

```
And I fill in "Text" with "Added a comment!"
  cannot fill in, no text field, text area or password field
  with id, name, or label 'Text' found (Capybara::ElementNotFound)
```

Oops! A web page from the `"Then show me the page"` step came up. Remove this step from your scenario now.

This failing step means that you've got work to do! The label it's looking for is going to belong to the comment box underneath your ticket's information.

Figure 10.2   The home page

10.1.2 *The comment form*

Let's continue building this comment form for the application, the same one to which you'll eventually add a state-select box to complete this feature. This comment form will consist of a single text field in which the user can insert their comment.

Add a single line to the bottom of app/views/tickets/show.html.erb to render the comment form partial:

```
<%= render "comments/form" %>
```

This line renders the partial from app/views/comments/_form.html.erb, which you now create and fill with the content from the following listing.

Listing 10.3   app/views/comments/_form.html.erb

```
<strong>New comment</strong>
<%= form_for [@ticket, @comment] do |f| %>
  <%= f.error_messages %>
  <p>
    <%= f.label :text %><br>
    <%= f.text_area :text %>
  </p>

  <%= f.submit %>
<% end %>
```

Pretty much the standard form_for here, except you use the Array-argument syntax again, which will generate a nested route. You need to do four things before this form will work.

First, you must define the @comment variable in the show action in Tickets-Controller so this form_for has something to work with.

Second, you need to create the Comment model and associate this with your Ticket model so you can create new records from the data in the form and associate it with the right ticket.

Third, you need to define the nested resource so that the form_for knows to POST to the correct URL, one similar to /tickets/1/comments. Without this, you run into an undefined method of ticket_comments_path when the form_for tries to generate the URL by combining the classes of the objects in the array for its action.

Finally, you need to generate the CommentsController and the create action along with it so that your form has somewhere to go when a user submits it.

Now set up your TicketsController to use the Comment model for creating new comments, which you'll create shortly afterward. To do this, you need to first build a new Comment object using the comments association on your @ticket object.

10.1.3 *The comment model*

The first step to getting this feature to pass is to set up the show action in your TicketsController to define a @comment variable for the comment form. To do this, change the show action, as shown in the following listing.

Listing 10.4   app/controllers/tickets_controller.rb

```
def show
  @comment = @ticket.comments.build
end
```

This will use the `build` method on the `comments` association for your `@ticket` object (which is set up by the `find_ticket` `before_filter`) to create a new `Comment` object for the view's `form_for`.

Next, you generate the `Comment` model so that you can define the `comments` association on your `Ticket` model. This model's going to need to have an attribute called `text` for the text from the form, a foreign key to link it to a ticket, and another foreign key to link to a user record. Let's generate this model using this command:

```
rails g model comment text:text ticket_id:integer user_id:integer
```

Then run the migration for this model on both your development and test databases by running these familiar commands:

```
rake db:migrate
rake db:test:prepare
```

With these done, your next stop is to add the associations to the `Ticket` and `Comment` models. For this, you add this line to app/models/ticket.rb directly under the `accepts_nested_attributes_for :assets` line:

```
has_many :comments
```

Add a validation to your `Comment` model to validate the presence of text for the records by adding this line to app/models/comment.rb:

```
validates :text, :presence => true
```

This will help your second scenario pass, because it requires that an error message is displayed when you don't enter any text. You also add a `belongs_to` association definition to this model, given that you have a `user_id` column in your `comments` table:

```
belongs_to :user
```

When you run your feature at this mid-point, you're told that it can't find the routing helper that `form_for` is trying to use:

```
undefined method `ticket_comments_path' for ...
```

This is because you don't have a nested route for comments inside your tickets resource yet. To define one, you need to add it to config/routes.rb.

Currently in your config/routes.rb you've got the tickets resource nested inside the projects resource with these lines:

```
resources :projects do
  resources :tickets
end
```

This generates helpers such as `project_tickets_path`. But for your form it's not important what comment the project is being created for, so you use `ticket _comments_path` instead. This means you need to define a separate nonnested resource for your tickets and then a nested resource under that for your comments, as shown in the following listing.

> **Listing 10.5 config/routes.rb**

```
resources :projects do
  resources :tickets
end

resources :tickets do
  resources :comments
end
```

The last three lines in listing 10.5 are the lines you need in order for `ticket _comments_path` to be defined, which will make your form work.

10.1.4 *The comments controller*

Now finally you need to generate the `CommentsController` so that your form has somewhere to post to. You can do this by running the following command:

```
rails g controller comments
```

A `create` action in this controller will provide the receiving end for the comment form, so you should add this now. You need to define two `before_filters` in this controller. The first is to ensure the user is signed in, because you don't want anonymous users creating comments; the other is to find the `Ticket` object. This entire controller is shown in the following listing.

> **Listing 10.6 app/controllers/comments_controller.rb**

```
class CommentsController < ApplicationController
  before_filter :authenticate_user!
  before_filter :find_ticket

  def create
    @comment = @ticket.comments.build(params[:comment].merge(:user =>
  current_user))
    if @comment.save
      flash[:notice] = "Comment has been created."           ❶ Redirect to
      redirect_to [@ticket.project, @ticket]                     ticket page
    else
      flash[:alert] = "Comment has not been created."
      render :template => "tickets/show"          ❷ Render template
    end
  end

  private

    def find_ticket
```

```
      @ticket = Ticket.find(params[:ticket_id])
    end
  end
```

In this action you use the `template` option of `render` when your `@comment.save` returns `false` to render a template of another controller. Previously you've used the `action` option to render templates that are for the current controller. By doing this, the `@ticket` and `@comment` objects will be available when the app/views/tickets/ show.html.erb template is rendered.

If the object saves successfully you redirect back to the ticket's page by passing an `Array` argument to `redirect_to` ❶, which compiles the path from the arguments passed in, like `form_for` does to a nested route similar to /projects/1/tickets/2.

But if the object doesn't save successfully you want it to render the template that `TicketsController`'s `show` action renders. You can do this by using the `render` method and passing it `"tickets/show"` ❷. Keep in mind that the `render` method doesn't call the action, and so any code within the `show` method of `TicketsController` wouldn't be run. This is fine, though, because you're setting up the `@ticket` variable the template renders by using the `find_ticket` before filter in your controller.

By creating the controller, you've now got all the important parts needed to create comments. Let's run this feature again by running bin/cucumber features/creating _comments.feature to see how you're progressing. You see that it's able to create the comment but it's unable to find the text within the #comments element on the page:

```
Then I should see "Added a comment!" within "#comments"
  Unable to find css "#comments" (Capybara::ElementNotFound)
```

This step is failing because you haven't added the element with the `id` attribute of `comments` to the `show` template yet. This element will contain all the comments for a ticket. Let's add it by entering the code from the following listing above the spot where you render the comment form partial.

Listing 10.7   app/views/tickets/show.html.erb

```
<h3>Comments</h3>
<div id='comments'>
  <% if @ticket.comments.exists? %> <co id='ch10_191_1' />
    <%= render @ticket.comments.select(&:persisted?) %>
  <% else %>
    There are no comments for this ticket.
  <% end %>
</div>
```

Here you create the element the scenario requires: one with an `id` attribute of `comments`. In this you check if there are no comments by using the `exists?` method from Active Record. This will do a light query similar to this to check if there are any comments:

```
SELECT "comments"."id" FROM "comments"
WHERE ("comments".ticket_id = 1) LIMIT 1
```

It only selects the id column from the comments table and limits the result set to 1, which results in a super-fast query to check if there are any comments. You used exists? back in chapter 8 when you checked if a ticket had any assets. You could use empty? here instead, but that would load the comments association in its entirety and then check to see if the array was empty. If there were a lot of comments, then this would be slow. By using exists?, you stop this potential performance issue from cropping up.

Inside this div, if there are comments, you call render and pass it the argument of @ticket.comments. On the end of that call, select on it.

You use select here because you don't want to render the comment object you're building for the form at the bottom of the page. If you left off the select, @ticket.comments would include this new object and render a blank comment box. When you call select on an array, you can pass it a block that it will evaluate on all objects inside that array and return any element that makes the block evaluate to anything that's not nil or false.

The argument you pass to select is called a *Symbol-to-Proc* and is a shorter way of writing this:

```
{ |x| x.persisted? }
```

This is a new syntax versions of Ruby >= 1.8.7 and used to be in Active Support in Rails 2. It's a handy way of writing a shorter block syntax if you're only looking to call a single method on an object.

The persisted? method checks if an object is persisted in the database by checking if it has its id attribute set and will return true if that's the case and false if not.

By using render in this form, Rails will render a partial for every single element in this collection and will try to locate the partial using the first object's class name. Objects in this particular collection are of the Comment class, so the partial Rails will try to find will be at app/views/comments/_comment.html.erb, but you don't have this file right now. Let's create it and fill it with the content from the following listing.

> **Listing 10.8   app/views/comments/_comment.html.erb**

```
<%= div_for(comment) do %>
  <h4><%= comment.user %></h4>
  <%= simple_format(comment.text) %>
<% end %>
```

Here you've used a new method, div_for. This method generates a div tag around the content in the block and also sets class and id attributes based on the object passed in. In this instance, the div tag would be the following:

```
<div id="comment_1" class="comment">
```

The class method from this tag is used to style your comments so that they will look like figure 10.3 when the styles from the stylesheet are applied.

admin@ticketee.com (Admin)
Hey look! A comment!

Figure 10.3   A comment

With the code in place not only to create comments but also to display them, your feature should pass when you run it with `bin/cucumber features/creating _comments.feature`:

```
2 scenario (2 passed)
23 steps (23 passed)
```

Good to see. You've now got the base for users to be able to change the state of a ticket. Before proceeding further, you should make sure that everything is working as it should by running `rake cucumber:ok spec`, and you should also commit your changes. When you run the tests, you'll see this output:

```
48 scenarios (48 passed)
492 steps (492 passed)
# and
32 examples, 0 failures, 15 pending
```

Good stuff! Let's commit and push this:

```
git add .
git commit -m "Users can now leave comments on tickets"
git push
```

With this form added to the ticket's page, users are now able to leave comments on tickets. This feature of your application is useful because it provides a way for users of a project to have a discussion about a ticket and keep track of it. Next up, we'll look at adding another way to provide additional context to this ticket by adding states.

10.2   *Changing a ticket's state*

States provide a helpful way of standardizing the way that a ticket's progress is tracked. By glancing at the state of a ticket, a user will be able to determine if that ticket needs more work or if it's complete, as shown in figure 10.4.

**Figure 10.4
A ticket's state**

To change a ticket's state, you'll add a drop-down box on the comment form where a user can select a state from a list of states. These states will be stored in another table called `states`, and they'll be accessed through the `State` model.

Eventually, you'll let some users of the application have the ability to add states for the select box and make one of them the default. For now, you'll focus on creating the drop-down box so that states can be selected.

As usual, you'll cover creating a comment that changes a ticket's state by writing another scenario. The scenario you'll now write goes at the bottom of features/ creating_comments.feature and is shown in the following listing.

Listing 10.9   features/creating_comments.feature

```
Scenario: Changing a ticket's state
  When I follow "Change a ticket's state"
  When I fill in "Text" with "This is a real issue"
```

```
And I select "Open" from "State"
And I press "Create Comment"
Then I should see "Comment has been created."
And I should see "Open" within "#ticket .state"
```

In this scenario, you follow a ticket's link from the homepage (which you go to in the `Background`) and go through the process of creating a comment, much like in the Creating Comments feature, only this time you select a state. This is the first part of the scenario that you can expect to fail because you don't have a state-select box yet. After the comment is created, you should see the state appear in the `#ticket .state` area. This is the second part of the scenario that will fail.

When you run this scenario by running `bin/cucumber features/creating _comments.feature:36`, it will fail like this:

```
And I select "Open" from "State"
  cannot select option, no select box with id,
  name, or label 'State' found (Capybara::ElementNotFound)
```

As you can see from this output, the "I select" step attempts to select an option from a select box. In this case, it can't find the select box because you haven't added it yet! With this select box, users of your application should be able to change the ticket's state by selecting a value from it, entering some comment text, and clicking the Create Comment button.

Before you do all that, however, you need to create the `State` model and its related table, which is used to store the states.

10.2.1 *Creating the State model*

Right now you need to add a select box. When you're done, you should have one that looks like figure 10.5.

Before adding this select box, let's set up the `TicketsController`'s `show` action to return a collection of states that you can populate the drop select box with. Change the `show` action to be like this now:

```
def show
  @comment = @ticket.comments.build
  @states = State.all
end
```

Here you call `all` on the `State` class, which doesn't exist yet. You'll be storing the states in a table because you'd like the users to be able to create their own states. For now, you define this `State` model to have a `name` field as well as two other fields: `color` and `background`,

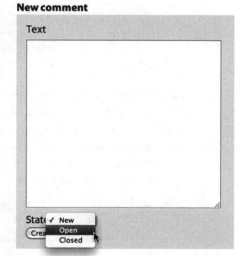

Figure 10.5 State select box

which define the colors of the label for this ticket. Later on, you'll add a `position` field that you'll use to determine the sort order of the states in the select box. Let's create this `State` model and the associated migration by running this command:

```
rails g model state name:string color:string background:string
```

Before running this migration, you need to define a way that states link to comments and to tickets, but there are a couple of things worth mentioning beforehand. For comments, you want to track the previous state so you can display that a comment has changed the ticket's state. For tickets, you want to track the state for which you'll use a foreign key. With all of this in mind, let's add these fields to the migration now. You also remove the `timestamps` call from within `create_table` because it's not important when states were created or updated. When you're done, the whole migration should look like the following listing.

Listing 10.10   db/migrate/[date]_create_states.rb

```ruby
class CreateStates < ActiveRecord::Migration
  def up
    create_table :states do |t|
      t.string :name
      t.string :color
      t.string :background
    end

    add_column :tickets, :state_id, :integer
    add_index :tickets, :state_id

    add_column :comments, :state_id, :integer
  end

  def down
    drop_table :states
    remove_column :tickets, :state_id
    remove_column :comments, :state_id
  end
end
```

In this migration you use the `add_index` method to add a database index on the `tickets` table's `state_id` field. By adding an index on this field, you can speed up queries made that search for this particular field. The side-effect of indexing is that it will result in slower writes and more disk space. It's always important to have indexes on nonprimary-key fields[2] because of this great read speed increase.

Let's run this migration now by running these two commands:

```
rake db:migrate
rake db:test:prepare
```

---

[2] Primary key in this case is the id field that is automatically created for each model by `create_table`. Primary key fields are, by default, indexed.

There you have it! The State model is up and running. Let's now associate this class with the Comment class by adding this line to the top of the Comment model's definition:

```
belongs_to :state
```

Figure 10.6
A ticket's state

The state method provided by this belongs_to will be used shortly to display the state on the ticket page, as in figure 10.6.

Before doing that, however, you need to add the select box for the state to the comment form.

10.2.2 Selecting states

In the comment form partial, add this select box underneath the text box, as shown in the following listing.

Listing 10.11   app/views/comments/_form.html.erb

```
<p>
  <%= f.label :state_id %>
  <%= f.select :state_id , @states.map { |s| [s.name, s.id] },
      :selected => @ticket.state_id %>

</p>
```

Here you use a new method, select, which takes its first argument as the foreign-key *attribute* of your Comment object, not the association. You also use the :state_id value for the argument passed to the label, but Rails is smart enough to know the text for this should be "State". select's second argument is a two-dimensional[3] Array that you create by using map on the State objects returned from the controller in the @states variable. The first element of each array is the value you want shown as an option in the select box to the user, whereas the second element is the value that's passed back to the controller.

Use the :selected option in the select call to select the current state of the ticket from the list. This value must match the value argument for one of the options in the select box; otherwise it will default to the first option.

Let's assume for a moment that you've got three states: New, Open, and Closed. For a ticket that has its state set to New, the select box generated by f.select would look like this:

```
<select id="comment_state_id" name="comment[state_id]">
  <option value="1" selected="selected">New</option>
  <option value="2">Open</option>
  <option value="3">Closed</option>
</select>
```

---

[3] A two-dimensional array is an array that contains arrays as elements.

The first option tag in the select tag has an additional attribute: selected. When this attribute is set, the option is the one selected as the default option for the select. This is achieved by using the :selected option for f.select. The value for this option is the corresponding value attribute for the option tag. In this case, it's the state_id of the @ticket object.

With the select box in place, you're almost at a point where this scenario will be passing. Let's see how far you've gotten by running bin/cucumber features/creating _comments.feature. It won't be able to find the Open option in your select box:

```
And I select "Open" from "State"
  No such option 'Open' in this select box. Available options:
➡ (Capybara::OptionNotFound)
```

This is because you need to add a state to your database! Let's add this line to the bottom of your Background in features/creating_comments.feature to do this:

```
Given there is a state called "Open"
```

Let's now run the scenario using bin/cucumber features/creating_comments .feature so you can get the step definition. Put this step definition in a new file called features/step_definitions/state_steps.rb using this code:

```
Given /^there is a state called "([^"]*)"$/ do |name|
  State.create!(:name => name)
end
```

By defining this step and rerunning the scenario you'll see that it's now failing at the last step:

```
And I should see "Open" within "#ticket .state"
  Unable to find css "#ticket .state" (Capybara::ElementNotFound)
```

This output means it's looking for any element with the id attribute of ticket that contains any type of element with the id of state, but it can't find it.

Rather than putting the state inside the TicketsController's show template, put it in a partial. This is due to the fact that you'll be reusing this to display a state wherever you need it in the future. Additionally, you'll apply a dynamic class around the state so you can style it later on. Let's create a new partial at app/views/states/_state.html.erb and fill it with this content:

```
<div class='state state_<%= state.name.parameterize %>'>
  <%= state %>
</div>
```

To style the element you need a valid CSS class name. You can get one by using the parameterize method. If, for example, you had a state called "Drop bears strike without warning!" and used parameterize on it, all the spaces and non-URL-valid characters would be stripped, leaving you with "drop-bears-strike-without-warning," which is a perfectly valid CSS class name. You'll use this later on to style the state using the color and background attributes.

You're now going to render this partial underneath the "Created by" line on app/views/tickets/show.html.erb using the following line:

```
<%= render @ticket.state if @ticket.state %>
```

You're using the short form of rendering a partial here once again, and you conditionally render it if the ticket has a state. If you don't have the if at the end and the state is nil, this will raise an exception because it will try to determine the model name of nil.

To get this state method for your Ticket, you should add the association method to the model. This method should go directly above the belongs_to :user line in app/models/ticket.rb:

```
belongs_to :state
```

If you run the feature again it will fail because there's nothing shown in the #ticket .state element:

```
And I should see "Open" within "#ticket .state"
<false> is not true. (Test::Unit::AssertionFailedError)
```

This is because you're updating the state on the Comment object you're creating, not the associated Ticket object! You're trying to get the new state to display on the ticket object so that the users of the application can change the state of a ticket when they add a comment to it. For this to work, you need to define a *callback* in your Comment model.

10.2.3 *Callbacks*

When a user selects a state from the drop-down box attached to the comment form on a ticket's page, you want that ticket's state to be updated with what that user picked.

To do this you can use a callback to set the ticket's status when you change it through the comment form. A callback is a method that's called either before or after a certain event. For models, there are before-and-after callbacks for the following events (where * can be substituted for either before or after):

- Validation (*_validation)
- Creating (*_create)
- Updating (*_update)
- Saving (*_save)
- Destruction (*_destroy)

You're able to trigger a specific piece of code or method to run before or after any of these events. The Saving item in the list refers to when a record is saved to the database, which occurs when a record is created or updated. For your Comment model you want to define a callback that occurs after a record has been created, and for this you use the after_create method at the top of your Comment model, as well as a ticket association, transforming this model into the code shown in the following listing.

Listing 10.12   app/models/comment.rb

```ruby
class Comment < ActiveRecord::Base
  after_create :set_ticket_state

  belongs_to :ticket
  belongs_to :user
  belongs_to :state
  validates :text, :presence => true
end
```

While you're here, you can also set it up so that you can access the `project` association that the `ticket` association has in this model by using the `delegates` method:

```ruby
delegate :project, :to => :ticket
```

If you call the `project` method on a `Comment` object, this method will "delegate" the project method to the `ticket` object, making a call exactly like `ticket .project`. This makes your code shorter and will come in handy later on.

The symbol passed to the `after_create` method here is the name of the method to call for this callback. You can define this method at the bottom of your `Comment` model using the code from the following listing.

Listing 10.13   app/models/comment.rb

```ruby
class Comment < ActiveRecord::Base
  ...
  private

    def set_ticket_state
      self.ticket.state = self.state
      self.ticket.save!
    end
end
```

With this callback and associated method now in place, the associated ticket's state will be set to the comment's state after the comment is created. When you run your feature again by running `bin/cucumber features/creating_comments.feature`, it still fails:

```
And I should see "Open" within "#ticket .state"
   Failed assertion, no message given. (MiniTest::Assertion)
```

Even though you're correctly assigning the state to the ticket, it still doesn't display as the state in the view. But why is this? You can attempt to duplicate this issue by running the server using the `rails server`. By visiting http://localhost:3000, you can follow the steps inside the scenario to attempt to duplicate the behavior you've seen in your feature.

Because you have no states in the development database, you won't be able to reproduce this problem right away. Your feature uses the "Given there is a state called..." steps to define states, but you can't use these in your development environment. It would be better if you added seed data to your database because then you'll have a repeatable way of setting up the states in your application's database.

10.2.4 Seeding states

If you add some states to the db/seeds.rb file, users will be able to select them from the State drop-down box on the tickets page rather than leaving it blank and useless, much like it is now. With these states in the db/seeds.rb file, as mentioned before, you will have a repeatable way of creating this data if you ever need to run your application on another server, such as would be the case when you put the application on another computer.

You're adding these files to the db/seeds.rb so you have some to play around with in the development environment of your application. You're attempting to figure out why, when a user picks Open from the State select box and clicks Create Comment, the state doesn't display on the ticket that should be updated.

When you go to the Ticketee Beta project to create a ticket and then attempt to create a comment on that ticket with the state of Open, you'll see that there are no states (as shown in figure 10.7).

You should add a couple of states to your seeds file now; they'll be New, Open, and Closed. Ideally, New will be the default state of tickets, and you'll set this up a little later on. Before adding these states, let's add a couple of steps to features/seed.feature to always ensure that your states are defined.

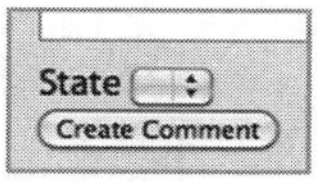

**Figure 10.7
Oops! No states!**

You extend this feature to go inside the Ticketee Beta project, create a ticket, and then begin to create a comment on that ticket. When it's on the comment-creation screen, you check to see that all your states are in the state box. To do this, modify the scenario in this file to what's shown in the following listing.

Listing 10.14   features/seed.feature, the basics scenario

```
Scenario: The basics
  Given I have run the seed task
  And I am signed in as "admin@ticketee.com"
  When I follow "Ticketee Beta"
  And I follow "New Ticket"
  And I fill in "Title" with "Comments with state"
  And I fill in "Description" with "Comments always have a state."
  And I press "Create Ticket"
  Then I should see "New" within "#comment_state_id"
  And I should see "Open" within "#comment_state_id"
  And I should see "Closed" within "#comment_state_id"
```

The #comment_state_id element referenced here is the State select box for your comments, and you're confirming that it's got the three states you're going to be seeding your database with. When you run this feature by running bin/cucumber features/seed.feature, it will fail because you don't have your states yet:

```
Then I should see "New" within "#comment_state_id"
  <false> is not true. (Test::Unit::AssertionFailedError)
```

Let's add these states to your db/seeds.rb file by using the lines shown in the following listing.

Listing 10.15   db/seeds.rb

```
State.create(:name       => "New",
             :background => "#85FF00",
             :color      => "white")

State.create(:name       => "Open",
             :background => "#00CFFD",
             :color      => "white")

State.create(:name       => "Closed",
             :background => "black",
             :color      => "white")
```

If you try to run `rake db:seed` now, you see that this task was aborted:

```
rake aborted!
Validation failed: Email has already been taken

(See full trace by running task with --trace)
```

When a rake task aborts, it means an exception has been raised. As the output suggests, you can see the backtrace by running the same command with `--trace`:`rake db:seed --trace`. You'll now be given the complete backtrace of your `rake` task and can determine what broke. The first line of application-related backtrace in the output provides a useful clue:

```
/home/you/ticketee/db/seeds.rb:1:in `<top (required)>'
```

It's the first line of db/seeds.rb that's causing the problem! This is the line that creates your admin user, and it's rightly failing because you already have a user with the email address `admin@ticketee.com`. Let's comment out these first couple of lines as well as the line that creates the Ticketee Beta project, because you don't want two Ticketee Beta projects. The only line left uncommented in your seeds file should be the line you've just added. When you run `rake db:seed` again, it will run successfully. Let's uncomment these lines that you've just commented out.

With these states now defined inside db/seeds.rb, your feature at features/seed .feature will pass:

```
1 scenario (1 passed)
10 steps (10 passed)
```

Also, with your states seeding, you can go back to your server at http://localhost:3000 and create a comment on your ticket with any status, because you're trying to figure out why the "Creating comments" feature is failing. After creating your comment, you should see that the ticket's

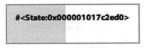

Figure 10.8   Ugly state output

state doesn't display as simple text like New, Open, or Closed, but rather as a standard `inspect` output, as shown in figure 10.8.

Well, isn't that ugly and not user-friendly? It flows off the end of the ticket box! Thankfully, you can fix this by defining the `to_s` method in your `State` model to call the `name` method:

```
def to_s
  name
end
```

By default, objects in Ruby have a `to_s` method that outputs the ugly version, the inspected version of this object, you saw earlier. By overriding this in the model to call the `name` method, you'll get it to display the state's name rather than its object output.

When you refresh the page in your browser, you should see the correct state, as shown in figure 10.9.

Great! This should mean that the last scenario in your "Creating comments" feature will pass. Let's run it with `bin/cucumber features/creating_comments.feature` and find out:

Figure 10.9
The correct state

```
1 scenario (1 passed)
14 steps (14 passed)
```

Indeed it's passing! This is a good stage to ensure that everything is working by running `rake cucumber:ok spec`. Blast, one of the features is failing:

```
Failing Scenarios:
cucumber features/
    creating_comments.feature:26 # Scenario: Creating an invalid comment
```

A broken feature often means a broken part of your code, so you should investigate this before continuing. If there are thoughts of "it's only one feature," think again. At what point do you draw the line? One? Two? Three failing scenarios? Let's have a zero-tolerance policy on these and fix them when they break.

10.2.5 *Fixing creating comments*

The entire reason why you write features before you write code is so that you can catch scenarios like this where something unexpectedly breaks. If you didn't have these scenarios in place, then you wouldn't be made aware of these scenarios until a user of your site stumbled across it. This isn't what you want. You want your users to assume that you're perfect.

You should look into why this feature is failing and fix it right away. This particular scenario is failing with this backtrace:

```
And I press "Create Comment"
  You have a nil object when you didn't expect it!
  You might have expected an instance of Array.
  The error occurred while evaluating nil.map (ActionView::Template::Error)
  ./app/views/comments/_form.html.erb:12
```

Here it claims you're calling `map` on a `nil` object, and that it's on line 12 of app/views/comments/_form.html.erb. The line it's referencing is the following:

```
<%= f.select :state_id, @states.map { |s| [s.name, s.id] } %>
```

Alright, the only place where `map` is being called is on the `@states` variable, so it's pretty straightforward that `@states` is the `nil` object. But how did it come to be? Let's review this scenario, as shown in the following listing.

Listing 10.16 features/creating_comments.feature:26

```
Scenario: Creating an invalid comment
  When I follow "Change a ticket's state"
  And I press "Create Comment"
  Then I should see "Comment has not been created."
  And I should see "Text can't be blank"
```

This scenario tests that you're shown the "Text can't be blank" error when you don't enter any text for your comment. In this scenario, you click the Create Comment button, which submits your form, which goes to the `create` action in `Comments-Controller`. This action looks like the following listing.

Listing 10.17 app/controllers/comments_controller.rb

```
def create
  @comment = @ticket.comments.build(params[:comment].merge(:user
  => current_user))
  if @comment.save
    flash[:notice] = "Comment has been created."
    redirect_to [@ticket.project, @ticket]
  else
    flash[:alert] = "Comment has not been created."
    render :template => "tickets/show"
  end
end
```

As you can see from this action, when the comment fails validation (when `@comment.save` returns `false`), then it rerenders the app/views/tickets/show.html.erb template. The problem with this is that, by rerendering this template, it calls the following line in the template:

```
<%= render "comments/form" %>
```

This inevitably leads you right back to app/views/comments/_form.html.erb, the source of the problem. Therefore, you can determine that you need to set up the `@states` variable during the "failed save" part of your action, and the best place for this is right after the `else` so that this part ends up looking like the following listing.

Listing 10.18 app/controllers/comments_controller.rb

```
else
  @states = State.all
  flash[:alert] = "Comment has not been created."
  render :template => "tickets/show"
end
```

Now that you're correctly initializing your `@states` variable, this scenario will pass. Let's run the whole feature now using bin/cucumber features/creating_comments .feature:

```
3 scenarios (3 passed)
39 steps (39 passed)
```

Awesome! Now let's try rerunning `rake cucumber:ok spec`. That should be the last thing you need to fix. You should see the following output:

```
49 scenarios (49 passed)
515 steps (515 passed)
# and
33 examples, 0 failures, 16 pending
```

Excellent, everything's fixed. Let's commit these changes now:

```
git add .
git commit -m "When updating a comment's status, it also updates
➥the ticket's status"
git push
```

It's great that you've now got the ticket status updating along with the comment status, but it would be handy to know what the timeline of a status change looks like. You can display this on the comment by showing a little indication of whether the state has changed during that comment. Let's work on adding this tidbit of information to the comments right now.

10.3 *Tracking changes*

When a person posts a comment that changes the state of a ticket, you'd like this information displayed on the page next to the comment, as shown in figure 10.10.

By visually tracking this state change, along with the text of the comment, you can provide context as to why the state was changed. At the moment, you only track the state of the comment and then don't even display it alongside the comment's text; you only use it to update the ticket's status.

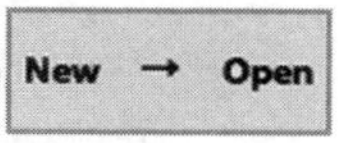

**Figure 10.10
State transitions**

10.3.1 *Ch-ch-changes*

What you need now is some way of making sure that, when changing a ticket's state by way of a comment, the "State: Open" text appears. A scenario would fit this bill, and luckily you wrote one that fits almost perfectly. This scenario is the final scenario ("Changing a ticket's state") in features/creating_comments.feature.

To check for the state change text in your "Changing a ticket's state" scenario, you add this single line to the bottom of it:

```
Then I should see "State: Open" within "#comments"
```

If the ticket was assigned the New state, this text would say "State: New ?' Open," but because your tickets don't have default states assigned to them the previous state for the first comment will be `nil`. When you run this scenario by using `bin/cucumber features/creating_comments.feature:33`, it will fail:

```
Then I should see "State: Open" within "#comments"
  expected there to be content "State: Open"
  in "\n    \n  user@ticketee.com (User)\n
     This is a real issue\n\n"
```

Good, now you've got a way to test this state message that should be appearing when a comment changes the state of the ticket. Now, you'd like to track the state the ticket was at *before* the comment as well as the state of the comment itself. To track this extra attribute, you'll create another field on your `comments` table called `previous_state_id`. Before you save a comment, you'll update this field to be the current state of the ticket. Let's create a new migration to add the `previous_state_id` field to your `comments` table by running the following command:

```
rails g migration add_previous_state_id_to_comments previous_state_id:integer
```

Again, Rails is pretty smart here and will use the name of the migration to infer that you want to add a column called `previous_state_id` to a table called `comments`. You only have to tell it what the type of this field is by passing `previous_state_id:integer` to the migration.

If you open up this migration now, you'll see that it defines a `change` method which calls the `add_column` method inside it. You can see the entire migration shown in the following listing.

Listing 10.19   db/migrate_[date]_add_previous_state_id_to_comments.rb

```
class AddPreviousStateIdToComments < ActiveRecord::Migration
  def change
    add_column :comments, :previous_state_id, :integer
  end
end
```

It's done this way because Rails knows how to roll back this migration easily. It's a simple call to `remove_column` passing in the first two arguments in this method.

You don't need to do anything else to this migration other than run it. Do this now by running `rake db:migrate` and `rake db:test:prepare`. This field will be used for storing the previous state's id so that you can then use it to show a state transition on a comment, as pictured in figure 10.11.

With this little bit of information, users can see what comments changed the ticket's state, which is helpful for determining what steps the ticket has gone through to wind up at this point.

To use the `previous_state_id` field properly, you're going to need to add another callback to save it.

Figure 10.11
A state transition

10.3.2 *Another c-c-callback*

To set this field before a comment is created, you use a `before_create` callback on the `Comment` model. A `before_create` callback is triggered—as the name suggests—before a record is created, but *after* the validations have been run. This means that this callback will only be triggered for valid objects that are about to be saved to the database for the first time.

Put this new callback on a line directly above the after_create because it makes sense to have all your callbacks grouped together and in the order that they're called in:

```
before_create :set_previous_state
```

Call the set_previous_state method for this callback, which you define at the bottom of the Comment model just before the set_ticket_state method, like this:

```
def set_previous_state
  self.previous_state = ticket.state
end
```

The previous_state= method you call here isn't yet defined. You can define this method by declaring that your Comment objects belongs_to a previous_state, which is a State object. Let's put this line with the belongs_to in your Comment model:

```
belongs_to :previous_state, :class_name => "State"
```

Here you use a new option for belongs_to: class_name. The field in your comments table is called previous_state_id and so you call your association previous_state. To tell Rails what class this associated record is, you must use the class_name option, otherwise Rails will go looking for the PreviousState class.

With this belongs_to defined, you get the previous_state= method for free and so your callback should work alright. There's one way to make sure of this, and that's to attempt to display these transitions between the states in your view so that your feature will potentially pass. You'll now work on displaying these transitions.

10.3.3 *Displaying changes*

When you display a comment that changes a ticket's state, you want to display this state transition along with the comment.

To get this text to show up, add the following lines to app/views/comments/_comment.html.erb underneath the h4 tag:

```
<%= render comment.previous_state %> &rarr;
      <%= render comment.state %>
```

This is almost correct, but there's a slight problem. Your callback will set the previous_state regardless of what the current state is, and in this case you can end up with something like figure 10.12.

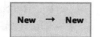

**Figure 10.12
State transition
from itself to itself**

To stop this from happening, you can wrap this code in an if statement, like this:

```
<% if comment.previous_state != comment.state %>
  <%= comment.previous_state %> &rarr; <%= comment.state %>
<% end %>
```

Now this text will only show up when the previous state isn't the same as the current state.

You can go one step further and move this code into a helper. Views are more for displaying information than for deciding how it should be output, which should be left to the helpers and controllers. Move this code into the app/helpers/tickets_helper.rb because this partial is displayed from the `TicketsController`'s `show` template. The entire `TicketsHelper` should now look like the following listing.

Listing 10.20   app/helpers/tickets_helper.rb

```
module TicketsHelper
  def state_for(comment)
    content_tag(:div, :class => "states") do
      if comment.state
        if comment.previous_state && comment.state != comment.previous_state
          "#{render comment.previous_state} &rarr; #{render comment.state}"
        else
          "&rarr;" + render(comment.state)
        end
      end
    end
  end
end
```

In this example, you check to see if the comment has an assigned state and then if it has a previous state. If it has a previous state that isn't the assigned state, then you show the state transition; otherwise you render the assigned state.

You can now replace the whole `if` statement in app/views/comments/_comment .html.erb with this single line:

```
<%= state_for(comment) %>
```

Now check to see if this is working by running your scenario using `bin/cucumber features/creating_comments.feature:33`:

```
Then I should see "State: Open" within "#comments"
expected there to be content "State: Open" in
  "\n   \n  user@ticketee.com (User)\n  \n
  Open\n\n  This is a real issue\n\n"
```

It's *still* failing? Are you sure you've set everything up correctly? Absolutely. Capybara (through Cucumber) is telling you that it still can't find this text on the page. Lucky for you there's a way to see the page that Cucumber is seeing: the "Then show me the page" step you saw a little earlier.

10.3.4   *Show me the page*

When you use this step, it saves the current page to a file and opens it in the browser so you're able to see exactly what Cucumber is seeing. Let's put this step as the second-to-last step in "Changing a ticket's state." The last three steps in this scenario should look like the following:

```
And I should see "Open" within "#ticket .state"
Then show me the page
Then I should see "Open" within "#comments"
```

When you run your scenario again, it should pop up a browser window that shows you the exact same page as Cucumber sees, shown in figure 10.13.

Here you can see the partials rendered with their HTML shown on the page. This is because code coming from a string in a helper is automatically escaped, which is helpful—but sometimes things like this happen. Better safe than sorry!

10.3.5 *Automatic escaping saves your bacon*

This automatic escaping of strings is one of Rails 3's big features. This saves your bacon because it stops malicious output being input into forms accidentally. This output would be things like your ticket's description or comment text, which comes from the users. Never trust the users with outputting nonmalicious content!

If this input wasn't escaped before it was output to the page, it could potentially contain HTML tags like <script>, which could contain malicious content. Rails 3 saves your bacon in this respect by automatically escaping all strings output to the view through ERB tags. Yes, sometimes it will be overzealous and escape things you don't want it to escape, like your state partials.

You can tell it that the string is safe by calling html_safe in your helper, changing it to this:

```
"#{render comment.previous_state} &rarr; #{render comment.state}".html_safe
```

The html_safe method effectively tells Rails, "It's cool, man," and Rails won't escape anything inside the string. When you run bin/cucumber features/creating_tickets .feature:33, your scenario will now pass:

```
1 scenario (1 passed)
17 steps (17 passed)
```

A browser window will appear, showing you the correct states, as shown in figure 10.14.

Let's remove the "Then show me the page" step from this scenario now, and you're done. You've got your application showing the users what state a comment has switched the ticket to. Now's a good time to check that you haven't broken anything. When you run rake cucumber:ok spec, you should see that everything is A-OK:

```
49 scenarios (49 passed)
516 steps (516 passed)
# and
33 examples, 0 failures, 16 pending
```

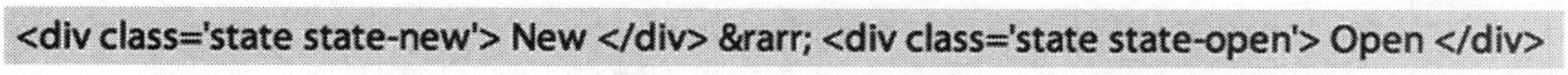

`<div class='state state-new'> New </div> &rarr; <div class='state state-open'> Open </div>`

Figure 10.13   The states aren't what they should be...

You have state transition showing in your application neatly, which is great to see. Let's commit and push this to GitHub:

```
git add .
git commit -m "Display a comment's state transition"
git push
```

Currently, your styles aren't distinguishable. Look at figure 10.14, and gaze upon their ugliness.

You could distinguish them by using the colors you've specified in the attributes. Earlier, you wrapped the state name in a special div that will allow you to style these elements, based on the class. For the New state, the HTML for the div looks like this:

Figure 10.14   The unescaped states

```
<div class="state state_new">
  New
</div>
```

The state_new part of this you can use to apply the colors from the record to this element. To do this, you put a style tag at the top of your application's layout and dynamically define some CSS that will apply the colors.

10.3.6   *Styling states*

The states in your system can change at any point in time in the future, and so you can't have set styles in public/stylesheets/application.css for them. To get around this little problem, put a style tag in your app/views/layouts/application.html.erb file, which will contain some ERB code to output the styles for the states. Directly underneath the stylesheet_link_tag line, put this code:

```
<style>
  <% for state in @states %>
    .state_<%= state.name.parameterize %> {
      background: <%= state.background %>;
      color: <%= state.color %>;
    }
  <% end %>
</style>
```

You need to define the @states variable in a place that will be accessible in all views of your application. This means you can't define it inside any controller other than ApplicationController. Lucky for you, this is like a normal controller, and you can use a before_filter to load the states. Underneath the class definition for Application-Controller, you can add this before_filter:

```
before_filter :find_states
```

Now you define the method under the authorize_admin! definition:

```
def find_states
  @states = State.all
end
```

With these few lines of code, your states should now be styled. If you visit a ticket page that has comments that have changed the state, you should see a state styled, as shown in figure 10.15.

While you're in the business of prettying things up, you can also add the state of your ticket to the listing on app/ views/projects/show.html.erb so that users can easily glance at the list of tickets and see a state next to each of them. Let's add this to the left of the ticket name so that the li element becomes

Figure 10.15 States, now with 100% more style

```
<li>
  <%= render ticket.state if ticket.state %>
  #<%= ticket.id %> - <%= link_to ticket.title, [@project, ticket] %>
</li
```

Now that's looking a lot better! You've completed all that you need to do to let users change the state of a ticket. They'll be able to select one from the State select box on the comment form, and when they create a comment, that ticket will be updated to the new state. Right next to the comment's text on the ticket page is a state transition shown, and (ideally) the comment's text will provide context for that change.

Why did you add states in the first place? Because they provide a great way of standardizing the lifecycle of a ticket. When a ticket is assigned a New state, it means that the ticket is up for grabs. The next phase of a ticket's life is the Open state, which means that this ticket is being looked into/cared for by somebody. When the ticket is fixed, then it should be marked as Closed, perhaps with some information in its related comment relating where the fix is located.

If you want to add more states than these three default states, you can't at the moment. Tickets can have two different types of Closed: one could be "Yes, this is now fixed" and another could be "No, I don't believe this is a problem." A third type could be "I couldn't reproduce." It would be great if you could add more states to the application without having to add them to the state list in db/seeds.rb, wouldn't it? Well, that's easy enough. You can create an interface for the admin users of your application to allow them to add additional states.

10.4 Managing states

Currently your application has only three states: New, Open, and Closed. If you want to add more, you have to go into the console and add them there. Admins of this application should be able to add more states through the application itself, not the console. They should also be able to rename them and delete them, but only if they don't have any tickets assigned to them. Finally, the admins should also be able to set a default state for the application, because no ticket should be without a state.

You'll start out by writing a feature to create new states, which will involve creating a new controller called `Admin::StatesController`. This controller will provide the admins of your application with the basic CRUD functionality for states, as well as the ability to mark a state as the default, which all tickets will then be associated with.

We're not going to look at adding an `edit`, `update`, or `destroy` action to this controller because it's been covered previously and should be left as an exercise for you.

10.4.1 Adding additional states

You have three default states from the db/seeds.rb file currently: New, Open, and Closed. If the admin users of your application wish to add more, they can't—not until you've created the `Admin::StatesController` and the `new` and `create` actions inside it. This will allow those users to create additional states which then can be assigned to a ticket.

You have this lovely `State` model, but no way for admins of the application to add any new records to it. What if they want to add more states? You'll create a new controller called `Admin::StatesController` and put a `new` and `create` action in it so that admins can create more states.

But before you write any real code, you'll write a feature that describes the process of creating a state. Put it in a new file called features/creating_states.feature, which is shown in the following listing.

Listing 10.21   features/creating_states.feature

```
Feature: Creating states
  In order to be able to specify other states for tickets
  As an admin
  I want to add them to the application

  Background:
    Given there are the following users:
      | email               | password | admin |
      | admin@ticketee.com  | password | true  |
    And I am signed in as them

  Scenario: Creating a state
    When I follow "Admin"
    And I follow "States"
    And I follow "New State"
    And I fill in "Name" with "Duplicate"
    And I press "Create State"
    Then I should see "State has been created."
```

Here you sign in as an admin user and go through the motions of creating a new state. When you run this feature through using the command `bin/cucumber features/creating_states.feature`, it will fail because it can't find the States link:

```
And I follow "States"
  no link with title, id or text 'States' found (Capybara::ElementNotFound)
```

The States link should take you to the `StatesController`'s index action, which is missing from the admin home page, located at app/views/admin/base/index.html .erb. You can add this link now by adding the following line to this file:

```
<%= link_to "States", admin_states_path %>
```

The `admin_states_path` method isn't defined yet, and you can fix this by adding another `resources` line inside the admin `namespace` in config/routes.rb like this:

```
namespace :admin do
  ...
  resources :states
end
```

With this line in the admin namespace, the `admin_states_path` method (and its siblings) are defined. Let's run the feature again now to see what you have to do next:

```
And I follow "States"
  uninitialized constant Admin::StatesController
```

Ah, that's right! You need to generate your controller. You can do this by running the controller generator:

```
rails g controller admin/states
```

When you run this feature again, you're told that you're missing the index action from this controller:

```
And I follow "States"
  The action 'index' could not be found for Admin::StatesController
```

You add this action to the app/controllers/admin/states_controller.rb file now, as well as making this controller inherit from `Admin::BaseController`. After you're done, the whole controller class will appear as shown in the following listing

Listing 10.22   app/controllers/admin/states_controller.rb

```
class Admin::StatesController < Admin::BaseController

  def index
    @states = State.all
  end
end
```

Next on the menu is defining the view for this action in a brand new file to be located at app/views/admin/states/index.html.erb. This view must contain the New State link your feature will go looking for, and it should also include a list of states so that anyone looking at the page knows which states already exist The code to do all this is shown in the following listing.

Listing 10.23   app/views/admin/states/index.html.erb

```
<%= link_to "New State", new_admin_state_path %>

<ul id='states'>
  <% for state in @states %>
    <li><%= state.name %></li>
  <% end %>
</ul>
```

With this view written, your feature will now whinge about the new action when you run bin/cucumber feature/creating_states.feature:

```
And I follow "New State"
  The action 'new' could not be found
  for Admin::StatesController (AbstractController::ActionNotFound)
```

Alright then, you should add the new action to Admin::StatesController if you want to continue any further. It should be defined like the following inside that controller:

```
def new
  @state = State.new
end
```

You now need to create the view for this action at app/views/admin/states/new.html.erb and fill it in with the following content:

```
<h1>New State</h1>
<%= render "form" %>
```

You're using a form partial here again because it's best practice and also just in case you ever wanted to use it for an edit action. In a new file for your partial at app/views/admin/states/_form.html.erb, you put the form that will be used to create new states. This form is pretty simple—it only needs a text field for the name and a submit button to submit the form:

```
<%= form_for [:admin, @state] do |f| %>
  <p>
    <%= f.label :name %>
    <%= f.text_field :name %>
  </p>

  <%= f.submit %>
<% end %>
```

Because the @state variable coming from the new is a new instance of the State model, the submit method will display a submit button with the text Create State, just like your feature needs. Speaking of which, with this form partial done, your feature should run a little further. You should check this now by running bin/cucumber features/creating_states.feature:

```
And I press "Create State"
  The action 'create' could not be found
  for Admin::StatesController (AbstractController::ActionNotFound)
```

Right, so you need to create the `create` action too, which you define inside `Admin::StatesController` as shown in the following listing.

Listing 10.24 app/controllers/admin/states_controller.rb

```ruby
def create
  @state = State.new(params[:state])
  if @state.save
    flash[:notice] = "State has been created."
    redirect_to admin_states_path
  else
    flash[:alert] = "State has not been created."
    render :action => "new"
  end
end
```

With the `create` action defined in your `Admin::StatesController`, you'll now be able to run `bin/cucumber features/creating_states.feature` and have it pass:

```
1 scenario (1 passed)
8 steps (8 passed)
```

Very good! By implementing a feature that lets the admin users of your site create states, you've provided a base to build the other state features upon. You shouldn't have broken anything by these changes but it won't hurt to run `rake cucumber:ok spec` to make sure. You should see the following summaries:

```
50 scenarios (50 passed)
571 steps (571 passed)
# and
25 examples, 0 failures, 9 pending
```

Good to see everything's still working. Commit and push this now:

```
git add .
git commit -m "Added Admin::StatesController for managing states"
git push
```

With this base defined, you can move on to more exciting things than CRUD, such as defining a default state for your tickets.

10.4.2 *Defining a default state*

A default state for the tickets in your application will provide a sensible way of grouping tickets that are new to the system, making it easier for them to be found. The easiest way to track which state is the default state is to add a boolean column called `default` to your `states` table, which is set to true if the state is the default, false if not.

To get started, you write a feature that covers changing the default status. At the end of this feature, you end up with the `default` field in the `states` table, and then you can move on to making the tickets default to this state. Let's create a new feature called features/managing_states.feature and fill it with the content from the following listing.

Listing 10.25   features/managing_states.feature

```
Feature: Managing states
  In order to change information about a state
  As an admin
  I want to be able to set a state's name and default status

  Background:
    Given I have run the seed task
    And I am signed in as "admin@ticketee.com"

  Scenario: Marking a state as default
    Given I am on the homepage
    When I follow "Admin"
    And I follow "States"
    And I follow "Make default" for the "New" state          ◄——❶ New step
    Then I should see "New is now the default state."
```

In this scenario you've got one new step ❶, which you need to define for this feature
to run. Let's run this feature now to get the step definitions for these steps by running
bin/cucumber features/managing_states.feature:

```
When /^I follow "([^"]*)" for the "([^"]*)" state$/ do |arg1, arg2|
  pending # express the regexp above with the code you wish you had
end
```

You put this step definition inside features/step_definitions/state_steps.rb and work on
getting the first definition to pass for now. This definition is used like this:

```
And I follow "Make default" for the "New" state
```

Which is a slightly modified version of the following:

```
And I follow "Make Default" within "#some_state"
```

You're not using the within variant here directly because you're not going to be using
a statically set id attribute for the state in the view but rather setting it to something
like state_3 using this code:

```
<li id='state_<%= state.id %>'>
  <%= state.name %>
  <% if state.default? %>
    (Default)
  <% else %>
    <%= link_to "Make Default", make_default_admin_state_path(state) %>
  <% end %>
</li>
```

But you use this step within your custom step. You're also not using the step When I
follow "Make Default" because this will follow the first Make Default link on the
page, which may or may not be the one that you want. With all of this in mind, you can
redefine your step as follows:

```
When /^I follow "([^"]*)" for the "([^"]*)" state$/ do |link, name|
  state = State.find_by_name!(name)
  steps(%Q{When I follow "#{link}" within "#state_#{state.id}"})
end
```

Now in this step definition you find the state by the name given to you by the step and then find the link using the "When I follow [x] within [y]" step provided by Capybara. When you run this feature again, you're told that it can't find the state element you're referencing:

```
And I follow "Make default" for the "New" state
  scope '//*[@id = 'state_1']' not found on page (Capybara::ElementNotFound)
```

This is because you haven't added the `id` attribute to your state `li` tags inside the app/views/admin/states/index.html.erb. You can do this now by changing the following line inside this view; while you're here, also add the Make Default link:

```
<li><%= state.name %></li>
```

To this:

```
<li id='state_<%= state.id %>'>
  <%= state.name %>
  <%= link_to "Make default", make_default_admin_state_path(state) %>
</li>
```

When you run your feature again you'll rightly be told that the `make_default_admin _state_path` method is undefined. This method should take you to the `make_default` action in the `Admin::StatesController`, much like `edit_admin_state_path` takes you to the `edit` action. You can define this method as a *member route* on your states resource. A member route provides the routing helpers and, more important, the route itself, to a custom controller action for a single instance of a resource. To define this, you change the `resources  :states` line inside the admin namespace inside config/routes.rb to the following:

```
resources :states do
  member do
    get :make_default
  end
end
```

Inside the `member` block here, you define that each `state` resource has a new action called `make_default` that can be accessed through a `GET` request. As stated previously, by defining the route in this fashion you also get the `make_default_admin_state_path` helper which you use in app/views/admin/states/index.html.erb. With this member route now defined, your feature will complain that it's missing the `make_default` action:

```
And I follow "Make default" for the "New" state
  The action 'make_default' could not be found for
  Admin::StatesController (AbstractController::ActionNotFound)
```

The `make_default` action will be responsible for making the state you've selected the new default state, as well as setting the old default state to not be the default anymore. You can define this action inside app/controllers/admin/states_controller.rb, as shown in the following listing.

Listing 10.26 app/controllers/admin/states_controller.rb

```ruby
def make_default
  @state = State.find(params[:id])
  @state.default!

  flash[:notice] = "#{@state.name} is now the default state."
  redirect_to admin_states_path
end
```

Rather than putting the logic to change the selected state to the new default inside the controller, you place it in the model. To trigger a state to become the new default state, you call the `default!` method on it. It's best practice to put code that performs functionality like this inside the model.

This `default!` method can be defined in the `State` model, as shown in the following listing.

Listing 10.27 app/models/state.rb

```ruby
def default!
  current_default_state = State.find_by_default(true)      ◁━━❶ Dynamic finder

  self.default = true
  self.save!

  if current_default_state                                 ◁━━❷ Change default state
    current_default_state.default = false
    current_default_state.save!
  end

end
```

The `find_by_default` ❶ method here is a *dynamic finder* method from Active Record. The `find_by_default` will either return the `State` object for the default state, or `nil`. If it doesn't return `nil` ❷ then you change its `default` state to `false` and save the record.

When you run your feature again with `bin/cucumber features/creating_states .feature`, you see that the `find_by_default` method isn't defined:

```
And I follow "Make default" for the "New" state
 undefined method `find_by_default' for State...
```

This dynamic method doesn't exist because you haven't yet defined the `default` column on your `states` table. If you had this column then Rails would have already defined the `find_by_default` method for you. To do this, you generate a migration that will add this column using the following command:

```
rails g migration add_default_to_states default:boolean
```

Don't run this migration just yet. With the `default` column being a boolean field, it's going to need to know what its default value should be: either `true` or `false`. To set a default for this column, open your newly created migration and change the line that adds the column to the following:

```
add_column :states, :default, :boolean, :default => false
```

With this small change, every `State` object that's created will have the `default` attribute set to `false` by default. You now run your migration using `rake db:migrate` and `rake db:test:prepare`:

When you run `bin/cucumber features/managing_states.feature` now, it will pass because you've got this `default` column allowing the whole process of making a state the default to complete:

```
1 scenario (1 passed)
7 steps (7 passed)
```

Great to see! When a ticket is created, the state of that ticket will default to the `State`, which is set to default. You should make New the default state in your application by adding a `default` attribute from where you create it inside `db/seeds.rb` to the following:

```
State.create(:name       => "New",
             :background => "#85FF00",
             :color      => "white",
             :default    => true)
```

When this seeds file is run later on, you'll have a default state for your tickets so that they display properly in your tickets listing.

You should now commit these change but, before that, you should make sure you haven't caused anything to break. Let's run `rake cucumber:ok spec` to find out:

```
51 scenarios (51 passed)
531 steps (531 passed)
# and
34 examples, 0 failures, 17 pending
```

There's nothing broken, so it's time to commit:

```
git add .
git commit -m "Admins can now set a default state for tickets"
git push
```

You're close to being done with states. So far, you've added the functionality for users to change the state through the comment form, to display the state transition on a comment, and (just recently) for admins to be able to create new states and toggle which state is the default.

At the moment, any user is able to change the state of a ticket, which isn't a good thing. You'd like some users to have the ability to leave a comment but not to change the state, and you'll look at creating this feature right now. This is the final feature you'll be implementing for states.

10.5   Locking down states

This feature is going to take a little more than hiding the State select box on the form; you also need to tell the application to ignore the state parameter if the user doesn't have permission to change the state. You implement this one piece at a time, beginning with ensuring the State select box is hidden from those who should be unable to change the state.

10.5.1   Hiding a select box

In previous chapters you've seen how you can hide links from certain users by using the CanCan-provided can? view helper. You can also use this helper to hide the state field in your comment form from users without the permission to change the state. First, you write a Cucumber scenario to ensure that the State box is always hidden from these users.

You add this particular scenario to the bottom of the features/creating _comments.feature because its operation is based around creating a comment. The scenario to ensure that you don't see this state field is a short and simple one:

```
Scenario: A user without permission cannot change the state
  When I follow "Change a ticket's state"
  Then I should not see the "#comment_state_id" element
```

This scenario contains two simple steps: one to go to the ticket page and another to assert that you don't see the State select box. When you run this scenario by running `bundle exec features/creating_comments.feature:44`, you see that the second step isn't yet defined:

```
Undefined step: "I should not see the "#comment_state_id" element"
```

As usual, the definition for this step appears at the bottom of Cucumber's output:

```
Then /^I should not see the "([^"]*)" element$/ do |arg1|
  pending # express the regexp above with the code you wish you had
end
```

To define this step, you put its definition inside of features/step_definitions/ application_steps.rb. To make it do the thing you want it to do, you can use one of Capybara's helper methods called `find`.

`find` can take many different forms, but in this case you'll be using the following form:

```
find(:css, css)
```

By passing these two options to `find`, Capybara will look for any element on the page that matches the CSS selector. In this case, that would be css. If `find` does find an element or even a collection of elements, it will only return the first element from this list. If it can't find anything, it will return nil. Using this knowledge, you can implement this step now as shown, putting it inside features/step_definitions/application_steps.rb:

```
Then /^I should not see the "([^"]*)" element$/ do |css|
  page.should_not(have_css(css),
    "Expected to not see the #{css} element, but did.")
end
```

Here you use Capybara's have_css matcher to see if the page has an element matching the CSS selector, which is passed to this step. You also use RSpec's ability to specify a custom message if this assertion fails, returning "Expected to not see the #comment_state_id element, but did" if this element is visible on the page.

If you run this feature using bin/cucumber features/creating_comments .feature:42, you see that this step is failing because it *is* seeing the element:

```
Then I should not see the "#comment_state_id" element
  Expected to not see the #comment_state_id element, but did
```

Right, now that you've got your feature to a good-enough point that it ensures that you shouldn't see this field, it's time to hide it and fix the feature. To do this, you use the can? method to check that the user has permission to change states for this project. If the user doesn't have this permission, then you'll hide the state field. With this change, the State select box code in app/views/comments/_form.html.erb will now look like the following listing.

Listing 10.28   app/views/comments/_form.html.erb

```
<% authorized?(:"change states", @project) do %>
  <p>
    <%= f.label :state_id %>
    <%= f.select :state_id, @states.map { |s| [s.name, s.id] },
                     :selected => @ticket.state_id   %>
  </p>
<% end %>
```

Here you use the authorized? method defined in chapter 8 to only display the fields if the user is authorized to changed the states.

This little change will make your scenario pass because the user you're signing in as doesn't have this particular permission set up. Let's run it now with bin/cucumber features/creating_comments.feature:42 to make sure:

```
1 scenario (1 passed)
10 steps (10 passed)
```

Good to see, but this view change has definitely broken the scenario in this feature, which *does* change the state. You can run this other scenario by running bin/cucumber features/creating_comments.feature:33; when you do that, you see that it's indeed broken:

```
cannot select option, no select box with id, name, or label 'State' found
```

You've done something similar to this before in chapter 8. Back then, you used a step that set the current user up with a permission to perform a specific protected action. This is no different. Let's write a new step underneath the title of the scenario on line

33 of features/creating_comments.feature, which should be the scenario title of "Changing a ticket's state":

```
Given "user@ticketee.com" can change states on the "Ticketee" project
```

With the step in your scenario using this step definition now, the scenario will pass when you rerun it using bin/cucumber features/creating_comments.feature:33:

```
1 scenario (1 passed)
16 steps (16 passed)
```

Good! All the scenarios in this feature should now be passing; you'll check that in a minute. Your next step was going to be to ensure that the state_id parameter wasn't passed through if the user doesn't have access to create a state, but you've just added a new permission to the system. You should ensure that this permission is assignable to users before continuing, which you can do by adding a scenario to the Assigning Permissions feature.

10.5.2 *Bestowing changing state permissions*

The features/assigning_permissions.feature file contains the Assigning Permissions feature, which you've used to ensure that permissions are assignable from the permissions page in the backend accessible by admins. Let's add another scenario now to test that you can assign this "change states" permission, as shown in the following listing.

Listing 10.29   features/assigning_permissions.feature

```
Scenario: Changing states for a ticket
  When I check "View" for "TextMate 2"
  And I check "Change States" for "TextMate 2"
  And I press "Update"
  And I follow "Sign out"

  Given I am signed in as "user@ticketee.com"
  When I follow "TextMate 2"
  And I follow "Shiny!"
  When I fill in "Text" with "Opening this ticket."
  And I select "Open" from "State"
  And I press "Create Comment"
  Then I should see "Comment has been created."
  And I should see "Open" within "#ticket .state"
```

When you run this scenario with the command bec features/assigning _permissions.feature:73, you see that it can't find the Change States select box for the TextMate 2 project:

```
cannot check field, no checkbox ... 'permissions_1_change_states'
```

This is fine. You haven't added it to the list of permissions inside of app/helpers/admin/permissions_helper.rb yet. You can add this now by adding this key-value pair to the Hash object in the permissions method's hash:

```
"change states" => "Change States"
```

With this added to the `permissions` hash, your scenario will move a little further toward success. When you rerun it, it will complain that it can't find the Open state from your select box:

```
And I select "Open" from "State"
  No such option 'Open' in this select box.
```

Ah, not a problem! This means that the Open state isn't yet defined in your test database. You need to create this state in the `Background` for this feature. You can do this by adding the following line at the bottom of the `Background`:

```
Given there is a state called "Open"
```

When you rerun this scenario using `bin/cucumber features/assigning_permissions` `.feature:74`,[4] it will now pass:

```
1 scenario (1 passed)
22 steps (22 passed)
```

That's good! Now admins are able to assign the "Change states" permission and users are able to see and touch the State select box on the comment form if they have this permission.

This is a great halfway point before you go diving into the final stage of this particular set of features to run your Cucumber features and specs to ensure that nothing is broken. Let's run `rake cucumber:ok spec` now; you should see that all your tests are passing:

```
53 scenarios (53 passed)
568 steps (568 passed)
# and
34 examples, 0 failures, 17 pending
```

Yay! Everything is in working order, which means you can commit and push these changes to GitHub:

```
git add .
git commit -m "Only users with the 'change states' permission
  ➥can change states"
git push
```

The final piece of your states puzzle is to stop the `state` parameter from being set in your `CommentsController` if a user passes it through and doesn't have permission to set states. First, you'll investigate how a user can fake this response. Afterward, you'll write a controller spec that duplicates this and ensures that the state isn't set.

---

[4] If you get no scenario and no steps running for this feature, are you sure you're running the right line? Check to make sure you're running line 75, not 74, which is now a blank line.

10.5.3 *Hacking a form*

Even if your `state` field is hidden from view, users are still able to submit a form containing this parameter, and your application will accept it. Let's now see this in practice.

The first things you need to do are to create a user and give it read access to a project, which you can do by starting `rails console` (or `rails c`) and running these commands:

```
user = Factory(:user)
user.confirm!
user.permissions.create(:object => Project.first,
                        :action => "view")
```

Let's quit the console by typing `exit` and then start up the application with `rails server`. Now you can sign in with the user@ticketee.com email and *password* password. Once you're in, you should see the page shown in figure 10.16.

Let's go into this project and pick any ticket in the list or create your own. It doesn't matter, you just need a ticket. When you're on the ticket page, save this page by choosing File and then Save or Save Page As, and save this file in a memorable location. You're going to be editing this saved file and adding a State select box of your own.

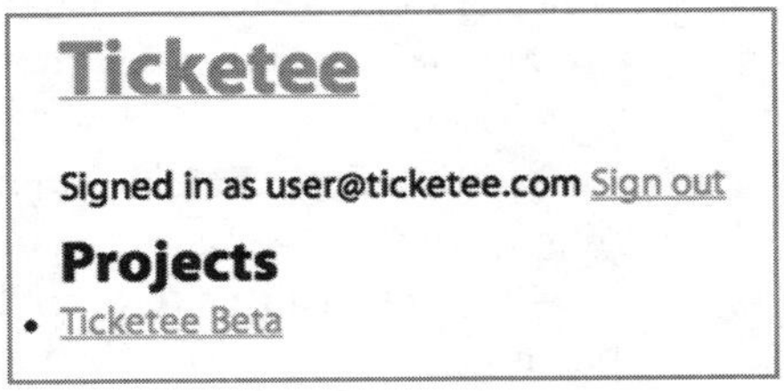

Open this saved file in a text editor, and look for the following lines:

Figure 10.16   **What the user sees**

```
<p>
  <label for="comment_text">Text</label><br>
  <textarea cols="40" id="comment_text" name="comment[text]" rows="20"></
    textarea>
</p>
```

These lines display the Text label and the associated `textarea` for a new comment. You're able to add the `state` field underneath the text field by adding this code[5] to the page:

```
<p>
  <label for="comment_state">State</label><br>
  <select id="comment_state_id" name="comment[state_id]">
    <option value="1" selected="selected">New</option>
    <option value="2">Open</option>
    <option value="3">Closed</option>
  </select>
</p>
```

When you save this page, you'll now be able to choose a state when you open it in a browser. The `action` of the `form` tag on this page goes to http://localhost:3000/tickets

---

[5] Assuming you know the IDs of the states.

/[id]/comments (where [id] is the id of the ticket this form will create a comment for), and this route will take you to the create action inside CommentsController.

Figure 10.17
Hacked state transition

Let's open this saved page in a browser now, fill in the text for the comment with anything, and select a value for the state. When you submit this form, it will create a comment and set the state. You should see your comment showing the state transition, as shown in figure 10.17.

Obviously, hiding the state field isn't a foolproof way to protect it. A better way to protect this attribute would be to delete it from the parameters before it gets to the method that creates a new comment.

10.5.4 *Ignoring a parameter*

If you remove the state_id key from the comment parameters before they're passed to the build method in the create action for CommentsController, then this problem won't happen. You should write a *regression test*. Regression tests are tests that save you from causing regressions.

You now open spec/controllers/comments_controller_spec.rb and set up a project, ticket, state, and user for the spec you're about to write by putting the code from the following listing inside the describe CommentsController block.

Listing 10.30 spec/controllers/comments_controller_spec.rb

```ruby
let(:user) { create_user! }
let(:project) { Project.create!(:name => "Ticketee") }

let(:ticket) do
  project.tickets.create(:title => "State transitions",
                         :description => "Can't be hacked.",
                         :user => user)
end

let(:state) { State.create!(:name => "New") }
```

The state you create is the one you'll attempt to transition to in your spec, with the ticket's default state being not set, and therefore nil. The user you set up is the user you use to sign in and change the state with. This user has no permissions at the moment and so they won't be able to change the states.

Your spec needs to make sure that a change doesn't take place when a user who doesn't have permission to change the status of a ticket for that ticket's project submits a state_id parameter. You put this code, shown in the next listing, directly underneath the setup you just wrote.

Listing 10.31 spec/controllers/comments_controller_spec.rb

```ruby
context "a user without permission to set state" do
  before do
    sign_in(:user, user)
  end
```

```
  it "cannot transition a state by passing through state_id" do
    post :create, { :comment => { :text => "Hacked!",
                                  :state_id => state.id },
                    :ticket_id => ticket.id }
    ticket.reload                              ←──❶ Reload Ticket object
    ticket.state.should eql(nil)
  end
end
```

This spec uses a before to sign in as the user before the example runs. Inside the example, you use the post method to make a POST request to the create action inside CommentsController, passing in the specified parameters. It's this state_id parameter that should be ignored in the action.

After the post method, you use a new method :reload ❶. When you call reload on an Active Record object, it will fetch the object again from the database and update the attributes for it. You use this because the create action acts on a different Ticket object and doesn't touch the one you've set up for your spec.

The final line here asserts that the ticket.state should be nil. When you run this spec by running bundle exec rspec spec/controllers/comments_controller _spec.rb, this final line will be the one to fail:

```
Failure/Error: ticket.state.should eql(nil)

expected nil
     got #<State id: 1, name: "New", default: false>
```

The ticket.state is returning a state object because the user has been able to post it through the parameter hash. With a failing spec now in place, you can go about stopping this state parameter from going unchecked. To ignore this parameter, you can remove it from the params hash if the user doesn't have permission to change states. At the top of the create action, inside of CommentsController, put the following lines:

```
if cannot?(:"change states", @ticket.project)
  params[:comment].delete(:state_id)
end
```

This code will remove the state_id key from the params[:comment] hash if the user doesn't have permission to change the states on the ticket's project, thereby preventing them from being able to change the state. If you rerun your spec using bin/rspec spec /controllers/comments_controller_spec.rb, you'll see that it passes:

```
1 example, 0 failures
```

Great! Now nobody without permission will be able to download the ticket page, make modifications to it to add a state field, and then be able to change the states.

You're done with this feature now so it's time to make sure you didn't break anything with your changes by running rake cucumber:ok spec. You should see that everything is squeaky clean:

```
53 scenarios (53 passed)
615 steps (615 passed)
# and
26 examples, 0 failures, 9 pending
```

Great! You now commit and push this to Github:

```
git add .
git commit -m "Protect state_id from users who do
              not have permission to change it"
git push
```

The `CommentsController` will now reject the `state_id` parameter if the user doesn't have permission to set it, thereby protecting the form from anybody hacking it to add a `state_id` field when they shouldn't.

The feature of protecting the `state_id` field from changes was the final piece of the state features puzzle. You've now learned how to stop a user from changing not only a particular record when they don't have permission to, but also a specific field on a record.

10.6 *Summary*

You began this chapter by writing the basis for the work later on in the chapter: comments. By letting users posts comments on a ticket, you can let them add further information to it and tell a story.

With the comment base laid down, you implemented the ability for users to be able to change a ticket's state when they post a comment. For this, you tracked the state of the ticket before the comment was saved and the state assigned to the comment so you could show transitions (as shown in figure 10.18).

You finished by limiting the ability to change states to only those who have permission to do so, much as you've previously limited the abilities to read projects and create tickets in previous chapters. While doing this, you saw how easy it was for somebody to download the source of your form and alter it to do their bidding and then how to protect it from that.

In chapter 10, you will add *tags* to your tickets. Tags are words or short phrases that provide categorization for tickets, making them easier for users to manage. Additionally, you'll implement a search interface that will allow users to find tickets with a given tag or state.

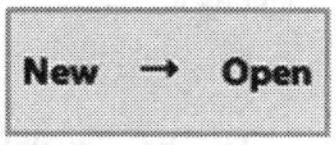

**Figure 10.18
Replay: state transitions**

Tagging

This chapter covers
- Tagging specific records for easier searching
- Restricting user access to tagging functionality
- Searching for specific tags or specific states of a ticket

In chapter 10, you saw how to give your tickets states (New, Open, and Closed) so that their progress can be indicated.

In this chapter, you'll see how to give your tickets tags. Tags are useful for grouping similar tickets together into things such as iterations[1] or similar feature sets. If you didn't have tags, you could crudely group tickets together by setting a ticket's title to something such as "Tag - [name]." This method, however, is messy and difficult to sort through. Having a group of tickets with the same tag will make them much, much easier to find.

To manage tags, you'll set up a `Tag` model, which will have a `has_and_belongs_to_many` association to the `Ticket` model. You'll set up a *join table* for this association, which is a table that contains foreign key fields for each

---

[1] For example, by using a process such as Agile, feature sets, or any other method of grouping.

side of the association. A join table's sole purpose is to join together the two tables whose keys it has. In this case, the two tables are the `tickets` and `tags` tables. As you move forward in developing this association, note that, for all intents and purposes, `has_and_belongs_to _many` works like a two-way `has_many`.

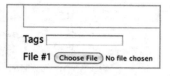

Figure 11.1 The tag box

You'll create two ways to add tags to a ticket. A text field for new tickets beneath the ticket's description field will allow users to add multiple tags by using a space to separate different tags, as shown in figure 11.1.

Additional tags may also be added on a comment, with a text field similar to the one from the new ticket page providing the tagging mechanism. When a ticket is created, you'll show these tags underneath the description, as shown in figure 11.2.

When a user clicks a tag, they'll be taken to a page where they can see all tickets with that particular tag. Alternatively, if the user clicks the little "x" next to the tag, that tag will be removed from the ticket. The actions of adding and removing a tag are both actions you'll add to your permission checking.

Finally, you'll implement a way to search for tickets that match a state, a tag, or both, by using a gem called `searcher`. The query will look like `tag:iteration_1 state: open`.

Figure 11.2 A tag for a ticket

That's all there is to this chapter! You'll be adding tags to Ticketee, which will allow you to easily group and sort tickets. Let's dig into your first feature, adding tags to a new ticket.

11.1 Creating tags

Tags in this application will be extremely useful for making similar tickets easy to find and manage. In this section, you'll create the interface for adding tags to a new ticket by adding a new field to the new ticket page and defining a `has_and_belongs _to_many` association between the `Ticket` model and the not-yet-existent `Tag` model.

11.1.1 Creating tags feature

You're going to add a text field beneath the description field on the new ticket page for this feature, as you saw earlier in figure 11.1.

The words you enter into this field will become the tags for this ticket, and you should see them on the ticket page. At the bottom of features/creating_tickets.feature, you add a scenario that creates a new ticket with tags, as shown in listing 11.1.

Listing 11.1 features/creating_tickets.feature

```
Scenario: Creating a ticket with tags
  When I fill in "Title" with "Non-standards compliance"
  And I fill in "Description" with "My pages are ugly!"
  And I fill in "Tags" with "browser visual"
```

```
And I press "Create Ticket"
Then I should see "Ticket has been created."
And I should see "browser" within "#ticket #tags"
And I should see "visual" within "#ticket #tags"
```

When you run the "Creating a ticket with tags" scenario using bin/cucumber features /creating_tickets.feature:50 it will fail, declaring that it can't find the Tags field. Good! It's not there yet:

```
And I fill in "Tags" with "browser visual"
  cannot fill in, no text field, text area or password field
    with id, name, or label 'Tags' found (Capybara::ElementNotFound)
```

You're going to take the data from this field, process each word into a new Tag object, and then link the tags to the ticket when it's created. You'll use a text_field_tag to render the Tags field this way. text_field_tag is similar to a text_field tag, but it doesn't have to relate to any specific object like text_field does. Instead, it will output an input tag with the type attribute set to text and the name set to whatever name you give it.

11.1.2 *Using text_field_tag*

To define this field, you put the following code underneath the p tag for the description in app/views/tickets/_form.html.erb:

```
<p>
  <%= label_tag :tags %>
  <%= text_field_tag :tags, params[:tags] %>
</p>
```

This field will be sent through to TicketsController as params[:tags], rather than the kind of attributes you're used to, such as params[:ticket][:title].

By specifying params[:tags] as the second argument to text_field_tag, you can re-populate this field when the ticket cannot be created due to it failing validation.

When you re-run this scenario again with bin/cucumber features/creating _tickets.feature:51, it no longer complains about the missing Tags field, telling you instead that it can't find the tags displayed on your ticket:

```
And I should see "browser" within "#ticket #tags"
  Unable to find css "#ticket #tags" (Capybara::ElementNotFound)
```

You now need to define this #tags element inside the #ticket element on the ticket's page so that this part of the scenario will pass. This element will contain the tags for your ticket, which your scenario will assert are actually visible.

11.1.3 *Showing tags*

You can add this new element, with its id attribute set to tags, to app/views/tickets/ show.html.erb by adding this simple line underneath where you render the ticket's description:

```
<div id='tags'><%= render @ticket.tags %></div>
```

This creates the `#ticket #tags` element that your feature is looking for, and will render the soon-to-be-created app/views/tags/_tag.html.erb partial for every element in the also-soon-to-be-created `tags` association on the `@ticket` object. Which of these two steps do you take next? If you run your scenario again, you see that it cannot find the `tags` method for a `Ticket` object:

```
undefined method `tags' for #<Ticket:0x0..
```

This method is the `tags` method, which you'll be defining with a `has_and _belongs_to_many` association between `Ticket` objects and `Tag` objects. This method will be responsible for returning a collection of all the tags associated with the given ticket, much like a `has_many` would. The difference is that this method works in the opposite direction as well, allowing you to find out what tickets have a specific tag.

11.1.4 *Defining the tags association*

You can define the `has_and_belongs_to_many` association on the `Ticket` model by placing this line after the `has_many` definitions inside your `Ticket` model:

```
has_and_belongs_to_many :tags
```

This association will rely on a join table that doesn't yet exist called `tags_tickets`. The name is the combination, in alphabetical order, of the two tables you want to join. This table contains only two fields—one called `ticket_id` and one called `tag_id`—which are both foreign keys for tags and tickets. The join table will easily facilitate the union of these two tables, because it will have one record for each tag that links to a ticket, and vice versa.

When you re-run your scenario, you're told that there's no constant called `Tag` yet:

```
uninitialized constant Ticket::Tag (ActionView::Template::Error)
```

In other words, there is no `Tag` model yet. You should define this now if you want to go any further.

11.1.5 *The Tag model*

Your `Tag` model will have a single field called `name`, which should be unique. To generate this model and its related migration, run the `rails` command like this:

```
rails g model tag name:string --timestamps false
```

The `timestamps` option passed here determines whether or not the model's migration is generated with timestamps. Because you've passed the value of `false` to this option, there will be no timestamps added.

Before you run this migration, however, you need to add the join table called `tags_tickets` to your database. The join table has two fields: one called `ticket_id` and the other `tag_id`. The table name is the pluralized names of the two models it is joining, sorted in alphabetical order. This table will have no primary key, because you're never going to look for individual records from this table and only need it to join the `tags` and `tickets` tables.

To define the `tags_tickets` table, put this code in the `change` section of your db/ migrate/[timestamp]_create_tags.rb migration:

```
create_table :tags_tickets, :id => false do |t|
  t.integer :tag_id, :ticket_id
end
```

The `:id => false` option passed to `create_table` here tells Active Record to create the table without the `id` field, because the join table only cares about the link between tickets and tags, and therefore does not need a unique identifier.

Next, run the migration on your development database by running `rake db:migrate`, and on your test database by running `rake db:test:prepare`. This will create the `tags` and `tags_tickets` tables.

When you run this scenario again with `bin/cucumber features/creating _tickets:48`, it is now satisfied that the `tags` method is defined and moves on to complaining that it can't find the tag you specified:

```
And I should see "browser" within "#ticket #tags"
  Failed assertion, no message given. (MiniTest::Assertion)
```

This failure is because you're not doing anything to associate the text from the Tags field to the ticket you've created. You need to parse the content from this field into new `Tag` objects and then associate them with the ticket you are creating, which you'll do right now.

11.1.6 *Displaying a ticket's tags*

The `params[:tags]` in `TicketsController`'s `create` is the value from your Tags field on app/views/tickets/_form.html.erb. This is also the field you need to parse into `Tag` objects and associate those tags with the `Ticket` object you are creating.

To do this, alter the `create` action in `TicketsController` by adding this line directly after `@ticket.save`:

```
@ticket.tag!(params[:tags])
```

This new `tag!` method will parse the tags from `params[:tags]`, convert them into new `Tag` objects, and associate them with the ticket. You can define this new method at the bottom of your `Ticket` model like this:

```
def tag!(tags)
  tags = tags.split(" ").map do |tag|
    Tag.find_or_create_by_name(tag)
  end

  self.tags << tags
end
```

On the first line here, use the `split` method to split your string into an array, and then use the `map` method to iterate through every value in the array.

Inside the block for `map`, use a *dynamic finder* to find or create a tag with a specified name. You last saw a dynamic finder in chapter 10, where you found a `State` record by using `find_by_default`. `find_or_create_by` methods work in a similar fashion, except they will always return a record, whether it be a pre-existing one or a recently created one.

After all the tags have been iterated through, you assign them to a ticket by using the << method on the tags association.

The `tag!` method you have just written will create the tags that you display on the app/views/tickets/show.html.erb view by using the `render` method you used earlier:

```
<%= render @ticket.tags %>
```

When you run this scenario again by running `bin/cucumber features/creating _tickets.feature:51`, you see this line is failing with an error:

```
Missing partial tags/tag ...
```

The next step is to write the tag partial that your feature has complained about. Put the following code in a new file called app/views/tags/_tag.html.erb:

```
<span class='tag'><%= tag.name %></span>
```

By wrapping the tag name in a span with the `class` of tag, it will be styled as defined in your stylesheet. With this partial defined, the final piece of the puzzle for this feature is put into place. When you run your scenario again by running `bin/cucumber features/creating_tickets.feature:51`, it passes:

```
1 scenario (1 passed)
15 steps (15 passed)
```

Great! This scenario is now complete. When a user creates a ticket, they are able to assign tags to that ticket, and those tags will display along with the ticket's information on the `show` action for `TicketsController`. The tag display was shown earlier in figure 11.2.

You now commit this change, but before you do you ensure that you haven't broken anything by running `rake cucumber:ok spec`:

```
54 scenarios (53 passed)
583 steps (583 passed)
# and
36 examples, 0 failures, 18 pending
```

Good to see that nothing's blown up this time. Let's commit this change:

```
git add .
git commit -m "Users can tag tickets upon creation"
git push
```

Now that users can add a tag to a ticket when that ticket is being created, you should also let them add tags to a ticket when they create a comment. When a ticket is being discussed, new information may come that would require another tag to be added to the ticket and group it into a different set. A perfect way to let your users do this would be to let them add the tag when they comment.

11.2   Adding more tags

The tags for a ticket can change throughout the ticket's life; new tags can be added and old ones can be deleted. Let's look at how you can add more tags to a ticket after it's been created through the comments form. Underneath the comment form on a ticket's page, add the same Tags field that you previously used to add tags to your ticket on the new ticket page. One thing you have to keep in mind here is that if someone enters a tag that's already been entered, you don't want it to show up.

You've got two scenarios to implement then: the first is a vanilla addition of tags to a ticket through a comment, and the second is a scenario ensuring that duplicate tags do not appear. Let's implement this function one scenario at a time. When you're done, you'll end up with the pretty picture shown in figure 11.3.

Figure 11.3   Comment form with tags

11.2.1   Adding tags through a comment

To test that users can add tags when they're creating a comment, you add a new scenario to the features/creating_comments.feature feature that looks like this listing:

Listing 11.2   features/creating_comments.feature

```
Scenario: Adding a tag to a ticket
  When I follow "Change a ticket's state"
  Then I should not see "bug" within "#ticket #tags"
  And I fill in "Text" with "Adding the bug tag"
  And I fill in "Tags" with "bug"
  And I press "Create Comment"
  Then I should see "Comment has been created"
  Then I should see "bug" within "#ticket #tags"
```

First, you make sure you don't see this tag within #ticket #tags, to ensure you don't have a false positive. Next, you fill in the text for the comment so it's valid, add the word "bug" to the Tags field, and click the Create Comment button. Finally, you ensure that the comment has been created and that the bug tag you entered into the comment form now appears in #ticket #tags.

When you run this scenario using bin/cucumber features/creating_comments .feature:47, it will fail because there is no Tags field on the ticket's page yet:

```
cannot fill in, no text field, text area or password
  field with id, name, or label 'Tags' found
```

You can fix this by taking these lines from app/views/tickets/_form.html.erb and moving them into a new partial at app/views/tags/_form.html.erb:

```
<p>
  <%= label_tag :tags %>
  <%= text_field_tag :tags, params[:tags] %>
</p>
```

Replace the code you removed from app/views/tickets/_form.html.erb with this line:

```
<%= render "tags/form" %>
```

This new line will render your new `tags` partial. In order to make the failing step in your scenario now pass, you re-use this same line inside the `authorized?` block inside app/views/comments/_form.html.erb underneath the code you use to render the State select box.

When you run `bin/cucumber features/creating_comments.feature:47`, you see that this step is indeed passing, but now it's the final step of your scenario that is failing:

```
Then I should see "bug" within "#ticket #tags"
  expected there to be content "bug" in ""
```

This feature is not seeing the word "bug" within the content for the ticket's `tags` (which is empty), and so the scenario fails. This is because the code to associate a tag with a ticket isn't in the `create` action of `CommentsController` yet. In the `create` action in `TicketsController`, you use this line to tag the ticket that was created:

```
@ticket.tag!(params[:tags])
```

You can use this same method to tag a comment's ticket. On the line immediately after `if @comment.save` in the `create` action inside `CommentsController`, you re-use the `tag!` line. That's all you need to get this scenario to pass, right? Run `bin/cucumber features/creating_comments.feature:47` to find out:

```
1 scenario (1 passed)
15 steps (15 passed)
```

Boom, that's passing! Good stuff. Now for the cleanup. Make sure you haven't broken anything else by running `rake cucumber:ok spec`:

```
55 scenarios (55 passed)
598 steps (598 passed)
# and
27 examples, 1 failure, 10 pending
```

It would seem your spec/controllers/comments_controller_spec.rb doesn't want to play nice.

294 CHAPTER 11 Tagging

11.2.2 Fixing the CommentsController spec

The `CommentsController` spec is failing with this error:

```
You have a nil object when you didn't expect it!
You might have expected an instance of Array.
The error occurred while evaluating nil.split
# ./app/models/ticket.rb:16:in `tag!'
# ./app/controllers/comments_controller.rb:12:in `create'
```

Ah, it seems to be from within the `tag!` method from the `Ticket` model. The sixteenth line of this model is

```
tags = tags.split(" ").map do |tag|
```

It's the calling of `tags.split` that is making the spec fail, but why? `tags` comes from the argument passed to this method from the `CommentsController`'s create action by this line:

```
@ticket.tag!(params[:tags])
```

You'd get this error if `params[:tags]` was ever `nil`, because you cannot call `split` on `nil`. Why is it `nil` in your controller spec, though? It's because you're not sending it through with the other parameters in your spec:

```
post :create, { :comment => { :text => "Hacked!",
                              :state_id => state.id },
             :ticket_id => ticket.id }
```

You can solve this problem in one of two ways. The first way is to check that `params[:tags]` is not `nil` before calling the `tag!` method by adding code to the `CommentsController`, or better still, by adding code to the `tag!` method in the `Ticket` model. The second way is to make the controller spec accurately reflect reality.

Because the Tags field is always going to be on the comments page, its value will be set to an empty string if it is left as-is. The second fix is therefore better, because it fixes the problem rather than compensating for an issue that will only happen in your tests. You can change the `post` method in the test in spec/controllers/comments_controller_spec.rb to this:

```
post :create, { :tags => "",
             :comment => { :text => "Hacked!",
                           :state_id => state.id },
             :ticket_id => ticket.id }
```

Due to this small change, all your specs will be passing when you run `rake spec` again:

```
27 examples, 0 failures, 10 pending
```

With all the specs and features passing, it's commit time! In this section, you've created a way for your users to add more tags to a ticket when they add a comment, which allows your users to easily organize tickets into relevant groups. Let's commit this change now:

```
git add .
git commit -m "Users can add tags when adding a comment"
git push
```

With the ability to add tags when creating a ticket or a comment now available, you need to restrict this power to users with permission to manage tags. You don't want all users to create tags willy-nilly, because it's likely you would end up with an overabundance of tags.[2] Too many tags makes it hard to identify which tags are useful and which are not. People with permission to tag things will know that with great power, comes great responsibility.

11.3 Tag restriction

Using the permissions system you built in chapter 8, you can easily add another type of permission: one for tagging. If a user has this permission, they will be able to add and (later on) remove tags.

11.3.1 Testing tag restriction

When a user without permission attempts to submit a ticket or comment, the application should not tag the ticket with the tags they have specified. You'll add this restriction to the `CommentsController`, but first you'll write a controller spec to cover this behavior. In spec/controllers/comments_controller_spec.rb, put this spec underneath the one you just fixed:

```
it "cannot tag a ticket without permission" do
  post :create, { :tags => "one two", :comment => { :text => "Tag!" },
                  :ticket_id => ticket.id }
  ticket.reload
  ticket.tags.should be_empty
end
```

You can then run this spec using `bin/rspec spec/controllers/comments_controller _spec.rb` and see that it fails because the tags are still set:

```
Failure/Error: ticket.tags.should be_empty
 expected empty? to return true, got false
```

Good! A failing test is a good start to a new feature. To make this test pass, you should use the `can?` method in `CommentsController` to check the user's permission. You now change this line

```
@ticket.tag!(params[:tags])
```

to these lines:

```
if can?(:tag, @ticket.project) || current_user.admin?
  @ticket.tag!(params[:tags])
end
```

---

[2] Such as the tags on the Rails Lighthouse account, at lower right of this page: https://rails.lighthouseapp .com/projects/8994-ruby-on-rails/overview.

Because the user that is set up in spec/controllers/comments_controller_spec.rb doesn't have permission to tag, when you re-run your spec it will now pass:

```
2 examples, 0 failures
```

Good! You have something in place to block users from tagging tickets when they create a comment. Now you're only missing the blocking code for tagging a ticket when it is being created. You can create a spec test for this too, this time in spec/controllers/tickets_controller_spec.rb. Underneath the "Cannot delete a ticket without permission" example, add this example:

```
it "can create tickets, but not tag them" do
  Permission.create(:user => user, :thing => project,
    :action => "create tickets")
  post :create, :ticket => { :title => "New ticket!",
                             :description => "Brand spankin' new" },
                :project_id => project.id,
                :tags => "these are tags"

  Ticket.last.tags.should be_empty
end
```

You can run this spec by running bin/rspec spec/controllers/tickets_controller _spec.rb:59, and you'll see that it fails:

```
Failure/Error: Ticket.last.tags.should be_empty
  expected empty? to return true, got false
```

Because there is no restriction on tagging a ticket through the create action, there are tags for the ticket that was just created, and so your example fails. For your TicketsController's create action, you can do exactly what you did in the CommentsController's create action and change the line that calls tag! to this:

```
if can?(:tag, @project) || current_user.admin?
  @ticket.tag!(params[:tags])
end
```

When you re-run your spec it will pass:

```
1 example, 0 failures
```

Great, now you're protecting both the ways a ticket can be tagged. Because of this new restriction, the two scenarios that you created earlier to test this behavior will be broken.

11.3.2 *Tags are allowed, for some*

When you run rake cucumber:ok you see them listed as the only two failures:

```
Failing Scenarios:
cucumber features/creating_comments.feature:45
cucumber features/creating_tickets.feature:48
```

To fix these two failing scenarios, you use a new step, which you first put in the "Creating comments" feature underneath this line in the Background for this feature

```
And "user@ticketee.com" can view the "Ticketee" project
```

Put this line:

```
And "user@ticketee.com" can tag the "Ticketee" project
```

With your all-powerful step defined in features/step_definitions/permission_steps.rb, you don't have to define a definition for this step to work. When you re-run this scenario using bin/cucumber features/creating_comments.feature:48, it will pass:

```
1 scenario (1 passed)
16 steps (16 passed)
```

One scenario down, one to go! The next one is the features/creating_tickets.feature:51 scenario. At the top of the feature, you can put the same line you used in the "Creating comments" feature, right under the view permission. Don't forget to rename the project:

```
And "user@ticketee.com" can tag the "Internet Explorer" project
```

This scenario too will pass:

```
1 scenario (1 passed)
16 steps (16 passed)
```

Great! Only certain users can now tag tickets. Let's make sure that everything is still running at 100% by running rake cucumber:ok spec. You should see this:

```
55 scenarios (55 passed)
608 steps (608 passed)
# and
38 examples, 0 failures, 18 pending
```

In this section, you have restricted the ability to add tags to a ticket—whether through the new ticket or comment forms—to only users who have the permission to tag. You've done this to restrict the flow of tags. Generally speaking, the people with the ability to tag should know only to create useful tags, so that the usefulness of the tags is not diluted. In the next section, you'll use this same permission to determine what users are able to remove a tag from a ticket.

11.4 Deleting a tag

Removing a tag from a ticket is a helpful feature, because a tag may become irrelevant over time. Say that you've tagged a ticket as v0.1 for your project, but the feature isn't yet complete and needs to be moved to v0.2. Without this feature, there will be no way to delete the old tag. Then what? Was this ticket for v0.1 or v0.2? Who knows? With the ability to delete a tag, you have some assurance that people will clean up tags if they're able to.

To let users delete a tag, add an X to the left of each of your tags, as shown in figure 11.4.

When this X is clicked, the tag will disappear through the magic of JavaScript. Rather than making a whole request out to the action for deleting a tag and then redirecting back to the ticket page, remove the tag's ele-

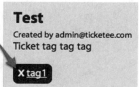

Figure 11.4   X marks the spot

ment from the page and make an asynchronous behind-the-scenes request to the action.

11.4.1 *Testing tag deletion*

To click this link using Cucumber, you give the link around the X an id so you can easily locate it in your feature, which you'll now write. Let's create a new file at features/deleting_tags.feature and put in it the code from the following listing.

Listing 11.3 features/deleting_tags.feature

```
Feature: Deleting tags
  In order to remove old tags
  As a user
  I want to click a button and make them go away

  Background:
    Given there are the following users:
      | email             | password |
      | user@ticketee.com | password |
    And I am signed in as them
    And there is a project called "Ticketee"
    And "user@ticketee.com" can view the "Ticketee" project
    And "user@ticketee.com" can tag the "Ticketee" project
    And "user@ticketee.com" has created a ticket for this project:
      | title | description      | tags              |
      | A tag | Tagging a ticket! | this-tag-must-die |
    Given I am on the homepage
    When I follow "Ticketee" within "#projects"
    And I follow "A tag"

  @javascript
  Scenario: Deleting a tag
    When I follow "delete-this-tag-must-die"
    Then I should not see "this-tag-must-die"
```

In this scenario, it's important to note that you're passing through the tags field as a field in the "created a ticket" step, just like the other fields. The tags field isn't in the tickets table. You'll get to that in a second.

In this feature, you create a new user and sign in as them. Then you create a new project called Ticketee and give the user the ability to view and tag the project. You create a ticket by the user and tag it with a tag called this_tag_must_die. Finally, you navigate to the page of the ticket you've created.

In the scenario, you follow the delete-this-tag-must-die link, which will be the id on the link to delete this tag. When this link has been followed, you shouldn't see this_tag_must_die, meaning that the action to remove the tag from the ticket has worked its magic.

When you run this feature using bin/features/deleting_tags.feature, you get this error:

```
undefined method `each' for "this_tag_must_die":String (NoMethodError)
./features/step_definitions/ticket_steps.rb:10 ...
```

This error is coming from ticket_steps.rb, line 10. Lines 8–11 of this file look like this:

```
table.hashes.each do |attributes|
  attributes.merge!(:user => User.find_by_email!(email))
  @project.tickets.create!(attributes)
end
```

The error is happening because the `tags` key in the `ticket` hash wants to pretend it's a field like the other keys. In this case, it's assuming that you're assigning a collection of tag objects to this new ticket, and is therefore trying to iterate over each of them so that it can generate the join between this ticket and those tags. Because you're passing it a string, it's not going to work!

You should extract this column out of this hash and use the `tag!` method to assign the tags, rather than attempting to create them through `create!`. You can modify these four lines now to look like this:

```
table.hashes.each do |attributes|
  tags = attributes.delete("tags")
  attributes.merge!(:user => User.find_by_email!(email))
  ticket = @project.tickets.create!(attributes)
  ticket.tag!(tags) if tags
end
```

On the first line of your iteration, you use the same `delete` method that you've used a couple of times previously. This method removes the key from a hash and returns the value of that key, which you assign to the `tags` variable. On the final line of the iteration, call the familiar `tag!` method and pass in `tags`, thereby tagging your ticket with the passed-in tags. You use `if tags` because otherwise it would attempt to pass in a nil object, resulting in the `nil.split` error you saw earlier.

When you re-run your feature using bin/cucumber features/deleting_tags .feature, it gets to the guts of your scenario and tells you that it can't find the delete link you're looking for:

```
When I follow "delete-this-tag-must-die"
  no link with title, id or text 'delete-this_tag_must_die'
```

Alright, time to implement this bad boy.

11.4.2 *Adding a link to delete the tag*

You need a link with the id of delete-this-tag-must-die, which is the word *delete*, followed by a hyphen and then the `parameterize`'d version of the tag's name. This link needs to trigger an asynchronous request to an action that would remove a tag from a ticket. The perfect name for an action like this, if you were to put it in the `TicketsController`, would be `remove_tag`. But because it's acting on a tag, a better place for this action would be inside a new controller called `TagsController`.

Before you go and define this action, let's define the link that your scenario is looking for first. This link goes into the tag partial at app/views/tags/_tag.html.erb inside the span tag:

```
<% if can?(:tag, @ticket.project) || current_user.admin? %>
  <%= link_to "x",
    :remote => true,
    :url => remove_ticket_tag_path(@ticket, tag),
    :method => :delete,
    :html => { :id => "delete-#{tag.name.parameterize}" } %>
<% end %>
<%= tag.name %>
```

Here, you check that a user can tag in the ticket's project. If they can't tag, then you won't show the X to remove the tag. This is to prevent everyone from removing tags as they feel like it. Remember? With great power comes great responsibility.

You use the :remote option for the link_to, to indicate to Rails that you want this link to be an asynchronous request. This is similar to the Add Another File button you provided in chapter 9, except this time you don't need to call out to any JavaScript to determine anything, you only need to make a request to a specific URL.

For the :url option here, you pass through the @ticket object to remove_ticket _tag_path so that your action knows what ticket to delete the tag from. Remember: your primary concern right now is disassociating a tag and a ticket, not completely deleting the tag.

Because this is a destructive action, you use the :delete method. You've used this previously for calling destroy actions, but the :delete method is not exclusive to the destroy action, and so you can use it here as well.

The final option, :html, lets you define HTML attributes for the link. Inside this hash, you set the id key to be the word *delete*, followed by a hyphen and then the name of your tag parameterize'd. For the tag in your scenario, this is the id that you'll use to click this link. Capybara supports following links by their internal text, the name attribute, or the id attribute.

When you run your feature with bundle exec cucumber features/deleting_tags .feature, you see that it reports the same error message at the bottom:

```
When I follow "delete-this-tag-must-die"
  no link with title, id or text 'delete-this-tag-must-die'
```

Ah! A quick eye would have spotted an error when the browser launched by Web-Driver tried going to this page; it looks like figure 11.5.

This error is coming up because you haven't defined the route to the remove action yet. You can define this route in config/routes.rb inside the resources :tickets block, morphing it into this:

Internal Server Error

undefined method `remove_ticket_tag_path' for #<#<Class:0x000001030...

WEBrick/1.3.1 (Ruby/1.9.2/2011-02-18) at 127.0.0.1:54141

Figure 11.5   Internal Server Error

```
resources :tickets do
  resources :comments
  resources :tags do
    member do
      delete :remove
    end
  end
end
```

By nesting the tags resource inside the ticket's resource, you are given routing helpers such as `ticket_tag_path`. With the `member` block inside the `resources :tags`, you can define further actions that this nested resource responds to. You'll define that you should accept a `DELETE` request to a route to a `remove` action for this resource, which you should now create.

Before you add this action to the `TagsController`, you must first generate this controller by using

```
rails g controller tags
```

Now that you have a controller to define your action in, let's open app/controllers/tags_controller.rb and define the `remove` action in it like this:

```
def remove
  @ticket = Ticket.find(params[:ticket_id])
  if can?(:tag, @ticket.project) || current_user.admin?
    @tag = Tag.find(params[:id])
    @ticket.tags -= [@tag]                    ◁——❶ Remove tag

    @ticket.save
    render :nothing => true
  end
end
```

In this action, you find the ticket based on the id passed through as `params[:ticket]`, and then you do something new. On the left side of `-=` ❶ you have `@ticket.tags`. On the right, is an array containing `@tag`. This combination will remove the tag from the ticket, but will not delete it from the database.

On the second-to-last line of this action, you save the ticket minus one tag. On the final line you tell it to return nothing, which will return a `200 OK` status to your browser, signaling that everything went according to plan.

When you re-run your scenario it will now successfully click the link, but the tag is still there:

```
When I follow "delete-this-tag-must-die"
Then I should not see "this-tag-must-die"
  Failed assertion, no message given. (MiniTest::Assertion)
```

Your tag is unassociated from the ticket but not removed from the page, and so your feature is still failing. The request is made to delete the ticket, but there's no code currently that removes the tag from the page. There are two problems you must overcome to make this work. The first is that there's no code. That part's easy, and you'll get there pretty soon. The second is that there's no unique identifier for the element rendered by app/views/tags/_tag.html.erb, which makes removing it from the page exceptionally difficult with JavaScript. Let's add a unique identifier now and remove the element.

11.4.3 *Actually removing a tag*

You're removing a tag's association from a ticket, but you're not yet showing people that it has happened on the page. You can fix the second of your aforementioned problems by changing the span tag at the top of this partial to be this:

```
<span class='tag' id='tag-<%= tag.name.parameterize %>'>
```

This will give the element a unique identifier, which you can use to locate the element and then remove it using JavaScript. Currently for the remove action, you're rendering nothing. Let's now remove the render :nothing => true line from this action, because you're going to get it to render a template.

If a request is made asynchronously, the format for that request will be js, rather than the standard html. For views, you've always used the html.erb extension, because HTML is all you've been serving. As of now, this changes. You're going to be rendering a js.erb template, which will contain JavaScript code to remove your element. Let's create the view for the remove action in a file called app/views/tags/remove.js.erb, and fill it with this content:

```
$('#tag-<%= @tag.name.parameterize %>').remove();
```

This code will be run when the request to the remove action is complete. It uses the jQuery library's $ function to locate an element with the id attribute of tag-this-tag-must-die and then calls remove()[3] on it, which will remove this tag from the page.

When you run your feature using bin/cucumber features/deleting_tags .feature, you see that it now passes:

```
1 scenario (1 passed)
```

```
11 steps (11 passed)
```

Awesome! With this feature done, users with permission to tag on a project will now be able to remove tags too. Before you commit this feature, let's run rake cucumber :ok spec to make sure everything is ok:

```
56 scenarios (55 passed)
619 steps (619 passed)
# and
39 examples, 0 failures, 19 pending
```

That's awesome too! Commit and push this:

```
git add .
git commit -m "Added remove tag functionality"
git push
```

---

[3] http://api.jquery.com/remove/.

Now that you can add and remove tags, what is there left to do? Find them! By implementing a way to find tickets with a given tag, you make it easier for users to see only the tickets they want to see. As an added bonus, you'll also implement a way for the users to find tickets for a given state, perhaps even at the same time as finding a tag.

When you're done with this next feature, you'll add some more functionality that will let users go to tickets for a tag by clicking the tag name inside the ticket show page.

11.5 Finding tags

At the beginning of this chapter, we planned on covering searching for tickets using a query such as `tag:iteration_1 state: open`. This magical method would return all the tickets in association with the `iteration_1` tag that were marked as open. This helps users scope down the list of tickets that appear on a project page to be able to better focus on them.

There's a gem developed specifically for this purpose called Searcher[4] that you can use. This provides you with a `search` method on specific classes, which accepts a query like the one mentioned and returns the records that match it.

11.5.1 Testing search

As usual, you should (and will) test that searching for tickets with a given tag works, which you can do by writing a new feature called features/searching.feature and filling it with the content from the following listing.

> **Listing 11.4 features/searching.feature**

```
Feature: Searching
  In order to find specific tickets
  As a user
  I want to enter a search query and get results

  Background:
    Given there are the following users:
      | email             | password |
      | user@ticketee.com | password |
    And I am signed in as them
    And there is a project called "Ticketee"
    And "user@ticketee.com" can view the "Ticketee" project
    And "user@ticketee.com" can tag the "Ticketee" project
    And "user@ticketee.com" has created a ticket for this project:
      | title | description     | tags        |
      | Tag!  | Hey! You're it! | iteration_1 |
    And "user@ticketee.com" has created a ticket for this project:
      | title   | description     | tags        |
      | Tagged! | Hey! I'm it now! | iteration_2 |
    Given I am on the homepage
```

---

[4] This gem is good for a lo-fi solution but shouldn't be used in a high search-volume environment. For that, look into full text search support for your favorite database system.

```
    And I follow "Ticketee" within "#projects"

Scenario: Finding by tag
   When I fill in "Search" with "tag:iteration_1"
   And I press "Search"
   Then I should see "Tag!"
   And I should not see "Tagged!"
```

In the `Background` for this feature, you create two tickets and give them two separate tags: `iteration_1` and `iteration_2`. When you look for tickets tagged with `iteration_1`, you shouldn't see tickets that don't have this tag, such as the one that is only tagged `iteration_2`.

Run this feature using `bin/cucumber features/searching.feature`, and it'll complain because there's no Search field on the page:

```
When I fill in "Search" with "tag:iteration_1"
   cannot fill in ... 'Search'
```

In your feature, the last thing you do before attempting to fill in this Search field is go to the project page for Ticketee. This means that the Search field should be on that page so that your feature and, more important, your users, can fill it out. You add the field above the `ul` element for the tickets list, inside app/views/projects/show.html.erb:

```
<%= form_tag search_project_tickets_path(@project),
             :method => :get do %>
  <%= label_tag "search" %>
  <%= text_field_tag "search", params[:search] %>
  <%= submit_tag "Search" %>
<% end %>
```

You've only used `form_tag` once, back in chapter 8. This method generates a form that's not tied to any particular object, but still gives you the same style of form wrapper that `form_for` does. Inside the `form_tag`, you use the `label_tag` and `text_field_tag` helpers to define a label and input field for the search terms, and use `submit_tag` for a submit button for this form.

The `search_project_tickets_path` method is undefined at the moment, which you see when you run `bundle exec cucumber features/searching.feature`:

```
undefined local variable or method `search_project_tickets_path' ...
```

Notice the pluralized `tickets` in this method. To define non-standard RESTful actions, you've previously used the `member` method inside of config/routes.rb. This has worked fine because you've always acted on a single resource. This time, however, you want to act on a collection of a resource. This means that you use the `collection` method in config/routes.rb instead. To define this method, change these lines in config/routes.rb

```
resources :projects do
  resources :tickets
end
```

into these:

```
resources :projects do
  resources :tickets do
    collection do
      get :search
    end
  end
end
```

The `collection` block here defines that there's a `search` action that may act on a collection of tickets. This `search` action will receive the parameters passed through from the `form_tag` you have set up. When you run your feature again by using `bin/cucumber features/searching.feature`, you see that it's reporting that the `search` action is missing:

```
And I press "Search"
  The action 'search' could not be found for TicketsController
```

Good! The job of this action is to find all the tickets that match the criteria passed in from the form as `params[:search]`, which is what you can use the Searcher gem for.

11.5.2 *Searching by state with Searcher*

The Searcher gem provides the functionality of parsing the labels in a query such as `tag:iteration_1` and determines how to go about finding the records that match the query. Rather than working like Google, where you could put in `iteration_1` and it would know, you have to tell it what `iteration_1` means by prefixing it with `tag:`. You use this query with the `search` method provided by Searcher on a configured model, and it will return only the records that match it:

```
Ticket.search("tag:iteration_1")
```

You'll use this method in the `search` action for `TicketsController` in a bit.

The first port of call to begin to use the Searcher gem is to add it to your Gemfile underneath `gem 'paperclip'`:

```
gem 'searcher'
```

To install this gem, you run `bundle install`. Now for the configuration. Searcher is configured by a `searcher` call in a class, just as associations are set up by using `has_many` and friends. In app/models/ticket.rb directly above[5] the first `belongs_to`, put this code:

```
searcher do
  label :tag, :from => :tags, :field => :name
end
```

---

[5] Code from gems or plugins should go above any code for your models, because it may modify the behavior of the code that follows it.

The :from option tells Searcher what association this label should be searched upon, and the :field option tells it what field to perform a lookup on.

The label method is evaluated internally to Searcher and will result in a by_tag method being defined on your Ticket model, which will be used by the search method if you pass in a query such as tag:iteration_1. This method will perform an SQL join on your tags table, returning only the tickets that are related to a tag with the given name.

With this configuration now in your model, you can define the search action directly underneath the destroy action in TicketsController to use the search method on Ticket:

```
def search
  @tickets = @project.tickets.search(params[:search])
end
```

Assign all the tickets retrieved with the search method to the @tickets variable, which you would render in the search template if you didn't already have a template that was useful for rendering lists of tickets. That template would be the one at app/views/projects/show.html.erb, but to render it you're going to make one small modification.

Currently this template renders all the tickets by using this line to start:

```
<% @project.tickets.each do |ticket| %>
```

This line will iterate through the tickets in the project and do whatever is inside the block for each of those tickets. If you were to render this template right now with the search action, it would still return all tickets. You can get around this by changing the line in the template to read

```
<% @tickets.each do |ticket| %>
```

With this change, you break the ProjectsController's show action, because the @tickets variable is not defined there. You can see the error you would get when you run bin/cucumber features/viewing_tickets.feature:

```
You have a nil object when you didn't expect it!
You might have expected an instance of Array.
The error occurred while evaluating nil.each
```

To fix this error, you set up the @tickets variable inside the show action of Projects-Controller, which you should place directly under the definition for the index action:

```
def show
  @tickets = @project.tickets
end
```

When you re-run bin/cucumber features/viewing_tickets.feature, you see that it now passes once again:

```
1 scenario (1 passed)
23 steps (23 passed)
```

Great! With the insurance that you're not going to break anything now, you can render the app/views/projects/show.html.erb template in the search action of Tickets-Controller by putting this line at the bottom of the action:

```
render "projects/show"
```

By rendering this template, you show a similar page to ProjectsController#show, but this time it will only have the tickets for the given tag. When you run your "Searching" feature using bin/cucumber features/searching.feature, you see that it all passes now:

```
1 scenario (1 passed)
13 steps (13 passed)
```

With this feature, users will be able to specify a search query such as tag:iteration_1 to return all tickets that have that given tag. You prevented one breaking change by catching it as it was happening, but how about the rest of the test suite? Let's find out by running rake cucumber:ok spec. You should see this result:

```
56 scenarios (57 passed)
632 steps (632 passed)
# and
39 examples, 0 failures, 19 pending
```

Great! Let's commit this change:

```
git add .
git commit -m "Added label-based searching for tags using Searcher"
git push
```

Now that you have tag-based searching, why don't you spend a little bit of extra time letting your users search by state as well? This way, they'll be able to perform actions such as finding all remaining open tickets in the tag iteration_1 by using the search term state:open tag:iteration_1. It's easy to implement.

11.5.3 *Searching by state*

Implementing searching for a state is incredibly easy now that you have the Searcher plugin set up and have the search feature in place. As you did with searching for a tag, you'll test this behavior in the "Searching" feature. But first, you need to set up your tickets to have states. Let's change the steps in the Background in this feature that set up your two tickets to now specify states for the tickets:

```
And "user@ticketee.com" has created a ticket for this project:
  | title | description    | tags        | state |
  | Tag!  | Hey! You're it! | iteration_1 | Open  |
And "user@ticketee.com" has created a ticket for this project:
  | title   | description   | tags        | state  |
  | Tagged! | Hey! I'm it now! | iteration_2 | Closed |
```

When you run your feature with bin/cucumber features/searching.feature, you see that you're getting an AssociationTypeMismatch:

```
State(#2178318800) expected, got String(#2151988680)
```

This is because, like the `tags` parameter, you're attempting to set a string value on a field that is actually an association. You must take the `state` key out of the parameters hash inside this step so that it is not parsed as a normal field of a ticket.

To fix this little issue, open features/step_definitions/ticket_steps.rb and change the step definition to be this:

```
Given /^"([^\"]*)" has created a ticket for this project:$/ do |email, table|
  table.hashes.each do |attributes|
    tags = attributes.delete("tags")
    state = attributes.delete("state")
    ticket = @project.tickets.create!(
      attributes.merge!(:user =>
                          User.find_by_email!(email)))
    ticket.state = State.find_or_create_by_name(state) if state
    ticket.tag!(tags) if tags
    ticket.save
  end
end
```

On the second line of this step definition, you remove the `state` key from the attributes hash, using the `delete` method again. On the second-to-last line you assign the ticket's state, but only if there was a state defined from `attributes`. The ticket would be saved if you had specified a tag in the attributes, but if you didn't then you need to call `save` again, as you do on the final line of this step definition.

With all the `Background` fiddling done, you can add a scenario that searches for tickets with a given state. It goes like this:

```
Scenario: Finding by state
  When I fill in "Search" with "state:Open"
  And I press "Search"
  Then I should see "Tag!"
  And I should not see "Tagged!"
```

This should show any ticket with the `open` state, and hide all other tickets. When you run this feature with `bin/cucumber features/searching.feature`, you see that this is not the case. It can still see the `Tagged!` ticket:

```
And I should not see "Tagged!"
  Failed assertion, no message given. (MiniTest::Assertion)
```

When a user performs a search on only an undefined label (such as your `state` label), Searcher will return all the records for that table. This is the behavior you are seeing right now, so it means that you need to define your `state` label in your model. Let's open app/models/ticket.rb and add this line to your `searcher` block:

```
label :state, :from => :state, :field => "name"
```

With this label defined, your newest scenario will now pass when you re-run `bin/cucumber features/searching.feature`:

```
2 scenarios (2 passed)
26 steps (26 passed)
```

You only had to add states to the tickets that were being created and tell Searcher to search by states, and now this feature passes.

That's it for the searching feature! In it, you've added the ability for users to find tickets by a given tag and/or state. It should be mentioned that these queries can be chained, so a user may enter a query such as `tag:iteration_1 state:Open` and it will find all tickets with the `iteration_1` tag and the `Open` state.

As per usual, commit your changes because you're done with this feature. But also per usual, check to make sure that everything is A-OK by running `rake cucumber :ok spec`:

```
58 scenarios (58 passed)
645 steps (645 passed)
# and
39 examples, 0 failures, 19 pending
```

Brilliant, let's commit:

```
git add .
git commit -m "Users may now search for tickets by state or tag"
git push
```

With searching in place and the ability to add and remove tags, you're almost done with this set of features. The final feature involves changing the tag name rendered in app/views/tags/_tag.html.erb so that when a user clicks it they are shown all tickets for that tag.

11.5.4 *Search, but without the search*

You are now going to change your tag partial to link to the search page for that tag. To test this functionality, you can add another scenario to the bottom of features/searching.feature to test that when a user clicks a ticket's tag, they are only shown tickets for that tag. The new scenario looks pretty much identical to this:

```
Scenario: Clicking a tag goes to search results
  When I follow "Tag!"
  And I follow "iteration_1"
  Then I should see "Tag!"
  And I should not see "Tagged!"
```

When you run this last scenario using `bin/cucumber features/searching.feature :33`, you're told that it cannot find the `iteration_1` link on the page:

```
no link with title, id or text 'iteration_1' found
```

This scenario is successfully navigating to a ticket and then attempting to click a link with the name of the tag, only to not find the tag's name. Therefore, it's up to you to add this functionality to your app. Where you display the names of tags in your application, you need to change them into links that go to pages displaying all tickets for that particular tag. Let's open app/views/tags/_tag.html.erb and change this simple little line

```
<%= tag.name %>
```

into this:

```
<%= link_to tag.name,
      search_project_tickets_path(@ticket.project,
      :search => "tag:#{tag.name}") %>
```

For this `link_to`, you use the `search_project_tickets_path` helper to generate a route to the `search` action in `TicketsController` for the current ticket's project, but then you do something different. After you specify `@ticket.project`, you specify options.

These options are passed in as additional parameters to the route. Your search form passes through the `params[:search]` field, and your `link_to` does the same thing. So you see that when you run `bin/cucumber features/searching.feature :35`, this new scenario will now pass:

```
1 scenario (1 passed)
13 steps (13 passed)
```

This feature allows users to click a tag on a ticket's page to then see all tickets that have that tag. Let's make sure you didn't break anything with this small change by running `rake cucumber:ok spec`. You should see this output:

```
59 scenarios (59 passed)
658 steps (658 passed)
# and
39 examples, 0 failures, 19 pending
```

Great, nothing broke! Let's commit this change:

```
git add .
git commit -m "Users can now click a tag's name to go to
                a page showing all tickets for it"
git push
```

Users are now able to search for tickets based on their state or tag, as well as go to a list of all tickets for a given tag by clicking the tag name that appears on the ticket's page. This is the final feature you needed to implement before you have a good tagging system for your application.

11.6 Summary

In this chapter, we've covered how to use a `has_and_belongs_to_many` association to define a link between tickets and tags. Tickets are able to have more than one tag, but a tag is also able to have more than one ticket assigned to it, and therefore you use this type of association. A `has_and_belongs_to_many` could also be used to associate people and the locations they've been to.[6]

You first wrote the functionality for tagging a ticket when it was created, and then continued by letting users tag a ticket through the comment form as well.

---

[6] Like foursquare does.

Next, we looked at how to remove a tag from the page using the `remove()` function from jQuery with the help of a `js` format template file, which is used specifically for JavaScript requests. This file allowed you to execute JavaScript code when a background asynchronous request completes, and you used it to remove the tag from the page.

You saw how to use the Searcher gem to implement label-based searching for not only tags, but states as well. Usually you would implement some sort of help page that would demonstrate to the users how to use the search box, but that's another exercise for you.

Your final feature, based on the previous feature, allowed users to click a tag name and view all the tickets for that tag, and also showed how you can limit the scope of a resource without using nested resources.

In chapter 12, we'll look at how you can send emails to your users using Action-Mailer. You'll use these emails to notify new users of new tickets in their project, state transitions, and new comments.

Sending email 12

This chapter covers

- Sending email with Action Mailer and the `mail` gem
- Subscribing via email to specific events within the system
- Connecting to a real-world email server to send emails
- Receiving emails using Action Mailer

In the previous chapter, you implemented tagging for your application, which allows users to easily categorize and search for tickets.

In this chapter, you'll begin to send emails to your users. When a user signs up to Ticketee, they use their email address as a way for the system to uniquely identify them. You then verify that the address is valid by sending the user a confirmation email. With a user's validated email address, you're able to send them updates for important events in the system, such as a ticket being updated.

Back in chapter 6, you changed a setting for the authentication engine Devise that would send a confirmation email to a new user when they signed up. To test this setting, you used a gem called email_spec, which only tested that the emails were delivered in a test environment, and not in the real world. This is how Action Mailer (the Rails component responsible for email) acts[1] during a test environment.

---

[1] It defaults to not truly sending out the emails, but rather keeping track of them in a variable that you can access by using `ActionMailer::Base.deliveries`, or by using the methods found in `email_spec`.

Before you go about configuring your application to send emails into the real world, you'll add two more features to Ticketee. The first feature automatically subscribes a user to a watchers list whenever that user creates a ticket. Every time this ticket is updated by another user, the creator of the ticket should receive an email. This is helpful, because it allows users to keep up-to-date with the tickets that they have created. The second feature will allow users to add themselves to or remove themselves from the watching list for a given ticket.

With these features in place, all users who are watching a ticket will be notified via email that a comment has been posted to the ticket, what that comment was, and any state change that took place. This email message will additionally contain a link to the ticket and a link to unsubscribe from further notifications regarding the ticket. If a user posts a comment to a ticket and they're not watching it, then they will automatically begin to watch it. They can unsubscribe later if they wish by following the unsubscribe link in the email. Email is a tried-and-true solution to receiving notifications of events such as this.

Once that's all said and done, you'll work on sending emails through an actual server—Gmail—which will test that your application is able to send out emails into the real world and that you're doing everything you can to let your users receive them. Gmail is great for low-volume sending,[2] but if you needed something with a larger capacity, other services such as SendGrid[3] and MailChimp[4] are acceptable alternatives. Although we don't look at how to use large-volume services in this chapter, it's always great to be aware of alternatives, should you ever need to scale up. To check for the emails on a Gmail account, you'll be using the (unofficial)[5] gmail gem.

After spending most of the chapter looking at how to *send* emails, you'll take a look at how to *receive* them using the gmail gem and Action Mailer. When a user receives an email notifying them that a comment has been posted to a ticket, they will be able to send a reply that you can read using both the gmail gem and Action Mailer. You'll also be able to create a new comment from their reply's text. Nifty stuff.

The first thing you're going to do is set up a way for users to receive notifications when a comment is posted to a ticket they've created. Let's dive into creating the feature and code for this functionality now.

12.1 Sending ticket notifications

The next feature of your application will provide users with the ability to watch a ticket. You'll build off this functionality to notify users by email that a ticket has been updated any time somebody posts a comment to it. This email will contain the name of the user who updated the ticket, the comment text, a URL to the ticket, and finally a link to unsubscribe from all future ticket updates.

---

[2] Gmail has a daily send limit of 200 emails.

[3] http://sendgrid.com.

[4] http://mailchimp.com.

[5] As in, not sponsored by Google.

To test all this, you'll use the `email_spec` gem, which you first used back in chapter 6. This gem provides very useful Cucumber steps (and RSpec helpers!) that allow you to easily verify that an email was sent during a test, and you'll be taking full advantage of these steps in the feature that you'll be writing right now.

12.1.1 Automatically watching a ticket

This feature will initially test that a user automatically watches a ticket when they create it. Whenever someone else updates this ticket, the user who created it (and later, anybody else watching the ticket) will receive an email notification. You put this new feature in features/ticket_notifications.feature and fill it with the content from the following listing.

> **Listing 12.1   features/ticket_notifications.feature**

```
Feature: Ticket Notifications
  Background:
    Given there are the following users:
      | email               | password |
      | alice@ticketee.com  | password |
      | bob@ticketee.com    | password |

    Given a clear email queue                       ⟵──❶ Clear received emails

    Given there is a project called "TextMate 2"
    And "alice@ticketee.com" can view the "TextMate 2" project
    And "bob@ticketee.com" can view the "TextMate 2" project
    And "alice@ticketee.com" has created a ticket for this project:
      | title        | description      |
      | Release date | TBA very shortly. |

    Given I am signed in as "bob@ticketee.com"
    Given I am on the homepage

  Scenario: Ticket owner is automatically subscribed to a ticket
    When I follow "TextMate 2"
    And I follow "Release date"
    And I fill in "Text" with "Is it out yet?"
    And I press "Create Comment"

    Then "alice@ticketee.com" should receive an email
    When "alice@ticketee.com" opens the email
    Then they should see "updated the Release date ticket" in the email body
    And they should see "[ticketee] TextMate 2 -
      Release date" in the email subject
    Then they click the first link in the email
    Then I should see "Release date" within "#ticket h2"
```

You use the "Given a clear email queue" step ❶ near the top of your `Background`, which will clear out any received emails from `ActionMailer::Base.deliveries` where the test deliveries are stored. This is important because two confirmation emails get sent out when you create the users, and you don't want your "should receive an email" step in the scenario to retrieve those instead.

You're not really sending emails

These emails aren't actually sent to these addresses in the real world, but captured by Action Mailer and stored in `ActionMailer::Base.deliveries`. You then access these emails using the helpers provided by `email_spec`. There's a setting inside config/environments/test.rb that goes like this:

```
config.action_mailer.delivery_method = :test
```

By default, this setting is set to `:smtp`, which means that Action Mailer will attempt to connect to an SMTP server that is running on localhost. You don't have one of these set up yet, nor will you. Later on, we'll look at how you can send real-world emails from your application using a Gmail account.

The setting in config/environments/test.rb will tell Action Mailer to store all sent emails internally in `ActionMailer::Base.deliveries`.

In this feature, you'll sign in as the second user and create a comment on the ticket that the first user created. After the comment has been created, the ticket creator should receive an email and click the View This Ticket Online Here link that will take them to the updated ticket's page to see the latest comment. When you run this feature using `bin/cucumber features/ticket_notifications.feature`, you see that everything up to the "should receive an email" step passes, because you've already implemented it all:

```
Then "alice@ticketee.com" should receive an email
  expected: 1,
       got: 0 (using ==) ...
```

When bob@ticketee.com updates the ticket, alice@ticketee.com doesn't receive an email, yet. That's why you wrote the feature: so you can test the behavior that you're about to create!

To make alice@ticketee.com receive an email, you're going to use what's known as an *observer.*

12.1.2 Using observers

An observer is a class that sits outside the model, watching it for specific actions such as a save to the database. If new instances of the model are created, then the `before_create` and `after_create` methods in the observer will be called. Observers are handy if you have complex logic for your callbacks, or for sending out email. Hey, isn't that what you want to do? Indeed it is!

In this instance, your observer will be called `CommentObserver`. It's named like that because it will observe the `Comment` model. Observers watch a model for specific changes and allow you to implement callback-like methods in them to order your application to do something when an action takes place in the model. Although you could use a callback in a model, abstracting out code such as this to an observer is much better because it can lead to reduced code clutter in the model.

Let's now create a new folder at app/observers so that you can also reduce clutter in the app/models folder. All the files inside the app directory are added to the load path, so they will be require'able by your application. Inside the app/observers folder you create a new file called comment_observer.rb that will hold the code for the observant observer. In this file, put this:

```
class CommentObserver < ActiveRecord::Observer
  def after_create(comment)
    (comment.ticket.watchers - [comment.user]).each do |user|
      Notifier.comment_updated(comment, user).deliver
    end
  end
end
```

This defines the observer that watches the Comment model and defines a method that will be called after a new Comment is saved to the database, more commonly known as the after_create callback.

At the top of the after_create method, you get the list of watchers for a ticket and remove the user who has just made the comment from that list, because they shouldn't receive an email for a comment they just created!

The Notifier referenced inside the after_create is something you'll create in a little while. Consider it similar to an Active Record object, but for handling emails instead. The comment_updated method will build an email for each of the users watching this ticket, and deliver will send it out.

There's a little bit of configuration you must do before this observer is used, however. You must open config/application.rb and put this line inside the Ticketee ::Application class definition:

```
config.active_record.observers = :comment_observer
```

By calling this method, you are telling Rails to load the CommentObserver class, which it will find without your help, because Rails will infer the name of the observer from the symbol passed in. When you run bin/cucumber features/ticket_notifications .feature, you're told this:

```
And I press "Create Comment"
  undefined method `watchers' for #<Ticket:0x...> (NoMethodError)
```

In this after_create method in your observer, you're calling the watchers method to get at the watchers for this ticket. It's failing because you haven't defined this association yet, so let's go ahead and do that now.

12.1.3 *Defining the watchers association*

The watchers method should return a collection of users who are watching a ticket, including (by default) the user who has created the ticket in the first place, so that in your feature alice@ticketee.com receives the email triggered by bob@ticketee.com's comment.

Here you must do two things: define the watchers association and add the ticket owner to the watchers list when the ticket is created.

You use another has_and_belongs_to_many association to define the watchers collection, this time in your Ticket model. To define it, put this code inside the Ticket model, along with the other has_and_belongs_to_many for tags:

```
has_and_belongs_to_many :watchers, :join_table => "ticket_watchers",
                                   :class_name => "User"
```

Here you pass the :join_table option to specify a custom table name for your has_and_belongs_to_many. If you didn't do this, then the table name would be inferred by Rails to be ticket_users, which doesn't really explain the *purpose* of this table as much as ticket_watchers does. You pass another option too, :class_name, which tells your model that the objects from this association are User objects. If you left this option out, Active Record would imply that you wanted the Watcher class instead, which doesn't exist.

You can create a migration that can be used to create this table by using this command:

```
rails g migration create_ticket_watchers_table
```

Unfortunately, the migration won't read your mind in this instance, so you need to open it and change it to resemble the following listing.

Listing 12.2   db/migrate/[timestamp]_create_ticket_watchers_table.rb

```
class CreateTicketWatchersTable < ActiveRecord::Migration
  def change
    create_table :ticket_watchers, :id => false do |t|
      t.integer :user_id, :ticket_id
    end
  end
end
```

Remember: you need to specify the id option here so that your join table doesn't have a primary key.

Let's save and then run this file using rake db:migrate, and let's not forget to run rake db:test:prepare either.

Now that you have your watchers method defined, you need to add the user who creates a ticket to the list of watchers for that ticket. You can do this by using an after_create callback on your Ticket model like this:

```
after_create :creator_watches_me
```

To define the creator_watches_me method, you put the following code at the bottom of the Ticket class definition:

```
private
  def creator_watches_me
    self.watchers << user
  end
```

Now that you have the user who created the ticket watching it, your `CommentObserver` will have something to act on. Let's see what happens when you run `bin/cucumber features/ticket_notifications.feature`:

```
And I press "Create Comment"
  uninitialized constant CommentObserver::Notifier (NameError)
```

This time, your feature is failing because it can't find the constant `Notifier`, which is actually going to be the class that you use to send out the notifications of new activity to your users. To create this class, you'll use Action Mailer.

12.1.4 Introducing Action Mailer

You need to define the `Notifier` mailer to send out ticket-update notifications using your fresh-out-of-the-oven `CommentObserver`'s `after_create` method. You can do this by running the `mailer` generator.

A *mailer* is a class defined for sending out emails. To define your mailer, you run this command:

```
rails g mailer notifier
```

When running this command, you see this output:

```
create  app/mailers/notifier.rb
invoke  erb
create    app/views/notifier
invoke  rspec
create    spec/mailers/notifier_spec.rb
```

The first thing the command generates is the `Notifier` class itself, defining it in a new file at app/mailers/notifier.rb. This is done to keep the models and mailers separate. In previous versions of Rails, mailers used to live in the app/models directory, which led to clutter. By separating mailers out into their own folder, the codebase becomes easier to manage. Inside this class, you define (as methods) your different notifications that you'll send out, beginning with the comment notification. You'll get to that in just a minute.

The second thing that is generated is the app/views/notifier directory, which is used to store all the templates for your emails. The methods in the `Notifier` class will correspond to each of the files in this directory.

The final thing that is generated is the spec/mailers/notifier_spec.rb, which you won't use because you've got your feature testing this notifier anyway.

In app/mailers/notifier.rb you see this code:

```
class Notifier < ActionMailer::Base
  default from: "from@example.com"
end
```

`ActionMailer::Base` defines helpful methods such as the `default` one, which you can use to send out your emails.[6] The `default` method here configures default options for

---

[6] Action Mailer had a revamp with Rails 3, switching to be based on the new `mail` gem rather than the old `tmail` gem. `mail`'s syntax is much nicer and won't crash when it parses a spam email, unlike `tmail`.

this mailer and will set the "from" address on all emails to be the one specified. Let's change this to be ticketee@gmail.com.

Now that you have the `Notifier` class defined, what happens when you run your feature? Let's run it using `bin/cucumber features/ticket_notifications.feature` and find out:

```
undefined method `comment_updated' for Notifier:Class (NoMethodError)
  ./app/observers/comment_observer.rb:3:in `after_create'
```

In this class, you need to define the `comment_updated` method, which will build an email to send out when a comment is updated. This method needs to get the email address for all the watchers for `comment`'s ticket and send an email to each of them. To do this, you can define the method like this:

```
def comment_updated(comment, user)
  @comment = comment
  @user = user
  mail(:to => user.email,
      :subject => "[ticketee] #{comment.ticket.project.name} -
    #{comment.ticket.title}")
end
```

Even though you're defining this as an instance method (the error complains about a *class* method), the `comment_updated` method is truly the method that is used by Action Mailer to set up your email. This is a little bit of magic performed by Action Mailer for your benefit.[7]

When this method is called, it will attempt to render a plain-text template for the email, which should be found at app/views/notifier/comment_updated.text.erb. You'll define this template after you've got the method working. You define a `@comment` instance variable as the first line of your method so that the object in `comment` will be available to your template.

You use the `mail` method to generate a new email, passing it a hash containing `to` and `subject` keys, which define where the email goes to as well as the subject for the email.

When you run `bin/cucumber features/ticket_notifications.feature`, you see that the user now receives an email and therefore is able to open it, but the content you're looking for is not there:

```
Then "alice@ticketee.com" should receive an email
When "alice@ticketee.com" opens the email
Then they should see "updated the Release date ticket" in the email body
  expected "" to include "updated the Release date ticket" ...
```

But why is this not seeing the content? Because you don't have a template set up just at the moment! It's good to know at this point that if you ever wanted to debug an email's content, there's a "Then show me the page" inspired step that you can use called "Then save and open current email." Let's add this on a new line right before

---

[7] By calling the method on the class, it's caught by `method_missing`, which initializes a new instance of this class and then eventually ends up calling your `comment_update` method.

the email body checking line in your scenario and rerun your feature. You should see the following:

```
Date: [date]
From: ticketee@gmail.com
To: alice@ticketee.com
Message-ID: [message_id]@[you].mail
Mime-Version: 1.0
Content-Type: text/plain;
 charset=UTF-8
Content-Transfer-Encoding: 7bit
```

This is a raw version of the email that alice@ticketee.com will receive when bob@ticketee.com updates the ticket. As you can see from this raw version, there's nothing else to this email, and therefore there's no content that will be displayed. To make this final step pass, you must define some content for your email, which you can do by defining a template.

12.1.5 *An Action Mailer template*

Templates for Action Mailer classes go in app/views because they serve an identical purpose as the controller views: they display a final, dynamic result to the users. Once you have this template in place, the plain-text email a user receives will look like figure 12.1.

As shown in the figure, you need to mention who updated the ticket, what they updated it with, and provide a link to the ticket. Let's put the template for your comment_updated method at app/views/notifier/comment_updated.text.erb, as shown in the following listing.

> **Listing 12.3 app/views/notifier/comment_updated.text.erb**

```
Hello!

<%= @comment.user %> has just updated the
<%= @comment.ticket.title %> ticket for
<%= @comment.ticket.project.name %>. They wrote:

<%= @comment.text %>

You can view this ticket on line by going to:
<%= project_ticket_url(@comment.ticket.project, @comment.ticket) %>
```

Wait, hold on! text.erb? Yes! This is the template for the plain-text version of this email, after all. Remember, the format of a view in Rails is the first part of the file extension, with the latter part being the actual file type. Because you're sending a text-only email, you use the text format here. A little further down the email road, you'll look at how you can send out HTML emails too.

> ☆ **Ticketee to me**
>
> Hello.
>
> alice@ticketee.com has just updated the Release date ticket for TextMate 2. They wrote:
>
> Posting a comment!

Figure 12.1
Your first email

The template is the final part for your feature: yay! When you run `bin/cucumber features/ticket_notifications.feature`, you see that it's now all passing:

```
1 scenario (1 passed)
18 steps (18 passed)
```

When the email is opened for this final time, you see that it has the content you're looking for:

```
Hello!

bob@ticketee.com has just updated the Release date ticket for TextMate 2.
➥They wrote:

Is it out yet?

You can view this ticket online by going to:
➥http://localhost:3000/projects/1/tickets/1
```

You've done quite a lot to get this little simple feature to pass.

In the beginning you created an *observer* called `CommentObserver`, which watches the `Comment` model for any specific changes. You defined an `after_create` method on this, which took the comment object that was being updated and then called `Notifier.comment_updated`, passing along the `comment` object.

`Notifier` is an Action Mailer class that is responsible for sending out emails to the users of your application, and in this file you defined the `comment_updated` method called in your `CommentObserver` and set the `recipients` up to use the `comment` object's related ticket watchers.

To define the `watchers` method, you used a `has_and_belongs_to_many` join table again. Your first experience using these was back in chapter 10, when you linked the `Ticket` and `Tag` models by setting one up on both of them. Back then, you used the `tags_tickets` table to link the two. This is the default naming schema of a `has_and_belongs_to_many` join table in Rails. In the case of your ticket watchers, however, your method was called `watchers`, and so would look for a class called `Watcher` to determine where it should find your watchers. This was incorrect, so you told your association that your join table should be `ticket_watchers` and that the related model was `User`, not `Watcher`. You used the `:join_table` and `:class_name` methods for this.

Finally, you defined the template for the `comment_updated` email at app/views/notifier/comment_updated.html.erb and filled it with the content you're expecting to see, including the link that you click to complete the final step of your scenario.

This scenario completes the first steps of sending email notifications to your users. You should now run all your tests to make sure you didn't break anything by running `rake cucumber:ok spec`:

```
60 scenarios (60 passed)
676 steps (676 passed)
# and
40 examples, 0 failures, 19 pending
```

Great to see everything still passing! You've added email ticket notifications to your application, so you should now make a commit saying just that and push it:

```
git add .
git commit -m "Add email ticket notifications"
git push
```

Now that you've got your application sending plain-text emails, let's bring it into the 21st century by getting it to send out HTML emails as well.

12.1.6 *Delivering HTML emails*

Emails can have multiple parts associated with them, which allows emails to have attachments and different content types. For instance, some email applications don't read HTML emails and will fall back to the text version of the template instead. More modern applications will render the HTML, presenting a prettier, formatted email.

With HTML, you're able to style your emails to include elements such as images, and HTML tags such as the a tag. By doing this, you can provide a much better-looking email than the plain-text version, as shown in figure 12.2.

You need to make only a couple of small changes to this email, such as the image at the top and the link that now reads View This Ticket Online Here. You could do more, but this will suit your purposes for now.

Some email clients don't support receiving HTML-only emails. Thankfully, Action Mailer has a solution to this problem. When you send your comment_updated email, it will arrive all in the same message, but that message will contain multiple *parts*. The first part of the email will be the text template that you set up earlier, and the second part will be the new HTML version that you'll code up in just a tad. Modern email clients are smart enough to detect an email such as this, and if they're capable of rendering the HTML version they'll do so; if not they will fall back to the plain-text variant.

To test that this works, you add another couple of steps right after the check of the email body in the scenario inside features/ticket_notifications.feature. These steps will check that you receive an email that contains two parts, with one of them having the content type of text/plain and the other of text/html:

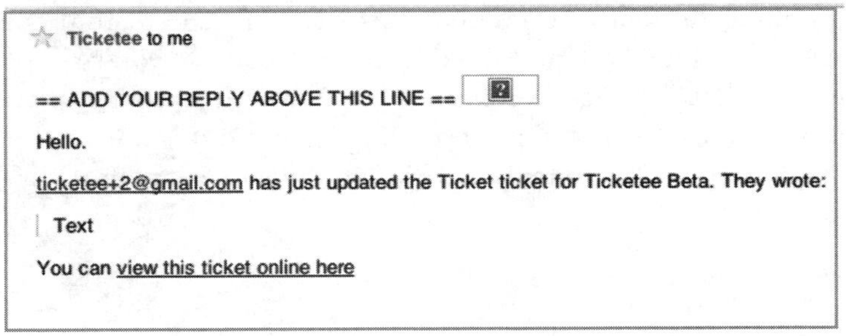

> ☆ Ticketee to me
>
> == ADD YOUR REPLY ABOVE THIS LINE ==
>
> Hello.
>
> ticketee+2@gmail.com has just updated the Ticket ticket for Ticketee Beta. They wrote:
>
> | Text
>
> You can view this ticket online here

**Figure 12.2
A better-looking email**

```
Then they should see "updated the Release date ticket" in the email body
And the email should contain 2 parts
And there should be a part with content type "text/plain"
And there should be a part with content type "text/html"
```

When you run this feature with bin/cucumber features/ticket_notifications .feature, you're notified that the two steps you've just used are undefined:

```
Then /^the email should contain two parts$/ do
  pending # express the regexp above with the code you wish you had
end
```

```
Then /^there should be a part with content type "([^"]*)"$/ do | arg1 |
  pending # express the regexp above with the code you wish you had
end
```

The email_spec gem doesn't provide any steps for this, so you must craft your own. The gem does provide some helper methods that you can use. You should define these steps in a file separate from features/step_definitions/email_steps.rb, because the next time you run the email_spec generator, it will overwrite this file. Let's instead put them in features/step_definitions/app_email_steps.rb and define them like this:

```
Then /^the email should contain (\d+) parts$/ do |num|
  current_email.parts.size.should eql(num.to_i)
end
```

```
Then /^there should be a part with content type "([^"]*)"$/
    do |content_type |
  current_email.parts.detect do |p|
    p.content_type == content_type
  end.should_not be_nil
end
```

In the first step here, the current_email method comes from email_spec and represents the currently opened email. You open this email with the "Then alice@ticketee .com opens the email" step in your scenario. This object is a Mail::Message object, which represents an email object. You check in this step that the email contains the number of parts you say it should contain, and convert the num variable to an integer using to_i because it comes in from the step definition as a String object.

In the second step, you iterate through the parts to the email, using detect to return the first part in parts, which matches the condition inside the block you specify. You don't care at this stage what *order* the parts appear in (that's something the different email clients will deal with), but you do care that there's more than one part.

When you run your feature using bin/cucumber features/ticket_notifications .feature, you see that the first of your two newest steps fails:

```
And the email should contain 2 parts

  expected 2
       got 0
```

So your scenario expected to see two parts, but got none. Why not even one? Well, the normal flavor of emails don't come with multiple parts, because the text is part of the message itself. For your multipart emails, the text and HTML versions will be split into two separate parts.

Defining a HTML version of your email is very easy. All you have to do is create another file that begins with `comment_updated` inside of app/views/notifier, and Action Mailer will automatically detect that you have a multipart message. If you use the `html` format in your template's filename, Action Mailer will do some more automatic detection and work out that the parsed content of this file should be sent as `text/html`. Inside of this new file you want to put the content from the following listing.

Listing 12.4   app/views/notifier/comment_updated.html.erb

```erb
<img src='http://ticketeeapp.com/images/logo.png' alt='Ticketee' />

<p>
  Hello.
</p>

<p>
  <%= @comment.user %> has just updated the
  <%= @comment.ticket.title %> ticket for
  <%= @comment.ticket.project.name %>. They wrote:</p>

<blockquote><%= @comment.text %></blockquote>

<p>
  You can <%= link_to "view this ticket online here",
    project_ticket_url(@comment.ticket.project, @comment.ticket) %>
</p>
```

Now that you have an HTML template, Action Mailer will send a multipart email containing both the HTML and text version of the mail without having to configure anything, which is always nice!

When you run `bin/cucumber features/ticket_notifications.feature`, you see that the feature fails:

```
Then they click the first link in the email
  No route matches [GET] "/images/logo.png'" ...
```

This is because the scenario is attempting to click the first link it comes across, which is the link to the image at the top of the HTML version of your email. What you really want it to do is to click the View This Ticket Online Here link, and you can make it do just that by replacing this line in the scenario

```
Then they click the first link in the email
```

with this one:

```
Then they follow "view this ticket online here" in the email
```

This will now make the scenario click the correct link. Let's re-run `bin/cucumber features/ticket_notifications.feature` to see that this feature is now passing:

```
1 scenario (1 passed)
21 steps (21 passed)
```

Great, so now your users will receive multipart emails; their email clients should attempt to render the HTML part of these first and, if they can't, then fall back to the text part. Such is the beauty of email these days.

Now is the time to commit these changes, but not before running your tests by running rake cucumber:ok spec:

```
60 scenarios (60 passed)
679 steps (679 passed)
# and
40 examples, 0 failures, 20 pending
```

Awesome! Everything is still going. Commit this change:

```
git add .
git commit -m "Send HTML ticket notification emails"
git push
```

Your ticket notification email will be sent out with two parts: an HTML version and a text version. This provides a way for email applications of all ages to render your email. Hopefully, more people will see the HTML version than the text version.

You learned how to generate a mailer and create a mailer method to it, and now you're going to move into how you can let people subscribe to receive these emails. You're currently only subscribing the ticket's author to the list of watchers associated with this ticket, but other people may also wish to be notified of ticket updates. You can do this in two separate ways: through a watch button and through automatic subscription.

12.2 Subscribing to updates

You'll provide other users with two ways to stay informed of ticket updates. The first will be very similar to the automatic subscription of a user when they create the ticket, but this time you'll automatically subscribe users who *comment* on a ticket. You'll reuse the same code that you used in the previous section to achieve this, but not in the way you might think.

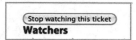

Figure 12.3   The watch button

The second will be a watch button on the ticket page, which will display either Watch This Ticket or Stop Watching This Ticket, depending on if the user is watching the ticket or not, as shown in figure 12.3.

We'll first look at implementing the automatic subscription when a user posts a comment to a ticket.

12.2.1 Testing comment subscription

You'll now implement a feature to make users automatically watch a ticket when they create a comment on it. This is useful because your users will want to keep up-to-date with tickets that they have commented on. Later on, you'll implement a way for these users to opt out.

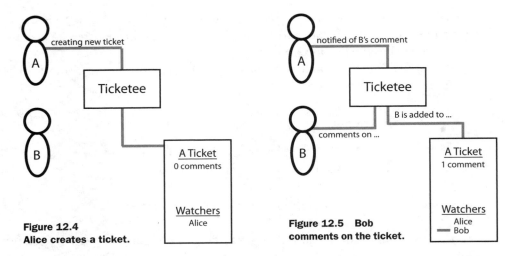

**Figure 12.4
Alice creates a ticket.**

**Figure 12.5   Bob
comments on the ticket.**

To automatically subscribe a user to a ticket of a new comment, use an `after_create`, just as you did in the `Ticket` model for only the author of that ticket. But first, you need to ensure that this works!

You'll add another scenario to the "Ticket notifications" feature, but first let's consider the current flow. A couple of diagrams help explain this process.

First, let's look at figure 12.4. Here, alice@ticketee.com creates a ticket that will automatically subscribe her to be notified of any comments posted to it.

Next, figure 12.5. Then bob@ticketee.com comes along and leaves a comment on the ticket, which should subscribe bob@ticketee.com to these ticket updates. This is the feature that you'll code in a short while. After Bob has commented on the ticket, Alice receives a notification telling her just that. Now that Bob is subscribed to the ticket, he should receive comment notifications every time somebody else—such as Alice—comments on the ticket, as shown in figure 12.6.

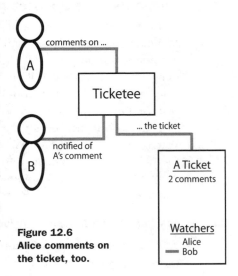

**Figure 12.6
Alice comments on
the ticket, too.**

In this case, alice@ticketee.com shouldn't receive a notification about a comment if she's the one posting it! With the scenario explained, you can write it in Cucumber-form at the bottom of the "Ticket notifications" feature, as shown in the following listing:

Listing 12.5 features/ticket_notifications.feature

```
Scenario: Comment authors are automatically subscribed to a ticket
  When I follow "TextMate 2"
  And I follow "Release date"
  And I fill in "Text" with "Is it out yet?"
  And I press "Create Comment"
  Then I should see "Comment has been created."
  When I follow "Sign out"

  Given a clear email queue

  Given I am signed in as "alice@ticketee.com"
  When I follow "TextMate 2"
  And I follow "Release date"
  And I fill in "Text" with "Not yet!"
  And I press "Create Comment"
  Then I should see "Comment has been created."
  Then "bob@ticketee.com" should receive an email
  Then "alice@ticketee.com" should have no emails
```

In this scenario, you're already logged in as bob@ticketee.com (courtesy of the Background). With Bob, you create a comment on the "Release date" ticket, check that alice@ticketee.com receives an email, and then sign out. Then you clear the email queue to ensure that alice@ticketee.com receives no emails after this point. You sign in as alice@ticketee.com and create a comment, which should trigger an email to be sent to bob@ticketee.com, but not to alice@ticketee.com. When you run this scenario using `bin/cucumber features/ticket_notifications.feature:36`, you see that Bob never receives an email:

```
expected: 1,
got: 0 (using ==) (RSpec::Expectations::ExpectationNotMetError)
...
features/ticket_notifications.feature:54
```

This is failing on the step that checks if bob@ticketee.com has an email. You can therefore determine that bob@ticketee.com isn't subscribed to receive comment update notifications as he should have been when he posted a comment. You need to add any commenter to the watchers list when they post a comment so that they're notified of ticket updates.

12.2.2 Automatically adding a user to a watchlist

To keep users up to date with tickets, you'll automatically add them to the `watchers` list for that ticket when they post a comment. You currently do this when people create a new ticket, and so you can apply the same logic to adding them to the list when they create a comment.

You can define another `after_create` callback in the `Comment` model by using this line:

```
after_create :creator_watches_ticket
```

Next, you need to define the method that this callback calls, which you can do by placing this code at the bottom of your `Comment` model:

```
def creator_watches_ticket
  ticket.watchers << user
end
```

By using the `tickets` association, you can add the creator of this comment to the watchers for this ticket. This should mean that when a comment is posted to this ticket, any user who has posted a comment previously, and not only the ticket creator, will receive an email.

You can see if this is the case when you run this scenario again using `bin/cucumber features/ticket_notifications.feature:36`. You see that Bob is now receiving an email and the entire scenario is passing:

```
1 scenario (1 passed)
23 steps (23 passed)
```

Perfect! Now users who comment on tickets are added to the watchers list automatically *and* the user who posts the comment isn't notified if they are already on that list.

Did you break anything by implementing this change? Let's have a look by running `rake cucumber:ok spec`. You should have this:

```
61 scenarios (61 passed)
702 steps (702 passed)
# and
40 examples, 0 failures, 20 pending
```

Every test that you have thrown at this application is still passing, which is a great thing to see. Let's commit this change:

```
git add .
git commit -m "Users are now automatically subscribed
              to a ticket when they comment on it"
```

You now have automatic subscription for ticket notifications when a user creates a ticket or posts a comment to one, but currently there is no way to switch notifications *off*. To implement this, you'll add a Stop Watching This Ticket button that, when clicked, will remove the user from the list of watchers for that ticket.

12.2.3 *Unsubscribing from ticket notifications*

You'll add a button to the ticket page to unsubscribe users from future ticket notifications. When you're done here, the ticket page will look like figure 12.7.

Along with implementing the ability to turn *off* the notifications by clicking this button, you'll also add a way for the users to turn *on* notifications, using what will effectively be the same button with a different label. This button will toggle users' watching status, which will allow them to subscribe to ticket notifications without 1) creating their own ticket or 2) posting a comment.

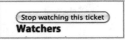

Figure 12.7 The "stop watching" button

You implement the on and off functionality simultaneously by writing a new feature in a new file at features/watching_tickets.feature. Let's start with the code from the following listing.

Listing 12.6   features/watching_tickets.feature

```
Feature: Watching tickets
  In order to keep up to date with tickets
  As a user
  I want to choose to subscribe to their updates

Background:
  Given there are the following users:
    | email             | password |
    | user@ticketee.com | password |
  Given there is a project called "TextMate 2"
  And "user@ticketee.com" can view the "TextMate 2" project
  And "user@ticketee.com" has created a ticket for this project:
    | title        | description      |
    | Release date | TBA very shortly. |

  Given I am signed in as "user@ticketee.com"
  Given I am on the homepage
```

In this example, you create a single user, a project, and a ticket. Because this user created the ticket, they're automatically subscribed to watching this ticket and therefore they should see the Stop Watching This Ticket button on the ticket page. You test this by writing the scenario from the following listing underneath your `Background`.

Listing 12.7   features/watching_tickets.feature

```
Scenario: Ticket watch toggling
  When I follow "TextMate 2"
  And I follow "Release date"
  Then I should see "user@ticketee.com" within "#watchers"
  And I press "Stop watching this ticket"
  Then I should see "You are no longer watching this ticket"
  And I should not see "user@ticketee.com" within "#watchers"
```

To begin to watch a ticket again, all the user has to do is click the Watch This Ticket button, which you can also test by adding the following code to this scenario:

```
When I press "Watch this ticket"
Then I should see "You are now watching this ticket"
And I should see "user@ticketee.com" within "#watchers"
```

See? *That's* how you test the watching/not watching function simultaneously! You don't need to post a comment and test that a user is truly watching this ticket; you can instead check to see if a user's name appears in a list of all the watchers on the right side of the ticket page, which will look like figure 12.8.

Figure 12.8   Who's watching

As usual, you see what you need to code *right now* to get your feature on the road to passing by running `bin/cucumber features/waching.feature`. You see that it's actually this watchers list, indicated by Capybara telling you that it can't find that element:

```
Then I should see "user@ticketee.com" within "#watchers"
  Unable to find css "#watchers" (Capybara::ElementNotFound)
```

To get this feature to continue, you're going to need this element! You can add it to app/views/tickets/show.html.erb underneath the `</div>` tag for `<div id='ticket'>` by using the code from the following listing.

Listing 12.8 app/views/tickets/show.html.erb

```
<div id='watchers'>
  <h4>Watchers</h4>
  <ul>
   <% @ticket.watchers.each do |watcher| %>
      <li><%= watcher %></li>
    <% end %>
  </ul>
</div>
```

You've created another `div` with the `id` attribute set to `watchers`, which is the element that your scenario looks for. In this `div` you iterate through all the watchers of the ticket and output a `li` tag for each of them, which will output a list of watchers when wrapped in a `ul` tag.

When you have this element and you run your feature again with `bin/cucumber features/watching_tickets.feature`, you see that your feature gets one step closer to passing by locating user@ticketee.com in the #watchers element, but it now can't find the Stop Watching This Ticket button:

```
Then I should see "user@ticketee.com" within "#watchers"
  And I press "Stop watching this ticket"
  no button with value or id or text 'Stop watching this ticket'
```

This button will toggle the watching status of the ticket of the current user, and the text will differ depending on if the user is or isn't watching this ticket. In both cases, however, the button will go to the same action. To get this next scenario to pass, you add the button to the `div#watchers` element you just created by using a helper, changing the first few lines of the element to this:

```
<div id='watchers'>
  <%= toggle_watching_button %>
  <h4>Watchers</h4>
```

This `toggle_watching_button` helper will only appear in views for the `Tickets-Controller`, and so you should put the method definition in app/helpers/tickets_helper.rb inside the `TicketsHelper` module, using the code from the following listing to define the method.

Listing 12.9   app/helpers/tickets_helper.rb

```ruby
def toggle_watching_button
  text = if @ticket.watchers.include?(current_user)
    "Stop watching this ticket"
  else
    "Watch this ticket"
  end
  button_to(text, watch_project_ticket_path(@ticket.project, @ticket))
end
```

On the final line of this method, you use a new method: button_to. This method works in a similar fashion as link_to does, providing a user with an element to click to go somewhere. In this case, the element is a button wrapped in a form that points to the specified action. When the user clicks the button, it submits this form through a POST request, with the only parameter passed through being params[:commit], which contains the text of the button.

Inside the button_to, you use a new route helper that you haven't defined yet. When you run bin/cucumber features/watching_tickets.feature, it will complain that this method is undefined when it tries to render the app/views/tickets/ show.html.erb page:

```
And I follow "Release date"
  undefined method `watch_project_ticket_path' for ...
```

This route helper points to a specific action on a project's ticket. You can define it in config/routes.rb inside the resources :tickets block, which itself is nested inside the resources :projects block, as shown in the following listing.

Listing 12.10   config/routes.rb

```ruby
resources :projects do
  resources :tickets do
    collection do
      get :search
    end

    member do                    ◁——❶ Define member route
      post :watch
    end
  end
end
```

The button_to's purpose is to toggle the watch status of a single ticket, meaning you want to define a member route ❶ for your ticket resource. You put it inside the tickets resource, nested under the projects resource, because for your watch action you want to confirm that the person has permission to view this project. You define the route to the watch action with post because button_to generates a form by default, and a form's HTTP method will default to POST.

When you run your feature again using `bin/cucumber features/watching _tickets.feature`, it will complain now because there is no `watch` action for your button to go to:

```
And I press "Stop watching this ticket"
  The action 'watch' could not be found for TicketsController
```

You're almost done! Defining this `watch` action is the last thing you have to do. This action will add the user who visits it to a specific ticket's watcher list if they aren't already watching it, or remove them if they are. To define this action you open app/ controllers/tickets_controller.rb and use the code found in the following listing.

Listing 12.11   app/controllers/tickets_controller.rb

```
def watch
  if @ticket.watchers.exists?(current_user)
    @ticket.watchers -= [current_user]
    flash[:notice] = "You are no longer watching this ticket."
  else
    @ticket.watchers << current_user
    flash[:notice] = "You are now watching this ticket."
  end

  redirect_to project_ticket_path(@ticket.project, @ticket)
end
```

The first thing to notice about this method is that you don't define the `@ticket` variable before you use it on the first line of this method. This is because you can add this action to the list of actions that the `before_filter :find_ticket` runs on by changing these lines at the top of your controller

```
before_filter :find_ticket,
              :only => [:show,
                        :edit,
                        :update,
                        :destroy]
```

to these lines:

```
before_filter :find_ticket,
              :only => [:show,
                        :edit,
                        :update,
                        :destroy,
                        :watch]
```

In this method you use `exists?`, which will check if the given user is in the list of watchers. If they are, then you use `watchers -=` to remove a watcher from a ticket. If they aren't on the watchers list, you use `watchers <<` to add them to the list of watchers.

The `watch` action now defines the behavior for a user to start and stop watching a ticket by clicking the button above the watchers list. When you run `bin/cucumber features/watching_tickets.feature`, it will pass:

```
1 scenario (1 passed)
15 steps (15 passed)
```

Great! Now you have a way for users to toggle their watch status on any given ticket. Let's make sure that everything is working by running `rake cucumber:ok spec`. You should see the following output:

```
62 scenarios (62 passed)
717 steps (717 passed)
# and
40 examples, 0 failures, 20 pending
```

Everything is still A-OK, which is good to see. Let's commit this change:

```
git add .
git commit -m "Add button so users can toggle
                watching on a ticket"
git push
```

You've now got a way that a user can start or stop watching a ticket. By watching a ticket, a user will receive an email when a comment is posted to the ticket. You're doing great in theoretically testing email, but you haven't yet configured your application to send out emails in the real world. Let's do that now.

12.3 Real-world email

You've just created the beginnings of a way to send email in your application, but there's still a part missing: the SMTP server that receives your mail objects and then sends them out to their recipients. You could spend a lot of time configuring one yourself, but many companies offer a free SMTP service, such as Gmail.[8] You'll use a Gmail account to send out tests of your emails, and you can use Action Mailer to connect to this service.

> **WARNING** You wouldn't use Gmail to send or receive your emails if you were running a much larger application, but rather another web service such as SendGrid. This is because Gmail has a limit of about 200 sent emails a day, and if there are 200 tickets updated in a single day then it's goodbye email cap. Gmail is great for light email usage, but if you want to scale up your usage, SendGrid is one of the best options out there.

Action Mailer has a setting that you can use to set up your SMTP connection:

```
ActionMailer::Base.smtp_settings = {
  :username = "youraccount@example.com",
  :password = "yourpassword"
  ...
}
```

Before you dive into setting this up, you're going to need a feature to ensure that it always works. When you set up your application to send emails in the real world, it may work from the get-go, and you can test it manually by sending out emails in your

---

[8] SendGrid offers one too that you *would* use, but you're going to need to receive emails next, and having a Gmail account will allow you to do that.

application through `rails server`. But how do you ensure that it works all the time? The feature will provide that insurance.

When you're done here, you'll have your application hooked up to Gmail's SMTP server so that you can send emails in the real world, and you'll have a Cucumber feature to ensure that it's never broken.[9] Let's jump into it.

12.3.1 *Testing real-world email*

In this section, you'll create a feature in which you set up Action Mailer to send out emails to Gmail's SMTP service. You'll then update a ticket's comment, which should trigger the emails to be sent to the real world. Finally, you'll check the Gmail account (using the `mail` gem on which Action Mailer is based), to make sure that the email was received. If it wasn't received, then the cause is most likely a configuration problem, such as an invalid password.

Let's write this new feature in a new file called features/gmail.feature a bit at a time. You start with just these few lines:

```
Feature: Gmail
  In order to send real world emails
  As the application
  I want to ensure my configuration is correct

  Background:
    Given there are the following users:
      | email                  | password |
      | alice@ticketee.com     | password |
      | youraccount@example.com | password |

    And Action Mailer delivers via SMTP
```

Here you have the standard feature setup on the first four lines, describing to any interested reader what this feature's purpose is. The final few lines begin your feature's `Background`, defining two users that you'll use and an as-of-yet undefined step. The two users set up here are for setting up the ticket a little later on in your `Background`. The youraccount@example.com should be your actual Gmail account's address[10] for reasons that you'll see later.[11]

The current undefined step on the final line will be used to tell Action Mailer not to capture all emails that are being sent, but rather to send them out through the SMTP configuration that you'll set up in a little while. When you run this feature using `bin/cucumber features/gmail.feature`, you're given the step definition for this step:

```
Given /^Action Mailer delivers via SMTP$/ do
  pending # express the regexp above with the code you wish you had
end
```

---

[9] That is to say, if you run all the tests and they all pass before you commit, then you know that your Gmail connection would be working, too.

[10] And if you don't have one, sign up! It's free and will only take a minute.

[11] We'd use youraccount@gmail.com as the example here, but we don't want to bombard the owner of this actual account with emails!

In this step definition, you need to tell Action Mailer to use SMTP to deliver your emails rather than capture them. You can define this new step definition in features/ step_definitions/app_email_steps.rb like this:

```
Given /^Action Mailer delivers via SMTP$/ do
  ActionMailer::Base.delivery_method = :smtp
end
```

Great! Now Action Mailer will set the delivery_method to :smtp before every scenario in this feature. The side effect of this setting is that it will be set for every scenario that runs after it, not only scenarios in this feature. This is a problem because you don't want every scenario to send email in the real world, only the ones contained in this feature. To make it revert this setting back to :test after every scenario, you can create a new file at features/support/after_hook.rb and put this content inside it:

```
After do
  ActionMailer::Base.delivery_method = :test
end
```

The After method here is provided by Cucumber, and its purpose is to execute any given block after each scenario has finished running. With this code, the setting will be reverted back to :test and you'll only be sending real-world emails in this particular scenario.

Let's continue writing your new feature. You need to set up a project that both alice@ticketee.com and you can see, and create a ticket on that project that is posted by you. In a short while, you'll get Alice to sign in and post a comment to this ticket, which should make an email appear in your inbox. You'll then check this email using the mail gem. Set up the project and ticket with these steps:

```
Given there is a project called "TextMate 2"
And "alice@ticketee.com" can view the "TextMate 2" project
And "youraccount@example.com" can view the "TextMate 2" project
And "youraccount@example.com" has created a ticket for this project:
  | title        | description       |
  | Release date | TBA very shortly. |
```

Here's another place where youraccount@example.com should be substituted with your real Gmail account. In these steps, you set up that alice@ticketee.com and your email both have the "view" permission on the TextMate 2 project. After this, you need a ticket that you've created so that Alice can post a comment to it and you can receive an email notification informing you of what Alice has posted.

Now you can get to the *meat* of your feature: the scenario itself. In this scenario, you want to log in as alice@ticketee.com, visit the "Release date" ticket inside the Text-Mate 2 project, and post a comment to it. After all that's said and done, you need to assert that your youraccount@example.com mailbox has one new message. The code for the scenario should therefore look like in the following listing.

Listing 12.12   features/gmail.feature

```
Scenario: Receiving a real-world email
  Given I am signed in as "alice@ticketee.com"
  Given I am on the homepage
  When I follow "TextMate 2"
  And I follow "Release date"
  And I fill in "Text" with "Posting a comment!"
  And I press "Create Comment"
  Then I should see "Comment has been created."

  When I log into gmail with:
    | username              | password      |
    | youraccount@gmail.com | your_password |
  Then there should be an email from Ticketee in my inbox
```

When you run this feature using bin/cucumber features/gmail.feature, you see that your feature fails when alice@ticketee.com clicks the Create Comment button:

```
And I press "Create Comment"
  Connection refused - connect(2) (Errno::ECONNREFUSED)
  .../net/smtp.rb:551:in `initialize'
```

Remember before how it was mentioned that Action Mailer would (by default) try to connect to an SMTP server running on localhost? That's what is happening here, because when a comment is updated a notification will be sent out. You didn't see this previously because it's only now that you've switched delivery_method to :smtp, You don't have one running locally[12] so it's unable to connect. You can tell that it's now using SMTP, because the first line of the stacktrace points to net/smtp.rb in Ruby's standard library, which is what Action Mailer (by way of Mail) uses to connect to SMTP servers. Therefore, you must change something in order to make this work once more.

12.3.2 *Configuring Action Mailer*

To fix this error, you must tell Action Mailer to connect to your Gmail server so that it has a way to send out emails. You can create a new file in config/initializers that provides Action Mailer with the necessary information it needs. But what would this information be? Well, let's hop on over to Google's "Configuring other mail clients"[13] page, where you'll see the table from figure 12.9.

You're trying to send email, so you want to use the Outgoing Mail section, which tells you to use smtp.gmail.com as the server. You'll connect to it using TLS, so you'll connect on port 587. The account name and password should be the Gmail address and password for your email address. With these settings, create a config/initializers/mail.rb file that looks like the following listing.

---

[12] Unless you've got it set up from some other place that's not this book.
[13] http://mail.google.com/support/bin/answer.py?hl=en&answer=13287.

Incoming Mail (POP3) Server - requires SSL:	`pop.gmail.com` **Use SSL**: Yes **Port**: 995
Outgoing Mail (SMTP) Server - requires TLS or SSL:	`smtp.gmail.com` (use authentication) **Use Authentication**: Yes **Port for TLS/STARTTLS**: 587 **Port for SSL**: 465
Account Name:	your full email address (including `@gmail.com` or `@your_domain.com`)
Email Address:	your email address (`username@gmail.com` or `username@your_domain.com`)
Password:	your Gmail password

Figure 12.9 Configuring other mail clients

Listing 12.13   config/initializers/mail.rb

```ruby
ActionMailer::Base.smtp_settings = {
  :user_name => "youraccount@gmail.com",
  :password => "password",
  :address => "smtp.gmail.com",
  :port => 587,
  :tls => true
}
```

With these settings in this file, you can rerun `bin/cucumber features/gmail.feature` to see that it passes now up to the last two steps, which are undefined:

```
When /^I log into gmail with:$/ do |table|
   # table is a Cucumber::Ast::Table
   pending # express the regexp above with the code you wish you had
end

Then /^there should be an email from Ticketee in my inbox$/ do
   pending # express the regexp above with the code you wish you had
end
```

With these step definitions, you'll be able to connect to Gmail using settings specified in a Cucumber table format and then check for the email, which should be sent by steps earlier in this feature. You need to define these now.

12.3.3 *Connecting to Gmail*

You've now sent the email to the server, but you don't have any steps in place to read these emails from your Gmail account and check that one of the emails is from Ticketee. As you can almost anticipate, there's a gem that can help you with this, called quite simply `gmail`. This gem will let you connect to a Gmail server using the username and password you just used to set up an SMTP connection, and also read the emails for that account. The code it uses looks like this:

```
Gmail.connect(username, password)
```

You'll also use this gem in the next section, when we look at how you can receive emails into your application. It's a pretty neat gem, and it's got a great README, which can be seen at http://github.com/nu7hatch/gmail.

To install this gem, you must first add it to the Gemfile by adding this line inside the group block for development and test, because you only want this gem used in those environments:

```
group :test, :development do
  gem 'gmail'
  ...
end
```

Then you need to run `bundle install` to install this gem so that you can use it. When `bundle install` is finished running, let's open features/step_definitions/app_email _steps.rb and add the "When I log into gmail with..." step by using this code:

```
When /^I log into gmail with:$/ do |table|
   details = table.hashes.first
   @gmail = Gmail.connect(details["username"], details["password"])
 end
```

In this step definition, you take only the first hash from the table (you're only going to be logging into one Gmail account at a time) and then you use the `Gmail.connect` method, provided by the `gmail` gem that you just installed, to start a connection to Gmail's servers using your username and password. By assigning this object to `@gmail`, you can use this connection in future steps to read emails from your Gmail account.

The second step you need to create will do precisely that, using the `@gmail` connection to read all the emails, find the emails that have a subject beginning with `[ticketee]` (there should only be one), and then delete the email after you've read it. The method you can use for this is the `find_and_delete` method, which will find emails matching a specific criteria, read them, and then delete them:

```
Then /^there should be an email from Ticketee in my inbox$/ do
@mails = @gmail.inbox.find(:unread,
            :from => "ticketee@gmail.com") do |mail|
   if mail.subject =~ /^\[ticketee\]/          ◄─① Check email subject

     mail.delete!
     @received_mail = true
   end
  end
  @received_mail.should be_true
end
```

In this step, you use the `@gmail` variable defined in the "log into gmail with" step you just defined. The `find` method here will find emails using the Gmail connection you've opened and then locate all emails from ticketee@gmail.com. The `mail` variable is an instance of the `Mail::Message` class, as are all messages parsed by the mail gem.

If there is an email with a subject that begins with "[ticketee]" ① then you set a `@received_mail` variable to `true`. You use this variable as the final line in this step, because it would only be set to `true` if the latest email's subject was what you were looking for.

When you run your feature using `bin/cucumber features/gmail.feature`, it will now pass:

```
1 scenario (1 passed)
15 steps (15 passed)
```

This feature checks that your real-world SMTP settings are valid by connecting to the real-world SMTP server, sending an email, and then checking that it arrived using `Mail::POP3`. Beautiful! If the password for this account were to change, however, then this feature would break.

Everything should still be working now. You haven't changed anything that would have broken your existing features or specs, but it's still great practice to run them just to make sure. Let's do this by running `rake cucumber:ok spec`. You see the following output:

```
63 scenarios (63 passed)
732 steps (732 passed)
# and
40 examples, 0 failures, 20 pending
```

Indeed, nothing is broken. But if you made a commit now, it would cause potentially private Gmail account details to be committed to the repository. You probably don't want to do this. To prevent this, you should copy config/initializers/mail.rb to config/initializers/mail.rb.example and change the details in it to be placeholders for real details. The same thing should be done for the features/sending_emails.feature feature.

After that, you must tell Git to ignore these files. You can do this by placing their names within a .gitignore file at the root of the Rails application, which is also the root of the Git repository. Create a new file called .gitignore now, and put these two lines in it:

```
config/initializers/mail.rb
features/sending_emails.feature
```

When you run `git add .` and then `git status`, the files with the real values should not appear in the "Changes to be committed" list. If they don't, then you can make a commit and push it:

```
git commit -m "Set up application to connect to Gmail to send emails"
git push
```

You've now got your application sending out emails in the real world using Gmail as the server. With these settings, the emails notifying users that tickets have had new comments posted to them, as well as the confirmation emails sent from Devise for new user signups, will be sent out through Gmail.

You have the *sending* emails part of your application done, but what about if you wanted to let users reply to comments by replying to the email notification they receive in their inbox? That would be cool. To do this, you're going to need to figure out how you can receive emails with Rails.

12.4   *Receiving emails*

You'd now like to add a feature to Ticketee where users can reply to the email notifications for a new comment on a ticket, and by replying create a new comment with their text. Many other applications do this by having an email such as this:

```
== ADD YOUR REPLY ABOVE THIS LINE ==
Bob has just updated the "Due date" ticket for "TextMate 2"
```

Text above the "ADD YOUR REPLY ABOVE THIS LINE" will be parsed out and turned into a new object. In Ticketee, this would be a comment.

In the previous section, you learned how you could connect to a Gmail account to check to see if there was an email that had a subject beginning with "[ticketee]." You can use the same method in order to check for replies to your emails too, but you need to make one small modification.

To determine what ticket and project the reply is directed at, you need to tag the emails in a certain way. The best way to do this is to add the tags to the email addresses themselves, so that an email address with a tag looks like ticketee+tag@gmail.com, where the +tag part of the email is ignored and the email arrives in ticketee @gmail.com's mailbox. For your emails, you'll set a reply-to address such as ticketee +61+23@gmail.com, where the first number is the project ID and the second number is the ticket ID.

You're not going to post comments straight from emails. You need to check to see if the user has permission to view the project where the ticket is, which means that they would be able to create a comment for that ticket too. If they're unable to post a comment to that ticket, you assume the user is trying to do something malicious and just ignore their email.

To parse these emails, you'll be using the `receive` method in an ActionMailer class, which takes an email object and allows you to process it.

A quick summary: you're going to use the `gmail` gem to check for emails in your inbox that are replies to comment notifications and then parse them using Action Mailer into new `Comment` objects. If a user is restricted from viewing a project, then you'll ignore their emails.

First, you want to check that the outgoing email contains the tag on the "from" address, so that when a user replies to it you know what project and ticket they're replying to.

12.4.1   *Setting a reply-to address*

By having a different "from" address set on the outgoing email, you'll be able to determine what project and ticket the user's reply comment should be created on. To ensure that all outgoing emails from the `comment_updated` method in `Notifier` have this set, you're going to write a simple test.

Let's open spec/mailers/notifier_spec.rb and change this whole file to what's shown in the following listing.

Listing 12.14   app/mailers/notifier_spec.rb

```
require "spec_helper"

describe Notifier do
  it "correctly sets the reply-to" do
    comment = Factory(:comment)
    mail = ActionMailer::Base.deliveries.last
    mail.from.should eql(["youraccount+#{comment.project.id}+" +
      "#{comment.ticket.id}@example.com"])
  end
end
```

Here you test that the `from` for the latest email sent out contains the ids of the project and ticket related to the comment you create. With this information contained in the email address, you'll be able to know what project and ticket to create the comment for when a user replies to that email.

When you run this spec using `bin/rspec spec/mailers/notifier_spec.rb`, you see that you need to define the comment factory:

```
No such factory: comment (ArgumentError)
```

Let's define this new factory in factories/comment_factory.rb like this:

```
Factory.define :comment do |comment|
  comment.text "A plain old boring comment."
  comment.ticket { |t| t.association(:ticket) }
  comment.user { |u| u.association(:user) }
end
```

Now when you run `bin/rspec spec/mailers/notifier_spec.rb`, you see that it fails with this error:

```
expected ["ticketee+1+1@gmail.com"]
        got ["ticketee@gmail.com"]
```

Right then! A failing test is a great place to begin, and now you need to fix it. Let's open app/mailers/notifier.rb and add a `:from` option to the `mail` call inside the `comment_updated` method:

```
:from => "Ticketee <youraccount+
#{comment.project.id}+#{comment.ticket_id}@example.com>"
```

This will change the "from" address on emails that go out to your users by tagging the addresses with the project and ticket id. When the user replies to this email, you can use this tag to find the project and ticket that you need to create a new comment on. Let's run `bin/rspec spec/mailers/notifier_spec.rb` again to see it pass:

```
1 example, 0 failures
```

Now you need to work on the actual receiving of replies directed at this tagged address!

12.4.2 *Receiving a reply*

With the correct reply-to set, you can implement the feature responsible for creating new comments from email replies. You create a new class for dealing with incoming email and call it `Receiver`, placing it in app/mailers by running this command:

```
rails g mailer receiver
```

This will generate the mailer you use for receiving email, as well as the RSpec file that you can use to write the tests for the class. To test this particular feature, you use a setup very similar to the spec/notifier_spec.rb test that you just wrote. This test needs to generate a comment and then a reply to the email you would receive from the comment. This new reply should have the same body as the original email, but prefixed with some text. This new text will become the new comment.

At this stage you only want to check that you can parse emails using this new class and a currently undefined method on it called `parse`. This method will take a `Mail::Message` object and create a new comment on a ticket. You'll do permission checking later on, but for now let's just get the basic functionality down.

You begin with these lines in spec/mailers/receiver_spec.rb:

```
require 'spec_helper'

describe Receiver do

  it "parses a reply from a comment update into a comment" do
    comment = Factory(:comment)
```

This will set up a comment and a ticket by using the factory, which will also cause a `comment_updated` notification to be delivered. You can retrieve this notification using this line:

```
comment_email = ActionMailer::Base.deliveries.last
```

This is possible because in the `test` environment, `ActionMailer::Base.delivery_method` is set to `:test`, which stores the emails that have been sent in `ActionMailer::Base.deliveries`. The last email that's been sent out will be the notification for the comment. With this email object, you can build a new `Mail::Message` reply to this email using these lines:

```
mail = Mail.new(:from => "user@ticketee.com",
              :subject => "Re: #{comment_email.subject}",
              :body => %Q{This is a brand new comment      ⬅━① Quoted string
                  #{comment_email.body}
              },
              :to => comment_email.from)
```

With these lines, you're constructing a new reply using the body ① from the original email to generate a multi-lined string with "This is a brand new comment" before the body of the first email. The first line in this first email will eventually be "== ADD YOUR REPLY ABOVE THIS LINE ==", which is how you distinguish what should be the new content for the comment and what's just from the old email.

The final step for this spec is to actually parse the thing using the `Receiver` class, and to check that it changes the related ticket's comment count by 1:

```
lambda { Receiver.parse(mail) }.should(
  change(comment.ticket.comments, :count).by(1)
)
```

The spec/mailers/receiver_spec.rb should now look like the following listing.

Listing 12.15   spec/mailers/receiver_spec.rb

```
require 'spec_helper'

describe Receiver do

  it "parses a reply from a comment update into a comment" do
    comment = Factory(:comment)
    ticket = comment.ticket

    comment_email = ActionMailer::Base.deliveries.last        ⬅──❶ Access email

    user = Factory(:user)

    mail =                                      ⬅──❷ Create new email
Mail.new(:from => user.email,
                 :subject => "Re: #{comment_email.subject}",
                 :body => %Q{This is a brand new comment
                     #{comment_email.default_part_body}        ⬅┐  Insert original
                 },                                            ❸  email content
                 :to => comment_email.from)

    lambda { Receiver.parse(mail) }.should(
      change(ticket.comments, :count).by(1)        ⬅──❹ Add I to comment count
    )

    ticket.comments.last.text.should eql("This is a brand new comment")

  end
end
```

In this spec, you build a comment and reference the ticket for it. By creating a comment, there will be an email going out that you can access using `Action-Mailer::Base.deliveries.last` ❶ because `ActionMailer::Base.delivery_method` is set to `:test`. Using this email, you can compile a new email using `Mail.new` ❷[14] and passing in some values using the original email's methods. One of these values—`:body`—is way more important than the others. For this value, you want to take the original content of the email and then above it put the new comment text. You use `default_part_body` ❸. From this new text, a comment should be created. That's exactly what you assert on the final few lines of this example by using RSpec's change ❹ method. On these final lines, you only want to make sure that the comments count has increased by one and that the latest comment has the text "This is a brand new comment."

---

[14] This functionality is provided by the `mail` gem, on which Action Mailer depends.

When you run this spec using `bin/rspec spec/mailers/receiver_spec.rb`, you'll be told this:

```
Failure/Error: lambda { Receiver.parse(mail) }.should(
  undefined method `parse' for Receiver:Class
```

To make this spec parse, you need to define this method. This method should take a `Mail::Message` object, read out everything from the body of that object above the line "ADD YOUR REPLY ABOVE THIS LINE", and create a comment from it. You can begin to define this method in app/mailers/receiver.rb like this:

```
def self.parse(email)
  reply_separator = /(.*?)\s?== ADD YOUR REPLY ABOVE THIS LINE ==/m
  comment_text = reply_separator.match(email.body.to_s)
```

Here you match the body of the email with the expected reply separator, getting back either a `MatchData` object (indicating the email is a valid reply to a comment) or `nil`. If you get back a valid reply then you do this:

```
if comment_text

  to, project_id, ticket_id =
    email.to.first.split("@")[0].split("+")
```

Here you take the list of `to` addresses for the email, get the first of them, and then `split` it on the @ symbol. This separates the username and the domain name in your email. The username contains the project id and ticket id, which you get by calling `split` again, this time separating the individual elements by the + symbol.

Next, you need to find the relative project, ticket, and user for this email, which you can do using these lines inside the `if` that you just opened:

```
project = Project.find(project_id)
ticket = project.tickets.find(ticket_id)
user = User.find_by_email(email.from[0])
```

Finally, you need to create the comment from the email body (stripping all extra spaces from it) and close the `if`, which is done with the following lines:

```
    ticket.comments.create(:text => comment_text[1].strip,
                           :user => user)
  end
end
```

The `[1]` here will get the first match for the `comment_text`, which will be the new comment's text, throwing `strip` on the end in case there are a couple of extra spaces / lines between the comment text and the separator. That's the final bit of code you need in the app/mailers/receiver.rb file. When you run this spec again with `bundle exec rspec spec/mailers/receiver_spec.rb`, it will still fail:

```
Failure/Error: lambda { Receiver.parse(mail) }.should(
  count should have been changed by 1, but was changed by 0
```

This is because your original comment notification doesn't have the reply separator, and therefore the `if` condition in the `parse` method you just wrote says "Oh, can't find it, so I'll just ignore this email," or something to that effect. In order to get this to work, you must add that line to the comment notification. You can do this by opening app/views/notifier/comment_updated.text.erb and its HTML compatriot and adding this line to the beginning of both files:

```
== ADD YOUR REPLY ABOVE THIS LINE ==
```

Now when you run your spec once more with `bundle exec rspec spec/mailers/ receiver_spec.rb`, it will pass because the `parse` method can find the separator:

```
1 example, 0 failures
```

Alright, now that you've got that feature passing, does everything else still work? Let's find out by running `rake cucumber:ok spec`:

```
63 scenarios (63 passed)
732 steps (732 passed)
# and
41 examples, 0 failures, 19 pending
```

Good! Everything is still going great. Let's commit the new feature:

```
git add .
git commit -m "Add Receiver class to receive emails"
git push
```

Right, this feature isn't complete quite yet, because it only takes mail objects but doesn't actually do any of the fetching itself. You'll revisit this feature in chapter 15 and complete it there. This is a great start, however.

12.5 Summary

That completes chapter 12! In this chapter, you learned how to send out your own kind of emails. Before that, however, you added two ways that users can subscribe to a ticket.

The first of these ways was an automatic subscription that occurred when a user created a ticket. Here, every time a comment was posted to a ticket, the owner of the ticket was notified through either a plain-text or HTML email, depending on what that user's email client supported.

The second of the two ways was to allow users to choose to subscribe or unsubscribe to a ticket. By doing this, all users, and not just those who created the ticket, can choose to receive emails when a ticket has had a comment posted to it. This way, all users can stay up to date on tickets they may be interested in.

Next, you made sure that you could actually send emails into the real world by connecting to a real Gmail account using Action Mailer's SMTP settings. You also ensured that when you send an email using the STMP setting, you can read it from the server by using the `gmail` gem.

By sending emails into the real world, you're bringing your application one step closer to being complete. Now you'll be able to put the application on a server, and it should work just as it does in your tests. But you're going to polish your application a little more before you do that.

The next chapter covers how you can use Rails to present your data to other developers so that they can create applications or libraries to parse it into new and interesting formats.

Designing an API

This chapter covers
- Building an API using new Rails 3 features
- Rate-limiting the API
- Versioning APIs

In the past chapters, you've created a great application that allows your users to manage projects and tickets through a web browser. In this chapter, you are going to create a way for your users to manage this content through what's known as an Application Programming Interface (API). As its name implies, an API is a programming interface (for your application) that returns either JavaScript Object Notation[1] (JSON) or XML[2] data for its requests, which are the two most common formats for modern APIs to return information in. People can then create programs or libraries (referred to as clients) to read and present this data in any way they see fit.

---

[1] http://json.org.
[2] http://xml.org.

One great example of how an API is used is Twitter. Twitter has had an API for an exceptionally long time now, and people have written Twitter clients for just about every operating system out there using this API. The functionality of the site is effectively the same, but people have come up with interesting ways of displaying and modifying that information, such as the Twitter for Mac clients.

There are many, many Rails sites out there that already provide an API interface, such as GitHub[3] and (as previously mentioned) Twitter.[4] Both of these APIs have exceptionally well-documented examples of how to use them and what can be done with them, which is a great way to convince people to start using your API. API documentation, however, is an exercise best left for you after this chapter's done.

APIs aren't unique to Rails. There are plenty of other sites out there that have implemented their own APIs, such as the StackExchange services that run on Microsoft.Net. Furthermore, APIs created in one language are not for exclusive use of API clients written in that specific language. For example, if you wanted to parse the data from the StackExchange API in Ruby, you could do that just fine.

In Rails, however, it's extremely easy to make a modern API for an application, as you'll see in this chapter. Your application will serve in two formats: JSON and XML.

Back to the Twitter and GitHub examples now, and one further thing to note is both of these APIs are also versioned. The point of this is that an API should be presented in a "frozen" state and should not be modified once it's considered stable. This way, a user is be able to use an API without fear of it changing and potentially breaking the code that they're using to parse the data from the API.

Twitter has a URL such as http://api.twitter.com/1/statuses/public_timeline.json that has the version as the first part of the URL after the site name and then the format as an extension at the end. Github's is slightly different, with a URL such as http://github.com/api/v2/json/repos/show/rails3book/ticketee having the version prefixed with a *v* as the second part of the URL, and the format as the part of the URL directly after. The *v* prefix here makes the version part of the URL clearer to those who are reading it, which is a good thing.

You're going to borrow ideas from both of these API designs, presenting your API at the base URL of /api/v1 and the format at the end of the URL, like most web requests. Your URLs will look like /api/v1/projects.json, which will be the URL to return a list of projects that the user is able to read. The reason for this versioning is so that you can always provide data that is predictable to your end users. If you wished to change the format of this data, you would create a new version namespace, which is the final thing we look at toward the end of this chapter. Really, these new version numbers can be whatever you wish, with minor versions such as 0.1 being the standard

---

[3] The octopi gem was built to interact with the GitHub API—you can see the source at http://github.com/fcoury/octopi.

[4] The (non-official) twitter gem was built to interact with the API that Twitter provides; you can see the source of this gem at http://github.com/jnunemaker/twitter.

for unstable APIs, and major versions such as 1, v1, or 1.0 being the standard for the stable, fixed APIs.[5]

To check what user is making a request to your API, you'll use a token-based authentication system, which is something that the Devise gem can be configured to provide. You'll require the token attribute to be passed through in every API request, because without it you cannot be sure of who is doing what with the API. You can then restrict things, such as the list of projects, based on the user's permissions. You can also use tokens to track the number of requests the user has performed on the API and then block them if they make more than 100 requests per hour, which is one of the final things you look at in this chapter. Twitter and GitHub both implement rate-limiting so that people do not spam the system with too many API requests.

Along the path of developing this API, you'll learn additional Rails goodies such as the `to_json` and `to_xml` methods, which will convert an object into JSON or XML representations of that object respectively, as well as the `respond_with` and `respond_to` controller methods, which are responsible for serving data in different formats.

When you're done with this chapter, you'll have a nice solid API that other developers can build upon. Other applications (be it Rails or not) will also be able to read the data from your application.

13.1 The projects API

To get started with Ticketee's API, you're going to write the projects part of it. In this section, you make extensive use of the `respond_with` and `respond_to` methods, which are new in Rails 3.

Before you go about implementing the first building blocks for your API, you'll learn about a module called `Rack::Test::Methods`, provided by the `rack-test` gem, which will allow you to easily test your API.

After that, you'll begin writing the API by creating the `index` action, which will be responsible for displaying all the projects in a JSON format. Next, you'll implement token-based authentication so you can know who's who when they access the API. This will allow you to restrict the list of projects shown in the `index` action to only those that the user should see. Later on, you'll get this action to return XML as well as the JSON output.

With an API, you don't need to provide a `new` and `edit` actions, because this functionality should be provided by the client that is accessing the API. Instead, you'll only write the action[6] parts of your API: the `create`, `show`, `update`, and `destroy` actions. Along the way, you'll be restricting the `create`, `update`, and `destroy` actions to administrators of the application.

When learning about these actions, you'll see a lot of reference to HTTP status codes, which are the standard for all pages of the web. These status codes play a

---

[5] Although logical (incremental) versioning is recommended to stave off questions such as, "What were they thinking?!" and "Are they crazy?" This is often referred to as Semantic Versioning, http://semver.org/.

[6] An absolutely terrible pun. Forgive us.

critical role in an API, providing key information such as if the request was successful (the 200 status code) or if the user is unauthorized (the 401 status code) to perform the request. These are standardized ways of quickly informing people of the result of their requests.

> **TIP** There's a handy gem called `cheat` that provides cheat sheets for a number of things, including one for HTTP status codes. You can install this gem using the `gem install cheat` command and then bring up the cheat sheet for status codes using `cheat status_codes`.
>
> But if you're on Windows, this won't work because Cheat requires a function not found on your system. Instead, go to http://cheat .errtheblog .com/b where you can view the list of all the cheat sheets.

To begin writing this API, you'll need to define the routes to it. Without routes, making requests to /api/v1/projects.json will forever be fruitless. If you recall from this chapter's introduction, the API URL that you'll be using looks like /api/v1/projects.json. Previously, when you wanted URLs to be prefixed with a name (such as back in chapter 7), you used a `namespace` method for them. You're going to do the same thing here, except you'll use a namespace within another namespace. Let's open config/routes.rb and add the code from the following listing to the top of the routes definition.

Listing 13.1   config/routes.rb

```
Ticketee::Application.routes.draw do
  namespace :api do
    namespace :v1 do
      resources :projects
    end
  end
  ...
```

This new route defines routes and routing helpers for the projects resources, such as /api/v1/projects, and `api_v1_projects_path` respectively. You're going to need to be serving content from this route, namely a list of projects. This list will be served in one of two forms: XML or JSON. Before you actually implement the code that makes these responses get served, you're going to write a new RSpec test that makes sure these routes return the right data. To help you along, you'll be using a feature provided by one of the dependencies of Rails: the `rack-test` gem.

This gem provides a module called `Rack::Test::Methods`, which contains methods such as `get`, `post`, `put`, and `delete`. Look familiar? They should. They're the four basic HTTP methods that you use when making requests. The methods from `Rack::Test::Methods` take a path on which to make a request and then return a Rack response (an `Array`) that consists of three parts: the HTTP status code, the HTTP headers (in `Hash` form), and the body. The simplest Rack response would look something like this:

```
[200, {}, "Hello World!"]
```

The first element of this result is the HTTP status code, and in this case it indicates that your fictional response was 200, or in human-terms: OK. The second element contains no special HTTP headers, but you'll see these as you progress in the next section. Finally, the third element contains a string, which represents the body of this request, returning the string "Hello World!"

Using `Rack::Test::Methods`, you can initiate requests to your application's API that then return these Rack responses, and you can then use these responses to check that your API is responding in the correct way. You're purposely not using the standard RSpec controller tests here to make sure that the precise URLs are responding in the correct manner, instead of only testing that the actions are doing what you tell them.

Let's get into writing this initial test for your API.

13.1.1 *Your first API*

You're going to continue on the running theme of "test everything" with your API, and with the `rack-test` gem you've got the necessary tools to test what your API's URLs are doing. Rather than testing this in Cucumber, you're instead going to use RSpec, which provides a nicer DSL for testing your APIs. To begin with, you're going to create a new folder structure at spec/apis/v1. You should name the apis directory as a plural for two reasons: first, it matches the consistency of the other directories in the spec directory; and second, it may one day contain more than one API version. Then you'll create a new file called spec/apis/v1/projects_spec.rb and begin to fill it with the following:

```
require "spec_helper"

describe "/api/v1/projects", :type => :api
 do

end
```

There's much more code to come after this short snippet, but it's a pretty good start.

In the `describe` block here you pass through an option of `:type => :api`. What does this do? Well, you can use it to modify the behavior of this `describe` block in many ways, such as including modules. The `Rack::Test::Methods` module you're going to use needs to be included into each test. Rather than doing this manually, you can use this `:type` option to do the `include` for you, as well as some additional behavior. Let's open a new file at spec/support/api/helper.rb and put the content from the following listing inside.

Listing 13.2   spec/support/api/helper.rb

```
module ApiHelper
  include Rack::Test::Methods

  def app
    Rails.application
  end
end
```

```
RSpec.configure do |c|
  c.include ApiHelper, :type => :api
end
```

Here you define a module called `ApiHelper`, which you include into any test marked as an API test with the `:type` option. Inside the module, you use the `Rack::Test::Methods` module, which provides useful methods that you'll see throughout this chapter for making requests to your application, such as the `get` method (not yet shown). You define the `app` method here so that the `Rack::Test::Methods` knows which application to act on. With this done, let's go back to your test.

Inside the `describe` block underneath this new method you're going to want to create a new user (an admin one at that, because later on you'll need it for the `create` and other actions) whom you'll use to make this request to the API. You can create this admin by adding a `let` inside spec/v1/api/projects_spec.rb:

```
let(:user) { create_user! }
```

You'll need to set up Devise to include the `token_authenticatable` module so that you can authenticate API requests from users by using a token they provide with each request. This is so that you will know what projects to show to your users, as well as any other authorization criteria that you need to apply to this user's request. For example, only users with permission to create projects in the application should be able to do so through the API.

To implement the change that you need, go into the `User` model (app/models/user.rb) and change the `devise` call to be this:

```
devise :database_authenticatable, :registerable, :confirmable,
       :recoverable, :rememberable, :trackable, :validatable,
       :token_authenticatable
```

Next, generate a migration to add a field called `authentication_token` to the users table, which will be used to store this token. You'll need to add this migration to both the development and test environments. To do this, run these three commands:

```
rails g migration add_authentication_token_to_users
➥authentication_token:string
rake db:migrate
rake db:test:prepare
```

The migration generator is smart here and will know to add the `authentication_token` to the `users` table based on the name you're passing through. The additional argument on the end tells Rails what type of field you'd like this to be.

With the migration created and run, you still need to add a callback to your `User` model, so that tokens are generated for users when they're created, or for when users are updated but don't have a token.[7] To do this, you'll put this line in your `User` model:

```
before_save :ensure_authentication_token
```

---

[7] A situation that is unlikely to happen (as you've got no serious users currently), but could potentially happen.

The before_save method here is run on a record whenever it is created or updated, as opposed to the before_create callback that you saw back in chapter 10, which only calls the specified method upon record creation.

With the callback to create the token in place, let's jump back to your spec and write a test to make a request with this token. Directly underneath the let(:user) in spec/api/v1/projects_spec.rb, you'll put the code from the following listing.

Listing 13.3 spec/api/v1/projects_spec.rb

```ruby
let(:token) { user.authentication_token }

before do
  @project = Factory(:project)
  user.permissions.create!(:action => "view", :thing => @project)
end

context "projects viewable by this user" do

  let(:url) { "/api/v1/projects" }
  it "json" do
    get "#{url}.json"                        ◁——❶ GET request

    projects_json = Project.for(user).all.to_json
    last_response.body.should eql(projects_json)
    last_response.status.should eql(200)

    projects = JSON.parse(last_response.body)

    projects.any? do |p|
      p["project"]["name"] == "Ticketee"
    end.should be_true
  end
end
```

You're using another let to define a token method that, when called, will return the authentication_token for the current user. You'll use this later for authenticating requests for your API. The get method ❶ you use here is provided by Rack::Test::Methods and simply makes a GET request with the provided URL. You put the URL in a let because you don't want to repeat the URL too many times if you have multiple tests, and the let stops you from repeating yourself in your code.

After the request is done in the test, you ensure that the last_response.status returns 200, which is the HTTP status code for OK and means the request was successful. The rest of this spec tests that the data contained within last_response.body contains the appropriate data. This to_json method will take the attributes for each project returned and turn them into JSON, resulting in an output such as

```
[
  {"project":
    {
      "created_at":"[timestamp]",
      "id":1,
      "name":"Ticketee",
      "updated_at":"[timestamp]"
    }
```

```
    }
  ]
```

This output can then be read with a JSON parser by the receiving user, which is what you do on the line directly after this by using the JSON.parse method that is provided by the json gem. This method takes the JSON string and converts it into a Ruby Array or Hash. On the final line of your spec, you check that there's anything in this array—anything at all—which returns true for p["project"]["name"] == "Ticketee", to make sure that the project you've created really shows up. You need the first key, project, because this is how elements are returned in JSON response so that their types can easily be identified. If something does match for the any? method, then your test passes.

Let's see what happens when you run bin/rspec spec/api/v1/projects_spec.rb now:

```
Failures:
  1) /api/v1/projects projects viewable by this user index JSON
       Failure/Error: get "#{url}.json", :token => token
       uninitialized constant Api::V1::ProjectsController
```

You haven't yet defined any controllers for your API, and so this test is going to quite obviously fail. To make it pass, you'll need to define the constant it requires, Api::V1::ProjectsController. This controller will be responsible for serving all the requests for your projects API.

13.1.2 *Serving an API*

To begin to define controllers for your namespace-within-a-namespace, you'll create a new file at app/controllers/api/v1/base_controller.rb. This file will serve as a base for all controllers within version 1 of your API, providing functionality (eventually) for authenticating and authorizing users, much like the ApplicationController currently does. In app/controllers/api/v1/base_controller.rb, you'll define the following:

```
class Api::V1::BaseController < ActionController::Base
  respond_to :json
end
```

Eventually you'll put in the token authentication code into this, but for now you're only trying to get the example to pass. The respond_to method here sets up any inheriting controller to respond to JSON requests, such as the ProjectsController that you're about to create. To make your test pass, you need to return JSON data from this action, which is much easier than it sounds. You can get the functionality you need from this controller by creating a new file at app/controllers/api/v1/projects_controller.rb and filling it with this content:

```
class Api::V1::ProjectsController < Api::V1::BaseController
  def index
    respond_with(Project.all)
  end
end
```

The `respond_with` method here will return the JSON representation of `Project.all` when you make a JSON request to this path by calling `to_json` on the object. Rails knows to return JSON data back from any request with the format (that's the bit after the dot in api/v1/projects.json) of JSON. Rails handles all of this internally for you, which is nice of it to do. Let's find out if this new controller and its only action make the spec pass with `bin/rspec spec/api/v1/projects_spec.rb`:

```
1 example, 0 failures
```

There you have it, your first API route and action are serving up data! Now you're going to need to restrict what this action returns to only the projects that the user can read, but you'll need to first authenticate a user based on their token, which is made easy with Devise.

13.1.3 *API authentication*

Your next task is authenticating the user who's making the request in your API. The first step is to do something with the token parameter that gets passed through with your request. A sensible place to check this token would be in `Api::V1::Base-Controller`, because you want to authenticate for all controllers in the API (although there's only one, for now). For this authentication, you'll find if there's a user with the token passed in by using a `before_filter` like this in app/controllers/api/v1/base _controller.rb:

```
before_filter :authenticate_user

private
  def authenticate_user
    @current_user = User.find_by_authentication_token(params[:token])
  end

  def current_user
    @current_user
  end
```

To check and see if this is working, you'll alter your test in spec/api/v1/ projects_spec.rb to generate another project, give the user read access to only that project, and check that the response from the API only contains that project. To do this, you'll add a new `before` to the "projects viewable by this user" context inside the spec, using the code from the following listing.

Listing 13.4   spec/api/v1/projects_spec.rb

```
context "projects viewable by this user" do

  before do
    Factory(:project, :name => "Access Denied")
  end

  ...
end
```

In the `before` block you create one project that the user should not have access to read. Inside the test itself, you're still using the `for` scope on the `Project` class to get only the projects that the specified user has access to. Let's add a couple more lines to your example now to check that this user cannot see the Access Denied project:

```
projects.any? do |p|
  p["project"]["name"] == "Access Denied"
end.should be_false
```

When you run this spec with `bin/rspec spec/api/v1/projects_spec.rb` you'll see that the JSON returned from your controller still contains both projects:

```
expected "[[Ticketee hash]]"
        got "[[Ticketee hash], [Access Denied hash]]"
```

To make this test pass, you're going to need to stop returning *all* the projects in the index action of `Api::V1::ProjectsController` and only return the projects that this user should be able to see. Let's now open app/controllers/api/v1/projects _controller.rb and change the `index` action to use the `for` method and pass in the current_user, rather than the `all` method:

```
def index
  respond_with(Project.for(current_user))
end
```

This will now return only the list of projects that the user should be able to see, which should be enough to get this test passing. You can find out with another quick run of `bin/rspec spec/api/v1/projects_spec.rb`:

```
1 example, 0 failures
```

Great, now you've got your API finding a user based on the token that you've gathered in your spec. One thing you haven't tested for yet is: what happens when an invalid (or no) token is given? Well, you should return an error when that happens. This is the final change you'll be making before you make a commit, because it's been a little too long since you've last done that.[8]

13.1.4 *Error reporting*

Something will inevitably go wrong in your application, and when that happens you're going to want to provide useful error messages to your users. One of the things that could go wrong in your API is that the user uses an invalid token to authenticate against your API. When a user makes a request with an invalid token, you should inform them of their mistake, which you can do by returning JSON that looks like this:

```
{ error: "Token is invalid." }
```

To test this behavior, you're going to make a request without a token and then fix up your projects_spec.rb test to pass in a token. You'll write your first test now in a new

---

[8] As a reminder: you should commit after every safe point so that if you stuff something up (it happens!) you won't have to roll back as much.

file at spec/api/v1/authentication_spec.rb, which will be filled with the content from the following listing.

Listing 13.5   spec/api/v1/authentication_spec.rb

```
require "spec_helper"

describe "API errors", :type => :api do

  it "making a request with no token" do
    get "/api/v1/projects.json", :token => ""
    error = { :error => "Token is invalid." }
    last_response.body.should eql(error.to_json)
  end

end
```

You're using Rack::Test::Methods in the spec again, and you've set up the token to be a blank string so get will pass this through as the token. Let's run this spec to make sure it's failing first with bin/rspec spec/api/v1/authentication_spec.rb:

```
Failures:
  1) API errors making a request with no token
      Failure/Error: get "/api/v1/projects.json", :token => ""
      NoMethodError:
        undefined method `admin?' for nil:NilClass
      # ./app/models/project.rb:13:in `for'
      # ./app/controllers/api/v1/projects_controller.rb:3:in `index'
      # ./spec/api/v1/
    authentication_spec.rb:6:in `block (2 levels) in <top (required)>'

1 example, 1 failure
```

Yup, definitely looks like it's failing. Line 13 of app/models/project.rb attempts to call admin? on the User object passed in to the for method. If you attempt to make a request without a valid token, the call to User.find_by_authentication_token will return nil, resulting in the error you see here. You should check if the user has been found, and if not then you'll show the error. To make your authenticate_user method do this in app/controllers/api/v1/base_controller.rb, you'll change it to what is shown in the following listing.

Listing 13.6   app/controllers/api/v1/base_controller.rb

```
def authenticate_user
  @current_user = User.find_by_authentication_token(params[:token])
  unless @current_user
    respond_with({:error => "Token is invalid." })
  end
end
```

If the @current_user variable is nil here, you set the response's body to be the JSON-form of { :error => "Token is invalid" } and respond_with that object. Does this work? Let's find out with bin/rspec spec/api/v1/authentication_spec.rb:

```
1 example, 0 failures
```

Booyah, it works! How about `bin/rspec spec/api/v1/projects_spec.rb` too?

```
1 example, 0 failures
```

All green there too, and so it's definitely time to do a commit now. You should run the customary checks before you commit by running `rake cucumber:ok spec`:

```
63 scenarios (63 passed)
732 steps (732 passed)
# and
43 examples, 0 failures, 19 pending
```

Great! Everything's still green. From now on you will only run the spec tests, because all you are going to be changing is the API, which will not impact anything that the features test. At the end of the chapter, you'll run it again to make sure that nothing is broken. Commit and push the changes that you've made:

```
git add .
git commit -m "Implemented token-based authentication API base"
git push
```

You've begun to implement the API now, and you've got the /api/v1/projects URL returning a list of the projects that a user can see. To check what user this is, you've implemented a basic token authentication using functionality built in to Devise.

There's still a little way to go before you're done with the API. For starters, this API only serves JSON requests, and some people who use it may wish for the data to be returned in XML. You've also only got the one action in your controller, and you need to implement a way for people to create, update, and delete projects through the API. Before you do that, you'll add in support for XML. This is incredibly easy to implement, as you'll soon see.

13.1.5 *Serving XML*

So far, you've been using the `respond_with` and `respond_to` methods to serve JSON responses. You can serve XML using these same methods while continuing to serve JSON. It's very, very easy. First of all, you're going to want to create a test to make sure that your new XML data is being returned correctly. You'll place this test in the `index` context for "projects viewable by this user" in spec/api/v1/projects_spec.rb using the code from the following listing.

Listing 13.7 spec/api/v1/projects_spec.rb

```
it "XML" do
  get "#{url}.xml", :token => token
  last_response.body.should eql(Project.readable_by(user).to_xml)
  projects = Nokogiri::XML(last_response.body)
  projects.css("project name").text.should eql("Ticketee")
end
```

In this spec you use the `nokogiri` gem to parse the XML (in chapter 6, you used it to parse HTML). Then you use the `css` method to find an element called `name` inside another called `project`, and then check to see if its `text` is equal to the name of your project, which it should be if everything works out fine. When you run `bin/rspec spec/api/v1/projects_spec.rb`, this spec will fail:

```
Diff:
@@ -1,10 +1,2 @@
-<?xml version="1.0" encoding="UTF-8"?>
-<projects type="array">
-  <project>
-    <created-at type="datetime">[timestamp]</created-at>
-    <id type="integer">1</id>
-    <name>Ticketee</name>
-    <updated-at type="datetime">[timestamp]</updated-at>
-  </project>
-</projects>
+
...
2 examples, 1 failure
```

The diff here shows that the expected XML is nowhere to be found in the response, and instead you're getting back a final line of absolutely nothing. This is because your `Api::V1::BaseController` doesn't yet respond to XML requests. So now with a failing test you can go right ahead and change this controller to fix it. To make your API serve XML requests, you'll change this line in app/controllers/api/v1/base_controller.rb

```
respond_to :json
```

to this:

```
respond_to :json, :xml
```

This simple little change will now make your spec pass, which you can see by running `bin/rspec spec/api/v1/projects_spec.rb`:

```
2 examples, 0 failures
```

Apologies if something harder was expected, but it really is this simple in Rails. You've only changed the API controller and spec, and it's all contained in itself, but even so it's still a good habit to run all the features and specs to make sure everything is fine:

```
61 scenarios (61 passed)
726 steps (726 passed)
# and
36 examples, 0 failures, 12 pending
```

Green is good. Commit this change:

```
git add .
git commit -m "Support XML & JSON with /api/v1/projects"
git push
```

Now that you've got your first action of your API responding to both XML and JSON, why don't you make some more actions, like the `create` action for creating projects in Ticketee?

13.1.6 *Creating projects*

In this section, you're going to implement a new API action that will allow you to create projects. The route for this action was provided by this code in config/routes.rb:

```
namespace :api do
  namespace :v1 do
    resources :projects
  end
end
```

You only need to implement the create action in your controller, which makes it all quite simple. When you make a request to this action and it passes validations, you will return the XML or JSON representation of the project that was created, along with a 201 Created HTTP status code, which indicates that a new resource has been created.[9] If the creation of the project fails any validation, then Rails will return a 422 Unprocessable Entity HTTP Status Code,[10] which will indicate that there are errors with the request. The body returned by this failing will contain those errors and look something like this:

```
{"name":"can't be blank"}
```

It's then up to the people receiving the status back from the API to choose how to display this information.

To make this request to the create action, you need to make a POST request to the /api/v1/projects path, and to do this there's the post method provided by Rack ::Test::Methods that you can use. You'll open spec/api/v1/projects_spec.rb now and add in another context block under the first for checking that creating a project through JSON works, as shown in the following listing.

> **Listing 13.8 spec/api/v1/projects_spec.rb**

```
context "creating a project" do

  let(:url) { "/api/v1/projects" }

  it "successful JSON" do
    post "#{url}.json", :token => token,
                        :project => {
                           :name => "Inspector"
                        }

    project = Project.find_by_name("Inspector")
    route = "/api/v1/projects/#{project.id}"

    last_response.status.should eql(201)
    last_response.headers["Location"].should eql(route)      ◁———❶ Check API route
    last_response.body.should eql(project.to_json)
  end
end
```

---

[9] This isn't unique to Rails, but is rather part of RFC 2616: http://tools.ietf.org/html/rfc2616#section-10.2.2.

[10] As described in RFC 4918, Section 11.2: http://tools.ietf.org/html/rfc4918#section-11.2.

In the normal `create` action for the normal `ProjectsController` in your application, you're restricting creation of projects to admin users. You'll do this for this API action in a bit—you're only trying to get the most basic example going first. Here you again set up the `url` in a `let` so that you can re-use it for the other tests you'll implement later.

You begin your test by making a POST request using `post` (provided by the `Rack::Test::Methods` module, just like `get`), passing through the parameters of a project as the second argument in this method. Then you check that the status of the `last_response` is set to 201, which is the correct reply if the resource was created successfully. Next, check that the `Location` ❶ in the header is set to the correct API route, which would be something such as http://example.com/api/v1/projects. You'll find out why when you go to implement this action. On the final line of the spec, check that the `last_response.body` contains the JSON representation of the project that should have been created.

When you run `bin/rspec spec/api/v1/projects_spec.rb` this test will fail, because you've yet to implement the `create` action for its controller:

```
Failure/Error: post "#{url}.json", :token = token,
  The action 'create' could not be found for Api::V1::ProjectsController
```

You'll need to implement this action to make the spec pass. Let's open app/controllers/api/v1/projects_controller.rb and add this action underneath your `index` action, using the code shown in the following listing.

Listing 13.9   app/controllers/projects_controller.rb

```
def create
  project = Project.create(params[:project])
  if project.valid?
    respond_with(project, :location => api_v1_project_path(project))    ◁┐
  else
    respond_with(project)                                 Set Location key ❶
  end
end
```

By using the `create` method of `Project`, Rails will attempt to create a new record. If this succeeds, then the status that will be returned will be 201 and you'll get back the proper representation (either JSON or XML) of the new project. On the final line of this action, you manually set the `Location` key in the headers by passing through the `:location` option ❶ so that it points to the correct URL of something such as http://example.com/api/v1/projects/1, rather than the Rails default of http://example.com/projects/1. People who are using your API can then store this location and reference it later on when they wish to retrieve information about the project. The URL that Rails defaults to goes to the user-facing version of this resource (/projects/1.json), which is incorrect.

If the project isn't valid (that is, if the `save` method returns `false`), then you simply let Rails return a response that will contain the errors of the project, without having a custom location set.

This should be all that you need in order to get your spec to pass, so let's see what happens when you run `bin/rspec spec/api/v1/projects_spec.rb`:

```
3 examples, 0 failures
```

Great! Now you need to write a test to check that when you attempt to pass through a project with no name you're given a 422 status code and an error along with it, indicating that the project wasn't created due to those errors. Directly underneath the previous test in spec/api/v1/projects_spec.rb, you'll add this test shown in the following listing.

Listing 13.10   spec/api/v1/projects_spec.rb

```ruby
it "unsuccessful JSON" do
  post "#{url}.json", :token => token,
                      :project => {}
  last_response.status.should eql(422)
  errors = {"name" => ["can't be blank"]}.to_json
  last_response.body.should eql(errors)
end
```

Naughty you, writing the test after the code is already there, but you can get away with it once. Let's run the spec and see how it goes now:

```
4 examples, 0 failures
```

Great success! With this URL working for valid and non-valid projects appropriately, you are now providing a way for your users to create a project through the API, and so it's time to make a commit:

```
git add .
git commit -m "Added API to create projects"
git push
```

Your next task is to restrict this action to only the admins of your application, as in the real `ProjectsController` controller. You want to limit the number of people who can change the projects to a select few who know what they're doing.

13.1.7 *Restricting access to only admins*

In app/controllers/projects_controller.rb you've got this line, which restricts some actions to only admins:

```ruby
before_filter :authorize_admin!, :except => [:index, :show]
```

As it says on the line, every action other than `index` or `show` has this filter run before it. This filter is defined in app/controllers/application_controller.rb like this:

```ruby
def authorize_admin!
  authenticate_user!
  unless current_user.admin?
    flash[:alert] = "You must be an admin to do that."
    redirect_to root_path
  end
end
```

You're not going to be able to use this same `before_filter` for your API because the API doesn't return flash messages. You have to return errors in a lovely little JSON or XML format. This particular error, for example, is "You must be an admin." Also, redirection doesn't make sense here, because it wouldn't tell users *why* they were redirected. Therefore, you'll implement a different `authorize_admin!` method in your `Api::V1::BaseController` instead. You'll take the time, however, to write a test to check for this error occurring. Let's open a new file at spec/api/v1/project _errors_spec.rb and add a test that if you attempt to make a POST request to api/v1/ projects using a token for a user who's *not* an admin, you get an error. Use the code from the following listing.

```ruby
require "spec_helper"

describe "Project API errors", :type => :api do
  context "standard users" do
    let(:user) { create_user! }

    it "cannot create projects" do
      post "/api/v1/projects.json",
        :token => user.authentication_token,
        :project => {
          :name => "Ticketee"
        }
      error = { :error => "You must be an admin to do that." }
      last_response.body.should eql(error.to_json)
      last_response.code.should eql(401)
      Project.find_by_name("Ticketee").should be_nil
    end
  end
end
```

With this spec, you test that a normal user who's using a valid authenticity token cannot create a project through the API because they're not an admin. Instead, the API should return a response of "You must be an admin to do that." This response should have a `code` of 401, indicating an Unauthorized response. When you run this spec using `bin/rspec spec/api/v1/project_errors_spec.rb`, it will not return the error as you expect:

```
expected "{\"error\":\"You must be an admin to do that.\"}"
    got "{[project hash]}"
```

To make this error happen, you'll go into app/controllers/api/v1/base_controller.rb and underneath your `authenticate_user` method add the `authorize_admin!` method shown in the following listing.

```ruby
def authorize_admin!
  if !@current_user.admin?
    if !@current_user.admin?
```

```
        error = { :error => "You must be an admin to do that." }
        warden.custom_failure!
        render params[:format].to_sym => error
, :status => 401
    end
  end
end
```

Here you use `warden.custom_failure!` to inform Warden (the Rack backend to Devise) that you're going to raise a custom 401 response. Without this, Devise would instead take over from this 401 response, showing a "You must be signed in to continue" error message.

You also use the `render` method in a unique manner here. You call it and pass in a hash with the key being a symbolized version of the format (in this case, `json`) and the value being the hash that contains the error. By calling `render` in this way, Rails will convert the hash to JSON, or if it were an XML request, to XML. The reason for doing it this way rather than using `respond_with` is because `respond_with` will attempt to do some weird behavior and doesn't work for POST requests, so you must work around that little issue.

By specifying the `status` option to the `render` here, your response's status code will be set to that particular status, which will let the code used to connect to the API know that the user is unauthorized to perform the specific request.

Now all you need to do is add this as a `before_filter` into app/controllers/api/v1/projects_controller.rb using this line:

```
before_filter :authorize_admin!, :except => [:index, :show]
```

With this line in the `ProjectsController`, any request to any action that's not the `index` or `show` action will have the admin check run before it. If a user doesn't meet this criteria, then you will return the "You must be an admin to do that" error. These pieces of code should be enough to get your test running, so let's find out with bin/rspec spec/api/v1/project_errors_spec.rb:

```
1 example, 0 failures
```

Now when people who aren't admins try to create a project, they will see the "You must be an admin to do that" error message returned from the API. Because this is the case, you'll need to set up the user in the projects API examples to be an admin when they attempt to create a project, which you can do by putting this `before` after the beginning of the "creating a project" context block:

```
before do
  user.admin = true
  user.save
end
```

When you run bin/rspec spec/api/v1/projects_spec.rb, all the examples will be passing:

```
4 examples, 0 failures
```

With this new authorization added you will make a commit, but before that you'll run a customary check to make sure everything is still alright by running `rake spec`, because all you've edited in this section is the API. You should see this output:

```
47 examples, 0 failures, 19 pending
```

Great, so let's go ahead and commit this then:

```
git add .
git commit -m "Only admins are able to create projects through API"
git push
```

In the response for your `create` action, the headers point to a location (you customized) of a project, something such as http://example.com/api/v1/projects/1. Currently, this URL doesn't *go* anywhere because it needs the `show` action to exist. You should probably get on to that.

13.1.8 A single project

You've got a link (http://example.com/api/v1/projects/1) provided by your `create` action that doesn't go anywhere if people try to access it. Soon this URL will show a particular project's attributes through the `show` action in your `Api::V1::Projects-Controller`. Within those attributes, you'll also show a `last_ticket` element, which will contain the attributes for the most recently updated ticket. To do this, you use another option of `respond_with`, the `:methods` option. Using this option will change the output of each project resource in your JSON API to something like this:

```
{
  "project": {
    "created_at": "[timestamp]",
    "id": 1,
    "name": "Ticketee",
    "updated_at": "[timestamp]",
    "last_ticket": {
      "ticket": {
        "asset_updated_at": null,
        "created_at": "[timestamp]",
        "description": "A ticket, nothing more.",
        "id": 1,
        "project_id": 1,
        "state_id": null,
        "title": "A ticket, nothing more.",
        "updated_at": "[timestamp]",
        "user_id": 2
      }
    }
  }
}
```

Using the `last_ticket` method, people using the API will be able to discover when the last activity was on the project. You could add other fields such as the comments too if you wished, but this example is kept simple for quality and training purposes.

To get started with this `show` action, you'll write a test in spec/api/v1/ projects_spec.rb for it inside the "projects viewable by this user" context block, as shown in the following listing.

Listing 13.13 spec/api/v1/projects_spec.rb

```
context "show" do
  let(:url) { "/api/v1/projects/#{@project.id}"}

  before do
    Factory(:ticket, :project => @project)
  end

  it "JSON" do
    get "#{url}.json", :token => token
    project = @project.to_json(:methods => "last_ticket")
    last_response.body.should eql(project)
    last_response.status.should eql(200)

    project_response = JSON.parse(last_response.body)["project"]

    ticket_title = project_response["last_ticket"]["ticket"]["title"]
    ticket_title.should_not be_blank
  end
end
```

You're using the `project` method that was set up by the "projects viewable by this user" context block earlier to generate the URL to a `Project` resource, as well as using it to create a new ticket for this project so that `last_ticket` returns something of value. You take this URL and do a JSON request on it, and you expect to get back a JSON representation of the object with the `last_ticket` method being called and also returning data. Then you check that the response's status should be 200, indicating a good request, and finally you check that the last ticket title isn't blank.

To make this test pass, open app/controllers/api/v1/projects_controller.rb and add in the `show` action, as shown in the following listing.

Listing 13.14 app/controllers/api/v1/projects_controller.rb

```
def show
  @project = Project.find(params[:id])
  respond_with(@project, :methods => "last_ticket")
end
```

In this action, you find the `Project` based on the `params[:id]` value and then `respond_with` this object, asking it to call the `last_ticket` method. If this method is undefined (as it is right now), then the method will not be called at all. When you run this test with bin/rspec spec/api/v1/projects_spec.rb, you'll see this error:

```
Failure/Error: ticket_title = last_response ...
  You have a nil object when you didn't expect it!
  You might have expected an instance of Array.
  The error occurred while evaluating nil.[]
```

The error occurs because you're attempting to call the `[]` method on something that is `nil`, and it's really likely that the something is the `last_ticket` key, which doesn't exist yet because the method is not defined. To define this method, open app/models/project.rb and add this method inside the class:

```
def last_ticket
  tickets.last
end
```

Why are you doing it this way? Well, `respond_with` doesn't let you chain methods, and so you'll work around this by defining a method that calls the chain in your model. When you run `bin/rspec spec/api/v1/projects_spec.rb`, this test will pass because the `last_ticket` method is now defined:

```
1 example, 0 failures
```

Great! Now the `show` action is responding with data similar to this:

```
{
  "project": {
    "created_at": "[timestamp]",
    "id": 1,
    "name": "Ticketee",
    "updated_at": "[timestamp]",
    "last_ticket": {
      "ticket": {
        "asset_updated_at": null,
        "created_at": "[timestamp]",
        "description": "A ticket, nothing more.",
        "id": 1,
        "project_id": 1,
        "state_id": null,
        "title": "A ticket, nothing more.",
        "updated_at": "[timestamp]",
        "user_id": 2
      }
    }
  }
}
```

How goes the rest of your API? Let's find out with a quick run of `rake spec`:

```
40 examples, 0 failures, 19 pending
```

Ok, that's good to see, time to make a commit:

```
git add .
git commit -m "Added API action for a single project with last ticket"
git push
```

Back in the main part of the application, you've got permissions on users that restrict which projects they can see. Currently in the API there is no such restriction, and so you need to add one to bring it in line with how the application behaves.

13.1.9 *No project for you!*

Currently, any user can see the details of any project through the API. The main application enforces the rule that users without permission to view a project are not able to do so. To enforce this rule in your API as well, you use the find_project method:

```
def find_project
  @project = Project.for(current_user).find(params[:id])
rescue ActiveRecord::RecordNotFound
  flash[:alert] = "The project you were looking for could not be found."
  redirect_to projects_path
end
```

Here you use the for method, which will return a scope for all projects viewable by the current user. By calling find on this scope, if the user doesn't have access to the project then an ActiveRecord::RecordNotFound exception will be raised. You then rescue this exception and lie to the user, telling them the project is mysteriously gone.[11] Much like the authorize_admin! method you ported over before, you can't set the flash notice or redirect here. Instead, you're going to have to present an API error as you did earlier.[12]

To test this new before_filter :authorize_user, write a new test in spec/api/v1/project_errors_spec.rb where a user without permission on a project attempts to view it, only to be rebuked by the server with an error. This test should be placed inside the "standard users" context block and is shown in the following listing.

Listing 13.15   spec/api/v1/project_errors_spec.rb

```
it "cannot view projects they do not have access to" do
  project = Factory(:project)

  get "/api/v1/projects/#{project.id}.json",
    :token => user.authentication_token
  error = { :error => "The project you were looking for" +
                      " could not be found." }
  last_response.status.should eql(404)
  last_response.body.should eql(error.to_json)
end
```

When the user attempts to go to the show page, they should receive the error informing them that the project has run away (or doesn't exist). The status code for this response should be 404, indicating the resource the user was looking for is not found. To make this work, you'll remove this line from the show action in app/controllers/api/v1/projects_controller.rb:

```
project = Project.find(params[:id])
```

---

[11] It's not really.

[12] Although this may seem like repetition (which it is), it's part of the project's API and will help you understand the concepts better. Practice, practice, practice! It makes perfect prefects.

Then you'll put this line under the `authorize_admin!` filter inside this controller's class:

```
before_filter :find_project, :only => [:show]
```

Next, you need to add the `find_project` after the `show` action as a private method, as shown in the following listing.

Listing 13.16 app/controllers/api/v1/projects_controller.rb

```
private

def find_project
  @project = Project.for(current_user).find(params[:id])
  rescue ActiveRecord::RecordNotFound
    error = { :error => "The project you were looking for " +
                        "could not be found."}
    respond_with(error, :status => 404)
end
```

Here you respond with the error message and set the status to 404 to tell the user that the project doesn't exist. When you run `bin/rspec spec/api/v1/project_errors _spec.rb`, your spec will pass:

```
2 examples, 0 failures
```

You're now restricting the projects that a user can access to only the ones they have permission to view. If the API user doesn't have the permission, you'll deny all knowledge of the project and return a 404 status code. It's quite grand how this is possible in such few lines of easy-to-understand code.

You'll run all the specs now to make sure everything's rosy with `rake spec`. You should see that it's all green:

```
40 examples, 0 failures, 12 pending
```

A nice round number this time. A commit you shall make:

```
git add .
git commit -m "Restricting projects API show to only users who have
  ➥permission to view a project"
git push
```

Currently you've got the `index`, `show`, and `create` actions implemented for your controller. What's missing? Well, you could say the `new`, `edit`, `update`, and `destroy` actions are, but you don't need the `new` and `edit` actions, because this should be handled on the client side of the API, not the server. It is the client's duty to present the new and edit dialogs to the user. Therefore, you only need to implement the `update` and `destroy` methods and then you're done with this API. So close!

13.1.10 *Updating a project*

To update a project in the API, people will need to make a POST request to the /api/v1/projects/:id URL with the project's new information contained in a `params[:project]` hash. Simple, really.

To test that this action works correctly, you'll add yet another spec to spec/api/v1/projects_spec.rb using the code from the following listing.

Listing 13.17   spec/api/v1/projects_spec.rb

```ruby
context "updating a project" do
  before do
    user.admin = true
    user.save
  end

  let(:url) { "/api/v1/projects/#{@project.id}" }
  it "successful JSON" do
    @project.name.should eql("Ticketee")
    put "#{url}.json", :token => token,              ⟵ ❶ put request
                       :project => {
                         :name => "Not Ticketee"
                       }
    last_response.status.should eql(200)

    @project.reload
    @project.name.should eql("Not Ticketee")
    last_response.body.should eql("{}")
  end
end
```

At the top of this new `context` block, you've defined that the user is an admin again. You could wrap the `create` and `update` tests within another context that sets this flag too, but you'll do it this way for now.

You need to make a `put` request to this action for Rails to accept it, and you can do that by using the `put` method ❶. Along with this request, you send the `token` and `project` parameters. The `project` parameter contains a new name for this project. Because it's a valid (non-blank) name, the response's status code will be 200, but the response will be an empty hash indicating no errors. This doesn't return an updated object, because what's the point? The client should be aware of the updates that have occurred, given it triggered them!

At the end of this spec, you use the `reload` method to find this object again from the database. This is because the object that the spec is working with will be a completely different Ruby object from the one in the `update` action in the controller. By calling `reload`, Rails will fetch the data for this object again from the database and update the object in the process.

To begin writing this action in `Api::V1::ProjectsController`, you're going to need to first modify the `before_filter :find_project` line to include the `update` action, changing it from this

```ruby
before_filter :find_project, :only => [:show]
```

to this:

```
before_filter :find_project, :only => [:show, :update]
```

Now in the update action you'll have a project that you can work with because this before_filter will find it for you. Next, you'll write this action into the controller using the code from the following listing.

Listing 13.18 app/controllers/api/v1/projects_controller.rb

```
def update
  @project.update_attributes(params[:project])
  respond_with(@project)
end
```

Well isn't this quite a difference from your standard update actions? You only need to call update_attributes here, which will save the object and return a valid object in the format that you've asked for. If this object fails validation, the status code returned by respond_with will be 422, which represents an Unprocessable Entity, and the body will contain only the validation errors that occurred. If the object is valid, respond_with will return a 200 status code, but an empty response. This is because the client should be aware of what changes it has made to the object, and so there's no need to send back the object.

So which is it? Does the update action work and return the 200 status code you want, or does it break? It's easy to find out by running bin/rspec spec/api/v1/ projects_spec.rb:

```
5 examples, 0 failures
```

All working, good stuff. You've now got a check that the update action responds correctly when a valid object is given, but what if invalid parameters are given instead? Well, the action should return that 422 response mentioned earlier. Although this is testing the already extensively tested[13] Rails behavior, you're making sure that this action always does what you think it should. No misbehaving allowed! You'll quickly whip up a spec for this, placing it right underneath the previous example, "successful JSON" that you wrote in spec/api/v1/projects_spec.rb. The code for it is shown in the following listing.

Listing 13.19 spec/api/v1/projects_spec.rb

```
it "unsuccessful JSON" do
  @project.name.should eql("Ticketee")
  put "#{url}.json", :token => token,
                     :project => {
                       :name => ""
                     }
  last_response.status.should eql(422)
```

---

[13] It's tested within Rails itself.

```
@project.reload
@project.name.should eql("Ticketee")
errors = { :name => ["can't be blank"]}
last_response.body.should eql(errors.to_json)
end
```

In this example, you attempt to set the project's name to a blank string, which should result in the 422 error you want to see. After you `reload` the project, the name should be the same. You should then get the 422 error as the response.

A quick run of `bin/rspec spec/api/v1/projects_spec.rb` should let you know if this is working:

```
7 examples, 0 failures
```

Indeed it is! Is everything else working? A run of `rake spec` will let you know:

```
51 examples, 0 failures, 19 pending
```

"51 examples, 0 failures" is exactly what you like to see. That means that your `update` action is all wrapped up, and now it's time for a commit:

```
git add .
git commit -m "Implement update action for projects API"
git push
```

You've now got three fourths of the CRUD of this API. You're able to create, read, and update project resources. With updating, clients authorized with an admin's token can send through updates to the project resource, which will update the information in the application. The one remaining action you've got to implement is the `destroy` action, for making projects go bye-bye. You're almost home!

13.1.11 Exterminate!

You need to create the `destroy` action, which allows admins of Ticketee to delete projects through the API. To do this, API clients need to make a DELETE request to /api/v1/projects/1.json or /api/v1/projects/1.xml. Upon making this request, the specified project will be deleted—gone forever, exterminated!

You'll write the final example in the spec/v1/api/projects_spec.rb to make sure that people are able to delete projects using this route. You'll use the code from the following listing to do this.

Listing 13.20   spec/v1/api/projects_spec.rb

```
context "deleting a project" do
  before do
    user.admin = true
    user.save
  end

  let(:url) { "/api/v1/projects/#{@project.id}" }
  it "JSON" do
    delete "#{url}.json", :token => token
```

```
        last_response.status.should eql(200)
    end
end
```

When you run `bin/rspec spec/v1/api/projects_spec.rb`, this spec will fail because the `destroy` action doesn't exist:

```
1) /api/v1/projects deleting a project JSON
   Failure/Error: delete "#{url}.json", :token => token
   The action 'destroy' could not be found for Api::V1::ProjectsController
```

You need to add the `destroy` action to the `Api::V1::ProjectsController`, which you can do with this code:

```
def destroy
  @project.destroy
  respond_with(@project)
end
```

The `respond_with` here will respond with a 200 status code and an empty JSON or XML response, which indicates the object was successfully destroyed. But where does `@project` come from? Your `before_filter` should set this up, but it doesn't right now. Let's fix it by changing it from this

```
before_filter :find_project, :only => [:show,
                                       :update]
```

to this:

```
before_filter :find_project, :only => [:show,
                                       :update,
                                       :destroy]
```

When you run `bin/rspec spec/api/v1/projects_spec.rb`, does it pass?

```
8 examples, 0 failures
```

It does, because you're great at what you do! That's the final piece of the projects API, and now people are able to create, read, update, and delete projects through it. The rest of your specs probably pass because you didn't change anything outside the scope, but it's still good to do a check. For old time's sake, you'll also run the features to make sure everything's ok there too. The full command that you'll now run is `rake cucumber:ok spec`. For this command, you should see this output:

```
63 scenarios (63 passed)
732 steps (732 passed)
# and
52 examples, 0 failures, 19 pending
```

All systems are go, so let's make a commit at this lovely point in time where everything is beautiful:

```
git add .
git commit -m "Projects can now be deleted through the API"
```

The entire projects API is now complete. What you've got at the moment is a solid base for version 1 of Ticketee's projects API. You'll now see how you can begin creating the nested API for tickets on a project.

13.2   *Beginning the tickets API*

In this section you'll begin to create an API for tickets on a project. You're only going to be creating the part of the API to list tickets for now, because the remaining parts are similar in style to what you saw with the projects API. This section will give you a taste of how to work with nested resources within the context of an API.

The first part you're going to need for this API is two tests: one to make sure you can get XML results back from this API and another for JSON results. Put these new tests in a new file at spec/api/v1/tickets_spec.rb, beginning with the setup required for both of these tests shown in the following listing.

> **Listing 13.21   spec/api/v1/tickets_spec.rb**

```
require 'spec_helper'

describe "/api/v1/tickets", :type => :api do
  let(:project) { Factory(:project, :name => "Ticketee") }

  before do
    @user = create_user!
    @user.update_attribute(:admin, true)
    @user.permissions.create!(:action => "view",
                              :thing => project)
  end

  let(:token) { @user.authentication_token }
```

In this spec you use a `before` block to set up your user, rather than using a `let` as you did in spec/api/v1/projects_spec.rb. The reason for this is when a `let` is referenced, the block is re-run. If you were to create five tickets and reference a `user` object set up with `let`, it would create five users. This problem becomes way more pronounced when you create 100 objects, each referencing the `let`.

With this setup, you can begin the `context` for your `index` action and then in a `before` block, create 20 tickets for the project by using these lines after the `let(:project)` line:

```
context "index" do
  before do
    5.times do
      Factory(:ticket, :project => project, :user => @user)
    end
  end
```

Finally, you can write the XML and JSON tests by placing the code shown in the following listing inside the `context` block you have written.

Listing 13.22 spec/api/v1/projects_spec.rb

```
context "index" do
  ...

  let(:url) { "/api/v1/projects/#{project.id}/tickets" }

  it "XML" do
    get "#{url}.xml", :token => token
    last_response.body.should eql(project.tickets.to_xml)
  end

  it "JSON" do
    get "#{url}.json", :token => token
    last_response.body.should eql(project.tickets.to_json)
  end
end
```

You've defined the let(:url) here to point to the nested route for tickets of a given project. This URL is currently undefined and so when you run this test with bin/rspec spec/api/v1/tickets_spec.rb, you're told that the route you're requesting doesn't exist:

```
Failure/Error: get "#{url}.json", :token => token
    ActionController::RoutingError:
      No route matches [GET] "/api/v1/projects/1/tickets.json"
```

You can define this route easily inside config/routes.rb by changing these lines

```
namespace :api do
  namespace :v1 do
    resources :projects
  end
end
```

to this:

```
namespace :api do
  namespace :v1 do
    resources :projects do
      resources :tickets
    end
  end
end
```

Now you've got the tickets resource nested within projects for your API again. When you re-run this spec you'll be told this:

```
uninitialized constant Api::V1::TicketsController
```

You can create this controller by creating a new file at app/controllers/api/v1/tickets_controller.rb. This controller needs to first of all respond to both JSON and XML, and find the project for each request using a before_filter. You can begin to define this controller using the code from the following listing.

Listing 13.23   **app/controllers/api/v1/tickets_controller.rb**

```ruby
class Api::V1::TicketsController < Api::V1::BaseController

  before_filter :find_project

  private
    def find_project
      @project = Project.for(current_user).find(params[:project_id])
      rescue ActiveRecord::RecordNotFound
        error = { :error => "The project you were looking for" +
                            " could not be found."}
        respond_with(error, :status => 404)
    end
end
```

In the beginning, you set up the controller to inherit from `Api::V1::BaseController` so that it inherits the basic behavior of your API. Then you tell it that this controller responds to both JSON and XML. Finally, you define a `before_filter :find_project` that will find a project, providing that the user is able to access it. If the user cannot access it, then you `respond_with` a 404 error.

Underneath the `before_filter` in this controller, you need to define the `index` action to return a list of tickets for your project. You can do that with the code shown in the following listing.

Listing 13.24   **app/controllers/api/v1/tickets_controller.rb**

```ruby
def index
  respond_with(@project.tickets)
end
```

That *feels* like you're getting too much for free, doesn't it? Rails is handling a lot of the actions here for you. When you run `bin/rspec spec/api/v1/tickets_spec.rb` specs again, your tests will now pass because you've got the controller defined correctly:

```
2 examples, 0 failures
```

This is a great start to generating a tickets API, and now with the skills you've learned a little earlier in this chapter you should be able to bash out the rest with little effort. Rather than covering that old ground again, it'll be left as an exercise for you.

Let's run all the tests with `rake spec` to make sure you didn't break anything:

```
54 examples, 0 failures, 19 pending
```

Nope, nothing broken there, which is awesome to see. Time for a commit:

```
git add .
git commit -m "Added beginnings of the V1 Tickets API"
git push
```

You should probably limit the number of tickets that are sent back through the API or, even better, cache the result. You'll see ways to do both of these things in chapter 15, and then you can apply them to the API when you feel it's right. For now, it would be fine for a project with a small amount of tickets, but if a project grew to something say, the size of the Rails project,[14] then it would be problematic because Rails would have to instantiate thousands of new Ticket objects per-request. That's no good.

Now that you're versed in the Ways of the API, you can tackle potential problems with it. One of the potential problems with this API is that you'll have too many users accessing it all at once, which may cause performance problems with the application. To prevent this, you'll implement the rate of requests people can make to your server.

13.3   Rate limiting

When a server receives too many requests, it can seem unresponsive. This is simply because it is too busy serving existing requests to serve the hoard of incoming requests. This can happen when an application provides an API to which many clients are connecting. To prevent this, you'll implement rate-limiting on the API side of things, limiting users to only 100 API requests per hour.

The way you're going to do this is to add a new field to the users table that stores a count of how many requests the user has made per hour. To reset the user's count back to zero, you'll create a method that finds only the users who've made requests in the last hour and reset their counts.

13.3.1   *One request, two request, three request, four*

Currently in app/controllers/api/v1/base_controller.rb you've got code that only checks if the token specified is correct, and if so, assigns a user to the @current_user variable:

```
def authenticate_user
  @current_user = User.find_by_authentication_token(params[:token])
  unless @current_user
    respond_with({ :error => "Token is invalid." })
  end
end
```

You'll now be able to do whatever you wish to this user object in an API request. First, you're going to make sure that it's incrementing the request count for a user whenever they make an API request. For this, you need a field in the database to keep a track of user API requests. You'll generate a migration using this command

```
rails g migration add_request_count_to_users request_count:integer
```

This migration will do exactly what you say it should do: add a field called request_count to the users table. You'll need to modify this migration slightly so that the field defaults to 0, which you can do by replacing this line in the new migration:

```
add_column :users, :request_count, :integer
```

with this:

```
add_column :users, :request_count, :integer, :default => 0
```

---

[14] 6000 tickets, as of this writing.

You can run these two commands to run this migration, and then you'll be on your way:

```
rake db:migrate
rake db:test:prepare
```

You can now write a test to make sure that the request count is going to be incremented with each request. You'll open a new file at spec/v1/api/rate_limit_spec.rb so that you can separate these tests from the others, because they are not part of the projects API or the errors from it. Into this file you'll put the code from the following listing.

Listing 13.25   spec/v1/api/rate_limit_spec.rb

```ruby
require 'spec_helper'

describe "rate limiting", :type => :api do
  let(:user) { create_user! }

  it "counts the user's requests" do
    user.request_count.should eql(0)
    get '/api/v1/projects.json', :token => user.authentication_token
    user.reload
    user.request_count.should eql(1)
  end
end
```

When you run this spec now with bin/rspec spec/v1/api/rate_limit_spec.rb, it's going to fail on the final line because the request count hasn't been incremented:

```
Failure/Error: user.request_count.should eql(1)

  expected 1
      got 0

  (compared using eql?)
```

Alright, now that you've got a failing test, you can make it work! Open app/controllers/api/v1/base_controller.rb and add in a new method called check_rate _limit right underneath the current_user method, using this code:

```ruby
def check_rate_limit
  @current_user.increment!(:request_count)
end
```

By calling the increment! method on the user object, the field specified will be incremented once. To call this method, you'll put it as another before_filter underneath the authenticate_user one at the top of this controller:

```ruby
before_filter :check_rate_limit
```

That's all there is to it, and so it will pass when you run bin/rspec spec/api/v1/rate_limit_spec.rb:

```
1 example, 0 failures
```

This is splendid. Before you run any more specs or make any commits, you'll do what you came here to do: limit some rates.

13.3.2 *No more, thanks!*

You've got the method called `check_rate_limit`, but it's not actually doing any checking right now, it's only incrementing. You should do something about this.

You'll begin by writing a test to check that people who reach the rate limit (of 100) receive a warning that tells them simply "Rate limit exceeded." You'll put this new test underneath the previous test you wrote in spec/v1/api/rate_limit_spec.rb using the code from the following listing.

Listing 13.26 spec/v1/api/rate_limit_spec.rb

```
it "stops a user if they have exceeded the limit" do
  user.update_attribute(:request_count, 200)
  get '/api/v1/projects.json', :token => user.authentication_token
  error = { :error => "Rate limit exceeded." }
  last_response.code.should eql(403)
  last_response.body.should eql(error.to_json)
end
```

In this spec, you set the request count to be over the 100 limit. If the user makes another request, they should see the "Rate limit exceeded" error. For the status in this spec, you're expecting the error to be set to a 403, which would indicate a forbidden request that is perfectly in line with the *no, we're not going to let you make any more requests* theme you've got going on.

To make this work, change the `check_rate_limit` method in app/controllers/api/v1/base_controller.rb to what is shown in the following listing.

Listing 13.27 api/controllers/v1/base_controller.rb

```
def check_rate_limit
  if @current_user.request_count > 100
    error = { :error => "Rate limit exceeded." }
    respond_with(error, :status => 403)
  else
    @current_user.increment!(:request_count)
  end
end
```

In this method, if the user's current `request_count` is greater than 100, then you respond with the "Rate limit exceeded" error and set the status code of the response to 403. If it's less than 100, then you'll increment their request count. This should be enough to make your spec pass now, so let's run `bin/rspec spec/api/v1/rate_limit_spec.rb` and find out if this is working:

```
2 examples, 0 failures
```

Your API is now limiting requests to 100 per user, but that's for all time right now, which isn't fun. You need a method that will reset the request count for all users who've made requests. It's the final step you need to complete the rate limiting part of your API.

13.3.3 *Back to zero*

You need to reset the `request_count` of each user who's made a request to your API. This will be a method on the `User` model, and so you'll put its test in a new file as spec/models/user_spec.rb file, inside the `describe User` block, using the code from the following listing.

Listing 13.28   spec/models/user_spec.rb

```
require 'spec_helper'

describe User do
  it "resets user request count" do
    user = Factory(:user)
    user.update_attribute(:request_count, 42)
    User.reset_request_count!
    user.reload
    user.request_count.should eql(0)
  end
end
```

With this spec, you set a new user's request count to something other than 0; 42 is a random number,[15] and you're quite fortunate for it to exist so that you can use it. The `reset_request_count!` method isn't defined, but as the remainder of the test implies, the user's request count should be 0. This test, unsurprisingly, will not pass when it runs, and so you should write the method to make it pass.

As the `reset_request_count!` method is called on `User`, you define this method in app/models/user.rb using the following code above the `to_s` method:

```
def self.reset_request_count!
  update_all("request_count = 0", "request_count > 0")
end
```

You're placing this code right above the `to_s` method because it is best practice to place class methods (such as `reset_request_count!`) above instance methods in a model, as some instance methods may refer to class methods. Also, if everybody puts their code in logical places, then you won't be confused when you look at it, which is what Rails is all about.

The `update_all` method here will set the `request_count` on all user records (the first argument) that have a `request_count > 0` (the second argument), or a `request_count` greater than zero. No point resetting counts that are zero back to zero.

Now that the `reset_request_count!` method is defined, does it work as your test says it should? Well, let's run `bin/rspec spec/models/user_spec.rb`:

```
1 example, 0 failures
```

Cool, so now you've got the request count being reset for all users whenever this method is called. You'll take a look at calling this method automatically when we look at background jobs in chapter 15.

---

[15] Not really.

That completes everything you need to do for rate limiting in your API. Before you make a commit, run all the specs with the `rake spec` to see if the API is still working:

```
56 examples, 0 failures, 18 pending
```

All good! You can commit this now:

```
git add .
git commit -m "Added rate limiting to the V1 API"
git push
```

You've implemented a way to stop people from making too many requests to your API, which will possibly stop your application from being overloaded due to excessive API requests. Next, we look at how you can implement versioning in your API.

13.4 *Versioning an API*

At the beginning of this chapter, we discussed how all your API routes would be under the /api/v1/ namespace. This was because you wanted to provide a predictable outcome of the requests to the URLs. If you go changing URLs to provide extra data or to take away data, some API clients may malfunction. So when you want to make changes to your API, you group them all up into logical versions.

With this separation, you can provide a link, such as /api/v1/projects.json, which will return the attributes you're already familiar with, as well as another path for the next version. This second version's path will be /api/v2/projects.json, and the difference between the two is that you'll change the `name` field to be called `title` instead. Although this is potentially a trivial example,[16] it's a great case to show off how to make two API versions different.

13.4.1 *Creating a new version*

To begin the versioning process, copy these routes from config/routes.rb in your application:

```
namespace :api do
  namespace :v1 do
    resources :projects
  end
end
```

And place them beneath, renaming v1 to v2:

```
namespace :api do
  namespace :v2 do
    resources :projects
  end
end
```

Now you'll need to create a new app/controllers/api/v2 directory, which you can do by copying app/controllers/api/v1 into that location. You've now got version 2 of

---

[16] Also a tiny fraction slower than v1, given you'll be calling a method from within another method rather renaming it.

your API. You'll need to open these controllers and replace the multiple occurrences of `Api::V1` with `Api::V2`.

Strangely, version 2 of your API is, right now, identical to version 1 of your API. That's intentional: a new version of the API should be an improvement, not an entirely new thing. With this separation, you can modify version 2 of the API as you please, leaving version 1 alone.

Before deprecating the `name` field in your project responses, you'll write a test to make sure that this is gone. This test will now test version 2 of the API, and so you'll copy over the spec/api/v1 directory to spec/api/v2, also replacing occurrences of v1 in these files with v2. The test for the new `title` field will now go in spec/api/v2/projects_spec.rb and will test that the `projects viewable by this user` action returns projects with `title`, and not `name`, using the code from the following listing to replace the JSON example in the `index` context.

Listing 13.29   spec/api/v2/projects_spec.rb

```
context "projects viewable by this user" do
  let(:url) { "/api/v2/projects" }
  let(:options) { { :except => :name, :methods => :title } }      ◁⏋  Pass
  it "JSON" do                                                         options to
    get "#{url}.json", :token => token                           ❶   to_json

    body = Project.readable_by(user).to_json(options)

    last_response.body.should eql(body)
    last_response.status.should eql(200)

    projects = JSON.parse(last_response.body)
    projects.any? do |p|
      p["project"]["title"] == "Ticketee"
    end.should be_true

    projects.all? do |p|
      p["project"]["name"].blank?
    end.should be_true
  end
end
```

At the beginning of this test, you need to pass the same options to `to_json` ❶ as you pass to `respond_with`, because the `respond_with` method generates the same output as `to_json`.

In the final lines of this test, you're checking that it's now `title` and not `name` that returns the correct project title, and that the `name` key on all projects is blank. You'll also need to change the XML test of this method to the code shown in the following listing.

Listing 13.30   spec/api/v2/projects_spec.rb

```
it "XML" do
  get "#{url}.xml", :token => token

  body = Project.readable_by(user).to_xml(options)
```

```
    last_response.body.should eql(body)
    projects = Nokogiri::XML(last_response.body)
    projects.css("project title").text.should eql("Ticketee")
    projects.css("project name").text.should eql("")
end
```

When you run this test using bin/rspec spec/api/v2/projects_spec.rb, it's broken:

```
Failure/Error: last_response.body.should eql(body)
  expected "[{[ticket hash without name key]}]"
  got      "[{[ticket hash with name key]}]"
```

This is because the name field is still being returned by your API. To exclude this field from your API, you can use the :except option to respond_with calls. In app/controllers/api/v2/projects_controller.rb the index method can now be altered to this:

```
def index
  projects = Project.readable_by(current_user)
  respond_with(projects, :except => :name, :methods => :title)
end
```

The :except option here will exclude the name field from the responses provided by this API, and the methods option will call the title method (you'll define it in a moment), providing that in your API response. You still need to have the name field in your database because it's used in quite a few places in your application. You could change it all now, but this example is purely to show off the :except option and API versioning. A change like that would be recommended over this example, however it's best left as another exercise for you.

To make your API respond with the title method, you need to define it in app/models/project.rb inside the Project class like this:

```
def title
  name
end
```

Now when you run bin/rspec spec/api/v2/projects_spec.rb, the tests that you edited will pass:

```
8 examples, 0 failures
```

You've seen how you can generate a new version of your API and alter the output of it, and the text *says* that your original API (v1) shouldn't be effected, but was it? A great way to check is a quick run of bin/rspec spec/api/v1:

```
15 examples, 0 failures
```

Great, that's all working! A quick run of rake spec will confirm your suspicions that nothing is broken:

```
71 examples, 0 failures, 18 pending
```

Awesome stuff. Let's make a new commit:

```
git add .
git commit -m "Implement v2 of the API,
```

```
                         renaming name to title for projects"
git push
```

Alright, so now you've got two versions of your API. Generally, there's much more than a single change in a new API version, but this is a good start. When you announce this API to the people who use your application, they can switch their libraries over to using it immediately, or, ideally, remain using the old version. After a while, you may elect to turn off the first version of the API, and you would do that by giving your users considerable notice such as a month, and then un-defining the routes and deleting the controllers and tests associated with that version. Out with the old and in with the new, as they say.

You've now seen how you can serve data from your application using an API, but how do you read it? The answer to that lies in a part of Rails called Active Resource.

13.5   *Summary*

You've seen in this chapter how you can use the `Rack::Test::Methods` module, given to you for free by the `rack-test` gem, to test that requests to URLs provided by your application return valid API responses in JSON and XML formats. Users will then be able to make these same requests for their own applications or libraries to get at the data in your system. What they come up with is up to their imagination. In this chapter, we only covered one aspect (projects) for your API, but with the knowledge found in this chapter you could easily create the other aspects for tickets, users, states, or tags.

In the second section of this chapter you saw how you can limit the request rate to your API on a per-user basis. Users can make up to 100 requests to your system, and when they attempt to make their 101st the application denies them the request and provides a relevant error message. This is to deter people from excessively using the API, as you do not want your server to become overloaded immediately.

Last, you saw how you can generate a new version of your API so that you can introduce a change, or changes, so as to not break the previous version of the API. Once an API has been released to the public, its output shouldn't be modified, as this may affect the libraries referring to it. The easiest way to introduce these modifications is through a new version, which is what you did. Eventually, you may choose to deprecate the old API, or you may not. It's really a matter of personal choice.

Your application's at a pretty great point now and is ready for prime time! To show it off to the masses, it's best that you put the code on a computer dedicated to serving the application, rather than running it on some local hardware. In chapter 14, you'll deploy your application to an Ubuntu 10.10 box, learning about the core components to a deployment software stack as you go.

14

Deployment

This chapter covers

- Deploying a Rails app to an Ubuntu server
- Using RVM and Ruby in a server environment
- Hosting a Rails app using the Passenger gem

In this chapter you'll deploy your Ticketee application to a new Ubuntu install. Ubuntu is the preferred operating system for deploying Rails applications, mainly due to its simplicity of use and easy package management. You don't need to install another operating system on your computer; you'll be using a product called Oracle VM VirtualBox.

You'll set up this machine manually so that you can see how all the pieces fit together. There are automatic tools such Puppet,[1] Chef,[2] Babushka,[3] and Git Pusshuten[4] that can do most, if not all, of this setup for you. To cover them all adequately in this chapter would turn the chapter into a book. Deployment is an enormous subject and different people have very different opinions of how it should be

---

[1] http://puppetlabs.com.
[2] http://opscode.com/chef/.
[3] http://babushka.me.
[4] http://gitpusshuten.com/.

done. This chapter will give you an adequate taste of what parts are involved in setting up a server, but shouldn't be considered as the be all and end all of deployment. There are countless ways to skin this cat.

This chapter covers the following processes:

- Setting up a server
- Installing RVM and Ruby
- Creating a user account
- Deploying an application using Capistrano
- Setting up a database server using PostgreSQL
- Running the application using Nginx and Passenger
- Securing the server

While this isn't an exhaustive list of everything that needs to be done for deployment, it is a great start. When you're done, you're going to have a server that's able to receive requests and return responses from your application like a normal web server. Let's get into it.

14.1   *Server setup*

Your first step is to set up the Oracle VirtualBox software on your machine. This software is free, works on all of the main operating system variants, and provides a virtual box (or environment) that you can run another operating system in while running your current operating system.

As an alternative to VirtualBox you could get a VPS with a paid service such as Linode,[5] Slicehost,[6] or Amazon EC2,[7] which allows you to set up a box with Ubuntu (or any one of a few other operating systems) pre-installed. You could also use Heroku,[8] which provides free hosting that has read-only access to the file system.[9] Each of these services have in-depth guides, which should be used as a primary reference if you're going to take this path.

Either direction is fine. If the latter path is taken, jump straight to section 14.2.

14.1.1   *Setting up a server using VirtualBox*

Oracle VirtualBox[10] is software that allows you to run another operating system inside your main operating system. Coupled with Vagrant[11]—a gem used for setting up VirtualBox servers—this is a perfect combination for getting an experimental server

---

[5] http://linode.com.

[6] http://slicehost.org.

[7] http://aws.amazon.com/ec2/.

[8] http://heroku.com.

[9] This would cause the file upload part of Ticketee to fail because it requires write-access. To fix this, you would upload images to Amazon S3. Amazon S3 and Paperclip have good enough documentation that this should be easily figured out.

[10] http://virtualbox.org.

[11] http://vagrantup.com.

up and running. Vagrant will allow you to download an operating system image and then set up VirtualBox in an exceptionally easy fashion.

To install VirtualBox, you must first download it from http://virtualbox.org and install it like a normal program.[12] After that, you need to install the vagrant gem, which you can do by running this command:

```
gem install vagrant
```

Now that you've got VirtualBox and Vagrant, you can install Ubuntu using Vagrant. This is the operating system that you'll use to run your server. This file is pretty large (over 500MB) and may not be good for some connections. As an alternative, we would recommend using a VPS, as suggested earlier. This command will download Ubuntu Lucid Lynx (10.04) which you can use as a perfectly fine base to set up your server:

```
vagrant box add base http://files.vagrantup.com/lucid32.box
```

To start up this server, you need to create a new folder called ubuntu (the name isn't important and could be anything), where the configuration of your server will be stored. You can then run vagrant up and vagrant ssh to boot it and connect to it through SSH. Altogether:

```
mkdir ubuntu
cd ubuntu
vagrant init
vagrant up
vagrant ssh
```

The up command will take a couple of minutes to run, but the ssh command should be instantaneous after that.

> **NOTE** If at any point you wish to shut down your server, you can use the vagrant halt command.

This is how you connect to servers in the real world, except you would use a command such as this:

```
ssh username@some-server.somewhere.com
```

The vagrant ssh is a good-enough analogy to that. By running vagrant ssh you connect to your server as the user vagrant. This user has administrative (or more commonly referred to as root) access on this box, and so you're able to install the packages that you need.

If you're using a non-Vagrant machine, you'll first need to set up a user for yourself rather than operating as the root user, as this can be dangerous.[13] To do this, use this command (replacing user with a username such as ryan):

---

[12] If you're on Windows XP you may encounter issues where it claims to have not been verified correctly. This is a known problem. If you skip the errors, it will still work.

[13] For example, if you were running a script as the root user and that script attempted to delete the /usr directory, the command would execute. By executing commands as non-root, you save yourself some potential damage from malevolent scripts. This is because the user will only have access to some directories, rather than root, which has access to everything.

```
useradd -d /home/user -m -s /bin/bash -G admin user
```

This command will create a directory at /home/user and set this user's home path to that directory. This is done with the -m and -d options, respectively. Next, the command sets the user's shell to /bin/bash—which is the default shell of UNIX operating systems—using the -s option. Near the end of this command, the -G option specifies that this user will be a part of the admin group, which will let the user execute commands using sudo, a kind of super-user command. This part is important because you'll need these permissions to set up your server. At the end of the command, specify the username of this new user.

Next, you need to set a password for this user, which you can do with this command:

```
passwd user
```

You need to enter the new password for this user twice, and then you're done. You mustn't forget the password, otherwise you'll have to reset it as the root user.

With that done, let's switch into this user by using this command:

```
su user
```

Now you're all set up to go about installing the different software packages you'll need to get your server up and running.

14.1.2 *Installing the base*

The majority of software packages are installed on Ubuntu using a system called Aptitude. You can install packages from their source code too, if you wish (with the help of a package called build_essential, which contains the build tools you need). These Aptitude packages are downloaded from a package repository and then installed for you. To ensure that the list of these packages are up-to-date, run this command:

```
sudo aptitude update
```

This command goes through the list of sources, connecting to each of them and downloading a package list that is then cached by Ubuntu. When you go to install a package (your next step), Ubuntu will reference these lists to find the packages and the necessary dependencies for them.

Once this command is complete, continue the set up by configuring RVM and creating a deploy user.

RVM is short for Ruby Version Manager and provides a simple way to install and maintain versions of Ruby on your system. You're going to be using it today to install a single Ruby version on your system, but it's good to learn it.

To get started, you're going to need to install some packages that will provide the necessary tools to use RVM. These packages are build-essential, git-core, and curl. RVM uses these packages to build the Ruby version for your server. The git-core provides the base Git functionality that RVM uses to stay up to date, and is also used to deploy your application because you're hosting it on GitHub. Finally, `curl` allows you to connect to a URL and download its content. You'll use this last package to install RVM.

To install these packages, run this command:

```
sudo aptitude -y install build-essential git-core curl
```

The `sudo` part of this command tells Ubuntu to run a command as a super-user (root).

14.2 RVM and Ruby

You could install Ruby by downloading the package manually, extracting it, and then running the necessary commands yourself, but that's boring. You could also install it using the package manager that comes with Ubuntu, but the Ruby that it provides is old and has been known to be broken.

Wouldn't it be nice if there was a tool that would install Ruby for you? There is! It's called RVM!

14.2.1 Installing RVM

RVM provides several benefits over a standard Ruby compile, such as the ability to easily install and upgrade your Ruby install using commands like `rvm install 1.9.2` to install Ruby 1.9.2. No digging for links on the http://ruby-lang.org site for you, no siree.

There are a couple of ways you can install RVM. The first is a user-based install, installing it in an .rvm directory within the user's own directory. But you're going to want to access gems at a system-level later on in this chapter, so it's best to install RVM at a system level.[14] To do this, run this command:

```
sudo bash < <(curl -s https://rvm.beginrescueend.com/install/rvm)
```

Once this script has finished executing you should see a lot of output, and part of it will contain installation instructions for packages you need to install before installing Ruby. Your version of Ruby is the standard Ruby 1.9.2, which is more commonly known as Matz's Ruby Interpreter, or MRI for short. The installation advises you to run a command to install the necessary packages for MRI. Do that, and add a couple of extra packages (`libpq-dev` and `libcurl4-openssl-dev`) that you'll need for later:

```
sudo aptitude -y install build-essential bison openssl \
libreadline6 libreadline6-dev curl git-core zlib1g \
zlib1g-dev libssl-dev libyaml-dev libsqlite3-0 \
libsqlite3-dev sqlite3 libxml2-dev libxslt-dev \
autoconf libc6-dev libpq-dev libcurl4-openssl-dev
```

With these packages installed, you'll experience minimum hassle when you install Ruby itself. To install Ruby using your current user, the user needs to be a part of the

---

[14] To install RVM at a user level, just remove sudo from the command.

rvm group, which is a group created by the installation of RVM. To add your current user to this group, run this command:

```
sudo usermod -a -G rvm user
```

The -a option here tells the command to append some groups to the list of groups that the user is in, and the -G option (like you saw before with useradd) specifies the group. You specify your username on the end of this command, telling it who you want this new group applied to.

To make the rvm command effective for all users, add a line to /etc/profile. Whenever new terminal sessions are launched, this file is read and run. Put a line in it using these commands:

```
sudo su
echo 'source "/usr/local/rvm/scripts/rvm"' >> /etc/profile
exit
```

The source command here will load the/usr/local/rvm/scripts/rvm file for each user whenever they start a new session. To make this change effective for the current session, exit out of your terminal and log back in. Once back in, you should be able to run rvm and have it output the help information.

If that's the case, then you are now ready to install Ruby.

14.2.2 *Installing Ruby*

Ruby 1.9.2 is considered the latest stable version of Ruby (at least, as of this writing). By installing it, you're on your way to being able to run your Rails application on this server. To install this version of Ruby, run this command:

```
rvm install 1.9.2
```

This command will take some time to run as it needs to download, compile, and then install Ruby. To switch to using this Ruby, use this command:

```
rvm use 1.9.2
```

When you type ruby -v into the terminal, you should see something like this:

```
ruby 1.9.2p180 (2011-02-18 revision 30909) [i686-linux]
```

The value may be different, but as long as it begins with ruby 1.9.2, you know that you've got the right Ruby version installed. To make this the default version of Ruby for your user, run the rvm use command again, but pass in an option:

```
rvm use --default 1.9.2
```

Now every time that you log in to this server you'll be using this version of Ruby. While you're doing Ruby things, let's install the Bundler gem, which you'll need for your application to install its gems on the server and rake for running Rake tasks:

```
gem install bundler rake
```

So now you've got the beginnings of a pretty good environment set up for your application, but you don't have your application on the server yet. To do this, you need to undertake a process referred to as *deployment*. Through this process you'll put your application's code on the server and be one step closer to letting people use the application.

When you deploy, you'll use a user without root privileges to run the application, just in case. Call this user the same as your (imaginary) domain: ticketeeapp.com.

14.3 Creating a user for the app

You're calling this user ticketeeapp.com because if you wanted to deploy more than one application to your server, there will be no confusion as to which user is responsible for what. When you set up a database later on, this username will be the same as your database name. This is for convenience's sake, but also because the database will be owned by a user with the same name, allowing this account and none other (bar the database super user) to access it. It's all quite neat.

To begin to set up this user, run these commands:

```
sudo useradd ticketeeapp.com -s /bin/bash -m -d /home/ticketeeapp.com
sudo chown -R ticketeeapp.com /home/ticketeeapp.com
sudo passwd ticketeeapp.com
```

You've used a couple of options to the `useradd` command. The `-s` option sets the shell for the user to /bin/bash (the standard shell found in most UNIX-based operating systems) and the `-d` option sets their home directory to /home/ticketeeapp.com, while the `-m` option makes sure that the user's home directory exists. The second command, `chown` (short for change owner), changes the owner of the /home/ticketeeapp.com directory to be the ticketeeapp.com user. The final command, `passwd`, prompts you to set a password for this user, which you should set to something complex (that you'll be able to remember) to stop people hacking your ticketeeapp.com user.[15]

To make this account even more secure, you can switch to key-based authentication.

14.3.1 Key-based authentication

In this next step, you'll set up a key that will allow you to log in as your user and `deploy` on your server without a password. This is called key-based authentication and requires two files: a private key and a public key. The private key goes on the developer's computer and should be kept private, as the name implies, because it is the key to gain access to the server. The public key file can be shared with anybody and is used by a server to authenticate a user's private key.

You'll use a key-based authentication for your server because it is incredibly secure versus a password authentication scheme. To quote the official Ubuntu instructions on this[16]:

---

[15] Even though this won't matter in a short while (when you turn off password authentication and switch to the more secure *key-based authentication*), it's still good practice to always secure any user account on any system with a strong password.

[16] https://help.ubuntu.com/community/SSH/OpenSSH/Configuring.

To be as hard to guess as a normal SSH key, a password would have to contain 634 random letters and numbers.

—OpenSSH Configuring

Not many people today would be willing to use a password containing 634 random letters and numbers! Considering the average password length is 8 characters, this a vast improvement over password-based authentication.

You're going to enable this key-based authentication for both your current user and your ticketeeapp.com. For now, use the same key generated for use with GitHub; however, it's recommended that a *different* key be used for the server.

Public keys are stored at a file called .ssh/authorized_keys located in the user's home directory, the user being the user you will connect as through SSH. When the user attempts to connect to the server, the private and public keys are used to confirm the user's identity.[17] Because the chances against two users having the same public and private key are so astronomically high, it is generally accepted as a secure means of authentication.

In this instance, you'll create two of these ~/.ssh/authorized_keys files: one for each user. In each case, create the ~/.ssh directory before creating authorized_keys. Begin with the user you're currently logged in as.

Let's create the ~/.ssh directory now using this command:

```
mkdir ~/.ssh
```

Now you need to copy over the public key from your local computer to the ~/.ssh directory on the server, which you can do by running this command on your local system:

```
# NOTE: Run this on your *local* machine, not the server!
scp ~/.ssh/id_rsa.pub user@your-server:~/.ssh/[your_name]_key.pub
```

If you're using Vagrant...

Vagrant already has a ~/.ssh/authorized_keys file, so there's no need to re-create it. Overwriting this file may cause `vagrant ssh` to no longer work.

You will also need to forward the SSH port from the virtual machine launched by Vagrant to a local port in order to connect without using Vagrant. While you're here, forward the HTTP port (80) as well so that you can access it from the outside. Go into the Ubuntu directory that you created at the beginning of this chapter, open Vagrant-File, and add this inside the `Vagrant::Config.run` block:

```
config.vm.forward_port "ssh", 22, 2200
config.vm.forward_port "http", 80, 4567
```

To connect to this server, use port 2200 for SSH and port 4567 for HTTP. When you use the `scp` command, the port can be specified using the `-P` (capital *p*) option and `ssh` using `-p` (lowercase *p*), with the port number specified directly after this option. In places where these commands are used, substitute `your-server` with `localhost` and `user` with `vagrant`.

---

[17] For a good explanation of how this process works, check this page: http://unixwiz.net/techtips/ssh-agent-forwarding.html#agent.

At this stage, you'll be prompted for a password, which is the complex one you set up a little earlier. Enter it here and the file will be copied over to the server.

Add this key to the ~/.ssh/authorized_keys file *on the server* by using this:

```
cat ~/.ssh/[your_name]_key.pub >> ~/.ssh/authorized_keys
```

This command will append the key to ~/.ssh/authorized_keys if that file already exists, or create the file and then fill it with the content if it doesn't. Either way, you're going to have a ~/.ssh/authorized_keys file, which means that you'll be able to SSH to this server without using your complex password. If you disconnect from the server and then reconnect, you shouldn't be prompted for your password. This means that the authentication is working.

Finally, change the permissions on this ~/.ssh/authorized_keys file so that only the user it belongs to can read it:

```
chmod 600 ~/.ssh/authorized_keys
```

With that set, change into the application's user account by running `sudo su ticketeeapp.com` and run the same steps, beginning with `mkdir ~/.ssh` and ending with disconnecting and reconnecting without password prompt. Remember to change `user` in the `scp` command to be the ticketeeapp.com user this time around.

If both of these accounts are working without password authentication, then you may as well turn it off!

14.3.2 *Disabling password authentication*

You've just implemented key-based authentication on your system for both the accounts you have, thus removing the need for any kind of password authentication. To secure your server against possible password attacks, it's a good idea to turn off password authentication altogether.

To do this, open /etc/ssh/sshd_config using `sudo nano /etc/ssh/sshd_config`[18] and add `PasswordAuthentication no` where it would otherwise say `#Password-Authentication yes` (the # symbol indicates a commented line, just like Ruby). You can find this line by pressing Ctrl+W, typing in `PasswordAuth`, and pressing Enter. This configures your SSH server to not accept password authentication.

Towards the top of this file there's a line that says `PermitRootLogin yes`. Change this line to read `PermitRootLogin no` instead, so that it blocks all SSH connections for the root user, increasing the security further.

> **NOTE** There is also /etc/ssh/ssh_config, which is a little confusing... two files with nearly identical names. The file you just edited is the file for the SSH *server* (or daemon, hence the d at the end), while the ssh_config file is for the SSH client. Make sure you're editing the right one.

Last, quit nano by pressing Ctrl+X and then Y to confirm that you do want to quit and save. Next, you need to restart the SSH daemon by using this command:

---

[18] nano is the basic editor that comes with Ubuntu.

```
service ssh restart
```

The server is now set up with key-based authentication, which completes the user setup part of this chapter.

The next step is to install a sturdy database server where you can keep the data for your application when it's deployed. At the moment (on your local machine) you're using the SQLite database for this. That's great for light development, but you probably want something more robust for your application, just in case it gets popular overnight.[19] That robust something is a database server called PostgreSQL.

14.4   *The database server*

PostgreSQL is the relational database[20] preferred by the majority of Rails developers. It will work perfectly with the Ticketee application because there's no SQLite3-specific code within the Ticketee application at the moment.[21]

To install, use the `aptitude` command again:

```
sudo aptitude install postgresql-8.4
```

This will install the necessary software and commands for the database server, such as `psql` (used for interacting with the database server in a console), `createuser` (for creating a user in the system), and `createdb` (for creating databases on the server).[22] You'll be using these commands to create a user and a database for your application.

14.4.1   *Creating a database and user*

To begin this, switch to the postgres user, which is another account that this postgresql-8.4 install has set up. To switch into this user, use this command:

```
sudo su postgres
```

This user account is the super user for the database and can perform commands such as creating databases and users, precisely what you want! Creating the database is easy enough; you only need to run `createdb` like this:

```
createdb ticketeeapp.com
```

Creating a user in PostgreSQL is a little more difficult, but (thankfully) isn't rocket science. Using the `createuser` command, answer no to all the questions provided:

```
$ createuser ticketeeapp.com
Shall the new role be a superuser? (y/n) n
Shall the new role be allowed to create databases? (y/n) n
Shall the new role be allowed to create more new roles? (y/n) n
```

---

[19] Chances are low, but this is more to demonstrate how to set it up with a different database server.

[20] http://en.wikipedia.org/wiki/Relational_database. Contrasts the NoSQL term: http://en.wikipedia.org/wiki/NoSQL.

[21] Some Rails applications are developed on specific database systems and may contain code that depends on that system being used. Be wary.

[22] For more information about how to configure PostgreSQL, read about the pg_hba.conf file: http://www.postgresql.org/docs/9.0/static/auth-pg-hba-conf.html.

Create the database and the user in PostgreSQL with the same name so that when the system user account of ticketeeapp.com attempts to connect to this database they are automatically granted access. There is no need to configure this at all, which is most excellent. This process is referred to as *ident authentication.*

14.4.2 *Ident authentication*

Ident authentication works by determining if the user connecting has an account with an identical name on the database server. Your system's user account is named ticketeeapp.com and the PostgreSQL user you created is also named ticketeeapp.com. You can attempt to connect using the `psql` command from the ticketeeapp.com user, after first exiting from the `postgres` user's session:

```
exit
sudo su ticketeeapp.com
psql
```

If everything goes well, you should see this prompt:

```
psql (8.4.8)
Type "help" for help.

ticketeeapp.com=>
```

This means that you're connected to the ticketeeapp.com database successfully. You can now execute SQL queries here if you wish. Exit out of this prompt by typing `\q` and pressing Enter.

That's all you need to do for your database for now. You've got a fully functioning server, ready to accept your tables and data for your application. Now you need to give it what it needs! You can do this by putting the application on the server and running the `rake db:migrate` command, which will create the tables, and then `rake db:seed`, which will insert the basic data found inside db/seeds.rb.

We're not going to make you manually copy over this application, as this can get repetitive and boring. As programmers, we don't like repetitive and boring. One of your kind is called Jamis Buck, and he created a little tool called Capistrano to help automate the process of deploying your application.

14.5 *Deploy away!*

Capistrano is a gem originally created by Jamis Buck that is now maintained by Lee Hambley and additional volunteers, as well as the growing community that use it. It was initially designed for easy application deployment for Rails applications, but can now be used for other applications as well. Capistrano provides an easy way to configure and deploy versions of an application to one or many servers.

You'll use Capistrano to put your application's code on the server, automatically run the migrations, and restart the server after this has been completed. This action is referred to as a *deploy.*

Before you leap into that however, you're going to set up a *deploy key* for your repository on GitHub.

14.5.1 *Deploy keys*

If your repository was private on GitHub, you would clone it with the URL of git@github.com:our_username/ticketee.git and would need to authenticate with a private key. You shouldn't copy your private key to the server because if a malicious person gains access to the server they will also then have your private key, which may be used for other things.

To solve this particular conundrum, generate another private/public key pair just for the server itself and put the public key on GitHub to be a deploy key for this repository. This will allow the server to clone the repository.

To do this, run the following command as the ticketeeapp.com user on your server:

```
ssh-keygen -t rsa
```

Press Enter to put the key at the default ~/.ssh/id_rsa.pub location. You can enter a password for it, but if you do this you will be prompted for it on every deploy. It's really personal preference whether or not to do this.

This command will generate two new files: a public and private key. The private key should remain secret on the server and shouldn't be shared with any external parties. The public key, however, can be given to anybody. You're going to put this key on GitHub now.

Run the `cat` command to get the contents of the public key file, like this:

```
cat ~/.ssh/id_rsa.pub
ssh-rsa AAAAB3NzaC1yc2EAA...
```

You should copy the output of this command into your clipboard. Your next step is to go to the repository on GitHub and click the Admin link in the bar in the view for the repository, shown in figure 14.1.

From here, press the Deploy Keys link and then paste the key into the box, calling it ticketeeapp.com to keep up with your current naming scheme, as shown in figure 14.2.

When you're done here, click the Add Key button, which will add the key you've specified to the list of deploy keys on GitHub. You should then be able to run a `git clone` command on the server using the private URL to clone your repository:

```
git clone git@github.com:our_username/ticketee.git ~/ticketee
```

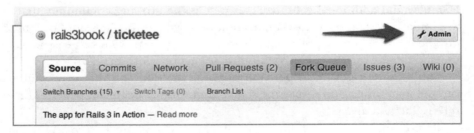

Figure 14.1   Admin button

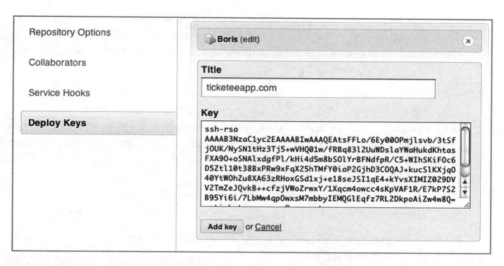

Figure 14.2   Paste in the key, and add a title.

If there is a ticketee directory at the current location of the server that contains the directories your application should contain, then this works. You can delete this directory now; you'll be putting the code on the server at another location using Capistrano.

Before that happens, you'll need to configure Capistrano.

14.5.2 *Configuring Capistrano*

To begin with, add the capistrano gem to your application's Gemfile using this code:

```
group :development do
  gem 'capistrano'
end
```

To install this gem, you (and other developers of your application) are able to run bundle install, which will keep those other developers up-to-date with all gems. Running gem install capistrano would only update them with Capistrano, and even then it may be a version that is incompatible with the one that you've developed.

When the gem is installed, you can set it up inside a Rails application by running this command from the root of the application:

```
capify .
```

This will create two files: Capfile and config/deploy.rb. The Capfile is a file containing setup for Capistrano in the application and the following default code that will be used to load your Capistrano configuration:

```
load 'deploy' if respond_to?(:namespace) # cap2 differentiator
Dir['vendor/plugins/*/recipes/*.rb'].each { |plugin| load(plugin) }

load 'config/deploy' # remove this line to skip loading any ...
```

The final line of this file is the most important, as it loads the config/deploy.rb file. This file contains the configuration for deploying your application. Everything in this file dictates how your application is deployed. We'll go through it with you line by line, beginning with these two lines:

```
set :application, "set your application name here"
set :repository,  "set your repository location here"
```

When you call `set` in Capistrano, it sets a variable you (or Capistrano itself) can reference later. The `application` variable here should be the name of your application and the `repository` variable should be the path to your application. Change these lines to this:

```
set :application, "ticketee"
set :repository,  "git://github.com/rails3book/ticketee.git"
```

Deploying a branch

When you deploy your application to the server, it will read from the `master` branch. If you'd like to change this, set the branch using this line in your configuration:

```
set :branch, "production"
```

You would also need to create this new branch in the GitHub repository called production with the `git checkout -b production` and `git push origin production` commands.

For a good branching model, check out this post: http://nvie.com/posts/a-successful-git-branching-model/.

On the next line of config/deploy.rb there's the `scm` setting:

```
set :scm, :subversion
```

You're going to use Git and not Subversion in this case, so change the line to this:

```
set :scm, :git
```

On the next few lines there are a couple of roles defined. These roles point to

- *web*—The server or servers responsible for serving requests for your application
- *app*—The server or servers where the application's code is hosted
- *db*—The server or servers where the database for the application is hosted

Right now we won't worry about multiple-server setups, focusing only on having everything on the one box. Your `web`, `app`, and `db` roles are all the same server in this instance. Therefore, you can replace those three lines with this:

```
role :web, "[your-server]"
role :app, "[your-server]"
role :db,  "[your-server]", :primary => true
```

Here you replace [your-server] with the address of the server, which is the same one that you've been SSH'ing to. If you're using Vagrant, this address is simply localhost and you'll need to add another line to specify the port:

```
set :port, 2200
```

Now that you've covered all the default options in config/deply.rb, you'll add some others to provide more information to Capistrano so that it can set up your application correctly.

The first two settings that you'll need to set up are the user and the path to which you'll deploy your application. Capistrano (unfortunately) can't guess what these are, and so you have to be explicit. The user will be the ticketeeapp.com user and the path will be /home/ticketeeapp.com/apps. Use the application name as the name of a subfolder of that application so the application will be deployed into /home/ticketeeapp .com/apps/ticketee. Underneath the set :scm line, put these settings:

```
set :user, "ticketeeapp.com"
set :deploy_to, "/home/ticketeeapp.com/apps/#{application}"
```

The ticketeeapp.com user doesn't have sudo privileges, so tell Capistrano not to use the sudo command by using this line:

```
set :use_sudo, false
```

When you deploy your application, you don't want to keep every single release that you've ever deployed on the server. To get rid of the old deploys (referred to as releases), put this in config/deploy.rb:

```
set :keep_releases, 5
```

This will keep the last five releases that you have deployed, deleting any releases that are older than that.

Last, at the bottom of the file there are a couple of lines for defining deploy:start, deploy:stop, and deploy:restart tasks for Passenger, which are commented out. Remove the comment hash from the beginning of these lines, transforming them to this:

```
namespace :deploy do
  task :start do ; end
  task :stop do ; end
  task :restart, :roles => :app, :except => { :no_release => true } do
    run "#{try_sudo} touch #{File.join(current_path,'tmp','restart.txt')}"
  end
end
```

This defines a blank start and stop task and a full restart task for your app role. This task will run the touch /home/ticketeapp.com/apps/ticketee/tmp/restart.txt command, which will tell your server (not yet set up) to restart the application, causing your newly deployed code to be started up upon the next request.

With the Capistrano configuration done, you can run the `cap` command, passing in the name of a task to set up your application, such as `deploy:setup`. This task is one of a group of tasks that are provided by default with Capistrano. To see a list of these tasks, use the `cap -T` command.

14.5.3 *Setting up the deploy environment*

You'll now use the `deploy:setup` task, which will set up the folder where your application is deployed, /home/ticketeeapp.com/apps/ticketee, with some basic folders:

```
cap deploy:setup
```

This command is in the same vein as the `rails new` command you've used previously because it sets up an identical, standard scaffold for every Capistrano. When this command runs, you'll see a large chunk of output that we'll now break down, one line at a time:

```
* executing `deploy:setup'
```

Capistrano tells you the name of the currently executing task, `deploy:setup`. The next line tells you what command it is about to execute.

```
* executing "mkdir -p /home/ticketeeapp.com/apps/ticketee
                       /home/ticketeeapp.com/apps/ticketee/releases
                       /home/ticketeeapp.com/apps/ticketee/shared
                       /home/ticketeeapp.com/apps/ticketee/shared/system
                       /home/ticketeeapp.com/apps/ticketee/shared/log
                       /home/ticketeeapp.com/apps/ticketee/shared/pids
```

These are the basic directories required for Capistrano. The first directory acts as a base for your application, containing several different subdirectories, the first of which is releases. Whenever you deploy using Capistrano, a new release is created in the releases directory, timestamped to the current time using the same time format as migrations within Rails (such as 20110205225746, or the full year followed by two digits each for the month, day, minute, hour, and second, or YYYYMMDDHHmmSS). The latest release would be the final one in this directory.

The shared directory is the directory where files can be shared across releases, such as uploads from Paperclip, that would usually go in the public/system directory, which would now be placed in shared/system.

The shared/log directory is symbolically linked[23] to the current release's log directory when you run a deploy. This is so all logs are kept in the shared/log directory (rather than in each release) so that, if you choose to, you can go back over them and read them.

The shared/pids directory is symbolically linked to the current release's tmp/pids up on deploy. This folder is used for process ids of any other parts of your application. At the moment, you don't have any of these and so this directory is of no major concern.

---

[23] http://en.wikipedia.org/wiki/Symbolic_link.

The next line after this makes these folders group writable with the `chmod` command:

```
chmod g+w /home/ticketeeapp.com/apps/ticketee
         /home/ticketeeapp.com/apps/ticketee/releases
         /home/ticketeeapp.com/apps/ticketee/shared
         /home/ticketeeapp.com/apps/ticketee/shared/system
         /home/ticketeeapp.com/apps/ticketee/shared/log
         /home/ticketeeapp.com/apps/ticketee/shared/pids
```

At the bottom of this command's output you can see what servers it will be executed on, with only your one server listed for now. It also tells you that the command is being executed and, faster than you can blink, that the command has finished. `chmod` isn't an intensive operation:

```
servers: ["your-server"]
[your-server] executing command
command finished
```

Once the `deploy:setup` Capistrano task has finished, you are returned to a console prompt. Now you can put the application on the server by deploying it!

14.5.4 *Deploying the application*

Capistrano has now been configured to deploy the Ticketee application and you've set up your server using the `cap deploy:setup` command, leaving it up to you now to deploy your code. Capistrano's `deploy` task will let you do this, and you can run this task with this command:

```
cap deploy
```

This command outputs an even larger output to `cap deploy:setup`, but again we'll go through it line by line. It's not all that intimidating when it's broken down into little chunks, really! The first output you'll see from a deploy is

```
* executing `deploy'
* executing `deploy:update'
** transaction: start
* executing `deploy:update_code'
```

These first three lines tell you the tasks which are being executed. The `deploy` task is going to be executed because you asked Capistrano to do that. This task depends on the `deploy:update` task, and so it will run that first.

The `deploy:update` task begins a transaction (the third line in the output), which is exceptionally helpful. If anything goes wrong in your deploy, Capistrano will roll back everything to the beginning of this transaction, deleting any code it's deployed. This transaction is a failsafe for your deploy.

The final part of the output is the `deploy:update_code` task, which is responsible for updating the application's code in your deployment environment. This task is responsible for the next chunk of output you see:

```
executing locally: "git ls-remote [git_path] HEAD"
 * executing "git clone -q [git_path] [release_path] &&
    cd [release_path] &&
    git checkout -q -b deploy [SHA1 hash] &&
    (echo [SHA1 hash] > [release_path]/REVISION)"
   servers: ["your-server"]
```

This task first runs `git ls-remote`, a lesser-known Git command, locally (not on the server), which will get the current SHA for HEAD, the latest commit to the `master` branch, unless you set a `branch` in Capistrano's configuration.

The next thing Capistrano does is put the current revision in a file called REVISION. If you like, you can alter the layout of your application to read the value from this file and put it in your application's layout as a HTML comment so that when you do a deploy to the server, you can check this hash to see if it is the latest code.

The next couple of lines output from `cap deploy` are from the beginning of the `deploy:finalize_update` task:

```
* executing "chmod -R g+w [release_path]"
  servers: ["localhost"]
  [localhost] executing command
  command finished
```

With this `chmod` command, Capistrano ensures that your new release's directory is group writable (g+w), allowing the user/group to make any modifications to this directory they like, barring all others.

Finally, the `deploy:finalize_update` then removes the log, public/system, and tmp/pids directories and symbolically links the shared/log, shared/system, and shared/pids directories (in your application's deployed path) to these paths respectively. It does that in this little series of commands:

```
* executing "rm -rf [release_path]/log
  [release_path]/public/system
  [release_path]/tmp/pids &&

  mkdir -p [release_path]/public &&
  mkdir -p [release_path]/tmp &&

  ln -s [shared_path]/log [release_path]/log &&
  ln -s [shared_path]/system [release_path]/public/system &&
  ln -s [shared_path]/pids [release_path]/tmp/pids
   servers: ["your-server"]
   [your-server] executing command
   command finished
```

Next, Capistrano will use the `find` command to touch every file in the public/images, public/stylesheets, and public/javascripts to update their last modified time. This is so that when a user visits your site they get the latest image, stylesheet, or JavaScript file rather than a cached file. It does this with this part of the output:

```
* executing "find [release_path]/public/images
               [release_path]/public/stylesheets
               [release_path]/public/javascripts
               -exec touch -t [timestamp] {} ';'; true"
```

```
  servers: ["your-server"]
  [your-server] executing command
  command finished
```

The second-to-last step for the `deploy:update` task is to run the `deploy:symlink` task, which symbolically links the new release directory to the current folder within your deploy path (in this example, /home/ticketeeapp.com/apps/ticketee/current):

```
* executing `deploy:symlink'
* executing "rm -f [current_path] &&

  ln -s [release_path] [current_path]
  servers: ["your-server"]
  [your-server] executing command
  command finished
```

The last action of the `deploy:update` task is to commit the transaction that began at the start, meaning your deploy was successful:

```
** transaction: commit
```

The absolutely final thing the `deploy` task does is call `deploy:restart`, which will touch the tmp/restart file in your new application directory (/home/ticketeeapp.com/ apps/ticketee/current), which would restart the server if you had one running:

```
* executing `deploy:restart'
* executing "touch [current_path]/tmp/restart.txt"
  servers: ["your-server"]
  [your-server] executing command
  command finished
```

And that's it! Your application is deployed for the first time; however, it's not quite ready for prime-time usage. For starters, the application's gems are not installed! On your development box you will do this by running the `bundle install` task, but you're no longer in Kansas[24] or on your own development box for that matter. Bundler has some pretty slick integration with Capistrano, which will run `bundle install` when you deploy. This functionality is provided to you by a file that comes with the gem.

14.5.5 *Bundling gems*

You can trigger the `bundle install` task to happen (in a slightly different fashion than usual) when you do a deploy by requiring the bundler/capistrano file in the config/deploy.rb of your application, right at the top:

```
require 'bundler/capistrano'
```

You'll also need to require RVM's `capistrano` configuration so that when you do a deploy it can locate the `bundle` command (provided by a gem that was installed using an RVM-provided Ruby install), which it will need to run `bundle install`. At the top of config/deploy.rb, put these lines:

```
$:.unshift(File.expand_path('./lib', ENV['rvm_path']))
require 'rvm/capistrano'
```

---

[24] Apologies for any Kansas-based readers out there. Let me assure you, you are still (most likely) in Kansas.

The first line here adds the lib directory of RVM to the load path (represented in Ruby by `$:`). This is required so that this file knows where to find rvm/capistrano. Without it, it may fail.

Now that you're requiring rvm/capistrano when you run `cap deploy` again, you'll see this additional output just after the stylesheets, javascripts, and images touching:

```
* executing `bundle:install'
* executing "ls -x /home/ticketeeapp.com/apps/ticketee/releases"
  servers: ["your-server"]
  [your-server] executing command
  command finished
* executing "bundle install --gemfile [release_path]/Gemfile
  --path [shared_path]/bundle
  --deployment
  --quiet
  --without development test"
  servers: ["your-server"]
  [your-server] executing command
  command finished
```

Bundler's added a `bundle:install` task to your Capistrano configuration which runs after `deploy:finalize_update`. This task runs `ls -x` command at the beginning to get the last release's directory (20110207202618, in this case), which it then uses to specify the location of the `Gemfile` using the `--gemfile` flag passed to `bundle install`. Rather than installing the gems to a system location which may not be writable by this user,[25] Bundler elects to install this to the /home/ticketeeapp.com/apps/ticketee/shared/bundler directory instead, specified by the `--path` flag.

The `--deployment` flag specifies that the repository must contain a Gemfile.lock file (meaning the gem versions are locked) and that the Gemfile.lock file is up-to-date according to the Gemfile. This is to ensure that you're running an identical set of gems on your server and local machines.

Last, the `--without` flag tells Bundler what groups to ignore. The `development` and `test` groups are ignored in this case, meaning gems specified in these two groups will not be installed at all.

With your application's gems installed, you're getting even closer to having an application running. When you deploy changes to your application, these changes may include new migrations, which will need to be run on the server after you do a deploy. You can deploy your code *and* migrate by running this lovely command:

```
cap deploy:migrations
```

After your code deploys, Capistrano will run the `rake db:migrate` task, which is of great use, because it sets up your database tables. You'll see output like this:

```
        ** [out :: [server]] (in [path_to_application])
        ** [out :: [server]] ==  CreateProjects: migrating ===
```

---

[25] This directory would be located within /usr/local/rvm, which is only writable by members of the `rvm` group. This member is not a part of this group and thus is unable to install any gems at a system-wide level.

```
** [out :: [server]] -- create_table(:projects)
** [out :: [server]] -> 0.0012s
...
```

This indicates that the migrations have happened successfully. Unfortunately, this is in the wrong database! You spent all that time setting up a PostgreSQL server and it's gone ahead and instead used SQLite3. The nerve!

14.5.6 Choosing a database

To fix this, you can make a little change to your application's Gemfile. Rather than having sqlite3 out there in the open and not in a group, switch it to only be used in development and test by moving it down into the group :development, :test block just underneath.[26] Beneath all of the content in the file currently, define a new group like this:

```
group :production do
  gem 'pg'
end
```

The pg gem provides the PostgreSQL adapter that you need to connect to your PostgreSQL database server on your server. If you run bundle install now it will install this gem for you. Now you can make a commit for this small change and push your changes:

```
git add Gemfile*
git commit -m "Added pg gem for PostgreSQL on the server"
git push
```

You haven't yet configured your production application to connect to PostgreSQL, which is somewhat of a problem. You would usually do this by editing the config/database .yml file in your application, but in this case you want to keep your development and production environments separate. Therefore, you'll set this up on the server.

Put this file in the shared directory of your application's deploy, so that all releases can just symlink it to config/database.yml inside the application itself. Connect to the server now with your user and then switch over to ticketeeapp.com using sudo su ticketeeapp.com so that you can add this file. Go into this shared directory now and open a new file for editing by running these commands:

```
cd /home/ticketeapp.com/apps/ticketee/shared
mkdir config
cd config
nano database.yml
```

Inside this file, put the database settings for the production environment of your application. These are as follows:

```
production:
  adapter: postgresql
  database: ticketeeapp.com
  min_messages: warning
```

---

[26] Generally, this is a bad idea. You should always develop on the same database system that you deploy on so that you don't run into any unexpected production issues. We're being lazy here because it's easier.

You can exit out of nano by using Ctrl+X and then press Y to confirm your changes.

Your next step is to get this file to replace the config/database.yml that your application contains upon deployment. For this, define a new task at the bottom of config/deploy.rb in your application:

```
task :symlink_database_yml do
  run "rm #{release_path}/config/database.yml"
  run "ln -sfn #{shared_path}/config/database.yml
      #{release_path}/config/database.yml"
end
after "bundle:install", "symlink_database_yml"
```

This task will remove the current config/database.yml located at the release_path and will then link the one from shared_path's config/database.yml into that spot. The final line that you have added tells Capistrano to run this task after the bundle :install task has been completed, meaning it will happen before anything else.

Now when you run cap deploy:migrations again, you'll see this additional output:

```
* executing `symlink_database_yml'
* executing "rm [release_path]/config/database.yml"
  servers: ["your-server"]
  [localhost] executing command
  command finished
* executing "ln -s [shared_path]/config/database.yml
             [release_path]/config/database.yml"
  servers: ["your-server"]
  [localhost] executing command
  command finished
```

It looks like your command is working! Another clue indicating this is the migration output just beneath. Check that the command is truly working by going onto the server as the ticketeeapp.com user and then going into the /home/ticketeeapp .com/apps/ticketee/current folder and running rake RAILS_ENV=production db:seed to load the default data into the production database. Then launch a PostgreSQL console by running the psql command. Inside this console, run SELECT * FROM projects;. You should see output like this:

```
ticketeeapp.com=> SELECT * FROM projects;
 id |     name     |        created_at         | ...
----+--------------+---------------------------+ ...
  1 | Ticketee Beta | 2011-03-05 12:05:55.447643 | ...
(1 row)
```

This output shows the data in the projects table that comes from db/seeds.rb, which means that your database configuration has been copied over and your database has been set up correctly.

Capistrano allows you to put the code on your server in a simple fashion. Once you make a change to your application, you can make sure that the tests are still passing, make a commit out of that, and push the changes to GitHub. When you're happy with the changes, you can deploy them to your server using the simple `cap deploy :migrations` command. This will update the code on your application, run `bundle install`, and then run any new migrations you may have added.

There's much more to Capistrano than this, and you can get to know more of it by reading the Capistrano Handbook[27] or by asking questions on the Capistrano Google Group at http://groups.google.com/group/capistrano.

To run this application and make it serve requests, you could use `rails server` like in development, but there are a couple of problems with this approach. For starters, it requires you to always be running a terminal session with it running, which is just hackish. Secondly, this process is only single-threaded, meaning it can only serve a single request at a time.

There's got to be a better way!

14.6 Serving requests

Rather than taking this approach, we're going to show you how to use the Passenger gem along with the nginx web server to host your application. The benefit of this is that when a request comes into your server, it's handled by nginx and an nginx module provided by the Passenger gem, as shown in figure 14.3.

When the client sends a request to the server on port 80, nginx will receive it. nginx then looks up what is supposed to be serving that request and sees that Passenger is configured to do that, and so passes the request to Passenger.

Passenger manages a set of Rails instances (referred to as a pool) for you. If Passenger hasn't received a request in the last five minutes, Passenger will start a new instance,[28] passing the request to that instance, with each instance serving one request at a time. The more instances you have, the more (theoretical)[29] requests you can do. If there has been a request within that timeframe, then the request is passed to one of the instances in the pool already launched by a previous request.[30]

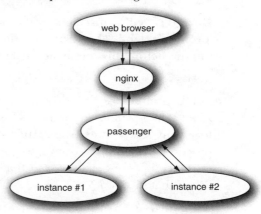

Figure 14.3 Nginx request path

---

[27] https://github.com/leehambley/capistrano-handbook/blob/master/index.markdown.

[28] The `passenger_pool_idle_time` configuration option is responsible for this: http://www.modrails.com/documentation/Users%20guide%20Nginx.html#PassengerPoolIdleTime.

[29] There's a hardware limit (when you run out of CPU and RAM) that will be reached if too many instances are started up. Things can get slow then.

[30] Passenger will scale up instances depending on the speed of requests coming to the application. The maximum number of application instances running at any one time by default is six, and can be configured by the `passenger_max_pool_size` setting: http://www.modrails.com/documentation/Users%20guide%20Nginx.html#PassengerMaxPoolSize.

Once Rails has done its thing, it sends the request back up the chain, going through Passenger to nginx and then finally back to the client as the response—most commonly HTML but it could be anything, really.

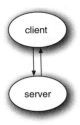

When you launch `rails server`, the process looks like figure 14.4.

In this example, there's only one instance of your application serving requests and so it's going to be slower than having the Passenger pool of them serving it. Additionally, nginx is super quick at serving files (like your CSS and JavaScript ones) and handles these requests itself,

Figure 12.4   Simplified client-server relationship

without Rails knowing about it. When you run `rails server`, it serves *every* request, and is definitely not web scale. nginx and Passenger are designed for speed and reliability, and so you should feel pretty confident in using them.

Enough talk, let's get into this! You're going to install the `passenger` gem now, and it's nice enough to set up nginx for you too!

14.6.1 *Installing Passenger*

To install Passenger, as your user on the box (`vagrant ssh`, if Vagrant) you can run the same `gem install` you've been running all this time:

```
gem install passenger
```

Once this gem is installed, install nginx and the Passenger module by running this lovely command. The `-i` option "simulates initial login," meaning that the RVM script will run before this command, making it available:

```
sudo -i passenger-install-nginx-module
```

At the prompt, press 1 for the install process to download and compile nginx automatically. When prompted for a directory (/opt/nginx), press Enter. This'll be the directory your server runs from. After this, nginx will be compiled and installed. This process takes a minute or two, so go grab something to eat or drink, or stretch.

Once it's done, you're told that Passenger inserted some configuration for you; wasn't that nice of it?

```
The Nginx configuration file (/opt/nginx/conf/nginx.conf)
must contain the correct configuration options in order for Phusion Passenger
to function correctly.

This installer has already modified the configuration file for you! The
following configuration snippet was inserted:

  http {
    ...
    passenger_root /usr/local/rvm/gems/ruby-1.9.2-p180/gems/passenger-
    3.0.4;
    passenger_ruby /usr/local/rvm/wrappers/ruby-1.9.2-p180/ruby;
    ...
  }
```

After you start Nginx, you are ready to deploy any number of Ruby on Rails applications on Nginx.

When you upgrade Passenger you'll need to edit the `passenger_root` line to point to the new version, and if you ever upgrade Ruby then you'll need to change the `passenger_ruby` line. Press Enter now to see the next bit of output, where you're told how to deploy a Rails application:

```
server {
    listen 80;
    server_name www.yourhost.com;
    root /somewhere/public;    # <--- be sure to point to 'public'!
    passenger_enabled on;
  }
```

This bit of configuration goes inside the /opt/nginx/conf/nginx.conf file. You can open this file with `sudo /opt/nginx/conf/nginx.conf`. It's already got a server block in there which is a default configuration for nginx that you can remove. In its place, put the code from the following listing (based on the advice offered by Passenger).

Listing 14.1   /opt/nginx/conf/nginx.conf

```
server {
    listen 80;
    server_name your-server.com;
    root /home/ticketeapp.com/apps/ticketee/current/public;
    passenger_enabled on;
}
```

You can now start the nginx server by running the `nginx` executable:

```
sudo /opt/nginx/sbin/nginx
```

You can make sure that requests to this server are working by accessing http://your-server or http://localhost:4567 if you're using Vagrant. You should see the sign-in page for your application, as shown in figure 14.3.

Figure 14.3   Sign-in page for Ticketee

This means your web server is now working seamlessly with your application and everything's almost ready. If the operating system of the server restarts, however, this nginx process will not. To fix this small problem, you need to create an *init script*.

14.6.2 *An init script*

An init script is a script that is run on startup (init) of the operating system and is usually used for launching applications or running commands. In Ubuntu, they reside in the /etc/init.d directory. Here, you're going to use one to start nginx. This script has already been prepared for you, and you can download it using this command:

```
sudo wget http://bit.ly/nginx-init-script -O /etc/init.d/nginx
```

This command will download the nginx init script and place it at /etc/init.d/nginx. This file won't automatically run on boot unless you tell Ubuntu it should, which you can do with these following commands:

```
sudo chmod +x /etc/init.d/nginx
sudo /usr/sbin/update-rc.d -f nginx defaults
```

If you were to reboot your operating system right now, nginx would start automatically along with it. You don't need to do it now, but it's good to know that it'll start nginx when the server boots.

There you have it: the application is deployed onto your Ubuntu server using Capistrano and is running through the power of nginx and Passenger.

14.7   *Summary*

In this chapter we covered one of the many different permutations you can use to deploy a Rails application to a server. This chapter covered the most commonly used software packages such as RVM, Capistrano, PostgreSQL, nginx, and Passenger, and therefore it should be a great starting ground for anybody learning about deployment.

There are plenty of other tools out there such as Puppet,[31] Chef,[32] Babushka,[33] and Git Pusshuten.[34] Different people prefer different ways of doing similar things, and so there's a wide variety of choice. To cover everything within one chapter is just not possible.

You set up your server with Ruby 1.9.2 running your Rails 3.0.5 application. You began by installing the essential packages you needed, then installing RVM, followed by Ruby.

Afterwards, you set up a user with the same name as your application. This was shortly followed by the locking down of SSH access on the machine: now nobody is able to access it with a password, because they need to have the private key instead. Disabling root access is just generally good practice. Nobody should ever need to use

---

[31] http://puppetlabs.com.
[32] http://opscode.com/chef/.
[33] http://babushka.me.
[34] http://gitpusshuten.com/.

the root account on this machine, as everything can be managed by your user or the application's user.

Then we had you set up a database server using PostgreSQL, one of the most popular relational datastores today. You discovered that giving your system user the same name as your database came in handy; PostgreSQL supports a kind of authentication that automatically grants a system user access to a database with the same name. That is of course provided a PostgreSQL user and database exist with that name. Very handy!

Second-to-last, you got down to the meat of the chapter: the first deployment of your application to your server using Capistrano. You saw that the config/deploy.rb file comes in handy, allowing you to specify the configuration of your deployment environment simply. With Capistrano, you distill everything you need to get your application's latest code onto the server down to one command: `cap deploy:migrations`. Every time you need to deploy, run this command, and Capistrano (along with your configuration) will take care of the rest.

Finally, you set up nginx and Passenger to serve your application's requests, as well as the static assets of your application. Generally, this is the setup preferred by Rails developers, and so there's a lot of useful knowledge out there. An alternative to this setup would be to use the Apache web server instead of nginx. Both work suitably.

That's your application done, really. From the first time you ran a test all the way up to deployment, you've covered a lot of important things within Rails. There's still much more to learn (which is why there are more chapters after this one), but right now you should have a firm grasp of what the process of developing and deploying a Rails application is. In the next chapter, we show you how you can let people authenticate to your application through either Facebook or Twitter.

Alternative authentication

15

Now that your application has been deployed to a server somewhere (or at least you've gone through the motions of doing that!), we're going to look at adding additional features to your application. One of these is OAuth authentication from services such as Twitter and GitHub.

When you sign into a website, you can generally use a couple of authentication methods. The first of these would be a username and password, with the username being forced to be unique. This method provides a solid way to identify what user has logged into the website, and from that identification the website can choose to grant or deny access to specific parts of the site. You have done this with your Ticketee application, except in place of a username, you're using an email address. An email address is an already unique value for users of a website that also allows you

412

to have a way of contacting the user if the need arises. On other websites, though, you may have to choose a username (with Twitter), or you could be able to use both a username and email to sign in, as with GitHub.

Entering your email address and a password[1] into every website that you use can be time consuming. Why should you be throwing your email addresses and passwords into every website?

Then along came OAuth. OAuth allows you to authenticate against an OAuth provider. Rather than giving your username/email and password to yet another site, you authenticate against a central provider, which then provides tokens for the different applications to read and/or write the user's data on the application.

In this chapter you're going to be using the OAuth process to let users sign in to your Ticketee application using Twitter and GitHub. You'll not only see how easy this is, but also how you can test to make sure that everything works correctly.

Rather than implementing this process yourself, you can use the OmniAuth gem in combination with the `devise` gem that you're already using. Although this combination abstracts a lot of the complexity involved with OAuth, it's still helpful to know how this process works. Let's take a look now.

15.1 How OAuth works

OAuth authentication works in a multi-step process. In order to be able to authenticate against other applications, you must first register your application with them. After this process is complete, you're given a unique key to identify your application and a secret passphrase, which is actually a hash. Neither of these should be shared. When your application makes a request to an OAuth provider, it will send these two parameters along as part of the request so the provider knows which application is connecting. Twitter's API documentation has a pretty good description of the process as an image, which you can see as figure 15.1.

First of all (not shown in the figure), a user initiates a request to your application (the Consumer) to announce their intentions to log in with Twitter (the Service Provider). Your application then sends that unique identifier and that secret key (given to you by Twitter when you register your application), and begins the authentication process by requesting a token (A). This token will be used as an identifier for this particular authentication request cycle.

The provider (Twitter) then grants you this token and sends it back to your application. Your application then redirects the user to the provider (B) in order to gain the user's permission for this application to access its data. When signing in with Twitter, your users would see something like figure 15.2.

The user can then choose to Sign In or Cancel on this screen. If they choose Sign In, the application then has access to their data, which authorizes the request token

---

[1] Ideally, a unique password per site is best for added security. If one site is breached, you do not want your password to be the same across multiple sites, because the attackers would gain access to everything.

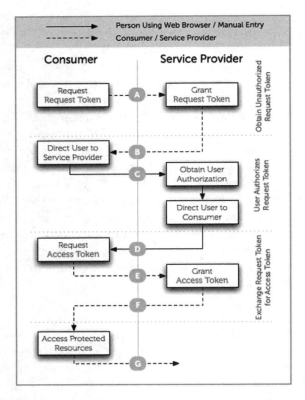

Figure 15.1   Twitter OAuth

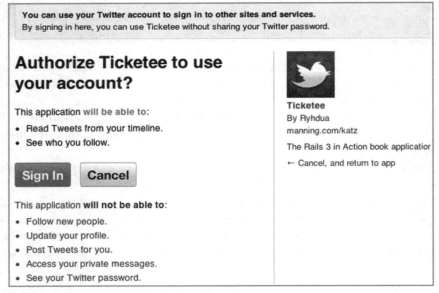

Figure 15.2   Twitter authorization

you were given at the beginning. If they click Cancel, it redirects the user back to the application without giving it access to the data.

In this case, you'll assume the user has clicked Sign In. The user is then redirected back to your application from the provider, with two parameters: an `oauth_token` and a `oauth_verifier`. The `oauth_token` is the request token you were granted at the beginning, and the `oauth_verifier` is a verifier of that token. OmniAuth then uses these two pieces of information to gain an *access token*, which will allow your application to access this user's data. There's also additional data, such as the user's attributes, that gets sent back here. The provider determines the extent of this additional data.

This is just a basic overview of how the process works. All of this is covered in more extensive detail in Section 6 of the OAuth 1.0 spec, which can be found at http://oauth.net/core/1.0/.

In the case of your application, you're going to be letting users go through this process with the intention of using their authorization with Twitter to sign them in whenever they wish. After this process has been completed the first time, a user will not be re-prompted to authorize your application (unless they have removed it from their authorized applications list), meaning the authorization process will be seamless for the user.

Let's see how you can use the OmniAuth gem to set up authentication with Twitter in your application.

15.2 Twitter authentication

You're going to be using OmniAuth to let people sign in using Twitter and GitHub as OAuth providers. We'll begin with Twitter authentication and then move on to GitHub.

15.2.1 Setting up OmniAuth

OmniAuth not only supports OAuth providers, but also supports OpenID, CAS, and LDAP. You're only going to be using the OAuth part, which you can install in your application by putting this line in your Gemfile:

```
gem "oa-oauth", :require => "omniauth/oauth"
```

The different parts of OmniAuth are separated out into different gems by an `oa-` prefix so that you can use some parts without including all the code for the other parts. In your Gemfile you're loading the `oa-oauth` gem, which will provide the OAuth functionality you need. The file to load this gem does not have the same name as the gem, so you need to use the `:require` option here and tell the correct file, omniauth/oauth, to load.

Next, you need to tell Devise that your `User` model is going to be using OmniAuth. You can do this by putting the `:omniauthable` symbol at the end of the `devise` list in your app/models/user.rb so that it now becomes this:

```
devise :database_authenticatable, :registerable, :confirmable,
       :recoverable, :rememberable, :trackable, :validatable,
       :token_authenticatable, :omniauthable
```

With OmniAuth set up, you can now configure your application to provide a way for your users to sign in using Twitter. Twitter first requires you to register your application on its site.

15.2.2 Registering an application with Twitter

You need to register your application with Twitter before your users can use it to log in to your application. The registration process gives you a unique identifier and secret code for your application (called a consumer key and consumer secret, respectively), which is how Twitter will know what application is requesting a user's permission.

The process works by a user clicking a small Twitter icon on your application, which will then redirect them to Twitter. If they aren't signed in on Twitter, they will first need to do so. Once they are signed in, they will then be presented with the authorization confirmation screen that you saw earlier, shown again in figure 15.3.

On this screen you can see that Twitter knows what application is requesting permission for this user, and that the user can either choose to Allow or Deny. By clicking Allow, the user will be redirected back to your application and then signed in using code that you'll write after you've registered your application.

To register your application with Twitter, you need to go to http://dev.twitter.com and click the Create an App link.

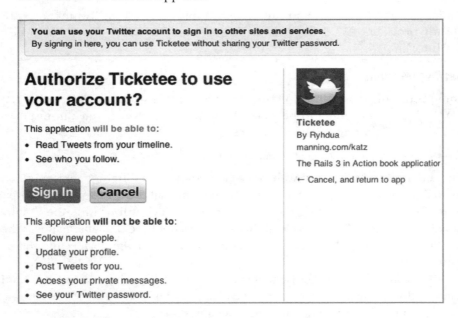

Figure 15.3   Twitter authorization request

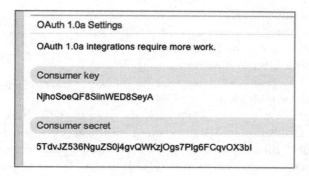

Figure 15.4 A brand-new application!

On this new page you need to fill in the name, description, and URL fields. The name should be [Your name]'s Ticketee because it needs to be unique; the description can be anything, and the URL can be http://manning.com/katz. When you click Create on this application, you'll see the consumer key and secret that you'll be using shortly, as shown in figure 15.4.

Although this screen isn't exactly the prettiest thing around, it does offer you the two key pieces of information that you need: the consumer key and the consumer secret. The other values on this page aren't important for you to know, as OmniAuth will take care of them for you.

You now need to set up your application to use this consumer key and consumer secret when authenticating with Twitter. You can do this in Devise's configuration file in your application, which is located at config/initializers/devise.rb. In this file, you'll see the following commented-out OmniAuth configuration:

```
# ==> OmniAuth
# Add a new OmniAuth provider. Check the wiki for more information on setting
# up on your models and hooks.
# config.omniauth :github, 'APP_ID', 'APP_SECRET', :scope =>
➥ 'user,public_repo'
```

This shows you how to add a new OmniAuth provider, using GitHub as an example. In this example, the APP_ID and APP_SECRET values would be the consumer key and consumer secret given to you by the provider. Set up a new provider for Twitter by putting these lines underneath the commented-out section:

```
config.omniauth :twitter,
  '[consumer key]',
  '[consumer secret]'
```

This will configure Devise to provide OmniAuth-based authentication for Twitter, but you're not done yet. You need some way for a user to be able to initiate the sign-in process with Twitter.

15.2.3 *Setting up an OmniAuth testing environment*

To provide a user with a way to sign in with Twitter, you'll add a small addition to your menu bar that lets people sign up and sign in using Twitter, as shown in figure 15.5.

When a user clicks this button, your application will begin the OAuth process by requesting a request token from Twitter, and then using that token to redirect to Twitter. From here, the user will authorize your application to have access to their data on Twitter, and then they'll be redirected back to your application. It's the user being redirected back to your application that

Figure 15.5
Sign in with Twitter

is the most important part. Twitter will send back the `oauth_token` and `oauth _verifier`, and then your application makes the request for the access token to Twitter. Twitter will then send back this access token and any additional parameters it sees fit, and you'll be able to access this information in a Hash format. For example, Twitter sends back the user's information in the response like this:

```
{
  ...
  "extra" => {
    ...
    "user_hash" => {
      "id" => "14506011"
      "screen_name" => "ryanbigg"
      "name" => "Ryan Bigg",
      ...
    }
  }
}
```

This is quite a stripped-down version of the response you'll be getting back from Twitter, but it contains three very important values. The first is the unique Twitter-provided `id` of the user, the second is their Twitter username, and the third is their display name. Currently in Ticketee, you've been using the user's email to display who you're logged in as. Because Twitter doesn't send back an email address, you'll have to change where you'd usually display an email address to instead display the user's display name or screen name if they've chosen to sign in with Twitter.

First things first though: you need to have a link that a user can click to begin this process, and to make sure that the link is working you're going to need to write a feature. With this feature, you shouldn't always rely on being able to connect to your OAuth providers like Twitter. Instead, you should create fake responses (referred to as mocks) for the requests you'd normally do. By doing this you can substantially speed up the rate at which your tests run, as well as not depend on something like connectivity, which is out of your control.

OmniAuth provides a configuration option for setting whether or not you're in a test mode, which will mock a response rather than making a call to an external service. This option is conveniently called `test_mode`. You can set this option at the bottom of your config/environments/test.rb like this:

```
OmniAuth.config.test_mode = true
```

With your test environment now set up correctly, you can write a feature to make sure that users can sign in with Twitter.

15.2.4　*Testing Twitter sign-in*

Next, you can begin to write your feature to test Twitter authentication in a new file at features/twitter_auth.feature as shown in the following listing.

Listing 15.1　features/twitter_auth.feature

```
Feature: Twitter auth
  In order to sign in using Twitter
  As a Twitter user
  I want to click an icon and be signed in

  Background:
    Given we are mocking a successful Twitter response

  Scenario: Signing in with Twitter
    Given I am on the homepage
    When I follow "sign_in_with_twitter"
    Then I should see "Signed in with Twitter successfully."
    And I should see "Signed in as A Twit (@twit)"
```

This is a simple little feature with a short, three-line scenario. The step in your Background will mock out a successful response from Twitter, which will be used by Omni-Auth because you declared that you're in test mode in config/environments/test.rb. Let's run this feature now with bin/cucumber features/twitter_auth.feature so that you can get the step definition for this new step:

```
Given /^I have mocked a successful Twitter response$/ do
  pending # express the regexp above with the code you wish you had
end
```

Put this step definition in a new file at features/step_definitions/oauth_steps.rb and define it as shown in the following listing.

Listing 15.2　features/step_definitions/oauth_steps.rb

```
Given /^we are mocking a successful Twitter response$/ do
  OmniAuth.config.mock_auth[:twitter] = {
    "extra" => {
      "user_hash" => {
        "id" => '12345',
        "screen_name" => 'twit',
        "display_name" => "A Twit"
      }
    }
  }
end
```

To generate a fake response for OmniAuth, you need to use set up a key OmniAuth .config.mock_auth hash that has the same name as the authentication provider, which in this case is :twitter. This mock response needs to contain the same kind of layout as the normal response would get back, including having each of the keys of the hashes be strings, because this is how your response will be accessed. Twitter's response hash, as stated earlier, contains an extra key that contains information about a user, which is what you'll use to track who has signed into your system using Twitter. You'll store these three attributes in new fields in your database when a user signs up using Twitter.

Run `bin/cucumber features/twitter.feature` again. This time you'll see that you're missing your link:

```
Scenario: Signing in with Twitter
  Given I am on the homepage
  And I follow "sign_in_with_twitter"
    no link with title, id or text 'sign_in_with_twitter' found ...
```

Rather than have a link that reads sign_in_with_twitter, you'll actually be giving the link an id attribute of `sign_in_with_twitter` and Capybara will still be able to find this link. The link itself is going to be a small button that you can get from https://github.com/intridea/authbuttons. You should download these images (just the 32 x 32px versions) and put them in the app/assets/images/icons directory of your application. Leave them named as they are.

To create this new link, open app/views/layouts/application.html.erb. This file contains the layout for your application and is responsible for displaying the Sign Up and Sign In links for your application if the user isn't signed in already. It's underneath these links that you want to display your little twitter icon, which you can do by making this small change to this file:

```
<%= link_to "Sign up", new_user_registration_path %>
<%= link_to "Sign in", new_user_session_path %>
<br>
Or use <%= link_to image_tag("icons/twitter_32.png"),
                 user_omniauth_authorize_path(:twitter),
                 :id => "sign_in_with_twitter" %>
```

With this link you use the downloaded icon as the first argument of `link_to` by using `image_tag`. The second argument to `link_to` is the routing helper method `user _omniauth_authorize_path` with the `:twitter` argument. This method is provided by Devise because you've told it your `User` model is `omniauthable`. This routing helper will go to a controller that is internal to Devise, because it will deal with the hand-off to Twitter.

When you run this feature again, the second step of your scenario will still fail, but this time with a different error:

```
And I follow "sign_in_with_twitter"
  The action 'twitter' could not be found
  for Devise::OmniauthCallbacksController
```

By default, Devise handles the callbacks from external services using the `Devise::OmniAuthCallbacksController`. Because different people will want this controller to perform differently, Devise provides a set of common functionality in this controller and expects you to subclass it to define the actions (like your `twitter` action) yourself. To do this, create a new controller for these callbacks by running this command:

```
rails g controller users/omniauth_callbacks
```

This command will generate a new controller at app/controllers/users/ omniauth_callbacks_controller.rb, but it's not quite what you want. You want this controller to inherit from Devise::OmniauthCallbacksController, and you also want it to have a twitter action. Before you do that, though, tell Devise to use this new controller for its callbacks. You can do this by changing these lines in your config/ routes.rb file

```
devise_for :users, :controllers => {
  :registrations => "registrations",
}
```

into this:

```
devise_for :users, :controllers => {
  :registrations => "registrations",
  :omniauth_callbacks => "users/omniauth_callbacks"
}
```

This will tell Devise to use your newly generated users/omniauth_callbacks controller rather than its own Devise::OmniauthCallbacksController, which you'll use as the superclass of your new controller. This Devise::OmniauthCallbacksController contains some code that will be used in case something goes wrong with the authentication process.

Now you need to define the twitter action in this new controller. This action is going to be called when Twitter sends a user back from having authorized your application to have access. Define this controller using the code from the following listing.

Listing 15.3   app/controllers/users/omniauth_callbacks_controller.rb

```
class Users::OmniauthCallbacksController <
  Devise::OmniauthCallbacksController
  def twitter
    @user = User.find_or_create_for_twitter(env["omniauth.auth"])
    flash[:notice] = "Signed in with Twitter successfully."
    sign_in_and_redirect @user, :event => :authentication
  end
end
```

When a request is made to this action, the details for the user are accessible in the env["omniauth.auth"] key, with env being the Rack environment of this request, which contains other helpful things such as the path of the request.[2]

You then pass these details to a currently undefined method called find_or_create_for_twitter, which will deal with finding a User record for this information from Twitter, or creating one if it doesn't already exist. You then set a flash[:notice] telling the user they've signed in and use the Devise-provided sign_in_and_redirect method to redirect your user to the root_path of your application, which will show the ProjectsController's index action.

---

[2] Covered in much more detail in chapter 17.

To make this action work, you're going to need to define `find_or_create_for` `_twitter` in your `User` model, which you can do using the code from the following listing.

Listing 15.4   app/models/user.rb

```
def self.find_or_create_for_twitter(response)
  data = response['extra']['user_hash']
  if user = User.find_by_twitter_id(data["id"])          ←——❶ Find user
    user
  else # Create a user with a stub password.                    Email ❷
    user = User.new(:email => "twitter+#{data["id"]}@example.com",  ←
                    :password => Devise.friendly_token[0,20])  ←
    user.twitter_id = data["id"]                              ❸ Password
    user.twitter_screen_name = data["screen_name"]
    user.twitter_display_name = data["display_name"]
    user.confirm!
    user
  end
end
```

You've defined this class method to take one argument, which is the response you get back from Twitter. In this response, there's going to be the access token that you get back from Twitter that you don't care so much about, and also the `extra` key and its value that you do really care about. It's with these that the application then attempts to find a user based on the id key ❶ within the `response["extra"]["user_hash"]` (here as `data` to make it easier to type). If it can find this user, it'll return that object.

If it can't find a user with that `twitter_id` attribute, then you need to create one! Because Twitter doesn't pass back an email, you make one up ❷, as well as a password, ❸ using Devise's very helpful `friendly_token` method, which generates a secure phrase like `QfVRz8RxHx4Xkqe6uIqL`. The user won't be using these to sign in; Devise needs them so it can validate the user record successfully.

You have to do this the long way, because the `twitter_` prefixed parameters aren't mass-assignable due to your `attr_accessible` call earlier on in this model, so you must assign them manually one at a time. Store the id of the user so you can find it again if you need to re-authenticate this user, the `twitter_screen_name`, and the `twitter_display_name`. Then you need to confirm and save the object, which you can do with the `confirm!` method, and finally you need to return the object as the final line in this `else` block.

These fields are not yet fields in your database, so you'll need to add them in. You can do this by creating a new migration using this command:

```
rails g migration add_twitter_fields_to_users
```

In this migration you want to add the fields to your table, which you can do by adding them to your migration, as shown in the following listing.

Listing 15.5 db/migrate/[timestamp]_add_twitter_fields_to_users.rb

```
class AddTwitterFieldsToUsers < ActiveRecord::Migration
  def change
    add_column :users, :twitter_id, :string
    add_column :users, :twitter_screen_name, :string
    add_column :users, :twitter_display_name, :string
  end
end
```

With this migration set up, you can run it on your development and test databases with `rake db:migrate` and `rake db:test:prepare` respectively. Now when you run your feature again with `bin/cucumber features/twitter_auth.feature`, you'll see that your new `User` object is being created and that you can see the "Signed in with Twitter successfully." message:

```
Scenario: Signing in with Twitter
  Given I am on the homepage
  And I follow "sign_in_with_twitter"
  Then I should see "Signed in with Twitter successfully."
  Then I should see "Signed in as A twit"
    Failed assertion, no message given. (MiniTest::Assertion)
```

The final step of your feature is now failing, but this is a pretty easy one to fix. You need to change where it would normally display a user's email to display something like "A Twit (@twit)" if the `twitter_id` attribute is set. To do this, define a new method in your `User` model above the `to_s` method, using the code from the following listing.

Listing 15.6 app/models/user.rb

```
def display_name
  if twitter_id
    "#{twitter_display_name} (@#{twitter_screen_name})"
  else
    email
  end
end
```

If the `twitter_id` attribute is set in this method, then you assume the `twitter_display_name` and `twitter_screen_name` attributes are set also and use those to display the twitter name. If it isn't set, then you'll fall back to using the `email` field. You'll be able to use this method later on to check if the `github_id` field is set and use the values for that instead.[3]

Now you need to change the occurrences of where `user.email` is referenced to use the `display_name` method. The first occurrence of this is in app/models/user.rb in your `to_s` method, which should now become

---

[3] Alternatively, you could add a feature to let the user pick which one they would like to display.

```
def to_s
  "#{display_name} (#{admin? ? "Admin" : "User"})"
end
```

The rest of the occurrences are found in a handful of views throughout your application, and you'll need to fix these up now. The first of these is the first line of app/views/admin/permissions/index.html.erb, which should now become this:

```
<h2>Permissions for <%= @user.display_name %></h2>
```

Next, there's one in the application layout at app/views/layouts/application.html.erb:

```
Signed in as <%= current_user.email %>
```

This needs to become simply

```
Signed in as <%= current_user %>
```

By placing an object like this in the view, the to_s method will be called on it automatically, which is of course the to_s method in the User model.

Finally, you'll need to update the app/views/tickets/show.html.erb page in the same manner, changing this

```
<%= @ticket.user.email %>
```

to this:

```
<%= @ticket.user.display_name %>
```

That's it! That's all the occurrences of calls to the email attribute in places where it's shown to users has been changed to display_name instead. So does this mean that your feature will now run? Find out with a quick run of bin/cucumber features/twitter_auth.feature:

```
1 scenario (1 passed)
5 steps (5 passed)
```

All green, all good. Now users are able to sign up and sign in by clicking the Twitter icon in your application rather than providing you with their email and password. The first time a user clicks this icon, they'll be redirected off to Twitter, which will ask them to authorize your application to access their data. If they choose Allow, they will be redirected back to your application. With the parameters sent back from the final request, you'll attempt to find a User record matching their Twitter ID or, if there isn't one, create one instead. Then you'll sign them in.

After that, when the user attempts to sign in using the Twitter icon, they'll still be redirected back to Twitter, but this time Twitter won't ask them for authorization again. Instead, Twitter will instantly redirect them back to your application; the whole process will seem pretty smooth, albeit with the delay that can normally be expected from doing two HTTP requests.

Go ahead, try launching rails server now and accessing the application at http://localhost:3000 by clicking the small Twitter icon on the sign-in page. You'll be redirected off to Twitter, which deals with the authentication process before sending you back to the application.

Did you break anything? Let's see by running `rake cucumber:ok spec`:

```
63 scenarios (63 passed)
737 steps (737 passed)
# and
72 examples, 0 failures, 19 pending
```

Nope, it seems like everything is functioning correctly. Let's make a commit:

```
git add .
git commit -m "Added OmniAuth-driven support for signing in with Twitter"
```

With the work you've done in this section, users will now be able to easily sign into your application using Twitter. You can see this for yourself by starting a server using `rails s` and clicking the Twitter icon if you've got a Twitter account.

If your users don't have a Twitter account, then their only other choice at the moment is to provide you with their email address and a password, and that's not really useful to anyone who has a GitHub but not a Twitter account. So let's see how you can authenticate people using GitHub's OAuth next, while recycling some of the Twitter-centric code in the process.

15.3 GitHub authentication

We've shown how you can let people authenticate using Twitter's OAuth. GitHub also provides this service, and the OmniAuth gem you're using can be used to connect to that too, in much the same way as you did with Twitter. Rather than re-doing everything that you did in the previous section again and changing occurrences of "twitter" to "github," you'll be seeing how you can make the code that you've written so far support both Twitter and GitHub in a clean fashion. When you're done, you're going to have a little GitHub icon next to your Twitter one so that people can use GitHub, Twitter, or email to sign in, making your sign in /sign up area look like figure 15.6.

As was the case with Twitter, your first step will be registering an application with GitHub.

Figure 15.6   GitHub login

15.3.1 Registering and testing GitHub auth

To register an application with GitHub, you must first be signed in. Then you can visit https://github.com/account/applications/new and fill in the form that it provides. After that, you'll need to copy the Client ID and Client Secret values and put them in your config/initializers/devise.rb file under your Twitter details, like this:

```
config.omniauth :github, "[Client ID]", "[Client Secret]"
```

With GitHub now set up in your application, you can write the feature to ensure that its authentication is working. To begin testing your application's ability to authenticate users from GitHub, you're going to write a new feature at features/github_auth.feature and fill it with the content from the following listing.

Listing 15.7   features/github_auth.feature

```
Feature: GitHub auth
  In order to sign in using GitHub
  As a GitHub user
  I want to click an icon and be signed in

  Background:
    Given I have mocked a successful GitHub response

  Scenario: Signing in with GitHub
    Given I am on the homepage
    And I follow "sign_in_with_github"
    Then I should see "Signed in with Github successfully."
    Then I should see "Signed in as A GitHubber"
```

Although it may look like all you've done here is replace all the references to Twitter with GitHub... actually, that's precisely what you've done! This is because there should be little difference in how the user interacts with your site to sign in with Twitter or GitHub. The differences should only be behind the scenes, as this is how a user would expect an application to behave.[4]

When you run this new feature with `bin/cucumber features/github_auth .feature`, you'll see that you've got an undefined step:

```
Given /^I have mocked a successful GitHub response$/ do
  pending # express the regexp above with the code you wish you had
end
```

Define this step in features/step_definitions/oauth_steps.rb underneath the one for Twitter. It goes like this:

```
Given /^I have mocked a successful GitHub response$/ do
  OmniAuth.config.mock_auth[:github] = {
    "extra" => {
      "user_hash" => {
        "id" => '12345',
        "email" => 'githubber@example.com',
        "login" => "githubber",
        "name" => "A GitHubber"
      }
    }
  }
end
```

GitHub returns a similar hash to that of Twitter, containing an `extra` key with a user_hash key nested inside. Within this nested hash you've got the three parameters that you'll be storing on your end: the id, the login, and a name.

---

[4] Also known as Principle of least surprise (POLS) or more colloquially, "keep it simple, stupid!" (KISS).

When you run your feature again, you'll be through this undefined step and now up to the next failing step:

```
And I follow "sign_in_with_github"
  no link with title, id or text 'sign_in_with_github' found
```

This means that your `sign_in_with_github` link doesn't exist yet, so you're going to need to create it like you did with your `sign_in_with_twitter` link. You could do this by copying and pasting the Twitter link code underneath itself in app/views/layouts/application.html.erb, ending up with something like this:

```
Or use <%= link_to image_tag("icons/twitter_32.png"),
                 user_omniauth_authorize_path(:twitter),
                 :id => "sign_in_with_twitter" %>
<%= link_to image_tag("icons/github_32.png"),
                 user_omniauth_authorize_path(:github),
                 :id => "sign_in_with_github" %>
```

This code in your application layout is going to get ugly as you add providers, and it's quite a lot of duplication! What would be more sensible is moving this code into a helper method in a new file such as app/helpers/oauth_helper.rb, defining it as shown in the following listing.

Listing 15.8   app/helpers/oauth_helper.rb

```
module OauthHelper
  def auth_provider(name)
    link_to image_tag("icons/#{name}_32.png"),
    user_omniauth_authorize_path(name),
    :id => "sign_in_with_#{name}"
  end
end
```

Then in place of the ugly code in your application layout, you'd put this instead:

```
Or use <%= auth_provider(:twitter) %> <%= auth_provider(:github) %>
```

How's that for simplicity? Well, you could make it even cleaner by accepting any number of arguments to your method, by turning it into this:

```
def auth_providers(*names)
  names.each do |name|
    concat(link_to(image_tag("icons/#{name}_32.png"),
    user_omniauth_authorize_path(name),
    :id => "sign_in_with_#{name}"))
  end
  nil
end
```

This helper uses the `concat` method to output the links to your view. If you didn't use this, it wouldn't render them at all. You could then write this in your application layout:

```
Or use <%= auth_providers(:twitter, :github) %>
```

Now isn't that way nicer? If at any time you want to add or remove one of the links, you only have to add or remove arguments to this method.

When you run this feature again with `bin/cucumber features/github_auth .feature`, you'll see that you're on to the next error:

```
The action 'github' could not be found for Users::OmniauthCallbacksController
```

As you did with Twitter, you're going to need to define a `github` action in the `Users::OmniauthCallbacksController`. This action will find or create a user based on the details sent back from GitHub, using a class method you'll define after in your `User` model. Sound familiar? You can duplicate the `twitter` action in this controller and create a new `github` action from it like this:

```
def github
  @user = User.find_or_create_for_github(env["omniauth.auth"])
  flash[:notice] = "Signed in with GitHub successfully."
  sign_in_and_redirect @user, :event => :authentication
end
```

But like the provider links in your application layout, this is not very clean and gets exceptionally more complex the more providers you have. Rather than doing it this way, you'll define a class method for your controller that will dynamically define these methods for you. Define this method in app/controllers/users/omniauth_callbacks _controller.rb by using the code from the following listing.

Listing 15.9   app/controllers/users/omniauth_callbacks_controller.rb

```
def self.provides_callback_for(*providers)
  providers.each do |provider|
    class_eval %Q{                        ⟵──❶ Evaluate code
      def #{provider}
        @user = User.find_or_create_for_#{provider}(env["omniauth.auth"])
        flash[:notice] = "Signed in with #{provider.to_s.titleize}
⟹successfully."
        sign_in_and_redirect @user, :event => :authentication
      end
    }
  end
end
```

As with your `auth_providers` method in `OauthHelper`, you can call this method in your controller (after removing the `twitter` and `github` methods already in it):

```
provides_callback_for :twitter, :github
```

The `provides_callback_for` method will iterate through each of the arguments passed in, defining a new method dynamically using `class_eval` ❶, which will evaluate the code you pass in within the context of the current class. The `%Q{}` encapsulation will provide a `String` object that you can put double quotes and single quotes in without having to escape them.

You then need to replace any occurrences that you previously had of either "twitter" or "github" with the `provider` variable from the current iteration, using interpolation to put it into the quoted string. The `provides_callback_for` method will then define a new action in your controller for the specified providers. This has greatly decreased the repetition in your controller's code, at the expense of a small easy-to-understand bit of `class_eval` "magic."

When you run your feature again with `bin/cucumber features/github.feature`, you'll see that it's now hitting your new `github` action, because it can't find a method that you use in it:

```
undefined method `find_or_create_for_github' for ...
(eval):3:in `github'
```

In this error output you're seeing that Rails is unable to find a `find_or_create_for_github` method on a class, which is the `User` class. You created one of these for Twitter, and unlike the provider links and the callback actions, you're not able to easily create a bit of smart code for your model. But you can separate out the concerns of the model into separate files, which would make it easier to manage. Rather than filling your `User` model with methods for each of your providers, you'll separate this code out into another module and then extend your class with it.

You can do this by creating a new directory at app/models/user and placing a file called app/models/user/omniauth_callbacks.rb inside it. You should put the content from the following listing inside this file.

Listing 15.10   app/models/user/omniauth_callbacks.rb

```ruby
class User < ActiveRecord::Base
  module OmniauthCallbacks
    def find_or_create_for_twitter(response)
      data = response['extra']['user_hash']
      if user = User.find_by_twitter_id(data["id"])
        user
      else # Create a user with a stub password.
        user = User.new(:email => "twitter+#{data["id"]}@example.com",
                        :password => Devise.friendly_token[0,20])
        user.twitter_id = data["id"]
        user.twitter_screen_name = data["screen_name"]
        user.twitter_display_name = data["display_name"]
        user.confirm!
        user
      end
    end
  end
end
```

In this file you define an `OmniauthCallbacks` module inside your `User` class. Inside this module, you've put the `find_or_create_for_twitter` method straight from your `User` model, except you've removed the `self` prefix to the method name. You can now go ahead and remove this method from the `User` model, making it temporarily unavailable.

By separating out the concerns of your model into separate modules, you can decrease the size of the individual model file and compartmentalize the different concerns of a model when it becomes complicated, like your `User` model has.

To make this method once again available, you need to extend your model with this module. You can do this by making the first two lines of your model into

```
class User < ActiveRecord::Base
  extend OmniauthCallbacks
```

The `extend` method here will make the methods available for the module on the class itself as class methods.

> **TIP** It's generally a good idea to put any `extend` or `include` calls at the beginning of a class definition so that anybody else reading it will know if the class has been modified in any way. If an `extend` is buried deep within a model, then it can be difficult to track down where its methods are coming from.
>
> By adopting a convention of putting things that can potentially seriously modify your class at the top of the class definition, you're giving a clear signal to anyone (including your future self who may have forgotten this code upon revisiting) that there's more code for this model in other places.

You can now define your `find_or_create_by_github` method in the `User::Omniauth-Callbacks` module by using the code from the following listing.

Listing 15.11   app/models/user/omniauth_callbacks.rb

```
def find_or_create_for_github(response)
  data = response['extra']['user_hash']
  if user = User.find_by_github_id(data["id"])
    user
  else # Create a user with a stub password.
    user = User.new(:email => data["email"],              ◁── ❶ Create user
                    :password => Devise.friendly_token[0,20])
    user.github_id = data["id"]
    user.github_user_name = data["login"]
    user.github_display_name = data["name"]
    user.confirm!
    user
  end
end
```

You're lucky this time around, as the form of the data you get back from GitHub isn't too different to Twitter, coming back in the `response['extra']['user_hash']` key. In the case of other providers, you may not be so lucky. The form of the data sent back is not standardized, and so providers will choose however they like to send back the data.

Included in the data you get back from GitHub is the user's email address, which you can use ❶ to create the new user, unlike with the `find_or_create_for_twitter` method where you had to generate a fake email. The added bonus of this is that if a user wishes to sign in using either GitHub or their email, they would be able to do so after resetting their password.

The final lines of this method should be familiar; you're setting the `github_id`, `github_user_name` and `github_display_name` fields to store some of the important data sent back from GitHub. You're able to re-sign-in people who visit a second time from GitHub based on the `github_id` field you save. Finally, you confirm the user so that you're able to sign in as them.

With the `find_or_create_for_github` method defined, has your feature progressed? Find out with a run of `bin/cucumber features/github_auth.feature`:

```
And I follow "sign_in_with_github"
  undefined method `find_by_github_id' for ...
```

Ah, it would appear that you're not quite done! You need to define the `github` fields in your users table so that your newly added method can reference them. Go ahead and create a migration to do this now by running this command:

```
rails g migration add_github_fields_to_users
```

You can then alter this migration to add the fields you need by using the code from the following listing.

Listing 15.12 db/migrate/[timestamp]_add_github_fields_to_users.rb

```ruby
class AddGithubFieldsToUsers < ActiveRecord::Migration
  def change
    add_column :users, :github_id, :integer
    add_column :users, :github_user_name, :string
    add_column :users, :github_display_name, :string
  end
end
```

Alright, you can now run this migration using `rake db:migrate` and `rake db:test:prepare` to add these fields to your users table. Now you can run your feature again with `bin/cucumber features/github_auth.feature` to see this output:

```
Scenario: Signing in with GitHub
  Given I am on the homepage
  And I follow "sign_in_with_github"
  Then I should see "Signed in with Github successfully."
  Then I should see "Signed in as A GitHubber (githubber)"
    expected there to be content "Signed in as A Githubber"
```

The third step of your scenario is now passing, but the fourth is failing because you're not displaying the GitHub-provided name as the "Sign in as ..." line in your application. You can easily rectify this by changing the `display_name` method in app/

models/user.rb to detect if the `github_id` field is set like it does already with the `twitter_id` field.

Underneath the display name output for the `if twitter_id` case in app/models/user.rb, add these two lines:

```
elsif github_id
  "#{github_display_name} (#{github_user_name})"
```

The entire method is transformed into this:

```
def display_name
  if twitter_id
    "#{twitter_display_name} (@#{twitter_screen_name})"
  elsif github_id
    "#{github_display_name} (#{github_user_name})"
  else
    email
  end
end
```

When you run `bin/cucumber features/github_auth.feature` again, you should see that it's all passing:

```
1 scenario (1 passed)
5 steps (5 passed)
```

Now users are able to use GitHub to sign in to your site, as well as Twitter or their email address if they please. Make a commit for the changes that you've done, but first make sure everything's running with a quick run of `rake cucumber:ok spec`:

```
64 scenarios (64 passed)
746 steps (746 passed)
# and
56 examples, 0 failures
```

All systems green! Time to commit:

```
git add .
git commit -m "Add GitHub authentication support"
git push
```

You've seen how you can support another authentication provider, GitHub, along with supporting Twitter and email-based authentication too. To add another provider you'd only need to follow these six easy steps:

1 Create a new client on the provider's website, which differs from provider to provider.

2 Add the new client's information to config/initializers/devise.rb as a new provider.

3 Write a test for your new provider to make sure that people can always use it to sign in.

4 Add the provider icon to your listed providers in app/views/layouts/application
.html.erb by passing another argument to the `auth_providers` helper method
that you defined in `OauthHelper`.

5 Add a callback to the `Users::OmniauthCallbacksController` by using the
`provides` method. Again, passing another argument to this method is all you
need.

6 Define the `find_or_create_for_[provider]` method in the `User::Omniauth-`
`Callbacks` module.

Due to the flexibility offered by Devise and OmniAuth, there's no provider-specific
configuration you need to do: it all works beautifully. For a full list of providers, check
out the `omniauth` project on GitHub: https://github.com/intridea/omniauth.

See for yourself if GitHub's authentication is working by launching `rails server`
again and going to http://localhost:3000 and clicking the GitHub icon.

15.4   Summary

In this chapter you've seen how easy it is to implement authentication using two
OAuth providers: Twitter and GitHub. You did this using the OmniAuth integration,
which is available in Devise versions after 1.2.

For the Twitter section, you implemented the complete flow in a very simple manner using the features given to you by Devise, such as the routing helper, which initially sends a request off to the provider. Before OmniAuth came along, this process
was incredibly tedious. It's truly amazing what OmniAuth offers you in terms of integrating with these providers.

When you got to the GitHub section, rather than copying and pasting the code
you created for Twitter, you saw how you could reduce repetition in your code by
using methods that iterate through a list of providers to display the icons or to provide callbacks.

Now that you've got multiple ways to allow people to sign in to your application,
the barrier of entry is lowered because people can choose to sign in with a single click
(after they've authorized the application on the relevant provider), rather than filling
in the sign-in form each time. You've also got a great framework in place if you want to
add any more providers.

Your application is at a pretty good state now, but you've not yet made sure that it
can perform as efficiently as possible. If thousands of users flock to your application,
how can you code it in such a way as to reduce the impact on your servers? In the next
chapter, we look at how you can implement some basic performance enhancements
to make your application serve requests faster, or even create a way by which a request
skips the application altogether.

Basic performance
enhancements

16

This chapter covers

- Implementing pagination for resources with the Kaminari gem
- Improving database query speeds with Active Record features
- Caching pages and fragments of pages
- Using the Delayed Job gem with background workers

When an application is written, it may be done in such a way that it will not perform ideally. A common situation is that an application with a small database will perform quickly because there is less data to retrieve, but starts to slow as the database grows larger. This problem can be fixed in many different ways.

The first way is to limit the amount of data retrieved in any one call to a fixed limit, a process known as *pagination*. At the moment, for example, you're not limiting the number of tickets shown in the show action of the ProjectsController. The more tickets that get added to a project, the slower the page that shows this data is going to perform because it will have to retrieve more data from the database and render it out to the page. By breaking the data down into a set of pages, you can

434

show 50 tickets per page. This will lessen the load on your database, but not completely eliminate it. That would only be possible if you were to run no queries at all. You could do exactly that if you cached the output of the page, or even just the part of the page that showed the list of tickets.

The first process involves saving a copy of the page in the public directory, which would then be used to serve this page. Any action on tickets, such as creating one, adding a comment, or changing a state would then wipe this cache and start afresh.

The second process is slightly different. Rather than storing the fragment as a file on the system, you will store it in memory and then access it through a key.

Finally, by adding indexes to key columns in your tables, such as foreign keys, you can greatly speed up the queries it runs too. If you had 10,000 tickets in your system and you wanted to find all the tickets which had `project_id` set to 123, an index would help speed up this process.

We'll show you examples of all of these approaches in this chapter, beginning with pagination.

16.1 Pagination

We'll discuss two different kinds of pagination here. The first kind paginates the interface that users can see, as shown in figure 16.1.

If this project had a thousand tickets, it wouldn't make sense to show all 1,000 at a time. It would also be terribly slow, because the database would have to retrieve 1,000 records. Rails would then have to instantiate 1,000 `Ticket` objects, render 1,000 tickets to the page, and send back that massive chunk of HTML.

The second kind of pagination has to do with your API. Back in chapter 13 you wrote the beginnings of the ticket API, and we promised you we'd revisit it in this chapter. Inside the `Api::V1::TicketsController`'s `index` action you have this innocuous-looking line:

```
respond_with(@project.tickets)
```

Again, if the database's `tickets` table contains 1,000 records for this project, it will have to send all of them to Rails. Rails will then have to instantiate 1,000 objects, parsing them all to JSON or XML before sending them off to the user. All of this would happen with each request, and if you were getting a lot of requests it would bring your application to its knees.

By paginating the result sets in both of these situations, you can change your application to return only 50 tickets at a time, which would theoretically make your application respond 20 times faster than if it were returning 1,000 tickets. Let's begin by installing a gem called Kaminari that will help you with pagination.

Figure 16.1   Tickets for a project

16.1.1 *Introducing Kaminari*

The Kaminari gem[1] is a new breed of pagination gem written by Akira Matsuda, and is considered the Rails 3 successor to the `will_paginate` gem,[2] which was the favorite for a long time.[3]

After you install this gem, you're given an interface on the models of your application, which allows you to make calls like this:

```
@project.tickets.page(2).per(50)
```

This call would ask for the second page of tickets, with each page containing 50 tickets. It's a very clean API. Those familiar with `will_paginate` will be used to a syntax like this:

```
@project.tickets.paginate(:per_page => 50, :page => 2)
```

The syntax is a little longer, but it's a little clearer what it's doing to those who are familiar with it. You'll use Kaminari here just for something different. In your views, you can use the same `paginate` method, which is made available by both gems:

```
<%= paginate @tickets %>
```

This little helper generates the output shown in figure 16.2.

To install this gem, add this line to your Gemfile underneath the `searcher` gem:

```
gem 'kaminari'
```

You'll then run the `bundle install` command to install the gem. With the gem installed, you can now begin to write a Cucumber feature to test that when you're on

Figure 16.2 Pagination helper

---

[1] http://github.com/amatsuda/kaminari.

[2] http://github.com/mislav/will_paginate.

[3] Since this original writing, `will_paginate` has been updated to be Rails 3 compatible.

the tickets page with more than 50 tickets in the system, you will see a pagination link somewhere on that page. You should be able to click Next and then see the next 50 tickets.

16.1.2 *Paginating an interface*

You're going to now implement paging for your tickets listing, showing 50 tickets at a time. Users will be able to navigate between pages by clicking the Next and Prev links. These two links will be provided by a helper from the kaminari gem.

TESTING PAGINATION

To test this, you'll write a new scenario at features/paginating_tickets.feature, shown in the following listing. If you create 100 tickets in this feature, you'll see the pagination links and can then make sure they're working.

> **Listing 16.1 features/paginating_tickets.feature**

```
Feature: Paginating tickets
In order to ease the load on the server
As the system
I want paginate ticket results
Background:
Given there is a project called "Internet Explorer"
Given there are the following users:
| email            | password |
| user@ticketee.com | password |
And "user@ticketee.com" can view the "Internet Explorer" project
And I am signed in as them
And there are 100 tickets for this project          ⟵─❶ Create tickets
When I am on the homepage
And I follow "Internet Explorer"
Scenario: Viewing the second page
Then I should see 2 pages of pagination
When I follow "Next" within ".pagination .next"
Then I see page 2 of tickets for this project
```

In this feature you use the "Given there is a project" step you've used many times before to create a project, and then a new step ❶, which will create a given number of tickets for the project. This is required so that the pagination links will appear on your tickets. If you didn't have enough tickets in your project to warrant pagination, then the links would not appear at all.

You then go through the motions of creating a user, giving them access to that project so that they can see into it, signing in as them, and then navigating to that project. On that project's page you should see the pagination links displaying two pages' worth of pagination. When you click the Next link within the pagination element, you should be on the second page.

You've got three undefined steps within this feature, and you can get the step definitions for these steps by running this feature using the bin/cucumber features/paginating_tickets.feature:

```
Given /^there are (\d+) tickets for this project$/ do |arg1|
pending # express the regexp above with the code you wish you had
end
Then /^I should see (\d+) pages of pagination$/ do |arg1|
pending # express the regexp above with the code you wish you had
end
Then /^I see page (\d+) of tickets for this project$/ do
pending # express the regexp above with the code you wish you had
end
```

The first step definition here has to do with tickets, and so you'll put it in features/
step_definitions/ticket_steps.rb using the code shown in the following listing.

Listing 16.2   features/step_definitions/ticket_steps.rb

```
Given /^there are (\d+) tickets for this project$/ do |number|
number.to_i.times do |i|
@project.tickets.create!(:title => "Test",
:description => "Placeholder ticket.",
:user => @user)
end
end
```

This small piece of code will create as many tickets as you've specified for the
@project object set up by the "Given there is a project" step, using the @user variable
set up by the "Given there are the following users" step. It's not important what the
title and description attributes are for these tickets, just that you have enough of them
to trigger the pagination links to appear.

The next two undefined steps can go into a new file called features/step
_definitions/pagination_steps.rb, as they're about the pagination more than any other
resource in your application.

The Kaminari paginate method you'll use in your view shortly will output a nav
element with the class of pagination. Inside this nav element there are a couple of
other elements. The first is a span element with the class of prev, which would contain
a Previous button if you're a page or two in with pagination. After that, there are a
couple more span elements, all with the class of page. The span tag representing the
current page has an additional class name of current, which we'll discuss a little later.
You can count these span.page elements easily, using the css method to find them
using a CSS selector and then using count on what that returns to count the number
of pages shown in pagination.

By gathering up these page elements and counting them, you easily assert that
there's pagination on this page. You can define the next step like this in features/
step_definitions/pagination_steps.rb:

```
Then /^I should see (\d+) pages of pagination$/ do |number|
pages = all(".pagination .page")
pages.count.should eql(number.to_i)
end
```

Here you use Capybara's `all` method, which will find all the elements matching the CSS selector specified and return them as an `Array` object. Then it's a simple matter of calling `count` on that `Array` and making sure it contains as many as you say it should.

You final undefined step asserts that you're on a specific page of the pagination. Write this step like this:

```
Then /^I see page (\d+) of tickets for this project$/ do |number|
  current_page = find(".pagination .current").text.strip
  current_page.should eql(number)
end
```

You use the `find` method rather than the `all` method because there is only going to be one current page element. This method will only return a single element, which matches the specified CSS selector. Calling `text` on this element will return the number inside it, and you can `strip` it (as it contains spaces) and then compare that to the number passed in for your step. If the two numbers are equal, then this step will pass.

With the last of your undefined steps now actually defined, let's see what happens when you run `bin/cucumber features/pagination.feature`:

```
Then I should see 2 pages of pagination
expected 2
got 0
```

IMPLEMENTING PAGINATION HELPERS

Your step that checks for two pages of pagination wasn't able to see any at all, most likely because you aren't showing any right now! To fix this, you'll have to display the pagination link in app/views/projects/show.html.erb by putting this line above the `ul` that displays tickets:

```
<%= paginate @tickets %>
```

This line will display the pagination links that your failing step currently requires. You're going to need to set up the `@tickets` variable for pagination in your controller so that these pagination links know what page you're on and that there are only 50 tickets displayed. You'll replace this line in the `show` action of app/controllers/projects_controller.rb

```
@tickets = @project.tickets
```

with this line:

```
@tickets = @project.tickets.page(params[:page]).per(50)
```

This `page` method will set `@tickets` to display only the tickets for the current page number, available in the `params[:page]` variable. The `per` method after it will retrieve 50 ticket objects rather than Kaminari's default 25. Your tickets don't take up much room on your page so you can bump this up.

When you run your feature again with `bin/cucumber features/paginating _tickets.feature`, it will pass because you've now got your pagination links showing:

```
1 scenario (1 passed)
10 steps (10 passed)
```

That's all there is to paginating a resource. You can also call the page and per methods on models themselves rather than associations; it was just in this case that you were calling it on an association.

Before you make a commit for this change, quickly make sure that everything's working by running rake cucumber:ok spec:

```
Failing Scenarios:
cucumber features/searching.feature:23
cucumber features/searching.feature:29
cucumber features/searching.feature:35
62 scenarios (3 failed, 59 passed)
736 steps (3 failed, 6 skipped, 727 passed)
```

Oh dear, it appears the feature in features/searching.feature has been broken by your changes! Good thing that you've got a feature to catch these kinds of things.

FIXING BROKEN SCENARIOS

All three scenarios in this feature failed with the same error:

```
undefined method 'current_page' for ...
```

This looks to be associated with the feature you just implemented, as it's trying to call a method called current_page. If you look a couple of lines down in the output, you'll see that there's a line in the stack trace that shows that this is from Kaminari:

```
...kaminari/helpers/action_view_extension.rb:21:in 'paginate'
```

Okay, so it looks to be a problem coming from Kaminari, but why? Well, if you look even further down in the stacktrace for this error somewhere in your application, probably from the app folder, you'll come across this line:

```
./app/controllers/tickets_controller.rb:60:in 'search'
```

What's so great about this line? Well, this line renders the projects/show view:

```
render "projects/show"
```

Above that, however, is the real culprit:

```
@tickets = @project.tickets.search(params[:search])
```

You're not calling either page or per on your search results, and so it's not going to be paginating them. You're going to call the same methods you called back in the ProjectsController's show action here so that you get paginated search results:

```
@tickets = @project.tickets.search(params[:search])
@tickets = @tickets.page(params[:page]).per(50)
```

With paginated search results, the feature in features/searching.feature will no longer complain when you run it with bin/cucumber features/searching.feature:

```
3 scenarios (3 passed)
39 steps (39 passed)
```

Alright, so that one's passing. Let's see what happens when you run `rake cucumber:ok spec` again:

```
66 scenarios (66 passed)
756 steps (756 passed)
# and
72 examples, 0 failures, 19 pending
```

All areas where you need pagination are working. You've called the `per` method twice, once in the `show` action of the `ProjectsController` and again in the `search` method of `TicketsController`. If you wish to change the number of elements returned for a list of tickets, you'd need to change both of these locations. Instead, you'll move the setting for the number of ticket objects returned on each page into the model.

CLEANING UP AFTER YOURSELF

Let's take the `per(50)` call out of this line in the `show` action of `ProjectsController`

```
@tickets = @project.tickets.page(params[:page]).per(50)
```

turning it into this:

```
@tickets = @project.tickets.page(params[:page])
```

Next, you'll do the same thing for the line that uses `per` in the `search` action of the `TicketsController`

```
@tickets = @tickets.page(params[:page]).per(50)
```

changing it into this:

```
@tickets = @tickets.page(params[:page])
```

To make 50 objects the default for this model, you can put this line directly under the searcher block in your `Ticket` model:

```
paginates_per 50
```

Now when your application is asked for a list of paginated tickets, you'll be given 50 tickets per page. You can make sure this is the case by rerunning your "Paginating tickets" feature by running `bin/cucumber features/paginating_tickets.feature`:

```
1 scenario (1 passed)
10 steps (10 passed)
```

Alright, that's still working, so that's good! Are your features and specs still working too? Another quick run of `rake cucumber:ok spec` will tell you:

```
66 scenarios (66 passed)
752 steps (752 passed)
# and
72 examples, 0 failures, 19 pending
```

Great, time to make a commit with this new feature:

```
git add .
git commit -m "Added pagination for tickets"
git push
```

SEEING PAGINATION FOR YOURSELF

Here you've seen an easy way to add pagination links to resources in your application by using the Kaminari gem. You could have used the `will_paginate` gem and that would have worked just as easily. It's really up to personal preference. Pagination allows you to ease the load on the database server by returning only limited amounts of records per page, and also doesn't overwhelm the user with choices.

Let's see how this works in a browser before you continue. First, you'll need to create 100 tickets for a project so that you can get two pages of pagination. To do that, launch `rails console` and put in this code:

```
project = Project.first
100.times do |i|
project.tickets.create!(
:title => "Fake ticket",
:description => "Fake description",
:user => User.first
)
end
```

Next, type `exit` and press Enter to exit out of the console, and then launch your application with `rails server`. You can log in using the email and password you've set up in db/seeds.rb, which are admin@ticketee.com and password, respectively. You can then click the Ticketee Beta page and you should see a page like figure 16.3.

The pagination here shows that you're on the first page and that there's a second page you can go to, by clicking either the 2 link or the Next link. By clicking this link, the page switches to the second page of tickets and the URL now becomes http://localhost:3000/projects/1?page=2. This `page` parameter is passed to the controller as `params[:page]` and then passed to the `page` method provided by Kaminari.

Figure 16.3 Paginated tickets

If you click the 1 link or the Prev link, you'll be taken back to the first page. All of that functionality was given to you by the `paginate` method in your views and the `page` call in your controller. You didn't have to code any of this yourself, which is great. Next, we'll look at how you can add this same kind of pagination to the tickets API.

16.1.3 *Paginating an API*

You've easily set up pagination for your tickets on the interface that a user sees, to ease the load on the database. However, for your tickets API you're still returning all the tickets for a project when they're requested, and therefore you'll run into the same problems you solved in the previous section.

Your API is different though. You can't provide a pagination link for the tickets returned by an API. Instead, you'll have to rely on people passing in a page number, which you'll then use to return that page of tickets.

To test this, you're going to go into your API spec file for tickets at spec/api/v2/tickets_spec.rb and add another test. This one should assert that when you pass in a page parameter to your requests, you receive that page of tickets, rather than all of the tickets or a different page.

In your API you'll limit requests to 50 per response, but you may choose to set this a little higher.[4] Therefore, you'll create 100 tickets, which should give you enough tickets to test that you can get the first and second pages of your API.

You'll add another `context` to spec/api/v2/tickets_spec.rb to test pagination, using the code shown in the following listing.

Listing 16.3   spec/api/v2/tickets_spec.rb

```
context "pagination" do
  before do
    100.times do
      Factory(:ticket, :project => project, :user => @user)
    end
  end

  it "gets the first page" do
    get "/api/v2/projects/#{project.id}/tickets.json",
      :token => token,
      :page => 1

    last_response.body.should eql(project.tickets.page(1).per(50).to_json)
  end

  it "gets the second page" do
    get "/api/v2/projects/#{project.id}/tickets.json?page=2",
      :token => token,
      :page => 2

    last_response.body.should eql(project.tickets.page(2).per(50).to_json)
  end
end
```

---

[4] 200 seems to be a common number to use for API return objects per request.

In this new context, you'll create 100 tickets using the ticket factory, referencing the @user variable set up in the spec's before block and also pointing it at the project object set up near the top of this file. Your first test makes sure that you're getting back the first 50 tickets for the project, and the second test checks for the second 50.

When you run this test using bin/rspec spec/api/v2/tickets_spec.rb:36, it won't pass because you've not got the pagination in place yet:

```
expected [small array of JSON'ified tickets]
got [larger array of JSON'ified tickets]
```

You can easily fix this by changing this line in the index action of app/controllers/api/v2/tickets_controller.rb

```
respond_with(@project.tickets)
```

to this:

```
respond_with(@project.tickets.page(params[:page]))
```

When you rerun the pagination context with bin/rspec spec/api/v2/tickets_spec.rb:35, both tests will pass:

```
2 examples, 0 failures
```

Now users can go to /api/v2/projects/:project_id/tickets.json to get the first page of 50 tickets, or specify the page parameter by putting it on the end of the URL as a query parameter (that is, /api/v2/projects/:project_id/tickets.json?page=2) to get to the second page of tickets.

You can now run rake cucumber:ok spec to check for any breakage:

```
62 scenarios (62 passed)
736 steps (736 passed)
# and
66 examples, 0 failures, 12 pending
```

By paginating the number of tickets shown both on the interface and in the API, you can ease the load on the server and provide a better interface to your users at the same time.

Sometimes when you're coding your application you may inadvertently call queries that aren't that performant. This could happen in a view if you were wanting to display all tags for each ticket as you iterated through them. In the next section, we take a look at how you can cause this problem to happen and at two ways to fix it.

16.2 *Database query enhancements*

What would you do without database queries? Well, you'd have a boring application, that's for sure! But it's database queries that can be the biggest bottleneck for your application once it grows to a larger size. Having a page that—in the beginning—only ran 5 queries and is now running 100 on each request will just not be webscale.

The most common place where performance degradation can occur in a Rails application is when an operation called *N+1 selects* takes place. Let's use your application as an example of this. Imagine that you have 50 tickets and want to display them all on the same page, but also along with these tickets you wanted to display all the tags for these tickets. Before you render this page, you know all the tickets but don't yet know what the tags are for the tickets. Therefore, you'd need to retrieve the tags as you are iterating over each of the tickets, generating another query to retrieve all the tags for each ticket.

This is the N+1 selects problem. You have an initial query for all of your tickets, but then *N* queries more, depending on the amount of tickets you're showing. This problem is not so much of a big deal now that you've got pagination, but it still can crop up.

16.2.1 *Eager loading*

In your app/views/projects/show.html.erb you can perform N+1 selects, asking for each ticket's tags just like in the example, by putting this line within the block where you iterate over each ticket:

```
<%= render ticket.tags %>
```

When you start your server using `rails server` and navigate to your first project's page, Rails will diligently run through each ticket in the `@tickets` array, performing a query for each one to find its tags. If you switch back over to the console, you'll see queries like this:

```
SELECT * FROM "tags"
INNER JOIN "tags_tickets" ON "tags".id = "tags_tickets".tag_id
WHERE ("tags_tickets".ticket_id = 1 )
```

There should be 50 of these little queries, and 50 adds up to a big number[5] when it comes to lots of requests hitting this page and running these queries. Fifty requests to this page would result in over 2,500 queries. Oh, your poor database server![6] It would be much better if you didn't have to run so many queries.

Thankfully, there's yet another thing in Rails that helps us be better programmers and better friends with our databases. This wonderful invention is known as *eager loading* and will allow you to run two queries to get all the tickets and all the tags, rather than one query for the ticket and *N* queries for all the tags for all the tickets.

There are two ways of doing this: you can use the `joins` or `includes` method when you attempt to grab all the tags for the tickets in app/controllers/projects _controller.rb. You're currently grabbing and paginating all the tickets for the current project using this line in the `show` action in `ProjectsController`:

```
@tickets = @project.tickets.page(params[:page])
```

The `@project.tickets` part of this line generates a query,[7] but doesn't eager-load the tags yet. To make it do this, you could use the `joins` method like this:

```
@tickets = @project.tickets.joins(:tags).page(params[:page])
```

---

[5] When used in a function that uses squares, or even worse, cubes.
[6] Yes, they're made for this kind of thing, but that's not the point!
[7] But doesn't run it! When it gets to the view and you call `each` on it, then it runs.

This line would generate an SQL query like this:

```
SELECT "tickets".* FROM "tickets"
INNER JOIN "tags_tickets" ON "tags_tickets"."ticket_id" = "tickets"."id"
INNER JOIN "tags" ON "tags"."id" = "tags_tickets"."tag_id"
WHERE ("tickets".project_id = 1)
```

The INNER JOIN parts of the query here mean that it will find all records in the tickets table that have tags only. It will also return a ticket record for every tag that it has, so if one ticket has three tags it will return three tickets. This is somewhat of a problem, given that you're going to want to display all tickets regardless of if they are tagged or not, and you definitely don't want three of them appearing when only one should.

To fix this, use join's brother includes, switching the line in the show action to this:

```
@tickets = @project.tickets.includes(:tags).page(params[:page])
```

When you refresh the page, Rails will generate two queries this time around:

```
SELECT "tickets".* FROM "tickets"
WHERE ("tickets".project_id = 1)
LIMIT 50
OFFSET 0

SELECT "tags".*, t0.ticket_id as the_parent_record_id FROM "tags"
INNER JOIN "tags_tickets" t0 ON "tags".id = t0.tag_id
WHERE (t0.ticket_id IN (1,2,[...],49,50))
```

Rails has run the query to find all the tickets first, then another query to gather all the tags for all the selected tickets as the second query. This query doesn't care if tickets have tags or not, it will still fetch them.

Here you've seen a way to cause an N+1 query and how to stop it from happening. You can remove the <%= ticket.tags %> from app/views/projects/show.html.erb now, because you're done with this experiment.

This is just one way your database can be slow. Another is more insidious. It creeps in slowly over months of the application seemingly running fine and makes it progressively slower and slower. The problem is a lack of *database indexes*, and it affects many Rails applications even today.

16.2.2   *Database indexes*

Database indexes aren't a Rails feature, they're a feature of your own database that can greatly improve its performance when used correctly. The absence of database indexes may not seem like a problem immediately, but when you're dealing with larger datasets it becomes more and more of a problem. Take for example if you had 10,000 tickets with 2,300 of them belonging to Project A. To find all the tickets for Project A, your database sans indexes would have to do a *full table scan*, searching through each ticket and determining if it belonged to Project A or not. That's a problem, because the more records you have, the longer this scan is going to take.

Indexing the data in your databases allows you to perform fast lookups and avoid full table scans. Imagine that your database is a phonebook and that the names are in no particular order. In this situation, it would be difficult to find all people with a name such as John Smith-McGee, because you'd have to scan the entire phone book to find out who has this name.

An index sorts this data into a logical order and allows for a much faster lookup. Ever seen how a phonebook that has the letter and the first name at upper left, and maybe the same or a different letter at upper right, with another name? That's an index. That allows you to easily find names because you know that the letter A comes before B, and C after B, and so on.

Indexes allow you to run much faster queries because you tell your database how to index the data. Although it may seem like premature optimization at this point, you're going to put an index on your `tickets` table to speed up finding collections of tickets for a project. It's common sense to have these from the beginning: adding them onto large datasets will take a long time, because you'll need to work out how to index each record.

To add this index, create a new migration with this command:

```
rails g migration add_project_id_index_to_tickets
```

This will generate a file at db/migrate that ends with the name you've given it. You're going to need to open this file now and add in the index, because Rails cannot (yet) read your mind. You'll add this index inside the `self.up` part of the migration using `add_index` and remove it in the `self.down` method using `remove_index`, like this:

```
def change
  add_index :tickets, :project_id
end
```

Run this migration using `rake db:migrate db:test:prepare` to run it on the development and test environment databases. You'll see this line in the output:

```
-- add_index(:tickets, :project_id)
   -> 0.0015s
```

Just to reinforce the message: it's better to add the indexes when the database is first being designed rather than at a later point because this 0.0015 seconds could easily become whole seconds on a larger dataset. This index will now group your tickets into groups of `project_id` columns, allowing for much faster lookups to find what tickets belong to a specific project.

You want the absolute best performance you can get out of your database because it's a key point in your requests. Indexes and eager loading are the two most basic ways you can get better performance out of your database.

If your database is performing optimally and your pages still aren't loading fast enough, you'll need to look for alternative methods of speeding them up. Two of these methods are page and action caching, which allow you to store the output of a page to serve it up rather than re-processing the code and hitting the database again.

16.3   *Page and action caching*

Rails has several methods of caching pages. The first of these methods serves a request and then stores the output of that page in the public folder of your application so that it can be served without going through the Rails stack by the web server. This is known as *page caching*

You'd cache a page if that page took a long time to process, or if there were a lot of requests to it. If either of these situations happens, the performance of the web server can be degraded and requests can end up piling up.

By caching a page, you take the responsibility of processing and serving it off your Rails stack and put it on the (usually) more-than-capable web server.[8]

The first time a page is requested, you store it as a file in your application. The next time the request is made, that static page will be served rather than having the action processed again.

This first type of caching is great for pages that don't require authentication. For pages that *do* require authentication you'll need to use a different kind of caching called *action caching*. This type of caching runs the before filters on a request before it serves the cached page, and you'll see a great example of this in this section.

Let's take a look at the first kind of caching, plain ol' page caching.

16.3.1   *Caching a page*

You're going to cache the page that's rendered when a user looks at Projects-Controller's show action. By caching this particular page, Rails will serve the first request to this file and then save the output of the request to a new file at public/projects/:id.html. This public/projects directory will be created by Rails automatically. This process is shown in figure 16.4.

On the next request, due to how the web server is configured, it will serve the file rather than hit the Rails stack, as shown in figure 16.5. This is absolutely a faster request, regardless of how little goes on in an action in Rails. If a request doesn't have to go down that extra level in the stack it's going to save a great deal of time, and again: modern web servers are *built* to serve these static files.

One of the downsides of this is that it will not cache the GET parameter on the request, like your page numbers. Earlier, when you used rails server to use your pagination, the URL became http://localhost:3000/projects/1?page=2. The page that's cached doesn't have this parameter at the end, and so it will always display the first page, because that's what will be stored at public/projects/:id.html.

Regardless of this, you'll at least see how this method works. In your Projects-Controller, underneath the before_filter lines, you can put this method to tell Rails to cache the page for the show action:

```
caches_page :show
```

---

[8]   Such as Apache or nginx, or any other HTTP server. Not WEBrick. There are some things that Ruby's made for, and being a fast/stable HTTP server ain't one.

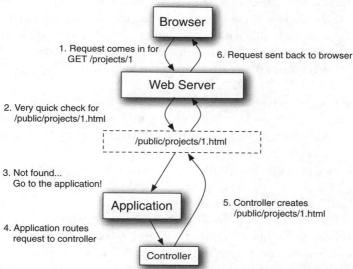

Figure 16.4 First request, no cached page

In development mode, caching is turned off by default. Obviously, in development mode you don't care so much about caching, as all requests are going to be local and not on a heavy-load server. You can turn caching on by going into config/environments/development.rb and changing this line

```
config.action_controller.perform_caching = false
```

to this:

```
config.action_controller.perform_caching = true
```

Without this option, you can still have `caches_page` in your controllers, it just won't do anything. With it turned on, your pages will be cached upon their first request.

Launch `rails server` again and this time go to http://localhost:3000/projects/1. In the server output, you'll see an additional line:

```
Write page /.../ticketee/public/projects/1.html (0.3ms)
```

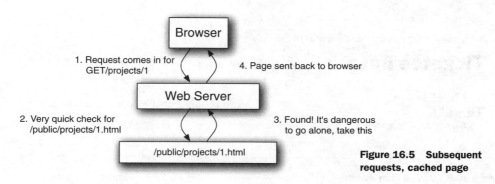

Figure 16.5 Subsequent requests, cached page

This time, rather than simply processing your action and sending the response body back to the server, Rails will save the body in a new file in your application at public/projects/1.html. The next time this route is requested, because the public/projects/1.html page exists, it will be served by your web server, rather than Rails. A side-effect of this means that your request will not show up in the Rails console, but at least it will be served faster.

Let's reload the page now; it should be a little faster because it's serving that static page. If you click the Next link on your pagination, you'll still be shown the first page. This is because the GET parameter was ignored, and the first page for this project's tickets was what was cached.

There's another problem too: this result is cached for *all* users of your application. At the top of the page, you'll be able to see the message that says "Signed in as admin@ticketee.com," as shown in figure 16.6.

To see this little issue in action, sign up as another user by first clicking the Sign Out link in the application to sign out, then the Sign Up link to be presented with a form to sign up. In this form, enter user@ticketee.com for the email and password for both the password and password confirmation fields. When you click the Sign Up button, this will create your new user account.

You currently require users to confirm their account through an email they receive, but because you're in development mode there will be no emails sent. To confirm this user, launch `rails console` now and run these commands:

```
user = User.find_by_email("user@ticketee.com")
user.confirm!
```

You'll also need to give this user access to the first project in your system, so that they can view the tickets too. To do this, run these couple of commands:

```
project = Project.first
user.permissions.create!(:action => "view", :thing => project)
```

Alright, now that your user is confirmed and has access to this project, let's see what happens when you sign in with the email and password you used to sign up, user@ticketee.com and *password*. At the top of the page you'll see that you're signed in as the new user, as seen in figure 16.7.

Figure 16.6   Signed in as admin

Figure 16.7   Signed in as a user

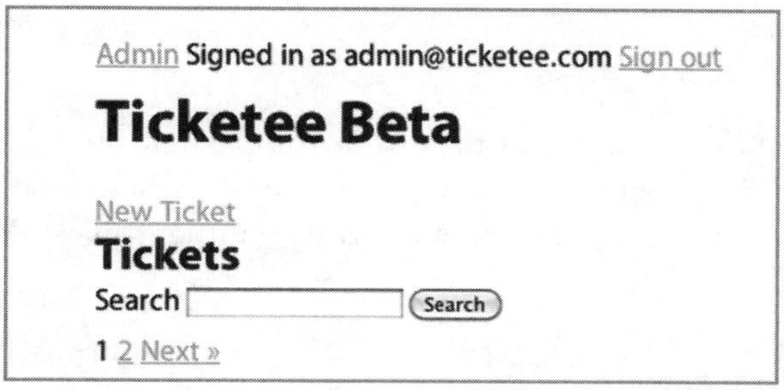

Figure 16.8   Still signed in
as admin@ticketee.com?

However, when you click the Ticketee Beta link to go to your first project, the page will change to saying that you're signed in as the admin@ticketee.com user again, as shown in figure 16.8.

You know better; you're actually signed in as the user! This is happening because Rails has cached the entire page, rather than just the tickets list. This page also ignores any kind of authorization you've set up in your controllers, making it available for every single person who wishes to access it, which is just a Very Bad Thing.

So it looks like `caches_page` isn't going to work in this situation. This method is better for pages that don't have dynamic elements on them, such as the place at the top that displays the currently logged-in user or the list of tickets.

This method has a brother called `caches_action` that will help you fix both the issue of the currently logged-in user display message, as well as the issue of it only showing the first page of pagination.

16.3.2 Caching an action

Caching an entire page is helpful when you don't have authentication, but if you have authentication then it's better to cache the response of the action on a per-user basis. Caching an action involves caching the response for a particular session, so that when that user requests it again they'll be shown it again.

Caching a page is great for a page that's accessible by anybody, as the body would be served as a static file from the public folder by the web server. Caching an action is best used for actions that take a long time to process (you don't have any at the moment) and that require some interaction with the Rails stack, such as a `before_filter` that authenticates your user.

There's a third way of caching, and that's *fragment caching*, where you'd cache just a bit of a page at a time, rather than the entire result. Before you get on to using that, let's see what `caches_action` provides you.

> **NOTE**   Before you do anything, you'll want to remove the old file that has been cached. To do this, delete the public/projects directory. Next time this page is requested, the cache will be re-created.

Let's replace this line in your `ProjectsController`

```
caches_page :show
```

with this line:

```
caches_action :show
```

For this change to take effect, you only need to refresh the page at http://localhost :3000/projects/1 or actually visit it again if you've closed the browser since the last time. If you switch over to the terminal where your server is running, you won't see the line that says this:

```
Write page /.../ticketee/public/projects/1.html (0.3ms)
```

Rather, you'll see this line instead:

```
Write fragment views/localhost:3000/projects/1 (40.3ms)
```

This time, Rails has written a *fragment* rather than writing a page. In this case, the fragment is actually the entire page, but it is the page available only for this user. When you request this page again, you'll see this line in the server's output:

```
Read fragment views/localhost:3000/projects/1 (0.3ms)
```

Upon the second request here, Rails has found the fragment pertaining to this request and served that instead. Rather than saving these files into the public directory, Rails instead saves them to the tmp/cache directory. Files that are in the public directory are automatically served by your web server without hitting the Rails stack, but cached responses in tmp/cache are served by the Rails stack itself. This may seem counterintuitive at first, but it's really helpful if you want to alter what cache fragments are served to what user.

Currently, the fragment is written to a file such as tmp/cache/CC6/080/ views%2Flocalhost%3A3000%2Fprojects%2F1. This location is simply a location in the tmp/cache folder with a hashed path, followed by the escaped name of views/ localhost:3000/projects/1. It's with this name that Rails can retrieve this fragment and show it again.

But you're still going to have the problem that both of your users are going to see the same page. Sign out of your current user, and sign in as the other one. Once you visit this page again, you'll see you're still signed in as the first user! It's doing the same darn thing as caches_page!

As stated before, caches_action is different. It runs the before_filters of your controller and has one more special benefit: you can change the path of where this file is cached by using the cache_path option passed to caches_action. You can then set this option to be a Proc object, which means it will be evaluated before every request made to the action (or actions) you are caching. In this Proc object you'll have access to the current controller instance, meaning you'll have access to current_user. With this access, you'll be able to customize the path where the cache is kept so that you can cache the same page for different users.

To do this, change your caches_action line in your controller to these lines:

```
caches_action :show, :cache_path => (proc do
  project_path(params[:id], :user_id => current_user.id)
end)
```

Here, you've passed the `cache_path` option to `caches_action`. This is a `proc` object, and you need to wrap the value for this option in brackets or Ruby will think the block is for the `caches_action` call.

This `Proc` object is evaluated within the context of an instance of this controller, and therefore you'll have access to the `params` and `current_user` methods usually available within an action or a `before_filter`. With these, you're building a string by combining the URL of the current project (provided to you by the helper `project_path`) and the `id` of `current_user`.

When you access this page again in the browser, Rails will re-process this action because the cache path has changed and then save the page in a new location. In the output for the server you'll see this new fragment has been written, indicated by this line:

```
Write fragment views/localhost:3000/projects/1/1 (4.4ms)
```

This time, the path to the file and the file itself have changed because you've changed the URL of the page; it's now the cached version of this page currently for this user. When you sign out as your current user and sign in as the other user and navigate to this project's page, you'll see that the "Signed in" message at the top of the page is now the correct one, as shown in figure 16.9.

This means that you've now fixed the problem where the same cached page was shown for all users, meaning that each of your users will see a slightly different version of this page. This is *almost* right, but not quite. When you click the Next link for pagination, you'll still only be shown the first page. This is because much like `caches_page`, your `caches_action` also ignores the *page* parameter.

You can fix this, however, by changing the path generated for the cached page to contain the current page number. To do this, change this line in `caches_action`'s `cache_path` option in `ProjectsController`

```
project_path(params[:id]) + "/#{current_user.id}"
```

Figure 16.9 Signed in as admin for a cached page

to this:

```
project_path(params[:id]) + "/#{current_user.id}/#{params[:page] || 1}"
```

The next time you request this page, it will again save a new version of it, this time outputting a line like this:

```
Write fragment views/localhost:3000/projects/1/1/1
```

The first 1 here represents the project's id, the second represents the user's, and the third represents the page number. This file is saved to a path such as tmp/cache/E62/3E0/views%2Flocalhost%3A3000%2Fprojects%2F1%2F1%2F1.

So in this section you've fixed the problem where all people would see that they were signed in as the first person who requested the page, as well as the case where only one page of your tickets was available. Now what happens when you update this page and the tickets change? These pages will still be cached, and your new tickets or updates to them will not be shown!

You're going to need a way to clear this cache, to expire the fragments that are created when these events happen. Right now, the number-one situation where that's going to happen is when you create a new ticket for a project. You can trigger this event to clear your cache by using a feature in Rails known as *cache sweepers*.

16.3.3 *Cache sweepers*

Cache sweepers are much like the observers you used back in chapter 12. In fact, the `ActionController::Caching::Sweeper` class *inherits* from `ActiveRecord::Observer`, effectively making them the same thing. The difference here is that you refer to the sweeper in the controller, telling it to run after certain actions have completed.[9]

In this case, whenever a ticket is created, updated, or destroyed in a project, you'll want your application to clear out the cached pages because they would be out of date at that point. This is precisely what you can use a sweeper for. To call this sweeper, put this line underneath the `before_filter` calls in `TicketsController`:

```
cache_sweeper :tickets_sweeper, :only => [:create, :update, :destroy]
```

You put this line in your `TicketsController` because you want it to run after the `create`, `update`, and `destroy` actions.

Now when you go to a project in your application and attempt to create a new ticket on it, you'll get this error:

```
uninitialized constant TicketsSweeper
```

Rails is looking for the `TicketsSweeeper` constant, which is supposed to define the cache sweeping behavior for your `TicketsController`, but can't find it because you haven't defined it yet. To define this, create a new folder at app/sweepers for this

---

[9] It uses `after_filter` to do this, which can also be used to run other actions after a controller's action has been processed, just like a `before_filter` can be used to run actions before a controller's action runs.

> ### Alternatively, pass a constant
>
> Rather than passing the symbolized version of the name along to the `cache_sweeper` method, you can also alternatively pass along a class:
>
> `cache_sweeper TicketsSweeeper`
>
> This doesn't perform any differently than passing in a symbol, but is really helpful if your sweeper was modularized:
>
> `cache_sweeper Ticketee::TicketsSweeper`
>
> You can't pass a modularized sweeper name as a symbol, and so the `cache_sweeper` method supports passing both a symbol and a constant reference as well.

sweeper and its brethren to live.[10] In this directory you'll create a new file called app/sweepers/tickets_sweeper.rb and fill it with this content:

```
class TicketsSweeper < ActionController::Caching::Sweeper
  observe Ticket
  def after_create(ticket)
    # expire fragment code goes here
  end
end
```

You'll get around to adding the expire fragment code in just a bit, but first a bit of explanation is needed. A sweeper looks and acts much the same as an observer. By calling the `observe` method at the top of the `TicketsSweeper`, you tell this sweeper to watch the `Ticket` class for changes. The `after_create` method here will be called after creation of a new `Ticket` object, but because you're in a sweeper, you'll have access to the controller's parameters also. With them, you can use what's usually available in the controller to expire the cached fragments.

To do this, you can call the `expire_fragment` method, passing it a regular expression. This regular expression will match all cached fragments for the ticket's project for all users, effectively wiping clean the slate for this project in terms of cached pages. Inside your `after_create` method you'll put this:

`expire_fragment(/projects\/#{ticket.project.id}\/.*?/)`

Now when you create a new ticket for a project, this `expire_fragment` method will be called. Let's try this out now, creating a new ticket by clicking the New Ticket link on a project's page and filling out the form. Once you've clicked the Create Ticket button on the form, you'll see this in the console:

`Expire fragment (?-mix:projects\/1\/.*?) (327.3ms)`

Rails has gone through and expired all the fragments associated with this ticket's project. If you now go into tmp/cache and into any one of the directories there looking

---

[10] Because it doesn't really belong in the controllers, helpers, models, observers, or views directory, but is still a vital part of your application.

for a file, you shouldn't see any. The directories (with names like E62 and 3E0) will still exist, but there aren't any files. This means that Rails has successfully cleared its cache of fragments for the project.

Let's get your sweeper to perform this same action when tickets are updated and destroyed. Move the expire_fragment call into another method and then call it in the after_create, after_update, and after_destroy methods in TicketsSweeper using the code shown in the following listing.

Listing 16.4 app/sweepers/tickets_sweeper.rb

```ruby
class TicketsSweeper < ActionController::Caching::Sweeper
  observe Ticket
  def after_create(ticket)
    expire_fragments_for_project(ticket.project)
  end

  def after_update(ticket)
    expire_fragments_for_project(ticket.project)
  end

  def after_destroy(ticket)
    expire_fragments_for_project(ticket.project)
  end

  private

    def expire_fragments_for_project(project)
      expire_fragment(/projects\/#{project.id}\/.*?/)
    end
end
```

Now you have Rails caching the pages of tickets for all projects in your application and clearing that cache when tickets are updated. This is a great demonstration of caching on a per-user basis, even if your project page isn't that intensive. If you had a system resource (CPU/memory) intensive action in your application that required user customization like this, you could use this same method to cache that action to stop it from being hit so often, which would reduce the strain on your server.

Expiring pages

If you were still using caches_page, you wouldn't use expire_fragment to expire the cache files that were generated. Instead, you'd use expire_page, which can take a hash like this:

```ruby
expire_page(:controller => "projects",
:action => "show",
:id => 1)
```

Or, better still would be to pass it the URL helper:

```ruby
expire_page(project_path(1))
```

Even though you're not caching pages any more, it's still handy to know how to clear cached pages and fragments.

Let's make a commit now for this:

```
git add .
git commit -m "Add fragment caching to ticket listings on a project"
```

Another way to ease the load on the server side is to use the browser (client) side caching by sending back a `304 Not Modified` status from your Rails application. In the next section, we'll look at a Rails controller method that'll help you with this.

16.3.4 Client-side caching

There's one more method in the controller you're going to see in this section, and that's the `fresh_when` method. This method will send an ETag[11] header back with the initial request to a client, and then the client's browser will cache that page with that ETag on the client's machine.[12] The ETag is the unique identifier for this page, or entity, at the current point in time.

In this situation, you'll use this type of caching for the `show` action on a ticket in a project, meaning the URL will be something like /projects/1/tickets/2. The first request to this action after you're done will follow the steps shown in figure 16.10.

The next time the page is requested, the browser will send a request with the ETag it received on the first request to the server, this time in a `If-None-Match` header. The server then regenerates the ETag for the page that's been requested and compares it against the `If-None-Match` incoming header. If these two match, then the server will send back a `304 Not Modified` header, telling the browser to use its cached copy. This means that, rather than having the server re-render the view and its pieces, the client does all the hard work of just re-showing the initial page. This whole process is shown in figure 16.11.

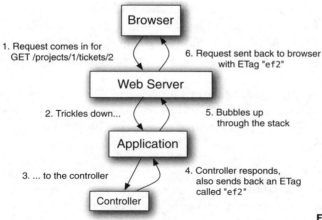

Figure 16.10 ETag caching

---

[11] The E stands for entity. More information is available on the Wikipedia page for this: http://en.wikipedia.org/wiki/HTTP_ETag.

[12] If Private Browsing is turned on in the browser, this wouldn't happen.

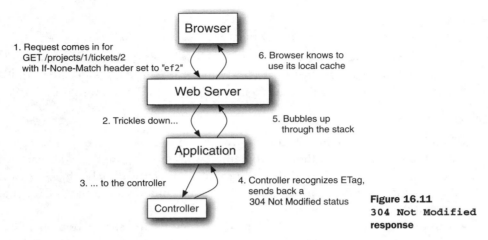

Figure 16.11
`304 Not Modified`
response

Even though this goes through the same series of events both times, what happens in the controller is the clincher: by returning a `304 Not Modified`, you can respond with a lightweight response and get the user's browser to render the page, rather than having your application do it again.

For your ticket page, you're going to want your application to send back this status only when your ticket hasn't been updated. When a ticket's information such as the title or description is updated, or when a comment is posted to the ticket, you'd want to send back a proper response rather than the `304 Not Modified` header. It's this timestamp that you're going to be using to determine if a page is either fresh or stale. A fresh page is one that's been recently updated, with a stale page being one that hasn't been.

You've got a column in your `tickets` table that you can use to determine if a ticket's been updated: the `updated_at` column. Each time a ticket's updated through your application, this field will be set to the timestamp automatically. But, when a comment is posted to the ticket, the `updated_at` field for the ticket will remain the same.

To fix this problem, you can configure the `Comment` model to touch the ticket object it's related to, which will update its `updated_at` timestamp. The way you do this is with an option on the `belongs_to` association in `Comment` called `touch`. Let's change the `belongs_to :ticket` line currently in app/models/comment.rb to this:

```
belongs_to :ticket, :touch => true
```

Whenever a comment is updated, created, or even destroyed, the related ticket's `updated_at` attribute will be updated. With the `touch` option, you can now confidently use this attribute to provide a reliable timestamp for your new form of caching. This particular form of caching uses a new method in your controllers called `fresh_when`.

To make the `show` action in `TicketsController` conditionally send back the `304 Not Modified`, put this at the bottom of the `show` method in app/controllers/tickets_controller.rb:

```
fresh_when :last_modified => @ticket.updated_at,
           :etag => @ticket.to_s + current_user.id.to_s
```

The `last_modified` option here sends back another header to the client: the `Last-Modified` header. This header is used by a browser to detect when the page was last updated, which provides a near-identical purpose to an ETag. A browser sends an `If-Modified-Since` header that contains the last `Last-Modified` time. If the server sees that the `Last-Modified` time is later than the `If-Modified-Since`, it will send a new copy of the page. Otherwise, it will send a `304 Not Modified` header.

The `:etag` option tells `fresh_when` to generate a new ETag for the resource. Until this resource changes, the ETag generated will be the same for each user. This wouldn't be the case if you didn't pass through the `current_user.id.to_s` to the ETag, but only for two user accounts accessed on the same computer. By using the `current_user`'s `id` attribute to seed the `etag` option, the tag will be different between users. How this ETag is generated differs from implementation to implementation; in Rails it's an MD5 hash, which is guaranteed uniqueness.

Even though these two options are nearly identical, some browsers may support one or the other. It's more of a way to cover your bases to pass through both headers, and it's a worthwhile thing to cover.

You can see this in action now if you attempt to visit a ticket's page. Your first request will have a final line that says something like this:

```
Completed 200 OK in 486ms (Views: 200.4ms | ActiveRecord: 5.6ms)
```

In this instance, the views have been rendered and the entire procedure has taken 486ms. Rather than refreshing the page (because in some browsers, this triggers them to *not* send the `If-Modified-Since` or `If-None-Match` headers), you'll go back to the project's page and then click back on the same ticket again. This time in the server output you'll see this output:

```
Completed 304 Not Modified in 267ms
```

The server has sent back a `304 Not Modified` response in a slightly quicker time than your original request, mainly because it didn't have to re-render the views for the application and send back all that HTML.

This is another way to ease the load on your server, by getting the browser to deal with the page caching and serving, rather than the server.

That wraps up this section. You've made a small change here you should probably commit. You can do that by typing these commands into the terminal:

```
git add .
git commit -m "Add ETag and Last-Modified
            support to ticket show page"
```

You've now seen many different flavors of controller caching, ranging from caching pages and caching actions (actually, fragments), to getting the browser to take care of the hard part of the caching process (storing a file and expiring it). All of these caching methods deal with caching entire pages, so what's a Railer supposed to do if they want to cache only a bit of a page at a time? For that, you can tell Rails to cache just these parts using an aptly named method: cache.

16.3.5 Caching page fragments

If part of a page takes a long time to render, then that's a problem. To fix this kind of problem, you can use fragment caching, which allows you to cache fragments of pages using the cache method in your views where appropriate. This method takes a block, like this:

```
<% cache do %>
  # some horribly long and complex thing
<% end %>
```

This way, when Rails attempts to load the page and comes across your cache call, it will check to see if there's an available fragment for it. Otherwise it will perform the code inside the block and then store it in tmp/cache, just like caches_action does for an entire page.

You don't have an actual use-case for this in your application at the moment, but you'll still use it just to see what it does. You're going to be using it back on the app/views/projects/show.html.erb view, meaning you're going to want to temporarily disable caches_action in ProjectsController for this action so that it doesn't cache the page before cache has a chance to run. You can do this by simply removing the lines in ProjectsController:

```
# caches_action :show, :cache_path => (proc do
#   project_path(params[:id]) + "/#{current_user.id}/#{params[:page] || 1}"
# end)
```

In the app/views/projects/show.html.erb, the primary content that's going to be changing is the list of tickets, and so you'll want to cache that and leave out the rest. To do this, you'll wrap the whole list of tickets, including the pagination link above it, in a cache block, as shown in the following listing.

> **Listing 16.5 app/views/projects/show.html.erb**

```
<% cache do %>
  <%= paginate @tickets %>
  <ul id='tickets'>
    <% @tickets.each do |ticket| %>
      <li>
        <%= render ticket.state if ticket.state %>
        #<%= ticket.id %> - <%= link_to ticket.title, [@project, ticket] %>
      </li>
    <% end %>
  </ul>
<% end %>
```

The next time you reload this page in your browser, you'll see this line in your server's output:

```
Write fragment views/localhost:3000/projects/1 (3.0ms)
```

Look familiar? It's exactly the same output generated by `caches_action`. The `cache` method that you just used assumes that it's only being used once per page and so will save it with the same path (more commonly referred to as the *cache key*). You had a problem with this initially, didn't you?

Yes, you did. It was saving the page name just fine, but it didn't care if you were on your first page of pagination or the last, it was always showing the first cached page. If you click the Next link on your pagination, you'll find that you've regressed this behavior accidentally. Not to worry, this is easy to fix. You need to tell your `cache` method that there's more than one type of this page. You can do that by passing a string containing the page number to the method to give it a unique name, or key. By making this key unique for each page, Rails will cache a list of tickets for each page rather than one for all.

To fix this, change the `cache` call in your app/views/projects/show.html.erb file to this:

```
<% cache "projects/#{@project.id}/#{params[:page] || 1}" do %>
```

When you refresh this page and switch back into the terminal where your server is running, you'll see this line of output:

```
Write fragment views/projects/1/1 (3.3ms)
```

You've specified the key that the cache now uses to store the fragment, and so you'll see that it's saved it as `views/projects/1/1` now, with the first 1 being the ID of your project and the second one being the page number. If you create, update, or delete a ticket, you'll see that this fragment gets cleared away.

```
Expire fragment (?-mix:projects\/1\/.*?) (1.9ms)
```

The next time you revisit the project's page, you'll see that it rewrites the fragment again:

```
Write fragment views/projects/1/1 (1.5ms)
```

In this section, you've seen that fragment caching is useful not only for caching dynamic actions with `caches_action`, but also for caching small chunks of pages by using the `cache` method. The latter allowed you to cache a small fragment of the page rather than the entire page, which is great if you have a small chunk of the page that takes a long time to render. You didn't, but it's always good to know what tools are available if you come up against this particular beast.

With the `cache` method in the view, you don't have to set the `cache_path` for the user because you're only caching the part of the page that is user-agnostic. Everything else in either the layout or elsewhere in this view would be processed each time the page is requested, but the part you have cached will be retrieved from that cache and added to the output, rather than re-processed. All in all, this solution is more elegant than `caches_action`. Another commit is in order!

```
git add .
git commit -m "Implement tidier caching for the tickets
➥list on the projects page"
```

That covers all the major methods for basic caching in controllers and views. You've seen ways to cache entire pages and parts of pages as cached files on the filesystem. In a Rails application there may be a lot of reading and writing to the filesystem, which can cause degradation of performance, so storing these files on the filesystem may not be the best idea. A speedier way of doing this would be to store these files in memory by switching the cache store that Rails uses. You can do this by putting this line in one of your config/environments files, probably production.rb:

```
config.action_controller.cache_store = :memory_store
```

Rather than storing the fragments on the file system, Rails will now store them in memory along with the code for the application. The retrieval time is faster here, but comes at the cost losing the cache if the server was ever stopped. If you want something more persistent, you may choose to use either Memcached (http://memcached.org) or Redis (http://redis.io). We won't go into these in this chapter, as they exceed the boundaries of what would be considered basic performance enhancements.

In this section you've learned how to use fragment caching to store parts of the view that may take a long time to process. This type of caching would store these fragments in the tmp/cache directory; they can be retrieved later on.

16.4   *Background workers*

There are other situations where requests can be slow for your application too. One of these cases would be if a ticket had a large number of watchers, and a comment was posted to that ticket. The reason for this slowdown would be because Rails would have to iterate through all the watchers and send out the update notification email to each of them individually, using the feature that you developed in chapter 12.

Rather than having a user make the request to create a comment in the application, having the server process the email notifications, and then send a response back, you can take the long-running task of sending these emails and move it into a job that runs in a background.

This will work by having your `CommentObserver` add the task of sending these emails to a job queue that runs in the background. You'll then have a background process separate from your application that will run these jobs as it receives them. This way, the hard work is done behind the scenes and the user receives the request back almost as if nothing of consequence happened.

To make this happen, you'll use a gem called `delayed_job`. This gem will allow you to create a table in your database where the jobs that the background worker needs to work off will be stored. The gem will also provide you with the ability to start a worker process. To add this to your application you'll put this line in your Gemfile:

```
gem 'delayed_job'
```

Then you'll need to run `bundle install` to install it. Once you're done there, you can run this command, which will generate a migration to create the `delayed_job` table:

```
rails g delayed_job
```

You can now run this migration with `rake db:migrate db:test:prepare`. That's all that's needed to set up the gem itself.

Your next task is to create a job. A job is any object that responds to `perform`. This method needs to perform the action of sending out the email to all the watchers of the ticket, which is currently the responsibility of the `after_create` method in `CommentObserver`, which uses this code:

```
watchers = comment.ticket.watchers - [comment.user]
watchers.each do |user|
  Notifier.comment_updated(comment, user).deliver
end
```

You'll take this code out of the `after_create` method and replace it with code to enqueue your job to be performed, using a method given to you by the `delayed_job` gem:

```
Delayed::Job.enqueue CommentNotifierJob.new(comment.id)
```

The `CommentNotifierJob` class here will actually be a `Struct` object. You can create the code by first creating a new directory called app/jobs and then a new file in it called comment_notifier_job.rb, using the code you stole from the `after_create` method as shown in the following listing.

Listing 16.6   app/jobs/comment_notifier_job.rb

```
class CommentNotifierJob < Struct.new(:comment_id)
  def perform
    comment = Comment.find(comment_id)
    watchers = comment.ticket.watchers - [comment.user]
    watchers.each do |user|
      Notifier.comment_updated(comment, user).deliver
    end
  end
end
```

In the `perform` method here, you find the comment based on the `comment_id` and then iterate through all the watchers of the comment's ticket who are not the commenter themselves, sending them each an email that the ticket has been updated with a new comment.

By enqueueing this job using the `Delayed::Job.enqueue` method, the `delayed_job` gem will store a *marshalled* format (actually a YAML string) of this object in the table, such as this:

```
--- !ruby/struct:CommentNotifierJob \ncomment_id: 1\n
```

When a worker reads this row, it will convert this marshalled object back into a real object and then call the `perform` method on it. The reason for making another class and using a `Struct` over using one such as the `Comment` is that a `Struct` object will always be lighter than a full-on class that inherits from `ActiveRecord::Base`. If you enqueued a `Comment` object instead, the result would be this:

```
"--- !ruby/
    ActiveRecord:Comment \nattributes: \n  text: This is a comment\n  ticket
    _id: 1\n  user_id: 2\n  created_at: &id001 2011-04-
    21 09:35:20.497749 Z\n  updated_at: *id001\n  state_id: \n  previous_sta
    te_id: \n  id: 1\n"
```

This contains a lot of useless information that you don't care about when you're enqueueing the job, and so you should not use it. When enqueueing jobs, you should always try for the lightest possible solution so that the job is queued quickly.

Now when a comment is created, a job will be enqueued to notify the watchers of the relevant ticket. This job is actually a record in a table called `delayed_jobs` that the worker reads from, running each job one at a time and working them off the queue. When there are no more jobs, it will simply wait.

To make sure that this is working, you're going to write a test for it. The test should check that a job is enqueued when a comment is created and that the watchers of the comment's ticket are notified by email when the job is run. Primarily, this test will check the `perform` method in the `Comment` model, and so you'll put it in spec/models/comment_spec.rb, using the code shown in the following listing.

Listing 16.7   spec/models/comment_spec.rb

```
require 'spec_helper'

describe Comment do
  let(:user) { Factory(:user) }

  before do
    @ticket = Factory(:ticket)
    @ticket.watchers << user
  end

  it "notifies people through a delayed job" do
    Delayed::Job.count.should eql(0)
    ticket.comments.create!(:text => "This is a comment",
                            :user => ticket.user)
    Delayed::Job.count.should eql(1)

    Delayed::Worker.new.work_off!
    Delayed::Job.count.should eql(0)

    email = ActionMailer::Base.deliveries.last
    email.to.should eql(user.email)
  end
end
```

At the beginning of the `describe Comment` block, you set up a user who will be the one to watch the ticket that you set up in the `before` block.

In the test itself you make reference to a `Delayed::Job` class, which is actually a model provided by the `delayed_job` gem which connects to the `delayed_jobs` table. You call `count` first up and make sure that's 0 because you don't want any jobs in the table before comments exist.

Next, you create a comment for the ticket, making it originate from the creator of the ticket (`ticket.user`). This way, you can be sure that the user you set up with the `let` block will receive the notification. After the comment has been created, there should be exactly one job in the table.

You then call `Delayed::Worker.new.work_off(1)` to create a new `Delayed::Worker` instance that will work off a single job on the queue and then finish.[13] When it's done, there will be no more jobs in the queue.

Finally, you check that the last email sent out (by referencing `Action-Mailer::Base.deliveries`, which stores the emails that have been sent but only in the `test` environment) has gone to the user who should have been notified, indicating that the job has run successfully.

This test should pass automatically because you've already implemented the feature. You can see this by running `bin/rspec spec/model/comment_spec.rb`:

```
1 example, 0 failures
```

Great! Now when a comment is created it should be created at the same speed, independent of the number of watchers on a ticket. Although the number of watchers on a ticket would have to reach a high number before a problem like this would arise, it is still a perfect example of how you can use `delayed_job` to queue jobs in the background.

One final thing. You've seen how you can enqueue the jobs and work them off using the `Delayed::Worker#work_off` method, but that isn't quite the way you'd do it in the real world or in a production environment. There, you'd run a command like this:

```
script/delayed_job start
```

This command will start a single delayed job worker,[14] which will check the database every five seconds for jobs and work them off as they come in. However, there is no monitoring in place for this, and so it is advisable that a tool such as Monit or God is used to monitor this process and restart it if it happens to go down.

You can stop this job runner by using this command:

```
script/delayed_job stop
```

---

[13] The default of this method is 100 jobs.

[14] Watch out: this loads the entire Rails environment again. On a low-memory system, a large number of Rails instances and job workers can suck up all the RAM of the system. It is advised to take care when deciding how many of each process are running on a machine. If this is outside the bounds of the system, then perhaps it is time to upgrade.

If you're using `delayed_job` extensively, you may wish to start more than one worker, which you can do by passing in the -n option to the command, like this:

```
script/delayed_job -n 2 start
```

This particular example will start two workers rather than one. For more examples on how to use this gem, check out the README on https://github.com/collectiveidea/delayed_job.

That does it for background jobs. You've learned how to take things that could potentially slow down a request and move them into the background, allowing the Rails application to continue serving the request.

Let's make a commit for these changes:

```
git add .
git commit -m "Ticket notifications are now a background job"
git push
```

Now you're done!

16.5 *Summary*

In this chapter you learned how to implement small, easy changes that help your application perform faster, beginning with pagination and ending with view-fragment caching and delayed jobs.

By using pagination, you're able to lighten the load on the database by retrieving smaller sets of records at a time. This is the easiest way to lessen the load on your application's infrastructure.

Database queries are often the bottleneck in the application because they may inadvertently be performed in excessive amounts, or they may not be indexed in the correct manner. You saw in the beginning how to implement eager loading for your queries so that rather than doing more requests than necessary, Rails will load all the necessary objects in a second, separate query.

The second way to improve database performance is to use an index similar to the page titles in a phonebook, but for a database. If you had a large number of records in your database, the index would allow for speed increases in the lookups for records for that index.

If your database speed can't be enhanced any further, then the next stop is caching the resulting pages from your actions. You first attempted to use `caches_page` but found that it came with a couple of problems: the page was available to all users regardless of their authorization, showing "Signed in as x" where "x" was the first user who requested the page, and it completely ignored your `page` parameter. So you moved on to the `caches_action` method, which allowed you to pass an option called `cache_path` to define where your file was saved.

Then you learned that you can cache specific parts of a view using the simply named `cache` method in them. This saves fragments of a view into the tmp/cache directory, allowing you to store the result of potentially computationally expensive parts of your view.

These are the basic concepts for enhancing the performance of your application. There is more you can do, like integrating with tools such as Memcached (http://memcached.org) and Redis (http://redis.io), and interacting with the `Rails.cache` variable which gives you fine-grained control over the cache that Rails uses to store fragments and can be used to store other pieces of information.

## 17

Engines

This chapter covers

- The importance of engines for Rails 3
- Building a new engine and exploring the base
- Using behavior-driven development to develop an engine
- Releasing the engine as a gem
- Integrating an engine with an app

Engines are a new feature for Rails 3.[1] They are effectively miniature applications that provide additional functionality to an application, and they function in much the same way as an application.

Back in chapter 6, you used the Devise gem, which itself is an engine. Other engines include the RailsAdmin[2] and forem[3] engines.

An engine allows you to share common functionality across applications in the form of a gem or a plugin.[4] This functionality could be an authentication system such

---

[1] Although in previous versions they were supported by a plugin written by the community: https://github.com/lazyatom/engines.

[2] http://github.com/sferik/rails_admin.

[3] http://github.com/radar/forem.

[4] In Rails 3, these two are basically interchangeable. One lives in vendor/plugins, the other is installed using gem. For all intents and purposes, they work in a near-identical manner. Developers should try to use gems where possible, as they are versioned and easy to upgrade to specific versions, where plugins are not.

as Devise, a commenting engine, or even a forum engine. If there's ever been a need to have the same features across an application, this is what engines were made for.

By installing an engine as a gem or plugin and then mounting it at a specific route in the config/routes.rb file of your application, you gain access to its features. Each engine will be different, so be sure to consult the README or other documentation that comes with it in order to figure out exactly how it works.

We'll begin by discussing the history of engines and why they're now a major part of the core ecosystem, as it's helpful to know the reasons why they weren't available in releases earlier than 2.3.

In this chapter we'll go through a little bit of the history of engines, why engines are useful, and how they work, and then you'll develop one of your own. At the end of the chapter, you'll integrate the engine with the Ticketee application you have developed earlier in the book.

17.1 *A brief history of engines*

On November 1, 2005, James Adam begun work on what would become the *engines* plugin.[5] Starting off crudely, engines eventually evolved into something much more useful, serving as the inspiration for the functionality within the Rails core today. There was a lot of controversy surrounding engines,[6] and James spent a lot of his time defending the decision to develop them. Since then, however, the community has grown to accept the idea of engines.

One of the major problems of having this engines plugin live outside of the core framework was that there wasn't a clearly defined place where it could hook into Rails code. Rails could potentially change and break the engines plugin, which would prevent people from upgrading to the latest version of Rails until the engines plugin was updated.

It was decided during the development process of Rails 3 that engines should be a core feature, and so a large chunk of work has gone into getting them right. By having them in core, it means that there is a clearly defined public API for engines and when newer versions of Rails come out, there's an almost-zero[7] possibility of things breaking.

Part of this work was added to Rails 2.3, and very basic engines were possible back then,[8] but things such as copying migrations and assets were not supported. Additionally, there was no way of running the Rails generator and so files had to be generated in a real application and then copied over.

Since then, engines have been dramatically improved. Rather than having to copy over migrations manually, there's a specific Rake task to do that. There is no need to

---

[5] http://github.com/lazyatom/engines.

[6] http://glu.ttono.us/articles/2006/08/30/guide-things-you-shouldnt-be-doing-in-rails and http://article .gmane.org/gmane.comp.lang.ruby.rails/29166 to name two such criticisms.

[7] In programming, the chances of things breaking over time approaches zero, but never truly reaches it.

[8] A good demonstration of engines in Rails 2.3 can be seen on Railscast #149: http://railscasts.com/episodes/ 149-rails-engines.

copy over assets from an engine into a Rails application any more either; they are served through the functionality of the Sprockets gem.

Finally, this ancient engine implementation didn't enforce namespacing of the controllers or models. This could potentially lead to conflicts between engines and the application code, where the application code would override an engine's code. If the application has a model called Forum at app/models/forum.rb, and the engine has the same model at the same location (relative to its root), the application's model will take precedence. Namespacing is something that you'll see has almost a zealot level of impact in the work that is done with engines today. It's absolutely important to keep the application and engine's code separate so that they do not conflict.

So today, we've now got engines as a core part of Rails 3.1, and they're better, and they're here to stay. Let's see why they're useful.

17.2   *Why engines are useful*

Engines allow Rails programmers to share common code between applications in an extremely easy fashion. It's entirely possible to use more than one engine in an application, and many people do. Engines are generally provided as gems, and so they are managed like every other gem your application uses: by using Bundler.

In previous (before 3.0) versions of Rails, we have seen that people had to use the engines plugin.[9] This was sometimes problematic, because whenever a new Rails version was released it could potentially break the compatibility of the plugin. By having this feature within Rails itself, this issue is fixed.

Alternatively, people could use generators. These would often generate controllers, models, and views in the application itself, which would allow people to change the code exceptionally easily. When new versions of these generators were released with changes to the previously generated code, however, there was no clean way to keep the changes.

One final, very hacky way, would be to copy over the controllers, models, or views into the application manually from a directory, which runs into the same problems as described, as well as making it difficult to know if you got it right or not.

With an engine, all the code is kept separate from the application and must be explicitly overridden in the application if that's what is needed. When a new version of an engine is released, it will only alter the code of the engine and not the application, making the upgrade process as easy as changing a version number in a Gemfile.

Even the routes for an engine are kept separate, being placed in the engine's config/routes.rb file rather than the application's. This allows you to namespace the engine's routes so that they don't conflict with the application.

The whole point of engines is to separate out chunks of functionality, and to be able to share it without it crashing into the code that already exists.

Let's generate your own engine and have a look at its parts.

---

[9] http://github.com/lazyatom/engines.

17.3   Brand-new engine

The layout of an engine is nearly identical to that of a Rails application, with the notable exception that all code that usually goes straight into the app directory now goes into a namespace. Let's take a look at the layout of the forem engine[10] at an early stage of its development, shown in figure 17.1.

You're going duplicate a little chunk of this code using the same practices that were used to develop forem. It's a good an example as any.[11]

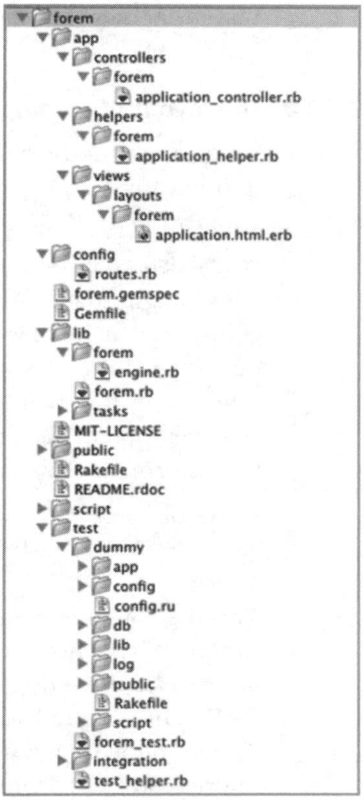

17.3.1   Creating an engine

Here you'll create your engine using a generator built-in to Rails.

> **WARNING**   You're going to need to use at least the Rails 3.1 version for this, which is what you should have installed from earlier chapters in this book.

You can run this executable file to generate the layout of your engine using this command at the root of the Ticketee application you created earlier:

```
cd ..
rails plugin new forem --mountable
```

Figure 17.1   The forem engine, directory structure

The `--mountable` option here is the magic incantation: it tells the plugin generator that you want to generate a mountable plugin, more commonly known as an engine. The output of this command is very similar to that of an application, containing an app directory and a config/routes.rb file. But that's what an engine is essentially: a miniature application! This command even runs `bundle install` automatically for you on this new engine, like the `rails new` command does when you generate a new application.

Before you go any further, run `bundle --binstubs` in this new directory so that you can use `bin/rspec` to run your tests, rather than `bin/rspec`.

Before you get too involved here, you're going to set this project up as a Git repository and create a base commit that you can revert back to if anything goes wrong. You'll first need to change back into the forem directory, then set up the git repository:

```
git init
git add .
git commit -m "Initial base for the forem engine"
```

---

[10] http://github.com/radar/forem.
[11] It also helps that one of the authors of this book has done extensive work on it.

With that safety net in place, let's go through the major parts of what this has generated.

17.3.2 *The layout of an engine*

You've now got the basic scaffold of your engine in the same directory of your application, and you can go back to that directory by using `cd  ../forem` from within the application. Let's go through the important parts of this engine.

FOREM.GEMSPEC

Each plugin that is generated using the new Rails plugin generator now comes with a gemspec, which allows it to be used as a gem.[12] This file allows you to specify information for your gem such as its name, a helpful description, and most important the other gems it depends on as either runtime dependencies using `add_dependency`, or as development dependencies using `add_development_dependency`. You can specify this information by lines like this in the `Gem::Specification` definition in this file:

```
s.add_dependency 'rails'
s.add_development_dependency 'rspec-rails'
```

GEMFILE

This file contains the `rails` and `sqlite3` gems, which provide the basis for your application. When, however, people install your engine using `gem install forem`, they'll not receive these dependencies. To fix this, you need to place them.

You need to tell your Gemfile to reference the forem.gemspec file too, as you specify gem dependencies in this rather than the Gemfile for engines. The Gemfile is not referenced at all when you install a gem, but the forem.gemspec file is. Therefore, you must put all dependencies in the forem.gemspec file and tell your Gemfile to reference it for all its dependencies. To do this, change the Gemfile to be this:

```
source :rubygems
gemspec
```

And add these lines to your forem.gemspec inside the `Gem::Specification` block:

```
s.add_dependency "rails", "3.1.0"
s.add_development_dependency "sqlite3"
```

When you run `bundle install`, it will install the Rails version specified in your Gemfile *and* any gem dependencies declared in forem.gemspec.

APP

This folder serves the same purpose as an application: to house the assets, controllers, helpers, models, views, mailers, observers, and whatever else is particular to your application.

Rails is automatically told about the app/assets directory contained within an engine, based on the class definition within a file you'll see a little later on, lib/forem/

---

[12] A great guide to developing a gem can be found here: http://github.com/radar/guides/blob/master/gem-development.md.

engine.rb. This folder works in the same way that it does in an application, providing a home for the images, JavaScript files, and stylesheets that are served by the `sprockets` gem. Providing that either the host application or the engine[13] specifies a dependency on CoffeeScript or Sass, you can use these as well.

Inside the app directory lies the app/controllers directory, which serves the same purpose as the app/controllers directory in a Rails application. This directory has a key difference though: the controllers should be placed into a forem namespace so that they do not clash with identically named controllers in the application. If you moved these controllers out of the namespace, they'd clash with controllers of the same name in the application, or in other engines that aren't using namespacing. By namespacing them, you prevent this error from happening. This also explains why the helpers in app/helpers are also separate.

Your `Forem::ApplicationController` currently inherits from `ActionController::Base`, but in the case of your engine you'll want it to inherit from `ApplicationController` instead. Therefore, you'll change app/controllers/forem/application _controller.rb from this

```
module Forem
class ApplicationController
```

into this:

```
module Forem
class ApplicationController
```

You must use the `::` prefix on the super `ApplicationController` so that it goes to the top-level `ApplicationController`, not the one inside the `Forem` model that you're defining! By inheriting from the `ApplicationController`, your engine will use the same layout as the application it's hosted within.

Within the app directory, you can define models which also go under a namespace. If you had a `Forum` model, it would live at app/models/forem/forum.rb and would be called `Forem::Forum`. By doing this, you separate the model class from any identically named class in the application or other engines. The default table name for this model would be `forums` if it weren't for some additional configuration in lib/forem/engine.rb that you'll see later.

With models also come migrations. When you create migrations in an engine, these are stored (again, like an application) in db/migrate. When you (or others) install the engine into an application, there's a `rake forem:install:migrations` task that will copy across these migrations, adding the migrations to the current list of migrations in the application's db/migrate folder. If a new version of the engine is released, the user can re-run `rake forem:install:migrations` and it will only copy across the newer migrations.

---

[13] It's best to specify this dependency in the engine if you wish to use either of these.

Obviously, you shouldn't alter the migrations at all after releasing the engine to the general public, as there is no clean way of copying the changes. If you wish to make an alteration to a migration after the fact, you should leave the ones already released alone and create new ones.

Finally, in the app directory you've got a app/views/layouts/forem/application .html.erb file. This file defines a basic layout for your engine, but you're going to want to use your application's layout, not this engine's, so you can delete it right away.

CONFIG/ROUTES.RB

This file defines the routes for your engine. You can use exactly the same helpers you'd use in an application's routing file, as you'll see later on this chapter when you develop a feature. We won't go into detail for the routing right now: we'll do that after we've gone through the directory structure.

LIB/FOREM.RB

This file is automatically required by Bundler when you're loading your engine as a gem, or by Rails if you're loading it as a plugin. This is the main entry point for everything your application does. This file is very simple:

```
require "forem/engine"
module Forem
end
```

By requiring the forem/engine (which is actually the lib/forem/engine.rb file in the engine), it triggers the process that loads your engine.

The module defined at the bottom of this file is there so that you can define any global behavior you wish. Right now, you don't need any.

LIB/FOREM/ENGINE.RB

This file is the heart and soul of the engine and defines the all-important Forem ::Engine. By inheriting from Rails::Engine, it sets in motion a chain of events to notify the Rails stack that an engine exists, providing a path to the assets within the engine. This file is pretty short:

```
module Forem
class Engine
```

By using the isolate_namespace method, you isolate this engine's routes from the application, as well as defining that models within the Forem module are to have a table prefix of forem_.

By isolating the routes, you allow a host application to have a forums_path routing method defined for the application, as well as for the engine itself. When you use forums_path within the application, it will point to the application's forums_path. If you use it in an engine, it will point to the engine's forums_path.

If you ever wanted to reference an engine's route from within your application, there's a helper defined for that too:

```
link_to "Forums", forem.forums_path
```

Calling the routing helper on the `forem` method automatically provided by this engine will generate the engine's `forums_path` rather than the application's. Note here that you're using a period (`.`) rather than an underscore (`_`). You're calling the `forem` method and then calling the `forums_path` method on that. If you wanted to reference the application's route from within the engine, you'd use `main_app` instead of `forem`.

Inside the `Forem::Engine` file you have access to the same config that an application would have. This is because the class that your application inherits from, `Rails::Application`, actually inherits from `Rails::Engine` as well. Applications and engines share much the same base functionality. This means that you'll be able to configure your engine to use RSpec as the testing framework by putting these two lines in the `Forem::Engine` definition:

```
config.generators.integration_tool :rspec
config.generators.test_framework    :rspec
```

RAKEFILE

This file loads the Rake tasks for your engine and any engine tasks Rails wishes to define. It also has one additional benefit: it loads your dummy application's Rake tasks too. But rather than loading them straight into the Rake global namespace and polluting it, it namespaces the application's tasks into the `app` namespace, so any defined task called `email` would become `app:email`.

The engine's tasks are much like an application; you can call `rake db:migrate` to run the migrations of the engine on your dummy application, and `rake db:seed` to load the seed data from the engine's db/seeds.rb directory.

SCRIPT/RAILS

When you run `rails` commands, it goes looking for the script/rails file. This is how `rails` knows if it's inside an application or not, based solely on the presence of one of these files. In your engine, its presence allows you to use the same generators you normally would in an application to generate your controllers, models, and whatever else you need.

TEST

No proper engine would be complete without tests, and it is, by default, the test directory where these would abide. You're going to be using RSpec because you're familiar with it. When tests in this directory run, they load the test/test_helper.rb file, which contains this code:

```
# Configure Rails Environment
ENV["RAILS_ENV"] = "test"
require File.expand_path("../dummy/config/environment.rb",
__FILE__)
require "rails/test_help"
Rails.backtrace_cleaner.remove_silencers!
# Load support files
Dir["#{File.dirname(__FILE__)}/support/**/*.rb"].each { |f| require f }
```

This file's second line of real code here requires the test/dummy/config/environment .rb file, which loads the application in test/dummy.

TEST/DUMMY

The application contained within this directory is purely for testing purposes, but you can set it up to act like a real application by creating controllers, helpers, models, views, and routes if you wish. When the tests run, this application is initialized like a real Rails application.

Your tests then run against this application, which has your engine mounted inside the test/dummy/config/routes.rb file with this line:

```
mount Forem::Engine => "/forem"
```

This line mounts the routes of your engine (not yet defined) at the /forem path of your application. This means that whenever you want to access this engine, you must prefix the route with /forem. If you are in code, you can use the `forem.` prefix for the routing helpers, as seen earlier with `forem.forums_path` or `forem.root_path` within the dummy application.

Even though there are a lot of files that are generated for engines—like there are when you generate an application—they all play a crucial role in your engine. Without this lovely scaffold, you'd have to create it all yourself, which would be no fun.

This routing may be a little confusing at first, but it's quite simple. Let's look into how this process works, and then you'll get into developing your first feature for this engine.

17.3.3   *Engine routing*

In an application, you need to define routes to an engine when you're using it. You can do that with this line in config/routes.rb:

```
mount Forem::Engine, :at => "/forem"
```

To understand how engines are routed, you must understand the concept of middleware within a Rails application.[14] Middleware is the term used for code that sits between the receiving server and the application; middleware can do a number of things, such as serve static assets and set flash messages. Rails 3 applications run on Rack, which uses a stack-based architecture to accomplish a request. A basic stack is shown in figure 17.2.

In this picture, a basic request cycle for a Rails application is shown. A request comes from a client and hits Rack first, which then goes through all of the middleware. If a middleware returns a 404 ("Not Found")

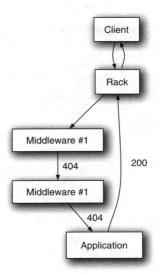

Figure 17.2
A simple middleware stack

---

[14] Additional information about middleware can be found in chapter 18.

HTTP status code, then Rack moves on to the next one, going all the way through each part of the stack, moving on to the next every time the current part returns a 404 until it hits the application. The application is the final stop of this request, and so whatever it returns goes. In this case, the application returns a 200 ("OK") request, which is then passed back to the client through Rack.

If a non-404 response was ever returned from a middleware object, then the digging would stop there, and the response would climb back to the surface.

In a Rails application, the routing is actually a piece of the middleware stack. As the request goes through the chain, it eventually comes to the routes, which then determine where the request should head. When routing requests to an application, the sequence looks like figure 17.3.

In this example, Rack still receives the request and goes through the middleware stack, with each middleware passing the buck until it comes up to the routes. This then handles the request, routing the request to (usually) a controller, which then executes the necessary code to get the job done and passes the result back up to the client.

An engine is served in much the same way; you mount it at a specific path in your application's config/routes.rb line with this line:

```
mount Forem::Engine, :at => "/forem"
```

Any request to the /forem path will not be passed to the application, but instead passed to the engine. The engine then decides how to route that request and returns a response exactly like an application. This process is shown in figure 17.4.

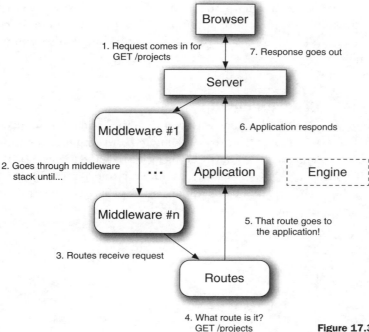

Figure 17.3 Application route cycle

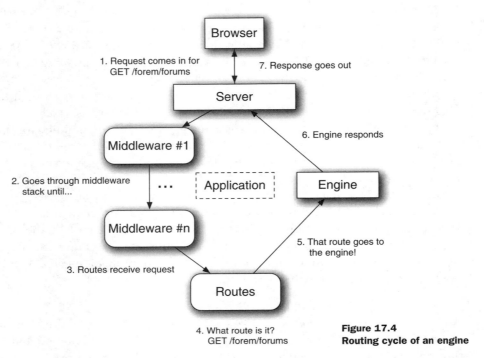

Figure 17.4
Routing cycle of an engine

It's the same cycle, except this time the routing code has determined this request should be handled by the engine, rather than the application.

We've talked long enough about the theory of an engine, and you've learned some key concepts. An engine is a miniature application that provides some functionality, and it's routed like a normal application would be, providing you've mounted it in your application's config/routes.rb file.

It's time to put all this theory into practice.

17.4   *Setting up a testing environment*

Before you can get down to writing any tests, you're going to need to set up the environment to do that. For a change, you're not going to be writing tests for your engine using Cucumber. Instead, you're going to be using RSpec and Capybara. It's always good to get a different perspective on testing, as not everyone agrees on the One True Way™ of doing things. The syntax for this RSpec and Capybara is still easy going, however, as shown by this example:

```
require 'spec_helper'

describe "topics" do
  it "creating a new one" do
    visit topics_path
    click_link "New Topic"
    fill_in "Subject", :with => "First topic!"
```

```
        fill_in "Text", :with => "First post!"
        click_button "Create Topic"

        within "#flash_notice" do
          page.should have_content("Topic has been created!")
        end

        within ".forem_topic #posts .forem_post" do
          page.should have_content("First post!")
        end
      end
    end

end
```

An obvious downside for writing this is that it's not as human-friendly as a Cucumber test is, but it's close enough. Anybody with an extremely basic understanding of Ruby should be able to understand everything here apart from the CSS selectors, which are another class of their own.[15]

There are a couple of benefits to using Capybara directly over using it in conjunction Cucumber. First, it's going to be faster because there's no parsing of the steps as there is in Cucumber—it's straight method calls to the very same methods that Cucumber uses. Second (and related), all the code for the feature is kept within one file.

You're going to need to make some changes to your engine to install RSpec and Capybara first.

17.4.1 *Removing Test::Unit*

At the moment in your application, you've got a test directory that uses Test::Unit for testing. We've avoided this throughout the book, and this chapter's not going to be any exception to that rule.[16] You're going to switch this over to using RSpec.

Inside this test directory, there is the test/test_helper.rb file that contains this content:

```
# Configure Rails Environment
ENV["RAILS_ENV"] = "test"

require File.expand_path("../dummy/config/environment.rb", __FILE__)
require "rails/test_help"

Rails.backtrace_cleaner.remove_silencers!

# Load support files
Dir["#{File.dirname(__FILE__)}/support/**/*.rb"].each { |f| require f }
```

---

[15] You could create a helper method here to help clarify what these mean, such as this `assert_seen` method from the real forem engine:
https://github.com/radar/forem/blob/87092925e8f7092723e07e0adbae44ad96a45d01/spec/integration/posts_spec.rb#L28

[16] For two reasons. First, the authors prefer RSpec. Second, RSpec is preferred by the majority of people in the community. There are still pockets of resistance though.

This is really helpful for Test::Unit, but you can also cannibalize it for your RSpec. Let's create a spec directory and put in it a spec /spec_helper.rb, which contains similar content to the test/test_helper.rb file:

```
# Configure Rails Environment
ENV["RAILS_ENV"] = "test"

require File.expand_path("../dummy/config/environment.rb", __FILE__)
require 'rspec/rails'

Rails.backtrace_cleaner.remove_silencers!          ←──❶ Remove backtrace cleaner

# Load support files
Dir["#{File.dirname(__FILE__)}/support/**/*.rb"].each { |f| require f }
```

It's about identical, except you've replaced the `require` to `rails/test_help` with `rspec/rails`. This spec/spec_helper.rb file will be loaded by RSpec when you run your tests.

One thing to note is the line `Rails.backtrace_cleaner.remove_silencers!` ❶. Rails has an automated backtrace cleaner, which it uses to shorten the resulting backtrace from errors so that it's easier to track down. You don't need this silencing going on in your tests, and so you can remove it using `remove_silencers!`.

You need to add one more thing to the end of spec/spec_helper.rb, which will reset your database back to a clean slate once all of your tests have finished running. It will do this by running the test's database queries inside a transaction, which is then rolled back at the end of the test. That would be this little configuration option:

```
RSpec.configure do |config|
  config.use_transactional_fixtures = true
end
```

Without this, test data would accumulate in your database, leading to undesired results.

Your next step in replacing Test::Unit with RSpec is to move the test/dummy directory to spec/dummy. This folder is the dummy application for your engine and contains the all-important config/environment.rb file, which is required in spec/spec_helper.rb.

With all this code moved over, you can remove the test directory completely, because you don't need it any more. The test/dummy directory itself is still referenced in the engine in a couple of places, and you'll need to replace these references with the new spec/dummy location.

The first of these locations is the Rakefile file at the root of the engine. This file is loaded when any `rake` task is executed and is responsible for loading those tasks. You need to replace this line in Rakefile

```
APP_RAKEFILE = File.expand_path("../test/dummy/Rakefile", __FILE__)
```

with this:

```
APP_RAKEFILE = File.expand_path("../spec/dummy/Rakefile", __FILE__)
```

This will now point to the correct location for your dummy application's Rakefile. If you had defined a custom task within this dummy application called `email_everyone`, it would be available in your engine as `app:email_everyone`. This is designed to stop the conflicts between the application and the engine.

Also in Rakefile, you need to replace the use of `Rake::TestTask` with the equivalent for RSpec. Let's remove these lines from Rakefile now:

```
require 'rake/testtask'

Rake::TestTask.new(:test) do |t|
  t.libs << 'lib'
  t.libs << 'test'
  t.pattern = 'test/**/*_test.rb'
  t.verbose = false
end

task :default => :test
```

Replace them with lines that will do the same thing, but for RSpec:

```
require 'rspec/core/rake_task'
RSpec::Core::RakeTask.new(:spec)

task :default => :spec
```

On the final line here you tell Rake to default to the `spec` task if there is no task specified. This means that, rather than running `rake spec` to run the tests, you can run `rake`.

The second and final location you need to change the test/dummy reference is in script/rails at the root of your engine. This contains this line:

```
load File.expand_path('../../test/dummy/script/rails', __FILE__)
```

This file would normally load the test/dummy/script/rails file directory, if you hadn't already moved it. This file is responsible for loading the subcommands for the `rails` command. You need to change this line to make it work again:

```
load File.expand_path('../../spec/dummy/script/rails', __FILE__)
```

With these changes complete, your move away from Test::Unit is also complete. Your next step is going to be installing the RSpec and Capybara gems and setting them up. With those done, then you can get down to writing some tests.

17.4.2 *Installing RSpec and Capybara*

To install these gems, you're not going to add them to your Gemfile, but instead to forem.gemspec. The established best practice for developing gems is to put the dependencies inside the gemspec. That way, when people install this engine as a gem using `gem install forem`, they'll get all the normal dependencies installed, and if they install it using `gem install forem --dev`, they'll get all the development dependencies as well.

Directly before the `end` of the `Gem::Specification.new` block, you'll put these two lines to declare that RSpec and Capybara are development dependencies of your application:

```
s.add_development_dependency "rspec-rails", "~> 2.5"
s.add_development_dependency "capybara"
```

You can run `bundle install` to install these two gems as dependencies because you've got the `gemspec` method call in Gemfile. Once that command is done, then you've got what you need in terms of gems.

Your next move is to set up Capybara to be used with RSpec. In spec/spec_helper.rb there's this line:

```
Dir["#{File.dirname(__FILE__)}/support/**/*.rb"].each { |f| require f }
```

This line will require all the files with a .rb extension within the spec/support directory or its subdirectories. You can use this to load Capybara for your tests by creating the spec/support folder and putting a file called spec/support/capybara.rb inside of it with this content:

```
require 'capybara/rails'
require 'capybara/dsl'

RSpec.configure do |c|
  c.include Capybara, :example_group => {
    :file_path => /\bspec\/integration\//
  }
end
```

The capybara/rails sets up Capybara to be used for your dummy application (which loads your engine), while the capybara/dsl gives you all the helpful Capybara methods that you're going to need in your tests.

The final chunk of code here includes the `Capybara` module within all tests that are within the spec/integration directory. This should provide a pretty big clue as to where your integration tests are going for your engine!

That's all that you've got to do for setting up Capybara and RSpec. Let's make a commit for this:

```
git add .
git commit -m "Remove Test::Unit, replace with RSpec + Capybara"
```

Now why don't we get into some real coding?

17.5   *Writing your first engine feature*

When they first start writing a Rails application, many people will attempt to create a forum system.[17] This is a great place to start, as a lot of people have used forum systems[18] and therefore they understand the basic concepts of how they work.

Generally, on the home page there's a list of forums that have topics inside of them and then posts inside of those topics. Each topic and post are created by a user, and there's a wide gamut of conversation (and, on larger forums, a great deal of trolling) that goes on in them.

---

[17] One of the authors attempted such a project and it grew into rboard: http://github.com/radar/rboard.
[18] Such as PHPbb and VBulletin.

Your engine is going to be a stripped-down version of this, showing only topics and posts. It's a great example of how you can implement engine functionality, and it's short enough to fit neatly into a chapter. You're going to be using the User model from the host application (Ticketee) for all of your authentication needs too, which is kind of neat.

Your first port-of-call is adding the ability to create a topic and the first post for that topic *at the same time.* This topic will then be displayed at the top of a topics listing, which will be the next feature you'll work on.

17.5.1 *Your first Capybara test*

You're going to need to generate a file to put your test in, and that particular file's going to be called spec/integration/topics_spec.rb. You need to place it inside the spec/integration directory so that you have access to the Capybara helpers that you set up earlier.

In this test, you want to navigate to the listing of all topics, then click the New Topic link, fill in your topic's details, and see that you've got a topic. You'll do this one step at a time, beginning with the code in the following listing.

Listing 17.1   spec/integration/topics_spec.rb

```
require 'spec_helper'

describe "topics" do
  it "creating a new one" do
    visit topics_path
    click_link "New Topic"
    fill_in "Subject", :with => "First topic!"
    fill_in "Text", :with => "First post!"
    click_button "Create Topic"

    within "#flash_notice" do
      page.should have_content("Topic has been created!")
    end

    within ".forem_topic #posts .forem_post" do
      page.should have_content("First post!")
    end
  end

end
```

Here you've defined a test like you would in an application. The test requires spec_helper (spec/spec_helper.rb), which sets up the environment for your test and then launches right into defining the test itself.

Inside the test, you use a Capybara method called visit that will navigate to the specified path in the application, which in this case is topics_path. This will take you to the index action on the TopicsController. You'll put the code that defines this method in your engine's config/routes.rb in a short while.

The `click_link` method here will do exactly that: it will click a link called New Topic, taking you to the `new` action in `TopicsController`. On this page, there will be a form with two fields, one called Subject and another called Text. You fill these fields in using the `fill_in` method, and when you click Create Topic with `click_button`, the form will post to the `create` action of `TopicsController`. This action sets a flash notice that you'll see within an element with its `id` attribute set to `flash_notice`. Finally, you should see the content of your post also within another element on the page. You use the `within` methods provided by Capybara for both of these.

When you run this spec with `bin/rspec spec/integration/topics_spec.rb`, you'll be told this:

```
1) topics creating a new one
     Failure/Error: visit topics_path
     NameError:
       undefined local variable or method `topics_path' for ...
```

This is missing the `resources` call for topics in config/routes.rb, which you must add now.

17.5.2 *Setting up routes*

You've not yet defined the route for this resource in your engine's config/routes.rb, and so you should do that now, transforming the file into this:

```
Forem::Engine.routes.draw do
  resources :topics
end
```

You'll also make it so the `index` action of the controller for this route (`Topics-Controller`) serves as the root page for this engine by putting this line within the `draw` block:

```
root :to => "topics#index"
```

When you run your spec again, you'll still be given the same error:

```
1) topics creating a new one
     Failure/Error: visit topics_path
     NameError:
       undefined local variable or method `topics_path' for ...
```

Even though you've defined the routes correctly in config/routes.rb, the routing helpers are not made available to your specs automatically like they are in a Rails application. This is an easy-to-fix problem though: you'll include them much like you did with the `Capybara` module earlier.

The routing helpers for a Rails application are actually available in a dynamic module that is accessible through the `Rails.application.routes.url_helpers`. Like an application, your engine's URL helpers will be available through `Forem::Engine .routes.url_helpers`. Let's include this module for all spec/integration tests by creating a new file in spec/support called spec/support/load_routes.rb, which contains the content from the following listing.

Listing 17.2 spec/support/load_routes.rb

```
RSpec.configure do |c|
  c.include Forem::Engine.routes.url_helpers,
    :example_group => {
      :file_path => /\bspec\/integration\//
    }
end
```

This will load the URL helpers, such as `topics_path`, that you need for your test.

One interesting thing to note here is that your `topics_path` method doesn't generate the normal /topics URL as would be expected. Instead, it generates the correct /forem/topics path. This is because your engine is mounted in spec/dummy/config/routes.rb under the forem path. When you `visit topics_path`, you're actually going to visit the correct path of this route, like you would in a real application.

The next time you run your spec, you'll see this error:

```
ActionController::RoutingError:
  uninitialized constant Forem::TopicsController
```

Now your `topics_path` helper is working and generating a route to the `index` action inside `Forem::TopicsController`, which you attempt to visit by using the `visit` method. This controller doesn't exist right now, and therefore you get this error. So let's generate this controller to proceed.

17.5.3 *The topics controller*

You've come to the stage where you need the first controller for your application, `Forem::TopicsController`. To generate this controller, you can run this command:

```
rails g controller forem/topics
```

You have to namespace your controller by putting `forem` before it so that Rails creates it correctly. This command will generate the normal controller stuff for your engine, such as the controller itself, a helper, and the app/views/forem/topics directory.

What's your spec tell you next? Let's find out with `bin/rspec spec/integration/topics_spec.rb`:

```
AbstractController::ActionNotFound:
  The action 'index' could not be found for Forem::TopicsController
```

You now need to create the `index` action in `Forem::TopicsController`.

17.5.4 *The index action*

Let's open app/controllers/forem/topics_controller.rb now. Inside this controller, you'll see this:

```
module Forem
  class TopicsController < ApplicationController
  end
end
```

This code has defined a `Forem::TopicsController`, which inherits seemingly from `ApplicationController`. This is actually `Forem::ApplicationController` because the class is being defined in the `Forem` module. The `Forem::ApplicationController` will be where you put all your engine's common controller things later on.

Right now, you need to define this missing `index` action. This action needs to retrieve a list of all topics and then show them in the view. You'll define this action by changing your `Forem::TopicsController` to what's shown in the following listing.

Listing 17.3   app/controllers/forem/topics_controller.rb

```ruby
module Forem
  class TopicsController < ApplicationController
    def index
      @topics = Forem::Topic.all
    end
  end
end
```

You're namespacing your reference to the `Forem::Topic` model because it's actually Ruby that will be loading this class. If you referenced it without the `Forem::` prefix, then it would go looking for a normal `Topic` model that may belong to your application or another engine.[19] At this point, you're not going to have the `Forem::Topic` model defined, and so you'll need to generate that too. It will need to have a `subject` attribute, as well has having a `user_id` attribute, which you'll fill out later:

```
rails g model topic subject:text user_id:integer
```

As when you generated the topics controller, this model will also be namespaced. The migration it generates is called `create_forem_topics` and will create a table called `forem_topics`. This means the migration, model, and table will not clash with any similarly named migration, model, or table in the main application.

To run this migration, run `rake db:migrate` as you would in an application. In an engine, this will run the migration against the dummy application's `development` database. There's no `rake db:test:prepare` in engines at the moment, and so you'll have to work around this by changing the dummy application's config/database.yml file to make the development and test databases the same. You'll do this by using the code in the following listing.

Listing 17.4   spec/dummy/config/database.yml

```yaml
shared: &shared
  adapter: sqlite3
  database: db/development.sqlite3
  pool: 5
  timeout: 5000

development:
  <<: *shared
```

---

[19] Although, in a perfectly sane world, this last scenario isn't possible. This isn't a perfectly sane world.

```
test:
  <<: *shared
```

This won't be too much of a problem, as you'll be doing the major part of your engine's development in tests anyway.

When you run your spec again with `bin/rspec spec/integration/topics_spec.rb`, you'll see that it's missing a template for this `index` action you have created:

```
ActionView::MissingTemplate:
  Missing template forem/topics/index ...
```

This means that you now need to create the view for this action, which goes at app/views/forem/topics/index.html.erb and uses the code from the following listing.

Listing 17.5 app/views/forem/topics/index.html.erb

```erb
<h1>Topics</h1>
<%= link_to "New Topic", new_topic_path %>
<% if @topics.empty? %>
  There are currently no topics.
<% else %>
  <table id='topics'>
    <thead>
      <tr>
        <td>Subject</td>
        <td>Posts count</td>
        <td>Last post at</td>
      </tr>
    </thead>
    <tbody>
      <% @topics.each do |topic| %>
        <tr>
          <td id='topic_subject'><%= link_to topic.subject, topic %></td>
          <td id='posts_count'>0 posts</td>
          <td id='last_post'>last post was at TIME by USER</td>
        </tr>
      <% end %>
    </tbody>
  </table>
<% end %>
```

In this view, you have the New Topic link that you're going to need to click in order to create a new topic. Underneath that link, you have the table for displaying all the topics, or a short message of "There are currently no topics" if that's the case.

In this `table` you've got a Posts Count and Last Post At heading, and you've set placeholder data for these. You'll come back to them a little later on.

With the view defined and the New Topic link in it, your spec will get a little further. Let's run it again with `bin/rspec spec/integration/topics_spec.rb`:

```
AbstractController::ActionNotFound:
  The action 'new' could not be found for Forem::TopicsController
```

You're missing the new action in your Forem::TopicsController. This action will provide the form that users can use to create a new topic.

17.5.5 *The new action*

You need to define the new action in the controller. This action and its related view will provide the form for creating a topic and its first post. In this brand new action, you can initialize a new topic and post with the following code underneath the index action:

```
def new
  @topic = Forem::Topic.new
  @topic.posts.build
end
```

There's no association definition or even a model for the posts association yet, and so you should create the model and then the correct associations. You can do this by running this command:

```
rails g model post topic_id:integer text:text user_id:integer
```

You can then run rake db:migrate to create the forem_posts table. Next, you need to set up both ends of this association, beginning with the Forem::Post model, which needs to have this line inserted:

```
belongs_to :topic
```

Here you don't need to tell Rails that the class of this association is Forem::Topic, Rails will figure that out itself. In the Forem::Topic model, you need to set up the other end of this association and accept nested attributes for it:

```
has_many :posts, :order => "created_at ASC"
accepts_nested_attributes_for :posts
```

You're putting the accepts_nested_attributes_for in the Forem::Topic model because when you submit the form for this action, you'll be passing through the attributes for the topic as well as nested attributes for the post. With the association now defined in your Forem::Topic model, your new action will work.

The next step here is defining the view for this action, which you can do by putting this code at app/views/forem/topics/new.html.erb:

```
<h1>New Topic</h1>
<%= render "form" %>
```

This view will render the partial at app/views/forem/topics/_form.html.erb, which you need to define using the code in the following listing.

Listing 17.6   app/views/forem/topics/_form.html.erb

```
<%= form_for @topic do |f| %>
  <p>
    <%= f.label :subject %>
    <%= f.text_field :subject %>
  </p>
```

```
<%= f.fields_for :posts do |post| %>
  <%= render :partial => "forem/posts/form", :locals =>
{ :post => post} %>
  <% end %>
  <%= f.submit %>
<% end %>
```

❶ Reference partial

Alright now, with the action, the view, and the form partial defined, you're almost there. In this partial though, you reference another partial called forem/posts/form ❶, passing through the local variable of the post form builder object as f to it by using the :locals option. You're using the long form here, as Rails cannot infer the name of it any other way.

This new partial will provide the text field that you'll use for posts. You're placing it into a partial because you may use it later on if you ever create a form for creating new posts, like a reply feature for a topic.

Let's create the file for this partial now at app/views/forem/posts/_form.html.erb and put these lines in it:

```
<p>
  <%= post.label :text %><br>
  <%= post.text_area :text %>
</p>
```

Even though this is an extremely short partial, it's good to separate it out so that it can be shared across the topic and posts forms, and also in case you ever decide to add any additional information to a post.

Your test should get a little further when you run bin/rspec spec/integration/topics_spec.rb again:

```
AbstractController::ActionNotFound:
  The action 'create' could not be found for Forem::TopicsController
```

Now you need to define the create action, the second to last action along this chain, with the show action being the last.

17.5.6 *The create action*

The create action will take the parameters passed from the form provided by the new action and create a new Topic object with a nested Post object. This action should set the flash[:notice] variable to inform the user that the topic could be created and then redirect to the show action.

This action needs to be defined using the code shown in the following listing, placing it under the new action.

Listing 17.7 app/controllers/forem/topics_controller.rb

```
def create
  @topic = Forem::Topic.create(params[:topic])
  flash[:notice] = "Topic has been created!"
  redirect_to @topic
end
```

> **NOTE**   We're purposely not including validations in this action. This is mainly to keep the chapter short, but it's also a good exercise to be left to you. Remember to write tests that the validations work before implementing the code!

When you run your spec again using `bin/rspec spec/integration/topics_spec.rb`, you'll get this error:

```
AbstractController::ActionNotFound:
  The action 'show' could not be found for Forem::TopicsController
```

You're getting closer to having your spec pass! When it clicks the Create Topic button, it's now going through the `create` action successfully and is then redirecting to the `show` action, which you need to define now.

17.5.7   *The show action*

The `show` action in `Forem::TopicsController` will be responsible for displaying a topic and its posts. Your first step will be defining this action, which you can do by putting this code inside app/controllers/forem/topics_controller.rb underneath the `create` action:

```ruby
def show
  @topic = Forem::Topic.find(params[:id])
end
```

You're then going to need to create the view for this action, which goes at app/views/forem/topics/show.html.erb and contains the short bit of code in the following listing.

Listing 17.8   app/views/forem/topics/show.html.erb

```erb
<% div_for @topic do %>
  <h1><%= @topic.subject %></h1>
  <div id='posts'>
    <%= render :partial => "forem/posts/post", :collection => @topic.posts %>
  </div>
<% end %>
```

You're using a long form of `render` here again to render the app/views/forem/posts/_post.html.erb partial for each of the posts. The shorter version goes like this:

```erb
<%= render @topic.posts %>
```

Unfortunately, due to the namespacing on your model, Rails will attempt to render the app/views/forem/forem/posts/_post.html.erb (double "forem") partial instead. You therefore have to be explicit. A short note: the long form's syntax was how it used to be done in earlier versions of Rails.

The partial that it renders hasn't been created yet, and so this will be your next step. Let's create a new file at app/views/forem/posts/_post.html.erb and fill it with this content:

```erb
<%= div_for(post) do %>
  <small>Written at <%= post.created_at %></small>
```

```
  <%= simple_format(post.text) %>
<% end %>
```

In this view you see the reappearance of the `div_for` method (last seen in chapter 10), which will create a new `div` HTML element with the `id` attribute set to `post_[post.id]` and a class attribute set to `post`. This is so you can easily style the element containing the post text if you wish. You're also using the `simple_format` method here too (also last seen in chapter 10), which converts line breaks in the text of the post to HTML `br` tags.

You're close to having your spec pass. Go to the `new` action, fill in the form, click the button, and then you're on the show page. But something's missing. Let's run `bundle exec rspec spec/integration/topics_spec.rb` to see what this is:

```
Capybara::ElementNotFound:
  Unable to find '#flash_notice'
```

Your spec is unable to find the element with the `id` attribute set to `flash_notice`, but why? This is because you haven't defined a way of displaying it in your engine's dummy application's app/views/layout/application.html.erb yet. You can do this by using this code inside spec/dummy/app/views/layout/application.html.erb, directly underneath the <body> start tag:

```
<% flash.each do |key, message| %>
  <div id='flash_<%= key %>'><%= message %></div>
<% end %>
```

This code will iterate through the `flash` hash, setting the keys to the `key` variable and the value to the `message` variable. For each message contained within `flash`, a new `div` element will be put on the page, outputting something like this:

```
<div id='flash_notice'>Topic has been created!</div>
```

Your spec should now see this element with the `id` attribute set to `flash_notice` and pass. Run `bin/rspec spec/integration/topics_spec.rb` and see for yourself:

```
1 example, 0 failures
```

Good! The test passes. This engine now sports the ability to create a brand-new topic, and that's a good start. Given that it's the only test in the engine at this point in time, you don't need to run all the tests at the moment. Let's make a commit:

```
git add .
git commit -m "Added the ability to create a new topic"
```

You've seen here that the basics of developing an engine's feature are very similar, if not identical, to developing a feature under a namespace in a normal application.

Before we move on to your next feature, you'll fix up the two placeholders that you left in app/views/forem/topics/index.html.erb. They were these two lines:

```
<td id='posts_count'>0 posts</td>
<td id='last_post'>last post was at TIME by USER</td>
```

You're probably going to want to replace these two lines with actual data, right? Absolutely! Let's start with the posts count.

17.5.8 *Showing an association count*

You're going to want to replace the "0 posts" in app/views/forem/topics/ index.html.erb with something actually useful. You can do this very easily. You've got a has_many association for posts in your Topic model, which gives you, among other things, a lovely method called count on the association that you can use. Let's replace this line in the view

```
<td>0 posts</td>
```

with this:

```
<td><%= topic.posts.count %></td>
```

This line will execute an SQL count query for all the posts with the topic id set to topic.id, a query like this:

```
SELECT COUNT(*) FROM posts WHERE topic_id = 1
```

This is great, but doing an extra query for every single topic on the page would be extremely hard on performance. If there were 100 topics, then there would be 100 extra queries.

Enter counter caching. Counter caching will allow you to store the number of posts on the topics table, and then you can use this cache to show the number of posts. It works like a normal attribute on a model, except that it's updated by Rails. This attribute's name is [association_name]_count, and so in this case it would be posts_count. To get started with this, you're going to need to add this attribute to the forem_topics table, which you can do by running this command to generate a migration:

```
rails g migration add_posts_count_to_forem_topics posts_count:integer
```

You need to open this migration and set the field to default to 0; otherwise the counter cache won't know where to start counting! You'll change this line in the brand-new migration

```
add_column :forem_topics, :posts_count, :integer
```

to this:

```
add_column :forem_topics, :posts_count, :integer, :default => 0
```

Next, you can run this migration using rake db:migrate. To let Rails know that you've now got a counter cache column on your table, you need to open up the app/models/ forem/post.rb and change this line

```
belongs_to :topic
```

to this:

```
belongs_to :topic, :counter_cache => true
```

It may seem counterintuitive to define the field on the table for the Forem::Topic model, but then have the counter_cache option in the Forem::Post model, but it's really simple. When a post is created, Rails will check for any associations with the `counter_cache` option set to `true`. It then gets the current count for this association, adds 1 to it, and saves the associated object. When a post is deleted, it will do the same thing, except instead of adding 1, it will subtract 1. This way, you're always going to have an accurate count of the number of posts each topic has.

In the app/views/forem/topics/index.html.erb file now, you'll change this line

```
<td id='posts_count'><%= topic.posts.count %></td>
```

to this:

```
<td id='posts_count'><%= topic.posts_count %></td>
```

Rather than inefficiently calling `posts.count` for each topic, Rails will now reference the `posts_count` attribute for the `Forem::Topic` object instead, saving you many queries for the `index` action when you have many topics. This also means that you'll have an accurate count of posts for your topics!

You'll commit this change now:

```
git add .
git commit -m "Add posts counter cache to topics"
```

You've fixed up one of the placeholder lines in the app/views/topics/index.html.erb view now, and when you get around to adding users to your engine, you'll fix up the second placeholder line.

In this section, you've created an interface for creating topics and their first post, which is the first feature of your engine and a well-tested one at that. You've seen how to use `fields_for` to yet again create nested resources. You first saw that back in chapter 8. You've also seen the `:counter_cache` option for `belongs_to` that you can use to cache the count of an association, so that you don't have to perform another query to get that number. That's a potential lifesaver if you're displaying a lot of objects at once and want to know an association's count on all of them, like in your topics view.

In the next section, you're going to add the ability to add posts to a topic, because what are topics without posts?

17.6 *Adding more posts to topics*

A forum system without a way for users to reply to topics is nearly useless. The whole point of having topics is so that users can reply to them and keep the topic of conversation going for as long as they wish!

The feature that you're about to develop will let people add these replies to existing topics. They'll click a New Reply link on a topic, fill in the post text, and click the submit button. They should then see their post within the list of posts in the topic. Simple, really!

You'll also see here more examples of integration testing with Capybara; you'll repeat some of the concepts, but it's a good way of learning.

You'll start out with a new spec file called spec/integration/posts_spec.rb and begin to fill it with the content from the following listing.

Listing 17.9 spec/integration/posts_spec.rb

```ruby
require 'spec_helper'

describe "posts" do
  before do
    @topic = Forem::Topic.new(:subject => "First topic!")
    @topic.posts.build(:text => "First post!")
    @topic.save!
  end
end
```

In order to reply to a topic, you're going to need to create one. You initialize a new `Forem::Topic` object by using `Forem::Topic.new` and then `build` a post for it. This means that when you navigate to the topic's page, then you'll see a post that will have a Reply link for you to click. You'll put the test underneath the `before` by using the code in the following listing.

Listing 17.10 spec/integration/posts_spec.rb

```ruby
it "reply to a topic" do
  visit topics_path
  click_link "First topic!"

  within ".forem_topic #posts .forem_post" do
    click_link "Reply"
  end

  fill_in "Text", :with => "First reply!"
  click_button "Create Post"

  within "#flash_notice" do
    page.should have_content("Post has been created!")
  end                                                          ❶ Find last
                                                                 .forem_post element
  within ".forem_topic #posts .forem_post:last" do  ⟵
    page.should have_content("First reply!")
  end
end
```

In this test, you go to `topics_path` and click the First Topic! link. Then within a post, you click the Reply link, which will take you to the form to create a new reply to this topic. On this new page, you fill in the text with a short message and click the Create Post button to create a new post. Once this is done, you'll be taken to the `create` action in `Forem::PostsController`, which will set the `flash[:notice]` to be "Post has been created!" and then redirect you back to the topic's page, where you should see First Reply! within a post.

You've used a slightly obscure selector syntax here; you're looking for the `#forem_topic` element, which contains a `#posts` element, which itself contains many `.forem_post` elements, of which you want the last one ❶. This will indicate to you that on the page, the post that has been created is now at the bottom of the posts listing for this topic, right where it should be.

Let's start with running this test using `bin/rspec spec/integration/posts_spec.rb`. It will get through the first two steps, but fail because it cannot find a Reply link:

```
Capybara::ElementNotFound:
  no link with title, id or text 'Reply' found
```

This link needs to go in the app/views/forem/posts/_post.html.erb, and you can do that by using this text and placing it inside the `div_for` in the file, as that's where your test is expecting the link to be:

```
<%= link_to "Reply", new_topic_post_path(@topic) %>
```

This Reply link will go to the `new` action within the `Forem::PostsController`. The nested route helper that you use, `new_topic_post_path`, will again reference only the engine's `new_topic_post_path` because the engine is isolated. To define this route helper and the relevant routes for it, you'll open config/routes.rb and alter this line

```
resources :topics
```

to now be these lines:

```
resources :topics do
  resources :posts
end
```

When you re-run your spec, you get this error:

```
ActionController::RoutingError:
  uninitialized constant Forem::PostsController
```

You need to generate this controller, which you can do by running this command:

```
rails g controller posts
```

Again, this will generate a namespaced controller because you've isolated your engine. In this controller, you're going to need to define a `new` action, as well as a `before_filter` to load the topic. You'll change your `Forem::PostsController` into what's shown in the following listing.

Listing 17.11   app/controllers/forem/posts_controller.rb

```ruby
module Forem
  class PostsController < ApplicationController
    before_filter :find_topic

    def new
      @post = @topic.posts.build
    end

    private

    def find_topic
      @topic = Forem::Topic.find(params[:topic_id])
    end
  end
end
```

Note that the `params[:topic_id]` here doesn't need to be namespaced yet again because you're isolated. This feature is really saving you a lot of useless typing! Now, with the action defined in the controller, you're going to need a view too. You'll define it with a couple of lines in a new file at app/views/forem/posts/new.html.erb:

```
<h2>New Post</h2>
<%= form_for [@topic, @post] do |post| %>
  <%= render :partial => "form", :locals => { :post => post } %>
  <%= post.submit %>
<% end %>
```

> ### Always specify options when using locals
> If, in this example, you used this line to render the partial
>
> ```
> { :post => post } %>
> ```
>
> the `:locals` option would be ignored by `render`. You must always use the `:partial` option in conjunction with the `:locals` option; otherwise it will not work.

With the code in the controller for the `before_filter`, the `new` action defined, and the view written, when you run your spec again with `bin/rspec spec/integration/posts_spec.rb`, you'll be shown this error:

```
AbstractController::ActionNotFound:
  The action 'create' could not be found for Forem::PostsController
```

You now need to define the `create` action within your `Forem::PostsController`:

```
def create
  @post = @topic.posts.create(params[:post])
  flash[:notice] = "Post has been created!"
  redirect_to topic_path(@topic)
end
```

This action will create a new post for the topic with the non-namespaced parameters that have been passed in, set the `flash[:notice]`, and send the user back to the `topic_path(@topic)` path. Hey, that's about all that your test needs, isn't it? Let's find out with another run of `bin/rspec spec/integration/posts_spec.rb`:

```
1 example, 0 failures
```

Awesome! That was easy, wasn't it? You've now got a way for users to post replies to topics for your engine in a couple of steps. You repeated a couple of the steps you performed in the last section, but it's good to have this kind of repetition to enforce the concepts. Additionally, having topics without posts would be kind of silly.

Before you run your specs, RSpec has generated controller tests incorrectly for your application, calling the classes inside the files at spec/controllers/forem/topics _controller_spec.rb and spec/controllers/forem/posts_controller_spec.rb Topics-Controller and PostsController, respectively. You will need to change these to

`Forem::TopicsController` and `Forem::PostsController` so that RSpec doesn't barf when you run your tests. There are also the helpers in spec/helpers and the models in spec/models, which need to undergo similar changes.

Did you break anything? Let's find out with `bin/rspec spec`:

```
2 examples, 0 failures
```

It doesn't look like it, and that's a good thing! Let's commit this change to provide yourself with a nice little checkpoint:

```
git add .
git commit -m "Added the ability to reply to posts"
```

Users of your engine are now able to add replies to topics created by themselves or other users.

You've got a nice couple of features going for your engine, but they're very inclusive. You haven't yet seen how to use the application's `User` model to add authorship to your topics and posts, nor any way of integrating this engine with your Ticketee application. But never fear! That's what the next two sections are for.

17.7 Classes outside your control

When creating an engine such as this one, you may want to rely on classes from the application. To relate posts and topics to users within the application, you could do this in the models:

```
belongs_to :user
```

But what if the concept of users in the application isn't kept within a `User` model at all? Then this would break. You could store a couple of common model names, such as `User`, `Person`, or `Account` and check for those, but that's prone to breakage as well.

Here we'll cover the theory behind configuration options, which you can use to let your engine know the application's `User` model.

17.7.1 Engine configuration

Within this engine you're going to want to reference the `User` model from your application so that you are able to attribute posts and topics to whomever has created them. However, there's a catch: within the application, the model that refers to the user in the system *may not* be called `User`! Therefore, you're going to need to create a way to inform the engine of what this class is called from within the application.

The best way to inform the engine about the `User` model would be to have a file called config/initializers/forem.rb which will run when the application loads like all other initializers. This file would contain a single line, which would tell the engine what class represents users within this application, like this:

```
Forem::Engine.user_class = User
```

This configuration setting will then be maintained by your engine across requests, and you'll be able to reference `Forem::Engine.user_class` wherever you need it within

your application. To add this setting to the engine, you can use a class-level
attr_accessor call within the Forem::Engine class, inside lib/forem/engine.rb:

```
class << self
  attr_accessor :user_class
end
```

The class << self syntax is known as a *metaclass*. The code inside of it defines additional functionality on the class it is contained within. The attr_accessor method
defines what's known as an *attribute accessor*. This consists of a setter (user_class=)
and a getter (user_class), which would usually be accessible on instances of this
class. Due to how you've defined it, it will now be available on the class rather than the
instances. These three lines are the equivalent of this:

```
def self.user_class=(obj)
  @user_class = obj
end

def self.user_class
  @user_class
end
```

Writing it using only three lines with a metaclass is definitely much easier!

Your engine shouldn't run if this variable isn't set, as it's a requirement for the
Forem::Post and Forem::Topic models to work. Therefore, you should get your
engine to raise an exception if this method is called and this @@user_class variable
isn't set.

To make this happen, you'll first write a test for that behavior in a new file at spec/
configuration_spec.rb, using the code from the following listing.

Listing 17.12   spec/configuration_spec.rb

```
require 'spec_helper'

describe 'Configuration' do
  it "user_class must be set" do
    config = lambda { Forem::Engine.user_class }          ◁——❶ Define code block
    error = "Please define Forem::Engine.user_class" +
            " in config/initializers/forem.rb"
    config.should raise_error(Forem::ConfigurationNotSet, error)
    Forem::Engine.user_class = User
    config.should_not raise_error(Forem::ConfigurationNotSet)     ◁——┐
  end
                                           Don't raise exception ❷
end
```

Within this test, you do a couple of new things. First up, you use a lambda ❶ to define
a block of code (a Proc object) that you can run later on. After that, you define an
error message, which should appear if you don't have this configuration setting set.
Finally, you get into the meat of your test, asserting that when the config block is
called, it will raise an exception with the class of Forem::ConfigurationNotSet and
the error message defined earlier in the test.

Once you set this configuration option to the User class and attempt to reference Forem::Engine.user_class again, you assert that it should *not* raise that exception ❷.

When you run this test using bin/rspec spec/configuration_spec.rb, it will fail with this error:

```
uninitialized constant Forem::ConfigurationNotSet
```

This is because your spec is attempting to reference the exception class before you've even defined it! No problem though, you can define this very easily within the lib/forem.rb file by using this code:

```
class ConfigurationNotSet < StandardError

end
```

The StandardError class is used for custom errors within Ruby and serves as a great base for this exception. If you run bin/rspec spec/configuration_spec.rb, you'll see this:

```
expected Forem::ConfigurationNotSet with
 "[error]" but nothing was raised
```

When you attempt to grab the user_class setting in your test, it's not raising this exception when it should. To fix this, you'll need to redefine the user_class method on the Forem::Engine class by putting this code underneath the attr_accessor line in lib/forem/engine.rb:

```
def self.user_class
  error = "Please define Forem::Engine.user_class" +
          " in config/initializers/forem.rb"
  @user || raise(ConfigurationNotFound, error)
end
```

Previously, the user_class method would have returned the @user variable whether or not it was set. In this method, you now define the message that will be shown if this class variable is not set. After that, if the class variable *is* set then it will be returned by this method, and if not then the ConfigurationNotFound exception will be raised, which seems to be all the criteria needed for your test to pass. Let's find out by running bin/rspec spec/configuration_spec.rb now:

```
1 example, 0 failures
```

Great! That's all passing. You've now got a class-level user_class method that you can set up in any applications that use this engine, so that you can notify the engine of the class that represents users within the application. If this setting is not set by the application by the time the engine gets around to referencing it, then the Configuration-NotFound exception will be raised, informing the owner of the application that they need to set this variable up in config/initializers/forem.rb.

Let's now set up the User model within your dummy application so that you can use this setting.

17.7.2 *A fake User model*

Your engine has been deliberately designed to have no concept of authentication. This is so it can be used with any application, independent of whatever authentication system the application uses, be it Devise (which is what your main application uses) or something else. In this section and the ones following, you're going to be associating topics and posts to users so that you know who's been posting what. In order to this, you're going to need to generate a dummy User model.

When you have this model correctly set up, you'll use it to restrict access to the new topic and new post actions to only logged-in users, as well as using it to assign ownership to posts and topics. You'll be able to do this using the current_user made available by the host application. It will be accessible in your engine's controllers, as Forem::ApplicationController inherits from ApplicationController.

To generate this new User model, you're going to have to run the generator from within the spec/dummy directory. This is so the generator will place the model code within the dummy application and not your engine. You don't need anything on this User model besides a login field, which you'll be using as the display value a little later on by defining a to_s method inside this class. Within the spec/dummy directory, run this command:

```
rails g model user login:string
```

To run the migration for this model, run rake db:migrate inside the spec/dummy directory as well.

In this fake model, you're going to need to define the to_s method your engine will use to display the user's name. Right now your users table only has a login field, and so you'll return that:

```
class User < ActiveRecord::Base
  def to_s
    login
  end
end
```

With the fake model generated and the to_s method defined in it correctly, the only thing left to do is to set up the initializer in your dummy application. Create a new file at spec/dummy/config/initializers/forem.rb with this simple line:

```
Forem::Engine.user_class = User
```

That is all the preparation you need to do to notify your engine of this class. To make your engine use this class, you'll put this line in *both* the class definitions of app/models/forem/post.rb and app/models/forem/topic.rb:

```
belongs_to :user, :class_name => Forem::Engine.user_class.to_s
```

This line will now reference the setting that's configured by config/initializers/forem.rb, thereby relating your posts and topics from your engine to the User class within the application, forming a lovely bridge between the two.

Next, you'll apply what you've done here to associate the users who are signed in with the topics they post. This is so people will be able to see who posted what.

17.7.3 *Authenticating topics*

By having a `belongs_to :user` association on the `Forem::Post` and `Forem::Topic` models, you'll be able to assign users to topics and posts when they create them so that other users can know who's been posting what.

You've got, on purpose, no authentication in your dummy application at the moment, and so you'll have to take a shortcut around this. Usually an application would provide a `current_user` method that returns a `User` object, but your dummy application doesn't do this right now. You need this method to sometimes return a user object (like with actions that require authentication), and to sometimes return `nil`.

A cool way to do this would be to dynamically redefine the `current_user` method yourself. A way to do this is to have two methods that you can call in your tests—a `sign_in!` method and a `sign_out!` method—which will redefine the `current_user` method in `ApplicationController` to either return the user object or `nil`, respectively. You'll also make this method a helper method by using the `helper_method` method, which is available in all controllers. This will mean that your fake `current_user` method can then be referenced by the controllers and views of your engine without any problems.

Define these two new methods in a new file at spec/support/dummy_login.rb using the code shown in the following listing.

Listing 17.13 spec/support/dummy_login.rb

```
def sign_out!
  ApplicationController.class_eval <<-STRING
    def current_user
      nil
    end

    helper_method :current_user
  STRING
end

def sign_in!(options={})
  ApplicationController.class_eval <<-STRING
    def current_user
      User.find_or_create_by_login("forem_user")
    end

    helper_method :current_user
  STRING
end
```

When you call the `sign_out!` method in your tests, it will call the `Forem::Application-Controller.class_eval` method, which will redefine the `current_user` to return nil. When you call the `sign_in!` method, it will find a `User` record with its `login` set to forem_user; if it can't do that, it will create one instead. This will then be the object that is returned when you reference `current_user` in your application.

The next function you're going to add to your engine is one that will redirect users who aren't logged in when they attempt to access the `new` action in `Forem::Topics-Controller`. Your test will also test that an unauthenticated user can't see the New Topic link on the`Forem::TopicsController`'s index action. You'll add this spec in spec/integration/topics_spec.rb by using the code in the following listing.

Listing 17.14 spec/integration/topics_spec.rb

```
context "unauthenticated users" do
  before do
    sign_out!
  end

  it "cannot see the 'New Topic' link" do
    visit topics_path
    page.should_not have_content("New Topic")
  end

  it "cannot begin to create a new topic" do
    visit new_topic_path
    page.current_url.should eql(sign_in_url)        ←—❶ Read current URL
  end
end
```

In the `before` block of this new `context`, you call the `sign_out!` method, which will set up the crucial `current_user` method that this test depends on. If it wasn't defined, then you'd get an undefined method when `current_user` attempted to access it.
In this spec, you use `page.current_url` ❶ to read what the current URL is; it should match whatever `main_app.sign_in_path`'s method points at. Remember: this is the `sign_in_path` method, which is made available in the application by a definition in its config/routes.rb file. This is not currently set up, and so you'll do that later.

First, let's see what the output has to say about your first test when you run bin/rspec spec/integration/topics_spec.rb:25:

```
Failure/Error: page.should_not have_content("New Topic")
  expected #has_content?("New Topic") to return false, got true
```

You're asserting in your test that an unauthenticated user cannot see the New Topic link, but they do. You can go into app/views/forem/topics/index.html.erb and change this line

```
<%= link_to "New Topic", new_topic_path %>
```

to these lines:

```
<% if current_user %>
  <%= link_to "New Topic", new_topic_path %>
<% end %>
```

When you run this example again with `bin/rspec spec/integration/topics_spec .rb:25`, you'll see that it now passes:

```
1 example, 0 failures
```

One down, two to go. Let's run the next spec down in this file with `bin/rspec spec/ integration/topics_spec.rb:30`. When you do, you'll see this output:

```
NoMethodError:
 undefined local variable or method `sign_in_url' for ...
```

Your test currently can't find the `sign_in_path` helper for your dummy application. You can define the helper by putting this line in spec/dummy/config/routes.rb:

```
match "/sign_in", :to => "fake#sign_in", :as => "sign_in"
```

When you run your test again with `bin/rspec spec/integration/topics_spec .rb:30`, you'll be shown this:

```
expected "http://www.example.com/login"
    got "http://www.example.com/forem/topics/new"
```

The page expected to be on /login, but was actually on /forem/topics/new! That's because you're not yet authenticating users when they go to the `new` action in `Forem::TopicsController`. You can add a `before_filter` to the class definition in app/controllers/forem/topics_controller.rb using this code:

```
before_filter :authenticate_forem_user!, :only => [:new, :create]
```

You'll put this `authenticate_forem_user!` method definition inside `Forem ::ApplicationController` so that you can use it for all the controllers of your engine. It'll go like this:

```
private

  def authenticate_forem_user!
    if !current_user
      flash[:notice] = "You must be authenticated before you can do that."
      redirect_to main_app.sign_in_url          ◄─┐
    end                                              ❶ Go to login path
  end
```

Now when you visit your `new` or `create` actions in `Forem::TopicsController`, you'll be sent away to the login path for your application, which you can access by calling `sign_in_path` on the `main_app` helper ❶. You must use `main_app` here so that you point to the application's routes rather than the engine's. The engine itself has no concept of `sign_in_path`.

When you run your spec again with `bin/rspec spec/integration/topics_spec .rb:30`, you'll see that this test is now failing because your application is missing the `FakeController` that your `sign_in_path` route uses:

```
ActionController::RoutingError:
  uninitialized constant FakeController
```

You don't need this controller to do much more than sit there and look pretty. Oh, and it needs to have a `login` action that responds in an OK fashion too. Let's define this controller in your dummy application by creating a new file at spec/dummy/app/controllers/fake_controller.rb and putting this content inside it:

```
class FakeController < ApplicationController
  def sign_in
    render :text => "Placeholder login page."
  end
end
```

This action will now render the text "Placeholder login page," thereby returning that OK status you're after, as well as some helpful text to indicate where you're at. When you run bin/rspec spec/integration/topics_spec.rb, you'll see that it passes:

```
1 example, 0 failures
```

This means now that any user attempting to access the `new` action in the `Forem::TopicsController` will be redirected to the login page. What happens when you run the whole spec file? Let's find out with bin/rspec spec/integration/topics_spec.rb:

```
ActionView::Template::Error:
  undefined method `current_user' for #<Forem::TopicsController:...>
  ...
  # ./spec/integration/topics_spec.rb:21:in ...

3 examples, 1 failure
```

Your final spec in this file is failing with an undefined method `current_user`, because you're not calling `sign_in!` before it. Move this code into its own `context` with a `before` like the other two tests have, using the code shown in the following listing.

Listing 17.15   spec/integration/topics_spec.rb

```
context "authenticated users" do
  before do
    sign_in!
  end

  it "creating a new one" do
    visit topics_path
    click_link "New Topic"
    fill_in "Subject", :with => "First topic!"
    fill_in "Text", :with => "First post!"
    click_button "Create Topic"

    within "#flash_notice" do
      page.should have_content("Topic has been created!")
    end

    within ".forem_topic #posts .forem_post" do
      page.should have_content("First post!")
    end
  end
end
```

When you run the whole spec with `bin/rspec spec/integration/topics _spec.rb` one more time, all three examples should pass:

```
3 examples, 0 failures
```

You've now got your engine using the concept of a current user from the application so that it can authorize users to perform certain actions when they're logged in. Are all the tests working still? A quick `bin/rspec spec` will tell you:

```
ActionView::Template::Error:
  undefined method `current_user' for #<Forem::TopicsController:...>
  ./spec/integration/posts_spec.rb:11:...
Finished in 1.16 seconds
6 examples, 1 failure
```

It would appear your spec/integration/posts_spec.rb test is failing because `current_user` isn't defined. You can fix this very quickly by throwing a `sign_in!` call in the `before`, turning it from this

```
before do
  @topic = Forem::Topic.new(:subject => "First topic!")
  @topic.posts.build(:text => "First post!")
  @topic.save!
end
```

into this:

```
before do
  @topic = Forem::Topic.new(:subject => "First topic!")
  @topic.posts.build(:text => "First post!")
  @topic.save!
  sign_in!
end
```

When you run your specs again, they'll all pass:

```
4 examples, 0 failures
```

Great success! Now it's time to commit:

```
git add .
git commit -m "Use application authentication to block
                unauthenticated users from creating topics"
```

Now that you've got an easy way to restrict access to the creation of new topics to only authenticated users, you can be sure you're always going to have a `current_user` object that you can use to associate users with topics. With this in mind, you're going to set the topic's and its first post's user when you create a topic.

17.7.4 *Adding authorship to topics*

You'll now associate topics and users. To make sure that this will work, add these lines to the example within the `authenticated` context in spec/integration/topics_spec.rb:

```
within ".forem_topic #posts .forem_post .user" do
  page.should have_content("forem_user")
end
```

This is the element in which you'll be displaying the user on the page, with the content being the name of the user that you set up in the `sign_in!` method. This user association is actually going to be set both on the topic and its first post. Right now this element doesn't exist, and so if you were to run this test it would fail.

Your first step is to associate the topic to a user when you create the topic in `Forem::TopicsController`. You can do this by changing this line of the `create` action

```
@topic = Forem::Topic.create(params[:topic])
```

to these two lines:

```
params[:topic].merge!(:user => current_user)
@topic = Forem::Topic.create(params[:topic])
```

This will set up the user association for the topic, passing it through with the other parameters inside `params[:topic]`. This will not set up the first post for this topic to have this user associated, which is what you need in order to make your test pass. To do this, create a `before_save` callback in the `Forem::Topic` by using the code from the following listing, placing it under the `accepts_nested_attributes_for :post` line in the model.

> **Listing 17.16   app/models/forem/topic.rb**

```
before_save :set_post_user

private
  def set_post_user
    self.posts.first.user = self.user
  end
```

With the `user` association now set for a topic's first post, you can display the user's name along with the post by putting this line under the `small` tag already in app/views/forem/posts/_post.html.erb:

```
<small class='user'>By <%= post.user %></small>
```

Here you use `Forem::Engine.user_name`, which is the method that you use to display the user's name. In this case, it would display the `login` attribute. When you run `bin/rspec spec/integration/topics_spec.rb`, all your tests will pass:

```
3 examples, 0 failures
```

That was easy! When a topic is created, the topic and its first post will now belong to the user who created it. Remember: your `User` model is in another castle, or rather, it is in your application, and so this is very cool.

Now you'll need to check that users are logged in before they create posts too, and then associate the posts to the users upon creation.

17.7.5 *Post authentication*

You've got the `authenticate_forem_user!` method defined in the `Forem::ApplicationController`, and so it's available for all controllers that inherit from it.

This includes `Forem::TopicsController`, where you just used it, and `Forem::Posts-Controller`, where you are about to use it to ensure that users are signed in before being able to create new posts.

Before you use this method, you'll add a test to the spec/integration/posts_spec.rb to check that a user cannot access the new action if they aren't signed in, and it will fail because you're not using it yet.

You're going to have two `context` blocks in your spec, one for unauthenticated users and the other for authenticated users. You can share the `before` block between these two contexts if you take the `sign_in!` method out and turn your spec into what's shown in the following listing.

Listing 17.17   spec/integration/posts_spec.rb

```
require 'spec_helper'

describe "posts" do
  before do
    @topic = Forem::Topic.new(:subject => "First topic!")
    @topic.posts.build(:text => "First post!")
    @topic.save!
  end

  context "unauthenticated users" do
    before do
      sign_out!
    end
  end

  context "authenticated users" do
    before do
      sign_in!
    end

    it "reply to a topic" do
      ...
    end
  end
end
```

With the `before` block now run before both of your contexts, you'll have the `@topic` object available in both of them. In the "unauthenticated users" context block, you'll write your test for the unauthenticated new action access under the `before` block, using the code from the following listing.

Listing 17.18   spec/integration/posts_spec.rb

```
it "cannot access the new action" do
  visit new_topic_post_path(@topic)
  page.current_url.should eql(sign_in_url)
end
```

Because you don't have the `before_filter :authenticate_forem_user!` line in `Forem::PostsController` when you run this spec using `bin/rspec spec/integration/posts_spec.rb:15`, you'll get this:

```
expected "http://www.example.com/login"
  got "http://www.example.com/forem/topics/[id]/posts/new"
```

With your test in place, you can add the `before_filter` line at the top of your class definition in app/controllers/forem/posts_controller.rb:

```
before_filter :authenticate_forem_user!, :only => [:new, :create]
```

When you run your example again with `bin/rspec spec/integration/posts_spec.rb:15`, this time it'll pass:

```
1 example, 0 failures
```

What happens when you run `bin/rspec spec/integration/posts_spec.rb` though?

```
2 examples, 0 failures
```

This is passing also, which is great to see! Right now though, posts do not belong to users when they are created, and so when you go to display a user's name for a reply post, nothing will appear. In order to fix this, you'll copy over the final couple of lines you put in spec/integration/topics_spec.rb and put them at the bottom of the "reply to topic" example you have in spec/integration/posts_spec.rb:

```
within ".forem_topic #posts .forem_post:last .user" do
  page.should have_content("forem_user")
end
```

Like last time, you're asserting that you can see the user's name within the final post on the page, which you can find using the `within` method. When you run this test using `bin/rspec spec/integration/posts_spec.rb`, it will fail because it cannot see the user's name on the page:

```
Failure/Error: page.should have_content("forem_user")
  expected #has_content?("forem_user") to return true, got fals
```

Now that you have a test ensuring that this behavior is indeed not yet implemented, let's fix it up. First, you're going to need to change the `before` block in your test to set up a user for the first post that it creates, changing it into this:

```
before do
  @user = User.create!(:login => "some_guy")
  @topic = Forem::Topic.new(:subject => "First topic!", :user => @user)
  @topic.posts.build(:text => "First post!")
  @topic.save!
end
```

That will solve it for the first post on this page, but you also care about the new post that you're creating. You can fix this one by changing this line in the `create` action in app/controllers/forem/posts_controller.rb

```
@post = @topic.posts.create(params[:post])
```

to these lines:

```
params[:post].merge!(:user => current_user)
@post = @topic.posts.create(params[:post])
```

We're putting this on separate lines to make the second line a little shorter for readability. When you run `bin/rspec spec/integration/posts_spec.rb` again, you'll see that it all passes:

```
2 examples, 0 failures
```

Now you're authenticating users before they can create new posts, and then assigning them as the user when they're authenticated. That means you're done here and should run all the specs to make sure everything works with a quick run of `bin/rspec spec`. You should see this:

```
7 examples, 0 failures
```

Good to see! Let's make a commit:

```
git add .
git commit -m "Authenticate users and link them to posts"
```

You've now got a pretty good starting feature set for your engine. Users are able to create topics and posts, but only if they're authenticated in the parent application, and that's a good start. You could generate further features, such as editing topics and posts, but that's an exercise best left to you.[20]

One thing you've still got left to do is fix up the second placeholder in app/views/topics/index.html.erb, which shows the last post for a topic. You'll do this now; it'll only take a moment.

17.7.6 *Showing the last post*

Currently in app/views/topics/index.html.erb you have this line:

```
<td id='last_post'>last post was at TIME by USER</td>
```

It would be extremely helpful to your users if this returned useful information rather than a placeholder. You've finished linking posts and users, and so now is a great time to fix this placeholder up.

To begin with, you're going to add a test to spec/integration/posts_spec.rb to ensure that you do indeed see the last post's information. It's the same function displayed to unauthenticated users as it is authenticated users, but you're going to need current_user set by either `sign_out!` or `sign_in!`. Therefore, you'll put this test inside the `context "unauthenticated users"` block to make things easy. The code for this test is shown in the following listing.

---

[20] Additionally, this is a long enough chapter already!

Listing 17.19   spec/integration/posts_spec.rb

```
it "should see the post count and last post details" do
  visit topics_path
  within "#topics tbody td#posts_count" do
    page.should have_content("1")
  end

  within "#topics tbody td#last_post" do
    page.should have_content("last post was less than a minute ago
    ➡by some_guy")
  end
end
```

This test ensures that the post count is showing the correct number of posts and that the last post details are displayed correctly. When you run this spec, it will pass the first assertion because of the posts count you set up a little earlier,[21] but it fails on the last assertion because it cannot find the content you've specified:

```
Failure/Error: page.should have_content("[content]")
  expected #has_content?("[content]") to return true, got false
```

The first part of your content is "last post was less than a minute ago." Let's focus on getting this working. There's a helper within Rails that can help you display this "less than a minute ago" text called time_ago_in_words. Let's assume that you've got a method called last_post that returns the last post for now. You'll define it later. You can use the time_ago_in_words helper within the last post table cell in app/views/forem/topics/index.html.erb:

```
<td id='last_post'>
  last post was <%= time_ago_in_words(topic.last_post.created_at) %> ago
</td>
```

This time_ago_in_words helper will display a humanized version of how long ago the post was. When you first create the post, the text would read "less than a minute ago," as this is the smallest granularity that this helper provides.

Before your test will pass, you're going to need the other half of this line. At the end of the %> on the line you just wrote, add this:

```
by <%= topic.last_post.user %>
```

This first uses a new method that you'll define shortly on the Forem::Topic model called last_post, which will return the last post for this topic. Then, you'll display who posted that post by calling user on that object.

When you run your test again, this time it will fail because the last_post method on topic is only defined in your imagination:

```
ActionView::Template::Error:
  undefined method `last_post' for #<Forem::Topic:0x00000100cfb498>
```

---

[21] Naughty of us not to write tests back then, but sometimes this happens.

It's time this method moved out of your imagination and into your engine. This method needs to return the last post for your topic, and because the `topic_id` lives on the `posts` table and you're wanting only one of these posts, this is a great opportunity to use a `has_one` association.

This association needs to find the chronological last post for your topics; you can do this by defining this association in app/models/forem/topic.rb like this:

```
has_one :last_post, :class_name => "Forem::Post",
                    :order => "created_at DESC"
```

The `class_name` option you've used before; it tells Rails that objects of this association are of that class, rather than the inferred class, which is a constantized version of the association name. In this case, that would be `LastPost`. The `:order` option, however, will order the posts by the `created_at` field in reverse chronological order. The `has_one` method will then execute this query and limit the results to one, returning only the first post.

With the association defined, you can re-run your test and see it passing:

```
1 example, 0 failures
```

You've now got a test that covers that a user can see the posts counter and the last post information on the topics page for a topic, which proves that this feature is working. Let's run all the RSpec tests to make sure that everything's working with `bin/rspec spec`:

```
6 examples, 0 failures
```

Great, everything's good. Time for a commit:

```
git add .
git commit -m "Add last post information to topics index"
```

This has been quite a long section and we've covered a lot of ground. The purpose of this section was to demonstrate how you could reference classes outside your control, such as those in the application or found in other engines. We opted for configuration options for some of the options, and a module for others.

You then asked users to authenticate before they could create new topics and posts, and after that you linked your engine's classes' objects to the objects from an application's class. This is kind of a big deal, as it shows that an engine is able to interact with an application without extravagant modification of the application's code.

Finally, you fixed up your topics `index` view to display information from these linked-in classes.

This has been only the beginning of linking your application and engine. In the final sections of this chapter, you'll see how you can release your engine as a gem and how you can integrate it into your application so that the users of Ticketee have a forum system they can use.

17.8 *Releasing as a gem*

By releasing your engine as a gem, you'll make it publicly available for anybody to download from http://rubygems.org. This will also allow you to share this engine across multiple applications. If people wish to use your engine, they would be able to put this line in their Gemfile of their application:

```
gem 'forem'
```

Then they would need to go about configuring the application to have a config/initializers/forem.rb file with the proper configuration options (only `Forem::Engine.user_class` for now, but possibly others). You'd usually put these steps in a README file at the root of the engine.[22]

To release your engine as a gem, you can use Bundler. Bundler provides some gem-management tasks in the form of Rake tasks that allow you to build your gem (basically, zip it up into a .gem file),[23] install the gem locally, and release it.

To make these tasks available for your engine, you can put this line at the bottom of your Rakefile:

```
Bundler::GemHelper.install_tasks
```

When you run `rake -T`, you'll see that you've got a few tasks for your engine, some of which you've already used. This line that you've put in the Rakefile will add the `build`, `install`, and `release` rake tasks.

Before you can release your gem, you must give it a unique name. To do this, you'll go into your application and rename forem.gemspec to your-name-forem.gemspec[24] to make it unique. Then inside this file, you'll need to change this line

```
s.name = "forem"
```

to have the same name as the gemspec:

```
s.name = "your-name-forem"
```

Now you're ready to release your gem. Let's run the `rake build` task first and see what does:

```
(in /Users/ryanbigg/Sites/book/forem)
your-name-forem 0.0.1 built to pkg/your-name-forem-0.0.1.gem
```

This command has built your gem and put it in a new directory called pkg. This new gem can be installed using `gem install pkg/your-name-forem-0.0.1` if you wish, but there's a problem: this gem doesn't contain all your files.

At the moment, the gem only contains the files specified by this line in your-name-forem.gemspec:

---

[22] This is so when you put it in GitHub, people will have a clear way of seeing what this engine's good for and how they can use it.

[23] Yup, .gem files are actually .zip files.

[24] A wise decision here would be to use your GitHub username, as that's bound to be unique, compared to your first name which is most likely not.

```
s.files = Dir["lib/**/*"] + ["MIT-LICENSE", "Rakefile", "README.rdoc"]
```

This line will only include files from the lib directory, as well as the MIT-LICENSE, Rake-file, and README.rdoc files. But you've got much more than that in your application, such as the app folder for starters! To fix this little problem, you'll replace that line with this one:

```
s.files        = `git ls-files`.split("\n")
```

This will add all the files that have been added to your Git repository to the gem. When you run `rake build` again, it will create your gem with all the files.

You'll also need to set up some authors for your gem, which you can do by putting this line underneath `s.version` in the forem.gemspec:

```
s.authors = ["youremail@example.com"]
```

The next task you can run is `rake install`. This can be run without having `rake build` first, as it will run the build code first, then install. This will actually install the gem onto your system so that you can use it. That's all well and good, but you want to show off your stuff to the world!

That's what `rake release` is for. This command will create a git tag for your current commit, then call `git push` to push your changes online. Next, it will call `gem push`, which will publish your gem to http://rubygems.org. You may have to set up an account on RubyGems.org first, though.

Once this is done, your gem is released out into the world as version 0.0.1. To bump the version, you need only to alter this line in your-name-forem.gemspec:

```
s.version = "0.0.1"
```

It's sensible to increment the last part of this number for minor corrections, such as typos or bug fixes, the middle part for minor breaking changes and additional feature releases, and the major version for major breaking changes or to represent the solidifying of the API.

With your gem now live and out there, you can use it in your application. Exciting times!

17.9 *Integrating with an application*

Now you get to the best part of this chapter: linking Ticketee, your Rails application that you've built throughout the earlier chapters of this book, to the engine that you have just written, forem. This is a pretty easy process.

The first thing you're going to need is to add forem to your application's Gemfile with this line:

```
gem 'your-name-forem', :require => "forem"
```

Then you'll need to run `bundle install` to install the gem. To install the migrations for this gem, you'll need to run this command:

```
rake forem:install:migrations
```

This task actually copies across the engines migration into the application's db/ migrate directory, with the first migration having a timestamp of the current second, the next migration having it one second in the future, and so on. This is so the engine's migrations are inserted after the current application's migrations and maintain the same order that they have in the engine. If you update the engine later on, you'll have to run this task again. To install these migrations, you'll run this:

```
rake db:migrate
```

After this, you'll need to mount the engine in your application's config/routes.rb, which you can do with this:

```
mount Forem::Engine, :at => "/forem"
```

You saw this line in your spec/dummy/config/routes.rb file earlier. Mounting your engine will make its routes available to the specified path. If you launch `rails server` now and go to http://localhost:3000, you'll be shown this error:

```
Please define Forem::Engine.user_class in config/initializers/forem.rb
```

You should follow the advice for this error and define `Forem::Engine.user_class` within the application's config/initializers/forem.rb, as you need to tell the engine what the user class is:

```
Forem::Engine.user_class = User
```

Because you've created a new initializer, you'll need to restart the `rails server` that is currently running so that Rails re-evaluates the files in the config/intializers directory. When you do this and refresh the page, you'll see this error:

```
undefined local variable or method `admin_root_path' ...
```

This is happening because your engine is using the application's layout and is trying to reference `admin_root_path` method from inside the engine, rather than the one that's defined in the application. To fix this, you'll need to first call `main_app` for these routing helpers and then call the helpers on that. You need to change the `root_path`, `admin_root_path`, `destroy_user_session_path`, `new_user_registration_path`, and `new_user_session_path` helpers in the app/views/layouts/application.html.erb file to all have the `main_app`. prefix on them.

These are all the changes you need to make in order to integrate your engine with your application. Click around a bit and try it out!

17.10 *Summary*

In this very long chapter we've covered quite the gamut! We've gone through the theory first of all, the history of engines, and why they're useful. After that, you saw the layout of one and how the routing for an engine works.

You then spent the rest of the chapter creating your own engine called forem, which provides the basic functionality of a forum: topics and posts.

We got into the nitty-gritty of adding configuration options to your engine, as well as a module called `Forem::UserExtensions`, which configured the two models in your engine with new associations. This module is exceptionally interesting, as it allows you to configure the engine's behavior regardless of the class that it's included into.

We then covered releasing your engine as a gem, which is the best way to get it out into the world.

In the final chapter, we look at how you can write lightweight applications using Rack and Sinatra, and hook them into your Rails application. In Rails 3, that's become easier than ever to do.

Rack-based applications

So far, this book has primarily focused on how to work with pieces of the Rails framework, such as application and engines. In this chapter, we'll look at how you can use Rack-based applications to respond more quickly than what you'd otherwise be capable of with your main application.

Rack is the underlying web server framework that powers the underlying request/response cycle found in Rails, but it isn't a part of Rails itself. It's completely separate, with Rails requiring the parts of Rack it needs. When your application is running, it's running through a web server. When your web server receives a request, it will pass it off to Rack, as shown in figure 18.1.

Rack then determines where to route this request, and in this case it has chosen to route to a specific application stack. The request passes through a series of pieces called *middleware* (covered in the final section of this chapter) before arriving at the application itself. The application will then generate a response and pass it back up through the stack to Rack, and then Rack will pass it back to the server, which will finally pass it back to the browser. All of this happens in a lightning quick fashion.

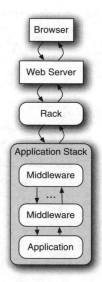

Separating Rack from Rails not only reduces bloat in the framework, but also provides a common interface that other frameworks can use. By standardizing the request/response cycle, applications that are built on top of Rack can interact with one another. In this chapter, you'll see how you can do this by making your Rails application work with applications built using Rack, but not Rails.

You'll build some Rack applications in this chapter that aren't Rails applications but will work just as seamlessly. You'll learn how Rack provides the request/response cycle underneath Rails and other Ruby frameworks, and learn how to build your own small, lightweight Rack-based applications.

With these lightweight applications crafted, you'll then create one more application that will re-implement the tickets API functionality you first created in chapter 13, using another Rack-based web framework called Sinatra. You'll then mount this Sinatra application inside your Rails application using methods that Rails provides. This will provide an apt example of how you're able to interact with classes from your Rails application from within a mounted Rack application.

Figure 18.1 Application request through the stack

Finally, we'll take a look at middleware within both the Rack and Rails stacks, and you'll learn how to use it to your advantage to manipulate requests coming into your application.

All Rack-based applications work the same way. You request a URL from the application, and it sends back a response. But it's what goes on between that request and the response that's the most interesting part. Let's create a basic Rack application now so that you can understand the basics.

18.1 *Building Rack applications*

Rack standardizes the way an application receives requests across all the Ruby frameworks. With this standardization, you know that any application purporting to be a Rack application is going to have a standard way for you to send requests to it and a standard way of receiving responses.

You're going to build a basic Rack application so that you can learn about the underlying architecture for requests and responses found in Rails and other Ruby frameworks. With this knowledge, you'll be able to build lightweight Rack applications that you can hook into your Rails stack, or even Rack middleware.

When you're content with the first application, you'll create another and then make them work together as one big application. First things first, though.

18.1.1 *A basic Rack application*

To build a basic Rack application, you only need to have an object in Ruby that responds to the `call` method. That `call` method needs to take one argument (the request) and also needs to return a three-element `Array` object. This array represents the response that will be given back to Rack, and looks something like this:

```
[200, { "Content-Type" => "text/plain"}, ["Hello World"]]
```

The first element in this response array is the status code for your response. In this case, it's `200`, which represents a successful response. You had a bit of a play with status codes back in chapter 13 when you were building your API, so these should be no mystery at this point.

The second element in this array are the headers that will be sent back. These headers are used by the browser to determine how to deal with the response. In this case, the response will be rendered as-is to the page because the `Content-Type` header is `text/plain`, indicating normal text with no formatting applied. Usually your Rack application would set this to `text/html` to indicate an HTML response.

Finally, the third element represents the response body, which is sent back along with the status code and headers to Rack. Rack then compiles it all into an HTTP response, which is sent back to where the request came from.

Let's see this in action now. You're going to create a light Rack application that responds with "Hello World" whenever it receives a request. This kind of application is often used to check and see if a server is still up and responding to HTTP calls. You'll create a new file inside your Ticketee's application's lib called lib/heartbeat.ru (you're checking the "heartbeat" of the server) and fill it with this content:

```
run lambda { |env| [200, {'Content-Type' => 'text/plain'}, ['OK']] }
```

The .ru extension for this file represents a Rack configuration file, also known as a Rackup file. In it, you call the `run` method, which needs an object that responds to

---

You already have a Rackup file

Your Rails application also has one of these .ru files, called config.ru, which is used by Rack-based servers to run your application. You can see this in action by running the `rackup config.ru` command, which will start up your application using the config.ru file's configuration.

If you look in this file, you'll see these lines:

```
# This file is used by Rack-based servers to start the application.
require ::File.expand_path('../config/environment', __FILE__)
run Ticketee::Application
```

The first line requires config/environment.rb for the application, which is responsible for setting up the environment of the application. Then it uses the `run` method—just as you are—except it's passing `Ticketee::Application`, which actually responds to `call`.

Cool stuff.

call. When Rack receives a request to this application it will call the `call` method on the object passed to `run`, which will then generate and return a response back to the server. The object in this case is a `lambda` (or `Proc`) object, which automatically responds to `call`.

When the `call` method is called on this `lambda`, it will respond with the three-element array inside it, completely ignoring the `env` object that is passed through. Inside this array, you have the three elements Rack needs: the HTTP status, the headers for the response, and the body to return.

To see your lib/heartbeat.ru in action, you can launch a Rack server by using the command you saw in the sidebar:

```
rackup lib/heartbeat.ru
```

This is now running a server on 9292 (the standard port for Rack) using the built-in-to-Ruby WEBrick HTTP server, as indicated by the server output you'll see:

```
[timestamp] INFO  WEBrick 1.3.1
...
[timestamp] INFO  WEBrick::HTTPServer#start: pid=... port=9292
```

You can now go to your browser and open http://localhost:9292 to make a request to this application. You'll get back "Hello World," and that's okay. You can also make a request to any path at the http://localhost:9292 application and it will respond in the same way, such as http://localhost:9292/status.

What you've done here is write one of the simplest Rack applications possible. This application receives a response to any path using any method, and always responds with `OK`. This application will respond very quickly because it hasn't loaded anything, but at the cost of being a one-trick pony.

You can make this little application respond differently in a number of ways. The easiest (and most fun!) would be to program it to change its response depending on the path it's given, like a Rails application does. For this, you'll use the `env` object. First up, let's see what this `env` object gives you by changing your script to do this:

```
require 'yaml'
run lambda { |env| [200,
  {'Content-Type' => 'text/plain'},
  ["#{env.to_yaml}"]]
}
```

The `to_yaml` method provided by the `yaml` standard library file will transform your env object (spoilers: it's a `Hash`) into a human-readable YAML output (like that found in config/database.yml in a Rails application).

To make this new change apply, you can't refresh the page like you would in a Rails application; you have to stop the server and start it again. You can press Ctrl+C to stop it, and rerun that command. This time when you go to your server, you'll see output that looks like this:

```
---
GATEWAY_INTERFACE: CGI/1.1
```

```
PATH_INFO: /
QUERY_STRING: ""
REMOTE_ADDR: 127.0.0.1
REQUEST_METHOD: GET
REQUEST_URI: http://localhost:9292/
...
```

This output is the YAML-ized version of the env hash, which comes from Rack itself. Rack parses the incoming request and provides this env hash so that you can determine how you'd like to respond to the request. You can alter the behavior of the request using any one of the keys in this hash,[1] but in this case you'll keep it simple and use the PATH_INFO key.

A lambda is great for one-liners, but now your Rack application is going to become more complex, and so you've probably outgrown the usefulness of a lambda. You don't have to use a lambda though, you only need to pass run an object that has a call method that responds with that three-element array. Your new code will be a couple of lines long, and so it's probably best to define it as a method (called call) on an object, and what better object to define it on than a class?

A class object would allow you to define other methods, and can be used to abstract chunks of the call method as well. For good measure, let's call this class Application and put it inside a module called Heartbeat, as shown in the following listing:

Listing 18.1 lib/heartbeat.ru

```
module Heartbeat
  class Application
    def self.call(env)
      [200, {'Content-Type' => 'text/plain'}, ["Hello World"]
    end
  end
end

run Heartbeat::Application
```

Here you've defined the Heartbeat::Application to have a call method, which once again returns OK for any request. On the final line, call run and pass in Heartbeat ::Application, which will work like your first example because Heartbeat ::Application has a call method defined on it. If this looks familiar, it's because there's a similar looking line in your application's config.ru file that you saw earlier:

```
run Ticketee::Application
```

Your Rails application is actually a Rack-based application! Of course, there's a little bit more that goes on behind the scenes in your Rails application than in your Rack application at the moment, but the two are used identically. They both respond in nearly identical ways with the three-element response array. Your Rack application is nearly the simplest form you can have.

---

[1] Yes, even the HTTP_USER_AGENT key to send users of a certain browser elsewhere.

Let's change your Heartbeat application now to respond differently to different request paths by referencing the PATH_INFO key within env. You'll replace the code inside your call method with this:

```
def self.call(env)
  default_headers = { "Content-Type" => "text/plain"}

  if env["PATH_INFO"] =~ /200/                    ◁──❶ Return requested path
    body = "Success!"
    status = 200
  else
    body = "Failure!"
    status = 500
  end

  [status, default_headers, ["#{env["PATH_INFO"]} == #{body}"]]
end
```

The env["PATH_INFO"] ❶ here returns the path that has been requested. If you made a request like http://localhost:9292/books to your Rack application, this variable would return /books. You compare this string to a regular expression using the =~ operator, and if it contains 200, you'll return "Success" in the body along with an HTTP status of 200. For everything else, it's "Failure" with an HTTP status of 500.

Let's restart the server once again and then make a new request to http://localhost:9292. You'll see this output:

```
/ == Failure!
```

This is because for any request to this server that doesn't have 200 in it, you're returning this message. If you make a request to http://localhost:9292/200 or even http://localhost:9292/this/is/a/200/page, you'll see the success message instead:

```
/this/is/a/200/page == Success!
```

Also, if you look in the console you can see a single line for each request that's been served:

```
127.0.0.1 - - [[timestamp]] "GET / HTTP/1.1" 500 - 0.0004
127.0.0.1 - - [[timestamp]] "GET /200 HTTP/1.1" 200 - 0.0004
127.0.0.1 - - [[timestamp]] "GET /this/is/a/200/page HTTP/1.1" 200 - 0.0004
```

This output shows the IP where the request came from, the local time the request happened, the request itself, the HTTP status contained within the response, and finally how long the page took to run. For the first request, it returned a 500 HTTP status, and for the other two requests that contained 200 in their paths, it returned a 200 HTTP status.

What you've done here is implement a basic router for your Rack application. If the route for a request contains 200, then you give back a successful response. Otherwise, you give back a 500 status, indicating an error. Rails implements a much more complex routing system than this, extracting the complexity away and leaving you with methods such as root and resources that you use in config/routes.rb. The underlying theory is the same though.

You've learned the basics of how a Rack application works and gained an understanding that your Rails application is a bigger version of this little application you've written. There's much more to Rack than providing this abstraction for the underlying request/response cycle. For example, you can build more complex apps with logic for one part of the application in one class and additional logic in another.

One other feature of Rack is the ability to build applications by combining smaller applications into a larger one. You saw this with Rails when you used the `mount` method in your application's config/routes.rb to mount the engine you developed in chapter 17. Let's see how you can do this with Rack.

18.2   *Building bigger Rack applications*

Your basic Rack application quickly outgrew the `lambda` shell you placed it in, and so you moved the logic in it into a class and added some more. With the class, you're able to define a `call` method on it, which then returns the response that Rack needs. The class allows you to cleanly write a more complex Rack application than a `lambda` would.

So what happens now if you outgrow a class? Well, you can abstract the function of your application into multiple classes and build a Rack application using those classes. The structure is not unlike the controller structure you have in a Rails application, because it will have separate classes that are responsible for different things.

In your new Rack application, you'll have two classes that perform separate tasks, but are still running on the same instance of the server. The first class is going to be your `Heartbeat::Application` class, and the second one will provide two forms, each with one button: one for success and one for failure. These forms will then submit to the actions provided within the `Heartbeat::Application` class, which will demonstrate how you can get your classes to talk to each other.

18.2.1   *You're breaking up*

Now that your Rack application is getting more complex, you're going to break it out into three files. The first file will be the `Heartbeat::Application` class, the second will be a new class called `Heartbeat::TestApplication`, and the third will be the Rackup file that will be responsible for combining these two classes into one glorious application.

Let's begin by separating out your application and the Rackup file into two separate files. In a new directory at lib/heartbeat.rb, add the code shown in the following listing to lib/heartbeat/application.rb.

Listing 18.2   lib/heartbeat/application.rb

```
module Heartbeat
  class Application
    def self.call(env)
      default_headers = { "Content-Type" => "text/plain"}

      if env["PATH_INFO"] =~ /200/
        body = "Success!"
```

```
            status = 200
        else
          body = "Failure!"
          status = 500
        end

        [status, default_headers, ["#{env["PATH_INFO"]} == #{body}"]]
      end
    end
end
```

Next, in lib/heartbeat/config.ru, add the code shown in the following listing.

Listing 18.3 lib/heartbeat/config.ru

```
heartbeat_root = File.expand_path(File.dirname(__FILE__))
require heartbeat_root + '/application'

run Heartbeat::Application
```

This new lib/heartbeat/config.ru sets up a `heartbeat_root` variable so that you can `require` files relative to the root of the heartbeat directory without having to specify direct paths to them. At the moment, this file still contains the run line from the old heartbeat.ru, but you'll be changing this shortly.

Before that change though, you're going to add your second application class, `Heartbeat::TestApplication`, to a new file at lib/heartbeat/test_application.rb by using the content shown in the following listing.

Listing 18.4 lib/heartbeat/test_application.rb

```
module Heartbeat
  class TestApplication
    def self.call(env)
      default_headers = { "Content-Type" => "text/html"}
      body = %Q{
        <h1>Success or FAILURE?!</h1>
        <form action='/test/200'>
          <input type='submit' value='Success!'>
        </form>

        <form action='/test/500'>
          <input type='submit' value='Failure!'>
        </form>
      }

      [200, default_headers, [body]]
    end
  end
end
```

This file follows the same style as the file that defines `Heartbeat::Application`, but in this class the body returned as part of the Rack response consists of two forms, each with its own button. The first form goes to /test/200, which should give you the response of "Success!", and /test/500, which should give you a "Failure!" response because the path doesn't include the number 200.

A keen eye may have noticed that you've nested the paths to the heartbeat responses underneath a path called test. This is because when you build your combined class application, you'll make your `Heartbeat::Application` sit under the /test route. When do you do this? Right now!

18.2.2 Running a combined Rack application

You're now going to change the lib/heartbeat/config.ru file to now create a Rack application that uses both of your classes for different functionality. For this, you're going to use the `Rack::Builder` class, which lets you build Rack applications from different parts. Let's fill lib/heartbeat/config.ru with the content shown in the following listing.

Listing 18.5   lib/heartbeat/config.ru

```
heartbeat_root = File.expand_path(File.dirname(__FILE__))
require heartbeat_root + '/application'
require heartbeat_root + '/test_application'

app = Rack::Builder.app do
  map '/test' do
    run Heartbeat::Application
  end

  map '/' do
    run Heartbeat::TestApplication
  end
end

run app
```

Rather than calling `run Heartbeat::Application` here, you're compiling a multi-faceted Rack application using `Rack::Builder.app`. The run method you've been using all this time is defined inside the `Rack::Builder` class, actually. A *.ru file is usually evaluated within the instance of a `Rack::Builder` object by the code the rackup command uses, and so you are able to use the run method without having to call `Rack::Builder.new` before it or wrapping .ru code in a `Rack::Builder.app` block.

This time, you're being implicit and building a new `Rack::Builder` instance using `Rack::Builder.app`. Inside this instance, you'll declare two routes using the map method. Within a block given to each of your map calls, you're calling the run method again, passing it one of your two application classes.

When a request comes into this application beginning with the path /test, it will be served by the `Heartbeat::Application` class. All other requests will be served by the `Heartbeat::TestApplication` class. This is not unlike the way certain requests in your Rails application beginning with /tickets are routed to the `TicketsController` and others beginning with /projects go to `ProjectsController`.[2]

Let's start this application and see what it can do by running this command:

```
rackup lib/heartbeat/config.ru
```

---

[2] In fact, the similarities are astounding.

Now remember, to make requests to the Heartbeat::Application class you must prefix them with /test; otherwise they'll be served by Heartbeat::TestApplication. Keeping that in mind, let's make a request to http://localhost:9292/test/200. You'll see something unusual: the path displayed on the page isn't /test/200 as you may expect,

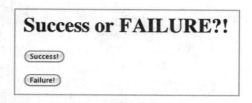

Figure 18.2   Success or FAILURE?!

but rather it's /200. The env["PATH_INFO"] key doesn't need to contain the path where your application is mounted, as that's not important for routing requests within the application itself.

If you make a request to another path not beginning with the /test prefix (such as http://localhost:9292/foo/bar), you'll see the two buttons in forms provided by the Heartbeat::TestApplication, as shown in figure 18.2.

When you click the Success! button, you'll send a request to the/test/200 path, which will be served by the Heartbeat::Application class and will respond with a body that says /200 == Success!. When you click the back button in your browser and click the Failure! button, you'll see the /500 == Failure!.

This is the basic foundation for Rack applications and a lightweight demonstration of how routing in Rack applications works. When you began, you were able to write run Heartbeat::Application to run a single class as your Rack application, but as it's grown more complex you've split different pieces of the functionality out into different classes. To combine these classes into one super-application you used the Rack::Builder.app method.

Now you should have a basic understanding of how you can build Rack applications to have a lightweight way of creating dynamic responses. So how does all of this apply to Rails? Well, in Rails you're able to mount a Rack application so that it can serve requests on a path (like you did with Rack::Builder), rather than having the request go through the entire Rails stack.

18.3   *Mounting a Rack application with Rails*

Sometimes, you'll want to serve requests in a lightning-fast fashion. Rails is great for serving super-dynamic requests quickly, but occasionally you'll want to forego the heaviness of the Rails controller stack and have a piece of code that receives a request and quickly responds.

Previously, your Rack application had done just that. However, when you mount your Rack application inside of a Rails application, you're able to use the classes (that is, models) from within the Rails application. With these models, you can do any number of things. For example, you can build a re-implementation of your tickets API, which will allow you to see an alternate way to craft the API you created in chapter 13. So let's do this.

This new API will be version 3 of your API (things move fast in this app!). It will be accessible at /api/v3/json/projects/:project_id/tickets[3] and—as with your original API—will require a token parameter to be passed through to your application. If the token matches to a user and that user has access to the requested project, you can send back a list of tickets in a JSON format. If the token sent through doesn't match to a user, then you'll send back a helpful error message explaining that; if the project requested isn't accessible by the authenticated user, you'll deny all knowledge of its existence by sending back a 404 response.

18.3.1 *Mounting Heartbeat*

Before you get into any of that though, you should probably look at how mounting works within Rails by using one of your basic applications first! Mounting a Rack application involves defining a route in your Rails application that basically says, "I want to put this application at this path." Back when you were doing a pure Rack application, you did this in the lib/heartbeat/config.ru file like this:

```
map '/heartbeat' do
  run Heartbeat::Application
end
```

Rails has a better place than that for routes: config/routes.rb. This location provides you with some lovely helpers for mounting your Rack applications. In your Rails application, to do the same thing as you did in your Rack application, you'd need to first require the application by placing this line at the top of config/routes.rb:

```
require 'heartbeat/application'
```

Then inside the routes block of config/routes.rb you'd put this line:

```
mount Heartbeat::Application, :at => "/heartbeat"
```

The mount method accepts an object to mount and an options hash containing an at option to declare where this should be mounted. Alternatively, you could use the match method in routes:

```
match '/heartbeat' => Heartbeat::Application
```

Both lines are identical in function. So let's make these changes to your config/routes.rb file and boot up your Rails server with this command:

```
rails s
```

You should now be able to go to http://localhost:3000/heartbeat/200 and see the friendly /200 == Success! message. This means that your Heartbeat::Application is responding as you'd like it to.

Rails has been told to forward requests that go to /heartbeat to this Rack application and it has done so diligently. Rather than initializing a new instance of a controller

---

[3] This URL closely resembles the URL that GitHub uses for v2 of its API, but the similarities are purely coincidental.

(which is what normally happens in a standard Rails request), a Rack class is much lighter and is perfect for serving high-intensity requests that don't require views, like the response from your `Heartbeat::Application` and the responses from your API.

So now that you've learned how you can mount your `Heartbeat::Application`, let's build this slightly more complex Rack application that will serve JSON API requests for tickets. To make sure everything works, you'll be writing tests using the same `Rack::Test::Methods` helpers that you used back in chapter 13. These helpers are designed for Rack applications, but they worked with your Rails application because... well, it's a Rack app too.

Rather than writing this application as a standard Rack app, let's branch out and use another Ruby web framework called Sinatra.

18.3.2 Introducing Sinatra

Sinatra is an exceptionally lightweight Ruby web framework that's perfect for building small applications, such as those that serve an API. Like Rails, it's built on top of Rack and so you'll have no worries about using them together. You'll use it here to create version 3 of your API. Building you app this way not only demonstrates the power of Sinatra, but also shows that there's more than one way to skin this particular cat.[4]

To install the `sinatra` gem, run this command:

```
gem install sinatra
```

You can make a small Sinatra script now by creating a file called sin.rb, as shown in the following listing.

Listing 18.6   sin.rb

```
require 'sinatra'

get '/' do
  "Hello World"
end
```

This is the smallest Sinatra application that you can write. On the first line you require the Sinatra file, which gives you some methods you can use to define your application, such as the `get` method you use on the next line. This `get` method is used to define a root route for your application, which returns the string "Hello World" for GET requests to /. You could also make it into a class, which is what you'll need to do for it to be mountable in your application:

```
require 'sinatra'

class Tickets < Sinatra::Base
  get '/' do
    "Hello World"
  end
end
```

---

[4] Although why anybody would skin a cat these days is unknown to the authors.

By making it a class, you'll be able to mount it in your application using the `mount` method in config/routes.rb. By mounting this Sinatra application, it will have access to all the classes from your Rails application, such as your models, which is precisely what you're going to need for this new version of your API. You won't use this code example right now; it's handy to know that you can do this.

To use Sinatra with your application, you'll need to add it to the Gemfile with this line:

```
gem 'sinatra'
```

Then you'll need to run `bundle install` to install it. So let's go ahead now and start building this API using Sinatra.[5]

18.3.3 *The API, by Sinatra*

Let's create a new file to test your experimental new API at spec/api/v3/json/tickets_spec.rb. In this file you want to set up a project that has at least one ticket, as well as a user that you can use to make requests to your API. After that, you want to make a request to /api/v3/json/tickets and check that you get back a proper response of tickets. With this in mind, let's write a spec that looks like the code shown in the following listing.

> **Listing 18.7   spec/api/v3/json/tickets_spec.rb**

```ruby
require 'spec_helper'

describe Api::V3::JSON::Tickets, :type => :api do
  let(:project) { Factory(:project) }
  let(:user) { Factory(:user) }
  let(:token) { user.authentication_token }

  before do
    Factory(:ticket, :project => project)
    user.permissions.create!(:thing => project, :action => "view")
  end

  let(:url) { "/api/v3/json/projects/#{project.id}/tickets" }

  context "successful requests" do

    it "can get a list of tickets" do
      get url, :token => token
      last_response.body.should eql(project.tickets.to_json)
    end
  end
end
```

This test looks remarkably like the one in spec/api/v2/tickets_spec.rb, except this time you're only testing for JSON responses and you've changed the URL that you're requesting to api/:version/:format/:path. When you run this spec with `bin/rspec spec/api/v3/json/tickets_spec.rb` you'll see that it's giving you this error:

```
... uninitialized constant Api::V3
```

---

[5] You can learn more about Sinatra at https://github.com/sinatra/sinatra/.

This is because you haven't yet defined the module for the `Api::V3` namespace. Let's create a new file at app/controllers/api/v3/json/tickets.rb that defines this module, as shown in the following listing.

Listing 18.8   app/controllers/api/v3/json/tickets.rb

```
require 'sinatra'

module Api
  module V3
    module JSON
      class Tickets < Sinatra::Base
        before do
          headers "Content-Type" => "text/json"          ◁─── 1  Before method
        end
        get '/' do
          []
        end
      end
    end
  end
end
```

Within this file you define the `Api::V3::JSON::Tickets` class that is `described` at the top of your spec, which will now make your spec run. This class inherits from `Sinatra::Base` so that you'll get the helpful methods that Sinatra provides, such as the `before` ❶ and `get` methods that you use here. You've already seen what `get` can do, but `before` is new. This method is similar to a `before_filter` in Rails and will execute the block before each request. In this block, you set the headers for the request, using Sinatra's `headers` method, so that your API identifies as sending back a `text/json` response.

Let's rerun it using `bin/rspec spec/api/v3/json/tickets_spec.rb`:

```
Failure/Error: get url, :token => token
    ActionController::RoutingError:
      No route matches [GET] "/api/v3/json/projects/1/tickets"
```

This is a better start: now your test is running and failing as it should because you haven't defined the route for it yet. Your test is expecting to be able to do a GET request to /api/v3/json/projects/1/tickets but cannot.

This route can be interpreted as /api/v3/json/projects/:project_id/tickets, and you can use the `api` namespace already in config/routes.rb to act as a home for this route. Let's put some code for v3 of your API inside this namespace now:

```
namespace :v3 do
  namespace :json do
    mount Api::V3::JSON::Tickets,
      :at => "/projects/:project_id/tickets"
  end
end
```

By placing this `mount` call inside the namespaces, the Rack application will be mounted at /api/v3/json/projects/:project_id/tickets rather than the /tickets URI if you didn't have it nested. Additionally, you've specified a dynamic parameter in the form of `:project_id`. With this, you'll be able to access the requested project id from inside your Rack application using a method very similar to how you'd usually access parameters in a controller.

If you attempted to run your spec again it would bomb out with another new error:

```
expected "[tickets array]"
got ""
```

This means that requests are able to get to your Rack app and that the response you've declared is being served successfully. Now you need to fill this response with meaningful data. To do this, find the project that's being referenced in the URL by using the parameters passed through found with the `params` method. Unfortunately, Sinatra doesn't load the parameters from your Rails application and so `params[:project_id]` is not going to be set. You can see this if you change your root route in your Sinatra application to this:

```
get '/' do
  p params
end
```

Then if you run your test, you'll see only the `token` parameter is available:

```
{"token"=>"6E06zoj01Pf5texLXVNb"}
```

Luckily, you can still get to this through one of the keys in the environment hash, which is accessible through the `env` method in your Sinatra actions, like it was available when you built your Rack applications. You saw this environment hash earlier when you were developing your first Rack application, but this time it's going to have a little more to it because it's gone through the Rails request stack. Let's change your root route to this:

```
get '/' do
  p env.keys

end
```

When you rerun your test, you'll see all the available keys output at the top, with one of the keys being `action_dispatch.request.path_parameters`. This key stores the parameters discovered by Rails routing, and your `project_id` parameter should fall neatly into this category. Let's find out by changing the `p env.keys` line in your root route to `p env["action_dispatch.request.path_parameters"]` and then re-running your test. You should see this:

```
{:project_id=>"3"}
```

Okay, so you can access two parameter hashes, but you'll need to merge them together if you are to do anything useful with them. You can merge them into a super params method by redefining the params method as a private method in your app. Underneath the get you'll put this:

```
def params
  hash = env["action_dispatch.request.path_parameters"].merge!(super)
  HashWithIndifferentAccess.new(hash)
end
```

By calling the super method here, you'll reference the params method in the superclass, Sinatra::Base. You want to access the keys in this hash using either symbols or strings like you can do in your Rails application, so you create a new HashWith-IndifferentAccess object, which is returned by this method. This lets you access your token with either params[:token] or params["token"]. This hash is quite indifferent to its access methods.

Let's switch your root route back to calling p params. When you run your test again, you should see that you finally have both parameters inside the one hash:

```
{:project_id=>"3", "token"=>"ZVSREe1aQjNZ2SrB9e8I"}
```

With these parameters you'll now be able to find the user based on their token, get a list of projects they have access to, and then attempt to find the project with the id specified. You can do this by putting two calls, a find_user and find_project method, in the before block you already have, using this code:

```
before do
  headers "Content-Type" => "text/json"
  find_user
  find_project
end
```

The find_user and find_project methods can be defined underneath the private keyword using this code:

```
private

  def find_user
    @user = User.find_by_authentication_token(params[:token])
  end

  def find_project
    @project = Project.for(@user).find(params[:project_id])
  end
```

This code should look fairly familiar: it's basically identical to the code found in the Api::V1::TicketsController and Api::V1::BaseController classes inside your Rack application. First you find the user based on their token and then generate a scope for all projects that the user is able to view with the Project.for method. With this scope, you can then find the project matching the id passed in through params[:project_id]. You are referencing the models from your Rails application inside your Sinatra application, and there's nothing special you have to configure to allow this.

Because you're not too concerned with what happens if an invalid `params[:project_id]` or user token is passed through at the moment, you'll fix those up after you've got this first test passing. With the project now found, you should be able to display a list of tickets in JSON form in your `call` method. Let's change your root route to return a list of JSON-ified tickets for this project:

```
get '/' do
  @project.tickets.to_json
end
```

Now your root route should respond with the list of tickets required to have your test pass. Let's see if this is the case by running `bin/rspec spec/api/v3/json/tickets_spec.rb`:

```
1 example, 0 failures
```

Great, this spec is now passing, which means that your Rack application is now serving a base for version 3 of your API. By making this a Rack application, you can serve requests in a more lightweight fashion than you could within Rails.

But you don't have basic error checking in place yet if a user isn't found matching a token or if a person can't find a project. So before you move on, let's quickly add tests for these two issues.

18.3.4 *Basic error checking*

You'll open spec/api/v3/json/tickets_spec.rb and add two tests inside the `describe` block in a new `context` block, as shown in the following listing.

Listing 18.9   spec/api/v3/json/tickets_spec.rb

```
context "unsuccessful requests" do
  it "doesn't pass through a token" do
    get url
    last_response.status.should eql(401)
    last_response.body.should eql("Token is invalid.")
  end

  it "cannot access a project that they don't have permission to" do
    user.permissions.delete_all
    get url, :token => token
    last_response.status.should eql(404)
  end
end
```

In the first test you make a request without passing through a token, which should result in a 401 (unauthorized) status and a message telling you the "Token is invalid." In the second test, you use the `delete_all` association method to remove all permissions for the user and then attempt to request tickets in a project that the user no longer has access to. This should result in the response being a 404 response, which means your API will deny all knowledge of that project and its tickets.

To make your first test pass you'll need to check that your find_user method actually returns a valid user; otherwise you'll return this 404 response. The best place to do this would be inside the find_user method itself, turning it into this:

```
def find_user
  @user = User.find_by_authentication_token(params[:token])
  halt 401, "Token is invalid." unless @user
end
```

The halt method here will stop a request dead in its tracks. In this case, it will return a 401 status code with the body being the string specified. When you run your tests again the first two should be passing, with the third one still failing:

```
3 examples, 1 failure
```

Alright, so now if an invalid token is passed, you're throwing exactly the same error as the last two iterations of your API did—good progress! Finally, you'll need to send a 404 response when a project cannot be found within the scope for the current user. To do this, change the find_project method in your app to this:

```
def find_project
  @project = Project.for(@user).find(params[:project_id])
  rescue ActiveRecord::RecordNotFound
    halt 404, "The project you were looking for could not be found."
end
```

When you run your tests for a final time with bundle exec rspec spec/api/v3/tickets_spec.rb, they should all pass:

```
3 examples, 0 failures
```

Awesome! This should give you a clear idea of how you could implement an API similar to the one you created back in chapter 13 by using the lightweight framework of Sinatra. All of this is possible because Rails provides an easy way to mount Rack-based applications inside your Rails applications. You could go further with this API, but this is probably another exercise for you later on if you wish to undertake it.

You've learned how you can use Rack applications to serve as endpoints of requests, but you can also create pieces that hook into the middle of the request cycle called *middleware*. Rails has a few of these already, and you saw the effects of one of them when you were able to access the env["action_dispatch.request.path _parameters"] key inside your Sinatra application. Without the middleware of the Rails stack, this parameter would be unavailable. In the next section, we look at the middleware examples in the real world, including some found in the Rails stack, as well as how you can build and use your own.

18.4 *Middleware*

When a request comes into a Rack application, it doesn't go straight to a single place that serves the request. Instead, it goes through a series of pieces known as *middleware*, which may process the request before it gets to the end of the stack (your application) or modify it and pass it onward, as shown in figure 18.3.

You can run the `rake middleware` command within your Rails application's directory to see the list of middleware currently in use by your Rails application:

```
use ActionDispatch::Static
use Rack::Lock
use ActiveSupport::Cache::Strategy::LocalCache
use Rack::Runtime
...
use ActionDispatch::BestStandardsSupport
use Warden::Manager
run Ticketee::Application.routes
```

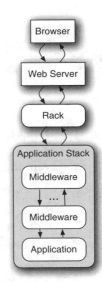

Figure 18.3   Full request stack, redux

Each of these middleware pieces performs its own individual function. For instance, the first middleware `ActionDispatch::Static` intercepts requests for static files such as images, JavaScript files, or stylesheets found in public and serves them immediately, without the request to them falling through to the rest of the stack. It's important to note that this middleware is only active in the development environment, as in production your web server (such as nginx) is better suited for serving static assets.

Other middleware, such as `ActionDispatch::BestStandards-Support`, sets additional headers on your request. This particular piece of middleware sets the `X-UA-Compatible` header to `IE=Edge,chrome=1`, which tells Microsoft Internet Explorer to "display content in the highest mode available" that is "equivalent to IE9 mode," meaning your pages should render in a "best standards" fashion.[6] The `chrome=1` part of this header is for the Google Chrome Frame, which again will support "best standards" rendering on a page.

Let's look at both of these middleware pieces now.

18.4.1 Middleware in Rails

In the case of the `ActionDispatch::Static` middleware, a response is returned when it finds a file to serve, and the request stops there. In the case of `Action-Dispatch::BestStandardsSupport`, the request is modified and allowed to continued down the chain of middleware until it hits `Ticketee::Application.routes`, which will serve the request using the routes and code in your application. The process of `ActionDispatch::Static` can be seen in figure 18.4.

When a request is made to /images/rails.png, the middleware checks to see if the public/images/rails.png file exists. If it does, then it is returned as the response of this request. This middleware will also check for cached pages. If you make a request to /projects, Rails (by default) will first check to see if a public/projects.html file exists before sending the request to the rest of the stack. This type of request is shown in figure 18.5.

---

[6] For more information about `IE=Edge` and the `X-UA-Compatible` header, see http://msdn.microsoft.com/en-us/library/cc288325(v=vs.85).aspx.

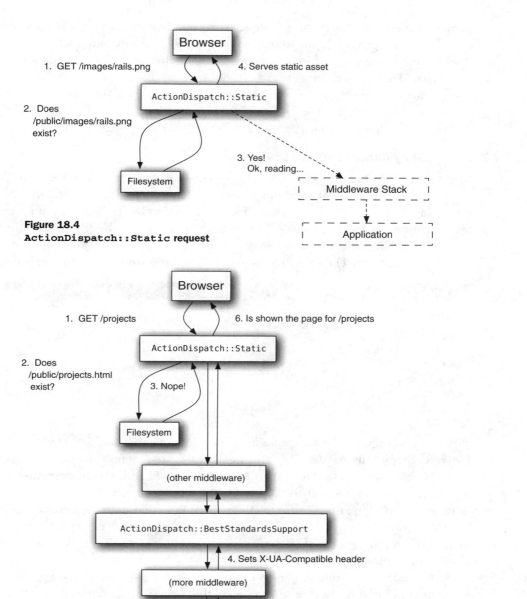

Figure 18.4
`ActionDispatch::Static request`

Figure 18.5
`ActionDispatch::BestStandardsSupport`
request

In this request, the `ActionDispatch::Static` middleware first checks for the presence of public/projects.html, which would be there if you had cached the page. Because it's not there, the request goes through the rest of the middleware stack being passed along. When it gets to `ActionDispatch::Best::StandardsSupport`, this middleware sets the `X-UA-Compatible` header and passes along the request to the application, which then serves the request like normal.

Let's dive into exactly how `ActionDispatch::Static` works.

18.4.2 *Investigating ActionDispatch::Static*

The `ActionDispatch::Static` class is responsible for serving static requests in the development environment for your application. The code for this piece of middleware can be found in the `actionpack` gem, which you can view by opening the path provided by the command `bundle show actionpack` in your editor. The file that defines the `ActionDispatch::Static` middleware can be found at lib/action_dispatch/middleware/static.rb. The first 10 lines in this file are shown inthe following listing.

Listing 18.10   Listing 18.10 lib/action_dispatch/middleware/static.rb

```
require 'rack/utils'

module ActionDispatch
  class Static
    FILE_METHODS = %w(GET HEAD).freeze

    def initialize(app, root)
      @app = app
      @file_server = ::Rack::File.new(root)
    end
```

The first line requires the rack/utilsfile, which contains the `Rack::Utils` module this file references a little later on. The next three lines define the `ActionDispatch::Static` class and a constant called `FILE_METHODS`. Finally, this middleware defines the `initialize` method, which takes two arguments, an `app` and a `root`. This method then assigns the `app` argument to the `@app` variable so that it can be accessed in methods called after this point. The `root` variable is passed to a call to `::Rack::File.new`[7] which is then assigned to the `@file_server` variable. The `Rack::File` class is actually a Rack application too, as you'll see later.

So why does this middleware begin in this particular way, and what is `app`? Well, `app` is the next piece of middleware in the stack that you can pass requests to if you wish. You'll see this `app` variable used later. The instance of your middleware is then cached by the Rails server so it can call the `call` method on it when a request comes into the stack. The `call` method in this middleware begins with this:

---

[7] Not-well-known Ruby fact: the double colon (`::`) of `::Rack::File` represents a top-level class, meaning that Ruby will get the `Rack::File` class defined at the top level of your application, rather than one (potentially) within the current class or module.

```
def call(env)
  path   = env['PATH_INFO'].chomp('/')
  method = env['REQUEST_METHOD']

  if FILE_METHODS.include?(method)
```

The env variable here is the same sort of style as the env variable that you used back in your Rack application. Rack middleware and Rack applications are actually designed almost identically. You saw the env["PATH_INFO"] key before—that's the one that contains the path of the request, something such as /images/rails.png. By calling chomp on this, it strips off any trailing forward-slashes on the end of this URL.

The env["REQUEST_METHOD"] key contains the HTTP request method used in this request. If this method is either GET or HEAD, then the code inside the if runs here. The next line after this one checks for the presence of a file:

```
if file_exist?(path)
```

This method is defined further down in this file, like this:

```
def file_exist?(path)
  full_path = File.join(@file_server.root, ::Rack::Utils.unescape(path))
  File.file?(full_path) && File.readable?(full_path)
end
```

This method uses the root method, which returns the fill path to the public directory of your application. This method then uses File.join to join the path to the public directory and the unescaped name of the file that's being requested. Finally, this method uses the File.file? and File.readable? methods to determine if the path specified is actually a file and if that file is readable. If it is indeed a file and is indeed readable, then this line is executed:

```
return @file_server.call(env)
```

This calls the call method on the Rack::File instance, which then (after some additional processing) serves the file.

So far, this has been the process this piece of middleware uses for an existing file. If the file doesn't exist, then it goes into the else for the if File.exists? line, which results in the following code being run:

```
cached_path = directory_exist?(path) ? "#{path}/index" : path
cached_path += ::ActionController::Base.page_cache_extension

if file_exist?(cached_path)
  env['PATH_INFO'] = cached_path
  return @file_server.call(env)
end
```

The first line here checks for a directory with the same name as the path you've requested. Imagine your request is now /projects and you have a public/projects directory. This directory_exists? method would then return true because this directory exists. The directory_exists? method is defined like this:

```
def directory_exist?(path)
  full_path = File.join(@file_server.root, ::Rack::Utils.unescape(path))
  File.directory?(full_path) && File.readable?(full_path)
end
```

It performs basically the same function as the `file_exist?` method, except that it uses `File.directory?` to check for the directory rather than `File.file?`. If this directory does exist, then the `cached_path` variable is set to /projects/index in your case. The second line in this `else` references the `::ActionController::Base.page_cache _extension`, which is a string that defaults to .html and makes your `cached_path` variable now projects/index.html, the alternate path where the page for /projects may be cached.

If this file exists, then the middleware sets `env["PATH_INFO"]` to be this path so that the `Rack::File` instance knows what's being requested, and then it makes a call to the `@fileserver.call` method and returns the response it gives back.

If everything fails and there's no file at the path you've requested, the middleware gives up and passes the request to the next piece of middleware by using this line:

```
@app.call(env)
```

The request then continues on down the chain of middleware until it hits a middleware that serves that request or the `Ticketee::Application.routes` endpoint. Either way, the browser (or whatever makes the request) is basically guaranteed to get a response from a piece of middleware or the application itself. For the first situation, a middleware can return a response itself:

```
return [200, { "Content-Type" => "text/html" }, ["Oh happy day!"]]
```

Or it can pass the buck to the next piece with the `call` method, passing through the (possibly modified) `env` variable representing this request's environment:

```
@app.call(env)
```

Now that you've got a nice grasp of how one piece of middleware works, let's build your own!

18.4.3 *Crafting middleware*

Soon you'll have your own piece of middleware that you can put into the middleware stack of a Rails or Rack application. This middleware will allow the request to run all the way down the chain to the application and then will modify the body, replacing specific letters in the text for links with other, equally specific letters. Create a new file for your middleware at lib/link_jumbler.rb and fill it with the content shown in the following listing.

> **Listing 18.11   lib/link_jumbler.rb**

```
require 'nokogiri'
class LinkJumbler

  def initialize(app, letters)
```

```
    @app = app
    @letters = letters
  end

  def call(env)
    status, headers, response = @app.call(env)
    body = Nokogiri::HTML(response.body)
    body.css("a").each do |a|
      @letters.each do |find, replace|
        a.content = a.content.gsub(find.to_s, replace.to_s)
      end
    end
    [status, headers, body.to_s]
  end
end
```

In this file you've defined the `LinkJumbler` class, which contains an `initialize` and a `call` method. The `initialize` method sets the stage, setting up the `@app` and `@letters` variables you'll use in your `call` method.

In the `call` method, you make a call down the middleware stack in order to set up your `status`, `headers`, and `body` values. You can do this because the `@app.call(env)` call will always return a three-element array. Each element of this array will be assigned to its respective variable. In a Rails application's middleware stack, the third element isn't an array but rather an instance of `ActionDispatch::Response`. To get to the good part of this response you can use the `body` method, like you do on the second line of your `call` method.

With this body you use the `Nokogiri::HTML` method (provided by the `require 'nokogiri'` line at the top of this file) to parse the body returned by the application into a `Nokogiri::HTML::Document` object. This will allow you to parse the page more easily than if you used regular expressions. With this object, you call the `css` method and pass it the `"a"` argument, which finds all a tags in the response body. You then iterate through each of these tags and go through all of your letters from `@letters`, using the keys of the hash as the `find` argument and the values as the `replace` argument. You then set the content of each of the a tags to be the substituted result.

Finally, you return a three-element array using your new body, resulting in links being jumbled. To see this middleware in action, you'll need to add it to the middleware stack in your application. To do that, put these two lines inside the `Ticketee ::Application` class definition in config/application.rb:

```
require 'link_jumbler'
config.middleware.use LinkJumbler, { "e" => "a" }
```

The `config.middleware.use` method will add your middleware to the end of the middleware stack, making it the last piece of middleware to be processed before a request hits your application.[8] Any additional arguments passed to the use method

---

[8] For more methods for `config.middleware` look at the "Configuring Middleware" section of the Configuring official guide: http://guides.rubyonrails.org/configuring.html#configuring-middleware.

will be passed as arguments to the initialize method for this middleware, and
so this hash you've passed here will be the
letters argument in your middleware.
This means your LinkJumbler middleware
will replace the letter *e* with *a* anytime it
finds it in an a tag.

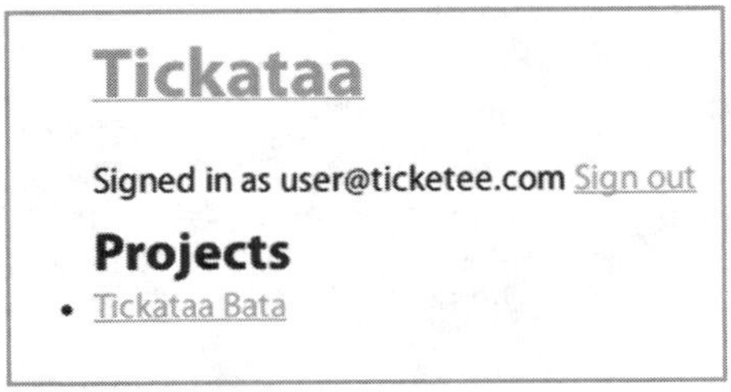

To see this middleware in action, let's
fire up a server by running rails s in a ter-

Figure 18.6   What's a Tickataa?!

minal. When you go to http://localhost:3000 you should notice something's changed,
as shown in figure 18.6.

As you can see in this figure, your links have had their *e*'s replaced with *a*'s and any
other occurrence, such as the user's email address, has been left untouched.

This is one example of how you can use middleware to affect the outcome of a
request within Rails; you could have modified anything or even sent a response back
from the middleware itself. The opportunities are endless. This time though, you've
made a piece of middleware that finds all the a tags and jumbles up the letters based
on what you tell it to.

18.5   Summary

You've now seen a lot of what Rack, one of the core components of the Rails stack, can
offer you. In the beginning of this chapter you built a small Rack application that
responded with OK. You then fleshed this application out to respond differently based
on the provided request. Then you built another Rack application that called this first
Rack application, running both of these within the same instance by using the
Rack::Builder class.

Next you saw how you could use these applications within the Rails stack by first
mounting your initial Rack application and then branching out into something a little
more complex, with a Sinatra-based application serving what could possibly be the
beginnings of version 3 of Ticketee's API. Sinatra is a lightweight framework offering
the same basic features as Rails.

Finally, you saw two pieces of middleware, the ActionDispatch::Static piece and
the ActionDispatch::BestStandardsSupport. You dissected the first of these, figur-
ing out how it worked so that you could use that knowledge to build your own middleware, a neat little piece that jumbles up the text on the link based on the options
passed to it.

A common question in the Ruby on Rails community from newcomers is, "Why Ruby?" or "Why Rails?" In this appendix, this question will be answered with a couple of key points about why people should be using Ruby on Rails over other frameworks, covering such things as the culture and community standards.

Ruby is an exceptionally powerful language that can be used for short scripts up to full-featured web applications, such as those built with Ruby on Rails. Its clean syntax and its focus on making programmers happy are two of the many major points that have generated a large community of people who use it. There are hobbyists who use it just for the sake of it right up to hardcore people who swear by it. However, Ruby (and by extension, Rails) should not be used as "golden hammers". Not all problems are solvable by Ruby or Rails, but the chance of running into one of these situations is extremely low. People who have used other languages before they have come to Ruby suggest that "Ruby just makes more sense."[1]

The speed at which that you can develop applications using Ruby on Rails is demonstrably faster than other languages. An application that has taken four months to build in Java could be done in three weeks in Rails, for example. This has been proven again and again. Rails even claims up front on http://rubyonrails.org that "Ruby on Rails is optimized for programmer happiness and *sustainable productivity.*"

The Ruby and Rails communities have a consistent focus on self-improvement. Over the last couple of years we've seen developments such as the improvements from Rails 2 to Rails 3, Passenger (covered in chapter 14), and Bundler. All of these have vastly improved the ease of development that comes naturally to Ruby. Other developments have focused on other areas, such as the RSpec, Capybara, and Cucumber[2] gems (featured prominently in this book), which focus on making testing exceptionally easier for Ruby developers. By consistently improving, things are becoming easier and easier for Ruby developers every year.

Along the same vein of self-improvement is an almost zealot-like focus on testing, which is code that tests other code. Although this may seem silly to begin with,

---

[1] Quote attributed to Sam Shaw from Railsconf 2011.
[2] A quick nod to the `aruba` gem: http://github.com/aslakhellesoy/aruba, which is used extensively to test RSpec's and Cucumber's command-line interfaces (CLI), but can also be used to test other CLIs.

it helps you make less silly mistakes and provides the groundwork for you to test the fixes for any bugs that come up in your system. Ruby, just like every other language, is no good at preventing buggy code. That's a human trait that is unavoidable.

The shift away from SVN to the wonderful world of distributed version control was also a major milestone, with GitHub (a Rails application!) being created in early 2008. Services such GitHub have made it easier than ever for Ruby developers to collaborate on code across cultures. As an example of this, you only need to look at the authors of commits on the Rails project to see the wide gamut of people.

Don't just take it from us. Here's a direct quote from somebody who had only been using Rails for a few days:

> *When I am programming with Ruby I think I'm making magic.*
> —New person

Although Ruby isn't quite the magic of fairy tales, you'll find young and old, experienced and not-so-experienced people all claiming that it's just a brilliant language to work with. As Yukihiro Matsumuto (the creator of the language) says: Ruby is designed to make programmers happy. Along the same lines, the Rails claim you saw earlier, "optimized for programmer happiness and sustainable productivity," is not smoke and mirrors either. You can be extremely happy and productive while using Rails, compared with other frameworks.

Let's dive a little deeper into the reasons why Rails (the framework) and Ruby (the language) are so great.

A.1   *Reason #1: the sense of community*

The Rails community is like no other on the planet. There is a large sense of togetherness in the community with people freely sharing ideas and code through services such as GitHub and RubyGems (see Reason #2). An example of this is the vibrant community on the Freenode IRC network (irc.freenode.net) where the main #rubyonrails channel is primarily used for asking questions about Rails. Anybody can come into the channel and ask a question and receive a response promptly from one of the other people who visit the channel. There's no central support authority: it's a group of volunteers who are voluntarily volunteering[3] their time to help strangers with problems, without asking for money or expecting anything else in return.

There's also a large support community focused around Stack Overflow (http://stackoverflow.com) and other locations such as the Ruby on Rails Talk mailing list (http://groups.google.com/group/rubyonrails-talk) and Rails Forum (http://railsforum.com). Not to mention, there's also the RailsBridge (http://railsbridge.org) organization, which aims to bridge the gap between newbies and experienced developers.

All of these different areas of the internet share a common goal: be nice to the people who are asking for help. One mantra in the Ruby community is, "Matz is nice

---

[3]   Too much "volunteer" usage, perhaps. It was voluntary.

always, so we are nice," often abbreviated to MINASWAN. People in the Ruby and Rails communities are incredibly nice to everyone.

Another example of the excellent community around Ruby on Rails is the number of conferences and gatherings held worldwide. The smallest of them are the intimate hack sessions where people work together on applications and share ideas in a room. Slightly bigger and more organized than that are the events such as Railscamps (http://railscamps.org) which have about 150 people attend and run from Friday–Monday, with interesting talks given on the Saturdays and Sundays. The largest however is Railsconf, which has about 2,000 people in attendance.

There are hundreds of thousands, if not millions of people using Ruby on Rails today, building great web applications with it and building the best web framework community on the planet.

A.2 Reason #2: the speed and ease of development

The speed of how quickly you are able to develop a Ruby on Rails application is definitely one of the main reasons that people gravitate toward (and stick with) the framework.

One documented case of this is that of a team that had developed an application using a Java-based framework, which took four months. When that application became difficult to maintain, alternative languages and frameworks were sought, with Ruby and Ruby on Rails found to fit the bill adequately. The team re-implemented *all* the features of the original Java-based application within three weeks, with less code and more beautiful code.

Ruby on Rails follows a paradigm known as *convention over configuration*. This paradigm is adopted not only by Rails, but also by other modern web frameworks. Rails is designed in such a way that it takes care of the normal configuration that you may have to do with other frameworks, leaving it up to you to get down to coding *real features* for your application.

One example of this convention over configuration is the mapping between classes designed to interact with the database and the tables related to these classes. If the class is called `Project` then it can be assumed by Rails (and the people coding the application) that the related table is going to be called `projects`. But this can be configured using a setting in the class if that table name is not desired.

A.3 Reason #3: RubyGems

This third point is more about a general boon to the community of Ruby, but it plays a key role in developing Rails applications.

As we stated before, the culture of the Rails community is one of self-improvement. There are people who are consistently thinking of new ways to make other people's lives better. One of these ways is the RubyGems system, which allows people to share libraries in a common format. By installing a gem, a user is able to use its code along with their own code. There are gems such as the `json` gem, which is used for parsing JSON data, `nokogiri` for parsing XML, and of course the Rails suite of gems.

Previously, gems were hosted on a system known as RubyForge which was unstable at times. In July 2009, Nick Quaranto, a prominent Rubyist, created the RubyGems site we know today: http://rubygems.org. This is now the primary nexus for hosting and downloading gems for the Ruby community, with RubyForge playing second fiddle. The site Nick created provides an easy way for people to host gems that other people can use, freely. Now isn't that just awesome?

Working with gems on a project used to be tough. To find out what gems a project used they had to be listed somewhere, and there were often times when the tools used to install these gems would not work, either installing the wrong gems or simply refusing to work at all. Then along came Bundler. The Bundler gem provides a standardized way across all Ruby projects for managing gem dependencies. It's a gem to manage the gems that projects use. You can list the gems you want your project to use in a special file known as the Gemfile. Bundler can interpret (when `bundle install` is run) the special syntax in this file to figure out what gems (and the dependencies, and their dependencies' dependencies) need installing and then goes about doing it. Bundler solves the gem dependency hell previously witnessed in the Ruby and Rails communities in a simple fashion.

In addition to this, having different Ruby versions running on the same machine used to be difficult and involve a lot of hacking around. Then another prominent Rubyist, Wayne E. Seguin, created a gem called Ruby Version Manager (RVM) that allows for simplistic management of the different

All in all, RubyGems and its ecosystem is very well thought-out and sustainable. It provides an accessible way for people to share their code in a free manner and serves as one of the foundations of the Ruby language. All of this work has been done by the exceedingly great community which is made up of many different kinds of people, perhaps one day even including people who are reading this appendix.

A.4   *Reason #4: emphasis on testing*

Within the Ruby and Rails community there's a huge focus on writing great, maintainable code. To help with this process, there's also a big focus on test-driven development along with a mantra of "red/green/refactor." This mantra describes the process of test-driven development: you write tests that are then failing (usually indicated by the color red), write the code to make those tests pass (indicated by green), and then clean up (refactor) the code in order to make it easier for people to know what it's doing. We covered this process in chapter 2.

Because Ruby is interpreted rather than compiled like other languages, you cannot rely on compilers to pick up errors in your code. Instead, you write tests that describe functionality before it's implemented. Those tests will fail initially, but as you write that functionality those tests will pass. In some situations (such as tests written using the Cucumber gem), these tests can be read by people who requested a feature of your application and can be used as a set of instructions explaining exactly how this feature works. This is a great way to verify that the feature is precisely what was requested.

As you write these tests for the application, you provide a safety net for if things go wrong. This collection of tests is referred to as a *test suite*. When you develop a new feature, you have the tests that you wrote *before* the feature to prove that it's working as you originally thought it should. If you want to make sure that the code is working at some point in the future, then you have the test suite to fall back on.

If something does go wrong and it's not tested, you've got that base to build upon. You can write a test for an unrealized situation—a process known as *regression testing*—and always have that test in the future to ensure that the problem does not crop up again.

appendix B
Tidbits

This appendix contains a collection of tidbits that we just couldn't fit into the rest of the book. They are designed to be read by themselves, although you are welcome (and encouraged!) to read as many of them at once as you wish.

B.1 Prettying URLs

In your application you've got a URL such as /projects/1/tickets/2, which really isn't that pretty. Let's take a look at how you can make the ticket's ID part of these URLs a little prettier, turning them into something like /projects/1/tickets/2-make-it-shiny.

Having URLs such as /projects/1/tickets/2-make-it-shiny will allow your users to easily identify what that URL links to without having to visit the page.[1] Rails allows you to very easily do this by overriding a method called to_param in the model where you want to have pretty URLs. This method is defined like this within ActiveRecord::Base, and so all your models inherit it:

```
def to_param
  id
end
```

This method is used to construct the URLs generated by the link helpers in your application such as project_ticket_path, if you use them like this:

```
project_ticket_path(project, ticket)
```

Rails does not care what the classes of the objects that are passed in here are; it just assumes you know what you're doing. What it does care about though is the output of the to_param method, which must not contain any slashes. To get the pretty URL you always wanted you can use the parameterize method on any String, which works like this:

```
"Make it shiny!".parameterize
= "make-it-shiny"
```

It does this by substituting any character that isn't *a* through *z*, the digits 0 through 9, a hyphen (-), or an underscore (_) into the - character. If the string ends in one

---

[1] It's also supposedly good for search engine optimization (SEO).

of these invalid characters then it will be removed completely. By doing this, it makes the name safe to be used as a parameter in the URL, hence the name `parameterize`.

Before you actually make this change, you're going to write a test for it to make sure that this feature of your code isn't accidentally changed or removed. Because this change is going to be for your `Ticket` model, you're going to put the test for it in spec/models/ticket_spec.rb, using the code from the following listing:

Listing B.1   spec/models/ticket_spec.rb

```
require 'spec_helper'

describe Ticket do
 it "has pretty URLs" do
   ticket = Factory(:ticket, :title = "Make it shiny!")
   ticket.to_param.should eql("#{ticket.id}-make-it-shiny")
 end
end
```

This code will use the factory you created in chapter 7 to create a new ticket with the title "Make it shiny!" Then you call `to_param` on that ticket, and you expect to see it output the ticket's `id` followed by the parameterized version of "Make it shiny": make-it-shiny.

When you run this test with `bin/rspec spec/models/ticket_spec.rb`, you'll see the following output:

```
expected "1-make-it-shiny"
    got "1"
```

This is happening because you haven't yet overridden the `to_param` method in your `Ticket` model and it is defaulting to just providing the `id`. To fix this, you can open the app/models/ticket.rb and add in the new method:

```
def to_param
  "#{id}-#{title.parameterize}"
end
```

When you run our test again, it will now be green:

```
1 example, 0 failures
```

You don't have to change anything else because Rails is still so incredibly darn smart! For instance, you can pass this "1-make-it-shiny" string to the `find` method, and Rails will still know what to do. Go ahead, try this:

```
Ticket.find("1-make-it-shiny")
```

If you have a record in the `tickets` table with an `id` value of 1, Rails will find this. This is because Rails will automatically call `to_i` on string arguments passed to `find`. To see this in action, you can do this in an irb session:

```
"1-make-it-shiny".to_i
```

You should get back the number 1 from this. If you didn't have the `id` prefix in your routes and instead had something like `make-it-shiny`, you would need to save this string to a field in the table called something obvious like `permalink` by using a `before_create` method; then rather than using `find` in places where you are searching for an object, you would instead use `find_by_permalink`.

B.2   *Attribute change tracking*

When working with Active Record, you have the ability to check if a field has changed since the last time you made reference to this record. Let's try this now with a `Project` object in the ticketee project by first launching `rails console`.

Within this console, let's create a new `Project` object:

```
>> project = Project.new
```

On any `ActiveRecord::Base` descendant, you can call the `changed?` method to determine if it has changed since it was created or found. Let's call it:

```
 >> project.changed?
=> false
```

In this case, the project hasn't changed from when it was created and so the `changed?` method returns `false`. If you set any attribute on this object, the `changed?` method will return `true`:

```
 >> project.name = "Ticketee"
=> "Ticketee"
>> project.changed?
=> true
```

Now if you want to know what fields have caused this change, you can just drop off the question mark at the end of `changed?`, like this:

```
  >> project.changed
 => ["name"]
```

As you can see here, this method returns an array containing the attributes which have changed on this object. If you changed another attribute on this project, such as `created_at`, it would also appear in this list:

```
 >> project.created_at = Time.now
=> [current time]
>> project.changed
=> ["name", "created_at"]
```

If you wanted to know only if a single attribute has changed, there's the `*_changed?` methods for all attributes on the model. For instance, if you wanted to know if the name attribute has changed, then you would call `name_changed?`:

```
 >> project.name_changed?
=> true
```

Of course this method will return `true`, because you changed your `name` attribute previously. In addition to this, you're even able to see what the value was before the change using the `*_was` method:

```
>> project.name_was
=> nil
```

This time, `name` was `nil` before you set it and so `nil` is returned. If it had a value before you created this object, it would return that instead. Finally, you can even get back an array containing the before and after values of the attribute by using the `*_change` method:

```
>> project.name_change
=> [nil, "Ticketee"]
```

Now, what would these methods be used for? Well, any number of things, really. You could use it for only running a certain callback if a specific field had been changed, or you could use the `*_change` methods to log the changes to attributes in another table if you wish.

index

S

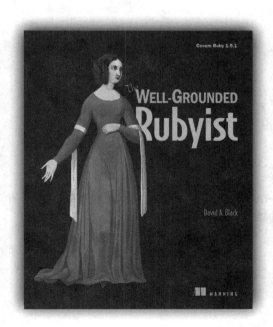